BARNSLEY
PALS

BARNSLEY PALS

The 13th & 14th Battalions

York & Lancaster Regiment

Jon Cooksey

Additional research
HUGO STOCKTER (Germany)
PETER TAYLOR

Pen & Sword
MILITARY

First published in Great Britain in 1986, 1988, 1996, 2006

In this edition 2008 and 2016 by Pen & Sword Military
an imprint of Pen & Sword Books Ltd
47 Church Street, Barnsley, South Yorkshire, S70 2AS

Copyright © Jon Cooksey 1986, 1988, 1996, 2006, 2008, 2016

ISBN 978 1 47389 198 2

Typeset in Sabon by Phoenix Typesetting, Auldgirth, Dumfriesshire

Printed and bound in England by CPI Group (UK) Ltd, Croydon, CR0 4YY

Pen & Sword Books Ltd incorporates the imprints of Pen & Sword Aviation, Pen & Sword Maritime,
Pen & Sword Military, Wharncliffe Local History, Pen & Sword Select, Pen & Sword Military Classics
and Leo Cooper.

For a complete list of Pen & Sword titles please contact
PEN & SWORD BOOKS LIMITED
47 Church Street, Barnsley, South Yorkshire, S70 2AS, England
E-mail: enquiries@pen-and-sword.co.uk
Website: www.pen-and-sword.co.uk

*Below: Non-commissioned officers of the First Barnsley Battalion (13th Battalion, York and Lancaster
Regiment) in the grounds of Noblethorpe Hall, Silkstone, early 1915. Not enough cap badges to go
rounds and some still awaiting the chevrons.*

Contents

And there went out another horse that was red: and power was given to him that was thereon to take peace from the earth, and that they should kill one another: and there was given unto him a great sword.

Revelations 6, verse 4.

Foreword

Sir Nicholas Hewitt, Bt.

'Your Country Needs You' – the 1914 Kitchener poster is still universally recognised today. People associate World War I with huge armies and mass slaughter, they forget that Britain relied on a volunteer army until 1916. Britain in 1914 was not prepared for war, only a small professional peace-time army existed. When the call came such was the popular feeling that one million volunteered in six weeks as compared with Kitchener's expectation of 500,000 in six months.

The army recruiting offices could not cope; in many areas local people and local councils got together to form their own Battalions. Friends all joined together and wanted to stay together. This is the story of Barnsley and the Barnsley Pals.

Often one does not take much interest in one's family's past but during the summer of 1982, as Managing Director of the Barnsley Chronicle, a proposal came forward to me that we should produce a nostalgia supplement to the paper. One of our researchers suggested, in view of a family connection with the Barnsley Pals, that I might ask around the family to see if anyone had any old photographs. I had an old album which had been rescued from a bonfire. Other material was quickly accumulated from a variety of sources.

Too much material was collected to go in the supplement. We decided instead to publish the story as a feature within the paper over a period of six weeks. The more I became involved in the research work the more I became gripped by this fascinating story.

The Barnsley Chronicle feature ran in the autumn of 1982 and we were quickly aware that we had only scraped the surface. The articles stimulated a number of enquiries for reprints. Material continued to accumulate but we lacked time to take it much further. As the local newspaper of Barnsley we are often contacted by people doing odd pieces of research on the town. One such person was Jon Cooksey who was also researching the Barnsley Pals and it seemed logical to get together and produce this book. Jon has worked like a detective on a difficult case leaving no stone unturned. Survivors have been interviewed; Regimental records, The Imperial War Museum, and The Public Record Office, along with relatives have all been consulted. The research also extended to France and Germany and whilst most German records were lost in the Second World War, Jon Cooksey was able to trace the records of the regiment which faced the Pals on 1st July, 1916.

This is a unique record of those who answered the call, an effort to chronicle their experiences which Barnsley can be truly proud of. Barnsley was exceptional in that it was able to raise two Battalions when one considers the size of the population being drawn on, especially as the Regular Army and Territorials were also recruiting. Their first major encounter was the Battle of the Somme about which much has been written. It remains the blackest day in the history of the British Army when the enthusiasm of this volunteer army was sacrificed.

Jon Cooksey recounts this extraordinary story of enthusiastic service for their country by the 'Pals', from their formation to the tragedy of the Somme. We hope that it will serve as a fitting memorial to all those who answered the call 'Your Country Needs You'.

Introduction

Every summer thousands of British tourists in search of the sun join in the annual stampede from the French Channel ports on their way to the Meditterranean coast. As they hurtle south down the 'auto-routes' the gently rolling countryside of Picardy barely merits their attention. During the first quarter of this century however, the vast majority of British people who landed at the Channel ports headed straight for Picardy and rarely ventured further south.

In the beginning Picardy was the only place they wanted to be. They wouldn't have wanted to go anywhere else, but there is a lifetime of difference between then and now. Then the British visitors, some of whom had never ventured further than the nearest town, were mostly men. Then they were dressed mostly in khaki and carried a rifle. Then it was wartime.

Picardy had been fortunate to have been blessed with many natural advantages which made it an area ideal for arable farming. The gently rounded contours of the rolling hills and the innumerable dry valleys which had furrowed the brow of many a slope were tell tale signs of the underlying chalk bedrock, making for excellent natural drainage. Large, open fields covered with a rich layer of fertile earth, grew corn and sugar beet. Here and there oddly shaped woods and copses, the last vestiges of the vast Arrouaise forest which had covered the country in the Middle Ages, were scattered on private estates or on slopes so steep that they had defied the use of the plough.

Scarcely any isolated buildings punctuated the horizon. Most of the building work had gathered small settlements of low red tiled houses around a village church. The villages, many of them safely tucked into the hollows of the landscape, were surrounded by orchards which were generous with their fruits at harvest time. What isolated buildings there were amounted to a few dispersed farmsteads with perhaps the addition of a windmill or a "sucrerie" for the refining of sugar beet; to relieve the monotony of the uplands.

Amiens was the principal settlement of the region with its magnificent cathedral, yet the much smaller town of Albert boasted a basilica which became more famous to thousands of British soldiers.

Albert, a town of 7,000 inhabitants, manufactured bicycles and sewing machines and was well known for this light industry, but it was the grand basilica that assured the town's lasting fame. Topping the spire was the 16 feet high gilded figure of the Virgin with outstretched arms holding the Child.

Three hundred miles away at the very heart of the South Yorkshire coalfield in Northern England, close

Below: *Looking from the old German positions at Serre towards the old British front line directly in front of the line of trees. In 1916 when the Sheffield, Accrington and Barnsley men attacked, there were four small copses named 'Matthew', 'Mark', 'Luke' and 'John' (Matthew copse has been farmed over).*

to the foothills of the flat topped moorlands which characterise the northern extremities of the Pennine chain, stands the town of Barnsley.

It would be hard to find another region which contrasted so starkly with the peaceful, predominantly rural setting of Picardy before the First World War.

It was difficult to imagine romance, or to hear distant echoes of any historical deeds amid the grim and unpleasant landscapes which were the hallmarks of the industrial age and Barnsley's close association with coal.

Picardy could boast the ancient battlefields of Agincourt and Crecy which lay between the River Ancre and the Channel coast. Barnsley had no such claims to fame. It was not impossible to find traces of tranquillity, for there were still some quiet agricultural backwaters which had managed to escape the obtrusive erection of pit headgears and grey 'muck-stacks' which had sprouted in profusion around the area.

In 1750 Barnsley's population numbered only 1,750 souls which rose gently to a total of 5,014 by the time of the census of 1811. A century later the figure had swollen to over 50,000.

There was one very simple reason for this rise – coal. The settlement of Barnsley had evolved quite slowly, unaware that it was placed on top of several rich seams of the very stuff that was to fire the industrial revolution. The best known of these seams was between seven and ten feet thick and high in calorific value. It was to this seam that the town gave its name. Not only had the local people taken to working underground for their daily bread, but tales of jobs and good wages beckoned from all over the land. Men from as far afield as Wales and the West Midlands packed what few possessions they had into trunks and cases and set out for Barnsley.

They soon became used to the town and the customs of the local people as they found lodgings in the villages around the district. On Saturday evenings they would tour the shops and wander in and out of the aisles between the market stalls on Market Hill.

Market Hill and the nearby thoroughfare of Cheapside had, for centuries, been at the very centre of life in the town. The Moot Hall and the Court of Justice had stood squarely in the middle of Market Hill and it was there in years gone by that the more serious transgressions of the law had been punished with a public flogging, while the less serious cases were placed in the stocks.

Market Hill had witnessed many scenes of rejoicing. Particularly joyous were the celebrations which followed the coronation of Queen Victoria and the parties which broke out spontaneously upon the proclamation of peace following the Crimea conflict and, almost half a century later, South Africa. It was to witness further scenes of passion just over a decade later as its menfolk formed up to receive the town's blessing before marching off to yet another war. It would see men standing upright in hastily procured khaki, cheering dignitaries, cheering children, wives and sweethearts sobbing silently into their handkerchiefs.

Amidst the pomp and pageantry of those emotional occasions, neither the men nor the watching crowds on the Barnsley streets would be able to conceive in their minds the sheer horror and ferocity of the struggle into which they had entered. They would never have believed it even if they were told, how for the first time in human history, a war could consume an entire nation and not just a few professional soldiers, as had been the case in the past. They would never have heard above the clamour of the brass bands.

Chapter One

1914 – Life will never be the same again

THE YEAR 1914 OPENED WITH A FLUSH OF OPTIMISM and promise for the 50,000 inhabitants of Barnsley. 1913 had been for the nation at large, a year 'over which to rejoice' according to the local chronicler of events, for it had heralded a great revival in trade.

Members of the Barnsley Traders' Association at their annual dinner spoke at length of the good times that local business people were experiencing. The wheels of industry appeared to be humming along despite a few dry squeaks which a little management oiling had smoothed over. The various retail outlets were doing a roaring trade backed by the buoyant state of the staple industries, and as a result money was said to be circulating freely in the economy.

The coal industry continued to prosper despite a long and gloomy history of fatal accidents in the area due to explosions underground and human negligence. Mining was an occupation fraught with uncertainty for the miners toiling in the Kent Thin seam, the Parkgate seam and the numerous other coal seams which had been opened up. Their working lives bore no relation to the lives they led above ground. When the engine winder dropped them down the shafts in the crude cages and the daylight gradually disappeared, they exchanged a life of light and certainty for one of darkness and danger.

For the experienced miners, it was easy to forget that they had what amounted to a fair sized mountain on top of them. "Hundreds of yards of solid rock, bones of extinct beasts, fossils, flints, subsoils, roots, green grass with cows grazing on it, the village you have just left – all suspended overhead and held back by a few wooden props as thick as the calf of your leg," commented an observer of the day.

Once they reached the black wall of coal, winking at them in the lamplight as so many black diamonds, they had to start work, often kneeling and sometimes lying on their sides. Everywhere there was the dust clinging to their sweating bodies causing them to merge with their grim surroundings. The dust, the physical difficulties presented by the work and the attendant dangers of being so far underground took their toll on the health of the colliers.

Lives were constantly being lost in the coalfields of the West Riding. Only six years previously seven Barnsley miners had plummeted over a hundred yards to their deaths when they were jolted out of the cage at the Parkgate level. This occurrence at Barrow Colliery was due to a mix-up of signals between that level and the pit top.

Even as the inhabitants of Barnsley prepared to let the new year in, a young man lost his life in similar circumstances at Wombwell Main. The report in the Barnsley Chronicle tells how 22 years old Frank

Opposite page: *Barnsley's population grew rapidly as men and their families moved in to work in the mines.*

Right: *Lives were constantly being lost in the coal-fields. One such disaster is commemorated by this post card. Seven miners were tipped out of the cage when there was a mix-up in signals.*

Wombwell Main at the turn of the century.

Hinchcliffe died: 'Killed by being crushed between the cage and the landing, through the cage being drawn up while the deceased was at work, in pursuance of a signal being given by some unknown person.'

The accidents, the dirty dangerous conditions and the low wages were giving rise to a groundswell of unrest in the pits, unrest which had not been calmed by the strike of early 1912.

Little wonder then that when the opportunity to escape from the mines presented itself, the colliers seized it with few second thoughts. They would leave the pits in numbers large enough to form two local battalions in the coming conflict. An amazing feat for a town of Barnsley's size, particularly as much larger centres of population such as Sheffield would raise only one battalion.

As 1914 was welcomed in it brought with it claims of prosperity in the coal fields, claims which drowned the cries for industrial reform.

Somewhat insensitively the Chronicle immediately followed the report of the young man's death at Wombwell Main with a report dealing with the boom time then being enjoyed by South Yorkshire Coal. This despite the fact that the mine owners were grumbling about the increased running costs forced upon them by the setting up of a minimum wage system for the miners. In fact the coal industry was alone in its export record, for nationwide other industries were showing signs of stagnation.

The economy had not really been helped by Britain's policy of keeping out of the various continental brawls in the Balkans and elsewhere. However a new spirit of diplomacy was commented on in the

Working conditions for thousands of men in the district.

editorial columns of the Chronicle where it was observed that the continued spreading of 'fraternal spirit' between nations would lessen the likelihood of the peace of the world being shattered by the Great Powers.

Fate was sorely tempted as the newspaper article concluded with the words, "1914 may be locally faced with a good heart."

The future indeed must have appeared rosy to our forebears as various claims were being made in relation to the development of applied science. Chronicle readers were assured that the scientists were on the brink of solving the age-old alchemists' dream of turning lead into gold. One Professor Soddy claimed enthusiastically that if an electric current of sufficient strength was passed through the lead then the miracle would occur.

Further claims for electricity were being made in connection with the working of the human body and more particularly with the operation of the digestive system. 1,500 volts passed through the body definitely improved the digestion!

In such an era of new found scientific awareness, a full description of the kind of life we could expect to find on Mars was given – and since the span of life was being predicted to increase from the 70 to 80 years allotted by the Bible up to a hundred, and eventually 250 years, everyone would presumably live long enough to make a visit.

Perhaps the general atmosphere of peace, prosperity and the hint of an age of plenty, was reflected in the reluctance of the Barnsley menfolk to join the locally based Territorial Army units.

Companies of the 5th Battalion the York and Lancaster Regiment with bases at Rotherham, Birdwell, Treeton, Wath and Barnsley were desperately short of recruits. Throughout the nation some 300,000 men were needed for the part-time army.

At the annual prize distribution in the Birdwell Drill Hall, the Commander of that detachment,

Outcropping for coal during the 1912 strike.

Captain H. P. Smith, in his address lamented the fact that the young men were not coming forward in the district as much as they might do, and went on to say: "Instead of silent sympathy the Territorials want practical help." To his mixed audience he appealed, "Think over what I have said, and I hope that you girls will use your influence with your sweethearts on behalf of the Territorial movement."

His remarks brought both laughter and applause from the assembled throng but nevertheless the companies were to remain seriously under strength up to the outbreak of war on August 4th.

However, the general feeling of optimism was about to suffer a blow and it began with the miners.

Working people all over the country were led to believe that a boom time was just around the corner, but their wages and conditions told them otherwise.

In February the general manager at Cortonwood Colliery, which employed 1,600 persons, made the following statement: "The Parkgate seam, which is at present being worked, will last 40 years and taking all seams into account there was coal to be got from 50 to 100 years."

The last shift to work at Cortonwood left the pit one Friday in late October 1985, the general manager's comments proving surprisingly near the mark.

Hot on the heels of this statement a strike broke out in West Riding over the issue of minimum wages for miners. In 1912 Sir Edward Clarke awarded a minimum wage ranging from two shillings and two pence a day for a 14 years old to seven shillings and three pence for a qualified face worker. In the event, the mine owners were dragging their heels in making the payments.

The unrest spread quickly until by April 170,000 miners were out on strike. One mine owner grumbled that because of the high minimum wage, 20 per cent of the miners were absent from the pit every day because, he claimed, they made enough to live on without attending for a full week.

Despite this unrest in Barnsley and District, local people sought their entertainment how they could. Knurr and spell or 'nipsy' was a popular pastime often attracting large crowds.

One Saturday afternoon a match was in progress on the Queens Ground when a crowd of 150 men were seen by two plain clothes constables to be preoccupied in another type of game. Cries of "Heads a dollar" signalled to the upholders of the law that an illegal gambling game was in progress. Coins were seen spinning in the air as the locals engaged in an illicit game of 'heads and tails'. Lookouts spotted the 'law' and the men scattered, attempting to disappear among the onlookers, but not before some of them were recognised. Thirty were later arrested and charged.

Indoor entertainment could be found at the 'Pavilion', the 'Empire', 'Princess Picture Palace' and the 'Theatre Royal', where films, live shows and plays were being performed.

At the Pavilion parents could take their children along to witness the marvellous feats of Pedro Pescador and his wonderful equilibristic double somersaulting dogs. Or laugh themselves silly at the antics of the four comedians who went under the name of McKinnons Scottish Meisters. Over at the Empire the boast was that there was never a dull moment in a programme which featured J. F. Sterling's 'Tango Mania' and an obvious stab at upstaging the Pavilion's gravity defying dogs by including 'The Four Flying Julians' on the

Captain Hugh Parry Smith, Commander of the Birdwell company of the Territorials.

13

Shambles Street, a thoroughfare with public houses where the working classes found their entertainment.

bill. This along with the amazing 'Edie', the only artiste in the world who, it was claimed, could turn 32 consecutive somersaults while playing mandoline solos.

The Theatre Royal angled for a different kind of audience by staging the musical comedy "The Dancing Mistress."

For the weekly cost of a penny for a copy of the Barnsley Chronicle, an excited reader could thrill at an on-running serial with the title "Old Mr Giffards Will" or "An Up To Date Wooing."

Reading the stories couched in post Victorian English a reader today could be excused from immediately misconstruing such notable lines as, "But Mademoiselle's intercourse with the gloomy faced master was not necessarily at an end."

Hidden among the Chronicle Church Notices a sombre warning was sounded to those religiously inclined. A certain Mr Kirkwood from Glasgow, a member of the International Bible Students Association was to deliver a lecture at the Arcade Hall with the chilling title of "End of the World and After."

His claim was that the year 1914 was marked as significant in Bible prophecy when the 'Horsemen of the Revelation' were due to ride out.

Could Mr Kirkwood have deduced that for many of his generation the world was indeed to come to an end in that year?

As the Summer of '14 began, the pit accidents continued. An explosion at the Wharncliffe Silkstone Colliery at Tankersley claimed another 12 lives.

With the onset of the warmer weather and the promise of a long hot summer, the annual incidences of drowning began to command the headlines, as the youngsters sought the cooling waters of the river Dearne and the canals.

The last month of world peace, July, began with a military display at Queens Ground. Six hundred red-coated soldiers marched through the streets with bayonets fixed. A show by the 5th York and Lancaster Regiment put on in the hope of attracting recruits prior to the Territorial battalion leaving for its annual camp at Whitby in August.

As the miners' strike petered out workers at Beevor Bobbin Works on Pontefract Road struck for an advance in their wages. Picketing became violent as some non-union workers attempted to go into work and police escorts had to be provided.

On page six of the July 4th edition of the Chronicle a story ran concerning the assassination of the Austrian Archduke Franz Ferdinand and his wife. The account told of the Duke fending off a bomb with his arm prior to the fatal shots.

The significance of that somewhat inaccurate account of the incident which took place in strife-torn

Above: *Trouble at the mill. As the miners' confrontation with the mine owners petered out a dispute arose at Beevor Bobbin Works, Pontefract Road. Non-union labour defy the pickets as they go into work under police protection.*

Right: *Detectives and uniformed officers keep their eyes on the strikers. The Great War a few weeks away, was to remove labour discontent for some months to come.*

A couple of middle-class girls enjoying the hot summer of 1914, Keresforth Road. They were to lose their brother in 1917 when he led his company into a German ambush.

Serbia would have been lost on the Chronicle readers. The Balkans were a world away.

An exhibition of flying at Queens Ground by a Mr. Manton, a mere youth at the age of 20, thrilled a paying audience of just 200. It was a small crowd for such a novel and thrilling event, but no doubt the local wags realised that the young lad's looping the loop could not be performed on the ground. There were plenty of local vantage points where the display could be viewed free.

Among the court cases for that last normal month of July was that of the 14 years old pony driver, Joseph Bennett of Monk Bretton, who was fined one shilling for playing bounce ball on the highway.

Margaret Harrington was charged with being drunk and disorderly at Dodworth. She admitted that she had drunk two gills and blamed the heat.

She had good cause to cite the heat in mitigation as one hot day followed upon another in the summer of 1914. Crowds flocked into Locke Park on Sundays free of the cares of work for at least one day. Tired parents lolled on the grass occasionally scolding their boisterous children. Couples strolled arm in arm to the accompaniment of popular tunes which floated from the bandstand. Opposition to Sunday music in the park came from those who feared that the free entertainment would empty the stuffy Sunday Schools. We read in the paper that £50 was allocated to the Parks Committee to pay them, and the band played on.

On the sporting side Barnsley Football Club, who had won the Football Association Challenge Cup in 1912, missed promotion to the first Division in 1914. This was due to an injury to their star player Dicky Downes, a much sought after exponent of the game, according to club officials at their annual meeting.

Matrimonial difficulties were in evidence as one George Tagg, miner of Lunn Wood cottage declared through the columns of the Chronicle that he would no longer be responsible for any debts contracted by his wife Maud. The following week Maud used the same medium to reply, "I Maud Tagg of Lunn Wood Cottage have never got George Tagg into debt and never intend to."

Readers were invited to see a genuine freak of nature at Joseph Wilkinson's Cock Inn Music Hall. Apparently a full grown calf could be viewed which had two heads, six legs, two tails and a rather intriguing "etc."

The Inspector of Nuisances at High Street, Monk Bretton, was inviting tenders for the removal of the contents of privies and ashpits. The work to be carried out 12 midnight to 8 a.m. The successful contractor would have to find some proper place to deposit the night-soil.

As the month of July came to a hot, sticky close, with no sign of a break in the heat wave, new baths were opened at Race Street. Alderman Rideal publicly stated his regret that there were no Turkish baths and ruefully declared that for a town of Barnsley's size Turkish baths were essential.

Members of the Barnsley Suffrage Society were visited by Australian Miss Matters, who addressed a gathering at Fairfield House and May Day Green. She gave an impassioned plea for equal conditions in the labour market for men and women.

August the First dawned and the talk of Barnsley was the dramatic escape from Wakefield Gaol of Walter Dargue, a 24 years old miner of Mason's Row, Carlton. Walter had been serving an 18 months' sentence for breaking and entering office premises. He had escaped by removing a window then bending the prison bars he had wriggled through and dropped to freedom. He was recaptured at home three days later, "I just wanted t' see wife," he explained.

The sun shone on but now there were proverbial dark clouds gathering on the future of the world. Life would never be the same again.

During the last golden week of July, 'C' and 'E' Companies, York and Lancaster Regiment, had left Barnsley Court House station under command of Captain Allport for their annual camp at Whitby. Hopes were high that the fortnight would be valuable, and that most of the men would stay in camp for at least fifteen days to earn their bounty of £1 plus their pay. Between the spells of training the men would be able to 'walk out' on an evening and enjoy the pleasures of the seaside town.

16

Officers of the 5th Battalion at their annual camp, Whitby, seen here in their 'blues'. Before the war ended four of them would be killed by enemy action.

The officers looked forward to the nightly ritual of the Officers' Mess. Every evening the battalion band would play selections of popular music outside the Mess tent, whilst inside the officers would attack a full menu on tables regaled with the regimental silver. Two servants scurried around serving champagne, gins, bitters and sherries.

The start of the annual camp was seen as an essential date in the Territorial calendar. For most of the year the local units of 'Terriers' devoted their evenings and weekends to military practices at the various drill halls around the district. The summer camp was the only real opportunity for the Barnsley companies to join with their comrades at Rotherham, Wath and Treeton to train as a complete battalion.

Training was hard but it was a welcome break from their full-time occupations, but the camp of July, August 1914 was to be the last for a few years. Rumblings of the political storm brewing over on the continent began drifting over the English Channel towards the end of July.

That 'fraternal spirit' between nations which the Chronicle had championed as being the key to world

Out on a route march near Whitby officers of the 5th. Their carefree days were about to be interrupted. Inset: Captain Parkinson enjoying a snooze in the Mess tent. Note the easy chair.

Lord Kitchener, hero of the Sudan is recalled to London for an appointment at the War Office. Tension is mounting.

peace at the start of the year, had been spread so thinly by the beginning of August that it did not even begin to fill the widening chasms that had appeared between the two armed camps of Europe. Everywhere on the continent national chests were heaving with pride and jaws were being thrust out in what had already been turned into a dangerous drama of juvenile bravado.

In the aftermath of the assassination of the heir to the Austro-Hungarian throne on June 28th, one declaration of war was quickly followed by another as the huge standing armies of Austria, Russia, France and Germany were mobilised. By Friday, 31st July Britain was becoming increasingly concerned by the crisis. For years she had been far too pre-occupied with her own industrial problems along with the deepening divisions in Ireland, to be unduly worried by the events taking place in Eastern Europe.

As the nation prepared for the August Bank Holiday weekend, on the Friday the fleet prepared to set sail in response to a French request to safeguard her Channel coasts from the attentions of the German fleet.

That afternoon the Kaiser prepared to make a speech from the balcony of the Knights' Hall in Berlin. Speaking to the attentive massed throng below, he informed them that, 'A dark day has today broken over Germany. Envious persons are everywhere compelling us to just defence. The sword has been forced into our hand.'

Since the sword had apparently been forced into her hand, it now appeared that Germany would use it, or at least, its threat. The Lancashire and Yorkshire Railway Company's steamer 'Dearne' which was due to sail from Hamburg to Goole on August 1st with a cargo of sugar, was impounded by the German port authorities.

The excitement then gripping Germany was recorded by H. W. Nevinson, correspondent for the London 'Daily News'. Travelling from England to Berlin on July 31st he witnessed the following scenes: 'Down the midnight Channel the searchlights were turning and streaming in long white wedges. Passing into Germany, we at once met trains full of working men in horse trucks decked with flowers and scribbled over with chalk inscriptions: 'Nach Paris,' 'Nach Petersburg,' but none so far as 'Nach London.' They were cheering and singing as people always cheer and sing when war is coming.'

In Britain the diplomatic heat generated by the House of Commons on Bank Holiday Monday was matched only by the weather. All day members of parliament, packed tight on the benches, debated the question of whether Britain should remain neutral in the crisis. It became clear to those assembled that at this late stage there was a certain air of inevitability about the proceedings as Lord Kitchener, the hero of the Sudanese skirmishes, was recalled to London to undertake certain administrative duties at the War Office.

It was the question of Belgian neutrality which was to decide Britain's fate once and for all.

The German General Staff shackled to the Schlieffen Plan which called for a wheeling invasion of France through Belgium with a final thrust for Paris, had already calculated Britain's response to their scheme. They suspected that she would rally round to preserve Belgium's neutrality.

On Tuesday, 4th August, the government delivered an ultimatum to Germany, and Mr Asquith,

The last days of peace trickle away, the military scene is about to undergo a severe change. The Yorkshire Dragoons seen here moving along Sheffield Road, are soon to be swallowed up in The Great War. "You had to be God Almighty to get into the Dragoons," comments an ex-Territorial officer.

The Barnsley Chronicle.

AND PENISTONE MEXBRO WATH AND HOYLAND JOURNAL.

Telegrams "Chronicle" Barnsley

Telephone, 67.

VOL. LV. NO. 3913 — THE BARNSLEY CHRONICLE. SATURDAY, AUGUST 8. 1914. — PRICE ONE PENNY.

GREAT EUROPEAN WAR.

KAISER'S DREAD DECISION.

GERMANY SUFFERING HEAVY REVERSES.

SIR E. GREY'S MEMORABLE SPEECH.

Germany having taken the final tragic plunge, the war cloud which for some time past threatened Europe has burst, and the country is plunged into what promises to be the greatest War which has ever occurred.

On Saturday night the German Ambassador, in the name of his Government handed to the Foreign Ministry a declaration of War upon France, and on Tuesday took the same drastic step with England.

The week has been one series of exciting events.

Here in Barnsley, like other towns, the gravest concern has been displayed on all hands, and the Reservists, Territorials, and other patriotic townsmen have willingly offered their services to their King and country.

The "signing on" process has been going on all week, and it is no exaggeration to say that the loyalty displayed has even eclipsed that shown when war was declared with South Africa.

In the "Chronicle" this week, we give extended details of the exciting events—locally and imperially—and in this issue, too, will be found a full list of the names of the Reservists, Territorials, and others who are open to do all in their power to resist the inexplicable action of Germany.

CONCISE HISTORY OF EVENTS.

HOW THE WAR HAS PROGRESSED FROM DAY TO DAY.

A WEEK OF INTENSE EXCITEMENT.

PLIGHT OF TOURISTS.

BOATS TO BE SENT FOR ENGLISH REFUGEES.

ESPIONAGE.

TOO MANY GERMANS IN ENGLAND.

GOVERNMENT AND FOOD SUPPLIES.

NO JUSTIFICATION FOR PANIC PRICES.

BRITAIN'S PART IN THE WAR.

DEFINED BY SIR E. GREY.

DIARY OF THE CRISIS.

WAR EDITIONS FORBIDDEN IN PARIS.

TIT-BITS OF THE WAR.

LOCAL POLICE FOR THE FRONT.

BARNSLEY GUARDIANS ANXIOUS.

RELIEF OF DISTRESS.

PRINCE OF WALES TO ISSUE AN APPEAL.

STRENGTH OF THE NATIONS.

THE NAVY AND LAND FORCES.

NEUTRALITY OF BELGIUM.

HOW TO HELP BRITAIN.

RUSSIANS PRAYING IN THE STREETS.

DURATION OF WARS.

Barnsley people's source of war news. Whilst the German army is sweeping through Belgium, the readers are being led to believe that they are "suffering heavy reverses". Truth is the first casualty of war.

19

the Prime Minister, announced to the Commons that Germany had been telegraphed that she should give an assurance whereby the demands made upon Belgium to allow German troops to cross her territory would not be pressed. The telegram ended 'We ask for an immediate reply.'

Britain held its breath as the hours advanced towards midnight and the time of the expiry of the ultimatum. Germany failed to acknowledge and crowds gathered in London at Parliament Square to witness the last minutes of peace tick by on the clock face of Big Ben. At 11 p.m., midnight in Germany, the ultimatum expired, Britain was at war.

Upon the final stroke of the hour of 11 o'clock it seemed as if the body of the nation convulsed with the first of the many shock waves of patriotism which were to flood the length and breadth of the land, submerging all but the most strongwilled of those who opposed the war. It was a rising tide which was to eventually engulf the young men of Britain and wash them away to France where it would leave them high and dry, facing the German Army on a lovely summer morning in 1916.

Events moved quickly after that last fateful stroke as the crowds dispersed excitedly from Parliament Square. Those Londoners who had been able to sleep during the night woke up to find the advertising placards of 'The Times' declaring "Britain at War" in striking black letters.

The famous cricket ground, the Kennington Oval, scene of many a sporting duel between batsman and bowler, had already been requisitioned for military purposes, while in the north, the home ground of Manchester City, then on Hyde Road, was taken over by the Territorial Artillery.

In Barnsley, the Chronicle played its part in raising the temperature of a nation already delirious with War fever by publishing intermittent reports issued by the Press Bureau in London. These reports did their best to encourage feelings of sympathy for the small nations of Serbia and Belgium, particularly Belgium, as tales of "Fiendish atrocities" committed by "Murderers in uniforms" were fed to the Barnsley public. The columns of the Chronicle promised to reveal all the "Horrible details" of the German advance and how drunken German soldiers were responsible for "Fire and Massacre". It was the first round in a bitter war of propaganda which accompanied the fighting and there was no doubt that the British had won it hands down. The Germans, set rocking on their heels, found that it was all they could do to reply with denial after denial to a barrage of accusations regarding their conduct of the War. With each fresh report the eyes and mouths of the readers gaped wider as the events grew more macabre. If anyone had been in two minds as to the righteous nature of Britain's decision to rush to Belgium's defence before August 4th then it was a good bet that they had made up their minds to support that decision after reading the papers.

The Prime Minister, Mr. Asquith, speaking to the House of Commons on August 6th, had said that Britain had entered the fray, ". . . to fulfill a solemn international obligation which if it had been entered into between private persons in the ordinary concerns of life, would have been regarded as an obligation not only of law but of honour." He went on, "Britain had a duty to Belgium; she was bound by honour to support France."

'Duty' and 'honour' soon began to emerge as the two key words in the early weeks of the war, words which manifested themselves in a rekindled warrior spirit which swiftly seized the nation. Nowhere was that warrior spirit more in evidence than in the National Reserve Clubs and Territorial Army drill halls up and down the country.

Before the War Britain had been alone among the nations of Europe in maintaining a system of voluntary military service. Being an island race with an island mentality she had not been inclined to a policy of conscription, preferring instead to build up a strong Navy to counter any

Territorial headquarters at Eastgate, the centre of activity in August 1914.

threats of aggression from over-seas and trusting her diminutive Army with the job of patrolling the distant outposts of her Empire. Despite its small size in relation to the forces of some of its continental neighbours the British Army had benefited from its close knit structure and had learned from the methods employed by the large Armies of the European powers, not least those of Germany. Subsequently the seven year regulars were proud of their traditions and of

Grim-faced officers of the 5th Battalion organise the premature return from summer camp.

their attention to basic military details such as accurate rapid rifle fire.

To supplement the professional full time force there were the volunteers of the National Reserve, trained ex-soldiers who had signed up to serve some time on the reserve lists and the part-time Territorial Army; a force which had superseded the old militia and who met for training in the evenings, at weekends and at an annual Summer Camp.

It was among the ranks of the local Barnsley ex-servicemen, reservists and Territorials that the words 'duty' and 'honour' were voiced most strongly in the early days of war and there the warrior spirit was nurtured. On August 8th the Barnsley Chronicle reported that reservists were hastening in their thousands to rejoin the colours nationwide and that offers of service were pouring in from all parts of the Empire.

In Barnsley the authorities had no trouble in recruiting men for the local volunteer units. One headline proudly boasted "Hundreds of volunteers", and the National Reserve Club was described as being a "hive of patriotic activity" as ex-Army men came forward anxious to be put back into uniform.

> "Clerks have been busy for hours daily taking names, and late last night there was no falling off in the number of Volunteers. The names of hundreds of men over and above the numbers required to complete the establishment of the 5th Battalion York and Lancaster Regiment, the 6th West Yorkshire Regiment, the Royal Horse Artillery, Wentworth, and the West Riding Field Ambulance Corps."

Volunteers were no problem, in fact there were so many that the sheer weight of their numbers caused an embarrassing hiccup in the bureaucratic process, as the Chronicle apologetically explained,

> "Such a noble response has been made for volunteers to go to the seat of the war that the supply of documents used for this purpose gave out on Wednesday. The recruiting officer and the magistrates of Barnsley have been inudated with applications from willing recruits, and the signing on was temporarily postponed until the arrival of another batch of papers."

Through the simple expedient of putting up a notice in the Reserve Club and another in the window of the Chronicle offices, Lt. Col. Bamforth, the commander of the Barnsley National Service Battalion, had acquired the names of 185 men, 25 more than he actually needed to top up the ranks of the four units involved. Of these 73 had been accepted for the 5th Battalion, the York and Lancaster Regiment, of which the Barnsley Territorials, the "Terriers", were a part.

All week members of the "Terriers" had been seen walking the streets in service dress, ever since their recall from Whitby Summer Camp on August 3rd, but no one had any inkling that by August 6th they would be leaving Barnsley and taking their first steps down the long trail which would eventually lead to the trenches of the Western Front at Fleurbaix.

A large and enthusiastic crowd gathered on that Thursday afternoon to witness the civic send-off from Market Hill. Once more, as had happened many times in the past, an atmosphere of pageantry, spectacle and anticipation descended on the centre of the town as the Mayor of Barnsley, Councillor William Goodworth England, bedecked with robes and chain of office, proceeded with his wife and other council luminaries to the steps of the Corn Exchange to await the arrival of the "Terriers".

They didn't have to wait long as Lt. Col. Fox, the commanding officer of the 5th battalion, York and Lancaster regiment, marched into the centre of Market Hill at the head of two companies of infantry, a signals and an ambulance corps, in all about 200 men.

"Their appearance was very smart and many expressions of approval were heard on all sides. The men, who carried their rifles, and were equipped for marching, looked eager and fit."

The mayor, surveying the ranks drawn up on the Hill could have been echoing the sentiments of the whole town as he delivered a speech brimful of hope, pride and patriotism.

"Officers, non-commissioned officers and men of the 5th Battalion York and Lancaster Regiment. On behalf of the citizens of this town, and speaking with a full sense of the responsibilities which rest upon me – on this momentous occasion – I have come to wish you God speed on the mission you have undertaken.

"The cloud which had for 40 years been gathering over our heads has suddenly burst and we as a nation are compelled to go into a war that has been forced upon us by the mad caprice of the German Emperor.

"But we know we are standing for the defence of the weak, the champions of the liberties of countries that for years have enjoyed our friendship and support. (Hear, hear).

"The marvellous manner in which the mobilisation of the forces has been accomplished, must have been an object lesson to the nations around us, for never in the history of our nation have our naval and military forces been ready at such short notice.

"The call has been made and it has instantly and willingly been obeyed. For some years you have played your part as citizens, but now at short notice you are soldiers of the King. See to it you acquit yourselves like men. (Hear, hear).

"And to quote 'The Times' of the other day, in this hour of national trial go into it united, calm, resolute, trusting in God – that is the mood in which our fathers fought – with the firm hope that in a just and righteous cause, the only Giver of all victory will bless our army.

"On behalf of our townsmen I sincerely wish you God speed, and a safe and speedy return to your native town." **Barnsley Chronicle, August 8th, 1914**

Mr. Joseph Hewitt, a well known local solicitor and himself an old Territorial officer, also addressed the men. In his speech he spoke of the 'duty' which was 'implanted' in the men, and intimated that Barnsley would re-generate its 'Patriotic Fund', first founded in October 1899 during the South African War, to care for the dependants

The first Wartime civic send-off for Barnsley soldiers. Dignitaries await the arrival of the Territorials on Market Hill. From the left: Councillor Chappell, Councillor Cockerill, Town Clerk W.P. Donald, Councillor England, Mrs. England, Mr. J. Hewitt and Rev. Huggard.

Three cheers for the King, the Regiment and Colonel Fox. The Barnsley Territorials are left in no doubt as to the rightness of their chosen course.

Colonel Fox and his 'weekend' soldiers listen to the fine speeches before leaving for Regimental Headquarters at Rotherham. After a few months' defence duty on the East Coast they are pitched into battle in April 1915.

of those Barnsley men called out of the Borough by the call to arms.

Perhaps in this way the town could also do its duty by caring for the loved ones of the men, who it seemed, were doing theirs.

The detachment moved proudly off from Market Hill to a lusty rendition of the National Anthem, and with three cheers for the King, the Regiment and Colonel Fox ringing in their ears they marched to the station to board the 3.30 Midland train to Rotherham, the home of the York and Lancaster Regimental H.Q.

The train moved off and disappeared down the line. The 'Terriers' had gone. The cheers and applause died away, hats were put back on heads and handkerchiefs pushed into pockets as the crowds left the station and went about their business. But it was not to be the last time that the people of Barnsley would congregate to give a rapturous send-off to their soldier sons. One of Britain's new heroes of the hour, Lord Kitchener, would see to that.

The Barnsley Terriers were not the only soldiers on the move in the first few days of war. Everywhere stations were filled with hordes of pushing, jostling people. Wives, children, sweethearts, and mums and dads all crowded round khaki clad figures, all of them wanting to wish their loved ones a fond farewell. Between August 12th and the 17th the small regular British Expeditionary Force, (known simply as the B.E.F.), was landed in France en route to their first action at the small Belgian town of Mons. Some of the officers of those regular units would, no doubt, have been sorry to miss the opening of the grouse shooting season on the "glorious twelfth", but there would be plenty of shooting where they were going and they would not find the Germans quite the defenceless game they had encountered on the moorlands of England.

Chapter Two

A change of life

Kitchener's Army, Join it to-day. Kitchener's Army, One 'Bob' a day, And if he grumbles, Sergeant will say: 'Put him in guard room; stop all his pay.'

IT WAS NOT DIFFICULT TO DEDUCE that the war was turning out to be a popular cause in almost every layer of society. It seemed as if the social unrest of the preceding years and the detached air with which Britain had for so long viewed events outside her Empire were, for the moment at least, suspended.

Nationally known politicians, provincial civic dignitaries and religious leaders joined together in filling the hearts and minds of their attentive audiences with their own particular variation on the theme of the 'good fight'.

In his sermon on Sunday 16th August the Reverend J. F. Walker, vicar of St. George's Church, Barnsley, declared that:

> "It was high time the flag of social and industrial war was hauled down, and a truce called . . . While there was war outside the country there was peace within. Long may that peace last."

The few who swam against the rising tide of Nationalism received short shrift from those who turned up to hear them speak. Labour M.P. Kier Hardie was interrupted many times as men and women mounted chairs in Aberdare Market Hall to sing 'Rule Britannia' and 'God Save The King' at an anti-war meeting. The Chronicle reported events at the meeting, Hardie shouting at the top of his voice amid the baying from the audience below the platform.

> "As your chairman has told you – (boos) – this meeting was organised before war was declared. Still, after the declaration of war I considered the meeting ought not to be postponed. (Cheers for the King). I came to the conclusion that my constituents – (disorder) – would like to hear information – (disorder and singing of 'The Boys of the Old Brigade') – Whatever I may be my constituents know there is no trace of the coward in my blood. (applause) And so I am here to endeavour to put before you a few of the reasons why the Labour Party . . ."

Above: 'We must help the girl that Tommy left behind him' had been a slogan for the Boer War. The York and Lancasters had a mere 17 volunteers from Barnsley for the South African campaign. Thousands are to volunteer and leave their families to hand out a sharp lesson to the Germans. Below: "Fear your God and defend your country," London Territorials are exhorted in a church parade prior to ceremonially depositing their colours at St. Pancras Church, August 1914.

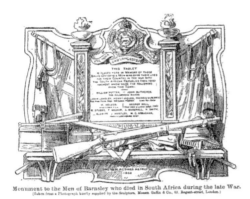

Monument to the Men of Barnsley who died in South Africa during the late War.
(Taken from a Photograph kindly supplied by the Sculptors, Messrs. Gaffin & Co., 63, Regent-street, London.)

Above left: *Memorial in St. Mary's Church, Barnsley containing Ernest Bell's brother's name.*
Above right: *As Britain and Barnsley in particular move on to a war footing the Germans continue their sweeping advance through Belgium. German infantry pictured here in Vise, the first village in Belgium they took.*

At this stage the meeting broke down with the crowd jostling Hardie's supporters below the platform. Hardie struggled on above the din and although he denounced the war in the interests of peace and civilisation, it seemed no-one wished to listen.

A great deal of the new national spirit was founded on a belief that the war would be a very short affair. Indeed a good many of the Reservists and Territorials were more concerned that they would not see action before Britain had handed out a sharp lesson in the art of soldiering to the Germans, and at the same time push them back down the international pecking order which they thought, in any event, was a good few places lower than that of Britain.

The Barnsley Chronicle had already published a list showing the duration of wars fought in the half-century previous to 1914, as if to reassure its readers that, at worst, the conflict would only last a year. Chronicle readers would have been well advised to scrutinise the eighth entry on the list marked "South African, October 1899 – May 1902." There was a sobering memory in there somewhere but by August 1914 even that had faded.

It had not faded quite so much for Ernest Bell and his family. Ernest was 21 years old in August 1914. He had been a child of 6 when the already strained links between the British and the Boers of South Africa finally snapped. The resulting military expedition was to prove less than conclusive for the British Army.

The innocent resilience of early childhood would have cushioned the impact of war on most children but Ernest was never to forget it for at the age of six he had experienced the trauma which accompanies seeing men off to fight. Ernest's brother George, along with 16 other Barnsley men, volunteered for service with the York and Lancaster Regiment in South Africa. George Bell contracted enteric fever during the campaign. He never came home.

The reason why the town of Barnsley is able to raise two battalions for Kitchener's new armies when a neighbouring city raises but one is perhaps explained by this picture. A youngster in the poor working conditions of the day.

For the Bell family life had to go on and by August 1914 Ernest was employed as a stonemason by the Barnsley Corporation. He enjoyed his work, having already served seven years of a long apprenticeship which all craftsmen of his day were expected to undertake before they were deemed to know their trade. What made his job even more enjoyable was the fact that his pal, Harry Gay, also worked with him. Ernest and Harry had been brought up together and when the time came, at the age of 13, for them to leave school and start work, they had both been lucky enough to secure apprenticeships as stonemasons. They had been through that together too. Yes, Ernest and Harry were very good friends.

Similar stories could have been told about scores of other young men of Ernest's age all over the Barnsley district.

In an age when hardship was widespread among a working class becoming increasingly disgruntled by what it saw as poor returns for sheer hard graft, it was rare for a child from such a background to gain access to further education in the shape of a Grammar school. In most cases the family budget could not

Uniforms, flags, marching and discipline of the Scouts and Church Lads Brigade lays a basis for future soldiers.

afford to feed an able mind when an able body could pay its own way and help the family finances into the bargain. Many of these young Barnsley men had been hard at work like Ernest Bell since their thirteenth birthday, but unlike Ernest, most of them ended up down the pits. Barnsley's continued growth was based on coal.

> *"I was about 13fi when I started work. I finished school at 13. You left school if you were good enough and received a Labour Certificate, that entitled you to go and get a job if you wanted one, 6 months before your time. I was pony driving to begin with, then I went on to haulage and finally to the coal face.*
>
> *I hated working down the pit when I first went but I got to like it. All the lads were there you see."* 13/440 Private Harry Hall, 'B' Company, 13th Y & L Regiment

All the lads were there plus two of Harry's brothers, Tom and Walter, and they all worked at Houghton Main pit. Having your mates with you counteracted the long hours and the heavy work. They were sharing the danger and the drudgery, laughing off the hardships of a working life spent underground. These were experiences which would be put to good use in the not too distant future.

In August 1914 Tommy Oughton was 18fi. He lived in Wombwell and worked at Mitchell's Main pit at Darfield.

> *"I was working on what they called 'tramming'. I know I was earning seven shillings a day and at that time I was earning a little bit more than my dad. That was good money for an 18 year old then."* Private Tommy Oughton, 14 Platoon 'D' Company, 13th Y & L Regiment

Being the eldest of seven children Tommy's wages were much appreciated by his financially stretched parents. A few miles away at Silkstone pit Oswald 'Ossie' Burgess was also 'tramming' but for one shilling

Ernest Bell, ex 13th Y & L

Harry Hall, ex 13th Y & L

Tommy Oughton, ex 13th Y & L

Ossie Burgess, ex 14th Y & L

BRITONS
"WANTS"
YOU
"TO"
JOIN YOUR COUNTRY'S ARMY!
GOD SAVE THE KING

Above and opposite page:
Pressure is on young men to
take up arms.

Below: Kitchener's Service
Record.

SECRETARY OF STATE FOR WAR.

LORD KITCHENER'S BRILLIANT CAREER.

The following are significant dates in Lord Kitchener's career:—

1850, 24 June.—Born at Ballylongford, County Kerry.
1868.—Entered Woolwich Academy.
1870.—Served as private in Army of Loire (French) against the Germans.
1871.—Became lieutenant in the Royal Engineers.
1874.—Under the Palestine Exploration Fund obtained survey work in Palestine.
1878.—Surveyed Cyprus.
1882.—Served as major throughout Egyptian campaign.
1885.—Nile Expedition for relief of Gordon; won Gordon's praise in his "Journal" as a "very superior officer."
1888.—Dangerously wounded in the jaw at Handub, near Suakim.
1892.—Sirdar (Commander-in-Chief) of the Egyptian Army.
1896, 8 April.—Dervishes defeated at the Atbara.
1893, 2 September.—Battle of Omdurman; rout of the Mahdi; fall of Khartoum.
1898, 19 September.—Meeting with Major Marchand at Fashoda; raised to the Peerage.
1899.—Chief of the Staff to Lord Roberts in South Africa.
1900.—Commander-in-Chief in South Africa.
1902.—Concluded peace at Vereeniging: received viscountcy and grant of £50,000.
1902-9.—Commander-in-Chief in India.
1905.—His insistence on his authority led to resignation of the viceroy, Lord Curzon.
1911.—British Agent and Consul-General in Egypt.
1914, 5 August.—Secretary of State for War.

a day less than Tommy was earning: "I worked with my two elder brothers and when they filled the tubs up I used to take a full one to the Pass by and bring an empty one back."

Patriotism was not a novel notion to these young working men of Barnsley and district when the tentacles of war finally wrapped themselves around Britain, for the elementary school curriculum, which they had all been subjected to, left enough room for a healthy respect of the Union flag and for the discipline of Physical Training.

"We were practically training for soldiering when we were seven years old. I went to Silkstone school and the parson used to come and say a few prayers. After he'd gone we'd do a few lessons like writing and then we went out. As you went out of the door you picked up some dumbells. Well we'd have a quarter of an hour on that, then we were out and the Union Jack would be flying. All the lads and lasses would stand around and sing songs like, 'Britannia the pride of the Ocean, Home of the Brave and the free.' When I got to 9 or 10 years old the Boy Scouts were starting, well we went into the Boy Scouts as well. All training for soldiering practically. It came in handy later on."

14/752 L/Corporal "Ossie" Burgess, 'D' Company, 14th Y & L Regiment

What with the P.T. and drill at school and the outdoor life which membership of the Boy Scouts offered it was little wonder that the boys of 9 and 10 when they grew into young men in their late teens and early twenties, should crave for the fresh air, the open space and the freedom which their work down the mines had stolen from them.

They were young, they were fit and they were enthusiastic. In team sports of all kinds they found an outlet for their energies which built up during the long hours underground.

"Before the war I was very interested in sport, football and cricket. We were attached to the Church at Broomhill. You had to go to Church if you wanted to be a member of the team. We used to enjoy going though," recalled Harry Hall.

It was with such men that Lord Kitchener would fashion a New Army. Lord Kitchener had accepted the seals of office as Secretary of State for War a few days after its formal declaration. He was one of Britain's new wave military heroes, his reputation heightened by an adoring British press for his exploits in the Sudan just before the turn of the century. Although he doubtless knew that the British regular and Territorial units would throw up a few heroes of their own in their first few hectic encounters with the Germans, he also knew that they were nowhere near a large enough force to withstand a war of three or four years' duration.

Kitchener had the foresight to realise that the war would last for much longer than people hoped, or indeed expected. He knew that the regulars, already on their way to France, and the Territorials who would follow them, would not be home in time for Christmas, nor would they be for several Christmases to come, if they came home at all.

He was not alone in his belief for Sir Joseph Walton, M.P. for Barnsley, had come to much the same conclusion. At a public meeting at the Harvey Institute on August 14th he said, "I fear it will be a most protracted struggle. I will not venture to predict how long. I pray to God it will not be half as long as I fear it will be; but I fear it will be. This war, in my judgement, will be the most protracted – the most awful war – the world has ever known."

Whatever the length he was adamant as to the final outcome, ". . . we have got to win!"

In Kitchener's mind there was nothing for it but to build a brand new army, an army which would be founded on the twin pillars of national pride and a sense of duty and having as its building blocks the young men of Britain. The plan was to raise an army of 500,000 men based on the already existing structure of the County regimental depots, but even in his wildest dreams he could never have imagined the enormous response to his appeal for the "First Hundred Thousand".

On August 8th the Barnsley Chronicle had published what it thought was a sneak preview of an official government notice.

"The following is a copy of a poster shortly to be published headed by the Royal Arms. An addition of One Hundred Thousand men to His Majesty's Regular Army is immediately necessary in the present grave National Emergency. Lord Kitchener is confident that this appeal will at once be responded to."

It was precise and to the point and didn't bear the immortal headings 'Your King and Country Need You', or 'A Call To Arms', but it was the prelude to an avalanche of slogans and posters which were designed at first to persuade, then to cajole and later to shame men into joining the colours.

Soon after the Chronicle's preview it became almost impossible for people to venture on to the streets without the steady stare of Lord Kitchener peering accusingly out from under the peak of his cap and following them down the road. Wherever they stood his huge, gloved finger searched them out and if it wasn't his image it was his name. By the end of August every motorbus in London displayed the huge, blue-lettered inscription: "Lord Kitchener's appeal; Enlist for the war. Discharged when it is over."

He wanted them and they heeded his call in their droves during the first two weeks of the war. Staff in the Central Recruiting Office in London burnt the candle at both ends to accommodate the influx of willing recruits and even that was not enough. They had to throw open their doors on Sundays to take down the seemingly endless list of names. News of the B.E.F. retreating from Mons with its tail well and truly between its legs helped to lengthen the queues.

While the recruiting staff in London certainly had their work cut out there was a different story to be told in Barnsley. There was no lack of willing volunteers, 53 men had turned up on the first day of the appeal and another 52 on the second day for the York and Lancaster regiment and The King's Own Yorkshire Light Infantry, which also recruited on Barnsley's doorstep. It was simply a matter of inadequate organisation. The recruiting mechanism was unable to cope with the steady stream of men wanting to serve King and Country. One lonely recruiting officer worked under taxing circumstances in one small room at the National Reserve Club. It was surprising that would-be recruits did not turn and go straight back home after observing the poky apology for a recruiting station in Barnsley.

It was hardly the most convincing start to building an army to beat the likes of the well organised and extremely efficient Germans. Not surprisingly, the military authorities became concerned that recruiting in Barnsley was not making the progress that they would have liked, and after certain discussions it was decided to send one more man plus two recruiting sergeants to Barnsley to work in the Territorial Drill

Rise and arm, your country needs you.
Rise and meet your country's foe,
Time is past for idle dreaming,
Time is come to strike the blow,
Let no clinging ties of kindred,
Blind you to your country's weal,
Peace for us and our children,
Now depends upon your steel.
Alice V. Norman, Ardsley.
The Barnsley Independent
August 29th, 1914.

TO THE SHOPKEEPERS OF ENGLAND!

Have you any young men serving at your counter who ought to be serving your Country?

Hall.

Other local authorities meanwhile did not seem to be suffering the same problems as Barnsley. Many cities, towns and County Boroughs, often spurred on by the urgings of local dignitaries, decided that they should take a hand in the recruiting of 'Kitchener's Army'. They would harness the still growing desire to get into khaki by giving Kitchener a ready made battalion of about a thousand men raised and maintained by the authority.

In this way they could also offer the lads from a particular district or from a similar occupation the chance to join a battalion with their mates and, perhaps more importantly, they would be allowed to stay with them. This simple scheme obviated the need for men to be dispersed into other units and proved to be a strong influencing factor in drawing groups of men who may have been put off by the idea of having to make new friends in a battalion far from home. Many young men had never travelled far and the thought of serving with their friends rather than travelling and landing among a regiment full of 'foreigners' would have appealed greatly to would-be volunteers.

Lord Derby, political stalwart of the commercial and industrial north west of England, was in the vanguard of the trend towards what became affectionately termed as the 'Pals' or 'Chums' battalions in the densely populated centres of Northern England.

The Barnsley Chronicle of September 5th published a report of lightning recruiting in Liverpool following an appeal for recruits by Lord Derby.

> *"In half an hour on Monday morning the battalion of Liverpool young men engaged in commercial pursuits – Lord Derby's "Battalion of Pals" – was officially enrolled. Lord Derby with his brother Mr. Ferdinand Stanley, who is to be the Commanding Officer of the new battalion, witnessed the assembling of the recruits and announced that the formation of a second one would immediately be proceeded with. Between 9 and 11 a.m. over 2,000 recruits presented themselves."*

Among the recruits were cotton workers, corn chandlers, shipping clerks, bank clerks, solicitors and Insurance men and they had all been drawn by the promise of being able to stay together. Most of them had a belief, however ill defined, that it was their duty to enlist to secure the future freedom of the British Empire. Some saw the new battalion as an open door which would lead to an exciting world of travel and adventure. There were still others, as there have been and still are in all groups of young men down the ages, who just went along with the crowd, and since the crowd was going to enlist they did too.

Altogether Liverpool was able to raise four battalions of soldiers which became known as the Liverpool 'Pals'.

Liverpool had pioneered a precedent which other cities and towns felt they had to follow and soon it appeared that every local authority from Glasgow to Grimsby and from Salford to Sheffield were attempting to raise their very own home grown battalions. Often they were raised so quickly that the War Office was taken completely by surprise. Pushed to the limits of its resources and far beyond it was unable to place all these new units into the existing system at the same time, so the 'Pals' battalions named themselves until they could be given a County regimental title.

The unofficial names stuck because the men took an almost perverse pride in their amateur status. They were not real soldiers yet, but they believed that they could finish the job that the regulars had started. Their names, Hull 'Sportsmen', Manchester 'Clerks and Warehousemen' and Newcastle 'Railwaymen' told much more about the calibre of the men who had come forward in their country's hour of need than any anonymous official title ever could.

The widespread reporting of the efforts of these unofficial 'raisers' was not lost on Barnsley's patriots and readers of the Chronicle were writing letters like this one published on September 5th, suggesting ways in which the town could enter the race for recruits.

"Pals" for Kitchener's Army.

To the Editor of the Barnsley Chronicle.
 Sir, Here are one or two things the people of Barnsley can 'get busy' with:
 (i) forming bodies of "Pals" to enlist in Kitchener's Army like they are doing in other towns,
 (ii) forming a kind of committee of men unable to enlist, who would help in any way required, any movement for the country's good.
 (iii) Using Cudworth range.
 Yours etc: "Tyke"

It was obvious that "Tyke" wanted to see some action on the recruiting front and in this way the seeds for the establishment of a Barnsley battalion were sown. Civic and local leaders knew there was an untapped reservoir of men in the surrounding area. The send-off which the 'Terriers' had been given was clear evidence that 'War fever' had seized the town and that Barnsley folk were as enthusiastic as any others when it came down to the question of patriotism.

The raising of a local Battalion of Pals would, they thought, attract the men in greater numbers and at the same time they could solve the problem of the poor enlisting arrangements which had so far dogged the recruitment locally. They would arrange that themselves.

Several meetings between the civic leaders and local employers had paved the way for the sending of a telegram to Kitchener offering to provide a battalion of 1,100 men to be recruited from Barnsley and district and although a formal reply had not been received by the beginning of September the spadework of organising a relentless recruiting drive, with public meetings designed to encourage men to take to uniform in the name of 'righteousness and freedom', had begun.

The first of these meetings took place in the Old Picture Palace at Mapplewell on September 1st. Locals from the villages of Mapplewell and Staincross packed the building to the doors to hear Mr. Joseph Hewitt, a man who was to be a prime mover in raising the Battalion, and other council members appeal to the men of the district to show their "true spirit of patriotism".

There in the Mapplewell district they had ample material for the army. Would they not come forward? Mr. Hewitt strenuously urged the youth of the district to "assert themselves in this most righteous cause."

The Mayor, Councillor England, introduced a chilling slant in his appeal for volunteers as he enlightened the audience that, ". . . in an eight or nine hours' journey they could meet the most formidable foe of modern times . . . they should look to their laurels to try and preserve the integrity of the Empire they so loved."

Another speaker, County Councillor J.W.F. Peckett, had evidently gauged the overall mood of the meeting. As he took the platform he said that he was convinced that it was up to every Englishman, "to do his individual part in the great life and death struggle", and he continued, "The Government asked for 500,000 men. In this country there are nine million men between the ages of 25 and 45, and the proportion asked for was

Local solicitor Joseph Hewitt, prime mover and first commander of the Barnsley Pals.

Admiral Lord Charles Beresford wins the hearts of Barnsley men with some well chosen words. Recruits for Kitchener's new volunteer army begin to pour in from Barnsley and District.

Cap badge of the York and Lancaster Regiment "Barnsley's Own". The regiment was raised in 1758 (65th and 84th Foot). During the South African War it formed part of Buller's army in Natal and took part in the battles leading up to the relief of Ladysmith. Barnsley was one of the towns from where it drew recruits.

only 50 in every 1,000. Would they give them?"

The audience were convinced too and speaking with one voice they replied with an emphatic cry of "Yes".

A week later at a meeting of the County Borough Council the Mayor revealed that Lord Kitchener had replied to his telegram and accepted the offer of a battalion of men to be raised in Barnsley.

Now the real work could begin. The councillors and other 'raisers' could talk themselves hoarse and wear out as much leather from the soles of their shoes as they could in travelling from village to village stamping out their message. And since the boats could now be pushed out in earnest to raise the one thousand or so men needed for the Battalion, who better to aid the appeal than a seafaring man?

The visit of Admiral Lord Charles Beresford, who came from London ostensibly to rally new recruits for Kitchener's Army, proved to be a fortuitous stroke of good luck for the local raisers, for his appearance would add weight to the call for a Barnsley Battalion. The attraction of a top flight military speaker, a man who had close contact with those who were conducting the war, drew the crowds like a magnet.

Admiral Beresford was up and out early on Friday 11th September. Leaving the country seat of his host the Earl Fitzwilliam at Wentworth Woodhouse, he had addressed meetings at Wombwell, Ardsley and Darfield before midday.

In Darfield, miners had obtained a field in which to hold the gathering and they sent out a brass band to meet the Admiral's motorcade as it entered the village. He was relaxed as he delivered his speech:

> *"I am doing a sort of light cruise round, and have come to the finest sporting county in England to get recruits. But I am beginning to find my campaign quite unnecessary in Yorkshire, because all the young men are only too eager to join the Colours."*

The phrase, "finest sporting county in England" clinched it. With these few well chosen words Lord Beresford had boosted the already well developed sense of pride which Yorkshiremen have regarding their involvement in sporting activities. How then could the listening miners refuse the call from a man who, in their eyes, obviously knew quality when he saw it.

Lord Beresford had been due to speak in Cudworth but his trip had been cancelled. It was perhaps a wise move on the part of the Admiral because one member of Cudworth council may have seen to it that his visit would have been anything but plain sailing as had been demonstrated at a Cudworth council meeting on September 8th. Discussing the advantage of a proposed Barnsley Battalion one of the council members, a Mr. Lambert, declared that if he were ten years younger he "should be off" to which Mr. Taylor, a Labour member, replied:

> *"To my mind it is a move on the part of Lord Kitchener to take away the young men who are helping to support homes with large families. Up to the present young men in lodgings or who have no direct dependants have gone, and I take it he wants the others now. There are homes to be kept up."*

A heated exchange took place and another voice of dissent was drowned out as the council accused Mr. Taylor of being unpatriotic and then voted to support the scheme. Needless to say when the Chairman asked for a show of hands for those in favour, Mr. Taylor's arms stayed firmly crossed.

Barnsley's Member of Parliament, Sir Joseph Walton, heard no such voices of dissent as he rose to speak on the political intrigue which had characterised international events in the decade or so before the war. Speaking in Wombwell's Congregational Schoolroom on September 14th he added his support for the raising of a 'home grown' battalion.

> *"Here in this district they are going to have a new Barnsley Battalion, and those who wished to go along with their pals would be given an opportunity of so doing. I hope this force will be speedily raised."*

September 17th, 1914 was to prove to be an historic date for the town of Barnsley for the new Barnsley Battalion was officially launched at a 'great' evening meeting at the Public Hall. The meeting drew one of the largest crowds ever recorded for a public gathering in the town. There were so many people that they spilled out into the open air into Peel Square where they were able to hold further speeches.

> "I swear, by Almighty God, that I will be faithful and bear true Allegiance to His Majesty King George V., his Heirs, and Successors, and that I will, as in duty bound, honestly and faithfully defend His Majesty, his Heirs, and Successors, in Person, Crown, and Dignity, against all enemies, and will observe and obey all orders of His Majesty, his Heirs, and Successors, and of the Generals and Officers set over me.
> So help me God."

Above: *The Soldier's Oath mouthed by new recruits whilst holding a Bible. Usually conducted by the chaplain.*

> *"The gathering in the Public Hall was thoroughly representative of Barnsley. Packed on the ground floor and in the galleries were men of every conceivable calling; many artisans had, perforce, to attend in their working attire but all were assembled as one united body for one common purpose and oppressive as the room became the enthusiasm of the mass of humanity never waned."*

The 'mass of humanity' heard a speech from Lord Beresford who had made a special return trip to launch the Battalion. He had also managed to squeeze in a trip to Hoyland to beat the drum before moving on to the Public Hall. At Hoyland Lord Beresford had again appealed to the Yorkshire spirit but confessed that although he had come to 'awaken enthusiasm', he had "never been in any place that less needed waking up."

The tone of his speech at the Public Hall was much the same and Sir Joseph Walton, Earl Wharncliffe, the Mayor and several other speakers only emphasised his views.

The Mayor pointed out that the response to Kitchener's call had been greater than in any other district, presumably since the attestation arrangements had been somewhat improved. He was sure that the men of Barnsley would respond immediately to a fresh call for recruits.

Meanwhile the German armies continue their advance through France. Seen here resting before the Battle of the Marne.

> "I have pledged your honour . . . to provide for Barnsley and district a Battalion to form a part of our own Regiment of the York and Lancasters. This offer has been accepted by Lord Kitchener and I know when asked – and I am going to ask you soon – you will respond, as Barnsley and district has always responded, with one voice."

Sir Joseph Walton followed Lord Beresford's example set a few days earlier when he had appealed to the sporting prowess of Yorkshire men and made a speech echoing similar sentiments. He was perfectly certain that, ". . . the Barnsley men would exhibit in the

33

Lieutenant Colonel Joseph Hewitt, commander of the First Barnsley Battalion.

field of battle the same dash and resolution and tenacity that they had exhibited so conspicuously on the football field."

What he failed to tell them was that war, unlike football, was not a game.

Two days later on Saturday, September 19th Mr. Hewitt seized the opportunity to appeal to a captive audience of sports fans as he made a half-time appeal during Barnsley's football match against Grimsby. Speaking to the crowd from one end of the grandstand at Oakwell Mr. Hewitt said, "You are here today enjoying a game of football while others, your brothers, are out at the front fighting your country's battles. Does it not appeal to your hearts that those of you who could go there to help them ought to go?"

In the days before large public address systems and dwindling numbers through the turnstiles other speakers gave forth from the four corners of the playing field to the masses thronging the terraces.

The idea proved to be effective as some young men followed the speakers back to the Public Hall after the game to enlist, although it was not as effective as the appeal made by the Lord Mayor of Leeds during the half-time break in Leeds United's game against Fulham. On that occasion a few weeks earlier, 200 men strode forward to receive an armlet of ribbon in the national colours from the Lady Mayoress and subsequently signed up for the duration.

While the Mayor, Mr. Hewitt and local councillors worked hard at thumping the tub in aid of the Barnsley Battalion, other forces equally effective in shaping the views of the Barnsley public were at work. The entertainments world had geared itself up to the patriotic cause by staging emotive productions designed to wring the last drop of duty and honour out of their audiences. One such production was "The King of Men", billed as a romantic military drama, which ran at the Theatre Royal twice nightly for six nights from the 7th September. It was bolstered on Tuesday and Saturday by a production called "A Soldier's Oath", in three scenes and a prologue.

At the Pavilion, "All the latest from the front" was the boast and if the "latest" included the whole truth about the Allied position on the eve of the Battle of the Marne then the audiences who turned up at the Globe Picture House would need every scrap of inner strength and courage which the cast of "Honour Awakened" could impart.

The Barnsley Battalion also had its rivals for the attentions of the young men of the district. The Chronicle may have been a champion of the cause to raise the 'Pals' but it still published a classified advertisement which was tucked away in the 'situations vacant' column. There, among the advertised vacancies for workers in the millinery trade and an appeal for a vocalist for Brierley Working Men's Club, (Sunday evenings, 7–10 p.m. – rate 7/6), was an advertisement which ran:

> "Recruits are needed for the 6th (Service) Battalion of the King's Own Yorkshire Light Infantry. The battalion is being formed at Woking under the command of Major C.R.I. Brooke."

Woking? Where was that? The advertisement never really stood a chance now that there was a local battalion to join.

After the official launch of the Barnsley 'Pals' Battalion there followed a frenzied round of public recruitment meetings in all the districts around Barnsley. The General Purposes Committee of the Borough Council reported in their minutes for the 22nd September the suggestion that:

> "... Ward Meetings for the purpose of recruiting for the Battalion be held in each of the Wards of the Borough on Friday the 25th instant".

Before that there were other unofficial meetings such as the one on Wednesday afternoon the 23rd September on the Recreation Ground at Little Houghton. Some 2,000 men were present, and as the day shift had just surfaced from the depths of Houghton Main colliery many men in the crowd were still in their pit muck. They heard their local branch representative of the Yorkshire Miners' Association, Mr. T.

At last it is official, the letter of appointment to command.

W. Illsley, who was also Chairman of Darfield Urban District Council, say that as a trades unionist he was ". . . heartily in favour of Lord Kitchener's recruiting campaign." He put his weight behind the drive and hoped that the miners would respond to the call.

Mr. Hewitt, the local solicitor who had expended so much time and energy rallying recruits, was rewarded for his efforts with the rank of Acting Colonel of the new Battalion of 'Pals' and he attended the meeting in his new capacity as Commanding Officer. He brought with him his new Acting Major and second in command, William Emsley Raley, an Alderman on the Council, and it was Raley who attempted to curry favour with the miners.

"You know very well that no-one makes better soldiers than the brave lads from our coal-fields. Why? Simply because every day you work down below, you are in danger. You know it. Who have done more good work, who have been greater heroes than those who have gone down the pit from time to time to rescue lads and men in these explosions? You men face death every day of your lives, and on the field of battle you will be braver than any there.

"I believe the lads who are coming forward now will be the cream of the Army and I believe we will show that we shall have a battalion which will rank among the very first so far as bravery is concerned."

Any further communication on this subject should be addressed to—

The Secretary, War Office, London, S.W.

and the following number quoted.

100/Infantry/551. (M.S.1.)

War Office, London, S.W.

20th November, 1914.

Sir,

I am directed to inform you that you have been appointed to command the Barnsley Battalion York and Lancaster Regiment, with effect from the 17th of September, 1914,

and I am to request that you will take up your duties as soon as possible.

You will be granted the temporary rank of Lieutenant Colonel in the Army.

The requisite notification as above will appear in the London Gazette in due course.

I am,

Sir,

Your obedient Servant,

Col.

for Military Secretary.

Lieutenant Colonel J.Hewitt,
Barnsley Battalion York and Lancaster Regt.
B A R N S L E Y .

After the speeches Mr. Illsley told the men: "Colonel Hewitt has just told me that if at Houghton we get a company's strength, or two companies' strength, that our men will be kept together. He assures me that just as you have worked together as men in the pit, you will be able to work together as soldiers."

After the singing of the National Anthem at the end of the meeting there was a rush for the colliery offices where almost 200 men handed in their names, over 50 more than had enlisted from Houghton Main since Kitchener's first appeal in early August.

The following morning the Houghton recruits were taken by motor bus to the Oaks colliery disaster memorial on Doncaster Road and from there they marched, as best they could, to meet the detachment of 120 men who had already enlisted with the 'Pals'. The ex-Houghton Main miners joined the company and marched with them back to the Public Hall, sometimes bursting into a spirited rendition of "It's a long way to Tipperary." For many of the ex-miners it was the first time they had sung the song on the

Raw recruits being knocked into shape at the Queen's Ground. Although used for military drill by the Territorials and now the Pals, it is far from ideal because of the sloping terrain.

march, but it would certainly not be their last. Many a long mile in England, and later France, would pass underfoot to the strains of that tune. There were no uniforms, there were no rifles. These were but promises. They were simply dressed in sober civilian suits; but there was one saving grace. Nearly all the men sported the large, floppy tweed flat caps so beloved of the men of 1914, and these at least gave the company a strangely comic uniformity.

That night, at another meeting at Hunningley Lane School in Stairfoot, another 20 men came forward to join the ranks of the 'Pals'. The snowball was well and truly rolling.

As Joseph Hewitt had spoken to the miners of Houghton Main the previous Wednesday afternoon, a letter was being drafted at the Headquarters of Northern Command at York informing the Mayor that the Army council had given its official blessing to the raising of a battalion in Barnsley. It was the news which many people in the town had been waiting for and like the proud parents of a newborn child, the late September issue of the Chronicle proclaimed the birth of "The Barnsley Battalion" to its readers and used the announcement to make a further appeal for recruits which tugged at the male ego:

> *"The enlistment of recruits in the Barnsley Battalion is rapidly progressing and all men are earnestly requested to join this Battalion, as it is an opportunity which will never present itself again for men to prove themselves men.*
> *"Enlistment in this Battalion, which of course will form part of Lord Kitchener's Army, takes place daily at the Harvey Institute between the hours of 10 and 1, and 2 and 5."* **Barnsley Chronicle, 26th September 1914**

The 100 or so recruits who had marched to meet the contingent from Houghton Main, later to become better known as the 'Houghton Main Mob', had a distinct advantage over the 'new boys'. Some of the very earliest volunteers were, after all, 'veterans' of almost a week's standing and had benefited from a little preliminary training.

Ninety of these amateur soldiers had been put through their paces early on the Tuesday morning at the Queen's Ground. For the curious crowd which had turned out to witness this first public airing of the much publicised Barnsley Battalion it must have appeared that a pre-requisite for joining Kitchener's New Army was the possession of a set of limbs which were independent of the brain's instructions as 90 pairs of 'left' feet tried valiantly to come to terms with the intricacies of parade ground drill.

Still, the Chronicle described their general physique and bearing as 'excellent' and once all the initial kinks had been smoothed over it confidently predicted that, ". . . before long they will prove themselves very efficient soldiers." The organisers had got started on the training before receiving the official orders from the War Office but as Kitchener had already accepted the Mayor's offer the Army Council's approval was a mere formality.

The lack of officers and training instructors with genuine military experience was certainly a problem for the new unit. The War Office had enough of a headache coping with the demands from the already large number of Service battalions which had apparently sprouted from nowhere almost overnight in response to Kitchener's first call. Along with this was the mountain of paperwork which accompanied the formation of so many locally raised battalions. Like a circus juggler who had just put one ball too many in the air, it could do little more than attempt to prevent the whole thing from coming to earth with a thunderous crash. Inundated by urgent pleas for supplies, equipment and advice on how to transform 1,000 or so assorted civilians into a well disciplined unit of the British Army, the War Office reply was to virtually give 'carte blanche' to people like the Mayor of Barnsley to make their own arrangements regarding the appointment of officers, non-commissioned officers and initial training schemes, until such time as the Army could absorb them.

Having no regular officers, and because the first Kitchener Battalions had taken the pick of the few experienced officers available, the Mayor went ahead and picked his own in consultation with other interested parties. When the first batch of battalion orders were published in the Chronicle, there appeared with them a list of temporary officers which reflected the work put in by various local councillors and businessmen.

Joseph Hewitt, because of his enthusiasm in rallying recruits and his knowledge gleaned from his time spent as an officer with the 'Terriers', was already established as the Commanding Officer. The Mayor himself became Honorary Colonel, while Alderman William Emsley Raley had been appointed acting Major and second in command. The local business and commercial interests were represented in the ranks of the junior officers. Thomas Guest, a prosperous local grocer and a man who had received three stripes and two wounds in the Boer War, was made a temporary Second Lieutenant alongside J. Normansell, in private life an engineer. G. H. Hudson, an antique dealer and P. H. di Marco the General Manager of the Barnsley Tram Corporation, were also appointed junior officers. Councillor Charles Plumpton Hon. Secretary and Treasurer of Barnsley Patriotic Fund was appointed temporary 2nd Lieutenant Supernumerary.

The Harvey Institute became the Battalion Headquarters, the Public Hall was requisitioned for military purposes, namely the accommodation and feeding of the men, while the Queen's Ground was reserved for drill and Drum Head Services, led by the Rev. Richard Huggard, acting battalion Chaplain.

The rank and file were for the most part miners, and over 70 years after the event recall quite clearly those heady joining-up days.

Above: *Popular officer of the First Barnsley Pals, Lieutenant, later Captain Tom Guest. Veteran of the war in South Africa where he served as a Sergeant, Tom Guest is invaluable, as an officer with combat experience. He is to be one of the first over the top on July 1st, 1916, Battle of the Somme.*

Tommy Oughton went down the pit at Mitchells Main on the afternoon shift on Tuesday 29th September, a day which was to radically alter his life. He had often thought of joining the Army, especially when the fever first took hold of the young men of Wombwell, and, during a slack time down the pit that

Left: *First headquarters and billets for the Pals, Harvey Institute on Eldon Street.*

afternoon, his thoughts turned to it again.

"We were waiting about for the tubs and of course the colliers were grumbling. It struck me that night there was a recruiting meeting down at the Wesleyan Chapel as it was then. Not long after, the deputy came round, they called him Watkins. I was sitting down and he said "Now then Tom, how's things?", I said "Oh not so good, we're waiting for the tubs and I don't feel so grand. I feel like going home." I expect he thought it would make a man less to wait on the tubs and he wrote me a note to go out of the pit because I was sick, course I wasn't sick at all it was this meeting I had thought about.* **Tommy Oughton, 13th Y & L Regiment**

P. H. di Marco, local businessman with military connections is appointed Second Lieutenant in the First Barnsley Battalion.

Tommy got home around six o'clock in the evening and with the meeting due to start at 7.30 he washed and dressed quickly and set out for Wombwell's Wesleyan chapel. Addressing the meeting were the, by now, usual selection of local dignitaries.

"Colonel Hewitt was there in uniform and there were one or two more. Then there were the local personalities, like Percy Miles Walker, who was the chief official in Wombwell, he was a solicitor, and various other local people. We had a Bulldog who was the Barnsley battalion mascot and this Bulldog was on the stage with Colonel Hewitt. When they asked for volunteers there must have been at least 30 of us straight away."

The keen young men were told to report at Wombwell Town Hall the following morning. Tommy duly turned up and joined the other recruits standing outside the Town Hall waiting for instructions before the trip to Battalion Headquarters in Barnsley.

"There was other recruiting going on and if there were any volunteers they used to get into Tommy Lee's charabancs and they would take them to Pontefract. They were riding free. We had to pay fourpence to go to Barnsley on the train. When Percy Miles Walker came up, I don't know what made me do it but I said, "Look here Mr. Walker, when volunteers have been going to Pontefract

An early Drum Head Service held at Queen's Ground. Officers and men of the First Barnsley stand bareheaded as Rev. Huggard leads the hymn singing.

they've had a free bus to take them. Have we got to pay our own fare to go to Barnsley?" Well he studied and said "I see what you mean." He put his hand in his pocket and pulled out a sovereign, an old gold sovereign. He said "I think this will pay for all your fares." He looked round us. Some of the lads cheered him.

"We knew what time the train came but as we were going down someone said "What about a pint?" It was only three or four pence at the time and they decided they would spend it on that. Well I had the money. We got down to the Railway Hotel and went in. Being teetotal I ordered a mineral water and 5 packets of Woodbines at 1d a packet. I put the sovereign on the table and told the landlord that it was for the beer for them. I had no idea how much it cost but nobody got any change. They all got their beer though. Everybody supped up and the train pulled in while we were going down the steps to the station. We got into the first carriage there and it was First Class. We hadn't booked any tickets just straight into the train.

"When this Porter came in none of us had a ticket so naturally he held the Train up and fetched the Stationmaster. When he came in our carriage he looked round and took four names, mine and three more besides. We told him we were recruits and that we hadn't had time to get tickets or notice which carriages we were getting into. I don't know whether he believed us or not."

The train then continued on its way and Tommy and the rest of the group promptly forgot about the incident. Others would not, as he was to find out later. On their arrival at the Public Hall they found another 30 men had reported from the surrounding districts. They were ushered inside and then began the solemn business of attestation.

"The parson was there, he was called Huggard. He swore us in. We got six at a time holding the Bible and we had to hold it and repeat after him until we were sworn in. We got the King's shilling then we were dismissed for the day and told to report next morning. Naturally I went home. I'll always remember that night. They had all gone to bed except me and my dad. I was just going to bed and I just turned round and said "Goodnight dad", and I can see him now. My mother had a sewing machine underneath the window sill and he was standing there with his hand on the sewing machine. He said "Goodnight lad but just think on, after tonight you're not always forced to have a bed to go to." I remembered those words many a time in the next three or four years."

Councillor Charles Plumpton is appointed Second Lieutenant for the First Barnsley. Editor of the Barnsley Chronicle, from 1909 to 1923.

The night after Harry Hall had enlisted he also heard his father's views on the subject of his joining the Army, although they were couched in terms a little different from those of Tommy Oughton's father.

Harry was 17 years old and he saw his joining the Barnsley Pals as being the passport to a tour of the continent of Europe at the Army's expense. War was still quite distant for the young Harry Hall, his thoughts were more on travel and escaping the haulage work at Houghton Main Colliery.

"There were four or five of us all at the same time all of an age. One followed another. We thought it was perhaps a holiday out of the pit, a change of life. I was under age but I was accepted. Wilf Paxton was with me. We'd always been pals from being at school.

He was with me when we all joined up together. There were four of us really near to each other. We'd do anything for each other. We stayed in the same platoon until the beginning of 1917."
Harry Hall, 13th Y & L Regiment

Harry and his friend tried the Territorial Drill Hall at Wath first but they were told that they could not take any more men. Perhaps being from the mining industry the Territorial recruiting officers were loath to take men who could assist the war effort just as effectively by producing coal, but when they tried

Left: Jack Normansell is preparing for his final examination for certificate of colliery manager. Drops the pen and takes up the sword, receives a wound in the face from a grenade in July 1916; returns to France at beginning of 1917 and is killed in March of that year.

Barnsley they found no such qualms there. Harry did have one slight problem but it was nothing to do with his job.

"We went to the Public Hall in Barnsley. The recruiting officer fixed my friends up then he got to me. He said "How old are you?", I said "I'm 17 and a half." He said "Have a walk round that table and see if you're not 18 when you come back."

All over the country thousands of boys, just like Harry all below what should have been the minimum age 19, were initiated into the strange new custom of walking round tables, or going out of doors and coming back in, to increase their age. Unprincipled recruiting sergeants, keen to fill the ranks, often seemed to hold the key to the miraculous addition of a year or two to the age of a lad, or an inch or two to the length of his body. It was a practice frowned upon by some commentators as an article in a late September edition of The Glasgow Herald reproduced in the Barnsley Chronicle proved:

"Apart from the moral aspect of the question there is a military view which is highly important and should not be disregarded and this is that only in very exceptional cases is a youngster at any rate 18 anything but a source of anxiety and trouble to an Army in the field . . .
"The War Office . . . would be well advised in its own interests to issue some sort of warning to this effect. For the trouble is that there is every chance that a bright youngster of 17 who enlists now may 6 months hence be sent to the front and have to face the rigours to which grown men may soon become inured but which will often send a boy quickly on the sick list, where, to put it bluntly, he is more trouble than he is worth."

The Hall family did not take the Glasgow Herald but it didn't need a newspaper to tell Harry's mother that he was only a boy and that he should not have joined the Army. Harry went back home after he had taken his oath as most of the local recruits were doing, and later that night he overheard a conversation between his parents.

"That night I was lying in bed and I could hear my mum and dad talking. My mum was saying "You'll have to go and get him back". My dad said "He's made his bed and he'll

The Hall family left to right: Tom, 9th K.O.Y.L.I. killed on first day of the Somme; Arthur, Canterbury Regiment, A.N.Z.A.C. killed at Gallipoli; Walter, 9th York and Lancaster Regiment. Kneeling in front of his dad is Harry who joins up under age in the Barnsley Pals.

Above: Rest between drill at Queen's Ground. Officers stand surrounded by seated recruits – caps off. Relatives and friends look on. Of the three standing officers, centre. Rev. Huggard would lose one son, 13th Barnsley; Raley, would lose two sons; and Lieutenant Colonel Hewitt, one son, killed in action.

> *lie on it". That was that. One of my brothers, Tom, had already enlisted. My other brother who went to New Zealand joined up out there and Walter joined up a bit later. There were four of us and we were all going. I should have had more sense because it was a big thing for mother."*

Harry however, at 17 young and enthusiastic and not then blessed with the benefits of hindsight, was a member of the Pals and he aimed to stay with them. Others gave in to parental pressure.

> *"There was a fellow with us, they called him Martin, he was a big hefty lad. When he went to be examined they said they'd never had a better specimen in front of them but 2 or 3 days later his mother came and chased him round the Public Hall with her umbrella. She 'brayed' him down the steps and he never came back again. He was twenty-ish. He got away with it. How he did it I don't know."* **Harry Hall, 13th Y & L Regiment**

Ernest Bell and Harry Gay, who had been brought up together and had worked together, naturally decided that they would join up together.

> *"Everybody felt that we really ought to join up in the younger age group. We joined on the 3rd October and enlisted at the Public Hall. We told the boss, the Borough engineer, that we were going to join and he was very pleased. We both passed 'A-1' and we'd to take our clothes and everything to the Public Hall."* **13/64 Private Ernest Bell, 'A' Company, 13th Y & L Regiment**

On the very day that Ernest and Harry Gay had thrown in their lot with the Pals, the Chronicle editorial noted that 'the progress made by our new recruits continues to be distinctly satisfactory. There seems to be no doubt that the infantry will be quite fit to take the field well within the limit of time prescribed by Lord Kitchener.'

The two Corporation stonemasons were just a very small part of the 150 men who had enlisted since the meeting at the Hunningley Lane Schools on September 24th, making the total number of volunteers near the 400 mark. But still the rallying and the speeches went on to rouse the groups of young men who were still to be seen promenading the streets of Barnsley on Saturday and Sunday evenings and queuing up to get into the Picture Palaces.

As the Barnsley Battalion reaches full strength in October 1914 the opposing armies reach the coast and dig in.

Left: A German advance patrol in Belgium takes time out to pluck some poultry.

The speakers on the platforms were aiming their message at the men of the town particularly. The response from the colliery districts had, so far, been favourable but then they had more of a reason to escape the shackles of the work. The men of the town, in shops or other commercial enterprises, needed more of a push to leave their jobs. One of the men of the town who needed no prompting was Harry Scargill, a well known and respected draper who carried out his business from a shop in Eldon Street. Upon his enlistment Harry Scargill saw fit to take up space in the Chronicle to deliver the following message to his loyal clientele.

EUROPEAN WAR

"Having joined the Barnsley Battalion of Lord Kitchener's Army my business will be left in the hands of Miss Scargill during my absence which, I trust, will only be for a short period. Customers can rely upon having the best attention and I take this opportunity of thanking all patrons for past favours." **Harry Scargill**

Few who read the message would remember it as little more than a courteous gesture by a local shop-keeper, but it was to take on a far greater significance than any would ever imagine.

By Friday October 3rd, 1,043 men of all ranks were enrolled in the Barnsley Pals. In a little over three weeks the small County Borough had recruited nearly all of the required troop strength of 1,100 men. It had not been quite the 'lightning recruiting' witnessed in the more densely populated cities of Liverpool, Manchester or, for that matter, nearby Sheffield, but then Barnsley was considerably smaller than her South Yorkshire neighbour.

The Barnsley Pals were the same as the many other local battalions of the New Army in almost every other respect. Most were sadly lacking in uniforms, rifles and other essential items of equipment usually associated with soldiering. Still that did not diminish the great sense of pride which went with being a new member of Kitchener's Army, even if in the early days, that soldier looked exactly the same as any other man walking the streets of Barnsley. These men had joined to do a job and they determined to go about it with a spirit that would stir the hearts of their fellow towns-people. The town of Barnsley had entered the struggle.

Left: The enemy are now just across the water, a beach patrol at Ostend.

Chapter Three

Silkstone camp

"The Barnsley Battalion"
"Company 'tion" the words ring out, each man in the blue clad line,
With head erect, stands smartly up, straight as a mountain pine.
"Left turn! Quick march!" They're off again, with firm and eager tread.
They wheel, deploy, and turn about, till the palest face is red.
But little reck these Barnsley lads, for though the training's tough,
With alacrity they've cast aside, the pick, the hammer, the pen,
Who wanted to stay inactive, when Britain had called for men?
The fighting blood of our fathers still courses through our veins,
And he who attempts to check the flow, the glory of England stains.
The Barnsley Battalion, Briton is ready to a man,
To meet your foes and show them to despise you's a silly plan.
When victory from the skies of Peace, dispels war's gloomy pall,
Barnsley's sons will take their place with the rest on honour's scroll."
                                        Barnsley Chronicle 28th October, 1914 A.C.

AN UNKNOWN BARNSLEY WAR POET wrote the above under the initials A.C. Did he, like other well known soldier poets of the Great War, change his patriotic tune to one of bitterness as the horror of it all sank in?

"As I'm an old regular, I'm not in the habit of asking anyone to volunteer for anything in the army, but I'm going to give you a bit of advice. In a week's time there will be a notice going up asking for volunteers for signallers. If you've any intelligence at all, I would advise you to volunteer for that. If you do I'll be your instructor and the only time that you'll do any parades is when the Battalion parades. You'll be excused all duties . . . you'll have no fatigues to do or guard duties."

With these few words of wisdom 'Old' Tom Lax had made Tommy Oughton think hard about the training which lay ahead for the raw recruits of the Barnsley Pals Battalion. Still flushed with feelings of patriotism, along with the hope that they would attract the admiring glances of the townspeople, few of the recruits would have troubled themselves with thoughts concerning military training; that age-old process of producing an effective fighting force from so much human raw material capable of giving battle.

Tom Lax knew otherwise. He knew that the life that lay ahead for Tommy Oughton would not be all uniforms and glamour, for he had given 21 years of his life in the service of the Regular Army during which time he had risen to the rank of Signals Sergeant. Old Tom Lax had heard the name Tommy Oughton mentioned as a small group of a dozen or so recruits trooped down Doncaster Road on their way to the Public Hall in Barnsley from Wombwell. He had turned to the eighteen-years-old youth and asked him if he were any relation to old Tom Oughton, the billiards player. Upon learning that Tommy was the eldest son of the local billiards champion the Signals Sergeant latched on to him and advised him to volunteer.

In the absence of officers with Regular Army experience, much of the responsibility for the initial work fell on the ageing shoulders of the 'old sweats' such as Tom Lax.

"The Sergeant Majors were all 'old timers' who had been called up to take charge of us. One was the caretaker at the Bank at the top of Market Hill, Company Sergeant Major Coates. The other chap came from Darton and he was the Battalion Sergeant Major." **Ernest Bell, 13th Y & L Regiment**

Sergeant Major Knapton had been made Acting Battalion Sergeant Major. These 'dug out' non-commissioned officers were past their military prime, indeed most of them had last seen service amid the parched panoramas of South Africa at the turn of the century. They had come out of retirement, or had left the jobs that would have occupied their last few working years, to serve the nation during the crisis. However, the military knowledge and experience which they had gained during their encounters with the Boers was to be of little use in the trench warfare of the next four years.

Sound reasons were given as to the purpose of the training which commenced as soon as the men had enlisted. These were pointed out by the regular contributor to the Barnsley Chronicle, a man who went by the pen name 'Old Volunteer'.

"The main objective is the development of a soldierly spirit, which enables a man to bear fatigue, privation, and danger cheerfully, a spirit which animates a man with a sense of honour, gives him confidence in his officers and his comrades; trains him to obey orders, or to act in the absence of orders for the advantage of his regiment under all conditions and gives him such a degree of courage that in the stress of battle he will use his weapons most effectively in order to defeat the enemy, success in battle being the supreme test and purpose of the present training." Old Volunteer went on further to expound . . . *"The formation of fours and elementary training in march discipline are all essential factors in the production of a competent soldier."*

There was also another very good reason for the whole emphasis at that period being placed upon squad drill and route marches – they had little else to occupy their time, for there were no weapons. No rifles, no machine guns, no ammunition, or for that matter, any other items of equipment with which to train. Marching could be easily executed without equipment, or even a uniform, which was just as well, for the Battalion had neither.

They were, however, enthusiastic and they needed to be to cope with their first chaotic weeks of army life. Most of the Battalion were billeted in the Public and Arcade Halls, but a few lucky men like Tommy Oughton and Harry Hall were allowed to sleep at home at first. They had to report every morning at their temporary headquarters where they joined the other men like Ernest Bell who, in the words of Colonel Hewitt were already, 'sleeping under the King's roof.

"You were more or less at liberty at first, as long as you were there for parade next morning. We used to come home three or four nights a week, as long as we caught the first train back in the morning. There was a train about half past seven from Wombwell." **Harry Hall, 13th Y & L Regiment**

For some members of the Barnsley Battalion the comfort of their own beds, for others the rigours of sleeping upon the hard boards of the Harvey Institute.

"We were sleeping on the floor, some in the main hall and some on the balcony. We just had a couple of blankets." **Ernest Bell, 13th Y & L Regiment**

Each man was issued with just one well-worn blanket which did little to ward off the draughts which whistled through and around the boards. It didn't take long for the men to realise that if they doubled up with a friend they could put one blanket on the floor and the other on top of them, thus making life a little more tolerable.

"We'd been there about a week and wondered what the devil we'd joined up for, just to spend our nights trying to sleep on that balcony. Later, we got a bag full of straw each and that made it a bit more comfortable." **Ernest Bell, 13th Y & L Regiment**

If the sleeping arrangements were primitive at least the feeding of the Pals was more tolerable. Working on a commercial basis the Barnsley British Co-operative Society organised the catering for the Battalion. This responsible task was entrusted to Mr. Walter Bates, the head of the Co-op's bakery department.

There were a variety of reports concerning the edibility of the food served up, some thought it poor,

The Pals are left in no doubt as to which side God favours in this conflict. Rev. Huggard conducts a Drum Head Service at Queen's Ground, September 1914. Huggard stands surrounded by Pals officers, none of whom will lead the Barnsley lads against the Germans.

others thought it first class. Such differing views were no doubt due to the individual's experience pre-enlistment. There is, however, one thing upon which they all agreed – there never seemed enough to satisfy their hearty appetites. Whatever the verdicts upon the quantity or quality of food there appeared to be more than enough to keep the youthful hunger pangs at bay, at least on paper. Interviewed by the Chronicle, the Co-op's gastronomic wizard, Mr. Bates, revealed that the Pals daily ate their way through 600 loaves of bread, half a ton of vegetables, 70 large plum puddings, a hundredweight of butter, and when beef was on the menu, 500lbs of it.

The Chronicle observer was particularly impressed with the speed of Mr. Bates and his staff of half a dozen 'expert' carvers and several serving ladies who managed to get the first meals for the 1,100 strong unit onto the tables within 45 minutes of orders being placed. The whole spectacle moved the reporter to remark, "What Mr. Bates does not know about the culinary arts is not worth knowing."

Even so the tempting aroma of baking pastry wafting down the Arcade from Raynor's cafe proved irresistible to Harry Hall and his group of Pals. When duties allowed they would slope off to purchase hot meat pies fresh from the oven. Mouths watering, they would stand at the counter and watch the baker pour thick gravy over the pies from a container resembling a watering can.

Each day the recruits were roused at 6 a.m. and after a brief wash in the few bowls provided, they would form up in the square, which was situated in Regent Street, opposite the County Court. From there they would march the short distance to the Queen's Ground to begin drilling at seven o'clock. Old Volunteer spent a day watching the Battalion hard at work and noted that this first session went on until breakfast time at 8.15. "Then from half past ten until twelve they are at it again and in the afternoon they have two hours more vigorous drill. In this way the Battalion promises to successfully exemplify their complete and practical grip of the theory and principles known as 'quick training in wartime'."

Old Volunteer seemed satisfied that the unit would not need more than the six months' minimum training before it was ready for active service.

Because of the nearness to Barnsley town centre spectators arrived daily at the sloping parade ground to watch the Battalion, wheeling, advancing, extending from the centre and then from the right . . . now at the double, executed with varying degrees of precision.

BARNSLEY BATTALION.

Y. and L.

✝

Order of Service.—Church Parade.

HYMN. "O God our help in ages past."

THE LORD'S PRAYER (all recite).

HYMN. "Fight the good fight."

4. ADDRESS.

5. HYMN. "Onward, Christian soldiers."

6. BENEDICTION.

GOD SAVE THE KING.

"Chronicle," Printers, Barnsley.

**Tommy Oughton
13th Y & L.**

After the exertions of the day a welcome tea was taken at 6 p.m., but the work was not over. There were duties and fatigues to perform between half past seven and 'lights out' at ten fifteen. Each night twelve men would be assigned guard duty at the Harvey Institute, keeping watch over the uncomfortable slumbers of their comrades. This was undertaken without the benefit of rifles and ammunition. One of the sentry posts was the Eldon Street entrance. Harry Hall recalls one night of sentry duty vividly:

"I had to stop any suspicious characters from entering the hall, but most of the suspicious ones were already inside. There was a big rubber mat that covered the whole entrance and I fell asleep on it. The next thing I knew there was somebody kicking me – it was a policeman and he wanted to know what I was doing there. I told him that I was supposed to be guarding the Public Hall." **Harry Hall, 13th Y & L Regiment**

Happily for Harry his misdemeanour was not reported. Preventing undesirables from entering the Public Hall was nevertheless a problem which any number of sentries, asleep or awake, did not appear to solve.

Several men complained that items of clothing had vanished while they were busy going about their duties or while they were out on route marches. The reason became apparent in a case which came before Mayor England, presiding over the Borough Court on December 31st. On trial was Joseph Allen, cuttingly described by the Chronicle as ". . . a young man of the ne'er do well type," charged with stealing a civilian overcoat belonging to Private Walter Stimson.

Leaving his coat in one of the rooms in the Public Hall, Private Stimson had gone on guard on the evening of December 18th. When he returned his coat had gone. It came to light a day later when Joseph Allen attempted to pawn it at the shop of John Guest and Sons but the manager, dissatisfied with Allen's explanation as to how he had come by the coat, kept it and refused to pay any money. Allen tried again four days later but this time the manager held him until the police arrived. The Chronicle reported the outcome thus:

"P.C. Meade deposed that prisoner in reply to the charge said, "I did not steal it. Someone gave it to me." The Chief Constable described prisoner as an associate of thieves and bad women, and a disreputable character generally. "He won't do honest work," added Mr. Butler – Fourteen days."

Every day there was drill but there was also the marching. Regularly the highways and byways of Barnsley and neighbouring districts were filled with the lilt and swing of breezy whistling as the men of the Battalion, bereft of a bugle band, added their own musical accompaniment to the strict tempo of their marching. The 'Houghton Main Mob' who made up the greater part of 'B' Company, had sung "Tipperary" on their way to take the oath at the Public Hall and were becoming accustomed to that tune's ability to raise flagging spirits. Other tunes were being added to the repertoire of the marching Pals such as, 'Life on the Ocean Wave', 'Boys of the Bulldog Breed' and strangely for Yorkshire men, 'Men of Harlech'. They became firm favourites as the columns toured the countryside.

"All we could do at first were route marches, marching round Cawthorne, round Silkstone and back into Barnsley. That was quite enough to start with." **Ernest Bell, 13th Y & L Regiment**

"Route marching was the big thing and I was taking size ten boots when I joined up. I can remember going home once with bad feet, they were giving me some stick. My dad asked what the matter was and when I told him that the boots were killing me, he said, "I'll get thee a pair of boots." Off he went and got me a pair with soft tops. He took mine to use at the pit. We used to march out as far as Kexborough and on the way back along Wakefield Road we'd have a stop at "The Sportsman" Smithies. Tommy Guest used to have a barrel laid on outside. There'd be a pint for all of us – he was a good old stick!" **Harry Hall, 13th Y & L Regiment**

With such gestures Second Lieutenant Guest won the respect of Harry Hall and the rest of 'B' Company. He quickly became a popular leader, this officer with his peaked cap permanently stuck at a jaunty angle. It would be as a Major, and the Officer Commanding 'B' Company that Tommy Guest would be among the first men to leave the assembly trenches when the time came for the Barnsley Pals to attack the German lines on July 1st, 1916.

It was while the Battalion was billeted at the Public Hall that Tommy Oughton's recent past caught up with him. He received his first taste of Army discipline. He had forgotten all about the incident when he and a group of would-be recruits had spent their train fare on beer and cigarettes, then travelled first class to Barnsley without a ticket. The railway company had a longer memory. At least a month after the incident Tommy found himself on a charge before Colonel Hewitt.

Beginning to look the part as equipment and rifles arrive.

"We were still in civvies and when we got back to the Public Hall for breakfast one morning, a sergeant got up and said that he had an announcement to make. Private Oughton and three others to report to the Orderly Room at 10 o'clock. We all wondered what was wrong, we had no idea. When we got to the Orderly Room the charge was read out: We had travelled in first class carriages from Wombwell to Barnsley on a certain date without paying the fare. Colonel Hewitt addressed us and asked us if we had anything to say. I told him the story and then he remembered the recruiting meeting. I then told him what had happened the following morning, that Percy Miles Walker had given us this pound and we had spent it. He turned round and smiled at the adjutant and said, 'I think if Mr. Walker can afford a pound, the railway company can also afford these fares.' He then gave us a bit of a dressing down and said that he didn't want to see us before him again on any other charge, or this incident would be taken into account." Tommy Oughton, 13th Y & L Regiment

The town centre accommodation at the Public and Arcade Halls was merely a temporary arrangement until a permanent, purpose-built camp was erected at New Hall, Silkstone. While the rest of the Battalion continued with route marching and drill at the Queen's Ground, some of the men such as Ernest Bell and his mate Harry Gay, whose pre-war occupations were in the building and the construction trades, were selected to work on the new camp. Men with such skills were a valuable asset to the firm who had won the contract to build the camp.

"One morning we paraded in front of the County Court in Regent Street and Colonel Hewitt called our names out to go and report to the Sergeant Major. Hall Burks, the contractors, were building a camp at Silkstone and being in the building trade me and my pal were sent to assist the surveyors setting the site out. Afterwards we helped to build the pillars to support the wooden huts. We also dug trenches for the water services and sewerage. Men from the Battalion were sent up in squads to help dig the trenches, and we were in charge of them. Some of the officers used to go up at the same time and we used to take sandwiches for them and for ourselves. There were two separate packages, one for the officers and one for us. Our sandwiches were real 'clog-hangers' – half an inch thick, theirs were cut nicely and cornered. One day we gave them ours by mistake. After that the sandwiches were all alike."
Ernest Bell, 13th Y & L Regiment

Because of the difficulty in obtaining khaki the new battalions have to make do with blue serge. Still Willy Dalton, formerly of Silkstone, manages to look smart in his new uniform.

Left: *George De Ville Smith, former vicar of Saint Thomas' Worsbrough Dale.*

Centre: *George Asquith, Redfearn Bros. Glassworks.*

Right: *Milton Asquith, brother of George.*

Everybody hoped that the camp would be ready in time for the Battalion to occupy the huts at New Hall on December 7th, but this turned out to be an optimistic estimate of the completion date. What with the construction work, the constant drill, marching and sleeping on floorboards, the men's own clothes were beginning to look shabby and threadbare. Before their suits finally fell apart at the seams they were issued with their first uniform in that Autumn of 1914. Alderman Rose described it as "a right smart suit" although it was not the standard issue khaki service dress complete with flat-topped peaked caps of the regulars and the Terriers.

> *"We were issued with a blue serge uniform with brass buttons and a little cocked hat."* **Ernest Bell, 13th Y & L Regiment**

Owing to the difficulty in obtaining khaki cloth, several of the New Army Pals Battalions received these navy blue serge outfits. Rumours abounded that the uniforms were made up from cloth which was surplus to requirements of the Post Office, but true or false, the men wore these, their first real uniforms, with much pride. They were not to receive khaki until Easter 1915 and so had to put up with the comments and wisecracks of the locals.

> *"I remember once marching through Stairfoot, we were in our blues at the time. There were some youngsters coming running to see us and I heard one voice shout, 'Oi! Come on there's some soldiers here.' And then another voice called out, 'Oh, it's only t' Barnsley Battalion'."* **Tommy Oughton, 13th Y & L Regiment**

A further affront to the dignity of the Battalion occurred on December 3rd when a Monk Bretton carter, Arthur Cawthrow, ran his horse and cart into the rear of marching 'A' Company. The case was brought before the West Riding Court at Barnsley. Second Lieutenant Di Marco claimed that Cawthrow "declined to turn back and used obscene and abusive language which could be heard by all of the men."

Sergeant Major Knapton told the court that a traction engine coming the other way had stopped to allow the Battalion to pass, but instead of doing the same the defendant simply, "drove into the ranks and pushed the men onto the causeway."

Cawthrow was found guilty of obstruction and of using obscene language – he was fined £2. The Chairman of the magistrates hoped that this severe fine would discourage others from committing similiar 'unpatriotic' breaches of the law as the Battalion marched through the Borough.

Despite such ego deflating experiences the 'postmen's' uniforms were welcome and much needed by the time they appeared, but the arrival of a batch of rifles was seen as much more of a milestone on the road to the Pals becoming a fully-fledged unit of Kitchener's Army.

> *"We got our rifles just after we got uniforms. The lot that came there might have been 30 or 40, and we had them occasionally."* **Tommy Oughton, 13th Y & L Regiment**

One thousand, one hundred men make up a battalion and for the Barnsley Battalion the 40 rifles had to be judiciously shared out on a daily basis between the four companies. In small batches other rifles were steadily acquired. Not for them the 'Short' Lee-Enfield so eagerly anticipated but a variety of weapons

Right, upper: Derfflinger, *battle cruiser completed in September 1914. As part of the High Seas Fleet its first action is the bombardment of the seaside town of Scarborough.*

Right, lower: Von der Tann, *battle cruiser, four years old when war broke out, it had already taken part in a previous raid on the British coast in November when Yarmouth was attacked. She. along with the* Derfflinger *sails into South Bay and opens fire.*

Below, left: *Scarborough Castle suffers twentieth century damage.*

Below, right: *Pals arrive at Newhall Camp, Silkstone. Here they are seen outside one of their huts with soup bowls. There is no dining hut, meals are eaten in the barrack rooms. Civilian shirts and waistcoats are still in evidence. Third from the left, front row is Samuel Oxley who is to become a drummer when the bugle and drum band is formed. Standing in doorway wearing side cap is Harry Gay. At other door post, hatless with centre parting, stands his best pal Ernest Bell.*

which included the older 'Long' Lee-Enfields, Lee-Metfords, and the Canadian Ross rifles. The latter were prone to jam after the first brief encounter with the mud of Flanders, and consequently were dumped by Canadian infantrymen in favour of the Lee-Enfields plucked from the battlefield.

Distribution of arms to the quickly forming units of the New Armies, seemed hardly fair to the Barnsley Pals, for over at Sheffield, at the end of October the Sheffield City Battalion (12th Battalion, York and Lancaster Regiment) took delivery of 600 rifles. Although not enough for the whole Battalion it was an amount that would have gladdened the hearts of the 13th, who were having to content themselves with broom handles at that time.

Along with rifles and uniforms the Barnsley Battalion acquired some more officers. These were always from the middle classes whose claim to leadership derived from the positions they held in Barnsley's society rather than any military skills or experience.

Tommy Oughton, who had been detailed to 'D' Company, found himself under the command of temporary Second Lieutenant George De Ville Smith, later to be appointed Captain. Tommy's new officer had been a curate in civilian life, ordained at Saint Ann's church, Birkenhead, he served there before travelling to Barnsley in 1912. He took the position of vicar at Saint Thomas', Worsbrough Dale. There he had been the life and soul of the Church Lads Brigade. Now as an officer with the Barnsley Battalion he found that he was the leader of a different sort of flock, a flock that became increasingly critical of his behaviour, especially the teetotal chapel lads like Tommy Oughton.

"He turned out to be a right rum customer and we weren't long in giving him a nickname. With being called De Ville Smith we gave him the name 'Devil Smith'. He was a chap who was very strict, but what hurt us more, he used to come out with a bit of swearing. With us knowing that he had been a parson, we thought that was all wrong, hence his nickname." **Tommy Oughton, 13th Y & L Regiment**

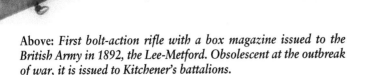

Above: *First bolt-action rifle with a box magazine issued to the British Army in 1892, the Lee-Metford. Obsolescent at the outbreak of war, it is issued to Kitchener's battalions.*

Right: *Colonel Hewitt addresses his men upon their arrival at the newly constructed camp at Silkstone.*

Another local man granted a temporary commission was George Asquith, whose father had been instrumental in founding Redfearn Brothers glass-works. Temporary Second Lieutenant Asquith, later to become a full lieutenant, was followed into the ranks of the Barnsley Battalion by his brother Milton, who became a Second Lieutenant.

Once the full complement had been reached the men were required to stay at the Public Hall "in the interests of discipline," and not travel home to sleep. This brought further problems as demands for more space were made. There were outbursts of ill-feeling and allegations between the Barnsley Chronicle on the one hand and some members of the Free Public Library Committee on the other over the application of Colonel Hewitt to press the reading rooms into service. The Free Library Committee found that they were unable to grant Colonel Hewitt's application under the terms of a special clause in the deeds of the Harvey Institute. Despite lively correspondence regarding what were seen as the 'unpatriotic acts of the Committee' the reading rooms stayed open to the public. This dispute over the use of the reading rooms was the only real set-back in the early development of the 13th (1st Barnsley) Battalion.

Because the response to the recruiting campaign had been so successful, Colonel Hewitt surprised many people in the town by hinting that a second battalion could be raised. In Colonel Hewitt's opinion he would soon have more recruits than he needed, and feared that if steps were not taken to create a second battalion, then these additional men would be shunted into other regiments. He made his views known to the Army's Northern Command at York.

The problem of the surplus recruits for the Battalion was addressed by a special Council meeting on November 27th. The Mayor was away on business in Brighton, but in a letter read out to the Council, he made it known that he doubted whether any attempts to raise a second battalion would be successful. After due deliberation the Deputy Mayor said that it "would not be fair to compel these men, who had left home to join the Barnsley Pals, to be draughted into various other regiments where they have no friends and know no one."

That sealed it – the Council voted to offer to Lord Kitchener another force which would be known as the Second Barnsley Battalion. Alderman William Raley, already associated with the First, was invited to become Acting Colonel. The offer was readily accepted by the War Office, subject to a reserve Company being formed for the First Barnsley's. Early December and that Company was nearing completion, conse-quently the Second Barnsley's was officially launched at a meeting at the Public Hall on December 9th. The Council may have foreseen some difficulty in raising another one thousand plus men, just as their Mayor had done, so they arranged for a tandem meeting to be held in the Regent Street Congregational Schoolroom. And this "for the purpose of securing the sympathy and co-operation of the women of the town and district in the Committee's Recruiting Scheme."

The whole recruiting bandwagon could once more begin to roll. So far the only contact that the majority of the people of Barnsley had had with the war was through the columns of the newspapers. Letters sent to the Chronicle from local men serving in France were published along with the occasional interview with one or another of the fortunate members of the British Expeditionary Force who had received a 'Blighty' wound during the retreat from Mons. Also a report of the not so fortunate Barnsley sailors who had gone down with the Battleship HMS *Bulwark*, in mysterious circumstances as it lay at Sheerness on the River

Medway. However, early in December the hand of war unexpectedly came closer home.

German cruisers sailing up the East Coast on December 16th fired several salvos at the resorts of Whitby and Scarborough. Further north along the coast Hartlepool in County Durham was also shelled.

During the half hour breakfast time bombardment of Scarborough, Miss Margaret Briggs, a native of Barnsley, lost her life as she was taking letters from the postman on the doorstep of the house where she worked. The postman was also killed.

Colonel Hewitt, as commanding officer of the First Barnsley's presumably expected to face German fire at some future date. His son George, a lieutenant in the 5th Battalion (Territorial) York and Lancaster Regiment, was eventually to come under fire in April, 1915. But it was the Colonel's daughter, Winnie, who was the first of the Hewitt family to experience the rain of enemy shells. She was at school in Scarborough when the Battle Cruisers *Derfflinger* and *Von Der Tann* sailed into South Bay and opened fire. Although shells hit houses on either side of the school buildings, she escaped unhurt.

The construction work at Silkstone camp continued through the early part of December and the general opinion was that the Pals would be out of the Public Hall by Christmas.

The appearance of a small black kitten which calmly walked through the front doors at the Public Hall, found its way upstairs, and then made itself at home in one of the rooms used by the officers was taken as an omen of good luck. The kitten remained and was christened 'Jeph'. Along with 'Buller' the bulldog they now had two mascots. In the same week the Pals heard the news that the War Office had graced them with the official title of the '13th Service Battalion (First Barnsley) York and Lancaster Regiment'. The superstitious few who had welcomed the arrival of Jeph the cat as some kind of happy omen must have been disturbed by the War Office's choice of number for them.

The town's other unit still in its infancy, was numbered the 14th Service Battalion (Second Barnsley). Both battalions were placed in the 115th Infantry Brigade along with the 12th Sheffield City Battalion, York and Lancaster Regiment, and the 10th Battalion Lincolnshire Regiment (the Grimsby Chums).

In the days leading up to Christmas 1914, the Pals found themselves packing their few belongings for the trip to Silkstone. At 11 o'clock on the morning of Sunday 20th December, the now officially designated 13th Service Battalion, with Cooper's Prize Band at its head marched from the Public Hall, along Eldon Street, Peel Street and up Dodworth Road to Newhall Camp.

When they reached the camp they were addressed by Colonel Hewitt. He informed them that the most important aspect of their training at Silkstone would be musketry, along with Company manoeuvres. "The sooner that was completed, the quicker the Battalion would be despatched to the front," he said.

Christmas morning 1914, brought a nip in the air and the promise of a day's celebrations ahead. The Pals slowly settled into their new surroundings, determined to make the best of it.

As a spontaneous unofficial truce spread peace through some sectors of the trench system in France and the killing ceased for a day, the Pals sat down to a Christmas dinner which was extremely lavish by Western Front standards.

The traditional fare of turkey and roast beef was supplemented with the addition of 100 pheasants, a seasonal gesture of goodwill fresh from the Stainborough Park estates of Captain Bruce Wentworth. His gift was only a part of the "Christmas Cheer" fund for the 13th York and Lancasters boldly initiated by the Chronicle two weeks before Christmas with the words,

". . . the public of Barnsley, it is hoped, will not forget the gallant men of their own district who have, at great sacrifice to themselves, left their homes, and in some cases their families, to fight for their country. By Christmas the Barnsley Battalion will probably have left the town for camp, and it is the wish of Colonel Hewitt and his officers that their Christmas shall be a happy and bright one." **Barnsley Chronicle, 5th December 1914.**

The fund, which realised a sum of £130, was made up of monies donated by various individuals or groups. Colonel Hewitt, as the men's commanding officer, had given £21, Miss Fountain, a friend of the Hewitt family who had shares in several local collieries, gave £20, and smaller amounts came from officers and their relatives. The fund enabled the camp cooks to be a little more adventurous than was usual. After dinner festivities continued in the Regimental Institute, where officers and men provided the entertainment.

The men must have been particularly delighted to find a new shilling added to their usual "one bob a

day" pay, the "new enlistment bob" as the troops were apt to call it. This bonus payment was made for the move to their new quarters, and as soon as the echoes of celebration had died away at Silkstone, a team of charwomen moved into the Public Hall in order to spruce it up in readiness for the men of the Second Battalion. The Raising Committee had jumped at the offer of the Public Hall on the First Battalion's departure for Silkstone, but promptly, on 4th January, the Harvey Institute Committee recommended that,

". . . an account be submitted to the War Office for the period during which the Battalion was accommodated at the Public Hall, and that a charge of 2d per head on the basis of 800 men accommodated for 87 nights be made."

Short-cut bridge to Newhall Camp is completed.

When it came down to the question of balancing the books, practicality tended to obscure patriotism.

Before they started their training in earnest there was one problem that had to be solved. Newhall Camp had been sited at the top of a steep hill with a deep ravine between it and the road from Barnsley. Entrance to the camp meant a long trip into the village of Silkstone even though the huts were tantalisingly close when approaching from Barnsley Road. The solution was simple.

"Our pioneers built a rough wooden bridge across a ravine. It was built on rough cut trees and must have been 70 to 80 yards long. It saved all that walk into Silkstone Village. When you got over the bridge you were 200 yards from camp. When we went across we had to break step. I've seen one or two officers go over on motor bikes. I bet they got a rough ride across there." **Tommy Oughton, 13th Y & L Regiment**

Winter weather coupled with the passage of many boots soon turned the thoroughfares between the huts into muddy tracks. But at least the Pals had beds, of sorts, to sleep in.

"We had three flat boards on trestles and mattresses full of straw. As a rule two of you used to get down together to make like a double. You each had two blankets, so when you got together you'd put one on the bottom and three on top. Me and Tom Bradbury kipped like that. We had a proper hut for meals and a cookhouse. Of course when we first got there the Barnsley British Cooperative Society was still feeding us. I expect that it all came out of the government later on, but they catered for us. You could see the big vans coming from Barnsley every day. I heard many men say, men older than me who were married, that they were better fed than in civilian life." **Tommy Oughton, 13th Y & L Regiment**

Once at Silkstone the training could be varied so that drill and marches could be interspaced with other activities usually associated with soldiering.

At Silkstone most of the men had some form of rifle, even if the majority of these were only to be used for drill purposes because of defects. It was for this reason and also because of the shortage of ammunition that bayonet drill featured heavily on the training programme. Colonel Hewitt was most emphatic in his views on the use of the bayonet, describing it as the ultimate weapon in battle.

Old Volunteer had already pre-empted Colonel Hewitt's views on the use of the bayonet in a November issue of the *Chronicle*. "It is a weapon," he wrote, "always popular with our men. The War Office knows what it is about when it directs that every encouragement should be given to the recruits to practise bayonet fighting. Not until they are thoroughly skilled in the use of this weapon can the men be sent on active service."

This creed passed down from on high, was strengthened by the old-timers acting as N.C.O.'s and, in the absence of experience to the contrary, was taken on by the Barnsley soldiers. It was a belief rooted in a time when soldiers with good fortune on their side and inefficient troops opposing them, could advance close enough to use the sharp edge of the bayonet. With the arrival of the machine gun with its ability to spray bullets at a rate many times faster than the most skilled rifleman, the doctrine of the 'ultimate weapon' was as outdated as the bow and arrow.

Rushing headlong towards a few dangling sacks filled with sawdust, and then thrusting the bayonets in with blood-curdling screams was only a part of the Pals' varied training at Silkstone.

The daily routine began with Reveille at 6 a.m. and, after the men tumbled from their trestle beds, they would receive a biscuit and a mug of coffee doled out by the Battalion catering unit. Physical drill followed under the expert eye of Sergeant Hayton, an instructor sent especially from Aldershot by the War Office to put the Pals through the mill. This early morning session sometimes took the form of a cross-country run along the muddy tracks of the woods surrounding the camp. They would return for breakfast at 8 a.m. There was barely time to digest the meal before they were at it again, this time falling in for Company training in Noblethorpe Park.

This took the form of instruction in the organisation of battle formations in attack and defence. Those sham battles usually consisted of an attack by individual companies against some pre-arranged objective, the men forming sections and deploying in extended order, all the time advancing towards their objective. On other occasions the companies would combine in a Battalion exercise which was on similar lines but on a much larger scale. These manoeuvres usually concerned themselves with the already dated tactics favoured by commanders in the South African campaign. In most cases the Battalion carried out this sort

At Silkstone Camp the Pals begin their training in real earnest with bayonet fighting. It is drummed into them that the bayonet is the ultimate weapon in warfare.

of training on relatively even ground with few obstacles barring their way.

Mock combat scenarios like these so painstakingly constructed by Colonel Hewitt and his company commanders, were being repeated at various locations dotted around Yorkshire. From Redmires Camp on the moors to the south of Sheffield, where the Sheffield City Battalion were in training, to Colsterdale near Masham in North Yorkshire, where several battalions of the West Yorkshire Regiment were based, similar manoeuvres were taking place.

On the Stray at Harrogate an incredulous subaltern of the 11th Battalion, York and Lancaster Regiment was ordered to storm a harmless, isolated kiosk which was supposed to represent an enemy stronghold. To the many intelligent young men of Kitchener's Army these exercises were a constant source of amusement as they failed to grasp the relevance of the whims of their elderly officers. This type of open movement that they were training so hard to perfect would be of little use to them in the siege warfare of the Western Front.

Elements of trench warfare had found their way into the training manuals. Trench siting and digging exercises were often combined with the ever popular route marches towards the moors west of Silkstone. These excursions were not without their surprises.

"We did the route marches more Penistone way and we went two or three times on the moors trench digging. On one occasion we set off at four in the morning to get there before daybreak. We as signallers, weren't trench digging, we were allotted places and we were using telephones. It was just breaking daylight and if I'd been on my own I would have run. This mist was rising and it just looked like water to me. I thought that water was flooding towards me – it only lasted a few seconds and then it suddenly cleared. I could see down into a valley below, that's where the mist must have come from. I'd never experienced anything like it before." **Tommy Oughton, 13th Y & L Regiment**

It was not unknown for some of those route marches to cover a distance of 20 miles. However, the Pals usually managed to get back to camp for lunch at 1 p.m. This was followed by afternoon parade, more forming fours, deploying, wheeling, extending. In the evenings the men were required to attend lectures, sometimes lantern slides, on topics such as map reading, rudimentary French and German, along with military history, guns and explosives.

The Pals had been hard at work for almost two months when Brigadier General Bowles, the commander of the 115th Infantry Brigade, whose headquarters was in Sheffield, paid them a visit. The Chronicle of February 27th reported cheerfulness and good spirits in the camp to welcome the Brigadier. It also noted the men's readiness for action:

Monckton men of the Barnsley Battalion. Uniforms are mixed, flat caps with blue serge, one bandsman and a rare khaki.

Third row, standing, first left, Sam Oxley. Fifth, same row, Harry Gay. Second row, second left, Ernest Bell. Part platoon of 'A' Company at Silkstone Camp.

"There is only one thing these men are waiting for and it is the opportunity of showing the stuff they are made of, and the love they have for King and Country. It will be a sorry time for any Germans who get in close touch with the Barnsley lads."

It was true that some of the men were itching to leave Silkstone, but it had nothing to do with wanting to show the Germans the stuff they were made of.

"After a few months' training we got a bit fed up. The feeling of wanting to do 'our bit' didn't last long. It was the regular routine that made us fed up." Tommy Oughton, 13th Y & L Regiment

Tommy, like many other Kitchener men, did not take naturally to the relentless routine which, day by day, attempted to reduce the individual spirit into some collective common denominator based upon a respect for discipline. Happily, the early training of the Pals was free of the more humiliating practices usually associated with turning wilful recruits into obedient soldiers. This was due to the avuncular interest which N.C.O.'s like Tom Lax took in their charges. Most of the officers too were free of traditional military prejudices and this resulted in a closer relationship between the officers and the rank and file. Friendships at times developed between junior officers and the men, a phenomenon which would have been unheard of in the strictly stratified Army society pre-1914. Close links between officers and private soldiers had obvious advantages, respect for the person rather than the uniform would be more of a motivating factor under battle conditions. But there were also disadvantages, as some officers were to find out when they tried to make the Battalion wags toe the line.

"We were coming back from Noblethorpe Park where we had been doing manoeuvres, and we were marching up the hill towards the wooden bridge which crossed to the camp. There were one or two lads in 'A' Company who were slouching about as we were marching to attention, so Lieutenant Asquith turned us around and marched us back again. 'Now we'll come up right,' he said. This happened twice and it got us all a bit worked up. We didn't make any to do about it at the time, but those two or three who were responsible copped it later." Ernest Bell, 13th Y & L Regiment

Surprisingly, little friction existed between the officers and men apart from the few clashes of personality,

Colonel Hewitt with his, then adjutant, Jack Brass (colliery manager, Houghton Main).

A Pal finds his girl. Right: Ernest Bell meets Bertha Hollingsworth at a local dance, they are to marry after the war.

Above, left: *Lt. di Marco with the Battalion football team.*

which were inevitable when bringing together so many individuals. In the main, the officers were viewed as 'a good set' although some of the men doubted their ability to come up to the mark when faced with command under fire.

Occasionally an officer would leave camp to attend a special course in commanding a company or platoon. Early in March Captain Wilkinson made such a trip to Hornsea and Colonel Hewitt spent a week on a course for commanding officers at Strensall, near York.

From the camp at Silkstone it was not easy to get to locations at the other side of Barnsley as there was no regular public transport system in operation. As a result the off-duty excursions of the Pals were restricted to within walking distance of the camp.

> *"We were invited to dances and functions at Keresforth school. We went down in our uniforms. There used to be a trio on, piano, violin and oboe, we used to dance waltzes and two-steps – it was lovely. That was every Saturday and sometimes during the week. It was there that I met my wife Bertha and I asked her for a dance – it was a waltz I think. I don't think that she had been to too many dances because she trod on my toes. After that we started to take notice of each other."* **Ernest Bell, 13th Y & L Regiment**

Bertha's family, Hollingsworth's, ran a small shop in Dodworth and Ernest found himself making an increasing number of visits to the village in his off-duty moments to do his shopping. Meanwhile, Tommy Oughton found that his chapel connections came in handy.

> *"It got so that people took an interest in you. People used to invite you to tea on Sundays, or suppers. I got to know a lot of nice people that way."* **Tommy Oughton, 13th Y & L Regiment**

Just after Colonel Hewitt had returned from his course at Strensall, Brigadier General Bowles ventured out of his Sheffield headquarters to pay another visit of inspection to Newhall Camp. The Pals initial training period was drawing to a close or so they thought – surely their removal to the front line was not far off. Battalion organisation was almost complete, four companies, each consisting of around 200 men, were fully formed and there was a fifth company acting as a reserve. There was a transport section and there were stretcher bearers.

True to his word Tom Lax had seen to it that his little band of signallers were relieved of tedious duties. Being an old soldier, Tom was steeped in the art of the flag signaller and he had duly passed on his expertise to Tommy Oughton and his colleagues in all good faith. He little realised that signalling with flags would be of little use in the trenches of the Western Front.

The machine gun was another modern development which, according to Ernest Bell, had not found its way to the camp; and yet a machine gun section was in the process of formation, Ernest being one of the

Signals Sergeant Tom Lax, with his signallers. A system that is obsolete in the trench warfare of France and Belgium.

first members. The absence of an integral item of equipment such as a machine gun for the Battalion is observed and yet an intriguing item appeared in the Barnsley Chronicle regarding a certain Reverend W. H. Elmhirst of Pinder Oaks ". . . interesting himself in providing an extra machine gun which he has offered to Colonel Hewitt for the acceptance of the First Barnsley Battalion." A total of £102 had been raised towards the purchase of a machine gun, yet there is no evidence to suggest that it ever materialised. In any event, it seems rather strange that at a time when weapons of any description were at a premium, a man of God should be in a position to lay his hands on a machine gun.

Everyone hoped that the promised khaki uniforms would appear soon and somehow they would set the seal on the Barnsley Battalion's training. Brigadier General Bowles had made several inspection visits and as he stood with Colonel Hewitt once more and witnessed the whole Battalion advance, one line of troops 'leap-frogging' over another he could not fail to be impressed. As the men made their final charge with fixed bayonets, shouting and screaming as they crossed the 'enemy' trenches, he could reflect that Colonel Hewitt's course at Strensall had been a complete success.

A full complement of officers for the Barnsley Battalion. Picture taken at Oakwell Football Ground. Four of them will be killed in the first action of the Pals, 1st July, 1916.

Chapter Four

Hell with the lid off

"On Thursday close upon 50 men left Newhall Camp, Silkstone, for Chatham, en route for the front. They are being required for special work, and the men who were chosen are of particular fine physique. Good luck to the Pals." **Barnsley Chronicle, 13th March 1915.**

GERMANY'S HIGH HOPES OF SEIZING PARIS within weeks of her armies sweeping through Belgium and northern France had been dashed, even as the idea to form the First Barnsley Pals Battalion had taken root. It was true that the small British force of regulars despatched so efficiently across the Channel in mid August, 1914 had played its part in checking the German advance at Mons and Le Cateau. It was true that the French had fought courageously, albeit with their hearts rather than their heads, on their eastern frontiers. It was also true that the small Belgian army had thrust a painful thorn into the German right flank from the fortress of Antwerp. Yet it had been the allied armies which had been forced into fighting a rearguard action to cover their long retreat.

By 2nd September the Allies had withdrawn to within 20 miles of the French capital. With the heart of France under direct threat and the position looking hopeless, the German Army on the right flank, instead of encircling Paris according to plan, instead marched across the front of the Paris garrison. Quickly gathering their wits, the exhausted Allies were able to go onto the offensive and for several days retreat turned into an advance, with the Germans falling back to the River Aisne. At that point the Germans dug in and the fighting spilled north leaving a belt of destruction as both sides raced to turn the flank of the other. It was all in vain, every manoeuvre was matched by one equally strong on the other side and the war of movement finally ceased when both sides reached the North Sea. They had run out of land over which to move their troops.

In a desperate bid to pick the lock which would open the gate to the Channel ports, the Germans attacked the Belgian town of Ypres. The British Expeditionary Force, helped by the French, fought to keep the gate closed and although it bowed under the tremendous onslaught, the line held. The cost to the British was very near extinction of the original B.E.F. After that First Battle of Ypres, with both sides temporarily spent, the heat of battle cooled as winter approached. The lines of feverishly dug trenches which the assailants had constructed to hold their ground, deepened and took on an air of permanence as the fluid warfare of the late Summer and early Autumn was gradually replaced by stalemate.

From the dubious shelter of their respective ditches the rival forces eyed each other across an unclaimed strip of No-Man's-Land, unsure as to what would happen next. Christmas was not far away and the boys were not yet home, something had gone seriously wrong. As the troops prepared to spend their first miserable Winter in the trenches, which threaded their way from the North Sea coast to the Swiss border, Kitchener's depressing prediction of a long hard war appeared to be turning into reality.

No one relished the thought of spending the long Winter months in stark and depressing dugouts, least of all the Indian troops of the Sirhind Brigade. Their trenches in the Festubert sector, some ten miles south of the Franco-Belgian border and at the southern extension of the British line, must have seemed a million miles from home. The very notion of endless weeks of soaking rain, snow, ice and biting winds which lay ahead, must have cut deep into their spirits. As if there weren't enough to worry about, the Germans, on the morning of December 20th, were intent on adding fire, in the form of high explosive, to the list of elements. Already cowed by the incessant buffeting of a ferocious artillery bombardment, at around half past ten the colonial troops suddenly felt the ground beneath their feet quiver for a moment as a loud growling spread along a 1,000 yard stretch of their trench. A split second later the very ground on which they stood belched flame, smoke and several tons of earth as it was violently thrown high into the air.

The Germans had renewed the attack. Unseen, and unheard from above, they had burrowed underneath the Indian lines to lay eleven explosive charges of which ten had blown. The shocked and dazed

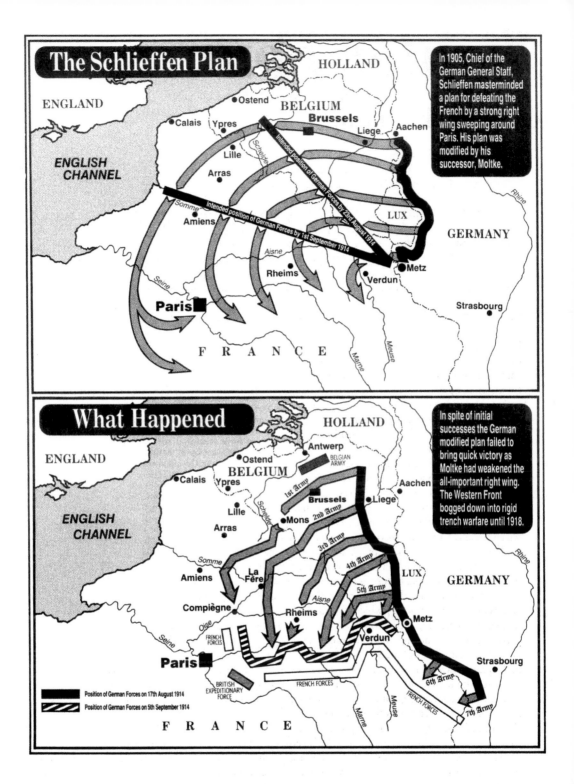

The Schlieffen Plan

HOLLAND

ENGLAND

Ostend

BELGIUM

Brussels

Calais

Ypres

Liege

Aachen

ENGLISH CHANNEL

Lille

Arras

Schelde

Intended position of German Forces by 23rd August 1914

Somme

Amiens

Intended position of German Forces by 1st September 1914

LUX

Rhine

GERMANY

Aisne

Rheims

Verdun

Metz

Paris

Strasbourg

Seine

FRANCE

Meuse

Marne

In 1905, Chief of the German General Staff, Schlieffen masterminded a plan for defeating the French by a strong right wing sweeping around Paris. His plan was modified by his successor, Moltke.

What Happened

HOLLAND

ENGLAND

Antwerp

BELGIAN ARMY

Ostend

BELGIUM

Calais

Ypres

1st Army

Brussels

Liege

Aachen

ENGLISH CHANNEL

Lille

Schelde

Mons

2nd Army

Arras

3rd Army

4th Army

Somme

Amiens

La Fère

5th Army

LUX

Rhine

GERMANY

Aisne

Compiègne

Rheims

Metz

FRENCH FORCES

Verdun

Oise

Seine

Paris

BRITISH EXPEDITIONARY FORCE

FRENCH FORCES

6th Army

Strasbourg

FRENCH FORCES

Meuse

7th Army

Marne

FRANCE

Position of German Forces on 17th August 1914

Position of German Forces on 5th September 1914

In spite of initial successes the German modified plan failed to bring quick victory as Moltke had weakened the all-important right wing. The Western Front bogged down into rigid trench warfare until 1918.

Loving husband and father John Davies, cycles to Barnsley from Croydon to find work. His wife and three sons join him; he goes to work at Wharncliffe Woodmoor Colliery in 1912. It is from there that he enlists in the First Barnsley Battalion, when the patriotic call goes out for men.

survivors struggled to get clear of the smoking debris and escape the swarm of German soldiers crossing No-Man's-Land in the wake of the explosions. The loss of men and their positions was indeed a severe blow, but the morale of the whole Indian Corps suffered long lasting damage.

Mining was not an innovative method of warfare. With the opposing lines of trenches lying so close to each other, the Germans had resurrected the centuries old art of subterranean warfare. If deadlock was the name of the game on the surface, then there was nothing to prevent vigorous German tunnellers undermining the British positions and, if successful in laying their charges, blowing the trenches and their unsuspecting occupants sky high. As well as the weather, the snipers, liberal doses of machine-gun bullets, and the indiscriminate pulverisation of shell fire, there was now the teasing uncertainty as to where and when underground charges would be blown. The Germans had grasped the initiative and intended to keep it.

In the new year two more mines were blown. One near the village of St. Eloi, a few miles south of Ypres, erupted under the feet of soldiers of the East Yorkshire Regiment. Only after these latest 'defeats' were calls for the formation of specialist mining units for the burrowing under the German lines, heeded. Up to that time, mining had been just another duty of the already hard pressed Royal Engineers. The ad hoc formation of mining sections, by a few far-sighted Brigadiers, lacked the training, the equipment and the large labour force required to mount mining operations on a scale which would match the German efforts, much less overtake them.

The drama of the German mining exploits and the paranoia of the British front line soldiers belonged to a different world from the one inhabited by young Johnnie Davies. As he slowly chewed his way through the greasy bacon served up by the camp cooks at Silkstone, he was more concerned with unpleasant feelings of nausea. It was a taste of Army life he wished he had not experienced. While the hungry soldiers of the First Barnsley Battalion polished off their breakfasts, fat and all, in double quick time, the bacon now wallowing in his stomach did not sit comfortably in the less robust digestive system of a ten-year-old boy.

Visitors, other than those with military connections, were not an unusual sight at Newhall Camp but Johnnie Davies' visit proved that the Army was in no position to make concessions for civilians, even if those civilians were the sons of Kitchener men and lads of tender years.

The eldest son of Private John Davies was at Silkstone to spend a few days with his father, and he certainly gained first hand experience of the type of life his father had been leading since he had left home in September. Accommodation for the boy was the same wooden hut shared by his father and nineteen other men of 'C' Company, while his 'bed' was the same type of low, three plank affair enjoyed by most of the Barnsley troop.

John Davies was a family man through and through, and it upset him a good deal that he had spent precious little time with young Johnnie and his other two sons; Charlie, aged seven and four-year-old George, since his enlistment. Like many more family men all over Britain, John Davies had felt it his duty to answer Kitchener's call for recruits and so he had joined the local Barnsley Battalion as soon as it had been formed. He had left his wife Esther, to look after the boys in his absence, but now as his eldest boy spent some time with him in camp he could at least make up for a little of the time he had lost with his family, even if his young son represented only a small part of it. For the Davies family however, time was short.

Brought up in Barnsley, John Davies had left the town in his early teens to find work in Croydon where he had joined the local militia. In 1908, cycling all the way from Croydon, he returned to Barnsley and

About to set off on a new adventure forty-two volunteers for newly formed tunnelling companies. John Davies is fourth from the right, standing, the man behind has his hands on his shoulders. Soon some will be engaged in a dangerous game of mining and counter-mining under Hill 60 in the Ypres Salient. Battalion mascot. "Buller" sees them off.

found work in the building trade with Flemings of Eastgate. With his wife and young sons following a little later, they all moved into a house in Vernon Street North belonging to his employers. They were allowed to stay there when John Davies left Flemings and took a job at the Wharncliffe Woodmoor Colliery at Carlton in 1912, where he worked up to the time of his enlistment.

If there was one thing John Davies had in abundance, it was knowledge of the mining and construction industries and it was men with such knowledge and practical skills that the War Office was recruiting. Special units were being quickly formed, units which were eventually to become known as the tunnelling companies.

There was a wealth of raw material for the new companies just waiting to be unearthed from a battalion such as the First Barnsley Pals. Many of the men had spent all their working lives underground and others, like John Davies, had a useful mixture of both mining and construction experience. It was logical that the Army should first scour the ranks of the Service Battalions which had sprung from the mining districts of Britain. From areas like the Yorkshire coalfield, from County Durham and from the valleys of South Wales, the tunnellers would emerge.

Late in February 1915, some 50 men of the First Barnsley Battalion were seconded to join the new tunnelling units which were to operate under the banner of the Royal Engineers, and Private John Davies was one of them. They left Silkstone on March 11th and were cheered on their way by some of their friends who were staying behind. Johnnie Davies was allowed to leave his classes at Eldon Street North school during the morning to wave goodbye to his father as the train carrying the party pulled out of the Court House Station. There would be no more visits to Silkstone Camp for the boy.

John Davies and his comrades were bound for the Royal Engineers depot at St. Mary's Barracks in Chatham. There they were officially absorbed into the Royal Engineers and prepared for active service overseas. Overnight, Private John Davies of the 13th Service Battalion, York and Lancaster Regiment found himself transformed into No. 86654, Sapper J. H. Davies, Royal Engineers.

It was never the Army's intention to allow the Pals to stay together and they were split up to assist in providing the uniformed nucleus of several tunnelling companies, along with ex-infantrymen from other regiments. Some of the Pals did however, end up in the same mob. With John Davies were several members of 'C' Company including Corporal Chambers who was later chosen to be in charge of the small group

The mound of earth to the left of the railway cutting and bridge is Hill 60. The Germans hold the mound and the British are tunnelling underneath. Although the landscape appears deserted, thousands of men are occupying the trenches and are keeping their heads down.

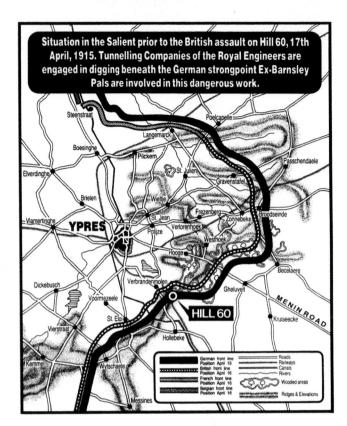

Situation in the Salient prior to the British assault on Hill 60, 17th April, 1915. Tunnelling Companies of the Royal Engineers are engaged in digging beneath the German strongpoint Ex-Barnsley Pals are involved in this dangerous work.

to which John Davies belonged.

On St. Patrick's day 1915, just six days after leaving Silkstone camp, John Davies was on his way across the Channel. His departure was a little later than he had anticipated, for in a letter to his wife on Saturday 13th March he wrote,

"If all is right we shall be off to France on Monday afternoon. It has all happened so suddenly that I can hardly take it in and I was very much down hearted at first. But it is now passed and we have to get ready for some grim work. I don't fear anything for it is all soldiering here. I want you to keep up a brave heart and let our boys pray for me until I come home again, as it may be a long time, and if I fall, don't fret, but work for the boys to grow up and honour the name of their father who fought for his country."

Soon after landing at Le Havre they made the long journey towards the already dreaded Salient which swelled out towards the German line jealously guarding the town of Ypres. There, some way behind the front line, they joined the 171st Tunnelling Company, a curious conglomeration of Royal Engineers, ex-infantrymen and also civilians who had come straight from the pits with little, or no, military training.

The grim work of which John Davies spoke in his letter, was helping to dig out the 'saps' which, inch by exhausting inch, were groping out to the bowels of the earth beneath Hill 60, as part of an elaborate plan designed to beat the Germans at their own game.

Hill 60, the name was as unimaginative as its gradual slopes were uninspiring. There was nothing in the name more sinister or complex other than the fact that a 60 metre contour had conveniently wrapped itself round the feature on maps of the area. The designation had been taken on board by Army cartographers, who were too busy charting trench maps to think up grand names for hills. In fact it wasn't really a hill at all, certainly nature had played no part in its formation. When the rail link between Ypres and the Franco-Belgian border town of Comines had been forged, the engineers had driven the track to the foot of the half-moon shaped crest of high ground which surrounds Ypres to the south. Blocked to the north by a thickening extension of that same rising ground and with the even trickier slopes of the Messines-Wytschaete ridge and Mount Kemmel to the south, the railwaymen had sliced clean through, pushing the route forward between the banks of a cutting some 2,000 yards long. The soil thrown up in excavating and laying the railway had been dumped, along with the waste from the Ypres-Comines canal cutting, in three piles nearby, and Hill 60 was the highest of these. In spite of its rather lack-lustre title its summit was one of the pinnacles at the northern extremity of the Messines-Wytschaete ridge, bursting out, as it did from the endless tedium that was the Plain of Flanders. To the commanders of both sides, the hill was a veritable mountain, a mountain whose lofty 'peaks' offered unrivalled observation for whoever gained its man-made heights. It was seldom out of the news. The French had tried valiantly to hold on to it in December 1914 but the countless bodies both French and German still strewn along its slopes told their own sorry tale of just how forcibly they had been pushed off.

When the 171st Tunnelling Company went to work, the trenches which seamed the hill, daily attracted

The town of Ypres beginning to suffer total destruction as the Germans make it their objective in attempts to straighten their line and get rid of the bulge.

the envious gazes of the British Generals, and for good reason as they were held in strong German hands. Looking north-west the Germans had a superb view of Ypres and a good stretch of the British line to the north and south. From the hill their artillery observers could signal the agonising destruction of Ypres and the men who held the trenches of the Salient. For the moment at least, it was the Germans who were the Kings of the Castle, but the British in their turn, were plotting to usurp them.

The plans for the destruction of the German trench system on the upper slopes of Hill 60 went far beyond anything envisaged by Guy Fawkes and his fellow conspirators. Several mines had been started by the time John Davies and the other Barnsley men joined the Tunnelling Company, and these, when completed were to be charged and fired prior to an overground assault by the infantry.

Barnsley's tunnellers found that they had landed amid a band of tense, nervous men, caught up in a race against time.

Less than a fortnight earlier the Germans had again blown three charges at St. Eloi, scattering the hapless British infantry before yet another German charge across No-Man's-Land, and days later the muffled but unmistakeable sounds of German countermining had been heard from the Hill 60 workings.

Little of that tension was allowed to show in a letter written by John Davies late in March on the eve of his front line initiation. Hastily scribbled in purple pencil, he appeared calm and still convinced of his purpose, his words reflecting almost exactly the mood of the British press.

"There are a lot of soldiers all over the country and what you read in the papers is all true. The Germans have spread death and destruction everywhere. I am in a Belgian town all in ruins. I shall have a lot of news to tell you when I come home, but I can't say how long that will be, but if the young men of England could see the ruined homes of these poor people they would come and avenge the fearful crimes. We have plenty to eat and I have had my shirt washed by a French woman and a shave as well. I hope my dear boys are well and good. Tell them their Dad often thinks of them when I see those little Belgian children here without homes. I haven't a lot of news, as you know the news is curtailed a lot, but I hope to have a few lines from you. I will conclude with all my fondest love and good wishes to you and the boys. I remain your loving husband and father. J. H. Davies"

Digging went on nervously despite the uncomplaining tone of John Davies' letter, even if it did disguise the hardships a relative newcomer to the front line had already faced. There was worse to come. Men with many years' experience of civilian mining behind them found the work loathsome. One of the problems was the thick layer of clay which underscored the whole of the region. The other was water, gallons of it, which trickled endlessly into the underground cavities due to Flanders' close proximity to sea level.

Life below the earth was a constant battle to drive the tunnels forward into the clay and then keep them clear of water. The only thing separating the men from a total deluge was the application of sturdy timbers to the walls and roofs.

Several yards deep, in tunnels sometimes less than a yard square, the men would toil at the working

Comfortable quarters for the Germans on Hill 60. The adventure has turned into a nightmare for the ex-members of the First Barnsley Pals as can be seen from the letter by Henry Fisher which appears in the Chronicle. Fisher gets his wish when a mine is exploded on April 17th.

face of the mine. There, two of them would huddle together in the red, oxygen starved glow of a candle. One would laboriously pick and pry into the heavy oozing clay with the point of a bayonet or bare hands. Another would scoop up the dripping waste and place it into sandbags or, in some cases, onto small trolleys. It would then be pulled towards the mine entrance and distributed carefully on the surface to prevent detection by German observers.

During their eight hour shifts the men would spend long periods working in painful cramp inducing postures, soaked to the skin in a vile smelling concoction of their own sweat suffused with muddy water. Whereas once they had been covered in coal dust from the mines of Barnsley they were now plastered from head to foot in a layer of slimy sludge.

The coal mines, with the ever present dangers of noxious gases, roof-fall and lung destroying dust had surely never been as injurious to the constitution as the dank, chilled atmosphere which pervaded those hell-holes beneath No-Man's-Land. There were no welcoming hearths or tin baths in Flanders. At the end of a shift the men had to dry out as best they could in the absence of a change of clothes.

The constant damp, coupled with the lack of oxygen played havoc with the men's health.

Still the digging went on but at times virtual silence had to be maintained. Any noises in the mine, the rhythmic squelch of a bayonet thrust into the clay by some over zealous sapper; or a hacking cough picked up in the wet underground passages, would signal the location of the tunnels to German counterminers.

It was not unknown for rival sappers to break into each other's tunnels and there, in pitch darkness, fight fierce claustrophobic duels. There was also the risk that the Germans would explode a small charge called a camouflet and collapse the gallery while men were still out working at the clay face.

In a letter to the Barnsley Chronicle in early April, Sergeant Stott of the 173rd Tunnelling Company wrote,

64

"I have charge of the 'pit' doing special work and am keeping all our party together as well as possible. Several of the Pals have been branched off to different companies but that, of course, is one of the events of war. I am sorry to say the officer who gave me first instructions in our work was killed this morning. We march two miles to our work and stay on for 24 hours, then back for 24 hours, and so on . . .

You know what service I have seen, but I can assure you that it is nothing compared to this. It is simply Hell with the lid off! Hoping to be remembered to the Pals. Excuse scribble as everything is done under difficulties here." **Sergeant P. Stott, 173rd Tunnelling Company, Royal Engineers.** Barnsley Chronicle, April 10th 1915

Corporal Chambers of the 171st Tunnelling Company was also a regular contributor to the pages of the Barnsley Chronicle. In a letter dated April 7th he wrote,

"Sir – I hope you will excuse me taking the liberty of writing to you, but I am writing at the request of the Boys of the Barnsley First Battalion, and I am pleased to inform you that we are all in the best of health. I am proud to be in charge of them. We received our first baptism of fire on March 28th, and I was quite surprised to see how they received their first experience in the firing line. They were just like old warriors. If the remainder of the Battalion come here with the same pluck – which I am confident they will, for they will all be triers for the honour of Barnsley and district – they will make a name for themselves. Out of the 1st Barnsley Battalion in my charge are Sapper Roberts, Billingham (late 'D' Co.), Davies, Buckley, Bell ('C' Co.), Gelder ('A' Co.), and Ather('D' Co.). They all send their best respects and a special request for a copy or two of the 'Barnsley Chronicle'. Anything which is sent in the form of cigarettes, socks or other wearing apparel will be shared honourably by me.

Will you kindly tell Captain Smith that E. Roberts would like to be remembered to all the boys, and to tell them that we often wonder how long it will be before we see some of them, for they are just the sort of lads who are wanted out here.

We have had some wet weather, but this will be a beautiful country when the nice weather sets in. All the country is in ruins – shelled by the Germans. We hope the war will soon be over and that all the boys will get safely back. I hope the old country is having no difficulty in getting recruits. If they could only get one glance of this country as it really is, I have no doubt all the slackers would enlist at once.

Remember me to the 'C' Co. and all the officers of the gallant 1st Barnsley Battalion." **Barnsley Chronicle, 17th April 1915**

Corporal Chambers, like John Davies, was simply adding his own little piece of fuel to the blazing bonfire of sentimental jingoism which had been started by the British press and was still being fanned daily. The truth appeared to be all but consumed. Corporal Chambers forgot to mention that British shells too were equally responsible for the ruination of the fair land of Belgium.

By 15th April 1915, the British tunnels beneath Hill 60 were empty and silent, empty that is except for the prodigious quantities of explosives which had been tight-rammed into 6 mine chambers. The German infantrymen were sitting on top of a 10,000 pound time bomb, fused, double fused and double fused again for good luck.

John Davies was not alone in praying that the timbers, shoring up the walls of the mines and holding back the whole weight of the Flanders subsoil, would keep the clay and the water at bay for just two more days. Two more days. It must have seemed like an eternity for the miners who had put so much labour into the tunnels. It was an agonising wait up to the proposed 'zero' hour of 7 p.m. on April 17th. Anything could have happened in two days, the water could have seeped into one or all of the firing systems or, worse still, it could have soaked the charges themselves. In both instances the whole enterprise would be rendered useless. The Germans, still active, could yet pip the British at the post and blow their mines first. Hours seemed like days until 'zero' and just when the daylight was beginning to fade in the evening of a pleasant Spring day the mines were blown. The shattered earth leapt skyward and the heart was ripped out of Hill 60.

OFFICERS OF THE 14TH SERVICE YORK AND LANCASTER REGIMENT 2ND BARNSLEY BATTALION.

BUGLES AND DRUMS PRESENTED BY BRETHREN OF FRIENDLY LODGE, 1513.

(TOP ROW.) 2ND LIEUT. SPENCER, 2ND LIEUT. DONALD, 2ND LIEUT. HARBORD, 2ND LIEUT. SAMES, 2ND LIEUT. MARSDEN.
2ND LIEUT. FITTON, 2ND LIEUT. FOULDS, 2ND LIEUT. BROOKS, 2ND LIEUT. FIELDING, 2ND LIEUT. BROOMHALL,' 2ND LIEUT. HIRST,
2ND LIEUT. BROOMHALL, 2ND LIEUT. GRAY, 2ND LIEUT. FOERS, 2ND LIEUT. KING.
LIEUT. NUTT, LIEUT. HANKINSON, LIEUT. CHALLIS, CAPT. SIDDALL, MAJOR CARRINGTON, LIEUT. COL. RALEY, CAPT. HUGGARD, LIEUT. QUEST.
LIEUT. McKENNA, LIEUT. ADAMS, 2ND LIEUT. ANDERSON.

Before the debris had fallen back to earth the Allied guns poured shell after shell into the thick clouds of smoke and dust which mushroomed out from the central columns of the explosions.

What few survivors there were, some still in shirt sleeves and without rifles, tripped, tumbled, and stumbled over each other in confused retreat down what remained of their communication trenches, towards the rear. Into that seething cauldron of chaos rushed the British infantry, traversing the yawning mine craters and taking the positions which had so recently been recognisable as the German trenches.

Corporal Chambers saw it all and wrote to the Chronicle.

"You will have heard about the great victory at Hill 60. I was one of the first twenty men to get there. We took the Hill with only two casualties (the West Kents).

It was quite an unnerving half hour, as when the enemy's trenches were going up it was like one large volcano. It was a wonderful and glorious sight to see the West Kents charge. They went at the Hill like a pack of wolves! The men of the 1st Barnsley Battalion who took part in the mining

The whole episode took little more than 25 minutes but it had proved that the Tunnelling Companies had come of age with devastating effect.

It wasn't quite the victory that Corporal Chambers had boasted of however, for even as the very edition of the Chronicle in which his letter appeared, hit the doormats of Barnsley's townsfolk, the Hill had been lost again.

For more than a fortnight the British had clung, limpet-like, to the crumbling lips of the craters on "Murder Hill", all the time being strafed by German guns ranged on three sides of their positions.

Time and again German counter-attacks would inch their way up the slopes and time and again the British would force them back. On each occasion another layer of British and German bodies would increase the height of the heap and add to its infamous reputation. In the middle of the siege 171 Tunnelling Company began work on three new shafts and throughly investigated the mines which had been left by the Germans.

On the morning of May 5th Corporal Chambers and the other Barnsley men were in the first British fire trench in one of the most advanced points of Hill 60 defences, when they saw something they had dreaded since April 22nd. On that day French-Algerian troops to the north of Ypres had watched dumbfounded as a yellow-green mist appeared above the German lines and crept across No-Man's-Land towards them. Baffled, they studied its approach until it was too late. Frothing at the mouth, vomiting and with eyes bulging they turned and fled, the first victims of chlorine gas in a shocking prelude to the Second Battle of Ypres. Some of that gas had wafted down on the northerly breeze right across the Salient as far as Hill 60, and although it tickled the throat and stung the eyes, on its arrival its effects had diminished as it had dispersed.

Now, as Corporal Chambers enjoyed the relative peace of an unusual lull in the German bombardment

Listening for sounds of underground mining. When the presence of a tunnel is determined the Germans will dig a short counter-mine in its direction and set off a charge – a camouflet.

he saw it. Gas, and a thick billowing mass this time.

"The gas came over in the form of a dirty green cloud. Davies, Roberts and Billingham were underground at the time in one of the old German mines, and the rest of us had to give them warning and retire." Corporal G. Chambers No. 86641, 171st Tunnelling Company, Royal Engineers. **Barnsley Chronicle, 22nd May 1915**

Sapper E. Roberts

Sinking down into the shafts the deadly vapours were inhaled, swelling the eyes and the linings of the throat and incinerating the lungs.

Gasping for breath the men retreated, and behind the gas came the Germans, hauling themselves once more to the top of the Hill.

John Davies escaped relatively lightly even though he had been caught underground as the gas had approached. He made it to a casualty clearing station suffering from the after effects of the gas, but after a brief rest at base he was able to resume his duties. Corporal Chambers was not so lucky. Making his way to the rear in "agonies absolutely beyond description", he was helped along by a Lieutenant who was himself carrying three leg wounds.

Corporal Chambers could not be treated at the first advanced dressing station he came to. The wounded from the fighting on the Hill had completely swamped their meagre resources and 'gassed' cases were being sent further back to the base hospital. He lay there for a week before being sent home to England.

Lance-corporal J. H. Davies

In little more than two weeks some 2,000 British soldiers had died, first in taking and then in attempting to hold Hill 60. There were countless more wounded and now 'gassed' cases as well. The Germans too had suffered dreadfully, all for a mound of earth that covered an area not much bigger than 3 full size football pitches.

On May 17th John Davies had recovered enough from the effects of the gas to write " . . . everything has come all right up to now. I am in good health," on a piece of paper his wife had enclosed in a parcel to the front. Not long afterwards he went back into the line and wrote another letter home. The Germans again controlled the "cemetery" that was Hill 60 and once again 171 Tunnelling Company had begun the long, hazardous process of worming their way beneath the German positions.

"I was thinking of you all on Whit Sunday. I was in the trenches. I am on duty again tonight, it is a long and tiring time but let's hope it will soon be over. No doubt Corporal Chambers will get a job at Chatham or at the base out here but I will let you know if he gets here. It's all right to get home but I don't want to come home in the same state as he was. How is my little George and Charlie. I guess they will be excited when we get the word to come home. Keep their little hearts up for my sake. I think I am a lot better in the Engineers than in the Barnsley Battalion for reasons I will explain if all goes well . . ."

He never disturbed his eldest son with any reason as to why he was better off in the Royal Engineers, but another letter to the boy was not without its serious side. In his Father's absence Johnnie Davies, at the age of 10 was the 'man' of the house.

"It is very good of you to offer that nice prayer for me and all the soldiers. Be a good boy, and look after your young brothers no matter what happens. Cheer your mother up till I come home and I will not forget you. 1 shall be pleased to get home again, but not till peace is proclaimed and we have won the day. So be a good boy Johnnie, and pray to God for us all that the war will soon be over and we shall be able to return home again and be happy together."

On June 17th, John Davies wrote what was to be his last letter to his wife and its contents make sadly pathetic reading in the light of the tragedy which loomed large for his family.

"The whole place looks grand in summer weather, but the boom of the guns and the constant traffic of men and horses spoils the peacefulness of Belgium. I always tried to lead a good life at home, but I think I shall lead a better one after this, as this war has taught me and a good many more, a lot that we shall never forget. If anything was to happen to me I should not wish you to fret at my loss but rather thank God that I had done my little bit for love and freedom, King and country."

Ironically, the date of that last letter, June 17th, is the same date which appeared at the foot of John Davies' Will.

Three days later he went down a shaft into the mines beneath Hill 60 for the last time.

It was well known that the Germans were also burrowing in the vicinity. Pushing the clay back silently by hand from man to man, John Davies paused and whispered, "listen".

There could be no mistake . . . somewhere, very close, the Germans were digging too, and for the Davies family time had run out.

A small camouflet explosion filled the straight-jacket confines of the gallery, collapsing it and burying John Davies.

The labyrinth of tunnels had become his tomb and Hill 60 had claimed another victim, this time in the separate underworld war waged by the miners. The Barnsley Chronicle had felt it its sad duty to publish news of the numerous local men who had been killed since the outbreak of hostilities and less than a week after the death of John Davies, the Editor included the following letter in its columns.

"Sir, – I have the painful duty to inform you that we have lost one of the finest men who came out with us from Newhall Camp, Silkstone – J. H. Davies, who belonged to 'C' Company. I dare not write to his wife, who resides in Vernon Street North, as he was a man whose whole heart was wrapped up in his wife and family, and it will be a severe blow to her to know of his death while at work yesterday, 20th June.

There was not a more willing or better liked man in the company than Davies; everyone thought the world of him and it has made a deeper impression on our minds than an ordinary death as we are used to that. But it seems so hard to lose such a good comrade as he was, a man who did his duty thoroughly. . . . I am sending this letter to you in the hope that you will know someone who will be able to break the news to his wife more gently than I can. I hope God will bless his wife and children in trouble as he was intensely fond of them and he often used to tell me of his lads.

There are not many of the Barnsley Battalion left here as they have been scattered about – some wounded, some gassed, and some with other companies. My home is at Royston and I used to belong to 'D' Company."
Yours obediently, Sapper E. Roberts. Barnsley Chronicle, 26th June 1915.

The white lies of the time. In order to save the family further pain the death of John Davies is described as "instantaneous" and that he looked peaceful "as he lay on the stretcher". His burial place is surrounded by corn-flowers. The truth is John Davies was buried alive or crushed and has no known grave. He is commemorated on Panel 9 of the Menin Gate Memorial to the missing, Ypres.

(4 27 1) W 8687—1338 250,000 11/14 H W V $\frac{21}{796}$

Army Form B. 104—82.

No. _Ref. R.(c). 36_
(If replying, please quote above No.)

Royal Engineers Record Office,

Chatham ~~Station,~~

9 July , 1915.

Madam,
~~Sir,~~

It is my painful duty to inform you that a report has this day been received from the War Office notifying the death of

(No.) 86654 (Rank) Sapper

(Name) J. H. Davies (Regiment) 141st. Coy.

Royal Engineers which occurred ~~at~~ while on Active Service with B. Exp Force on the 20th day

of June 1915 , and I am to express to you the sympathy and regret of the Army Council at your loss. The cause of death was

"Killed in Action".

If any articles of private property left by the deceased are found, they will be forwarded to this Office, but some time will probably elapse before their receipt, and when received they cannot be disposed of until authority is received from the War Office.

Application regarding the disposal of any such personal effects, or of any amount that may eventually be found to be due to the late soldier's estate, should be addressed to "The Secretary, War Office, London, S.W.," and marked outside "Effects."

Mrs E. Davies,
15, Vernon St, North,
Barnsley.

I am,
~~Sir,~~ Madam,
Your obedient Servant,

Arthur L. Marten
Capt

for Officer in charge of Records.

Chapter Five

Into khaki

EARLY IN MARCH 1915, "OSSIE" BURGESs, along with his two elder brothers, turned up as usual for the day shift at Silkstone pit. It didn't turn out to be quite the normal day they had expected.

"There had been an explosion and we couldn't get to the place where we were working. I said, "I'm not having this, I'm going to 'list". They said, "If you're going to 'list, we're going as well". They were asking for volunteers then, Lord Kitchener was asking. We all three went to the Public Hall to join up. One failed due to his eyesight. The eldest brother joined the same lot as me. He was married and had two or three bairns. There was a parson that swore you in. He said, "My word, I wish we'd a battalion like you."' **752 L/Corporal "Ossie" Burgess, 'D' Company, 14th Y & L Regiment**

The parson was none other than the Rev. Richard Huggard, the man who had sworn in so many of the First Barnsley Battalion and his remark was not without foundation. Ever since recruiting for the Second Battalion had been announced it had become a constant source of anxiety for Col. Raley, the Commanding Officer and the Corporation Raising Committee, that the Battalion was not growing as fast as they would have liked. In fact the response of married men, in circumstances similar to those of "Ossie" Burgess' elder brother Sam, had been greater than that of young, single men with fewer responsibilities.

"Of the recruits enlisted for the 2nd Barnsley Battalion this week more than half are married men. It is astonishing that more single men don't enlist. On the whole we should have expected this opportunity to be more attractive to those who have not yet had the chance of displaying their valour. Surely there are at least as many brave single men as married ones who are anxious and willing to respond to their country's call. We hope to report in this column next week that the single men of Barnsley are in a great majority." **Barnsley Chronicle, 16th January 1915**

The Chronicle's hopes appeared to be in vain.

"The Barnsley Second Battalion is not making the progress which it deserves. This is all the more strange when one looks about the streets and picture palaces in an evening, where hundreds of young men, quite eligible to serve in the Army, are whiling away their time. There is no sense of fairness in conduct such as this, and, to use the words of a returned wounded soldier, "It is disgraceful." Men are wanted, badly wanted, and if the single men did their duty the Battalion would be completed within a week." **Barnsley Chronicle, 23rd January 1915**

Certainly the feeling was that the first hot flushes of "war fever" had worked their way through the Nation's system and that a great many young men were shirking their responsibilities. In order to redress the balance as far as married and single men were concerned, Col. Raley hit upon a scheme which he called the 'chum system'. In reality it was little more than a bounty hunt. His idea was to give all the recruits a day's holiday in the hope that each man would return with at least one physically fit specimen who was willing and able to enlist. A first prize of £3 was offered as a reward for the man who brought in the

As recruitment begins to drop off advertisements are run in the Chronicle along with editorial urgings to join up.

Play a Man's part, and enlist to-day.

BARNSLEY SECOND BATTALION
YORK AND LANCASTERS
———
MEN, JOIN AT ONCE,
AND
"LEND A HAND."

71

Captain R. Huggard, 14th Y & L

most volunteers. As a recruiting exercise however, it was not a great success. Although Company Sergeant Major Gallagher claimed the £3 prize by "bagging" 40 recruits, and a further 50 were introduced by Sergeants Bailey and Bullock, the strength of the Battalion was nowhere near doubled as had been hoped.

Recruiting went on slowly and was still lethargic when, late in March, Barnsley's M.P. Sir Joseph Walton, visited the town to inspect the First Battalion at Silkstone and help with the rallying of men for the Second. In the three months since the beginning of January a total of 963 men had joined the Second Battalion, a figure the First Battalion had reached in three weeks, and a further 140 were still required. As he had done several months previously Sir Joseph gave a colourful speech to the audience at the first house at the Empire theatre. Fresh from a three week fact-finding tour of the Western Front, his speech was full of the rhetoric of death and destruction. He closed with the words,

"I beg of you ladies and gentlemen, to use your influence to get likely men to join Colonel Raley's Battalion soon, and complete it without further delay. I am sure I shall have from a patriotic Barnsley audience a very practical response."

Col. Raley, following Sir Joseph, took a rather more down-to-earth approach.

"Don't wait till after Easter, because the two or three days we have before then can be well spent, and you can get into uniform immediately after Easter. You will have a better holiday if you come to us than if you stay at home, as we are proposing that the men shall have holiday from Thursday night until Wednesday morning. Now lads, you can come to the Empire, you can go to your football matches, you go to your clubs and pubs – I don't blame you for it – only don't leave us in the lurch. Show what Barnsley can do." **Barnsley Chronicle, April 3rd 1915**

Frank Lindley ex 14th Y & L

If the town's elders thought that the youth of Barnsley was slow in showing what it could do, they must have appreciated the help of the 28 recruits who had come forward from outside Barnsley and district.

One of those 28 was Frank Lindley. Sheffield born and bred, Frank was just 8 days into his fifteenth year when he joined the Second Barnsley Pals on March 20th. Although he had been with them a mere 9 days when Col. Raley had made his speech, he was no skrimshanker, far from it. Frank had in fact, enlisted before the end of 1914, he had then graced the ranks of the 2/3rd West Riding Royal Field Artillery. Technically he was a deserter.

While some recruits had enlisted out of a sense of duty or patriotism and others had looked for a way out of the daily round

Left: *Frank Lindley with his elder brother Harry, who is among the first casualties of the war. as his ship, HMS Hawke (right) is torpedoed in the North Sea. Harry's death starts 14-year-old Frank on the vengeance trail. Under age he joins the Royal Artillery at Sheffield.*

with the hope, perhaps, of a European holiday at the Army's expense, Frank Lindley was driven by a much more powerful and uncompromising motive, namely revenge.

"I lost my brother in one of the first ships to go down in the 'Big War'. Harry had come home from the Mediterranean Fleet exercises. He hadn't been home a few days when war broke out. They fetched him back, shoved him on a scratch cruiser HMS Hawke *out in the North Sea, and down they went, torpedoed.*

"Me and my dad were getting ready to go to work one morning and a knock came at the door and there was a telegram, sudden like that, October time. We read the bugger and we both collapsed. That finished my dad, he died in 1918. Of course his grinding didn't help it, but it nearly killed him that morning." **949 Private Frank Lindley, 1 Platoon 'A' Company, 14th Y & L Regiment**

Frank Lindley 14th Y & L.
An under age deserter from the Royal Artillery joins up at Barnsley.

It nearly killed the fourteen-year-old Frank too. He had thought the world of his brother and his brother, in turn, had thought the world of Frank. As a pre-war naval rating Harry Lindley had sailed the globe aboard his ship HMS *Dido*. Each time he returned home on leave he would bring with him exotic tales of foreign countries and always there would be a present for his younger brother. One such present was an unusual travelling compendium, beautifully finished in cedarwood veneer which Harry brought home from Jerusalem. Harry's adventure yarns would not have shamed the pages of the Boy's Own paper, a journal which featured prominently on Frank's reading list. The heady mixture of fact and fiction had a profound effect on such an impressionable mind.

"I had itchy feet fired by Harry's travels. While he was on leave we used to talk because we used to sleep in the same bed. He said, 'Now Frank, I've got it all planned. We're refitting for the Far East and when I get to Australia I shall jump ship and go and take a tract of land, then I'll send for you'. That was the very last thing he said to me. We were pals me and him. We used to go all over. He even used to send money to clothe me. I had rather a posh job, a dental mechanic, and I had to have an appearance because I was dealing with titled people. That's what made me go to war, I wanted to avenge Harry's death."

Frank had made up his mind and although only fourteen years of age, no one was going to change it.

"Goodness knows what my mum and dad thought about me going. I never gave it a second thought because I meant to go. My parents realised I'd made up my mind and that was that. Dad put his foot down once. When I was 13 I wanted to join the Navy and it needed parental consent, but he wouldn't consent. I resented it because I was full of adventure. My brother had been to all these foreign parts and I thought I wouldn't mind having a go myself. Well that fell through and then Harry was killed . . . it made me think a bit. Everybody was wanting us, Kitchener was pointing at us, so I joined along with some of my pals." **Frank Lindley, 14th Y & L Regiment**

One of Frank's favourite pastimes was frequenting the local billiard halls and it was with a bunch of his billiard-playing friends that he went to join up.

"We tried the Sheffield City Battalion but it was full, so we decided we'd have to join something, and I joined the artillery at Edmund Road Drill Hall with one or two others."

Being a strong, muscular lad of twelve and a half stones, Frank had no trouble convincing the recruiting sergeant that he was twenty years old. It was while he was at the Edmund Road Drill Hall that Frank became friendly with Ethelbert Hobson who, for obvious reasons, much preferred to be known by his nickname of "Hoppy". "Hoppy", a Territorial, had just returned from annual camp and soon he and Frank were on the move again.

"We lived in a school called Carter Knowle Council School and moved from there to a village called Duffield near Derby. We did our training on the golf course there, riding school, bareback and all the tricks for our spurs, and it was a rough business. Some of the officers were time serving men and they sent them to drill us. There was one in particular, Sgt. Major Muffins, he used to bend down, get a handful of horsemuck and if you didn't suit him, if you weren't riding correctly, he'd ride up at the side of you and say, 'hey you', and you'd get it in your face. There were tricks like that which we didn't altogether swallow. We'd such a rotten lot of N.C.O.'s that we decided to clear off and find somewhere a bit more soldier-like. We weren't getting anywhere messing around with horses and all that. It was the slow hanging on, mucking out and all that business. Of course we saw a gun or two, but we didn't have much training on them. We thought we'd shove off, chuff the rough N.C.O.'s and join the foot soldiers."

Frank, along with "Hoppy" Hobson and a few others who had had the misfortune to be the recipients of a none too fragrant dollop of what passed for artillery discipline, decided to vote with their feet.

Above and below:
Ossie Burgess 14th Y & L

"We walked from Duffield to Belper one Friday evening and jumped on a train to Sheffield and told the ticket man we were on special duty back at the artillery drill hall and they hadn't had time to give us warrants. We reached Sheffield and agreed to meet the next morning. On Saturday morning we met and there was only me and 'Hoppy' Hobson turned up, so we shot off to Barnsley."

Before they did however they had to rid themselves of the last vestiges of their previous military existence.

"We were strutting about in our artillery gear in Sheffield on the Saturday morning, so what we did was to shove all our stuff, spurs and the lot, into a kit bag when we got into Victoria Station and we bunged it in a truck. We said 'You can have that lot'. We put on some 'civvies' that we had left at home. I had a suit. I think it was the first pair of long trousers I had to mean anything."

They could have gone anywhere but they chose Barnsley. For one thing it was quite close and for another the fare was cheap.

"We were in Barnsley and saw these placards hanging across the road saying 'Join the Barnsley Pals', so we decided we'd have a go with them. We signed on and lived in the Public Hall which was a Music Hall affair. My pal 'Hoppy' signed on under the name of Bert Hobson. He'd said to me 'If tha' calls me Ethelbert in front of this lot I'll kill thee'. We lived on the stage and slept all over the place. We slept in our shirts. We had blankets but the trouble was that they all used to be piled in a heap in the middle of the floor. It didn't matter whose blankets you got. In fact I got some eczema on my 'clock' and on my neck. I was daubed with yellow ointment for a week or two."

The bright yellow preparation went under the inglorious title of Dr. Stagg's ointment, recommended for, "Itch, bad legs and eruptions of the skin." Nash's chemist on Queen Street had probably done a brisk trade in half-crown pots of the stuff as eczema swept through the ranks. Not surprisingly Frank Lindley soon tired of the nightly scramble for blankets.

"Finally I took my blankets up into a limelight box. I could 'scrim' up this post and get into this little box away from everybody else. That was my kip." **Frank Lindley, 14th Y & L Regiment**

On the other hand "Ossie" Burgess had found no such cosy spot on his first night at the Public Hall.

Charlie Swales
ex 14th Y & L

"We slept right at the top in the School of Art. There were 3 or 4 of us together right next to some steps. They pushed me nearest to the steps and I rolled down them during the night." **'Ossie' Burgess, 14th Y & L Regiment**

"Ossie's" parents had voiced their misgivings about his enlistment, misgivings which emanated more from the Burgess family's financial situation rather than from any particular fears for his personal safety.

"My parents didn't like me joining up. I was between 18 and 19 and at that time you used to work for them until 21 and then you used to pay board. Of course with not being 21 I did what you called 'tipped up', I gave my parents all the money and they gave me pocket money. They lost some money when I joined up." **'Ossie' Burgess, 14th Y & L Regiment**

James Bennett
ex 14th Y & L

The Easter holidays of 1915 were somewhat of a milestone for both battalions of the Barnsley Pals. With the second Battalion reaching a round one thousand, it had begun to outgrow its accommodation at the Public Hall. Fortunately for the members of the Raising Committee, tearing their hair out wondering where to house a further 100 volunteers plus a reserve Company numbering some 250, the Trustees of the Regent Street Congregational Church came forward with the generous offer of its schoolroom for use by one of the Companies. The offer got the Raising Committee out of a tight spot. Most of the members of 'D' Company duly picked up a few blankets from the pile in the middle of the floor of the Public Hall and made the short trip across to Regent Street.

Easter proved to be more of a memorable occasion for the First Barnsley's, or at least it was for half their number. They had been training for a little over 6 months and the Navy Blue 'postmens' uniforms were showing definite signs of deterioration. Half the men had been granted 5 days' home leave for the holiday period while the remainder, who stayed at Silkstone, were served out with khaki service dress. The arrival of these long awaited uniforms was a real tonic for the men, who were eager to escape the routine of Silkstone and get on with the real business of fighting the war. It was, after all, one of the reasons why they had joined up. When the rest of the Battalion returned to camp after their short break, they too received their uniforms and at last the whole unit began to look and feel just like "real" soldiers of the British Army.

Their feelings were understandable. They had been told many times that they were a fine body of men and that they would be ready for the front well within the prescribed training period for New Army units. Now they had their uniforms they naturally wanted to know why they weren't preparing to go to France. They were innocent in their ignorance. The plain truth was that they still lacked experience in the basic military details on which the regular soldiers had prided themselves. Small-arms ammunition was still in short supply, a fact which seriously limited shooting practice. In any event no one was really sure how some of the older "drill pattern" rifles would react when called upon to fire live rounds. The men of the machine-gun section had never set eyes on a real machine gun, let alone been given the opportunity to handle one. The Battalion had also dug a few trenches in Noblethorpe and Wentworth Parks, and had even ventured on to the moors to construct neat lines of ditches, to the very latest specifications as set out in neat diagrams in the Field Service Pocket Book of 1914. Specifications were all very well but digging trenches in the countryside around Silkstone was a far cry from digging in under hostile fire.

In spite of their verve and self belief they were far from ready, a fact which would become increasingly

National fervour is kept on the boil with patriotic songs.

clear to the Army's top brass as the months progressed.

While the men of the First Barnsley's thought themselves ready for action after 6 months, there were others who were only just embarking on a military career. On April 6th, the last day of Easter leave for half the men of the First Barnsley's, Charlie Swales eventually managed to join the Barnsley Pals.

When war broke out Charlie was 16 years old and working for Cutt's horse and cart business, mainly employed in hauling canal barges. He was no stranger to working with horses for his first job on leaving school had been as a pony driver at Carlton pit. Charlie was a keen amateur footballer and one Sunday afternoon the lads who made up the local team decided that they would all join up together.

"We thought it was going to be a bit of fun – some wanted to get away from the pit. At that time we weren't worried about the Germans, the only thing that bothered us was that the war might be over before we got there." **1022 Private Charles Swales, 'C' Company, 14th Y & L Regiment**

Because it was a Sunday when the football team turned up at the Public Hall the lads were told by the recruiting officer to come back the next day.

"He told us he would take us all but we had to go to work the next day and we couldn't get there. After that me and another lad fancied the Navy but you had to go in for 12 years. Sammy was 2 years older than me, he being 18. They noticed that I was limping and asked me what was the matter – I had a nail up in my shoe and a big blister under my foot. They said, 'You'll have to get that better before I take you or you'll be straight in sick bay.' Sammy told them that he would only join up for the duration if I couldn't join and he signed up there and then. He wrote to me later and said, 'Don't come into the Navy or you'll have to come as a boy – we can't be together because of our ages'." **Charlie Swales, 14th Y & L Regiment**

The Navy's loss was the Pals' gain. The rest of Charlie's footballing friends had by that time joined the Second Barnsley Battalion.

"They were all in 'C' Company. When I couldn't go in the Navy I went to sign up with the Battalion. I told them I was 21 and asked if I would be in 'C' Company. Their regimental numbers were about 300 and something and mine was 1022, but I got with them and we were together then. In our section they were all under age. On enlisting we had all said that we were 21, but they knew bloody

well that we weren't. There were some younger than me, one of them, 'Lijah Wright from Cudworth was 15. There were a lot of young uns. We slept on the stage at the Public Hall on the boards with just a blanket. We were in ordinary clothes first before they dished khaki out." **Charlie Swales, 14 Y & L Regiment**

Young and single Charlie was just the type of recruit the raisers were looking for having turned a blind eye on the question of his age. Even so married men were still coming forward. *"I joined up at the Public Hall. I was living in Darfield and working in the pit at Dearne Valley. We all joined up because we took a fancy to doing our share. I went with one or two to join up. My wife thought nothing about it, she knew I was joining. She knew all the young chaps from Wombwell and Darfield were going. She evidently didn't mind at all. It was all arranged for her to be paid a marriage allowance. I remember talking it over with her but it was the general thing to join up. When we reported at the Public Hall we formed up in the back yard. I remember it was a sloping back yard, perhaps for the rain to run into the gutters. We formed up into a squad and there were different groups from different villages. They came from all over – some from Darton, some from Wombwell and us from Darfield. We moved about in different sections and platoons and eventually they formed us up into a Company."* **1096 Private James Bennett, 'C' Company, 14th Y & L Regiment**

Increased Separation Allowances

for soldiers' wives and children.

FROM MARCH 1st the Separation Allowances paid by the Government to the wives and children of the soldiers have been increased, so that the total weekly payment to the family, if the soldier makes the usual allotment from his pay, is now as follows:—

	Corporal or Private.		Sergeant
Wife................... per week	12/6	....	15/-
Wife and 1 child .... per week	17/6	....	20/-
Wife and 2 children, per week	21/-	....	23/6
Wife and 3 children, per week	23/-	....	25/6

and so on with an addition of
2/- for each additional child.

Each Motherless child................ 5/-

To wives living at the time of enlistment in the London area, a further sum of 3/6 per week is paid as long as they continue to live there,

From February 1st, 1915, Separation Allowance is payable for all children up to the age of 16 years. This includes adopted children.

Allowances for other Dependants.

If an unmarried soldier has supported a dependant for a reasonable period, and wishes the support he gave to be continued, the Government will help, during the war, by making a grant of Separation Allowance, provided he will contribute part of his pay.

Full particulars can be obtained at any Post Office.

God Save the King.

An inducement for family men to enlist is published in the Chronicle showing the recent Government increase in allowances. Many of the Pals were family men. a selection is shown here. Above: James Haywood, High Street, Royston, five children. Below: Edwin Coe, High Street, Barnsley, two children.

The marriage allowance, better known as the separation allowance, had been increased to 12 shillings and sixpence on March 1st 1915, for the wife of a Corporal or Private without children. The amount was more substantial for the wives of Sergeants and for mothers with children to support. Whatever the payment it always included a sum which had been deducted from the soldier's weekly pay. Single men too usually saw to it that their mothers received part of their pay, 6d a day being the standard payment. What with these deductions, plus other stoppages, the Pals were left with little scope for extravagant living.

The Raising Committee had hoped to clothe the recruits in khaki as soon as they enlisted, and certainly a number of the earlier recruits were into uniform quite quickly.

"We were measured for uniforms straight away and we got them 3 or 4 days after. The only thing was you didn't get boots because you had to be measured for them and had to wait until they came." **'Ossie' Burgess, 14th Y & L Regiment**

It did not work out as easily as that for the rest. One of the first tasks of the Raising Committee had been to attempt to place the contracts for the khaki uniforms with local firms, thereby assisting the local economy. Clearly the committee had come to the conclusion that if there was money to be made in the clothing and equipping of Kitchener's Army then it should be made by local business men. They would, after all, be clothing and equipping a locally raised battalion.

Early in January 1915 the Chronicle announced that,

Left: *Henry Watson, Woolley Colliery, one child.*

Right: *Ernest Reid, Pleasant View, Smithies. His little girl is to die of meningitis whilst he is away.*

"*Colonel Raley and other members of the Corporation interviewed the military authorities in London and secured their assent to clothe the Second Battalion in khaki service dress – exactly the same attire as will be used when the men go on foreign service. The khaki which the War Office has approved of has been woven at the Mills of Messrs. Thos. Taylor and Sons, Barnsley.*" **Barnsley Chronicle, 2nd January 1915**

The Committee didn't just stop at the uniforms. They managed to place the contracts for boots, drawers, shirts, braces, toothbrushes, combs, entrenching tools and the greater part of the contract for overcoats, with local firms. The trouble was that the committee only sanctioned the manufacture of uniforms and equipment in batches of 50 and consequently some of the men had to wait a considerable time for their outfits. For the men from outside the district this fact posed a problem. Frank Lindley's one and only Sunday best suit had taken a severe battering. He ate, drank, drilled and marched in the same suit he had enlisted in.

"*I wore that devil out in Barnsley. The other lads who lived in Barnsley could rustle different things up but we were more or less threadbare. By the time we finished, our breeches were out at the behinds. That's how we got our name 'The Ragged Arsed Battalion'.*"

When the uniforms did appear their quality did nothing to enhance the reputation of the local textile industry, but the quick-witted Frank Lindley was able to turn the situation to his advantage.

"*We got some khaki but it was shoddy at the side of the real stuff. I spent a bit of time taking up, sewing and making the trousers a bit tighter. I did one or two blokes. I'd slit the trousers and pull them tight so they fit nicely over their puttees. You had your trousers on and you put your puttees on over them starting at the bottom and tying them just below the knee. You pulled your trousers up first, so far, so that they made a little overlap and you folded that bit down over the top of your puttees. I used to get 'bacca' and fags as a treat for all my tailoring.*" **Frank Lindley, 14th Y & L Regiment**

Vernon Atkinson, a 19-year-old Barnsley Main miner who enlisted towards the end of April, had much the same problem with his uniform when he finally received it.

> *"It was a hard life at the beginning. I went in 'civvies' at first. Broomhalls on Sackville Street, they made our uniforms for us. As long as you got hold of one it was all right. They used to turn them out any road."* **1135 Vernon Atkinson, 'A' Company, 14th Y & L Regiment**

Vernon was placed in the Reserve Company, and again a shortage of space meant that after a brief stay at the Public Hall he and his comrades were moved to new quarters. The move was not without its compensations.

> *"I used to sleep in the gallery at the Public Hall and then they moved some of us to Blucher Street Chapel. It wasn't so bad there, it was next to Mrs. Leatham's 'boozer'."* **Vernon Atkinson, 14th Y & L Regiment**

Lieutenant J. W. Challice 14th Y & L

Mrs. Leatham was well used to the soldier fraternity trooping in from the United Methodist Church schoolroom, for her cousin Lance Corporal J. Barlow was one of the Barnsley 'Terriers' who were already, 'somewhere in France.'

As had been the case with the 13th Battalion, the first officers for the 14th were, in the main, local men nominated by the Raising Committee on behalf of the Corporation. During the month of January 1915, one acting Captain and eight acting subalterns were offered commissions. Several more officers quickly followed. Some of them had a depth of military experience, however antiquated, which put the 'old sweats' of the 13th Battalion to shame. Others were fresh-faced young men from well to do families, or with secure professions in the Barnsley area, whose budget would stretch to their purchasing the full officers' regalia, Sam Browne belt and all.

Right and below: *Vernon Atkinson 14th Y & L*

At one end of the scale were men like Lieutenant and Quarter-master J. W. Challice whose army career had begun as far back as 19th December 1883, when he had enlisted in the Yorkshire Regiment. Ten years and several promotions later had seen him transferred to the Indian unattached list as a Sergeant-Major with the Coorg and Mysore Rifles. The bulk of his career, 17 years, had been spent in the hot, sticky climates of India and Upper Burma. He was discharged on a pension on New Year's Day 1906 after 22 years' service. When war broke out he had responded quickly and by the end of September 1914 he was back as a Sergeant-Major with the 9th Battalion, the Yorkshire Regiment. On 25th January 1915, nine years after his 'retirement' he was appointed to serve with the 14th York and Lancasters.

At the other end were men like Frank Lindley's platoon commander, Second Lieutenant William Hirst. Before the war 30-year-old William Hirst had built himself a promising career in mine surveying. As the proud holder of the Bronze Medal of the City and Guilds of London Institute of Surveying he had been the consultant surveyor to the Wombwell Main Colliery Company and had lectured in the subject at Sheffield University as an assistant to Professor Hardwick.

In stark contrast to Lieutenant Challice, the only 'service' Second Lieutenant Hirst had seen, prior to joining the Second Barnsley Battalion in its early stages, had been as Captain of the Wombwell Church Lads Brigade.

*Lieutenant
McKenna
14th Y & L*

"*He was a very quiet gentlemanly chap who didn't shout and bawl. The young officers weren't the old regimental people, they weren't regulars. They were all amateurs. He was a real nice fellow.*" **Frank Lindley, 14th Y & L Regiment**

There were other amateurs too, like Walter Kell, described by Vernon Atkinson as a "big man in the Corporation". He was in fact with the Electricity Department and a keen rugby player in his spare time. He became a Lieutenant along with 26-year-old Duncan Fairley, a first class honours graduate of Leeds University and the youngest son of the headmaster of St. John's school in Barnsley. Fairley had been an assistant English master at the Scarborough Municipal Secondary school at the time of the German naval bombardment in December 1914. Yet another man from a scholastic background was Second Lieutenant R. Dudley Anderson, the 20-year-old youngest son of the Principal of Wakefield Academy. With a few notable exceptions, they all had one thing in common. They were devoid of hard military experience, a fact which for all their idealism regarding service to King and country, had not been overlooked by the Battalion jokers.

"*One officer called McKenna used to drill us at Queen's Ground and he didn't understand rifles properly. We had a Lance Corporal called Button and he was the head man. He'd give us our drill orders like, 'right incline', which meant, follow the Corporal. My mate, Cooper said, 'bugger him Vern, come down here'. Instead of following the Corporal we used to cut down to the bottom of the Queen's Ground and this Corporal was still going forward. The officer would shout to him and say, 'What the hell are you doing? Look where the men are going.' Well the Corporal was right, we were wrong. We were going wrong on purpose for a bit of a lark. We used to get him into trouble.*" **Vernon Atkinson, 14th Y & L Regiment**

It wasn't so simple to pull the wool over the eyes of the 'old-timers' like Sergeant Bullock, brought in, like the veteran N.C.O.'s of the 13th Battalion, to help with the training. They had probably witnessed almost every trick that the 'rankers' could pull. It was on the parade ground that Frank Lindley and "Hoppy" Hobson had displayed the dark secrets of their past life for worldly N.C.O.'s to view at their leisure. Again the army proved that it had a nasty habit of pulling old skeletons out of the private soldier's cupboard.

"*Eventually we were marched in 'clink'. We knew what it was for, they'd caught up with us. They'd sifted us out. We never wrote home, how they found out goodness knows. We were having dinner in the Public Hall when this orderly Sergeant came up and said, 'Come on here you two, in 'clink'.' The unfortunate thing was that the lad whose number came between mine and "Hoppy's" on the roll was called Lindley as well. They tapped him and "Hoppy" on the shoulder and took them in. Well, when I'd done my dinner I went to the guard room and said,*

Sergeant William Colbourne, 14th Battalion, antagonist of Vernon Atkinson. 'One day they blew the bugle and we fell in for pay parade. Q.M. Snowden and Capt. McKenna were sitting inside the hut with the money. I needed to go to the toilet and I went on my own. I didn't ask the Sgt. When I came back he said, "Where have you been Atkinson?" McKenna called in Sgt. Colbourne and asked what the matter was. Sgt. Colbourne said I had broken the rank and Capt. McKenzie said I hadn't, that I was quite in order to go to the toilet because they hadn't started paying. Sgt. Colbourne kept saying, "I shall get thee" and I used to say, "Yes, and I shall get thee back, them stripes don't bother me". Later they put me on guard at Woodend. The trees were rustling and I was a bit nervous being a new recruit. I called the guard out and Colbourne was the Sergeant of the guard. He said, "What's tha called the guard out for Atkinson", and I said, "I don't feel so clever". He said, "You'll just have to stick it". Oh, we cursed him upside down.'

Carefree days at Silkstone, 13th officers share a joke outside the Officers' Mess.

'Here's their dinner, I've brought it. It's me you want.' The sergeant of the guard said, 'I thought it was, I recognised the way you drilled on the Queen's Grounds when you were forming fours.' He was a very old soldier was Sergeant Bullock, he recognised the way we were moving. He used to say, 'What the hell are you two doing? That's artillery formation.' When the artillery moved across in echelon they moved in fours and you brought your four with you, but in the infantry the men just came round as they pleased. You broke from the four and moved around by yourself. We were put on a charge, a court martial and the old man in charge said, 'What would you like to do boys, go back or stay here? We want you here because we're forming a battalion.' We said we'd stay and that was that. We had three months' pay stopped and got 28 days in 'clink'. We did that but that black mark stayed with us all the way. We were labelled bad lads." **Frank Lindley, 14th Y & L Regiment**

Frank's crime of desertion was a misdemeanour which carried the maximum punishment of death for troops on active service. Although not on active service Frank's punishment seemed a little harsh when compared with that meted out to Private Robert Priestley who, in the process of deserting the 14th Battalion, took with him 11 knives, 5 forks and a tablespoon belonging to the Barnsley British Co-operative Society. He was caught by the police and appeared in court before the Mayor on 1st April 1915. Pleading guilty he said, "I am very sorry. It's my first time", to which the Mayor, Honorary Colonel of the 13th Battalion, replied,

"It is very sad for us to see a man wearing the King's uniform here on such a charge, and to know that he had done such acts as these. So far as our local battalions are concerned we are proud to think that they are composed of honourable men, of gentlemen, but evidently you are not of that class. The least we can do for you is 14 days' hard labour." **Barnsley Chronicle, 3rd April 1915**

Although Priestley went to jail, he was released two weeks earlier than Frank Lindley whose crime had been to try and find a regiment which was likely to see action.

Late in April, Brigadier General Bowles, commanding the 115th Infantry Brigade, intimated that the 13th Battalion were to be transferred to Castleton in Derbyshire early in May, leaving the 14th to continue their training at Silkstone. These plans were, however,

The 13th Battalion Bugle and Drum Band, pictured at Oakwell Football Ground.

Thirty officers of the 13th. Nine will not survive the war in Europe.

cancelled and instead both Battalions were given orders to prepare for a move to Penkridge Bank Camp near the market town of Rugeley on Cannock Chase in Staffordshire. There they would join the rest of the Brigade for what the Chronicle called the "finishing touch to their thoroughly successful training."

Shortly afterwards the 115th Brigade were re-numbered the 94th and that wasn't the only change. The Grimsby 'Chums' (the 10th Lincolnshire Regiment) were exchanged for 'Pals', the Accrington Pals, formed, like the First Barnsley Battalion, in September 1914. They were officially known as the 11th East Lancashire Regiment. Now there were four 'Pals' battalions in the same Brigade, spiritually straddling the Pennines even if the South Yorkshiremen did outnumber the Lancastrians by 3–1.

The Raising Committee of the 2nd Barnsley Pals were highly delighted with this surprise item of news.

"The Committee feel that it is a high compliment to be paid to the men that they should be thought fit to be brigaded with other Battalions having a much lengthier period of training, and speaks volumes for the energy and enthusiasm displayed by the Officers and men in connection with the work of the Battalion." **Minutes of the Report of the Sub-Committee Appointed to Superintend the Raising and Equipment of the Second Barnsley Battalion. 11th May 1915**

13th Battalion en masse in Noblethorpe Park, Silkstone.

13th Battalion football team.

There were compliments also for certain members of the 13th Battalion at a farewell luncheon given by Colonel Hewitt at Silkstone, on the eve of the Pals' departure for pastures new. It was a sumptuous occasion to mark an historic moment in the town's military endeavours.

Anybody who was anybody in connection with the raising of the two Battalions was present to take advantage of Colonel Hewitt's hospitality and listen to the after dinner back slapping of the local raisers. All the officers of both units were there, among them the newly promoted Major Guest and Captain DeVille Smith, along with wives, mothers and fathers, friends and members of the Corporation. The Regimental Institute had been specially adorned with the Union Jack and the flags of the Allies by a group of men of the 13th Battalion, and comments were passed that the decorations reflected great credit on their taste. Taste, that was a word which the often hungry lads of both battalions didn't readily associate with notions of aesthetic judgement. To them taste meant food and they never had a chance to savour the like of the fare offered to the guests of Colonel Hewitt. The menu, consisting of Salmon, Chicken, Ham, Roast Beef, Saddle of Lamb, Tongues, Champagne, Apple Tart, Blancmange, Port, Coffee and Liqueurs, far exceeded even the best efforts of the catering staff of the Barnsley British Co-op.

The speeches which followed the meal were reminiscent of those made by doting male relatives when a young man leaves home to find his fortune. Pride shone through. From Colonel Hewitt:

> "I am proud to be able to say that our lads in the 13th York and Lancaster Regiment and the sister Battalion are the finest lads you can have. We are proud of them – proud of them one and all."

From the Mayor:

Visiting Staff Officers inspect the 13th Battalion shortly before it leaves for Rugeley. Signallers led by Sergeant Lax cross the foreground to the accompaniment of the bugle and drum band.

> "... we can boast of having recruited two of the finest Battalions of manhood in this or any other country. The people of this district might well be proud of their Battalions, and now that they are about to depart from our midst we shall watch with unceasing interest their progress."

And from Major Guest:

> "I am quite sure that the Corporation and the town will have every reason to be proud of the First Barnsley Battalion."

They had presided over the birth of the local Battalions, fed them, clothed them and nursed them through their growing pains. Now they celebrated what was seen as their coming of age. In reality they were only just starting to walk.

One of the last pictures taken at Silkstone. Early morning parade.

Chapter Six

Poachers' rest

"Camp life is much enjoyed by the 'Pals', whose exposure to the climate has wrought a big change in their countenances. Scores of lads who constitute the battalions earned their livelihood in the pits, a class of work which does not tend to bring roses to the cheeks, but rather conduces to an anaemic-looking countenance. See these same pit lads now and note the change!"
Barnsley Chronicle, 21st August, 1915

THE DAY FOLLOWING THE FAREWELL LUNCHEON at Silkstone, May 13th was, according to the Chronicle, "The day of all days for Barnsley". Once more Market Hill was to bear witness to Civic celebrations as the town prepared to bid farewell to both its local Battalions.

It was quite an important day for the Sheffield City Battalion too for they were also Staffordshire bound. The departure of "Sheffield's Own" was however, marred by the ridiculously early hour fixed for the move by the railway authorities. As a result the men had to parade at 5 a.m. in order to reach the station in time to catch their trains. The Barnsley public were more fortunate that the time chosen for the departure of the Pals was at a much more sensible hour, affording them the opportunity of taking an active part in the send-off. Realising this, the Education Committee had wisely decided to close all the schools for the day to allow the children to go and wave to their fathers, their brothers, uncles and friends and by half-past nine people had begun to assemble in the Market Hill and Court House areas. Others, living in the vicinity of Dodworth Road, kept a keen eye on the thoroughfare so as not to miss the 13th Battalion which they knew, at some time, would have to march along it from Silkstone into town.

As the day wore on, cloudy and unusually cold but thankfully without rain, the scenes on Market Hill so stirred the heart of the Chronicle's observer that he felt inspired to draw classical parallels.

"A forest of faces confronted one everywhere – in the streets, at windows, from doorways, and even up lamp posts. Brilliant and moving was the spectacle of Barnsley's warrior sons, bronzed, hardy and eager for the firing line. The striking picture was as imposing in its way as was that historic gathering of the hosts by the shores of the Scamander, while the sunlight glistened on the golden pomegranates of the Immortal Guard and the gorgeous robes of the Thracians fluttered in the wind." **Barnsley Chronicle, 15th May, 1915**

Frank Lindley, with the aid of his four month stint with the artillery, had taken to soldiering fairly quickly, and had picked up the 'knack' of tying a decent

The Sheffield City Battalion receive a civic send-off as they prepare to entrain for Cannock Chase in Staffordshire where they will join the Barnsley Pals in the 94th Brigade. Colonel Mainwaring (centre) is in command.

Officers and men of the 13th at Barnsley Court House Station awaiting orders to board their train en route for Rugeley, Cannock Chase. The Mayor, Colonel England, in his scarlet Chief Magistrate's robes sees the Barnsley Battalions off; with him is Colonel Hewitt.

looking pair of puttees. Given the rough and ready quality of the uniforms he looked as smart as he could. With his expertise he had even helped to "dress" some of the other recruits, unused as they were to such strange rituals. Now, parading with the rest of his Battalion at half past eleven, loosely tied puttees, drooping equipment and yards of ill fitting khaki gently flapping in the breeze, it was difficult to imagine any similarity with the "gorgeous fluttering robes" featured in the Chronicle's report. Frank could have been forgiven for thinking he had turned up at an entirely different gathering.

> *"I can't remember any really big send off. That was probably for the 13th Battalion. They had already skimmed the cream off Barnsley and we were just the dregs. You never saw such a rag tail, bob tail mob in all your life. We just sort of sloped off, down to the station."* Frank Lindley, 14th Y & L Regiment

What the Chronicle's man on the spot had taken to be bronzed skin from some distance, would probably have turned out to be a rather generous application of Dr. Stagg's ointment under closer inspection.

With the 14th Battalion well on their way by half past two, it was the turn of the 13th to parade on Market Hill. Marching all the way from Silkstone Camp via Dodworth Road to Barnsley, they had been cheered on their way by the people lining the route.

As he had done nine months previously when the Barnsley 'Terriers' paraded before leaving home, the Mayor, his scarlet Chief Magistrate's robes covering his Colonel's uniform, wished the men "God speed". By four o'clock the town had said its last goodbye to its last Pal, as two Great Central 'specials' steamed out of the station bound for Rugeley via Manchester and Crewe. Barnsley was to see them together just once more before they left England for overseas service.

Rugeley Camp, 1915. home for three months for the 11th East Lancashire Regiment (Accrington Pals) and the 12th, 13th and 14th Battalions York and Lancaster Regiment. These four battalions make up the 94th Brigade.

Towards evening the various companies of Pals arrived at their destination to find that the weather had taken a turn for the worse.

"When we arrived at Rugeley it was throwing it down. We had to march up hill from Rugeley to Penkridge Bank Camp. We were wet through when we got there and we had to go straight to the huts, no change of clothing." **Ernest Bell, 13th Y & L Regiment**

It was a four mile hike from the station to the camp, and the men, wet, cold, tired and hungry after the exertions of the day, found the Camp far from complete.

"As you marched from Rugeley up to the camp our huts were the first lot upon the right. Marching up we passed a notice board on the right hand side which said 'site for cinema'. That was all very well but some of our huts had no roofs on." **Frank Lindley, 14th Y & L Regiment**

The first night at Penkridge Bank was an uncomfortable experience for the Pals but at least they were well used to privation by that time. When fully erected, the camp with huts much like those at Silkstone, a canteen and a hospital, was intended to accommodate up to 70,000 troops. As the first occupants however, the 94th Brigade, some 4,000 men in all, paid the price for blazing the trail.

There were insufficient beds for the Barnsley lads and, to the chagrin of the Officers of the 13th, no cutlery or furniture in the Officers' Mess. While the wet and weary troops scoured the empty huts for spare trestles, planks and mattresses with the help of several kindly members of the Army Service Corps, the Officers of the 13th had to endure the indignity of eating hastily made sandwiches standing up. The following day the missing essentials were procured and the Pals busied themselves tidying up and settling in. By the weekend they were off, marching across the high parts of the Chase, over the rough gorse moorland where wild deer still roamed free.

The onset of pleasant Spring sunshine during the first two weeks of the Pals' stay at Penkridge Bank Camp was dulled by the sad news from France that Col. Raley's youngest son, 21-year-old Lieutenant Walter Hugh Raley. had been killed on May 14th. He had been a fellow officer of Captain George Hewitt, the son of Col. Hewitt, both of them serving with the 1/5 York and Lancaster Regiment. Walter Raley had the tragic distinction to become the first officer of the Barnsley 'Terriers' to lose his life. As a signals officer he had been out inspecting his wires a full 800 yards behind the front line trench, alas well within the range of the patient German sniper who was waiting for just such a target.

Humour of the day; a picture postcard.

Votes of condolence and expressions of sympathy were passed at the meetings of the many Barnsley Borough Committees during the week following the tragic news, but they could not prevent Col. Raley's grief impinging on his health.

As the Spring of 1915 blossomed into the beginnings of a steaming Summer to rival that of the previous year, the Pals' training intensified with full Battalion and Brigade operations. Of course there were always the old trusty favourites of route marching and bayonet drill to fall back on, and yet, with the first anniversary of the outbreak of war just over the horizon, it seemed as though the training programme was content to stick to time honoured principles of infantry movement.

"FULL MARCHING ORDER" WHAT YOUR KIT FEELS LIKE AFTER TEN MILES !

Ernest Bell
13th Y & L

Charlie Swales
14th Y & L

Frank Lindley
14th Y & L

"On Cannock Chase we used to do a lot of route marching and manoeuvring in the formations of the old type of South African campaigning, with wings of scouts out to the side. We were practising open warfare. It was a burning Summer was 1915, we knew that when we were marching. They used to fill our water bottles and you had to show it at the end of the march, still full, because you couldn't drink on the march. In fact we should have been able to run a full mile with a full pack on without being out of breath. That was training!" Frank Lindley, 14th Y & L Regiment

Training could also commence on the firing ranges. The receipt of 400 rifles and a little 'spare' ammunition towards the end of May meant that at last more men could begin to familiarise themselves with the infantryman's closest friend.

"We were dished out with our 'short' Lee Enfield rifles with a long bayonet. Previous to that we'd scuttled around with an odd Ross rifle. We got real handy with the rifles." Frank Lindley, 14th Y & L Regiment

Some turned out to be handier than others.

"Most of the lads were pretty good at shooting. We were told that what we could see we could hit, but when we got on to the ranges I must have been a bit on the exceptional side because I passed the marksman course. I didn't think any more about it until one of the signaller Sergeants wanted me as a signaller but I wasn't keen. I said that I didn't want it, but he said he was going to ask for me. I said 'you've no need 'cos I'm not going,' but he went to ask anyway. When he came back I asked him how he'd gone on and he said 'I can't have you, you're earmarked for sniping.' Just after that I had to go on a sniping course which was altogether different from firing at big targets. You had to judge your own distances and you had different targets to shoot at – perhaps there would be a couple of sandbags, then, all of a sudden, there would be a 'face' in between. You had difficulty spotting some of them. You would have four seconds to shoot and we didn't have telescopic sights then. I must have got through the course because that was it. Some of the sights we got later weren't much good. The proper telescopic sight – there was only one per Company. When we got into the lines we always tried to get hold of that rifle because it was a deadly weapon that." Charlie Swales, 14th Y & L Regiment

Meanwhile the men in the specialised sections were also finding that life was becoming a little more interesting. Ernest Bell and the rest of the 13th Battalion machine-gun team finally got their hands on a real working machine gun. Now they could practise stripping it down, studying its innards and reassembling it again to their hearts' content.

"I was put in charge of the machine-gun section and made into a Lance-Corporal, unpaid. Not that it made a lot of difference, it was only 3d a day extra. I didn't get paid that until I went to France. We got an old Vickers machine gun and it was a bit outdated. I don't think the Army were intending to keep the Vickers as the main machine gun because the Lewis appeared a bit later. The Vickers was heavier than the Lewis, it stood on a

The Chase is burning! The hot Summer of 1915 turns the heath land surrounding the camp into a constant fire threat.

Inhabitants of the 'Poachers' Rest' pose for the official picture. Frank Lindley is standing, back row, fourth from left.

big tripod. You couldn't carry it by yourself when it was assembled. We had no special training on it, just cleaning and operating it. We never fired it though, there wasn't any ammunition." **Ernest Bell, 13th Y & L Regiment**

Tommy Oughton and his mates in the signals section were placed in a separate hut away from the other companies, a state of affairs which would be repeated at every other training camp they visited in England. There would be many times in the future when Tommy would have occasion to count his blessings, thanks to Old Tom Lax.

As the training and the weather warmed up so too did the dense scrubland which surrounded the Camp. The golden rays of the early Summer sun were so intense that the tinder-like heather ignited spontaneously, and in the first blaze a large area of an extensive fir wood disappeared amid 20 foot flames. There were real fears for the future of the timber huts and so the Pals turned their hand to firefighting.

"There were everlasting fires. They'd 'mush' us out at all hours with shovels and we'd dig a trench around the camp to stop the fire jumping over, otherwise we'd have been burnt up. Then we'd grab the branch of a tree and start beating. It was that hot it smashed the windows in the huts." **Frank Lindley, 14th Y & L Regiment**

Another example of 'christening' the hut. George Armitage, formerly of Dillington Square, Worsborough Common stands outside his hut, 'The Abode'. George, father of six, will die from a knee wound in May 1917.

The efforts of the whole Brigade in tackling the numerous conflagrations endeared them to the locals of Rugeley, Hednesford and Cannock. Drawn by the dense clouds of smoke visible for miles, they flocked to the Chase to witness the spectacle of the sweaty and smoke-blackened soldiers beating out the flames with their broken branches.

The men were seeing action, of a sort, although it kept them from the real business of their training, still there were those who felt it their duty to rekindle the Pals' desire for front line action. Barnsley's M.P. Sir Joseph Walton, attired in service dress, visited Penkridge Bank early in June and told them:

"I am confident you will not flinch from resolutely facing what lies before you, and that you will fully uphold the highest traditions of the British Army. In doing this remember that foolhardiness is not bravery and you owe it to yourselves and to your families that, whilst not hesitating to discharge the most dangerous duties, you should avoid needless risks in doing it." **Barnsley Chronicle, 12th June, 1915**

He went on to give a lesson on how best to resist a chlorine gas attack using a respirator soaked in a solution of bicarbonate of soda, and

proposed to give each man a small tin of the white powder to take overseas. For those men who had already gulped down several lungfuls of smoke from the burning Staffordshire flora, the offer came a little too late.

Combatting the recurring fires was tiring, thirsty work but for every dark cloud which billowed from the Chase, there seemed to be a silver lining.

"Cannock Chase was full of wildlife. There were snakes roaming about, blasted adders, grouse and other animals like hares and rabbits. They kept rushing out with all the fires. We used to snare the rabbits. That was poaching. 'Poachers' Rest' was painted on the side of one of the huts by one of the lads, one of the poachers. Most of them had been poaching in their time. It was the miner's prerogative." **Frank Lindley, 14th Y & L Regiment**

Above and below: George Armitage Nichols 14th Y & L Regiment

The lads in Number 8 hut were also partial to the taste of fresh rabbit. George Armitage Nichols, a glassblower in civilian life, enlisted with the 14th Battalion after its removal from Barnsley. Instead of joining the Reserve Company, he went straight to Penkridge Bank.

"At Cannock, Number 8 hut were noted for getting into scrapes. At night we'd go out catching rabbits with a snare, and then coming back we'd use any old container as a stewpot and stew them. It was 'wick' with rabbits on the moors there. We were always in trouble, we were more on 'jankers' than anything else. Anything that were going off we'd have a go at it. I wasn't an innocent bairn. We used to get into a lot of trouble for having lights on at night, playing cards. The orderly sergeant would come round at 10 o'clock for 'lights out'. As soon as he'd gone we'd put 'em back on. Of course when he came back he'd see us and report us. We'd go in front of the Colonel the next morning and get 14 days 'C.B.', confined to barracks." **14/24075 Private George Armitage Nichols, 'A' Company, 14th Y & L Regiment**

Gambling, along with a deep affection for smoking tobacco, were two of the enduring pastimes of the soldier wherever he happened to be. Cooped up in a wooden hut, a score or more khaki-clad warriors, most of them hovering on the brink of personal bankruptcy and several miles walk from the nearest entertainment in Rugeley or Hednesford, quickly got into the habit of making their own amusement.

Centre of Rugeley where members of the 94th Brigade spend some of their free time.

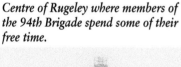

"I used to draw me 'bob', walk out and go straight to the hut where they were gambling and stick it on a card. If it came up it was all right and I'd carry on and make myself a little 'poke'. 'Crown and Anchor' and 'Bank' and 'Pontoon' were all very popular. 'Crown and Anchor' men carried a piece of linen with squares on it and they had a dice marked with 'Crowns' and 'Anchors'. When they chucked it, if a 'crown' came up and your money was on the 'crown' you drew off it. There were some crazy blokes. They'd have that roll in their pockets and wherever they were it'd be, 'Come on lads', and out it'd come. They made their cash like that. Wherever you stopped, even in the trenches, you had a gamble. There was always a pack of cards for 'twenty-one up' or 'brag', or anything like that." **Frank Lindley, 14th Y & L Regiment**

For the unlucky majority it was a different story.

"I only got a 'bob' a day and out of that I gave my mother 3/6d. We used to go and draw 3/6d., come back down to the hut, get the

cards out and play pontoon. In two minutes you were 'skint'." George Armitage Nichols, 14th Y & L Regiment

Kitchener's New Army had undoubtedly attracted its fair share of the cream of the crop, but inevitably there were elements within who had a souring effect. These were the 'wide boys' who, blessed with sleight of hand and loaded dice, commenced to 'fleece' many a raw recruit who had staked their last penny on the 'old lucky 'ook.'

Gambling was a disease which, seen through the devout eyes of General Douglas Haig when he assumed overall command of the B.E.F. in December 1915, had assumed epidemic proportions. Quite apart from the monetary problems faced by innocent, and not so innocent young recruits losing all their wages, there were fears that feelings of jealousy aroused in the losers would lead to fighting and localised breakdowns in discipline.

General Haig made it a penal offence to be caught playing 'Crown and Anchor' with a court martial after three convictions, but he fought a losing battle. He might just as well have tried to make the Earth spin in the opposite direction, than try to prevent soldiers from gambling.

Number 8 hut at Penkridge Bank was not the only one to be involved in high jinks. When the day's training and fatigue duties were completed, or in free time at weekends, some of the men who had a little money left and favoured a walk, would head for the night life offered by the nearby towns.

Lt. Colonel Raley relinquishes command of the 14th when news arrives of the death of another son at the front.

"We had what was called a town picket, and I used to be in that mostly fetching the lads out of the 'boozers' in Rugeley and Hednesford. That's how I got my beer, when I'd fetched them out. Some of them were rough fellahs. One time there was this man called 'Little' Tommy who'd been a 'trammer' at the pit. Them fellahs used to 'tram' the corves with their heads. He came into the hut one night 'blindo' and he said 'I'm a bloody 'trammer' I am', and he put his head down against the trestle table, shoved, and shot all the pots all over the place. We had to pay barrack damages after that. Another bloke who got blind drunk got hold of the stove in the hut and slung it over his shoulder. We had to scuffle around trying to put out the fires that the hot ashes had started on the blankets." Frank Lindley, 14th Y & L Regiment

Occasionally some of the men were surprised and delighted to find that they had visitors. Making use of the long hours of daylight whole families would make the long trek from Barnsley to see their menfolk. One such excursion came as quite a shock to Harry Hall.

"The Charabancs had just started running and all the parents from Wombwell organised this trip one Sunday to come and have a look at us. We didn't know they were coming. I was on my bed and I'd just lit a cigarette when the hut door at the bottom opened and they came trooping in, my dad and my mum. I never dared smoke at home and when I saw them I 'diffed' my cigarette. I had some nude pictures on the wall so I whipped them down and pushed them under the pillow. The old lad came up and said 'Nay, tha' can leet thi' cig' nar; tha' doin' a man's job.'" Harry Hall, 13th Y & L Regiment

While Harry's relationship with his father moved onto a different plane, another Barnsley father lost another son. Towards the end of June, Colonel Raley was devastated by the news that his eldest son, 30-year-old Captain 'Harry' Raley of the 3rd Yorkshire Regiment, had been killed on June 15th. Back in Barnsley, at a Thursday morning session of the Borough Court, the Mayor told the magistrates,

"It is a most regrettable thing for me to have to say what I am going to say now. One of our

Commander of the 94th Brigade, Brigadier-General Bowles, centre, with his Brigade officers. Two Military Police from each of the four Battalions provide escort.

colleagues has lost his eldest son. It seems strange for me to realise that on Tuesday week at the Corporation meeting when I referred to the loss of his youngest son, that probably at that very time Colonel Raley's first born son had been shot down in action. Words fail me to express my sympathy with Colonel Raley. I am sure this latest blow is almost enough to turn him into an old man all at once." Barnsley Chronicle, 26th June 1915

There was no 'almost' about it. Colonel Raley's health broke and he left Penkridge Bank to return to Barnsley and the ministrations of a local doctor. After the death of Walter Raley in May he had expressed his readiness to stand down and make way for a Commanding Officer with greater military experience and now his failing health made that appointment inevitable. As a stop-gap measure, Major T. Carter Clough, the second in command of the Sheffield City Battalion, filled Colonel Raley's shoes admirably until a successor to Colonel Raley could be found.

At a Battalion parade on July 9th Brigadier General Bowles informed the men that they were about to receive a new, permanent Commanding Officer. His name was Walter Backhouse Hulke.

"He was called Hulke and he was a hulk as well He was a big bloke. He didn't shoot his mouth off though, he left that to others, but he was a very unapproachable man. You couldn't get near him. He was a proper 'regular' bloke, a time server." Frank Lindley, 14th Y & L Regiment

Obviously the men's views of their new Colonel depended on their past experience of Army authority.

"The old Colonel, he was a grand fellow. He was a regular Army man and he knew his job." 'Ossie' Burgess, 14th Y & L Regiment

The Reserve Company going on parade at Barnsley.

In their pen-picture of the new C.O., the Chronicle, as always, went further, much further.

> *"To look at Colonel Hulke is to see trouble – tall, rugged and muscular, his big features mark the fighting man. He is no respecter of persons and calls a spade a spade – sometimes.! His men understand him and he understands them. He does more: he admires them, is proud of them, wrapped up in them. To him they are the finest fighting stuff on earth. He thinks so and says so, and he does not care a tinker's curse who he fights with or against for he fears comparison with no regiment at the Front. If I judge him rightly the 14th are in for no soft job. He will fight – can't help it – and they will fight with him to the last man. They know it, and knowing care not. For as one said, "There's summat about Hulke; he'll get us into a feight, and there's summat about him he'll get us aht."* Barnsley Chronicle, 1st January 1916

The newly appointed Lieutenant Colonel Hulke's military career had begun in 1892, when, at the age of 20 he had secured a commission as a Second Lieutenant with the Lincolnshire Regiment. After a varied Army life which mixed such diverse roles as a Captain in the Chinese Regiment of Infantry with the position of Eastern District Gymnasia Superintendent, he retired from the Lincolnshires in 1903. Recalled in 1914, he had, since November of that year, served as Adjutant of the 9th Service Battalion of his old regiment, based at Lichfield. At 43 years of age he was not the doddering, white whiskered, antique C.O. so beloved of cartoonists. Although the men may have held conflicting views with regard to his character, they all agreed that he epitomised the values of the regular Army.

Vernon Atkinson (standing left), with three Pals in the Reserve Company, two are from Wombwell, Ernest Allen and Walt Cooper.

Four days after the news of Lt. Col. Hulke's appointment both Barnsley battalions lined up for inspection as the responsibility for the care and equipment of the Pals passed formally into the hands of the War Office. It was a bittersweet moment for Col. Hewitt and the local raisers. Although the battalions were, at last, absorbed by the War Office, most of the local ties were being severed in the process. The raisers would no longer have a say in the future welfare of their battalions. There weren't even any members of the Second Battalion Raising Committee present at the official handover since the date clashed with a meeting of the Borough Council and the Annual meeting of the Licensing Committee.

One or two bonds still linked the town of Barnsley with its home battalions but these were their Reserve Companies.

Recruiting for a sixth Reserve Company of the 14th Battalion had already begun, and at least the original raisers could reflect that they were still charged with

responsibility for the rallying and equipping of the sixth companies of both Barnsley Battalions.

What's more, the original reserve companies of the 'Pals', although officially taken over by the War Office, were in fact still encamped at Silkstone along with the Depot companies of the Sheffield City Battalion who had moved up country from Redmires Camp.

All this activity was in accord with Army Northern Command Order Number 1228 which decreed that any reserves of a locally raised battalion were to remain behind in the event of a unit moving away to join its Brigade. Further to this reserve Companies of Battalions of the same regiment were to be grouped together wherever possible.

With the prospect of six companies, each of 250 men, descending on Silkstone it was certainly no ghost-camp after the removal of the 13th Battalion, and since four out of those six Companies were connected with Barnsley, the Raising Committee felt it quite within their rights to nominate a Barnsley man for the position of Camp Commandant. Who better, they thought, than Colonel Raley, a man already with experience of the pressures of recruiting and of commanding a large body of men. Perhaps they thought it would engage his mind and move its focus from his recent grief. In any event, the position was close to home and near to his doctor should Colonel Haley require medical attention.

Their appeals worked. Colonel Haley was appointed Lieutenant Colonel to command what became known as the 15th (Reserve) Battalion of the York and Lancaster Regiment formed out of the Reserves up at Silkstone.

Silkstone Camp in the high Summer of 1915 was a vastly different place from the damp, muddy home the 13th Battalion had known. From the camp on top of the hill the men of the Reserve Companies could see the vast expanse of the moors of the Pennines to the west. In the valley below the camp to the east was the neat and pretty little village of Silkstone and a little higher to the south, the village of Hoylandswaine. Looking north the village of Cawthorne could just be seen through the gently swaying branches of the trees which surrounded the camp. Making a visit to see the reserves at work a Chronicle reporter noted,

> "... nature is in its merriest mood and of course the effect on the spirits of the young soldier in training is the very happiest. All the boys one saw at Camp, whether at drill or at play, were in the brightest spirits." **Barnsley Chronicle, July 10th 1915**

As one of the 14th Battalion reserves Vernon Atkinson's spirits were always bright and he was always ready to indulge in a spot of fun.

> "On Thursday afternoons we'd have afternoon break and they'd take perhaps 250 of us to the golf course. We had a little officer called Lt. Marsden from Sheffield, a nice little chap. He marched us from the camp to the golf course and halted us. 'Now Atkinson' he said, 'I want you to take my watch and whistle, and when it gets to five minutes to four I want you to blow the whistle and fall the men in.' He then went back to the mess because he liked his whisky. Two chaps from Wombwell, being married, came to me and asked if they could get off so I let them go. The officer came back at five to four so I blew the whistle, fell 'em in and numbered 'em off. Because a few were missing I used to ask some of the men to say more than one number. Well, they numbered off and I told

the officer they were all present and correct. The officer said 'Are you sure? Number them again', so they numbered off as before. Of course they were all laughing under their shirts because there was nowhere near 250 there. They'd all scarpered to Wombwell. I'd let umpteen lads go." **Vernon Atkinson, 14th Y & L Regiment**

Sheffielders show the Barnsley lads the way in the inter-Battalion sports.

In Vernon's company were a few others who were not averse to pulling a fast one and supplementing their income into the bargain, all at the expense of the Raising Committee. They were quick to take advantage of the arrangement whereby 50 per cent of the men were given passes from noon on Saturday until 9.00 a.m. on Monday morning so that they could spend some time with their families.

> "The Co-operative was supplying us with food and it was four to a loaf then. There were these lads from New Street, we called them the Cross 'mob', they used to take bread home at weekends. They'd stay at home all weekend with their wives and they'd come in Monday morning with pit clogs on. They'd 'flogged' their bloody Army boots. Captain Broderick called them soldiers, he knew they'd sold their boots. He used to drill me at Racecommon Road School. We did musketry at school then. He used to say 'I wonder if any of them are in my company. If they are I'll have them in the office and I'll give them all 7 days' leave and give them another pair of boots'." **Vernon Atkinson, 14th Y & L Regiment**

Unfortunately for the 'Cross Mob', Captain Broderick, an old 'sweat' with 34 years' service, including South African experience behind him, was in command of the reserve company of the 13th Battalion.

Back at Penkridge Bank Camp the Barnsley contingent had obviously been imbued with the spirit of a Brigade Camp and the letters of Officers and men, written to the Chronicle, displayed a fair degree of inter-battalion rivalry.

They never missed an opportunity to make it clear that the lads from Barnsley and district were more than a match for any of the other troops on Cannock Chase in matters military, or otherwise. The performance of the Battalion bugle bands, and their attempts to outblow all the others must have given rise to a veritable cacophony of competitive music making.

> "As I pen these few notes 'retreat' is being sounded throughout the Brigade. The brisk Battalion band of the 13th is marching round its own parade ground holding its own against other bands here. It is difficult to believe from the smart appearance of these soldiers, that only a few months ago they were mostly Barnsley collier lads. The change has been wonderful." **Letter to the Chronicle** from Captain G. De Ville Smith, Officer Commanding 'D' Company, 29th May 1915

> "The bugle band attached to the 13th is going on splendidly and we are holding our own against all comers. We played capitally in front of Brigade

A typical Section of Barnsley Pals, made up mainly of ex-miners.

In sharp contrast, men of the City Battalion seen here in a dignified sing-song, the 'elite of Sheffield' the 'Coffee and Bun Boys'.

Headquarters the other night, every man doing his best." Letter to the Barnsley Chronicle from Bugler G. Lewis, 12th June 1915

It wasn't only the bugle bands who were in competition. When the 13th held their Battalion Sports in Hagley Park, Rugeley, there were several events which were open to the Brigade.

In the 100 yards, 13th Battalion sprinter, Private Harrison, breasted the tape in front of Sergeant Taylor of the Accrington Pals but that was where Barnsley's successes ended. The athletic abilities of the Sheffield City Battalion, in the shape of Privates Allen and Woodward, allowed them to clean up in the 440 and 880 yard events, while Private Tasker of the Accrington Pals trotted out an easy winner in the 'Musical Chairs on Mules' competition. In the inter-battalion relay race the Sheffielders took the honours, and with the Accrington team in second place the Barnsley lads had to content themselves with the third and final position.

Although they had not starred in the sporting arena there was still an almost constant urge to trumpet how well the Pals were conducting themselves at work or play, perhaps inflamed by just a hint of envy, especially where the Sheffielders were concerned. In the early days of their formation the Vickers Company had bestowed several favours upon them, including the loan of rifles and a machine gun which gave them a head start on many other locally raised battalions. It seemed, in fact, that they wanted for nothing.

"I'll always remember the Sheffielders with their handkerchiefs stuffed up their sleeves and their wristwatches flashing in the sun. They were the elite of Sheffield. We were the 'Ragged Arsed Battalion' but they were the 'Coffee and Bun Boys'." Frank Lindley, 14th Y & L Regiment

After little less than three months at Cannock the Pals were informed that they were about to be moved again. To their delight they learned that they were heading back to Yorkshire, in fact to a camp at Ripon, the Headquarters of the 31st Division, to which the 94th Brigade had been posted. For the lads born within a few miles of Barnsley they had already seen as much of the world than they would reasonably have dared to expect during the course of their normal working lives. For some, the dream of travel and a fresh air life was coming true. Advance parties of the 13th and 14th Battalions under the promoted Captain Di Marco and Lieutenant Fitton arrived in the small cathedral city on July 27th, followed by the rest of the men three days later.

They had left Rugeley in the early hours of the morning and in spite of their early departure the

Popular posting for the Pals. Ripon, where the 94th Brigade joins the 92nd and 93rd along with a Pioneer Battalion to form the 31st Division. A New Army Division under the Command of Major-General Wanless O'Gowan.

locals turned out in large numbers to wave goodbye. Due to restrictions on street-lighting, the passage of the Pals through the streets of Rugeley became almost a torchlight procession as the civilians armed themselves with lighted candles to get a last look at the soldiers. The Pals, and indeed the whole Brigade, must have made quite an impression upon the people of South Staffordshire, not least for their heroic conduct in fighting the fires on the Chase. The Rugeley Urban District Council even went so far as to write a letter to the Brigadier complimenting the men of the entire Brigade on their "excellent conduct". It was perhaps just as well that the members of the Council had never made a point of touring the Barnsley huts after "lights out".

A full service kit layout. The personal military issue for each soldier. Rifle is an obsolete Lee Metford suitable for drill purposes only.

Arriving in Ripon the 'Pals' found that the Army was busying itself in attempting to construct a second Aldershot amid the tranquil rural setting at one of the gateways to the Yorkshire Dales. Ripon, once a quiet agricultural centre, its peace disrupted only on market days, now fairly teemed with life. The quaint narrow thoroughfares seethed with off duty troops displaying an interesting mish-mash of regimental insignia. Every day became a market day as a plague of khaki locusts descended on the shops and stores, signalling a bonanza to the tradesmen of Ripon.

For a start there were the 13,000 or so men in the 31st Division. Composed exclusively of thirteen locally nurtured New Army Battalions, it represented, in its ranks, a fair proportion of the heavy industrial and commercial heartland of Northern England. Yorkshire alone had given eleven of the thirteen battalions, and those had been fostered by just six towns and cities. It was, in essence, a 'Pals' Division. Along with the Barnsley, Sheffield and Accrington Pals in the 94th Brigade, there was the 93rd Brigade with its contingent of Leeds Pals, two Battalions of Bradford Pals and the Durham Pals, while the whole of the 92nd Brigade, all four battalions, originated in Hull. To cap it all the Divisional Pioneer battalion was the 12th K.O.Y.L.I. which also went under the unofficial title of the Halifax 'Pals'.

George Hewitt (hatless) son of Colonel Hewitt, in his dug-out on the Yser Canal with Captain Colver; neither are to survive the war. Shortly after this picture is taken George receives his head wound.

There were also troops settled close by at Studley Royal Camp, and the whole lot had to be fed and watered by the good tradespeople of Ripon. How they must have rubbed their hands as the tills rang out their merry tunes.

A few minutes' walk south along the Harrogate Road from the ancient market place would have brought the casual rambler to the outskirts of a huge military base. There, scanning the horizon from east to west, the eye was greeted by an almost endless vista of standard Army huts, much like those at Silkstone and Penkridge Bank, with more appearing daily. The Barnsley Pals were placed in what was known as the 'South Camp'.

Life in the camp was little different to life in the other camps the Pals had known. The huts were slightly larger, taking 30 men and an extra comfort was the presence of purpose-built dining halls which meant the men no longer had to eat in huts where they also slept. This was indeed a luxury but much more of a priority was getting hold of a copy of the Chronicle. Some of the lads' mums, anxious for their sons to keep abreast of local news, religiously wrapped up

A Section of the 13th. At this stage they do not consider themselves as 'old soldiers' as is evidenced by the fact that none of them have removed the wire stiffeners in their caps. Seated on ground sheet, right, is Ernest Reid. He will be gassed during the Somme battle and discharged as unfit in 1917.

copies in brown paper and posted them off, but there were others who missed out on this maternal benevolence. The problem was solved when a representative of the Chronicle struck a deal with Messrs. W. H. Smith and Sons, booksellers. In a stroke of pure business enterprise, Smith's had opened up a number of kiosks to supply the soldiers' demands for reading matter and they agreed to sell copies of the Chronicle transported to Ripon from Barnsley every Friday evening.

One of the stories which the Pals would have read with great interest in their weekly journal hot from the presses in Barnsley, concerned Col. Hewitt's frantic search for his son, languishing in some unknown French hospital suffering from a scalp wound.

It just so happened that both Col. Hewitt and Col. Hulke had been away in France and Flanders on a Commanding Officers' course when the Pals had made their move to Ripon. The brief two week tour was intended to familiarise them with actual conditions of trench warfare and as if to make a point, 'fate' chose to synchronise Col. Hewitt's trip with the wounding of his son George, an incident which occurred on August 1st. Hearing the bad news from Col. Fox, C.O. of the 1/5 York and Lancasters, when he visited their stretch of the line, Col. Hewitt forgot the tour and commenced to dash around France, visiting hospital after hospital in search of his son. It was an unenviable task, for the whereabouts of wounded soldiers seemed to be a secret known only to the drivers of the ambulances shipping them from the forward aid stations to hospitals well behind the lines. After a long and trying search Col. Hewitt struck lucky and found his son, head swathed in bandages, in the Westminster Hospital in Le Touquet. The case notes at the foot of his bed told their own grisly tale of how George Hewitt had cheated death by the merest whisker.

"Large gutter wound in occipital region, splitting scalp right down to the bone, exposing skull."

"The official description of the wound is bad enough, but I do not think it is as terrible as it sounds, and I am simply not worrying about anything now – except coming home when I am fit enough. I was 'sniped' in the trenches and it was very annoying for it was the last time and place I would have expected to get hit. I was just on my way to have some food in my dug-out, when suddenly I saw millions of stars and found myself on my knees, clawing air." **Letter to his mother from George Hewitt dated 6th August, 1915**

Obviously grateful that his son was alive and apparently making a remarkably swift recovery, Col. Hewitt disguised any misgivings he might have had due to either his son's injuries or his tour of the battlefields. On the contrary Col. Hewitt's typically "John Bull" manner was once more in evidence as he spoke to the Chronicle before rejoining the Pals at Ripon.

"We were out to gain knowledge of warfare and we got it unmistakably. We saw the trenches – many of them. We dropped across Col. Fox and were recognised right and left by the lads whom I particularly have known under different circumstances and in far different spheres. I saw young men whom I knew when they were earning their livelihood in Barnsley and the immediate district – lads who were formerly in the pits and in the workshops here, and who, like the sensible lads they were, devoted their leisure time to military training. I saw the Sergeant Major, and another who

came forward with a joyous smile just as he might have done had he been in the Barnsley Drill Hall, was Sergeant Goodyear, and he sent messages, through me, to his friends at home assuring them of their rejoicings in taking the step they had to assist in the smiting of the Huns. Yes it was an inspiring sight!" **Barnsley Chronicle, 14th August 1915**

Colonel Hewitt had obviously not seen enough.

Probably due to the mining background of many of the Pals, it seemed that wherever they were sent they were called upon to perform extra little jobs for the Army. No sooner had they settled in at Ripon than they were allotted the task of constructing a rifle range, along with other troops of the 31st Division, five miles from South Camp, upon which they would fire the first part of the General Musketry Course. For the ex-colliers, working under the supervision of the Halifax Pals' Pioneer battalion, neither the spade-work nor the working hours presented a problem. The digging and raising of embankments was no hardship for men who had spent many a long hour at the coal face, while they were well used to the two-shift system of working "mornings" and "afternoons". Just as they had done in peacetime, the "days" shift would rise early and march to the site of the range at Wormald Green, do half a day's work and then march back to camp, on their way passing the men on "afters" who worked for the rest of the day.

When the work was completed each battalion commenced to "loose off" a few rounds at the targets on the ranges. When it came to the 14th Battalion's turn at the "Butts" Frank Lindley's pal found the musketry course much harder than he had anticipated.

"Poor old 'Hoppy' had a defective right eye and he used to shove his head over to shoot with his left eye. The instructor would say 'What the bloody hell is that man doing?' and he'd come up and kick him." **Frank Lindley, 14th Y & L Regiment**

"Hoppy" must have had an inordinate amount of skill or luck or both, because he passed the course. His antics on the ranges were not the only source of hilarity.

"There was a fellow called Clark with us on the range and he fired a round. Our officer Hunter had his field glasses on and said, 'That's right Clark, keep them all there. That's the bull', so Clark fired another 4 rounds, we were allowed 5. Hunter looked again and said, 'Where's the other 'buggers' Clark, you haven't hit the target man'. Clark replied, 'I have, they've all gone through the first hole'." **Harry Hall, 13th Y & L Regiment**

No. 2 Platoon, 13th Battalion. Note the number of caps that have now gone floppy.

The Pals' training stretched further than the rifle ranges. Apart from the shooting practice and the drilling in sections between the wooden huts to keep the hot sun's rays off the men's backs, they took part in more ambitious 'sham' engagements. Now they had been "Divisioned" they could combine with other arms of the military in an attempt to emulate real battle conditions. Sometimes the Divisional Commander himself, Major General Wanless O'Gowan, who had recently taken over from Major General Fanshawe, would observe the proceedings.

Marching out at dawn into the damp fields surrounding little villages like Mickley, a few miles north west of Ripon, the Pals would have breakfast "alfresco" cooked by Field Kitchens. Breakfast out of the way, they would be "shelled" by some obliging Artillery Brigade and in return the Pals would attack the Artillery positions just as they had been instructed to do at Silkstone and Penkridge. Towards late evening, battle won, the General's retinue would shake hands with the commanding officers of infantry and artillery, congratulate them on their men's performance and then speed back to base for evening dinner. The men meanwhile, would have to trudge wearily, back to Camp, tired and dirty from 12 hours of throwing themselves around the fields of North Yorkshire.

They were even given their very own "Hill 60", which they could attack and defend with great vigour. Someone, somewhere, obviously had a twisted sense of humour. It would perhaps have brought a wry smile to the lips of Corporal Chambers, who had seen the original poisonous mound go up in smoke in April and had been "gassed" when the Germans recaptured it in May. In September Corporal Chambers, home on leave, visited his old Pals of the 13th Battalion at Ripon. When he got back to France he wrote to the Chronicle,

"I enjoyed my trip to Ripon and thank the men very much for the way they entertained me. I rode up to the camp in the Barnsley Battalion mule chariot! I also carried out the R.S.M.'s Commission correctly. Now I must close wishing the officers, N.C.O's and men at Ripon every success."
Barnsley Chronicle, 25th September 1915

He seemed surprised with the new mode of transport acquired by the Pals, and so too had the people of Ripon, as an increasing number of mules were being used to pull transport wagons. Guarding them was yet another task for the men of Kitchener's Army.

"Each Battalion had several mules and carts for luggage and the like. One time our mules were tethered on the main road, and there were two of us on this job one night looking after them. The Sheffield City Battalion were just across the field and they had their mules tied up. Next morning, when we woke up, six of ours were missing, six mules had gone. Somebody had taken them. They'd perhaps had some missing so they took ours. Well we went across to the Sheffield camp and took six of theirs and brought them back." **Harry Hall, 13th Y & L Regiment**

Civilians visit the camps; the Colonel's son and daughters chat with the officers.

"They used to tie the mules in a line. If you were doing the picket on 'em at night sometimes they'd start falling out. The red mules were shockers. If you went by 'em you'd get a great lump chewed out of you and a lashing with their hooves. While we were at Ripon I saw they wanted some drivers for the transport limbers so I took it on and had a couple of grey mules. Grand. I used to go and fetch bread for the troops from Ripon. I used to enjoy going down the country lanes with the

wagon, picking new nuts out of the hedges and having a good feed." **Frank Lindley, 14th Y & L Regiment**

It was while he was at Ripon that Harry Hall heard some distressing news from home.

> *"Mr. and Mrs. Walter Hall, 102 Park Street, Wombwell, have been officially informed that their son, Private Arthur Hall, who was in the New Zealand Expeditionary Force in Gallipoli, is missing. Private Hall is well known in the Wombwell and Darfield districts. Two years ago he emigrated to New Zealand. He was formerly employed at Houghton Main Colliery. He enlisted in New Zealand at Christmas. The Halls have four children, all sons, and three have enlisted since the outbreak of the war."* **Barnsley Chronicle, 4th September 1915**

Harry's mother had never wanted all her boys to enlist and although she had protested to her husband when Harry had joined the Pals, she had been able to do little about it. She had been able to do less about Arthur who joined the Canterbury Regiment half a world away.

Don't be alarmed ! We're on guard at HURDCOTT.

> *"Mother and Father saved up so that Arthur could go away. He emigrated with a few of his friends. When they got to New Zealand they took a job here and one there so that they could travel around. When the war broke out he joined up out there. It was a nasty smack for Mother when Arthur went missing in the Gallipoli 'do'. He was missing a long time before he was posted, 'missing believed killed'. She clung to that missing for a long time."* **Harry Hall, 13th Y & L Regiment**

Even as Harry Hall's parents received the dreadful tidings from the authorities, the comrades of the missing Arthur Hall in the Australian and New Zealand Army Corps (ANZAC) were still breaking their fingernails trying to claw their way up the steep, scrub-covered gullies of the forbidding lump of rock called the Sari Bair Range.

They had been there for a little more than four months, long enough for the late Spring perfume of crushed wild thyme to give way to the stench of long dead human flesh. In all that time they had progressed a scant thousand yards inland and yet had suffered heavy casualties, despite the aid of two of the earliest New Army Divisions with Barnsley men among them.

As well as the brave and hardy Turkish troops the ANZACs had struggled on against relentless heat and thirst, dysenteric diarrhoea, jaundice and open, septic sores. They were to remain in roughly the same positions for the best part of another four months. There they lived and died, in wretched holes scratched into the dusty earth, before the only really effective decision of the whole campaign pulled them off the Gallipoli Peninsula in an almost bloodless evacuation.

By the middle of September the 'grapevine' was heavy with rumours of yet another move for the Pals. It was not to be the long awaited trip to France and active service, but to yet another training camp in England. The rumours proved to be correct and by the end of September they were installed at Hurdcott Camp on the edge of Salisbury Plain, seven miles from Salisbury and three from Wilton. As usual they had a job to do. This time they set to as hay-makers, and built up several haystacks by chopping down the unruly grass which grew between their huts.

Almost as soon as they had landed at Hurdcott an unknown First Barnsley Battalion soldier wrote a 'special' for the Chronicle.

> *"We are at last on Salisbury Plain and there is a feeling of subdued excitement, a subconscious thrill passing over the Barnsley lads during this period, probably the eve of their departure for the Front. It is a feeling that the task they originally volunteered to do, when they gave up their work to join the New Army, is about to commence; the task of actually doing their bit for King and Country.*
>   *The year that has gone (for the premier Battalion is now a year old) has been lived every moment*

of it. We never thought, a year ago, that we should be here now. A great deal has been accomplished; our lads are no longer collier lads, but part of a great New Army of fighting men, trained and skilled in the new and latest devices of modern warfare.

We look back with pleasant memories upon the several camps we have been in. Each camp had its outstanding feature, and by its outstanding feature we think of it. We remember Silkstone for its mud. It was essentially the "Mud" Camp. We walked in mud. We sometimes tumbled in it. We lived in it. We did our work in it. We learnt to be soldiers in it, and we look back upon that mud with a certain affection. We loved the Silkstone Camp – and the mud – and its days are full of happy memories.

Then came Penkridge – the Camp of the fires and of the smoke, when we were christened the "Fire Brigade". How well we remember the Bugle sound of the "Fire Alarm". On its first note, we ran like hares or Indians, hatless, coatless, with hatchets in hand – like little devils running to the mouth of Hell – and we attacked the fires – fierce and solemn and in dead earnest we went to those fires.

Next came Ripon – the most featureless of all camps, from our point of view, unless one can call "Red hats" a feature. There was a feeling that we were being watched by those "red hats", who watched to see if we were fit, if we had learnt the real thing, if we had "stamina" and grit in us, if we were real soldiers, and soon we were moved to Salisbury Plain, the great playground of the British Army; the finishing school of the country's trained troops.

Not much can be said of our new Camp at Salisbury Plain, as yet, for we have only just arrived – but it is the most perfect camp we have ever been in – almost surrounded by the gentle slopes of a ridge of a hill (which the men have already christened 'Hill 120') it offers ample room for movement." **Barnsley Chronicle, 2nd October 1915**

And move they did, with manoeuvres across the Plain, more rifle practice and novel courses of training for all the ranks.

"The Lewis gun came in and I volunteered for it. We got one and got on it and I took charge of the gun. They'd made me a Lance Corporal on the Lewis at Ripon. I had a pal called Bill Walker and they used to call us the 'Siamese Twins'. They said 'What about the Siamese twin here, he'll want to be a Lance Corporal as well'. So they made him one too. We were on two different guns. There were six on a gun and we all had different jobs." **Ossie Burgess, 14th Y & L Regiment**

"There were six in a team. You had the gunner, you had the feeder, you'd got the 'ammo' carriers and two 'fillers' who used to fill the magazines by hand. The Lewis had a pan that fitted on the top of the gun. The assistant used to take off a spring clip, and whip that pan off. That was his job, to take the magazine off and 'clomp' another on. He'd always one in his hand ready. He could put one on in no time. There was a 'knack' to filling the drums. They held about 48 rounds. We used to have little bets to see who could fill a drum the quickest. It was a very good gun. One of the best and very reliable. The only time a Lewis jammed was when a bullet was out of place. The Vickers was prone to jam with the cartridge belt, and it was heavy. The Lewis was very light, only about 28lbs. In fact you could pick it up in your arms and fire from the 'hip' but it was very erratic that way. When you rested it on its bracket and fired from the prone position, there was no missing. Being a Lewis gunner didn't get us off duties, we weren't signallers. They got off all duties. We still had to do the fetching and carrying." **Ernest Bell, 13th Y & L Regiment**

It appeared that signalling was the job to have and Frank Lindley seized his chance.

"At Hurdcott they wanted some signallers. I knew a bit that I'd learned as a kid in the Boy Scouts and the Boys Brigade. We did semaphore and that sort of thing. I joined the signals section. We used to go away from camp at night and signal with flash lamps. We learnt how to move with the stars, that came in handy later on." **Frank Lindley, 14th Y & L Regiment**

There were also courses in the use and abuse of the Mills bomb, a weapon very much like the modern grenade to look at. It became a very effective weapon when one side got into the same trench system as the opposition. An accurate straight-arm 'lob' could 'plop' one of these bombs straight into the German positions, causing havoc among the occupants. There was a right, and a wrong way to throw the missiles and these skills had to be taught on 'bombing' courses. The first thing to learn was to treat the bombs with due reverence, for tragedy stalked the inexperienced and unsuspecting soldier. On a weekend bombing course in late November, tragedy finally placed its hand on the shoulder of ex-Barnsley Main Blacksmith's striker Lance Corporal Sam Buckley of the 14th Battalion.

A telegram delivered to 30 Ash Row, Hoyle Mill on Saturday November 20th, contained the news that Sam Buckley lay seriously ill in the Fargo Military Hospital as a result of an 'accident'. The news was taken badly by Sam Buckley's mother and his ailing step-father Mr. Riley, but worse was to come. By Sunday night Sam was dead, and the entire Hoyle Mill area was stunned. They gleaned a little more information from another Hoyle Mill Pal of the 14th Battalion.

"I am sorry to say that poor Sam Buckley is dead. He was in the same squad of bomb throwers as me. Only the day before we were using live bombs and we had no accident, but when we were using dummy ones he got killed. Poor Sam! He was well liked by us all. The officer is trying to get us off for the funeral and he wants to go as well. You will see what dangerous work it is when things like that happen with dummy ones. It seems to be dangerous to even look at them." **Letter to his parents from Private J. Hargate, reproduced in the Barnsley Chronicle 27th November, 1915**

Mrs. Riley had lost her boy, the Barnsley lads at Hurdcott had lost a Pal and they hadn't even left England. Watching in solemn silence a few days later as the earthly remains of Sam Buckley were committed to the soil of his native town, his relatives and 20 of his Second Battalion Pals were served with a grim reminder of the trappings of modern warfare.

More trench digging was on the menu, and for most of the Pals these exercises on Salisbury Plain gave them their first opportunity to run out flimsy barbed wire defences, a skill which had been hitherto neglected. At Hurdcott however, many of the Barnsley lads had but one burning desire. It wasn't for new guns, bombs, or even barbed wire – it was for melodians, and lots of them.

"Now that the long nights have set in our evenings are spent in the hut when not out on night operations, guards etc. Like all soldiers, we are fond of music and can produce talent capable of handling anything from a tin whistle to a piano, but unfortunately no musical instrument can be found in our midst. It is suggested that should you be kind enough to publish this letter, some friend may be able to send us, say, a melodian, which is a favourite instrument, or perhaps a good mouth organ." **Letter to Barnsley Chronicle from Corporal Harman, 'D' Company, 14th Y & L Regiment**

Time and again, letters appeared in the Chronicle pleading for a melodian to fill the long, empty evenings with music.

From No. 14 hut and No. 16 hut the requests flowed in. Even "Ossie" Burgess and his brother Sam got their names in the paper.

"The lads of No. 31 hut, 'D' Company, 2nd Barnsley Battalion, would be very glad if you could help them in any way to get a melodian to pass a few of the dreary hours at night. The majority of the boys can play one, but they can't really buy one as it takes the largest portion of their weekly wage of 3/6 to buy a few cigs. We are nearly all readers of your valuable paper and we would very much appreciate any assistance you can give us. We remain yours etc. Sergeant A. W. Frost, Lance Corporal L. Smith, Gunner O. Burgess, Privates G. E. Padgett, R. H. Lowe, G. Atkinson, J. Finan, T. Ross, J. Hicks, E. Hirst, H. Shepherd, J. Burgin, S. Burgess, R. Heaversedge, G. Senior, T. Witto, W. Beevers, T. Berry, J. Drinkwater, F. Findlowe, W. Walker, W. Whitfield, H. Heffer, W. Winter, J. Rotchell, C. Gummerson, F. Sherry, T. Siddaway, H. Hannah." **Barnsley Chronicle, 23rd October 1915**

With just over a month's training at Hurdcott under their belts the Pals were feeling fit and ready for

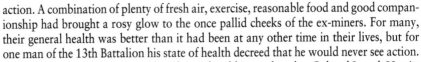

action. A combination of plenty of fresh air, exercise, reasonable food and good companionship had brought a rosy glow to the once pallid cheeks of the ex-miners. For many, their general health was better than it had been at any other time in their lives, but for one man of the 13th Battalion his state of health decreed that he would never see action.

On November 13th the Barnsley Chronicle told its readers that Colonel Joseph Hewitt had reluctantly been compelled to resign his command of the First Barnsley Battalion. The local solicitor with shares in several of the district's collieries had been with the 13th Battalion from the start. At times it had appeared that he had been a one-man recruiting machine appearing at countless meetings, his patriotic fervour always to the fore. As Colonel and C.O. he had been with the Battalion at Silkstone and Penkridge, at Ripon and at Hurdcott, but the pressures of command had taken their toll.

"Inability to physically stand the strain of an overseas campaign is the primary cause of Lt. Col. Hewitt taking the step", reported the Chronicle somewhat regretfully. Being a leading authority on colliery law, Col. Hewitt was offered a position with the Coal Commission and his dreams of command faded.

Colonel Hewitt was not the only Commanding Officer of a 31st Division, New Army Battalion to relinquish his position late in 1915. He merely trod the same path taken a month earlier by Lieut. Col. Richardson of the Hull "Commercials", (10th Battalion, East Yorkshire Regiment); and, two weeks before that, by Col. C. V. Mainwaring of the Sheffield City Battalion. Both men were replaced by Officers who had seen action in France. To the cynical observer it may have appeared that the War Office was getting rid of the old men with tired old legs in favour of younger, but nevertheless experienced substitutes.

Colonel Hewitt's place was amply filled by the striking figure of Lieut. Col. Edmund Ernest Wilford.

Exit Colonel Hewitt, raiser and commander of the 13th for one year.

"Colonel Wilford joined us five or six weeks before we went to Egypt. He'd been a Colonel in the Indian Army. He didn't seem a bad sort of a chap. He was a big fellow. I don't know how his horse carried him." **Tommy Oughton, 13th Y & L Regiment**

Exit Colonel Mainwaring, 12th Sheffield 'City' Battalion commander.

" 'Bullfrog' was Colonel Wilford's nickname. He was a man's man. A big smart fellow he was. We once had a parade at Hurdcott and Colonel Hewitt rode in on his little cob. It was only small. 'Old Joe' used to sit like a dumpling on this pony, his legs were nearly trailing on the floor. Wilford came in on his big horse. It was called 'Jerry M', and it used to run the hurdles. I bet you could find it in the racing columns. Wilford had his 'Lancer' chains on his shoulders. When he got up to Colonel Hewitt he said, 'Take that bloody cob away from mine will you'. Wilford proved himself a good fellow." **Harry Hall, 13th Y & L Regiment**

Colonel Wilford had all the dash and confidence one would have expected from an ex-Squadron Officer of the 30th Lancers (Gordon's Horse), a unit which had become part of the Indian Cavalry Corps in December 1914. Most of his military career had been spent in India, in fact he had only been promoted to the rank of Major in the Indian Army a month after the outbreak of war the previous year. He was to become respected by the men for his no-nonsense approach and his willingness to see for himself how things were going at the 'sharp end' of operations.

On November 16th, five days after Colonel Wilford had taken over command, the Pals marched 16 miles across Salisbury Plain past Stonehenge to Canada Lines and a place called Camp No. 2 at Larkhill.

It was to be their last home in England. Here they would polish their training before being sent overseas. At Larkhill the Pals spent most of their time, whole days, on the Durrington rifle ranges, getting their eyes in on Parts III and IV of the General Musketry Course. By that time the weather had broken and Number 2 Camp was awash with sludge. Vernon Atkinson who had joined the 14th Battalion in a draft of reserves from Silkstone had good cause to remember the ranges.

"One day we had this rifle course and it was 'siling' it down. The whole Battalion was there and we had to shoot at targets from 100-5,000 yards. It rained all day, it never ceased. The field kitchen came on with our dinner. I said to one of the cooks, 'Who's going to eat this then?' and the cook said, 'Well you'll have to eat it, water and all.' We had to eat it. If you threw anything away there was hell to pop." **Vernon Atkinson, 14th Y & L Regiment**

"We went for shooting practice at Larkhill, where the old druids had been. There was a camp up there notorious for men falling ill. In one of these camps there were a lot of Colonial soldiers and they fell ill. I don't know why but according to what we heard they had an epidemic of some sort." **Ernest Bell, 13th Y & L Regiment**

The story was that an influenza epidemic had taken the lives of some 200 Canadians who had been at the camp before the 'Pals', and these rumours were fuelled by the fanciful tale of a dead Canadian soldier who had been dug out of the mud in an upright position with full kit on and rifle at the slope.

By now the Pals were itching to see some sort of action. Surely they were as ready as they ever would be. It began to look as if they would never get away, but their disappointments disappeared when they were told, early in December, to prepare for an imminent move to a theatre of war.

All talk of melodians and mouth organs evaporated and the main topic of conversation in the huts at night revolved around their ultimate destination. They were however, given one huge clue.

"We didn't know where we were being sent, but they did issue us with sunhats." **Charlie Swales, 14th Y & L Regiment**

"We got dished out with Pith helmets and a label for the gun. It was a gummed label and you put your name and rank on it and stuck it on the butt. It was so you could identify it when you stacked your gun on-board ship. The old sweats used to say 'Take care of them guns lads, they're your main object.' They called 'em 'Bondooks'. The old blokes who'd been in India had different phrases. At night they'd say, 'Get in your "charpoy" and "chub-barow".' That meant, get in your bed and shut up!" **Frank Lindley, 14th Y & L Regiment**

Pith helmets only meant one thing, sun. That ruled France out. Perhaps they thought they were bound for the sniper-ridden ravines of the Gallipoli Peninsula, quite unaware of a higher decision to abandon that particular theatre of operations. Perhaps they were off to Mesopotamia to assist in the relief of General Townsend's force so recently surrounded by Turkish hordes at Kut-el-Amara. Whatever the place their excitement increased, the only fly in the ointment being the exasperating ritual of wrapping their newly acquired puggarees round their helmets.

"The puggarees were yards and yards of khaki linen and you had to bind them around the crown of your hat to protect it against the sun. You had to fold it neatly, back and front as the Indians do with turbans. You had to have the knack of turning it and folding it to make it look neat, and you had to keep a gap between folds. That gap had to stay the same all the way round. If you got stuck, you'd get a thick one and a thin one. I used to do it for some of the others." **Frank Lindley, 14th Y & L Regiment**

A picture to send home to his wife and child before proceeding abroad, Private Arthur Edon, 13th Battalion, of 41 Grafton Street is to die of wounds at the age of 21 in May 1917.

Their expectations were dashed when they were not sent away immediately after being given their new items of kit. Still, the delay gave them time to master these new military skills and get down to some serious 'spit and polish'. It also gave them time to march back across the Plain to Hurdcott.

Rumours concerning the destination of the Pals were by now bouncing from hut to hut, as orders were received, then revoked, received and revoked yet again. The suspense became almost intolerable.

Colonel Hewitt, although no longer in command of the 13th Battalion, was determined to bid 'au revoir' to 'his lads' before the final order for them to leave came through. He visited Hurdcott early in December and was greeted with ringing cheers when he announced his intention to give £100 to Colonel Wilford as a going away present for the men.

The cheering grew louder when Colonel Wilford told the parading soldiers that the comforts fund was being boosted by further gifts of £200 from Major and Mrs. Guest and £100 from Miss Fountain of Birthwaite Hall, Barnsley. More presents followed. Colonel Wilford and Colonel Hulke were eager to form Battalion bands before they left for overseas service and Councillor cum Second Lieutenant Plumpton duly obliged the 13th with the promise of a complete set of brass instruments. These would be added to the existing bugles which had served the Battalion well during the previous months. Councillor Plumpton hoped that the formation of a band would give the Pals the means of "cheering themselves up whenever occasion permitted."

The next day Councillor Plumpton and Major Guest drove to Salisbury, caught the train to London and went straight to the Regent Street showrooms of Messrs. Boosey. They purchased a piccolo, two saxophones, seven cornets as well as several horns and trombones, with a couple of drums thrown in for good measure. It was a generous gift. The whole lot was packed and despatched a day later and it arrived at Hurdcott at half past one in the afternoon. By 3 o'clock, Sergeant Danforth was conducting the newly formed 13th Battalion band, through "Jock o' York", the Regimental March and, ironically, "When the Boys Come Back". Not to be outdone, on hearing the 13th Battalion band strike up, Colonel Hulke was prompted into sending a telegram to the Barnsley Corporation Raising Committee.

"From O.C. 14th Battalion 7th December, 1915
As a farewell gift to the Battalion a complete set of brass and reed instruments and some music will be highly appreciated. This Battalion is the only one in the Brigade without a band. Would like them in time to proceed with us overseas on Thursday."

'Old Soldiers' some 13th Battalion men on Salisbury Plain. With overseas service imminent more wire stiffeners are being removed.

1 Platoon 'A' Company, 14th York and Lancaster Regiment. Issued with Short Lee Enfield rifles and pith helmets, destination unknown. The officer, centre, William Hirst, recently married his finacee Bertha Lockwood of Wath-on-Dearne. He is to die on 1st July, 1916. Along with William Hirst, Sergeant Draisey (8th from right, front row) will also die on that day.

The Committee acquiesced.

> *"To O.C. 14th Battalion from Raising Committee. Mayor and Raising Committee will authorise purchase set of instruments for 14th Battalion. Wire if you can obtain same, and approximate cost."*
> *"From O.C. 14th Battalion 9th December 1915*
> *All ranks greatly appreciated your gift band instructions and have purchased Hawkes estimate £130. Writing." Minutes of the Report of the Sub-Committee Appointed to Superintend the Raising and Equipment of the Second Barnsley Battalion, January 1916.*

A few days later a deputation consisting of Barnsley's new Mayor, Alderman H. Holden, Col. Raley and several members of the Raising Committee, visited Hurdcott to wish the men of both Battalions a safe journey.

Their first stop was the 14th Battalion camp and in a gesture which might have allayed any feelings of envy regarding the comforts fund for the 13th, Colonel Raley handed a cheque for £400 to Colonel Hulke. The money had been donated by an anonymous Barnsley "gentleman", whose desire was that "both Battalions should proceed overseas similarly provided for."

December 9th, the day Colonel Hulke had stated as the day of departure, came, and still they were kicking their heels in the huts of Hurdcott. Everybody cheered up however when they were told that they were being given 48 hours' leave. They all got away, but thanks to the ditherings of the Army authorities some went further than others.

> *"About the middle of December we were granted leave to go home. We got halfway home, to Basingstoke, and we noticed we were going back. They'd turned us round and they took us back. Well, I don't know why to this day."* **Ernest Bell, 13th Y & L Regiment**

> *"We passed out and they decided to give us 48 hours' leave for those who had the money to pay. We were all covered in sludge from trench digging. 'Hoppy' had had a remittance from home but I was 'skint'. 'Hoppy' went in and got his ticket and pass and when he came back to the door he handed me his money and I went in and got mine. You didn't pay, you just showed 'em that you had the money to pay at the railway. We got home for the weekend because we shot off that evening.*

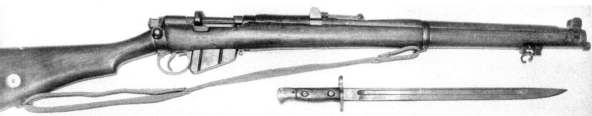

The Short Lee-Enfield scorned by many experts when introduced in 1903, it is eventually to become one of the finest bolt-action rifles ever developed. It is issued to the Pals battalions prior to their leaving for active service.

When we got back we'd been away over 48 hours and we were in 'clink' for going A.W.O.L. We found out that the majority had hung on until the next morning to clean up and when they got to Basingstoke they turned 'em back. From then on we called it 'Bastardstoke'." Frank Lindley, 14th Y & L Regiment

The Chronicle of December 11th had first mentioned Egypt as the probable theatre of operations for the Pals and on his return from his 'extended' leave, Frank Lindley found that particular rumour to be the most prevalent.

Finally, a few days before Christmas, it became known that the Pals were to move on Boxing Day. Everybody held their breath and waited for the order to be cancelled, but it wasn't. Instead, as if to confirm the order, the Pals were given a last spell of leave and they all rushed back to Barnsley before anyone in a position of power had a chance to change their minds. At least the men would have the opportunity of enjoying the pre-Christmas celebrations at home.

On Christmas night, their leave officially over, the Pals assembled in Barnsley town centre ready to catch the trains back to Salisbury.

Saturday, December 25th 1915, had been a cold miserable day. Dark clouds had drifted over Barnsley all day and towards evening showers added to the gathering gloom.

Above: *Widow Mrs. Edon with her three sons, William, Arthur and Alfred. Beginning with 13th 'Pals' Battalion member, Arthur in May 1917 Mrs. Edon, of Grafton Street, loses all three of her boys.*

The weather however, failed to dampen the ardour of the Barnsley public as they turned out in force to see their soldier sons depart. The townspeople had witnessed one or two farewells during the course of the war and the Pals had featured in at least one of them, but the farewell of Christmas Night 1915 eclipsed all the rest. The traditional feelings of goodwill were laced with the happy, sad emotions of parting. It all added up to an historic event the like of which Barnsley had never seen.

"The streets in the town centre were for some hours besieged by men, women and children. Market Hill, Eldon Street, Cheapside and May Day Green were never so densely packed with human beings in the history of the Borough, and it would seem as though every inhabitant not only of the town, but of the district too, had turned out to give the 'boys' a hearty send off. Orders had been given for the 13th Service Battalion to parade on Market Hill at 10p.m., the men of the 14th Service Battalion to assemble about the same time on May Day Green: but the density of the crowd completely prohibited any organised procession of the troops taking place, and finally the men moved off to Court House Station in sections surrounded by their friends. There were mothers, wives and sweethearts looking sorrowful, as the hour approached for their dear ones to depart." Barnsley Chronicle, 1st January 1916

"When we came home on that 48 hours leave, I think all of Barnsley turned out when we went back. There were tears from the young ladies. I think we were all worked up really." Ernest Bell, 13th Y & L Regiment

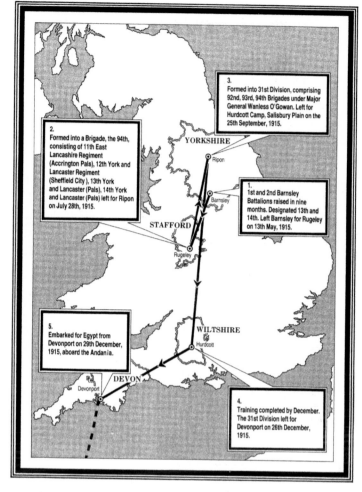

3.
Formed into 31st Division, comprising 92nd, 93rd, 94th Brigades under Major General Wanless O'Gowan. Left for Hurdcott Camp, Salisbury Plain on the 25th September, 1915.

2.
Formed into a Brigade, the 94th, consisting of 11th East Lancashire Regiment (Accrington Pals), 12th York and Lancaster Regiment (Sheffield City), 13th York and Lancaster (Pals), 14th York and Lancaster (Pals) left for Ripon on July 28th, 1915.

1.
1st and 2nd Barnsley Battalions raised in nine months. Designated 13th and 14th. Left Barnsley for Rugeley on 13th May, 1915.

5.
Embarked for Egypt from Devonport on 29th December, 1915, aboard the Andania.

4.
Training completed by December. The 31st Division left for Devonport on 26th December, 1915.

YORKSHIRE
Ripon
Barnsley
STAFFORD
Rugeley
WILTSHIRE
Hurdcott
DEVON
Devonport

Last kisses and final words were snatched in the streets outside the station. To the strains of the 13th Battalion band, playing their hearts out in the station yard, the men hauled themselves aboard the trains laden with presents and with every pocket bulging with extra home comforts. The trains left just after midnight to tumultuous cheers but all too soon they had gone. The crowds began to melt away and by 1 a.m. the streets, which had so recently held a noisy multitude, were empty and silent.

The Pals didn't spend too much time at Hurdcott once they arrived. In fact for the next three days they were to be mercilessly marched and transported towards the docks at Devonport with little time for anything resembling a good night's sleep.

On Boxing Day evening, with the rain falling in torrents, the Pals formed up in full kit and endured an unpleasant march to Dinton station. They were, in the main, glad to see the back of Hurdcott. It hadn't turned out to be such a perfect camp after all, for it had rained almost incessantly since the day they had first set foot inside the perimeter. The only memory they would retain was of mud, but of much more mud than Silkstone ever had. There was mud all over camp, it was trailed into their huts, it covered their uniforms and their bodies. They little realised that the lessons learned in the mire of Hurdcott would be a boon later on.

Not all the Pals marched to Dinton. Some 92 members of the 14th Battalion hadn't even made it to Barnsley on Christmas night. A disastrous combination of spirits of both the bodily and alcoholic varieties had conspired to provide a thumping hangover for a few of that number; 28 of these absentees were picked up in taxis at Salisbury, some of them still the worse for wear almost 24 hours later, and were transported to Dinton. 2nd Lieutenant Fairley was given the task of staying behind at Hurdcott to organise the rest of the stragglers and accompany them overseas on a later ship if necessary.

From Dinton the Pals were transported by train to a Rest Camp at St. Budeaux near Plymouth. The term 'Rest Camp' was a complete misnomer as far as the tired troops were concerned. They were there for less than four hours before they were herded out again, this time a thankfully short march down to Devonport docks and a rendezvous with His Majesty's Transport vessel *Andania*, described by Vernon Atkinson as 'a bloody old ship'.

All day it seemed, soldiers and stevedores alike tramped up and down the countless gang planks fetching and carrying cartons of this and crates of that, along with other pieces of military equipment. By mid-afternoon the *Andania* had swallowed up a total of 2,212 troops, comprising the 13th and 14th York and Lancaster Regiment and a few members of the Royal Engineers and Army Service Corps plus all their paraphernalia.

They sailed on 29th December. At last they were on their way, they had considered themselves equal to any task they might be asked to perform for quite some time but they had always been delayed a little.

Few of them had considered, when they had sworn their oath in the company of the Rev. Huggard, quite what their feelings would be when the time came for them to leave the shores of dear old England far behind. They had come a long way since sleeping in their shirts at the Public Hall and their first clumsy attempts at drilling on the Queen's Ground.

For the Pals, the adventure that most of them had dreamed of was only just beginning, and yet the sight of the soil of their native country slipping slowly by, touched a string in all but the most hardened heart.

"We went down the Sound at the side of the Hoe and there were some folks there as had got the 'whiff, that we were going. They were waving their handkerchiefs at us. We all waved our pith helmets. If you'd have seen that ship, full of these pith helmets all going round. You couldn't see anything on that ship but pith helmets all over. It was a sight to be seen. And then it started; someone singing 'Homeland' and it was ringing and echoing from the Hoe."

> *Homeland, homeland, land of my birth.*
> *The dearest place on earth.*
> *It may be for years,*
> *It may be forever,*
> *Dear homeland goodbye.*

And there weren't many of us came back."   Frank Lindley, 14th Y & L Regiment

Chapter Seven

My little grey home in the east

*"There is a nasty wind bringing in a choppy sea. The transport is now rounding
Drake Island and dropping the hawser from the tug. I can see your lads crowding
the bulwarks, having a look at the beautiful Bay – perhaps the most beautiful and
the most interesting in England. They are passing the very spot where Drake played
his famous game of bowls, sailing on the very waves where Howard gathered the
fleet to smash the Armada. They can see the monuments commemorating both and
three centuries of English history look down on them. They are so near I could
almost speak to them. But now she is heading for sea. No – she turns – she is
dropping her anchor in the bay. Why? 'Some trouble', says a tar, 'for see, one of the
destroyers told off to escort her returns and speaks to her. Perhaps a submarine
knocking about – perhaps waiting for orders.' But as dusk came she made for sea."*
Barnsley Chronicle. 1st January 1916

GUIDING HIS VESSEL CAREFULLY down the
busy English Channel towards the open waters of
the Bay of Biscay, the Captain of the *Andania* could
have counted himself extremely fortunate to be carrying so
many ex-colliers on board. After all, if it hadn't been for
the timely assistance of half a dozen men of Frank Lindley's
Company, the *Andania* would still have been wallowing at
anchor near Plymouth breakwater.

The ship had sailed without its full complement of stokers
and it had been a red-faced Chief Engineer who had been
forced to recruit some part-time stokers from the ranks of
the 14th Battalion. Now, with the six volunteers from 'A'
Company shovelling coal for all they were worth down in
the bowels of the ship, the *Andania* was, at last, on her way.

There was little time for mixed thoughts of melancholy or
adventure however as the cliffs of England receded into the
distance. The 13,000 ton *Andania*, by now pitching and
rolling in the increasingly heavy seas, held a few seafaring
surprises in store for the land-lubbers of Barnsley.

Crammed like sardines into cabins with wire netting
bunks so short that their heads hung over the ends, many of
the Pals were suddenly gripped by a different feeling – but
this time it was in the pit of their stomachs. The proud boast
of the younger lads on board was that they could eat
anything, anywhere, anytime, but on this occasion their
boasts were to prove as empty as their stomachs were soon
to be. The offer of a King's ransom would not have
persuaded them to touch a scrap of food.

*The first posting in a war zone for the Pals,
that vulnerable link between East and West –
the Suez Canal, under threat from the Turks.
Below: A popular publication portrays the
heroic defenders of the British Empire on its
front cover.*

The Modern Empire rallies in the shadow of the Ancient Sphinx   No. 24

*"The furthest I'd been prior to that trip was Cleethorpes, maybe Blackpool. I was as sick as a dog.
I lay on the top deck for three days, I daren't go down to eat. I remember the first day I went down,
I got to the top of the gangway steps going down and I met this fellow with a trayful of Quaker*

Oats. When I saw that tray of Quaker Oats, that was enough. I went back." **Harry Hall, 13th Y & L Regiment**

The loss of so many hefty appe-tites was a blessing in disguise for those who got off relatively lightly.

"*It was our first trip on a ship. I was seasick for the first two days and then I was all right. Some of them were 'off it' until we got into the Mediterranean. We got plenty of 'snap' because a lot of them couldn't eat.*" **Charlie Swales, 14th Y & L Regiment**

"*When we got into the Channel we hit the bad weather straight away. We were going up and down. I don't think half our men went down for meals for two or three days. We used to have a good time of it because there was food to spare. After they started to come down we hardly used to*

Keeping German intelligence up to date with troop movements, some of the Pals send postcards home depicting their troop transport ship, the "Andania". Both Barnsley Battalions on one ship, the Andania steams out en-route for the 'Med.' and the U-boat menace.
Written in pencil on the back is the following:
"*Dear wife and children, I am on this ship at Devonport and sail tonight 28th. Wishing you a happy new year. Hoping to see you again some day, from your husband, Herbert.*"
Herbert Hibbert, 13th Battalion

get any at all they were so hungry." **Ernest Bell, 13th Y & L Regiment**

For some of the worst affected cases any fate was better than the suffering they were now being subjected to.

"*I got out of my bunk one morning and I saw this bloke and he was heaving. He said, 'I wish this boat would go down'. I said, 'Steady on, I hope it doesn't go down yet, I can't swim all the way back'.*" **Vernon Atkinson, 14th Y & L Regiment**

The practical jokers in both Battalions had a field day with the helpless, green-faced victims.

"*I'd been on boats before but never so far. There were a lot seasick. Sometimes I used to imitate 'em and pretend to be sick. We used to do all sorts to make 'em be sick and sometimes they would be. They'd heave their hearts up. I never had any trouble at all.*" **James Bennett, 14th Y & L Regiment**

To make matters worse, apart from the full dixies of stew and porridge which cluttered the troop decks, the army chose those first few days of the voyage to immunise the men against cholera. It was a common practice for troops bound for warmer climes, but the timing left a lot to be desired.

"*When we got out into the Bay of Biscay it was really rough. The best of it was that they decided to inoculate us on the ship. We had to go down below, near the engines. Talk about hot down there, with the ship pitching and them jabbing needles in. Oh! Crikey! There was a bathroom at the side and that bath was full of spew. To top it all we had to line the deck and watch for submarines. You could see an odd destroyer nipping about as if they were looking after us, and there were all these porpoises going like hell up and down in front of the ship. It was a good sight, but with us staring out at the water it made you ill. There was me and 'Hoppy' hanging over the side and an old deck hand came up to us and says, 'Now boys you can spew and spew to your hearts content, but if you feel a ring in your throat swallow hard cos its your arsehole."* **Frank Lindley, 14th Y & L Regiment**

There was only one thing for it; the afflicted had to devise strategies to quell their restless innards and that usually entailed taking up a supine position as Harry Hall had already found out. It helped if one could dredge up any tips from dim memory, and if those tips were good enough for the Royal family then surely they were good enough for the Pals.

"I used to conquer it by lying down on my back on the deck. I once saw in a paper that the Prince of Wales always plugged his ears with cotton wool when he went on a boat. The other lads thought I was talking daft." **Vernon Atkinson, 14th Y & L Regiment**

Frank Lindley and his friend 'Hoppy' considered the sleeping arrangements to be less than adequate, so, just as he had done at the Public Hall, Frank went up in the world to find his 'kip'.

"We used to sleep up on the boat deck. Down below they'd made shelves with wire netting and to get in you had to swing in with your feet first and your head was out at the end. It was stuffy and filthy down below, burning hot and what with the stink of the bilge, we carted all our tackle up onto the top and we slept there. We sometimes slept in the lifeboats covered in tarpaulin." **Frank Lindley, 14th Y & L Regiment**

New Year's Eve aboard the *Andania* was a very subdued affair but as the sun rose on New Year's Day 1916, it brought with it a calmer sea, much to the relief of the Pals.

By now the Andania was well on its way around the Iberian Peninsula and heading for the warmer waters of the Mediterranean. The improving climate did much to raise the men's spirits.

"This morning, January 2nd, is one of the finest of mornings I have ever seen. It was beautiful to get up and see the sun shining. The water is nice and calm now and the ship is sailing grand. Today we have had our Church parade and we have had a few selections from 'Plumpton's Brass Band' and if you had heard it you would have thought it was Black Dyke playing at Crystal Palace." **Letter to the Barnsley Chronicle of 22nd January 1916 from an anonymous First Barnsley Battalion soldier**

It sounded as if the voyage had the makings of a very pleasant trip but since the Pals were now feeling bright and breezy their officers lost no time in reminding them that it was to be no pleasure cruise. Physical drill, kit inspections and inter-company contests, ranging from boxing to tug-of-war were organised to keep muscles toned up and prevent spirits from stagnating. Those men who were deemed handy with mop and hosepipe were volunteered for the unenviable task of swilling away the widespread results of the seasickness which had so recently gripped the ship.

New Year's Day had been celebrated with a full scale lifeboat drill and it was no idle exercise considering the present location of the *Andania*.

Moving troops by ship in the

First port of call, the Grand Harbour, Valletta, Malta. The Andania *drops anchor among the many warships.*

waters of the British Isles and beyond was a risky business given the German Navy's predilection for prowling the ocean depths in their submarines. In view of the U-Boat menace, the decision to cram some 2,000 men from Barnsley and district onto the same vessel could have been a recipe for catastrophe on a far greater scale than any which awaited them in the shell-torn fields of France. Added to this the *Andania* was now sailing alone, her destroyer escort having turned back after shepherding her out of British waters, but she was not entirely defenceless. Sitting astern was a single 4.7 inch naval gun which, in the hands of the ship's Captain, was a formidable deterrent to any U-Boat willing to chance its arm on the surface.

> "One day the Captain said he'd show us how to shoot. He threw a box into the water and he let fly. He blew this box into the air first time." **Vernon Atkinson, 14th Y & L Regiment**

As an extra measure the men of both Battalions, seven armed with a rifle and a bandolier of ammunition, continued their endless vigil of the water's surface.

In the early hours of January 3rd the ship slipped past Tangier, its many lights shining brilliantly in the darkness, and by 5 a.m. with the Straits of Gibraltar successfully negotiated, she entered the Mediterranean.

The voyage had entered a dangerous phase, as the Mediterranean was well known to be the watery graveyard of many an Allied vessel.

> "We'd always got our eyes open for them 'subs'. When we got through 'Gib' into the 'Med', we passed some wreckage of some ship that had gone down. We thought we saw some bodies floating in the 'Med'." **Frank Lindley, 14th Y & L Regiment**

Fortunately for the Pals the next three days of the voyage passed uneventfully. Free from the close attentions of submarine commanders the *Andania* steamed serenely through calm waters under clear blue skies while the Pals were put through their paces with practice fire drills and more physical jerks.

Malta was sighted early in the morning of January 6th and although the sunshine had turned to rain when the *Andania* anchored in the Grand Harbour at Valletta, the Pals crowded onto the boat decks to catch a glimpse of their first port of call.

Their view of Valletta was quite unlike any sight they had seen before. Scanning the skyline the Pals were struck by the closely packed flat roofed buildings which seemed to tumble down almost into the water.

For men used to the linear terraces of the smoke-stained 'back to backs' of home, the pale washed walls and the many angular designs of the houses of Valletta, came as a complete surprise. Up above were the large, low Government buildings and above them commanding the whole bay, were the steep and forbidding battlements of the harbour defences.

No sooner had the *Andania* dropped anchor among the many warships which already filled the harbour, than she was surrounded by a plethora of small craft, fussing and dodging around her massive bulk. These were the "bum boats", ably steered by lithe, olive skinned youths who willingly ran the gauntlet of the harbour police to display their wares to the serried ranks of troops peering down at them.

> "Out came the 'bum boats' selling their fruit and whatever, and there were these little lads who would dive for coins. You could chuck a coin in there and the little lads could go down and fetch it and show it to you when they brought it up." **Frank Lindley, 14th Y & L Regiment**

Breaking the voyage at Malta meant that the *Andania* could replenish her fuel supplies but it also meant that the rank and file were never allowed the opportunity of sampling the delights of Valletta. While some men contented themselves by watching the native Maltese dockers go about their business, others rekindled old Barnsley acquaintances in a Mediterranean setting.

> "We stopped at Malta to take on coal and these 'coolies' used to bring it up in baskets on top of their heads. They only had a thin plank to walk over and they were in bare feet." **Vernon Atkinson, 14th Y & L Regiment**

We stayed at Malta 'coaling', but we weren't allowed on land. Dr. James Foley from Wombwell was our family doctor and he was stationed in Malta. Of course he got to know the Barnsley Battalions were coming in and he came on board. I happened to be on deck and he saw me and came across for a chat." **Tommy Oughton, 13th Y & L Regiment**

The pleasures of shore leave were reserved for officers and warrant officers alone, and they too met old medical friends as well as witnessing scenes of high drama in the Grand Harbour.

"At Malta the officers and warrant officers went ashore and met an old friend of ours – Captain Russell, R.A.M.C., who was very pleased to meet the officers of the old 13th. There we had a little excitement. The vessel broke away from her moorings and nearly crushed a French

View of the Grand Harbour from the Saluting Battery, looking towards Isola Point and French Creek. The men were not permitted to go ashore during the 'coaling' of the Andania. The privilege of shore leave goes only to officers and sergeants.

destroyer which was underneath the bow of the vessel like a little cock boat. Happily there were two tugs which got hold of the ship after the siren had blown and secured her to another buoy." **Letter to the Barnsley Chronicle from Sergeant A.E. Greaves, Machine-Gun Section, First Barnsley Battalion, 19th February, 1916**

The stay in Malta was a brief one, with her stocks of coal topped up the *Andania* set sail in the afternoon of January 7th. 'Plumpton's Brass Band' played them out into the Mediterranean once more.

On leaving Malta, Company commanders were at last able to put an end to the speculation concerning the Pals' final destination. The sight of the shining white domes of Alexandria, which the *Andania* touched fleetingly on January 10th, confirmed the rumours which had swept through Hurdcott Camp in mid-December, Egypt was indeed to be journey's end.

At breakfast time the following day the ship sailed past the imposing statue of Ferdinand De Lesseps standing guard at the entrance to one of his greatest engineering triumphs, the Suez Canal. A short time later the *Andania* found a berth at one of the quays of Port Said.

The voyage had spanned 13 days. It had begun in the dreary depths of a miserable English Winter and had been concluded under the searing sun of the land of the Pharaohs. The Arab dhows slowly criss-crossing the harbour, somehow managing to avoid the carved figureheads and high prows of the Egyptian fellucas, set the seal on the atmosphere of the East.

Port Said itself was to prove rather less exotic than the Pals may have first imagined, but it still held immense interest for the pit lads of Barnsley. The men were kept waiting on the quayside until all their equipment had been unloaded by Arab deckhands, but the first attempts at coming to terms with the ways and customs of the native Egyptians did nothing to further the cause of international diplomacy.

"When the boat stopped at Port Said some of the natives were coming on row boats. They wore fezes and they had like a long smock on down to their ankles. One of the lads said, 'Are they lads or lasses?' Suddenly one of the lads had a bright idea. 'There's only one way to find art,' he said, 'tipple the bugger upside darn,' so one was upended to see if it was a lad or a lass, it was a lad! It was all in fun, they were just typical collier lads." **Charlie Swales, 14th Y & L Regiment**

In contrast to the poor soul whose world had been turned upside down due to the curiosity of some of Charlie Swales' section, the dress of the Arab dockers seemed to consist entirely of Army issue cast-offs. Cap-comforters and tatty tunics covered by long, flowing army shirts, seemed to be the order of the day.

With other vessels in the harbour the *Andania* was not the only ship to be attended by hordes of busy

workers. The Arabs' capacity for hard work drew admiring glances from the watching Barnsley Pals.

"We saw barges coaling the odd Navy ship. They had planks between the boats and the Arabs were filling baskets and running up these planks and tipping coal into the hold. They were going like hell and all the time they were singing 'Allah, Allah Hai-a-lee'. They were strong them Arabs. We used to see them carrying nearly full bell tents on their 'rigs'." **Frank Lindley, 14th Y & L Regiment**

With the unloading completed the men took their leave of the ship that had been 'home' for almost two weeks and marched to a new 'home', a flat expanse of sand upon which had sprouted tents and bivouacs. This uninspiring spot was Rest Camp number 7 and they were to be there for the next nine days, sleeping under canvas with a blanket

Disembarking in Egypt the Pals get a close look at the natives. Here some 13th Battalion men are introduced to the bargaining wiles of the Arabs.

separating their bodies from the sand.

"When we got off at Port Said we went to a camp just outside where we were all told to strip. We were all stark naked, we didn't have a stitch on. This officer marched us down to the sea and he said, 'Now get in there all of you and swim back to bloody England'." **Vernon Atkinson, 14th Y & L Regiment**

Situated at the entrance to the Suez Canal, Port Said was the very gateway to the Far East, India and Australasia, and it was there that East clashed with west in a hustling, bustling, Babel's Tower of a town. Now that the holiday had begun and they were so far from home, the men were naturally eager to explore the strange country they had landed in. As soon as duties allowed they escaped the dusty environs of the camp and headed for the town.

"On Saturday afternoon along with five pals I went into the town and the first item on the programme was a swim in the 'Med'. The water was splendid, but the waves were too big and conse-quently we did not venture out too far. The water was warm too. We afterwards took a very pleasant walk around the European quarters and ultimately succeeded in getting into conversation with a few French people. Thus the little French I know enabled me to talk to the people in their own language. These French folk can speak English and Egyptian fluently and it is impossible to find, even in lads of 12 or 13 years of age, a foreign accent when speaking any language other than their own." **Letter to the Barnsley Chronicle from Private Amos Quinnell, 'A' Company, 13th Y & L Regiment 29th January, 1916**

Little wonder that the children were fluent in so many tongues for the very act of walking the wide, airy avenues of the European quarter was an education in itself. All manner of languages and accents bounced back and forth between the members of the cosmopolitan crowd gathered there.

Due to its strategically sensitive position, Port Said played host to countless foreign servicemen along with many other international travellers. Australians mixed with Arabs, Sudanese with Japanese, and the sight of small groups of French sailors striding along, arm-in-arm at the same time belting out a lusty Gallic rendition of 'Tipperary', stopped the 'Pals' in their tracks.

In Port Said at least, that well-loved British air was as popular as it had ever been. From the dark and mysterious depths of the many saloons and cafes, young female voices with a distinctly French or Italian flavour, could be heard grappling vainly with the melody against the overpowering squeal of a solo violin.

There was a drinking shop on almost every street corner and, be they owned by French, Egyptian or Turkish businessmen, they all sported a sign in English. Some of the less salubrious of establishments dispensed with the vocal entertainments as they pandered to the baser desires of the packs of servicemen on the loose.

"I went into one place and these lasses were dancing round with bits of lace on and not much else. There'd be a bowl of monkey nuts on the table and we'd get a glass of wine while these lasses danced around us." **Frank Lindley, 14th Y & L Regiment**

As well as frequenting the bars, many men spent their time browsing round the street markets and bazaars, hunting for souvenirs of their visit. The memories of the rough and ready methods of the street vendors in displaying their produce were to last a lifetime.

"We had a look round Port Said but it was a dirty place. I've never touched a date since. You went into the market place and they'd spread all their stuff on the ground. The dates were in a square block and you couldn't see the dates for flies. They were absolutely covered. I've never fancied dates since." **Harry Hall, 13th Y & L Regiment**

"We were once walking round and we saw this bloke with a barrow full of 'canes'. He said 'Good for de belly, good for de stomach.' It gave us the runs. There were germs all over the place." **Frank Lindley, 14th Y & L Regiment**

Everywhere they went the Pals were offered items for sale. Beggar children, wise beyond their years through a lifetime spent on the streets, pestered the soldiers in the hope of earning a crust. High pitched cries of 'mangaree Tommee', were accompanied by armfuls of tomatoes, oranges or small cakes thrust under the men's noses as they walked along. The more hardened Arab children who dared to offer Harry Lauder and Jimmy Mackenzie matches for sale to British soldiers ran the risk of a painful clout around the ears.

The Pals quickly mastered the native art of bartering for fresh fruit, bread or other items of food they wished to purchase. Army rations in the rest camp were so dreadfully poor and unappetising that the men were left with little choice but to do business with the wily Arabs who loitered around the tents.

"Tomatoes are one of the cheapest fruits – 1d per pound. The natives eat a lot of sugar cane. Although we do not like the habits of the natives we are forced to buy something. For instance, they bake white bread in long loaves (French fashion), which we buy and find them very fair – that is if you have the luck to get them fresh." **Letter to the Barnsley Chronicle from Private Tom Bradbury, First Barnsley Battalion, 29th January, 1916**

A memento from one of the many bars in Port Said.

Playing mobile-shop to the soldiers was a lucrative venture for the natives, since it was the Pals' only means of supplementing their monotonous and unwholesome diet. Even so, from the Pals' point of view, there were risks in allowing the sharp-eyed and argumentative traders into the camp.

"We were dished out with hard biscuits and 'bully beef'. The biscuits were big round ones and full of bloody maggots. We had to dig 'em out with our bayonets. There were these lads who used to sell hard boiled little eggs. They used to come round the tent lines and if you didn't watch 'em they used to pinch things. One time there was this lad nosing around our tent and a 'bobby' rode up, a big Nubian bloke with white trousers and big black boots and a fez. They always carried a cane. Well he grabbed this lad and upended him and lashed his bare feet. He chucked him down but the lad was up, made a sign

European quarter of Port Said.

to the policeman and he was off. Their feet were like iron. If there was a 'barney' and we were involved the 'bobbies' used to ignore us and lash the others with the stick. They never asked who was in the right or anything like that, they used to lash their own kind." Frank Lindley, 14th Y & L Regiment

To the Pals it appeared that every native Egyptian male was doing his level best to 'twist' the soldiers out of what little loose change they had, or charging double the price for anything they wanted. Many a heated exchange hinged on disputes over sums of one penny while many a letter home complained of the ridiculously exorbitant prices of the more luxurious items for sale. Cigarettes, at 2fid for two packets of Woodbines, were about the same price as in England, and eggs and oranges were 1d each, but everything else seemed to be beyond the shallow pockets of the Barnsley troops.

They never saw much of the local beer ranging from a shilling a pint to 1/3d for a 3 gill bottle, a 2lb tin of golden syrup cost 1/3d and tinned peas were an astonishing 1/6d.

In the bazaars too, it was the same frustrating story. Ornamental spears, sword sticks, fancy brooches and the ever popular 'lucky scarabs' glittered tantalisingly on the stalls but they were priced well beyond the finances of Kitchener's 'one bob a dayers'. Reduced to a humbling Egyptian version of window shopping, the Pals could but look on enviously as others picked the stalls clean.

"The one disadvantage in Egypt was that there were a lot of other troops there as well as us. There were Australians, Indians, and Gurkhas. The Australians were paid a lot more than us, about 7/6d a day, and we only had a shilling, 6d when I allowed for my mother. Well they could buy what they wanted and we could only look at them." **Ernest Bell, 13th Y & L Regiment**

Partly due to the Australian habit of getting into everything, one part of Port Said was officially out of bounds to British troops. On Christmas Eve several casualties to 31st Division troops who had arrived in Egypt prior to the Pals, had been sustained in the native quarter. This area, better known as Arab Town, was the exact opposite of the European quarter. Ugly rumours of soldiers being drugged with hashish and their contorted bodies turning up down narrow alleys at dawn, were taken very seriously indeed.

"The dirtiest of all quarters here are those whose buildings are all ramshackle and are, like the streets, in a very filthy condition. The stench is enough to bowl one over! There are rumours here – men are being killed by the Arabs nearly every day, but as to the truth of that we cannot say." **Letter to the Barnsley Chronicle, from Private Amos Quinnell, 'A' Company, 13th Y & L Regiment 29th January, 1916**

"Port Said was a terrible place. We weren't allowed to go out alone. There were a lot of murders there." **Vernon Atkinson, 14th Y & L Regiment**

"Soldiers are not allowed in some parts of the town as thousands of the natives are not in sympathy with the English. The other day we were marched through a part of the town where we dare not go on our own, and we were glad when we got through I can tell you. The smells are awful and it is wonderful how the people live in such surroundings." **Letter to the Barnsley Chronicle from Private Tom Bradbury, 'D' Company, 13th Y & L Regiment 29th January, 1916**

"We were vetoed from Arab Town but me and 'Hoppy' had a run round. Arab Town had filthy hovels. People would be smacking chapatis on the floor. The blokes got a bit aerated when they

Wishful thinking on the part of the Germans, a postcard depicts the Turkish forces in strength on the Suez Canal. The fear that this could become a reality causes the British High Command to commit a large force to Canal defence.

saw two soldiers coming. We didn't go right in, we'd never have got out because there were stories there of 'Aussies' getting garrotted." **Frank Lindley, 14th Y & L Regiment**

In spite of the insanitary conditions and the grim tales of Arab Town, it appeared that the British and colonial troops concentrated in Egypt in early 1916 were leading a very cushy existence. Far from the incessant rumble of guns, the only thing the Pals had to worry about, apart from getting a square meal and keeping out of trouble, was avoiding being burnt by the scorching Egyptian sun. It was a far cry from knee-high mud and the ever present dangers of life on the Western Front, deep in the throes of another sullen Winter.

Despite appearances to the contrary the Pals had a duty to perform in Egypt and at 5 a.m. on January 20th they struck tents to begin the job.

Almost exactly a year earlier a large Turkish force under German direction had traversed the drifting dunes and rocky outcrops of the Sinai Peninsula to launch an attack on the Suez Canal from three different points in Syria. The advance to the banks of the canal was hailed as a glorious crusade. By seizing the waterway the Turks hoped to sever Britain's artery to the east and the vital supply lines to her Russian ally. If, with the same action, they could liberate their Moslem brothers from grinding British oppression, then their mission would have been complete.

Just crossing the peninsula was in itself a considerable feat of arms but, on reaching the eastern banks of the canal the

A unit of the elusive enemy, Turks equipped by the Germans, prepare to move against Egypt and the Suez Canal.

Egypt's hundred-mile barrier against Turkish invasion, the Suez Canal, looking along it from Port Said.

Turkish attacks faded like a mirage on the desert and with them went their dreams of initiating a 'Holy War'.

By early February 1915 the Turkish troops had vanished into the sands of the Sinai. All that remained of their campaign were a few burnt and bullet-riddled huts at El Kantara on the banks of the canal, some 30 miles south of Port Said.

The Turkish offensive may have failed in attaining its material objectives but it succeeded in planting the seeds of paranoia in the minds of the British commanders in Egypt.

Somewhere, out on the desert, they believed the Turks to be massing for an effort on a much grander

Off to construct and man defences, the 13th Battalion travel in open carriages alongside the Canal. Officers in the rear carriage settle down for the snail-pace journey.

scale at a later date. The start of the sad episode at Gallipoli, with the consequence of drawing Turkish troops to defend the Dardanelles, allayed British fears only slightly. The answer was to keep the canal defences strong. Ironically in making that decision the British played right into the hands of the Germans. Backed by Germany, the Turks adopted the cat and mouse ploy of applying sporadic pressure to the sensitive canal zone, keeping the British guessing as to their next move and pinning down men who could have been used elsewhere.

All through the Summer and Autumn of 1915 the British chased fleeting shadows in the desert to the east of the canal as the Turks resorted to small scale hit and run tactics. The decision to abandon the Gallipoli adventure towards the end of 1915 brought widespread relief to the troops who had fought there but caused another headache for the British Chiefs of Staff. Kitchener in particular, feared for the future of Egypt once Turkish hands were freed, but it was not only Egypt which was at risk. Turkey could just as easily strike in Mesopotamia or possibly in the Balkans. To counteract these fears, and until the picture in the east and near east became clear, the troops from Gallipoli were sent to bolster the force already manning the defences of the Suez Canal. Steaming all the way from England to join them, came the Pals of the 31st Division. Together they formed a reserve pool of troops who could be moved quickly to any likely trouble spot from a central position in Egypt.

The 31st Division was unique in that it was the only division to come straight from the United Kingdom to join the Mediterranean Expeditionary Force (M.E.F.) gathering there.

At last the Barnsley Pals were about to embark on the task they had come such a long way to execute.

Towards the end of 1915 the British commanders in Egypt were not content to simply sit tight on the banks of the Suez Canal and wait for the Turks to strike. With only the natural desert barrier of the Sinai to check their advance, there was nothing to prevent a determined Turkish force from wheeling their guns to within shelling distance of the Canal and causing considerable damage before vanishing into the desert. The answer to such a threat was to pursue a vigorous policy of active defence and construct a stumbling block to any Turkish advance. Such a substantial shift in strategy spelled sweat for the Pals, for their part in the scheme was to help dig and man a small section of an extensive system of defences some six miles out on the Palestine side of the canal, and roughly parallel to its eastern banks. On the morning of their move from Rest Camp number 7 in Port Said both Barnsley Battalions were introduced to the joys of troop travel Egyptian style. Marching to the station they came face to face with what the Egyptian State Railway called carriages, but what looked like large open crates on wheels. The Pals climbed aboard and at half past eight in the morning the train set off for El Ferdan, a settlement on the banks of the Suez Canal, 40 miles to the south. That 40-mile journey was to take four hours and fifty minutes.

'We were taken on a truck train and it was a laughable sight. Troops are never moved in England as they are here. We went that fast that one of our men who dropped his pipe on the permanent way was able to get out of the truck, gather it up and get back in the same truck. We passed a spot where the Turks had been 12 months before.' Letter to the Barnsley Chronicle from an anonymous First Barnsley Battalion Private, 12th February 1916

Above and below: *A halt at one of the five stations on the way to El Ferdan. The inevitable native vendors appear with fruit for sale.*

There was plenty of time for the Pals to take in the sights on their leisurely trip down the west bank of the Suez Canal. Stretching out to their right were the blue waters of the salty Lake Manzala while on their immediate left large ocean-going vessels and various small craft glided up and down the Suez

Canal beyond the verdant, palm-tree lined margins of the Sweet Water Canal. Passing the key position of El Kantara the Pals could see for themselves the damage wrought by the Turkish advance, still unrepaired a full year later. After El Kantara came El Ballah and finally, well after lunch time, they arrived at El Ferdan, but first they had to cross the canal to take up their posts on its eastern bank. Once more they were helped on their way by a gang of hefty Arabs whose job was to haul on the heavy chains and pull the flat bottomed ferry across the water. Since there were no tents on that first night out from Port Said the men of 'A', 'B' and 'C' Companies found spots in the open air or took shelter under sheds, while 'D' Company mounted guards and patrolled the settlement.

Tom Bradbury, Tommy Oughton's friend in 'D' Company, was now sending letters by the sackful, both to his wife off Dodworth Road and to the Editor of the Chronicle. He perhaps thought it his duty to act as the Near East correspondent for his local weekly paper. Seldom a week passed, while the Pals were in Egypt, without a piece by Tom

Eastern bank of El Ferdan, the Pals have ferried across and prepare to take up their positions at Abu Aruk, out in the desert.

Bradbury gracing the Chronicle's columns. His impressions of the stay at El Ferdan were duly conveyed to England.

> *"I have had my first experience of outpost duty in a hostile country and I have spent a very cold night I can tell you. It makes you feel that you are a soldier when you stand with a loaded rifle and fixed bayonet, out in the desert at night, gazing into the sandy wastes towards the Turkish lines. You can guess daylight comes very welcome. We are indeed roughing it now. We get our precious drinking water from a tank-boat and do our toilet and washing in the salty water of the canal. It is a very funny thing trying to get a lather in sea water. We have a fair number of camels with Arab drivers and they come in very useful for carrying goods. We got a very good view of the surrounding countryside in travelling by train in open trucks. When we stopped at stations the natives came and wanted to sell us all kinds of fruit, such as dates, figs, oranges etc., and the fruit tastes surprisingly good out here."*
> Barnsley Chronicle, 12th February 1916

For Tom Bradbury, Tommy Oughton and Harry Hall, El Ferdan was to be their base for almost a week, but for Ernest Bell and the rest of 'A' Company, even the dubious pleasures of washing in the canal were denied them.

At 6 o'clock on the morning following their arrival at El Ferdan they marched off into the desert. It was one of the hardest marches 'A' Company had ever known. Each step felt like ten as increasingly leaden Army boots plunged ankle deep into the soft, yielding sand. As the sun climbed higher into a clear blue sky the temperature soared and the men soon found out that thick, khaki service dress was not the most ideal outfit for a campaign conducted under such trying climatic conditions.

> *'We went out to a place on the desert called Abu Aruk. We went there digging trenches for quite a while. In the daytime we were roasted, at night time we were frozen. When we were in the trenches we had no cover. We were in the trenches all night you see. Didn't see any tents until we got back to Kantara. We had a few dug-outs where we got in to have a sleep and we could hear the wild dogs howling all night, but we couldn't shoot them. When we were digging the trenches we had matting to hold the sand back and we used to peg that down. If we had any machine-gun emplacements they were built up with sandbags, built up like brickwork."* Ernest Bell, 13th Y & L Regiment

122

Katib Abu Aruk was what could be described as a small frontier settlement way out on the first line of the canal defences. In fact there was no such thing as a line at all. The difficulties presented by the landscape rendered the construction of a continuous line of trenches a physical impossibility.

What existed were numerous small outposts or redoubts, each one linked to the next in the chain by frequent patrols. Each outpost consisted of a number of trenches which, according to instructions received and including parapets, were supposed to provide seven feet of cover. In practice the almost liquid properties of the free-flowing grains of sand made it impossible to maintain any trenches for more than a few hours at a stretch, let alone follow instructions. Even when supplied with nails, stakes and matting for revetting purposes the

Lieutenant Hunter, 13th Battalion (First Barnsley) about to set out from El Ferdan with a camel train.

task was utterly frustrating. Upon the removal of each shovelful the sand would roll back in and fill up the hole almost immediately. There was perhaps one consolation, there was more than enough of the right material with which to fill the many sandbags the men were supplied with.

Back at El Ferdan the rest of the Battalion were employed in patrolling the canal banks during the night or making up working parties during the day. Despite the front line outposts and the sentries on the canal itself, there were still fears that Turkish night raiders would somehow wriggle through and cut the railway lines or lay charges to destroy the canal banks.

Fatigue duties were an important part of the Battalion's time at El Ferdan. All the food, water, ammunition and trench-building equipment for the units like 'A' Company on the desert were brought up the canal from Port Said. Water pipes and narrow 2'6" and metre gauge railways were being constructed to convey supplies to the forward troops but a much more reliable method was by means of a different kind of train. This type of train had nothing to do with the Egyptian State Railway, although it travelled at about the same pace, it was the camel. In a land where airborne sand clogged the filters of early petrol engines and extremes of heat and cold played havoc with pipelines, using these 'ships of the desert' was the only sure way of getting the supplies through. Even then it was becoming increasingly difficult to acquire camels not affected by mange. Heaven help the poor Arab driver who failed to discharge his duty and care for his animal.

"The Arabs here have a fairly large camp and a great number of camels. You would think it cruel to see an Egyptian soldier hitting an Arab across the shoulders with a thick stick, but it is necessary to be cruel to be kind in this case. The Arabs have to be watched that they do not neglect their camels. It is easy to tell when a camel is short of food or water. We can tell by his hump! When an officer comes along and finds a camel running short of food the Arab responsible gets it hot. Considering the heavy weights the camels have to carry it is only likely they should be well cared for. One day we go loading camels and another we go unloading boats or railway trucks. You would be surprised to see the huge quantities of food unloaded on the banks of the Suez Canal together with tons of firewood for cooking purposes. We had a picnic the other day. A large English liner anchored down the canal, near our camp and the crew and officers threw loaves of bread, tins of biscuits, tobacco, cigs and bottled beer on shore. It was fine fun scrambling for some of the articles which, of course, we shared." **Letter to his wife from Tom Bradbury dated 26th January 1916, reproduced in the Barnsley Chronicle of 19th February 1916**

Like Tom Bradbury, some of the "Houghton Main Mob" in 'B' Company found that their labours on fatigue duty were rewarded with unexpected surprises.

"They used to bring provisions up to the camp in a barge and the boxes had been broken into. Our lads wouldn't sign for them. The barge stayed there all night and we put a guard on it. Some of the

Narrow-gauge military railway transports men and Abo supplies to 'Railhead'. This form of conveyance is unreliable and the petrol driven engine suffers numerous breakdowns.

fellows decided they'd like some stuff because they didn't know who'd taken it or how much had gone. We were only camped 200 yards from the canal side, under canvas, so we got some beers and liquors and covered it up. Nobody found it. It was heading for the Officers' Mess." **Harry Hall, 13th Y & L Regiment**

By the end of January, with fresh troops like the 6th York and Lancaster Regiment arriving from Gallipoli, the whole of the 13th Battalion had left El Ferdan. 'D' Company had joined 'A' Company at Abu Aruk while 'B' and 'C' Companies had moved to number 5 post on the desert. When 'C' Company, along with Battalion Headquarters left El Ferdan on January 28th, their baggage was conveyed on a camel train numbering 51 animals strung out in an extended line across the sands. The men of both Battalions were to have many more encounters with the camel before their time in Egypt came to an end.

For the 14th Battalion there had been no rest at El Ferdan. From Port Said they had crossed the canal at El Ferdan by means of a narrow pontoon bridge and without a pause had set off for Railhead. As the name implied this point, a few miles south of Abu Aruk, was the end of the line as far as the 14th Battalion were concerned. Beyond the buffers of the narrow gauge, military railway lay the few scattered outposts which had already been constructed. Beyond those lay sand, sand and more sand.

Charlie Swales and the rest of 'C' Company were the first men of the 14th Battalion to be assigned to outpost duty, and on January 23rd they set out with a camel train to a point two and a half miles south of Abu Aruk.

"From El Ferdan we marched out into the desert and in that stuff you used to march forward a yard and slip back two feet, so you were only moving a foot at a time. You were marching in the sun with full equipment on and it were hard work. Eventually we got out into the desert and we laid down because it were hot. Then we had to put tents up. We had an Australian officer called Best and on this occasion something must have got at him. He wanted things doing exact and, if something wasn't to his liking he would make us do it again. Rest of the Company had been dismissed bar our platoon. We were putting up the tent, and we must have got it 'bowed' and so he made us stand to attention to see if we could stand still for a minute. But somebody fidgeted inside that minute so he'd stand us at ease then bring us back to attention for another try. Now one in the platoon was a big Staffordshire bloke who was tall and thin, we called him 'Staff' Mason – he broke it up. For the umpteenth time Best brought us up to attention and started timing us, watch in hand. Suddenly 'Staff' broke wind from t' bottom end. All the platoon collapsed laughing, it were

a beauty! 'Staff kept a straight face but Best couldn't. 'What can I do with you lot, clear off!' There were some great characters." **Charlie Swales, 14th Y & L Regiment**

Charlie's task was exactly the same as the one being performed by Ernest Bell and the Pals of his Company of the 13th Battalion a few miles to the north.

"We were out there in case the Turks tried to attack again as they had done in 1915. We would scoop a large hole out in the soft sand and we put up like palisades with wood and coconut matting like, and then you put sandbags on and formed a trench. They made a perfect defence post. Remember your Barnsley Battalions were colliers and they were adept at it. We didn't used to like digging, in fact Lt. Best used to say, 'I've never seen men like you, you're always grumbling. Everybody else gets started before you, but then, you get started and you've finished before anybody else. When you've done a job, it is done'. The colliers were used to the pick and shovel. It was Best who discovered that our section was all under age. One night on the desert he came round to examine our post. We knew it was him and he was trying a fast one. The one who challenged him was John Hooson, he dropped on one knee and belted out 'Halt . . . or I'll fire!' Best called out that it was him and came in to us telling us we shouldn't do this and shouldn't do t'other. Then he got sat chatting, telling us that he would like to take us to Australia, then he said, 'I would love to test some of you lads on a route march,' to which we replied, 'Right, thee put same pack on as us, never mind a map case and revolver – put 220 lbs. on and a nine pound rifle and we'll take thi' on.' He never did. We used to chat back to them everything was easy. They used to hand cigarettes round. It was that night Best said to us, 'Now come clean boys, I know damn well that there's not one of you old enough to be here, and I know that it's too late to do anything about it now.' We all said how old we were and all of us were under 21 apart from one bloke called Kilner, and he were over age, he were 50 odd. There were around a dozen in a section all were under age but one and he was over. When Best asked him why he didn't want to be with men closer his own age he said, 'I'm all reight wi' t' young 'uns, they look after me.' 'But you're over age,' Best insisted, 'what be that, they're all under'." **Charlie Swales, 14th Y & L Regiment**

While the young and not so young and lovelies of 'C' Company were getting to know their colonial commander much better, the other three companies were not idling their time away. As well as constructing defensive sites for the Railhead and battalion camp they had other jobs to do.

"Our daily routine was scouting up on the peninsula. The main body were down but we were out there. The Turks were supposed to be coming across to take the canal because they'd licked us at Gallipoli. We were up there in case." **Frank Lindley, 14th Y & L Regiment**

As a signaller Frank Lindley's job, as well as scouting, was to help run out telephone lines from Railhead

Digging defences in the soft sand poses problems for the Pals, seen here working at Abu Aruk.

Above: *Keeping cool and clean presents a constant problem. Here an officer in the 13th gets a close military cut at the hands of the Battalion barber. The barber, Private Crossley is to lose his razor, shaving soap and lather brush on 1st July, when he is wounded by shrapnel in the 'advance'.*

to establish contact with 'C' Company near Abu Aruk. Apart from an unusually rare and notable storm bringing hail and violent winds which demolished the tents at Railhead camp towards the end of January, the brilliant sunlight also allowed the signallers to play with their heliographs. Like children with new toys the signallers flashed messages from the outpost to Headquarters and back again.

It was about this time that the Pals first noticed they were perhaps paying more attention to their bodily irritations than they had done before, but it wasn't prickly heat or sweat-stiffened khaki causing the discomfort.

Without firing a single shot in defence the Pals had been overwhelmed by an invading host far greater in number and endurance than the Turks who, every day, were rumoured to be advancing on the canal. With an itch here and a scratch there the Pals came to realise that their bodies were now being used as mobile homes for whole colonies of tiny travelling companions.

"It was red hot in Egypt but it was lousy, filthy. Our Captain, Moxon, came up to me and said, 'Corporal, are you lousy?' I said, 'Yes Sir, a bit', and he said, 'I am, they're carrying me about'." Ossie Burgess, 14th Y & L Regiment

"I first got lousy on the desert. You could see 'em walking about on you. One poor chap, he seemed to breed 'em rapidly and they used to walk out of the back of his collar and up his neck. They dragged him out onto the sand and pegged all his clothes out for the sun to kill all the 'chats'. At night when you were cold on the desert, the chats used to come out and form fours on your belly to keep warm. We used to bury our shirts at night and then put 'em on inside out in the morning. We used to allow the 'chats' to get through in a day and then turn our shirts round." Frank Lindley, 14th Y & L Regiment

For reasons of personal comfort the Pals now had yet another ritual to perform along with the umpteen other tasks in the soldiers' daily routine. Apart from burying infested clothing in the sand there was little the Pals could do to rid themselves of the bloodthirsty little beasts. Thumbnails, matches and lighted cigarettes were among the few weapons at the soldiers' disposal in an attempt to eject or cremate the creatures concentrated in the seams of shirts and tunics. Alas each method brought only temporary relief, and although some men developed their skills in 'chatting' to a fine art they fought a losing battle. Their new-found bosom buddies were there to stay.

"It is jolly hot out here. We are going about dressed in short khaki polo knickers. The heat tends to bring some none too welcome visitors, no matter how you combat with them. I think this is the only fighting we have ever done or shall ever do out here." Letter to the Barnsley Chronicle from Sergeant Arthur Wainwright, First Barnsley Battalion, 18th March, 1916

A far more serious consequence of the insanitary conditions encountered during the Pals' time on the desert was the increasing proportion of men beginning to suffer from dysentery. The reason behind this alarming development were the almost criminally unhygienic conditions of the rations given to the Pals. In most cases the food on the desert was even worse than that in Port Said.

Here come the supplies! The most reliable form of transport, but when it comes to food, not the most hygienic.

There the men could at least break the monotony of their army diet with fresh fruit bought from native pedlars, but now they were left with no choice. They got what they were given. The most precious of all commodities in such an arid environment was fresh water for washing and cooking. Their meagre allowance was one bottle a day for drinking and washing and two bottles for cooking. Fresh water came up the Suez canal on tank boats and was either stored in containers at stations like El Ferdan, or transferred into large tins which were then taken out to the Pals on the desert by camel train. The rough and ready methods of conveying such supplies as water and bread were bound to have an effect on the health of the Pals.

> *"Camel trains used to bring all our 'snap' up. It was figs and dates, sometimes apples and oranges. You couldn't eat anything hot. Water came up in camel trains as well, about ten in a train."* **Ossie Burgess, 14th Y & L Regiment**

> *"They used to bring up bread in these rope nets slung on the sides of camels and ten-to-one there'd be carnel 'chats' in the bread. We had to dig at it at times. At each side of the camel there'd be a tank of water. When you got the water out it was nearly boiling with the sun on it. We used to fill our bottles and that bottle had to last you two days. We used to shave in the dregs of our tea."* **Frank Lindley, 14th Y & L Regiment**

The grains of sand themselves were another risk to the health. Quite apart from forcing its way into every nook and cranny, seizing rifle bolts and Lewis guns; it landed on every scrap of food making each mouthful a crunchy one.

> *"All we had was bully beef stew. It was all mushed up in the dixie with sand blowing in and when you ate it you ate grit all the time. We had to clean our dixies out with the sand, get it full of sand and scrape it round till we thought it was clean. It'd clean it but you didn't know what was left with the residue of the sand. Still it didn't matter. I had a touch of dysentery now and again. I know a lot of 'em had when we went to France."* **Frank Lindley, 14th Y & L Regiment**

Life on the desert followed a fairly unexciting pattern well into the February of 1916. Work on the outpost defences went on and more men went sick with dysentery but still nothing happened. It left plenty of 'slack time' which the men had to fill somehow.

> *"We spent our time playing football or cricket or playing cards. We never met any Turks although they were supposed to be coming to attack us."* **Ernest Bell, 13th Y & L Regiment**

Boxes of ·303 ammunition for the 13th Battalion being loaded up at El Ferdan.

Part of a detachment of Indian cavalry whose job it is to patrol out in the desert looking for the rumoured Turkish advance.

One Private who had obviously been involved in a rather boisterous game of football, felt the sharp edge of Colonel Wilford's tongue.

"They told us the Turks were coming at any time so we dug trenches to wait for them, but they never came. One day we were digging trenches and there was one fellow had been playing football the day before and he got lamed. He was hobbling round the camp with two sticks and he met 'Bullfrog' and he said he'd sprained his knee or something. Anyway 'Bullfrog' said 'Drop those sticks; run, run, run. I don't want anybody here only dead, dying and digging,' and the bloke dropped his sticks and went." **Harry Hall, 13th Y & L Regiment**

Frank Lindley spent his time either playing cards all night under the bright moonlight or being tattooed by Jones, the platoon tattoo artist.

"He had just a row of needles at first but then he got a little battery machine and traced 'em out with that. He had a book with patterns in. I got several, a butterfly, there were all colours in that, and a dancing sailor. We tried to get a clientele up. I fancied one on my chest. It's a bloody good job we cleared off or else I'd have finished up with a big dragon on my chest or something. It was crazy but there it is." **Frank Lindley, 14th Y & L Regiment**

Not all of Frank's time was taken up with the card schools or in trying to drum up trade for his joint venture with Private Jones. The black mark which he felt he had picked up after his self imposed transfer from the Artillery kept creeping up on him. During the 14th Battalion's spell of duty at the Railhead, he had the misfortune to suffer the discomfort and humiliation of 'Field Punishment Number One'.

"I was fastened to the back wheel of a limber on the sand and another fellow was fastened on the other side of me. He scraped all the sand away to let his wheel down so that he could sit, and I was propped up on my wheel and my bloody hat fell off. It was only a couple of hours but with the sun

I couldn't see for three or four days after, only blue lights. I hadn't done anything really bad. I admit I was a bit arrogant against the 'stripeys' because I realised I'd dressed some of 'em when they were first in; then they got a stripe and they worked it at you. They had to show their authority." **Frank Lindley, 14th Y & L Regiment**

Stakes for building trenches in the sand are unloaded from the ferry on the Canal and packed onto camels.

Spurred on perhaps by the budding journalistic career of his friend Tom Bradbury, Tommy Oughton's creative talents also began to flourish on the desert. Some of the men would have argued that unlike other units of the New Army they did not belong to 'fancy' battalions. They did know how to dig, however, and as far as they were concerned when orders were given to do just that, they were more than a match for any battalion of the British Army. That was not to say that when it came down to inspiration, ideas were thrown out on the end of a shovel. Tommy Oughton's attempts to relieve the tedium of the long hours on outpost duty proved that his wits were razor sharp. Taking popular tunes of the day he would replace the well known lyrics with words of his own choosing.

"I wrote bits of songs before I went into the Army. I know I wrote quite a few, and I did some more when I joined up. One was called 'Alma Square', all about Wombwell. There was a song at the time about Leicester Square and I used that. The song was sung on the march because so many men from Wombwell knew the places in it. It went something like,

Alma Square, Alma Square,
What will they say when they miss me there?
What of the fashions in High Street?
What will become of New Guinea and Low Valley?
Oh what a blow to Pat-a-Cake Row,
When I go over the sea.
I know I can do without Wombwell,
But can Wombwell do without me?

Tommy Oughton, 13th Y & L Regiment

Sitting in a trench at Abu Aruk with time on his hands Tommy took another favourite with the title, 'My Little Grey Home in the West', composed by Herman Lohr and first performed by a Mr. Thorpe Bates; and altered the lyrics to fit the situation.

In my little grey home in the east,
On bully and biscuits we feast,
We live in a tent,
And pay 'nowt' for rent,
And we don't give a damn in the least.
We're out on the desert all day,
With Arab kiddies we play,
But oh dear, oh dear,
We've no bloody beer,
In my little grey home in the east.

"I was tee-total at the time, but I knew the lads' feelings. We'd no canteens on the desert."

Tommy Oughton, 13th Y & L Regiment

For Tommy's parodies there was to be no immortality. The words of 'Alma Square' and 'My Little Grey Home in the East' would not fall readily from the lips of thousands of British soldiers winding their way down the narrow pavé roads of Belgium and France. They were however, enjoyed by whole sections of 'D' Company of the 13th Battalion. For those men at least, Tommy was the undisputed Battalion Bard.

When it came to creativity the 14th Battalion were quick to show that the 13th had not cornered the market. Reading the many letters from members of the 13th in the Chronicle stirred Private Frank Woolten of the 14th to paint a picture of the joys of outpost duty in colourful prose.

"I have read in your paper a letter from a Private of the 13th Y & L giving an account of his experiences on outpost duty, and I must say his letter had pleased us all in the 14th Y & L more than a copy of 'Punch'. We have all to do some time in our turns, so perhaps my expressions will not be out of place as a contrast.

Two men, one N.C.O., and myself were told off to be a water guard for 24 hours, mounting at

5 p.m. The sun was just setting and many camels with drivers were returning towards camp, making a lovely picture, along with the yellow sand and the golden sky. The reflection of these colours in the water was beautiful. Presently the first evening star appears, the others following in quick succession, till the sky is covered with jewels. The cool air is nice after the heat of the day. The moon rises nearly full making a light one can easily read a letter by, and how clear it seems here, no smoke to veil it and no houses to restrict the vision – a vast expanse of sand and sky to meet the eye everywhere you turn. The night goes on; no sounds, everything is calm and still. The breeze, how cool and nice it feels. Nearby, while I am on duty, my chums sleep. We have no thoughts of Turks, or other hostile country. Why should we, knowing they will not come this night? On such a night indeed, sleeping out is no hardship. My two hours are nearly over and I hand over my duties to another. He can now witness this wonderful pageant of the stars." **Barnsley Chronicle, 18th March 1916**

Left and below: *An area used for bathing at El Kantara where some dramatic rescues from drowning occurred.*

After the slow hours of the night, all the men in the outpost trenches would 'stand to' during the dark, uncertain hour before dawn. As the first pink blush of daylight tinted the eastern horizon all eyes would scour the unbroken drift sand of the desert for any sign of the Turks. When the sun appeared in all its crimson glory they would relax a little. The Turks would not come for at least another day.

Effectively cut off from the outside world wild rumours tended to circulate of imminent moves to Mesopotamia, to India, or of the Kaiser's abdication. Occasionally, very occasionally, blood pressures would rise at the news of Turkish patrols sighted on the desert by detachments of the Indian Cavalry or the Australian Infantry Force, only to subside when it became known that the hostile Turks had been nothing more dangerous than Army surveyors on camels. Sergeant F. Nowell of the 13th Battalion recounted a similar occurrence.

"We were having dinner one day when the report went round that the enemy were coming, so out we came leaving our dinner, eager for the fray. It was a false alarm; it was merely another battalion being moved elsewhere. We returned to dinner, grumbling because we could not fire a shot."
Barnsley Chronicle, 26th February 1916

Someone, it seemed, had got their communication wires crossed.

In the middle of February four German aeroplanes were reported as being sighted at El Arish on the Mediterranean coast, 90 miles to the north-east. To meet the threat posed by such information, the 14th Battalion constructed four new machine-gun emplacements and the men were issued with clear instructions to lie down and resist the temptation to take pot shots at the planes. Only collective fire under the control of an officer was to be allowed.

After being out on the desert for a month the scattered companies of both battalions were relieved by troops of the 5th Dorsetshire Regiment, and made their way back to El Ferdan.

The 14th arrived on 20th February and relieved the Sheffield City Battalion of all canal patrol and picket duties. The 13th arrived on the following day along with a convoy of 110 camels carrying their camp equipment.

The next day they marched the 11 or so miles along the banks of the Suez Canal to El Kantara. For a week they stayed at Kantara, dividing their time between rifle practice on the ranges which they constructed six miles to the north-east, or in trying to gain revenge in various sporting events against the Sheffielders. Another popular pastime during the week was taking advantage of their proximity to the waters of the Suez Canal. Almost everyone ventured down to the water for a dip. If they couldn't swim already, now was the time to learn.

"I always used to be in the Suez Canal. I used to take officers and teach them how to swim, backwards, forwards and upside down. Those that couldn't swim I used to take on my back and tell them to watch my arms until they got the knack." **James Bennett, 14th Y & L Regiment**

"We swum in the Canal and we used to stand up in parts. It was about four feet deep. We thought it was like that all the way through. One day someone said, 'Do you know, that's about 150 feet deep.' That was my last day in there." **Ossie Burgess, 14th Y & L Regiment**

The unexpected depths of the canal were not the only source of danger, danger which elicited outstanding feats of heroism.

"We used to go swimming in the canal down at Kantara. One of our fellows nearly drowned there. A chap called Reg Dunk fetched him out. There used to be a building firm in Barnsley called Dunk's and he was one of the sons." **Ernest Bell, 13th Y & L Regiment**

"We are on the banks of the Suez Canal once again, and I had a lively experience last night when on fatigue work. We were unloading one of the boats when one of our fellows fell into the water. I jumped in after him with all my clothes on and got him out. Captain Wood is giving me a new suit of clothes, for these are not fit to put on now. My wristlet watch was spoilt. The water was 35 feet deep where I jumped in and there was a five-mile current, so you will see I had something on my plate to swim against the tide with another fellow clinging to me. But never mind, I saved him and that was all I went in for. He's a very nice fellow and he thanked me to all the extent he could besides offering to pay for my watch, but I told him that was all right." **Letter to his father from Sergeant Reg Dunk, 'A' Company, Second Barnsley Battalion. Reproduced in the Barnsley Chronicle, 11th March 1916**

"The man would have drowned but for the fact that your son jumped in and rescued him. And if that was not enough, on the Monday morning bathing parade another of my men, whilst swimming, was seized with cramp in the middle of the canal, and I fear it would have gone badly with him if your son had not swam out and brought him ashore. I am proud he is in my

Barnsley Battalion's Heroic Sergeant.

Who Rescued Two Comrades from Suez Canal.

Recognition Proposed.

Details Sent to Royal Humane Society.

In connection with the plucky and heroic rescues from drowning in the Suez Canal, effected by Sergt. Reg. Dunk, of the Second Barnsley Battalion, and reported in our last week's issue, it is interesting and pleasurable to hear that steps have been taken to bring the facts before the notice of the Royal Humane Society, with a view to securing suitable recognition from the Society for the sergeant's gallant deeds. The matter was considered at a meeting of the Barnsley Swimming Club and Humane Society on Monday night, and the members heard with pride the details of the praiseworthy part which the sergeant, as one of the club's members, had played, and the decision was quickly arrived at to forward to the Society the facts, as given a little more fully in a further letter received and published below.

The following details are from a letter received by Mr. E. W. Buswell, the manager of the Barnsley Corporation Baths, from Capt. Alphonse Wood:

"In my opinion," writes Captain Wood, on February 23rd, "he (Sergt. Dunk) saved two of our men from being drowned," and, describing the gallant deeds performed, says:—"The other night in the dark whilst at work one of our men fell into the Suez Canal. He had his clothes on, and couldn't swim. Sergt. Dunk with his clothes on, dived in and managed to bring him to shore. He (Sergt. Dunk) told me that thought he was never coming to the top again when he dived in; his clothes were so heavy."

"The very next morning, whilst the men were bathing, one of the men (who could swim) was seized with cramp in the middle of the Canal. I should say he would be about 80 yards from shore. Sergt. Dunk swam out to him and brought him in. I think this fully illustrates the value of people being taught to swim. I feel very proud he is in my Company."

Sergeant Dunk, who is 24 years of age, is the fifth son of Mr. W. Dunk, builder and contractor, of Hopwood street, Barnsley. Before joining the Barnsley Battalion, he was in the same business as his father—Messrs. W. Dunk and Sons, builders, Peel street. He is an able swimmer, and has won many prizes in swimming competitions. Mr. W. Dunk has received many messages of congratulation on his son's conspicuous gallantry.

Reproduced from the 'Barnsley Independent'. Barnsley is looking for heroes and finds one in Reg Dunk. He is to die in four months' time on the 'Big Push'.

Officers of the 13th, Tom Guest, seated in deck chair, and Lieutenant Braithwaite standing right become casualties on 1st July.

Company and I am glad to be able to tell you what he has done." Letter to Mr. Walter Dunk from Captain Alphonse Wood, Officer Commanding 'A' Company, Second Barnsley Battalion. Reproduced in the Barnsley Chronicle, 11th March 1916

It was fortunate for the two Pals Reg Dunk rescued from a watery grave, that he was able to draw on a depth of swimming experience gained through his long and happy association with a local Barnsley swimming club. By his swift actions he brought distinction, not only to the Dunk family, but also to his swimming club. "We are not in the least surprised to hear of his gallantry," said a fellow member, "because we know him and it was just like him."

Tommy Oughton too, took to the waters with almost fatal results. For some of the Barnsley Pals it appeared that their bathing sessions were dogged by bad luck.

> "When we got to Egypt it seems that some time in 1915 when the Turks were advancing, part of the desert had been flooded as an obstacle to them. That's where I learned to swim, in that overflow. I went in with a pal of mine called Arthur Dearden from Grimethorpe. It was only supposed to be four feet deep. The different depths were posted up and I could see a board up not far from me. Anyway I went down. There had been a trench there and as I went down I got my foot caught in a roll of barbed wire. I should have drowned but Dearden came and dragged me out. I had cuts and scratches all over me and had medical attention for a week or two. They used to run a little battalion newspaper. It wasn't a regular thing, maybe once every two or three weeks, and there was one column called 'Things We Want to Know', by my pal Tom Bradbury. In the next edition he wrote in broad Yorkshire, 'Who'd 've been a deard 'un if it hadn't been for A. Dearden?'"
> Tommy Oughton, 13th Y & L Regiment

By the end of their fortnight at Kantara it was becoming obvious that something important was in the wind.

> 'We had a 'whiff' we were moving. We rumbled it on the 'bush telegraph'. It was surprising how news got around. You got to know things you didn't read about. It just seemed to filter through. Some said India but it wasn't India it was the other way. It was France. We got to know that at Verdun the French were getting a smacking." Frank Lindley, 14th Y & L Regiment

They were indeed. On the very day the 13th Battalion marched back to El Ferdan from their positions on the desert, the Germans had delivered a crushing blow against the French fortress of Verdun. The murky pool of military strategy had suddenly and violently become crystal clear.

Even before the German attack, allied plans to stage a combined Franco-British effort in France, sometime during the coming Summer had been greeted with nods of approval, but now the Germans had well and truly turned the spotlight on the western theatre.

There was now no doubt, no uncertainty as to which arena would play host to the major struggles of 1916. It was France, and to France the Pals would go.

> "It suited us when we knew we were going to France. I didn't know of any objections. I don't know if they thought they were getting a bit nearer home or what!" Tommy Oughton, 13th Y & L Regiment

"The Barnsley team has donned its colours and entered the field, but its opponents have not yet left the dressing-room. It's too bad of them, for our men have travelled far, and are spoiling for a fight on the enemy's home ground. The appearance of their 'Brassmen' in the form of a mounted patrol yesterday, raised both hope and spirit, but up to the time of writing there's 'nothing doing'. The fight is sure enough, because in the present activities and preparation, which I am not allowed to mention, the Barnsley's have excelled themselves and received commendation from high quarters. They have done splendid work, work that has tested their endurance and patience, and done it on 'Bully' and biscuits, washed down with sandy tea, tasting strongly of smoke chlorine. But they look fit – I have never seen a fitter-looking lot of men in my life, and that's saying a good deal, for we are neighbours with the Australians, who have already won fame. The boys are now experts at moving camp. Reveille at six a.m., breakfast over, tents struck, folded up and packed, haversacks and kit cleared, packed, camels loaded with tents, stores, ammunition, and all the necessary camp equipment, and away on the desert march 'ere ten has chimed. The new camp site reached, marked out, tents pitched, telephone wires laid, guards set, and we are sitting down to tea at 4.30 as though nothing had happened. A few more finishing touches after tea, chiefly sanitary arrangements, and you would think the boys had dwelt in this spot for years. It is on occasions such as these that organization and discipline count, coupled with learning what you can do without, so as to march as light as possible. Frankly, and without, I hope, prejudice, remembering the previous experience, or lack of experience, and general environment of our men, with their inherent love of 'snap', plenty and good, with the 'best' to wash it down, I am amazed at their efficiency, cheerfulness and discipline. Many contributory causes have been at work to shape and mould our boys. They have been fostered to the fullest extent by the officers. I referred first to the esprit de corps of a regiment, roughly as a Tommy understands it, Pride in his Regiment." Anonymous letter sent to the Barnsley Independent

Of one thing they were assured. At long last they were to be given the opportunity of doing what they had felt able to do for a long time. With two months of having their bones warmed by the Egyptian sun, of swimming and sports, the Pals felt on top of the world. Their morale was as buoyant as it had been at any time during their short Army careers. Few of them cared to speculate that their work in Egypt had little in common with the day to day goings on of the war then being waged in France. Fewer still harboured any doubts as to their ability to cross that particular bridge when they came to it.

Early on the morning of March 8th both Barnsley Battalions, along with the Sheffield City Battalion, marched out of Kantara bound for embarkation at Port Said. They took with them the best wishes of their Corps Commander in Egypt.

"The Corps Commander, in wishing the 31st Division farewell and good luck, expresses his gratitude to all ranks for the good work they have done for him. It has been a great pleasure to him to be associated with such a capable body of officers and men. They have borne the brunt of the work in the XV Army Corps sector and have done wonders, and there exists a very fine spirit in the Division. He wishes all ranks the best of luck and hopes soon to have the pleasure of being associated with them again. He is confident that they will fight as well as they have worked."

The Pals' pride was further boosted by the following message from Brigadier General Carter Campbell who had taken over command of 94 Brigade on the retirement of Brigadier General Bowles.

"The work got through testifies to the industry and keen spirit of the officers and men – their fine efforts have been appreciated."

The march for the 13th Battalion was a very short one, in fact only as far as Kantara station where they boarded the same wooden trucks that had brought them down the canal, and were shunted away to the north.

For the luckless men of the 14th their march was much longer, the full 27 or so miles to Port Said.

Presumably put out by this gross act of unfairness on the part of the authorities, Colonel Hulke appeared to be in much more of a hurry to reach their destination than the men's legs could cope with.

"This call came for us to shift to France so we struck tents and had a night's 'kip' on the raw sand. Next morning we were frozen stiff but we marched off up the side of the canal. It was a forced march. As we were on the march the sun got hotter as the day came on. We were exhausted most of us but the Colonel kept on his horse in front. Usually we'd march so far and have a rest, but he kept at it until the Adjutant rode up from the back and told him we were about knackered. He got off then." Frank Lindley, 14th Y & L Regiment

Arriving in Port Said much earlier than the 14th, the 13th Battalion were marched to a seedy looking transit camp to await the arrival of the exhausted soldiers of the 14th. They weren't there for long. On March 10th two Companies of the 14th left Port Said on board the patriotically named troopship *Briton* with the Sheffield City Battalion. A day later the remaining two Companies of the 14th and the whole of the 13th sailed on the H.M.T. *Megantic* bound for Marseilles.

As the last rope was cast off the quayside at least one of the Pals had quite literally missed the boat. Private Vernon Atkinson was still at large somewhere in Egypt. Vernon had never got further than Port Said when the Pals had first arrived two months earlier. He had become one of the first victims of the germs which lurked in the waters of the Mediterranean, when he came down with an infection picked up on bathing parade.

"I was left behind in Port Said and they took me to Cairo. We went to an old palace they'd turned into a hospital. I was in just over a fortnight then I went back to my mob. I thought I was all right but I wasn't. They took me away again to a hospital in Alexandria, to a place where all the troops were." Vernon Atkinson, 14th Y & L Regiment

Vernon's malady had caused him to miss the whole of the 14th Battalion's stay in Egypt. He had missed the digging, the duties and the miserable rations. Still recuperating in Alexandria as the rest of his comrades steamed for France, he was left to ponder how on earth he would ever find them again.

The majority of the men did not perhaps appreciate it at the time but the *Megantic* had, in the past, carried a far more notorious cargo than the one which now stuffed her up to the gunwales.

Built in 1909, the *Megantic* was owned by the Oceanic Steam Navigation Company of Liverpool. Measuring 550 feet from stem to stern and 67 feet across, her chief claim to fame was that she had returned the infamous Dr. Crippen to Britain. Now she was laden up to every ounce of her 14,878 tons gross weight with quite a few more characters, albeit not quite as sinister as Dr. Crippen.

The voyages for both batches of Pals were, in the main, almost a carbon copy of the outward journey to Egypt. There were the inevitable drills and the inevitable seasickness but the journeys were largely unremarkable. There was however, one notable incident aboard the *Megantic* when, on March 14th, a little while after glimpsing Mount Etna off the starboard bow, the whole vessel was brought to action stations. Excitedly the Pals rushed on to the boat decks where they were informed that the tell-tale white streak of a periscope had been sighted slicing through the water 1,000 yards ahead.

Signalling 'full ahead' the Captain steamed over the spot but nothing more was seen or heard of the alleged submarine.

With that bout of frenzied activity out of the way the young Frank Lindley settled down to indulge in the one activity which now kept his mind from thoughts of submarines or anything else for that matter.

"We got on the ship and I had my birthday and I spent that birthday burning the 'chats' out of the linings of my clothes. We all did. Clothes were spread out all over the decks, scraping these 'chats' out and killing all their eggs. They used to get full of blood and when you popped 'em you used to get an eyeful of blood." Frank Lindley, 14th Y & L Regiment

That rather sanguinary experience was just a foretaste of much worse to come.

Chapter Eight

Somewhere in France

STEAMING UP THE GULF OF LYONS the Pals sensed they were not far from their destination. On their right, in the distance, they could just make out the hazy, snow-dusted peaks of the Alpes-Maritimes. Much closer on their left they passed the ageing island fortifications of the Chateau D'If, once more pressed into service to give extra protection to the port of Marseilles, already safely tucked between towering white cliffs on either side.

The two companies of the 14th Battalion who had sailed independently of their comrades, were the first Barnsley soldiers to set eyes on the busy harbour on March 15th, but a day later the rest of the 14th Battalion and the whole of the 13th lined the rails to watch as the *Megantic* dropped anchor out in the bay.

As ever, the Barnsley Chronicle was keen to chart the progress of its town's sons, and through its columns it informed its readers that having left Egypt they were now, "Somewhere in France". Where exactly, they were not at liberty to disclose, for in publishing a letter from "one of the lads", it appeared to adhere to the same code of conduct displayed by a zealous Army censor not wishing to reveal the movements of British troops to vigilant German spies.

"This morning we arrived at M. . . . . The weather was cold and it was raining a nasty drizzle, and the sea was quite choppy. From our place in the harbour little can be seen. On both sides we are surrounded by shipping and in the distance we can just make out a dome capped building and further in the gloom a very high hill on top of which is a church with a high spire. Tomorrow we land at seven in the morning when we entrain for a place much further north. Today we received smoke helmets." **Barnsley Chronicle, 25th March 1916**

Any German agent who happened to have a Chronicle fall into his lap, and was still scratching his head to think of a large seaport somewhere in France, beginning with the letter 'M' and boasting domed buildings and spired churches, then the staff of the newspaper seemed only too willing to lend a hand. Directly beneath the letter they published the following editorial comment,

"It might interest many in the battalions to know that the dome shaped roof mentioned in the letter above is the Cathedral. It stands quite close to the harbour. The building on the hill in the magnificent situation described is the church of 'Notre Dame de la Garde' or 'Our Lady of the Watch'. Overlooking the sea it is the first and last sight seen by the sailor inward or outward bound. For it the sailors of all nations have a great veneration and to it have come seamen's gifts from all parts of the world. It contains many tablets commemorating providential escapes of the donors from disaster at sea, some paintings depicting the terrible dangers from which others escaped, and suspended from the roof are many models of all kinds of ships, the simple offering of grateful sailors who attribute their survival to 'Our Lady of the Watch'."

The agents of Major Walter Nicolai's German intelligence fraternity were spread all over Europe and were extremely effective, but just to make sure they really got the message the Chronicle journalist really hammered it home.

"Really there are two churches, one above the other. Both are decorated in the warm Latin style. The flag post they would see before the church is really the signalling station of the coastguards – two of whom may be seen at the church door doing sentry duty any hour of the day, or night, for that matter."

No doubt the Barnsley soldiers would have been interested in the information supplied by the Chronicle, for it read like a visitors' guide to the Mediterranean seaport which was already noted for its traditional

The Mediterranean seaport of Marseilles where the Pals land March 17th, en route to the trenches and the coming 'Big Push'.

fish dish of bouillabaisse as a culinary speciality.

They had little time in which to savour any local delicacies or use any newly acquired knowledge of the sights, even if they had been able to receive their Chronicles from home in time, for their stay was to be a very short one.

With the ship riding the waves at anchor, the men spent their last uncomfortable night on their bunks in the crowded cabins. They were roused bright and early for breakfast at 5 a.m. and two hours later the vessel was nudging its way gently towards its berth. The process of disembarkation began at 9 a.m.

"I remember when we landed in France. I'll always remember the date, it was St. Patrick's day, the 17th March." **Tommy Oughton, 13th Y & L Regiment**

As the troops filed slowly down the gangways leaving their sea legs behind them, they could survey the bustle and apparent confusion on the quayside. Some of them had time to accept the plaudits of the enthusiastic French crowd which had gathered to welcome them.

"When we landed in Marseilles it was absolutely packed with people. Didn't they cheer when we got off." **Ossie Burgess, 14th Y & L Regiment**

The scenes which followed the disembarkation were chaotic as the accumulated possessions of several battalions were disgorged onto dry land by teams of roughly dressed French deckhands.

Finally the harbour was left behind as they were marched to the station for the train journey which was to take them nearer to the fighting zone.

Once more the whole performance of loading stores and other equipment onto flat cars and other forms of rolling stock was undertaken, and by eleven o'clock the men were able to take a short break and cast a critical eye over their travelling accommodation.

James Bennett was faced with a form of transport, the like of which he had never seen on the little branch lines around the Barnsley district. His first job at the tender age of 12, had been at Wortley station between Barnsley and Sheffield, and his father too had worked on the railways as a relief signalman on the line between Doncaster and Penistone. Never before had he seen such transports detailed for passenger conveyance. It was a sight which he and his friends were to become all too familiar with in the months that followed.

Standing by the platform were a row of covered wagons built up of wooden slats and featuring a large sliding door. On the door, painted in large, white block letters was the inscription, "HOMMES. 32/40, CHEVAUX (EN LONG) 8." To many this legend was a complete mystery, however Ernest Bell could see that there were no cushioned seats, and to him they looked just like cattle trucks.

No doubt some of the more linguistic of the men, or at least some of the officers, were able to enlighten their comrades that they were in fact the "Hommes", and that the "Chevaux" were horses. The state of the straw covering the floor, only served to convince the Pals that as the "hommes" were bundled in, the "chevaux" had recently trotted out. The more philosophical of the Barnsley contingent were left to ponder as to whether in a war directed by a preponderance of Generals with a cavalry background, that this was a comment on the relative worth of man and beast.

Each man tried to make himself as comfortable as he possibly could under the circumstances, but at least one member of the 13th Battalion had managed to find much more appealing surroundings. Tommy Oughton found himself in a carriage with seven other men and they all had seats. Tommy's luck was indeed, still holding. At any rate it appeared that he was travelling in carriages at least as good as those shared by the officers. His turn in the cattle trucks would however, come soon enough.

At last all was ready. The last piece of equipment was loaded up and the last khaki behind was shoved into yet another truck whose sides swelled in protest at its load.

The engine pulled off. The chains which joined the rolling stock, each took up the strain in turn making the carriages leap forward in an effort to catch up with the one in front and throwing the occupants rearwards in the process. The journey annoyed the Pals intensely, for the train moved very slowly but not at a constant speed. It would pick up a little speed and then slow to walking pace, and, because the linking chains were of an unalterable length, the men inside were thrown first one way as the chain tightened, and then the other as the buffers came into violent contact when the chain slackened.

"The train kept stopping and going, and stopping and going. They would shunt us into a siding for five or six hours at a time." **Ernest Bell, 13th Y & L Regiment**

The standards of French rail engineering were also brought into question and judging from the bone clattering received by the "other ranks", it seemed as if every section of rail they encountered did not quite meet the one preceding it. The men found themselves asking if the wheels were really round at all.

The train crawled northwestward across the region of Provence and the patchwork fields of the broad valley of the River Rhone, towards Tarascon. From there, it clanked and rattled its way up the Rhone valley, inching its way through towns which centuries before had witnessed the passage of the legions of the Roman Empire along their streets.

Avignon with its strikingly beautiful Papal Palace, and its bridge forever immortalised in song, came and went, as did Orange where Red Cross nurses served tea to the weary troops. For Private Wilfred Cleverley of the 13th Battalion the obvious discomforts of the journey were overshadowed by this tour of the gentle agricultural lands of southern France with a notable lack of young male workers tending the crops.

"The French people everywhere gave us a good welcome; they were most enthusiastic, especially in the south where, I suppose, they will not have seen very many English soldiers. We passed through many places which I have so often wanted to see in years gone by. That is one advantage of entering the country from the south." **Barnsley Chronicle, 8th April 1916**

The advantages gained by this route did not however, prevent the temperature falling, as the distance between the train and the waters of the Mediterranean lengthened.

"It is much colder here than in Egypt naturally, but the sea voyage sort of toned us down to it so that we don't feel the difference very

Postcard of the French village of Les Laumes-Alesia, typical of those sent home by some of the Pals to inform their families, and any other interested parties, of their progress through France.

much, and the nights here at any rate are no colder than we experienced in Egypt." **Wilfred Cleverley, 13th Y & L Regiment**

It was a view which was not shared by some of the other members of his unit.

"For the next fortnight I bet half the battalion were stuffed up with colds due to the difference in climate." **Tommy Oughton, 13th Y & L Regiment**

The men passed their time by talking or joined the ever present card schools. Others dozed as much as their uncomfortable crouched sitting position and the jerking, would allow. Occasionally the tedium was broken by halts for tea using boiling water from the engine, and simple rations like bully beef and hard biscuits, to keep the hunger at bay.

Passing through the smaller stations old porters would stop their work to shout 'bon chance' to the newly arrived defenders of France.

It was soon discovered that other forms of life were sharing their cramped quarters. Some men, like Ossie Burgess and Frank Lindley had become acquainted with them in Egypt. The straw upon which the men were sitting was alive with lice and other insects. The lice soon found that the soldiers' uniforms made far better homes than the straw on the floor of the van.

"When you got a little irritation that was bad enough, but when you got them all over it was a real pantomime. You used to feel like getting up against a wall and rubbing yourself. Everybody was alike, nobody could say they were clean and decent." **Ernest Bell, 13th Y & L Regiment**

It was certainly true that the body louse was no respecter of rank or privilege, as had been proved to Ossie Burgess and Frank Lindley, officers and other ranks alike were fine targets for its close attentions. It was a problem which the British Army was to address many times in the ensuing years, with little success. All the destructive power of modern warfare, in the hands of those conducting the struggle, met with meagre results when confronted by the humble louse. They colonised the seams of the men's garments and multiplied with such speed that all attempts to dislodge them were simply temporary measures. Although many claims of victory were made by the armies of all sides during the conflict, the only real and lasting victory belonged to the louse.

The train continued to chug along through Lyons, Dijon and Paris, and finally at a quarter to two in the afternoon of March 19th, it pulled into the station at Pont Remy, a few miles south-east of Abbeville. It had been a little over 50 hours since the train had first lurched into life at Marseilles, and by now the Pals were weary beyond words. The battalions detrained, and unloading their equipment once more, they prepared for a march which would take them closer to the front, following in the footsteps of the two companies of the 14th Battalion, the Accrington Pals and the Sheffield City Battalion, who had passed that way before.

The 94th Infantry brigade of the 31st Division had not sailed to France together and their passage to the front divided them still further. The Accrington Pals had arrived at Pont Remy on the 11th March, and had marched to the village of Huppy. Situated well away from the destruction wrought by heavy artillery, Huppy still displayed a certain country charm. Unlike the dishevelled villages nearer to the fighting, which were fortunate to have a few houses still standing, Huppy had houses, and what's more they still had roofs. Some were thatched and some were covered with red tiles, contrasting vividly against their bright whitewashed walls. The presence of village wells with their canopies of logs turning green due to the accumulated moss only added to its rustic atmosphere.

A week after the Accrington Pals had arrived the Sheffield City Battalion, along with two companies of the 14th Battalion were welcomed by the villagers. They quickly filled the billets vacated by the Accrington lads who had already moved on.

When the final contingent of the 94th Infantry brigade consisting of the rest of the 14th and the whole of the 13th Battalion detrained at Pont Remy on March 19th, the plans of the higher authorities took the Barnsley Battalions apart temporarily, for someone had a special duty in mind for the men of the 13th.

While the rest of the 14th marched to Fresnes to join their comrades, the members of the 13th picked

13th Battalion Band, which accompanied the men on their long marches through the French countryside to the front.

up their heavy valises, the large field packs in which they carried all their equipment, shrugged them up high onto their backs and prepared to march to the village of Doudelainville, a distance of just over six miles.

As the men began to form up for the march most of them were pleased that they were going into action at last, even though the Winter weather was not quite what they had become accustomed to in Egypt. Privately though, a few started to wonder as to the nature of the war they were about to march towards, a state of affairs the Barnsley Chronicle called "Nearing the Goal".

> *"There was a touch of apprehension as to what was going to happen next. You'd start thinking about things then, the real thing, because you knew it was there and you knew you had to go in. You started thinking then."* **Harry Hall, 13th Y & L Regiment**

They reached Doudelainville at half past six in the evening and billets were found in houses and barns. The old ladies, left alone in their houses, tried to make the men as comfortable as possible, caring for the young lads in the Battalion as they hoped others were caring for their sons, also far from home and fighting with the French Army. For several days the 13th stayed in Doudelainville and during their time there they were engaged in what their war diary called 'general routine', and what in fact meant rifle drill, route marching, physical training and the spit and polish of kit cleaning and inspection. It was amazing how time spent on this task made the men feel like 'real' soldiers again no matter how tired or dirty they had been before.

One night some of the men chanced upon an old French sergeant who enthused about an early end to the war. As confident as the Barnsley men were, they thought that his prediction, that they would be in Germany in May, was perhaps just a little optimistic.

On March 22nd an order came for 50 men to report for fatigue duties nearer the front line: Private Benson and twelve more men of his platoon volunteered quickly.

> *". . .We walked to the Divisional H.Q. eight miles away from our billets and reported, but owing to a misunderstanding we had to return to our original billets much to our disgust. In the morning we had been sent off gallantly and it was very unpleasant to have to return the same day."* **Barnsley Chronicle, 8th April 1916**

All was not lost however. Fifty keen men were an asset to any fatigue party and the Army laid on three special charabancs at tea time to whisk the men off nearer their 'goal'. Fifty men hauled themselves aboard accompanied by Lieutenant Sharp on a trip to Marieux.

> *". . . we spent about 10 hours in the charabancs, travelling at a rattling pace all the time and arriving at our destination at 3 a.m. It is a good sized village we are in with one or two cafes where we spend our evenings in order to keep warm, because we are not allowed fires in our billets."* **Barnsley Chronicle, 8th April 1916**

For these men, receiving their first taste of military fatigues a few miles behind the firing line, it was a trip that was to stand them in good stead when they entered that line in their own right.

One thing which remained constant for the men of both battalions was their close acquaintance with that much loved mode of infantry transportation, 'Shanks' Pony'. The 14th Battalion also found that the French were only too willing to show kindness to their allies, as they marched along.

"We footslogged for a long way when we got off the train. When we were walking, if we passed through a village, the ladies used to come out and give us a quaff of cider or whatever. They'd hand it to us as we were marching." Frank Lindley, 14th Y & L Regiment

For their part the soldiers of the 14th would spruce themselves up as they crossed the boundary of each new village.

"Between towns and villages they used to say 'walk as you please', but as soon as you came to a town or a village you had to walk in a soldier-like manner and the band used to strike up. Once you got through you'd flop back down to the plodding. We could last all day and night walking. It made no difference to us." Frank Lindley, 14th Y & L Regiment

It made no difference to Frank Lindley and his mates because they had picked up a useful tip from the old sweats marching alongside them. The trick was to lie back on their packs and prop their feet up against any hedge they could find, every time they had a rest break. This prevented the blood from pounding around their feet and seemed to cool them off just enough for them to resume the march when the order came to 'fall in' again.

The Western Front
Approximate line at end of 1914

It was a trick which some men of the 13th Battalion would have been wise to have picked up, for six of their number failed to complete the march to Doudelainville and another score were to drop out during the later stages of the trek.

The battalion diary attempted a diagnosis of the problem and concluded that the, 'many sore feet were accounted for by softness owing to the march and wearing no boots whilst on board ship'. The medical officer went further and stated clearly that he felt the time spent in Egypt had been a contributory factor.

Whatever the cause, those who were still able to march must have appeared somehow slightly odd to the villagers brought to their doors by the sound of bands and the tramp of marching feet. Certainly the men looked like soldiers and yet something was not quite right. It was only upon a closer inspection of their headgear that the mystery was solved, for there still perched precariously were the exotic pith helmets swathed in the troublesome puggarees. The helmets looked strangely out of place among the fields and country lanes of northern France which were here and there covered with stubborn patches of snow. The remnants of a harsh continental Winter were still biting hard on the battlefields of northern France and heavy snow fell on Doudelainville on the 24th March making the men shiver and pull their greatcoats tighter as they burrowed deeper into the straw, trying to rest after their day's labours.

These adverse conditions did not freeze the enthusiasm of Private Leonard Key of the 14th Battalion who, in a lull between musketry practice and route marches around the districts of Abbeville, had time to write the following letter to friends in Wombwell.

"You will have heard that we have had another pleasant voyage on the briny ocean, so you will see that they have had to fetch the old Barnsley boys to put the finishing touch on the Germans. We went to Egypt to meet the Turks, but I think they got to know where we came from and thought it best not to bother. Nevertheless what we have had to face has been no easy task. Keep on smiling until the boys come home again and that won't be long. We are all expecting to be at Barnsley Feast. We shall not be long in bowling Kaiser Bill out. You can depend on me not letting my heart drop in my shoes. A man who keeps on smiling gets on a lot better." **Barnsley Chronicle, 1st April 1916**

Despite Private Key's cheery optimism, all the smiling in the world was not going to help the Pals. 'Barnsley Feast' week was traditionally the last week in August. Whole firms closed their doors and the mining industry in the surrounding districts virtually came to a standstill as the people of Barnsley took their annual holiday.

Some of the very lucky families took advantage of similar charabancs to the ones used for transporting the troops nearer the battlefront, and these were hired by groups from a village or a number of streets to take them on outings. For a very few others old and young alike, it was a once in a lifetime chance to go to the seaside. A westward adventure to the distant shores of Blackpool in Lancashire or an expedition out to the east, to Filey, Bridlington or Scarborough. Private Key was confident that they would all be home to join their families and their friends on the late summer break which everyone looked forward to all year long.

One thing which Private Key had not taken into account however, was the already advanced planning of the Allied commanders for a 'Big Push' in France before the summer of 1916 was spent and before Barnsley 'Feast' had come and gone. It was this planning which was to make the Barnsley Feast of August

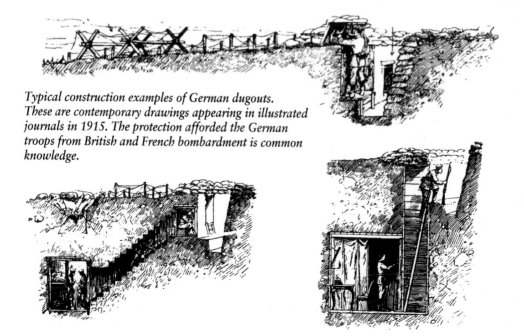

Typical construction examples of German dugouts. These are contemporary drawings appearing in illustrated journals in 1915. The protection afforded the German troops from British and French bombardment is common knowledge.

The dreaded German wire. Engineers laying a barbed wire entanglement in front of their reserve trenches. The British comment is, "Shell fire quickly disposes of entanglements of any kind, whether the wire be thick or thin." This will be found to be in error on the morning of July 1st, 1916.

1916 much more memorable for the people of the town than any trip to the seaside ever would, for the plans were destined to hand a key role to the Pals of the 31st Division and to the 14th Battalion would go one of the hardest tasks of the lot.

Although the Barnsley Battalions had not gone straight to France from England, that had not been their decision. The fact was that at last they had arrived and both battalions believed they were as fine a body of men as any that had set foot on French soil, with a collective enthusiasm to match that belief.

Although they had been admired by the women and cheered by young children as they had marched through England, although they were viewed by many as being among the cream of the nation's crop of manhood, the stark truth was that the vast majority of Kitchener's Army, the Pals included, were still unprepared for a major action.

For many of the Pals their time in uniform, be it blue or khaki, had been just less than two years, for others less than a year, and in all that time they had never fired a shot in anger. Now they were to be pitted against a German army of conscripts in which every man over the age of twenty had been trained as a soldier for at least a year prior to the outbreak of war, each one secure in the knowledge that their defences on the Somme were as strong as any which existed on the Western Front.

The German Army was justifiably proud of the complex maze of excavations it had carved out of the open chalk downland of the Somme. By the early spring of 1916 they had been given ample opportunity to work on their defences having come to the ridges and spurs overlooking the valley of the Ancre amid the late September mists of 1914.

After the bitter disappointments of the Marne and the deadlock on the Aisne, German eyes had turned to the north and to a means of breaking the stalemate. During the last few days of September the German cavalry rode north clearing a path for their infantry to follow. On September 27th German reserves newly arrived from Alsace-Lorraine, had fanned out along the upper slopes of the Thiepval Ridge, to within spitting distance of the Golden Virgin of Albert. With French troops scurrying north just in time to prevent the Germans from seizing Albert and pushing on to Amiens, Abbeville and their objective of the Channel coast, they were squeezed further north, across the marshy Ancre valley, up and over the broad plateau towards Gommecourt and beyond. It was there that German spades had first bitten into the red earth of Picardy. The Germans were on the Somme.

With typical teutonic diligence their soldiers immediately set to work to gain every natural advantage that the ridges and valleys of the Somme region had to offer. Where the ground rose, their front line followed to take in the high ground, where it fell away into the smooth bare slopes of some long dry watercourse their line retreated to stand guard at the head of the valley.

Their front line fire trenches hewn from the easily worked chalky subsoil were deep and secure. The angles and lines were clean and precise and during the very heaviest rainfall German boots were seldom soaked as the rain drained away naturally through the chalk to the lower ground. Compared with the dank, rat-infested ditches of Flanders, digging trenches on the Somme was almost a joy. The trenches themselves were dug to a depth of up to ten feet and for their dug-outs they just kept going down, down to a depth of twenty, thirty and sometimes forty feet in places. Some of the larger galleries housed small self-contained communities, being electrically lit, ventilated, and complete with piped fresh water. Down in those underground caverns, units of over 50 men could rest comfortably on their own wire bunks and stack their rifles in purpose built racks at the foot of the 30 or 40 steps leading to the trenches above.

Often the dug-outs were so elaborate and luxurious that the men put up curtains at the entrance, while their officers furnished their quarters with ornate tables and chairs or decorated them with trinkets picked up while on leave in Germany.

Behind the deep dug-outs of the front trenches lay several more support and reserve lines which, when connected by an intricate system of communication trenches, completed their first line system.

Some two miles further back lay their second line system, equally daunting and equally effective, and in front of every trench, like sleeping black serpents, lay thick unbroken coils of barbed wire. At important strategic points where their lines crossed the crown of a slope or clung to the higher contours of a spur that gently poked its nose into a valley below, the Germans had constructed strongly fortified positions called redoubts. These sites were carefully selected so as to provide the maximum field of observation and gunfire in any given direction. Each redoubt was a veritable warren of dug-outs and galleries, with trenches facing in every conceivable direction. As if these were not enough, then there was the question of the villages and woods which were integrated into the system of defences. Situated just behind the first complete line of trenches the villages, which before the war had been the homes of farmers, farm labourers and their families were now joined irrevocably in the cause of defensive warfare. The simple country folk had however, long since disappeared from their homes and fields in the face of a reaper of a different kind. Behind them they had left their farm buildings with deep cellars which later comfortably concealed rifles and machine-gun nests.

The term 'village' no longer applied to the settlements, they had become citadels which the British Army would have to storm over open ground and usually up a slope, to break through to objectives further afield. Sounding quaint and vaguely romantic in peace time, their names were to become branded into the memories of a generation of men who fought and fell in front of them and who lived to tell the tale. For the men of London and the Midlands the name would be Gommecourt; for the men of Ulster it would be Thiepval; for the Geordies, La Boisselle; but for the lads of Barnsley it would be Serre.

With characteristic zeal, the Germans had applied themselves just as effectively by turning the woods behind their lines into leafy strongholds.

Before the first British units had taken over the trenches of the Somme the French had held the sector, along with some 380 miles of defences which threaded their way down to the Swiss frontier. The British Army, to the north of the French, held a further seventy of the 475 mile trench line which stretched in the opposite direction towards the North Sea.

By the late summer of 1915, the French High Command were becoming increasingly worried about the strain that such a responsibility was having on their troops. They had broad shoulders but they felt their knees bending. The answer was to adjust the load, and so British troops found themselves moving south to man 18 miles of trench line resembling a rough and ready letter 'L' from Hebuterne down to the looping meanders of the Somme River itself. The river formed the natural boundary dividing the British and French Armies and its name was assured to link it forever with the most tragic episode in British military history.

The sector which the British inherited from the French could not be regarded as exuding the "offensive spirit" much beloved of the British military hierarchy. It seemed as if the French and German soldiers had entered into an unspoken agreement of "live and let live". This meant that any aggressive activity was kept to a level which would allow trench life to go on with as little disturbance as possible to both sides.

To their delight the British troops realised that they had stumbled across what they called a 'cushy' front. Far from the damp vapours of the Ypres salient and the glum, smoky skies of the British front south of the Belgian frontier, the trenches on the Somme were a welcome change of environment.

Even so this was war, and being on a cushy sector did not mean that carelessness would go unpunished.

Brief exchanges of rifle, machine-gun and artillery fire served to remind those whose thoughts had wandered home, that there was a war on, and in this comparatively quiet stretch of the line those exchanges could still exact a grim toll of dead and wounded. The soldiers soon learned that to look over the top was suicide. Sometimes the parapets were anything but safe and they could not be guaranteed to keep out stray bullets. In such a fashion were battalion 'Rolls of Honour' lengthened.

On the Somme sector, the British Generals were at pains to see that the "laissez-faire" attitude that had existed, albeit tacitly, between the French and the Germans was brought to an abrupt halt. In short, it could not and would not be allowed to continue.

The Army commanders fostered this doctrine and hoped that a policy of continual offensive activity would filter down through the chain of command to the private soldier and that the message of "the fighting spirit" would lose none of its potency on its long downward journey. That policy was still being pursued when the Pals arrived in France.

"They'd drilled it into us so much. Different Generals would come down and have a word with you. I remember one fellow coming, the Divisional Commander he was then, he finished by saying: 'If any German you see has a wife and four children, make sure that he doesn't get five.' That was his message. I'll always remember that." **Harry Hall, 13th Y & L Regiment**

The British Army had to be seen to be gaining the upper hand in this sector as it had attempted to do in sectors to the north.

To prove that the British had arrived, offensive activity all along the front was stepped up. Snipers were told to 'snipe' at any German who may have forgotten that the British had taken over. Raiding parties and fighting patrols crawled across No-Man's-Land to leave their mark on the German trenches. Since the British were not content to let sleeping dogs lie, the German artillery growled in retaliation to every British salvo which rained down on their wonderful earthworks. The result was that the Germans dug ever deeper, adding to the awesome strength of the positions they had already completed.

No doubt those soldiers of the New Army who had faced the well established German units since the summer of 1915 had a healthy disdain for troops like the Pals arriving from Egypt. Naturally they felt they'd seen it all and done it all. While the Barnsley Battalions had been digging and re-digging trenches in the yielding sands of Egypt, waiting for the Turks to sweep across the Suez Canal, some of the less fortunate of Kitchener's men had been taking their chances holding the Somme line for more than seven months. Although some of the Barnsley lads had not exactly taken Egypt or the Egyptians to their hearts, the vast majority of Tommies who had so recently endured their first Somme Winter, and indeed, were still suffering its icy consequences; would have eagerly exchanged the mud for the drifting sands of the desert. The early arrivals on the Somme had spent the greater part of that Winter in lousy dug-outs and had sloshed through the mud and the filth to take their turn "standing to" on the firestep of some God-forsaken trench, half filled with icy water. They had been posted as sentries in the long cold hours of the night and had stared so hard into the blackness that their eyes had seemed to revolve in their sockets.

Germans are in France to stay. An air of permanence about these officers' quarters constructed deep underground just half a mile from the opposing forces.

Those warriors who were also natives of Barnsley but who were serving in other battalions of the York and Lancaster Regiment already in France, could not help feeling more than a little superior and not a little envious of the Pals who, in their eyes, had had a 'cushy' time. Their letters home could not help but reveal their true feelings, and they also provided the opportunity to signal a warning to the new boys.

"All the boys out here from Barnsley are in the best of health, though they are not enjoying themselves as the troops are doing in Egypt where they seem to have it nice with band selections and bathing. I hope they will

continue to enjoy themselves for the fun will end when they get to this country. I have been in France since September last and I have not heard or seen a band of music all the time but have had to stand above the knees in water for over three months. All the music we get is from the German shells which burst over our heads." **Letter to the Barnsley Chronicle from Private J. W. Donner, 10th Y & L Regiment dated 3rd April 1916**

It was suitably ironic that on the very day Private Donner composed his letter, the Second Barnsley Pals, unbeknown to him, were moving into the front line trenches for their first tour of duty.

The commanders of the British forces in France knew that the volunteer spirit was willing but were less sure of the combat capabilities of their troops than the men obviously were. Some men, like Private Donner, felt that they had endured enough of the rigours of life and death on the Western Front to have been transformed into battle hardened veterans, but the preparations for the Somme offensive were clouded by the fact that for all their vigour the vast majority of the New Army were simply not ready to undertake such an enterprise. As the days grew slowly warmer and the hour of the coming battle approached, the General staff found themselves asking for more time in which to prepare the men and complete their training. By the Spring of 1916, time was a commodity in very short supply to the British planners and their French allies due to the struggle still raging at Verdun.

Nebulous plans for a joint Anglo-French campaign astride the River Somme sometime in the summer of 1916, had been aired at a conference between Sir John French, the then Commander-in-Chief (C. in C.) B.E.F. in France, and General Joffre, (his French counterpart), at Chantilly in December 1915. When the next Chantilly conference took place in January the British had gained a new C. in C.

General Sir Douglas Haig had assumed overall command of the B.E.F. at mid-day on December 19th, 1915, his criticism of Sir John French's handling of the war in France as well as having direct contact with the King, had placed him in a favourable position to accept the reins of command when they were duly offered. Indeed it was a pleasant surprise with which to fill his Christmas stocking, particularly as his appointment coincided with the elevation of Sir William Robertson to the position of Chief of the Imperial General Staff, (C.I.G.S.) a move which was the result of some delicate political chicanery designed to remove the overall control of British war strategy from Lord Kitchener.

In "Wully" Robertson, Haig discovered a kindred spirit. Both men were confirmed 'Westerners' with a heartfelt belief that the war would only be won by a decisive result against the German armies on the Western Front. Robertson was eager to put every available man, horse and gun into the effort in France. He particularly disliked the idea of vast numbers of men tied down in what he saw as "sideshows" dreamed up by "amateur strategists". Valuable men and arms were, according to Robertson, being wasted in theatres such as Salonika and Mesopotamia when they could be better used to furnish a substantial British success in the most decisive theatre of all. After all, that was where the bulk of the German army was concentrated, and that was where they would have to be defeated to gain a lasting result.

Nine Divisions had thus been transferred from Egypt, among them the 31st, with its contingent of Barnsley Pals. It would have cheered them to know that of the fourteen divisions that had been sent to or formed in Egypt to counter a threatened Turkish invasion, the nine that were eventually dispatched to France were seen as being of better military quality. It would have cheered the Pals but it would not have surprised them. In their minds, their quality was never in any doubt.

The French agreed wholeheartedly with the policy of the British C.I.G.S. but for reasons more to do with national pride rather than political or military intrigue. They felt the need for a decision on the Western Front much more keenly than the British, for most of the 475 miles of twisting, turning trench line, ran across their homeland, and the Germans were deeply entrenched upon their sacred soil. With every issue of every newspaper and with every meeting of people the length and breadth of unoccupied France, they were reminded of the presence of an invading host violating the sanctity of their beloved country.

The French were patriotically bent on driving the Germans back at the very least to the frontiers as they had existed before August 1914, while at best they yearned for the utter destruction of any force which was allowed to remain upon the face of France.

With this in mind the plans for the Summer operations crystallised and the French were handed a star-ring role in the campaign. The original plan called for a major French assault with 60 divisions over a 30

New commander of the British Expeditionary Force in France, General Sir Douglas Haig. He takes over to mastermind the coming big offensive in 1916 that he is convinced will break through the German defences and soundly defeat the enemy.

mile front south of the River Somme. Joffre wanted the British to instigate a number of smaller, and tactically more limited attacks, beyond the northern bank and straddling the valley of its tributary, the River Ancre, with a force of at least 25 divisions. The whole plan floated on a belief that a saturation of the German lines by an artillery bombardment so awesome that its like had never been witnessed before and supplied by an increased, unhindered flow of shells, would pave the way to victory.

Although Haig approved of the plan in principle, he was not altogether pleased with its intricacies. He had spent Boxing Day with Admiral Bacon discussing the strategic value of a combined Army and Navy operation in the north with the aim of securing the Belgian ports of Ostende and Zeebrugge from the Germans. He was also in no mood to allow Joffre's plans to dampen the enthusiasm of his untried troops of the New Army simply by using them as decoy forces in what could become costly actions, designed to divert German attention from the main thrusts of the French.

Despite his misgivings the British Supreme War Council left Haig in no doubt as to what was required of him in his dealings with the French. Not wishing to give the impression of disunity with their Allies they urged him to make every effort to support and co-operate with them, and indicated that his governing policy must be to move towards 'a united army'. Taking into account the different approaches to the twin arts of discussion and problem solving exhibited by the commanders of the two armies, the instructions were by no means always easy to carry out.

Although Haig was in no position to refuse the proposals made by Joffre, the Supreme War Council had given him room to bend them for it was also made clear that he would, 'in no case come under the orders of any Allied General further than the necessary co-operation with our Allies above referred to'.

When the two men met again at Chantilly in February, Haig again affirmed his willingness to co-operate with a joint offensive on a broad front, mentioning July as a possible date for its launch. Joffre in turn, acquiesced to the proposal that any preliminary 'softening' of the German defences should be made just before the main attack and not earlier as he had wished. He also agreed to stretch the French left wing just across the River to Maricourt.

United army or not, Haig was more than a little perturbed by what he perceived as a state of near exhaustion on the part of the French forces and he seriously doubted their ability to be a contender in any future rounds of the dour brawl of attrition beyond one more Winter. He was convinced that the hammer blow that he and Robertson longed for would be struck, ". . . by the forces of the British Empire".

Unwittingly it was the Germans who were to give Haig the chance to vindicate the thoughts that he had committed to his diary. A week after the Franco-British campaign had been settled in theory, the Germans had launched their own murderous onslaught upon the ancient, eastern fortress of Verdun. The German Commander-in-Chief, Falkenhayn, knew full well that the French would throw themselves headlong into this carefully calculated war of attrition as a point of honour. He knew also, that Verdun itself was of little importance tactically. The French commanders had dithered and had virtually removed the teeth from Verdun and its protecting ring of Forts, feeling that their garrisons would be trapped under heavy howitzer fire as had happened at Liege and Namur in August 1914. There was no conceivable way that the Germans could ever drive for Paris more than 130 miles distant even if Verdun fell. In terms of the general trend of the front the taking of Verdun would, at best, have flattened out a rather annoying salient.

What was under attack was a myth, a name which had come to symbolise French pride. The name of a bastion which, for years, had stared haughtily beyond France's eastern borders, taunting German military thinkers.

Falkenhayn saw Verdun as a psychological prize. He knew the French could not refuse the challenge and if he could succeed in smashing the myth and the flower of French manhood into the bargain, then victory would be within his grasp, but as the weeks turned to months and the struggle wore on, the nature of the battle changed. The French did not capitulate but held on, exchanging blow for bloody blow with the Army of the Crown Prince of Germany and the Germans, in their turn, found themselves enmeshed in the same web of honour which held the French. It became a matter of military pride for them to take Verdun, as it was a matter of pride for the French to hold it.

By the time April 1916 came around, the furnace had been stoked relentlessly with the bodies of the German assailants and the French defenders, and although it did not appear to directly interfere with the everyday work of the troops holding the Somme line, the episode of attrition being played out around Verdun's ring of Forts was to have much more of an effect on the future of every man of Kitchener's Army than any could have anticipated.

A simple calculation of French manpower sacrificed on the altar of Verdun revealed that it was quite impossible for France to fulfill her original obligations, and that Britain would have to take the leading part. On the other hand the urgings of Haig and Robertson had ensured that the British forces were increasing in strength. The build-up of the Kitchener battalions of General Rawlinson's newly formed Fourth Army was augmented by the influx of troops released by the closure of the forlorn escapade in the Dardanelles and who, like the 31st Division, were fresh from wintering in Egypt. The build-up of manpower was however, by no means complete for the job the Fourth Army would be asked to perform.

Commander of the French armies in the field, General Joffre. Under pressure from the German offensive against the French fortress of Verdun he constantly calls for the British to launch their offensive so as to bring some relief to his hard pressed divisions.

The longer the French held on the more German reserves would have to be drawn to Verdun to make them lose their grip. The British command believed this to be in their favour, for it gave them valuable extra time in which to complete their preparations and when the attack came on the Somme the Germans, they believed, would be much the weaker side, in terms of strength and morale.

Clearly the balance of the attacking forces would have to change and the scales came down heavily on the British side, but it was not turning out quite the way Haig had envisaged. He had set his heart on a victory in the west, planned and executed at his time of choosing, when all factors were in his favour. Now, although he had agreed to an attack being launched alongside the seasoned warriors of the French Army in the hope that this would bolster his untried troops of the New Army, he now found that circumstances had contrived to place him in a delicate position.

Haig's plans for an attack in Flanders had been greeted with a frosty reception by the King of the Belgians, and although he still hoped for an attempt to break the deadlock in that region he knew that now, it would have to wait.

Due to the German attack on Verdun the time was not of his choosing. As more and more French Divisions disappeared up the 'Sacred Way' from Bar le Duc, into the Dante-esque horrors of the battlefield never to return, the French demands on the British to launch the campaign earlier than

French soldiers moving up a communication trench to the front line.

planned became more frequent and ever more frenzied. Already the French had drastically reduced their share in the overall plan over an attack front which seemed to diminish daily. Joffre had calculated the loss of up to 200,000 troops before the end of May and gave July 1st as the last possible date for the launch of the attack before the French finally buckled under the pressure.

The Pals may have thought themselves fit for the job but they were not yet ready and the still weary and disillusioned units from Gallipoli needed more time to rest and retrain.

The battleground also was not entirely to Haig's liking. It had been suggested by Joffre, seemingly on the flimsy premise that the British would be bound to take an active part in an attack where the flanks of their Army extended its arms across the marshy curves of the Somme, to join hands with its French ally in driving the Germans back. Joffre very much wanted the British to commit themselves to more active fronts. Like a nervous lover betrothed but not yet married, the old General wanted a token that the British would finally give themselves wholly to a struggle which he felt the French had been engaged in for far too long without adequate assistance.

The Somme campaign was the way in which he would secure that commitment once and for all. If nothing else, Haig was certainly committed in spite of his reservations. He would have been hard pressed to rethink the nature and value of the British effort on the Somme even if he could have, for having once been set in motion, the slowly turning wheels of fate and the plans, would have been difficult, if not impossible, to arrest.

The Germans knew that the British would be forced to accept at least some responsibility in relieving the pressure on her beleagured ally at some time, but as an initial trickle of information turned into a steady stream of intelligence reports regarding British preparations on the Somme, they simply could not or would not believe it.

German balloonists suspended precariously in their baskets high above the lines, reported large clearings appearing in the woods around Albert and hutments being erected within them. They saw working parties digging, sawing, fetching and carrying, as existing roads were strengthened and new rail links were forged behind the frontal positions. Endless work on new trench construction was observed as mile upon mile of communication trenches were dug and made secure. Certainly these unstinting, overt labours appeared to herald the build-up to an attack.

The sighting of the renowned French 'Iron Corps', diverted from Verdun to the trenches south of the Somme, puzzled the Germans still further. Why, they asked, should the British choose to attack the strongest portion of their entire frontage in the west, alongside an ally already showing severe symptoms of war weariness and demoralisation?

As the evidence mounted, the German staff could ignore the facts no longer. The preparations were not merely a diversion, they were too elaborate for that. They knew an attack was coming and they knew it was coming on the Somme.

French soldiers return with a captured German gun..

Chapter Nine

The real thing

"You don't know how pleased we all are to receive news from good old Barnsley. Let it be known far and wide that we are all in the best of health and spirits. The beautiful weather which we have been looking for for some time now has at last arrived, and the sunshine has made us forget all about the nasty slushy days and nights of the past. It came for Easter and it made things look ever so much brighter than the dull, miserable, and rainy days which we have had on visits to the trenches. But we have kept smiling, and accepted the uncomfortable conditions with a good heart. After all, it was a pretty tall order after basking in the sunshine on the plains of Egypt. All our thoughts were of Easter, as of old, all the week before it came, and then it suddenly dawned on us that we had to put up with such disappointments at times. . . I have heard it said that high tributes have been paid to the two battalions on the manner in which we go about our work and the soldierly appearance of the men in general. Our duties are hard, but we tackle them cheerfully, and whether we have to wade through water in going to and from the trenches, we are ever cheerful. Sometimes things are lively, but we take it all in good part, and by this time we have become seasoned Tommies, feeling quite at home. You can rest assured that if ever the two Battalions get the chance of making a name like the good old Terriers have done, they will go for the stuff. It is very little that any of the Boys fear, now they have got to the real thing." **Private Harold Emson, 13th Battalion Y & L Regiment**

WITH MARCH 1916 DRAWING TO A CLOSE, the men of the 13th Battalion found themselves on the move once more. This time they marched in several gruelling stages of between ten and twenty miles culminating in their arrival at the village of Mailly Maillet, a little way behind the front line.

"We marched for about an hour and then rested for ten minutes. We carried everything. You used to carry everything you had in your valise, blankets, shaving tackle, all the paraphernalia a man wants. You used to carry your gas mask, water bottle and everything. The Lewis guns were on the trailers but we carried all our kit and rifles." **Ernest Bell, 13th Y & L Regiment**

'Everything' included a holdall carried in the pack, complete with toothbrush, razor and case and extra laces. There was a mess tin, extra socks, a towel and a 'housewife' kit for darning holes in socks or repairing the uniform. A small haversack was carried which held a knife, fork and spoon. A canvas bag containing iron rations was thrown in, for emergencies, and these consisted of hard biscuits, 'bully beef', tea, sugar and salt. Added to this not inconsiderable load was the rifle, bayonet and scabbard, a bandolier of ammunition and an entrenching tool. With full service dress included and various leather pouches and personal accoutrements hanging about their persons, all topped with the greatcoat, an indispensable luxury in the freezing conditions, the total weight carried by the marching soldier was upwards of 66 pounds. Little wonder that some feet didn't last the course.

The battalion had passed through many villages on its journey from Doudelainville and one of them, Beauquesne, was destined to become important as the location of General Haig's advanced H.Q. at the Chateau de Valvion, for the duration of the coming Battle of the Somme.

Mailly Maillet had suffered its fair share of damage at the hands of the guns. A few hopeful shells had demolished a wall here or thumped a gaping hole in a roof there, but there were still some buildings left standing in which the men could find billets.

"We got to Mailly and were billeted all over the place. Some houses with half a roof on, some with none. Of course, we were among the shells then. We were in firing distance." **Ernest Bell, 13th Y & L Regiment**

The men's experiences in the cattle trucks on the train journey from Marseilles had acquainted them with the way of life usually reserved for farmyard animals. It was the bitterly cold weather, still playing tricks on them, which they disliked.

> *"We were billeted in old barns and farms. The village was battered but some places were habitable. There was plenty of straw in the tops of the barns. It was a terrible winter that first winter there. I remember one night I'd taken my boots off. You took your boots off at night because you'd been walking all day. We got up one morning and we had to chip our boots off the ground the frost had been that keen."* Harry Hall, 13th Y & L Regiment

The men of Kitchener's Army, congregated in the rear areas between the River Somme and the village of Hebuterne to the north, knew something big was afoot. The Barnsley Pals had arrived quite late in France but still they knew. With every step they had taken nearer to the front, they had been reminded of the passage of an ever increasing number of men. Each village they passed through had seemed to have a tired, more cynical air about it. They could almost feel the expectancy in the stale, smelly atmosphere of every billet they found in the abandoned houses and barns. They could see the telltale signs of recently departed troops littering their new quarters, and, although their surroundings were far from luxurious, they were glad to be moving at last.

This was, after all, why they had walked from the pits at Dodworth, Silkstone and Houghton Main to join the colours. This was why they had slipped away from the artillery camps in Derbyshire and had clambered aboard trains from the outlying districts like Wombwell and Darton to enlist at the Public Hall. They had certainly come a long way since their early days in Barnsley and they carried with them the expectations of the whole town, for they were "Barnsley's Own". Their testing time was at hand.

Nevertheless, the Barnsley Pals, along with the other New Army battalions of the 31st Division, were just one small section of a giant military jigsaw being pieced together by the British on the Somme.

Early in March the Fourth Army had been created under the leadership of General Sir Henry Rawlinson and when the Pals arrived in the Somme region towards the end of that month, Rawlinson's army contained troops from four Army Corps, numbered thirteen, three, ten and eight.

Three of those Corps, thirteenth, third and tenth, held a twelve mile stretch of the line which ran west from the River Somme, swung sharply north around the German-held village of Fricourt, up and over the Thiepval Ridge and down into the valley of the Ancre. The remaining Corps, the 8th, held a further five miles north of the Ancre, from a point just north of the village of Hamel up to Hebuterne and the junction with the Third Army.

Lieutenant-General Sir Aylmer Hunter-Weston commanding 8th Corps.

The Pals of the 31st Division became part of the 8th Corps and found themselves alongside the 4th and 48th Divisions on the extreme left wing of the entire Fourth Army.

The infant Fourth Army was, however, growing quickly. Not long after the Pals had been absorbed by the 8th Corps, the 29th Division, also from Egypt, joined them. Even more divisions and yet another Army Corps were also on their way. The Pals, newly arrived and eager to enter the fray, had already sensed that something was in the wind, but few, if any, realised that when the time came to attack the German lines they would be part of an Army half-a-million strong.

The Pals' Corps Commander was Lieutenant-General Sir Aylmer Hunter-Weston, a Scotsman who sported a heavy moustache and a weathered complexion, which was hardly surprising, since he had spent three months in Gallipoli before being evacuated to England with sunstroke in mid-July, 1915. It was in Gallipoli that Hunter "Bunter" Weston had first taken command of the 8th Corps when the three British Divisions at Cape Helles had been grouped together. Now, feeling fit and well, he was back to take command of a new-look 8th Corps in France.

On the face of it Hunter-Weston's command stood out among the other Corps of the Fourth Army, for it embraced a mixture of divisions, each having an apparently different military pedigree. Apart from the 31st, composed entirely of New Army Service Battalions, it also boasted two divisions of the Regular Army, the 4th, which had been one of the famous 'First Five' of the original B.E.F., and the 29th, Hunter-Weston's old division from the Gallipoli days.

Although two more regular divisions and two more of the Territorial Force were to be sprinkled among the remaining corps the greater proportion of the Fourth Army were, like the Barnsley Pals, composed of Service Battalions of the New Army.

Kitchener had dreamed of his great New Army being used 'en masse' and had doggedly resisted any suggestions that it should have been intermingled with Regular and Territorial units to balance its lack of experience in any future battle.

Looking at the make-up of the Fourth Army it seemed that his wishes were about to be granted, despite the handful of Regular and Territorial Divisions. Sadly, even those Divisions were now in no position to shore up the efforts of their New Army colleagues, for they had undergone a crucial transformation since the outbreak of fighting in 1914. Their titles were no longer an indication of their military expertise, for they had borne the brunt of the initial struggle and in doing so had lost a good many well trained troops. The reinforcements which had topped up their numbers were, on the whole, just as short of real battle experience as were the New Army volunteers.

The 29th Division was a telling example. Before being ordered to France via Egypt it had taken part in the fighting at Gallipoli, an experience which not only earned its 'incomparable' reputation and gained it a clutch of V.C.s, but also succeeded in draining its strength.

In the space of just seventeen days after the April 1915 landings its total casualties had amounted to more than half its officers and half its rank and file.

In the words of Sir Ian Hamilton, Commander-in-Chief of the Gallipoli forces, the men of the 29th Division during that period had been, '. . . illuminating the pages of military history with their blood'.

As Corps Commander, Hunter-Weston was proud to have his old division under his wing once more, but there was no doubt that its fabric had changed as the flow of regular reinforcements had begun to dry up and wartime volunteers had been sent to fill up the gaps.

That said, there were still a few veterans of the 29th who had seen a thing or two, in stark contrast to the lads of the Barnsley Pals, who had seen a good deal of sand and precious little else.

For the most part, the Pals were blissfully unaware of their part in the grand scheme of things, or indeed which troops made up the 8th Corps. As far as the men were concerned, orders came from a non-commissioned officer in charge of their particular section, or occasionally from their platoon commander, but the orders handed to the 13th Battalion towards the end of March came from a source much higher than either of those.

Since most of the Pals had been coalminers in peace time, it was perhaps logical that the Army should choose one of the Barnsley Battalions to assist with the intensive tunnelling operations which were to be carried out under the 8th Corps' front. The job fell to the 13th Battalion and, with certain exceptions, that particular task was to occupy the men for the best part of three months.

Mining was not a novel pastime on the Somme front. In the days when the sector had been held by the French both they and the Germans had burrowed underneath each other's lines, laid charges and blown them; often as a thunderous curtain raiser to a local assault. What usually ensued was a bloody hand to hand struggle to dominate the lip of the resultant mine crater which lay nearest their own front line trench. There were several such mine craters, each one in various stages of defence, along the 8th Corps' front.

When the British had relieved the hard pressed French by taking over the Somme sector in the late summer of 1915, they also inherited the desire to continue with the mining operations and since the 13th Battalion were detailed as special Corps troops, they would have to be prepared to go where they were needed, and they were needed near Beaumont Hamel.

No date had, as yet, been fixed for the start of the coming offensive but General Rawlinson had been told to be ready for June or early July and so, as the preparations for the attack gathered momentum, plans to deal the Germans holding the village of Beaumont Hamel a very heavy blow on the opening day, were taking shape underground as well as on the surface.

Looking down on the British lines from a rise of higher ground to the west of the village, the Germans had excavated a tangled knot of deep dug-outs and trenches which was known as the Hawthorn Redoubt.

It was a miniature field fort which effectively dominated the surrounding countryside and barred the way into Beaumont Hamel from the west. It was obvious that the stronghold would have to be dealt with before the village itself could be captured. To this end deep mine galleries had been initiated under cover of a sunken road and slowly, laboriously they were reaching out to the very roots of the Hawthorn Redoubt. Although members of a Royal Engineers Tunnelling Company were driving the mines forward, the Pals were sent to help, and the men of the 13th found their experiences in the private underground war no less nerve-racking.

"When we got to France we were a mining battalion. The R.E.s were doing a lot of mining and we were attached to them. We were billeted well behind the lines, but we were in the lines 24 hours and had 48 hours out, helping to dig the mines with the R.E.s, 'sapping'." **Tommy Oughton, 13th Y & L Regiment**

"Our lot were occupied in mining under the German lines. They were going to blow Beaumont Hamel up. The Germans were mining as well. At one time during the process I was down there and you could hear the Germans working. I didn't think much to that." **Ernest Bell, 13th Y & L Regiment**

Although the Pals of the 13th were not holding the front line in their own right, they were still very, very close indeed, and their duties were no less onerous. It was certainly heavy work. For every period of 24 hours the Royal Engineers required three shifts of 100 men to help remove all the waste from the mines. Captain Normansell and Lieutenants Butterley and Cooke were to see that all the galleries were kept free of dirt. Most of the men who made up the 13th were well used to the principles employed by the Royal Engineers who, a year earlier, had poached 50 of their number to help in forming the specialist mining units of the Royal Engineers.

To men like Harry Hall, the ex-Houghton Main collier, mining was mining be it Beaumont Hamel or Barnsley, the difference was that now they were exchanging the shining wall of coal for the chalk beneath the Picardy hills and now their journey to work was accompanied by the music of flying shells.

The 13th Battalion arrive at the front and are billeted at Mailly Maillet one-and-a-half miles from the front-line trenches.

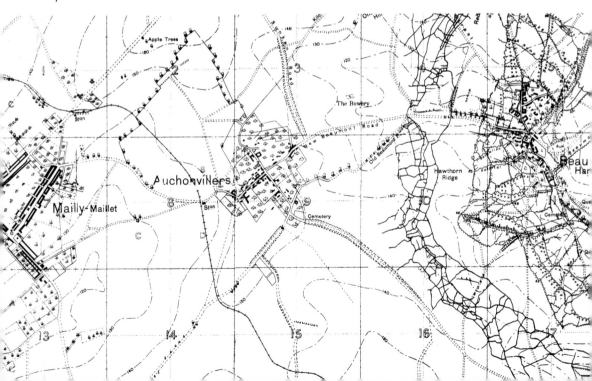

The chalk was undoubtedly much easier to work than the heavy clay and stinking sludge of the mines in Flanders, and the tunnels needed less in terms of support, but the waste still had to be removed from the galleries. The Pals' uncomfortable task was to carry or drag the dirt along the tunnels in sandbags and then conceal the tell-tale chalk deposits well away from the mine entrance so as not to reveal its position.

"It was chalk but it wasn't easier than coal mining because it was all hand moved, there were no trucks to bring the muck out. It was all damned hard work for our chaps. We weren't digging, there was a special company to do that." **Ernest Bell, 13th Y & L Regiment**

Lady Luck however, continued to smile down on Tommy Oughton, the same Lady Luck who had saved him from the squalid conditions of the cattle trucks on the long journey from Marseilles to Pont Remy. Because of his position as a signaller he was spared the hard graft.

"I didn't dig myself, I was on the phones. As you went into the mine about thirty yards or so there was a phone. You went further and there was another telephone. We were on telephone duty. For everyone to take a turn, 24 hours in and 48 hours out, Sergeant Wainwright had to take his turn and he was doing his turn with me." **Tommy Oughton, 13th Y & L Regiment**

With only 300 men being employed in the mines every day, the Army were certainly not about to let the other 600 or so of the Battalion idle their time away in rest billets in Mailly Maillet. Although for the British, there had been no major clash of arms in the Western theatre since the closure of the ill-starred affair at Loos in the Autumn of the previous year, the British General Staff were at pains to keep their troops active. For the soldiers on both sides of No-Man's-Land, confined to their trench systems for long periods, immobility had been the order of the day, a state of affairs punctuated only by spells of front-line duty and relief, desultory shelling, the odd mine here or a trench raid there.

To the British Generals however, immobility didn't mean indolence. In keeping with their policy of attempting to raise morale by inculcating the 'offensive spirit', the British Lion, if its teeth were to be kept sharp, had to be kept busy, and the same principles applied to the 'Tigers' of the York and Lancaster Regiment.

With many of their colleagues straining and heaving in the mines, several large parties of officers and men were attached for short periods to units then holding the front line, to receive brief insights into life in the trenches. The journey from their billets in Mailly Maillet towards the front line was usually made at night to confound German observers looking for the movements of troops and supplies.

Since the men detailed for these familiarisation exercises were making their way forward, they were put to good use as beasts of burden, bringing up rations, ammunition and other vital supplies from the dumps in the rear areas.

Buckling under their various loads, the Pals stumbled along in the dark, up what seemed like interminable lengths of communication trench.

"We went in at night the first time. It was about a mile and a half to the trenches from Mailly and it was up to your neck in muck. Up to May it was rough. There was a lot of snow and bad weather. The trenches were in an awful condition; they were filthy. You had to be very careful because there were sump holes dug into the trench bottoms to drain the water away. If you weren't careful, and some of the boards covering them had gone rotten, you used to go through, up to your knees in water. I fell into one called "Surrey's Hill" and it wasn't very comfortable when you were wet through.

"It was the natural duty of everybody when you came up from your base to carry ammunition with you. Each of us carried a box of ammunition which was no mean load. It was a real toil of a pleasure – it weighed about half a hundredweight! We had to take the machine gun as well, we never had to leave that anywhere. We had to carry it. Fortunately it wasn't a heavy gun wasn't the Lewis. Being machine gunners we were put into a listening post, well out between the lines. My listening post came out of a trench that our lads were mining under. We had to go down this mine to get to the listening post. If there was any danger, anything out of the ordinary, you had to notify people in the rear. You had your machine gun to try and stop an attack if one came. We were in

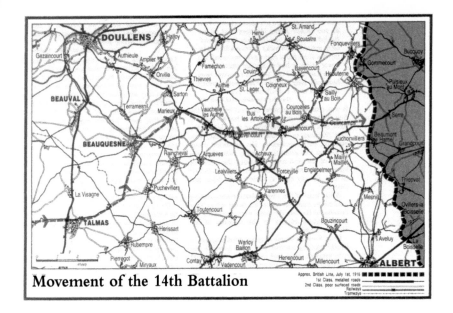

Movement of the 14th Battalion

Approx. British Line, July 1st, 1916 ■■■■■■■■■
1st Class, metalled roads
2nd Class, poor surfaced roads
Railways
Tramways

Whilst the 13th Battalion are situated at Mailly Maillet and engage in mining operations under the Redan and Hawthorn Ridges, the 14th march northwards towards the village of Serre.

48 hours and then out for 48 hours. You passed your time the best you could in the trenches. You always had to look out, keep your eyes open, but the men doing the mining were doing the hard work." Ernest Bell, 13th Y & L Regiment

For Harry Hall the first trip to the trenches proved to be an unnerving experience.

"It was all a bit new to us. We weren't quite sure if we were firing at them or they were firing at us. There were two or three batteries of our artillery just behind Mailly Maillet and what with their stuff coming over, you couldn't decide whether the shells were coming or going." Harry Hall, 13th Y & L Regiment

The first casualty to be sustained by either of the Barnsley Battalions occurred almost immediately after the 13th had received orders to start work in the mines. On March 29th, Corporal F. Bennett of 'D' Company, found out exactly which shells were coming and which were going. In a letter to his parents at Godley Street, Royston, Corporal Bennett wrote,

"Just a few lines to tell you that I am recovering in fine style and hope to be back with the boys in a few days. I am in a convalescent hospital about 16 miles from the trenches. I am not expecting to be sent to the Base now as my wound is not severe as was expected. The shot has gone in the back of my shoulder, but has missed the bone, so there is no danger, only of blood poisoning and I have been injected against that. What do you think? I was the very first in our Battalion, also in our Division, to be wounded in action! I was lucky not to get hit worse, for the shell burst right over my head, but never mind, it had to be, and thank God it wasn't serious. I can tell you I haven't been here very long but I have seen some stormy incidents that I shall never forget." Barnsley Chronicle, 22nd April 1916

It was true that Corporal Bennett had been the first Pal to be wounded in action, but his claim to have also been the first man in the whole of the 31st Division to be marked by the war, was, perhaps, pure speculation. His somewhat proud deduction was probably nothing more than the result of the good news regarding the nature of his wounds, and his wish to tell his parents that he had already done a 'little bit' for King and Country.

While most of the 13th Battalion were getting used to the hard toil and sweat in the mines near

Beaumont Hamel, the 14th were preparing for their baptism of fire in the trenches of the Western Front.

From Fresnes, where they had been engaged in steady training consisting of route marches and rifle practice, they had marched to Vignacourt and then on to Bertrancourt, finally arriving at a village called Courcelles Au Bois on the 2nd April. Colonel Hulke had already visited the trenches to make arrangements for the takeover of the line but the rest of the battalion had to make the most of their bivouacs in the woods between Courcelles and Colincamps.

"I don't remember any billets anywhere. We used to kip where we dropped. I can't remember seeing inside a blinkin' bed or a house anywhere all the time." **Frank Lindley, 14th Y & L Regiment**

Obviously the 14th Battalion were not as fortunate in their billeting arrangements as their sister battalion in Mailly Maillet, but unlike the men of the 13th, most of whom were to work in the mines, they were almost in the trenches and there wasn't a man among them who would have changed places with any of the 13th.

As they spent that last night under the open sky they reflected on all that had befallen them up to that point. They could hear the muffled thuds of the not too distant gunfire as some unknown battery, British or German, loosed off a defiant round somewhere to the north, perhaps near Gommecourt or to the south on either side of the valley of the Ancre. The sounds were enough to remind the men that their long period of relative inactivity was about to come to an end.

On April 3rd, the 14th Battalion marched out from Courcelles Au Bois for their first tour of duty in the front-line trenches opposite the German-held village of Serre. For several of the Pals that first trip was destined to be their last. Their particular responsibility was to be a 1,300 yard stretch of the line on the Colincamps sector. Two days earlier a party of four officers, four non-commissioned officers and sixteen men from each of the four companies, had visited a part of the line near Fonquevillers; which, due to either inability or unwillingness to grasp the subtleties of French pronunciation, became known universally to the men as "Funky-Villas". During that time the advance party had received initial instruction in the art of trench warfare as guests of the Royal Warwickshire Regiment in the hope that any tips picked up would be passed on to the rest of the battalion. As the 14th marched out for the trenches they little realised that they were soon to be handed a far more memorable piece of instruction, courtesy of the German artillery.

The approach to the battlefront took the battalion around the battered village of Colincamps, a settlement in an advanced state of decay due to the close attentions of German heavy guns. The village had suffered a pounding as recently as April 1st when German batteries had attempted to locate two British 9·2 inch guns in an orchard near the church. Not surprisingly the church tower was removed.

As they left the pock-marked roads of Colin-camps behind, the Pals came across what looked like a series of shallow ditches dug into the ground. Perhaps because they were new at the game, or because they were trying to make life easier for themselves, some of the men dispensed with the protection offered by the cramped conditions of the communication trenches at the start of the trench network.

"I can remember going up into the line for the first time. We were camped in the woods near Colincamps. We marched up so far and then dropped into small parties, passing through the guns and then up to where the trench system began. At first we tried walking on't top, but there must have been one of their artillery observers watching us because some of their 'whizz-bangs' started falling. We jumped into t' trenches as sandbags and muck was being blown all around us. None of us was hurt – I don't know how the hell we were missed. We never tried it again, we always got in at the right spot after that. It was in that area that we finally went

Tunnelling in the chalky soil of the Somme. The officer is using a stethoscope to listen for countermining operations by the Germans.

The trenches in front of Serre seen here with the French in occupation. The British take these trenches over and tidy them up. It is from this area that the Barnsley, Sheffield and Accrington men will attack on July 1st.

over." **Charlie Swales, 14th Y & L Regiment**

Lessons learnt, the men of the 14th Battalion soon got used to meeting the guide from the unit already holding the line and were led, single file, along the narrow duckboards towards the front.

Even with such a scare still fresh in their memories, it was with an undiminished sense of adventure that the Pals carried out the relief of the 1/8 Worcesters and the 1/6 Gloucesters, for their nerves at that time were still relatively resilient.

> *"I can't remember being nervous at the time, in fact I don't think that any of us were really nervous until July 1st. Before that date it was a disgrace to duck. After that you ducked at the slightest thing – you ducked automatically."* **Charlie Swales, 14th Y & L Regiment**

The countryside to the east of Colincamps was, in terms of chalk downland, largely unremarkable. One distinctive feature which broke up the gently sloping monotony was an interesting cleft running roughly

Sugar factory on the Serre Road with its cemetery to accommodate the steady trickle of casualties from this part of the front. The trickle will become a flood when the Battle of the Somme gets under way.

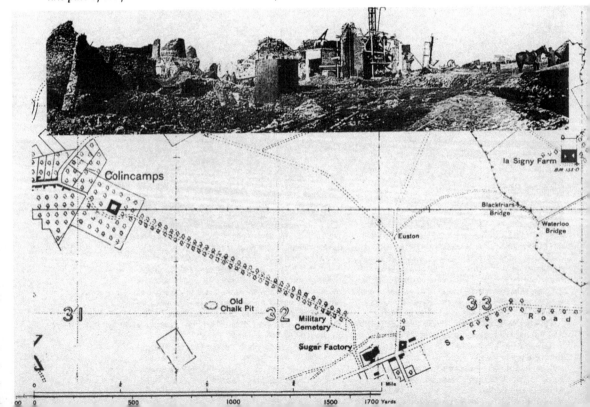

north to south marking the lowest point of a shallow valley separating Colincamps from Serre, some two and a half miles to the east. From Colincamps, just over two miles behind the British lines, the land fell gently into the dell and then, within 50 yards, a steep bank ran up to mark its eastern limits.

Four distinct clumps of trees had once gathered together in copses on the eastern slopes of this rise and had been christened with the names of the four writers of the Gospel. Running from north to south there was John Copse, then Luke, Mark and Matthew. When the 14th Battalion first made their way towards them they were copses in name only, for they had been destroyed by shellfire and only sadly splintered stumps and broken branches remained. It was at this point that the British front line positions ran just in front of the

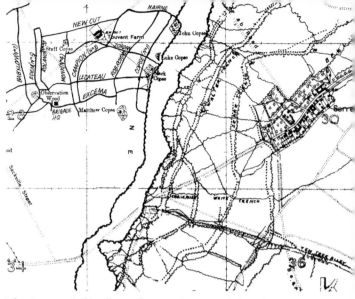

The German-held village of Serre, objective of the Pals on the first day of the 'Big Push', shows the British trench system behind the four copses, named 'Matthew', 'Mark', 'Luke' and 'John'.

shattered tree-trunks and it was there that the men of Barnsley were to live and work on their visits 'up the line'.

Charlie Swales and his friends in 'C' Company may not have been unduly worried by the hostile fire

Photograph of the terrain looking towards the German lines. The Leeds and Bradford Pals will attack across this ground.

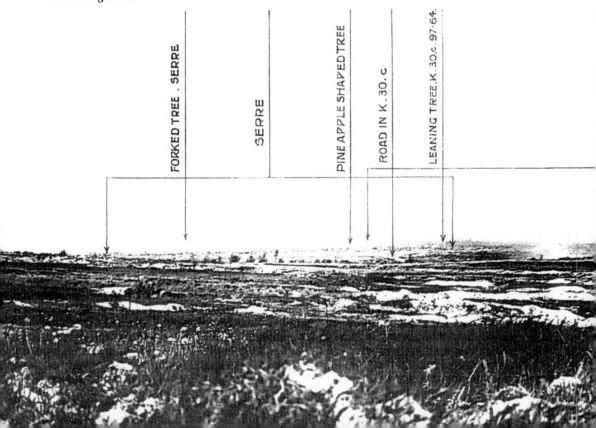

they had been exposed to, but, like Harry Hall of the 13th, they were still quite unaccustomed to the sights and sounds of the trenches. They too found it difficult to tell who was firing at who, and since at this early stage they could not identify the origin of the shells, it was a useless exercise to try and differentiate between the various calibres.

They could however differentiate between certain types of trenches as they stumbled nearer to the front line. Instead of the rather simple, hastily dug communication trenches, running at right angles to the front line, and which the German artillery had so recently tried to obliterate, the trenches became deeper and more elaborate in construction. There were signposts at some of the junctions and these were painted with the names of the particular routeway to which they pointed, an indispensible feature among the myriad lines of communication in what was, after all, a city below the level of the ground.

The custom of naming trenches had been initiated by the Pals' Corps Commander, General Hunter-Weston, who, as a Brigadier General commanding the 11th Infantry Brigade on the Aisne in late 1914, had taken to christening trenches and outposts for ease of identification.

Continuing the practice, the early British occupants of the sector had given each trench a name. They were an incongruous mixture, reflecting the often caustic humour of the front line soldier and a yearning for some reminders of home, however small, in their hostile environment. The Pals found themselves passing Sackville Street, a name which immediately conjured up visions of Barnsley, they then filed up Nairne Street, and it was here that they parted company with their topis and exchanged them for a much more useful form of headgear under the circumstances.

"We gave our pith helmets in at Nairne Street end, stuck a tin hat on and up we went. Nairne was one of the main communication trenches down at Railway Hollow. There was a light railway down there and later on us defaulters used to take 'ammo' up while the others were resting." **Frank Lindley, 14th Y & L Regiment**

It appeared that there had been a strong religious element among the erstwhile occupants of the trenches, for their names were heavily influenced by references taken from the Bible. Extending the theme of Biblical links begun with the christening of the four copses after the Four Evangelists, there was 'Jordan' trench, 'Eden' trench and behind that 'Babylon' trench. Some wag with a perverse sense of humour had gone so far as to name one trench 'Paradise'. Other trenches were more commonly titled, but the man who gave 'Eczema' trench its name must have been in a particularly vitriolic mood on that day.

On reaching the front line they could see that it had been dug to a depth of between six and seven feet and that the earth had been piled on top of the wall which faced the Germans to form a parapet, and in the rear to form a parados. The parapet was supplemented with the addition of a few sandbags. The earth walls were revetted with an odd assortment of woven wickerwork sections and sparse timber supports. It was about five feet wide at the bottom and the floor was covered with a thick layer of filthy, brown, slushy mud, the result of the passage of many pairs of booted feet churning the earth and rainwater into a foul smelling, sucking mire. Although deep drainage sumps had been dug at intervals along the floor to take the excess water, they were totally inadequate to cope with the weather conditions prevalent during the Spring of 1916, as Ernest Bell had already found out to his discomfort.

Looking right and left along the trench the men found it impossible to see beyond a distance of between six to ten yards for there was a buttress blocking their view. The sections they were standing in, constituted what were known as fire bays, projecting slightly out towards the German lines. The fire bays gave the trenches their characteristic zigzag appearance when viewed from above. The design of the fire bay was extremely utilitarian, for it minimised the blast effects of a direct hit by a German shell or trench mortar bomb. In theory, the traverses at either end would prevent most, if not all, of the blast and shrapnel from penetrating the bay on either side.

Two feet from the floor of the trench in the fire bay, a raised step could be seen cut into the wall facing the German line. This was the fire step, built to enable the troops to shoot over the parapet and for sentries to man at night on the lookout for possible German raiders and fighting patrols. Looking around still further the men's eyes noticed lengths of black wire hanging from the walls and apparently disappearing into holes dug down into the rearward sides of the trench. These holes were the dugouts, the supposedly shell-proof shelters which housed the lucky few whose job it was to organise the trench routine and its defence. Each company had a dugout for officers, and nearby, one for the Company Sergeant Major. Signallers would also have their own dugout to enable them to contact Battalion H.Q. a little way to the rear. The trenches were surprisingly clear of debris, even after almost eighteen months of fighting. Any accumulation of rubbish, old ammunition boxes, broken spades or items of unwanted kit, were unceremoniously dumped on the top, usually behind the parados as the trenches had to be kept clear for ease of passage.

Drooping from the walls a waterproof sheet would be pegged here and there, the flimsy shelter of some soldier. Scanning the scenes in the trenches the Pals were learning fast, but obviously not as fast as the Germans, ever alert in their trenches on the other side of No-Man's-Land, out beyond the belts of British barbed wire and the thicker coils of their own.

Lieutenant Colonel Hulke's report to Brigade Headquarters upon completing his inspection of the sector to be occupied by the 14th Battalion.

"As we went into the front line there was a bloke from over the German side shouted, 'When's them Yorkshire bastards coming?' They started then and they bunged everything they could at us." **Frank Lindley, 14th Y & L Regiment**

Any feelings of exhilaration at being in the front line at long last were quickly dispelled as the Germans, knowing they had raw troops opposite them, tried their level best to put the wind up the Pals. Frank Lindley and the other members of 'A' Company, on the right flank of the Battalion front, were treated to an introductory bombardment by canister bombs. These were frighteningly lethal weapons, also familiar to Robert Graves, then serving with the First Battalion, the Royal Welch Fusiliers in the trenches opposite Fricourt, seven and a half miles to the south-east and on the elbow of the Fourth Army front.

"Our greatest trial was the German canister — a two gallon drum with a cylinder containing about two pounds of an explosive called ammonal that looked like salmon paste, smelt like marzipan, and, when it went off, sounded like the Day of Judgement. The hollow around the cylinder contained scrap metal, apparently collected by French villagers behind the German lines: rusty nails, fragments of British and French shells, spent bullets, and the screws, nuts, and bolts that heavy lorries leave behind on the road. We dissected one unexploded canister, and found in it, among other things, the cog wheels of a clock and half a set of false teeth. The canister could easily be heard approaching and looked harmless in the air, but its shock was as shattering as the very heaviest shell."

The Barnsley Pals had a less eloquent description for the German weapons.

"Canister shells? 'Piss cans' we called 'em. They were big cans full of rubbish and what not. They used to spin across and flop and then, 'whoosh' everything went up. We used our rifles that first time in. We gave them some rapid rifle fire, we were good at that. That seemed to quieten them down." **Frank Lindley, 14th Y & L Regiment**

The canister was only the first item in an extensive arsenal which the Germans were to throw at the Barnsley Battalions. The welcoming bombardment did not last too long but it was long enough for the Pals to witness at first hand the havoc that the canister bombs could cause. Isolated sections of trench had been all but flattened and consequently some of the fire bays were almost unrecognisable. These would have to be repaired and rebuilt during the night.

As the Pals became ever more accustomed to the trenches in the lull after the German canister bombardment, they were quickly organised and a routine began to emerge. No one had been hurt as yet, but the tremendous damage to the trenches as a result of the brief barrage left no one in any doubt as to what would happen to a man should a canister land close by. With such thoughts already making a deep impression on the minds of the Pals they found that, even in the trenches there were jobs to do, and they were the men to do them. The work was not without its gloomy side for there were constant grisly reminders of the former occupants of the trenches.

"There was a job for everybody repairing, repairing, repairing all the time. When we first went in we took over what had been French lines and they were in a terrible state. We had to start straightaway with the old pick and shovel and we straightened things up. We had to deepen the trenches and build the parapets up, get sandbags and square 'em up. We had to make the front line zig-zag and build fire steps. It was continuous dig, dig, dig. The French had wickerwork sections on the sides of their trenches and sometimes when you pulled the wickerwork down you'd pull out a 'Froggy' as well. If you were digging in the trench bottoms you'd sometimes come across one there. There was plenty of mud. You'd be plodding about in the trenches. You'd dig a sump and stick a duck board across it but there was still that slimy sludge all round, and the stink and the rat holes. You could hear the rats gnawing at bones inside their holes. They'd plenty to feed on." Frank Lindley, 14th Y & L Regiment

"There were always bits of jobs to do during the day, and there was always someone on sentry. You had periscopes or a little mirror that you could fix on the top of your bayonet on your rifle. You stood your rifle up on the back of the trench, then you sat on the fire step and looked into No-Man's-Land through your mirror. On night duty, there was always somebody on the fire step with a mate sat dozing beside him. At 'Stand-to' at night and 'Stand-to' at morning everybody 'stood to'. If there were to be any attacks they were always at that particular time, daybreak or nightfall." Charlie Swales, 14th Y & L Regiment

It was after 'Stand to' at dusk that the real repair work could begin. From the front position No-Man's-Land stretched enticingly to the German front line which, at its closest point opposite Matthew Copse, was only a hundred and fifty yards away. By day it was inviolate, but by night it became a hive of activity as working parties of both sides beavered away in repairing the shattered breastworks, sentry posts and broken barbed wire obstacles which had been damaged by the artillery and mortar fire during the day. Occasionally a flare would soar high into the night sky before bursting like a firework into a brilliant white light illuminating the whole sector as bright as day.

"At night it was a picture. There were all these hanging lights going off. They used to hang in the sky, and light everything up. They'd make the place look a picture with all the barbed wire and all the tops of the trenches. If you were caught up there in the light you had to stand still and keep still. If you shifted you'd had it. If you stood still you were part of the landscape, but if you moved, the least movement, it was 'rat-tat-tat' and that was it." Frank Lindley, 14th Y & L Regiment

As soon as the last flickers of light had faded, the statues would come back to life and carry on with the fatigues they had been detailed to perform, each man a cog in a nocturnal machine which slowed gradually to a halt before the first streaks of daylight bleached the sky behind the German lines.

For British snipers like Charlie Swales those last few minutes before 'Stand to' at dawn was a time of special significance.

160

"We were in the second line and we were shooting from there, about 400 yards. We were in a dugout with a curtain at the back so that no light showed through. The sniping position at the front was an iron plate with two apertures, one for the rifle and one for the observer. There were two of you, one with a pair of binoculars, the other with the rifle. You used to catch them early before daybreak. This 'ere day we could see smoke rising from the German lines where they were cooking and we could see the head and shoulders of this chap bobbing about. I told 'Lijah Wright, who was with me, to slip back t'dugout and fetch telescopic rifle. When he came back he told me that one of the lads was sleeping on it and he didn't like to disturb him. 'Tha should have kicked the bugger awake then,' I told him. 'Anyway, there's only one thing to do 'Lijah, we'll use what we've got, I'll aim at the smoke and thee just tell me when he bobs up agean.' I took first pressure ont' trigger and waited while 'Lijah used t' binoculars. Suddenly he shouted 'Reight!' I squeezed the trigger and t' bullet went. 'Lijah slapped my shoulder and yelled, 'Thas gorrim!' He'd seen the bullet skim the parapet kicking up the dust. He was still looking through the binoculars when he swore, 'Bloody 'ell! He's waving thee a washout.' In a split second the German had jumped up and waved a white cloth and bobbed back down again. 'He deserves to get away with it for his blasted cheek,' I told 'Lijah. I bet I'm the only man in the British army to be waved a washout by a German. We must have done some damage because the Germans tried up with dummies, but you could always tell they weren't the real thing, it was one of those things we were taught. They were trying to see where we were firing from. We went further up the trench and shot from there. They must have located the section of trench we had used at first because they shelled and destroyed our sniping post, but no one was hurt." **Charlie Swales, 14th Y & L Regiment**

It was a miracle that no one had been killed up to that point, although the Battalion had suffered its first casualty on the night of April 3rd, when at 10.30 p.m., just six hours after they had relieved the 1/8 Worcesters and 1/6 Gloucesters, a German patrol of six men had entered the Pals' front line trench and stabbed the second in command, Major G. A. Sanford. The wound was serious enough for the Major to be returned to England aboard the hospital ship *Saint Patrick* on the 19th April. If, after that incident the men of Barnsley still harboured dreams of a 'cushy' existence at the front, then they were made to think again, for on April 5th the unspeakable occurred.

Within 48 hours of the Pals entering the front line the first name of many was being etched forever on to the 14th Battalion 'Roll of Honour'. The death of Private Thomas Burns, whose home was in Brittania Street, Barnsley, struck a chord with the people of the town as he was the first soldier in either of the two local Battalions to lose his life as they served together in France. Several ex-First Barnsley Battalion men, like John Davies nine months earlier, had already lost their lives in the service of the Royal Engineers. Their loss had been taken no less lightly by the people at home, but the news of the loss of a Pal, one raised and nurtured by the town, whilst their battalions were on active service together, was received with sorrow.

Thomas Burns had been born in Wolverhampton but had lived in Barnsley for most of his thirty-six years. He had been employed as a miner at Barrow Colliery where he had spent the greater part of his working life before deciding to enlist in the Second Barnsley Battalion early in 1915. The regimental number that he held bore witness to the fact that he had been among the first to join the Second Barnsley, having taken the oath and accepted the shilling on the 12th January, 1915.

Private Thomas Burns, 14th Battalion, of Brittania Street, Barnsley. The first Pal to die as the First and Second Barnsleys enter the arena in France, April 1916.

News of his death reached his wife in a letter written by the Battalion Chaplain, the Rev. William Field, upon whose shoulders fell the sad duty to inform Mrs. Burns.

"It happened last night and without a doubt it was a machine gun shot which penetrated the steel helmet he was wearing at the time. Death was instantaneous. He never suffered for a single second. In fact he knew nothing whatever about it. His head was up just that fatal fraction of a height to receive a dropping shot." **Barnsley Chronicle, 15th April 1916**

In one split second of carelessness borne of unfamiliarity with the vagaries of trench warfare, Thomas Burns had made the ultimate sacrifice and Mrs. Burns was left to face the future as a widow, without the comfort of a family to support her in her hour of need. She was left with these final words from the Rev. Field to cling to in her sorrow:

"God knows your sadness; creep close to Him and let Him help you in His wonderful way. I am sure that He had special help for our stricken womenfolk today. Remember you are shoulder to shoulder with thousands of other poor sisters who are silently suffering a similar loss." **Rev. Field**

Indeed they were, for the newly widowed Mrs. Burns was but the first of many local women to receive such news of their menfolk in the Barnsley Battalions.

In the days following the death of Thomas Burns, the Germans showered the Pals' positions with an array of projectiles of all shapes and sizes. As well as the canister bombs the Pals had to endure the Minenwerfer, a trench mortar which fired a shell much in the same way as the canister bombs were fired, and which exhibited about the same powers of destruction. Everyone came to view the Minenwerfer with loathing, but none more so than the Battalion signallers.

"I had a phone in the front line and unfortunately a Minenwerfer dropped on the top of the little dugout I'd been in and busted it in. It threw me about along with the telephone and the explosion damaged the tapping key. It also busted the wire and I had to go and find it so that it could be repaired. I went up on top of the parados, it was quite dark, and I found that I was walking about amongst a load of dead French soldiers, all decomposing. They'd just been covered with a bit of soil and the Minenwerfer had uncovered them. They were just like jam – my puttees were sodden." **Frank Lindley, 14th Y & L Regiment**

Succour for the bereaved families, cards that can be sent to the mothers and wives encouraging them to view their loss as a sacrifice on a par with that of Jesus Christ's. Thus the rightness of the cause is perpetuated as the deaths begin to mount.

"I was a signaller and went up with the phones. You used to lay your wires out from the dugouts to headquarters and then, when there was a 'blitz' on you'd stop with your wires. If they got broken you had to go out and repair them no matter what. You had to keep your lines intact. The other men used to think we had a cushy number. Of course it was cushy when there wasn't a 'blitz' on because you were in a dugout and they were on the outside. But we had the roughest part of it when they were shelling because we had to go out in it." **George Armitage Nichols, 14th Y & L Regiment**

The rifle grenade was another weapon to which the Pals took an instant dislike. These were small bombs attached to shafts which were then dropped down the modified muzzle of a rifle; in much the same way that a sky rocket might be placed in a milk bottle. They were then fired into the British trenches. Although not quite as potent as the canister or Minenwerfer, in the close confines of the trenches they were nevertheless feared. Shellfire was another hazard which the Pals had to contend with and in that respect being in the immediate vicinity of Matthew, Mark, Luke and John Copses, was a distinct disadvantage. This was because the German gunners behind Serre had had plenty of time to establish the range and to zero in on those likely targets.

"The copses didn't have leaves on them, they were just bits. Our trenches were more or less on the edge of the copses. The main trenches were just

in front. Communication trenches came up to the copses but the copses themselves were open. The Germans had them marked though because they could drop a few shells into them. The 'Jerries' had been there before. They'd had a dugout in one of the copses. It had been steep down under their parapet. There were steps down, then like a big chamber with bunk places in it. They'd been there long enough to do that. They'd probably been shifted by the French and gone on to the higher ground above us. They could overlook us all the time with their observation balloons and they could spot everything that went off in our lines. They knew every inch of that land, for the reason that they had been ploughed in there a long time before we appeared." Frank Lindley, 14th Y & L Regiment

For every second that Frank Lindley spent in the front line his senses were absorbing valuable lessons in the game of survival. Gradually he began to distinguish between the British and the German guns, and then between the various types of shell which the Germans employed.

"You soon got used to the different noises, you could hear 'em all coming. Their 'whizz bangs' were laid just on top of our trenches. When you were in the front all you heard was, 'bang . . . whoosh . . . bang.' The howitzers used to go 'shoosh', and some of our sharp-eyed types claimed that they could see the shells that were fired high. Some of the big heavy shells we called 'coalboxes' for when they hit and exploded it was like a load of slack going up." Frank Lindley, 14th Y & L Regiment

Between the death of Thomas Burns on the 5th April and the Battalion's relief in the early evening of the 12th April, the Second Barnsley's had lost a further five men killed and suffered eight casualties with wounds sustained from trench mortar bombs, shellfire and rifle grenades. Two of the wounded men, Private W. Haigh and Lance Corporal William Knowles of Carlton, subsequently died due to the severity of the wounds received.

It was fast becoming clear that this type of warfare was not quite what the Battalions had trained many a long hour at their training camps in England for. If the men had expected an immediate face to face showdown with the German army then they were mistaken. Apart from Charlie Swales and 'Lijah Wright, most of them hadn't seen the slightest flicker of a field grey uniform let alone a real German soldier, they had been far too busy keeping their heads down. Even so they were still losing comrades due to the tormenting uncertainty as to when and where the next lethal projectile would fall, but that was not the end of the sorry tale.

The tour of duty also served to give warning that the dangers faced by the front line soldier did not always come from the other side of No-Man's-Land. Accidents could and did happen, often with fatal results.

The mysterious circumstances surrounding the death of Private William Russell, the day after the death of Thomas Burns, was perhaps the saddest blow to the 14th Battalion up to that time. William Russell, an ex-Littleworth miner whose wife and

SATURDAY, APRIL 22, 1916.

BARNSLEY BATTALIONS IN THE TRENCHES

VICTIMS OF A GERMAN BOMB.

BARNSLEY AND DISTRICT MEN KILLED AND WOUNDED.

PTE. H. ARDRON (BARNSLEY.)

PTE. H. W. WALTER (CUDWORTH

PTE. J. BEEVORS (MAPPLEWELL.) | LCE.-CPL. W. KNOWLES (CARLTON.)

163

PTE. A. HEPWORTH

Victim of a German night raiding party, he is 'blown to smithereens' when a grenade is lobbed into the trench.

Pictures reproduced from the Barnsley Chronicle.

young child lived in Worsbrough Bridge, had joined the Second Barnsley Battalion on 2nd February, 1915, just two days after his brother Arthur had enlisted. They had both been posted to 'B' Company where Arthur had become a stretcher-bearer.

The brothers travelled to Egypt together, quite a feat for lads born and brought up in Monk Bretton, and they had gone into the trenches together for their first taste of action in France.

On April 6th, William Russell was on sentry duty guarding his section of the trench system against possible attack by a German raiding party, when someone made a dreadful mistake. Perhaps a code word was confused, or maybe the strict code of challenge and response was ignored, but a shot was fired and William Russell lay dead, a victim of the confusion and disorientation that those early days in the trenches had wrought.

As a Company stretcher-bearer, Arthur Russell was called upon to carry the lifeless body of his brother away from the scene of the accident, an act which must have required an immense amount of courage and self-control under such painful circumstances. The war was over for William Russell but for his wife and child the struggle against hardship was just about to begin. For his brother, Arthur, there were more bizarre twists of fate to come.

Ten days after making their way up to the front line for the first time, the Pals of the 14th Battalion, buffeted by high winds and soaked by a heavy rainfall, squelched their way back down the muddy communication trenches towards a well earned rest in the village of Bertrancourt. There were now fourteen gaps in the ranks where there had once been Pals. Half of that number could count themselves as the lucky ones, men like Private Gawthorpe of Worsbrough Dale, whose wrist wound ensured him of a trip back to 'Blighty' with the clean sheets of a hospital bed in Exeter at the end of it. For the time being at least, he would take no further part in the war. For the other seven there would be no 'Blighty' and clean sheets, only a final journey to a small military cemetery near a ruined sugar factory, halfway between Colincamps and the front line.

Meantime the 13th Battalion had also begun to draw up a steadily growing list of casualties. During the ten days that the 14th Battalion had spent in the line, the 13th had also lost their first Pal, 21 years old Harold Ardron of King Street, followed by several more killed and wounded.

Since most of the 13th were involved in mining operations the majority of their casualties were due to shellfire, particularly shrapnel, as they made their way towards the mines.

"I regret to say that a young man named Wilmot, of Darfield has been killed, and Walter Wright, also of Darfield, has been wounded. A shell killed four of our men, besides wounding two officers and ten men." **Letter to the Barnsley Chronicle from Private Walter Broadhurst, 10th April, 1916**

The two officers who had been among the party to be injured by shrapnel on April 9th were Captain N. W. Streat and Lieutenant George Asquith.

"George Asquith was wounded soon after we got to France. When I saw him he was laying on the floor outside the place where we were in Mailly ready for taking down the line. I asked where he had got it and he told me that he had been wounded in the shoulder. The first man I remember dying was a man called Hepworth. He was blown to smithereens when a grenade was thrown into the trenches during a German night raid. I knew him well." **Ernest Bell, 13th Y & L Regiment**

For both Battalions life out of the line was much the same. There were always fatigues to perform and large working parties were detailed for duties under the instruction of the Royal Engineers Field Companies. Somehow the men found time to wander around the villages where they were billeted. These excursions provided ample opportunity for them to sample the limited delights offered by the local traders, and also for them to get to grips with the French language.

"When you got into a little village like Mailly there used to be a local baker – remember, while we'd been in the trenches there'd been as many as ten men sharing a loaf of bread – he used to make these long loaves, what they called 'doo pan'. If we'd a few coppers to spare we used to go and buy one and have a real birthday. You learnt French as you went along. . . you got into it so that you could make yourself understood. 'Kel-er et eel?' What time is it? But we never had any real cause to speak French to anybody much, because we were mainly among our own party. The French shop-keepers weren't bad, it was the farmers that were the trouble. Many a time they'd take the bucket out of the well so that you couldn't get water. They thought that it was going to run dry for them-selves. They did that many a time but we always contrived to get another bucket from somewhere." **Ernest Bell, 13th Y & L Regiment**

"Some of the French were alright, but I found that a lot of them wanted to make too much out of you. Small shopkeepers would rob you anytime. In some places I've known it where the handles of water pumps had been fastened so that you couldn't pump water out. The pumps would then get smashed up because they had made it so we couldn't draw water." **Tommy Oughton, 13th Y & L Regiment**

"There were happy times if you got near an estaminet when you were out of the line. You could get 'erfs and pom-di-tares,' – that was egg and chips. Champagne was only one franc a bottle." **George Armitage Nichols, 14th Y & L Regiment**

"We went out one night and one lad, Jimmy Allen drank over the mark. We came out of the bar and it was snowing like blazes. He dropped down on the floor and we rubbed him with snow and shoved it down his neck to sober him up. We got back to our billets and in the garden was a big cold frame. We lifted it up and it was full of liquors and wines of all sorts. It had been the store for the house. We took a bottle each, three bottles of whisky – we drank one before we got down to sleep. I warned them to put the rest out of Jimmy's way or he'd be up in the night and at it. During the night Jimmy did get up whilst the rest of us were asleep and took our boots and put them on the billet fire. Next morning three of us without boots and a parade coming up – we didn't know what to do. I went down to see George Wardle to see if he could do anything for us. George asked Buswell, the Quarter Master Sergeant if we could have some boots. George straightened it out, and I came back with three pairs." **Harry Hall, 13th Y & L Regiment**

It was in Mailly Maillet that some of the 13th Battalion Pals received a pleasant surprise. Soldiers of the Barnsley Terriers' who had been on the Western Front since April 1915 and were therefore veterans, as they had seen action in the Ypres salient, heard that the Pals were in France.

"We may tell you that every one of us were just killing ourselves to get to see them. At first we were a bit unlucky but we were determined that we would see them somehow. We had a hunt round for a bit and then discovered that the Pals were in a village seven or eight miles away. Then, what a hurry there was! No tea; no, we must see our Barnsley friends and off we went. My word we shall never forget that meeting! Going up the streets where the Pals were billeted the first man we saw was one of the First Battalion – a trammer. One of us yelled out, 'Bring a tub in Tommy' and my word you should have seen his face. They all wanted to know the news at once and we had to tell them this over a drop of French beer. It was just like being in Barnsley without the tram and how happy we all did feel!" **Letter to the Barnsley Chronicle from Pioneer C. Anderson and Private MacKelvey, 1/5 York and Lancaster Regiment, 8th April, 1916**

No doubt the roof of some local estaminet was raised a few inches as several beery choruses of a good old Barnsley song filled the air.

The period of relief was also the time for a wash and brush up. Even after such a relatively short period of service at the front, almost two weeks of slopping up and down through the slime had left them feeling decidedly ragged and much lousier than usual. There had been no shortage of water in the front line but unfortunately most of it had been filling up the bottoms of the trenches.

"You couldn't keep clean it was an impossibility. To try and keep clean we had to cut all our hair off. We used to try delousing ourselves by running the flame from a lighted candle up the seams of our clothing, but the blankets were never clean. They were thrown all over the place. They were loaded onto transports when you went out of the line and you picked them up when you went back. Those blankets were lousy so you were just kept in the same state." George Armitage Nichols, 14th Y & L Regiment

"Our uniforms were scruffy – the dirt had to wear off. You just rubbed the sludge off when it dried, which was seldom. When you were in the trenches you were up to your knees in water and you'd rear up at the side of the trench and have a doze. One day the order came that we were going to be 'stoved'. We marched to Colincamps and in the woods there they had big tanks boiling. You stripped off and chucked all your clobber in these tanks. They had big tubs cut in half with hot water poured in and we all mucked in. Then you all had to scramble for your 'togs' as they were all thrown out of the 'stover', but it wasn't long before you were bung full again, perhaps hatching out other bloke's chats." Frank Lindley, 14th Y & L Regiment

"When we came out of the trenches we used to have a bath and a change of underclothes. You didn't change your uniform, just your underclothes. There was an old brewery in Mailly and there'd be a vat that they used to brew beer in that was full of water. They used to give you ten minutes. You used to dump your underclothes at one side before you got in. They used to burn those, you couldn't do anything with that lot. Then fifty or sixty of us used to get in the vat and have a good wash down. You didn't think about the colour of the water. That was trivial after the state we'd been in. You used to feel better for it after a good swill down. That's all it amounted to – you were lucky if you had any soap." Ernest Bell, 13th Y & L Regiment

Nicotine addiction receives an enormous boost because of the war. Barnsley folks are encouraged to send tobacco as gifts for the troops.

SMOKES FROM HOME
Barnsley Chronicle Tobacco Fund.

" Barnsley Chronicle " Tobacco Fund
(Amalgamated with the " Chronicle " Comforts Fund,)
FOR ALL SOLDIERS.

Ordinary Cost,	**9/10**	Parcel and Postage for	**3/-**	Special by Coupon.

CONTENTS OF PARCEL:—
¼-lb. United Service Tobacco, usually sold at 8d. per oz. ; 200 Cigarettes (Woodbines) ; Carriage 1/-. Or—

Z. —280 Wills' Woodbine Cigarettes 3/-
X.—575   Ditto   Ditto 5/-
W.—3 pounds Wills' United Service Mixture 5/-
V.—280 Wills' Gold Flake Cigarettes 5/-

A Postcard ready addressed back to you for your friend's acknowledgment is enclosed in every parcel.
One Coupon for each Parcel.

By the middle of April preparations for what was to be hailed as 'The Big Push' were in full swing, but the vast numbers of men required for such an endeavour were the cause of considerable concern for the military hierarchy. On the one hand they needed as many men as they could lay their hands on to carry out their initial objectives and to press home any advantage, should one present itself. On the other hand every new battalion which trudged wearily towards the Somme brought with it yet another set of problems. Every single man in the Fourth Army would have a job to do when zero hour rolled around and before then they would have to know that job inside out and back to front.

If General Haig was of the opinion that those New Army troops who had been in France for several months were in need of further training then the case of the Pals, with less than two weeks of trench warfare under their belts must have been verging on the desperate.

In the case of the 14th, as soon as they were out of the line, small parties left their rest billets for courses at the Brigade bombing school at Colincamps. Others were given a demonstration of the Flammenwerfer, literally, flamethrower, first used at Hooge in Belgium in the summer of 1915. While still more were trained in the use of the Lewis gun.

With all these extra men requiring specialist training and more arriving every week, the Army needed many more instructors to deal with them, but with so few Regular battalions in the Fourth Army the men with the requisite skills and knowledge of their subject were extremely thin on the ground. In their search for sufficient instructors, men had to be taken from the New Army battalions, and, by virtue of the fact that he had been one of the first members of the 13th Battalion machine-gun section, later graduating to the Lewis gun, they took Ernest Bell too.

"During the period that I was in France I instructed three or four hundred men on how to use a Lewis gun and my pal Harry Gay was one of them. After I'd trained them they were sent back so that if there were any casualties in the Lewis gun teams they could replace them. Harry wasn't a machine gunner. I didn't see him much because he had been a servant to George Asquith. After he'd had his course I saw very little of him." **Ernest Bell, 13th Y & L Regiment**

Unfortunately, the Army could not afford to let men train without calling on them to help with the immense amount of work still to be carried out on all manner of tasks. There was the digging of assembly trenches, the re-surfacing of roads and the ferrying of essential supplies to the various dumps that were being set up.

Invariably the men in rest were called upon to do the work. If the men trained then they couldn't work or relieve the troops at the front, which in turn meant that the physical preparations would take longer to complete; yet if they worked or held the line, they could not train. With that dilemma in mind the Pals trained as they fought and worked. Hardly the most effective way of making ready for such a momentous occurrence as the Battle of the Somme.

During the 14th Battalion's stay at Bertrancourt, some of the 13th Battalion Pals had ventured into the trenches opposite Serre to begin work on five tunnels on the front of the 31st Division. Two of the tunnels were cut in the rising bank behind the British front line at John and Mark copses. The other three named 'Eczema', 'Grey' and 'Bleneau', originated under cover of the trenches from which they took their names. Unlike the deep mined galleries under the Hawthorn Ridge, the object of which was to destroy the Hawthorn Redoubt, the tunnelling in the area of the copses was to serve a different purpose. If the infantry did their job and captured the German trenches on the day of the attack, then the shallow thinly covered tunnels would be broken out to provide an instant means of communication with the assaulting troops. They would also save the Pioneers a lot of digging.

Several of the 13th Battalion officers meanwhile had developed a dangerous liking for patrolling No-Man's-Land on the Redan Ridge; part of a high spur jutting out from the Hebuterne plateau and falling sharply into the valley of the Ancre, separating Serre from Beaumont Hamel. The Redan and the extension of the plateau to the north was a much desired tract of land, for it offered a commanding view of the spurs and valleys to the south and a large area of territory behind both the British and German lines. In its time the Redan had witnessed many a horrific struggle as both the French and Germans had blown mines in attempts to secure the vantage point for their observers. It was towards the old mine craters on the Redan that Lieutenant Cooper and Lieutenant Maleham were drawn, towards the end of April.

Just after dark on April 18th, Lieutenant Cooper and three men slipped over the top from post Number 3 and crawled into No-Man's-Land to find out if an old mine crater, some 33 feet across and six feet deep, had been absorbed into the German system of defences. They later returned safely with the news that the Germans had not defended the far lip of the crater.

Ten days later, at 9.00 p.m. Lieutenant Cooper again went out from Number 3 post, this time accompanied by Lieutenant Maleham. They were still out when a German machine-gun opened fire, but they returned unharmed three hours later.

Even though the Battalions had not been called upon to serve in the line for an extended length of time, the desultory shelling of the 8th Corps' front and communication trenches took a steady toll of men.

On April 28th the 14th Battalion marched from Bertrancourt for their second tour of duty in the trenches. Passing through Colincamps, one particular spot impressed itself on Frank Lindley's mind more than any other.

"There was a crucifix on the bend of the road. Our lads used to cross themselves as they passed by on their way back to the front." **Frank Lindley, 14th Y & L Regiment**

Relieving the Leeds Pals, the 14th took over the same length of line that they had manned before, with the addition of a further 300 yards extending north from John copse to Nairne Street. Like Ernest Bell a few weeks before, Frank Lindley found himself on duty in a forward sap which snaked out cautiously towards the German lines. He was hoping to pick up early clues as to the movements of German working parties and patrols.

"I was on a listening post right up against their wire and under ours in like a little sap. I don't know just how long I was stuck there, but I thought that they had forgotten about me. There was no system, you were on your own. You could smell their cigar smoke wafting across, and you could smell their booze. They were playing accordians and piccolos, and I could hear them rattling their beer bottles – they were 'hoch hoching' but I couldn't understand a dickie bird of what they were saying." Frank Lindley, 14th Y & L Regiment

The second spell in the line was much shorter than the first had been, but the duties to be performed varied very little, with the odd artillery duel during the day along with working and wiring parties at night.

The Germans too were busy working on their front line between Matthew and John copse. The parapets of the British trenches marked the limits of the Pals' world, but if any of them had been tempted to raise their heads, or had a good look through a trench periscope they would have seen the land rise steadily between them and the Germans, right up to their front line trench. They would have seen the parados of that trench clearly visible on the horizon, a long line of earth dusted with a white icing of chalk thrown up from twelve feet below ground. Just in front of the trench, contrasting starkly against the white of the chalk was a thick belt of black barbed wire piled up to three feet high.

"We could see their trenches if we were quick, but we had to move fast for there was a sniper waiting for you. But I've used a little periscope, and you couldn't have one of them up too long before it was knocked off you. No-Man's-Land was pretty flat before our guns started ripping it all up. It was still green in places and of course there was the German wire which stretched for miles in either direction. Their wire was about four times as wide as ours. The quantity of wire they had! You couldn't have got through that in a month of Sundays. Our wire was narrow when compared to theirs." Frank Lindley, 14th Y & L Regiment

"The ground sloped up to the village of Serre. It was like any ordinary countryside but you knew that they were there. You could see their line of trenches in the daytime if you were so minded to risk a quick look. I once had my hat knocked off. I didn't try it anymore – I didn't know that my head had been up so high." Ernest Bell, 13th Y & L Regiment

Little else could be observed beyond the parados of the German front-line trench, what did lay beyond was Serre, standing defiantly atop its knoll a thousand yards away, behind three more lines of trenches and yet more barbed wire.

In addition to these daunting obstacles the village itself was tied into the German intermediate trench network, and if that wasn't enough had its own village defences, consisting of several strongpoints standing guard to the front, each corner and the rear.

Surrounded by trees and with guns poking from every nook and cranny, Serre was a village fortress of amazing strength, completely dominating the positions of the 31st Division. It would certainly be a tough nut to crack.

The second tour of duty, just four days, was much shorter than the first, but it proved to be far more costly in terms of casualties. Five men had been killed and another twenty-seven wounded. It was not uncommon for men in the front line, pinned down under the roaring cannonades, to lose their powers of speech and hearing temporarily. Later on some would lose their power of reason permanently. It was hardly surprising then, with the grim prospect of death or mutilation lurking around the corner of the next traverse, that the survivors should adopt a stoic attitude to loss of their comrades. If nothing else the hardening of their feelings went some way to preserving their own sanity.

"Leading up to July 1st you always had a few casualties from shellfire. Every time that you went into the front line there always seemed to be a few more. A shell dropped among a party from A Company and knocked out about three or four of them living in a dugout." **Charlie Swales, 14th Battalion, Y & L Regiment**

"I know when the Minenwerfers and whizz-bangs came over I wondered what we'd got here, but you had to live with it. I remember once carrying ammo up to the trenches, they were trench mortar bombs. We used a little wagon on a light railway line. When we got as far as Nairne Street there were a bunch of lads folded up in their blankets ready for sticking down in the holes. We couldn't get

The Germans are thorough in their construction of defences. Against these efficiently prepared positions the British Army is to hurl itself on July 1st, 1916.

past them, they were all piled in the trench. We had no choice we had to walk over them. As we did so carrying the ammo we'd get a belch here and a belch there, of course we'd say 'sorry lads' but we had to carry on. I can remember on another occasion one fellow got blown up by a Minenwerfer. This thing dropped into one of the bays and he'd gone. We had to scrape him up. Strange as it may seem he'd had a postal order sent him and as they were scraping him up they were looking for it – pity to let it go to waste. When you were dealing with dead 'uns and bits of 'em you had to get on with it. It was there, it was a job and you had to do as you were told. Get there and sort it out as it came. You got into a state of mind that you didn't care either way, you didn't think about getting it. They used to mumble to each other, 'well if thi name's on it thas got it.' You just used to hope that your name weren't on it." **Frank Lindley, 14th Y & L Regiment**

"I was frightened sometimes . . . if I said that I wasn't then I should be a liar. You knew that you had to go out in it, so you simply went out . . . and that was all there was to it." **George Armitage Nichols, 14th Y & L Regiment**

"There's been times when we thought that we wouldn't live above two hours, but things came right. I've never panicked much. There used to be shells bursting all over the place, but you just had to do the best that you could, getting out of difficulties and helping others to do the same. You had to fall in with the conditions." **James Bennett, 14th Y & L Regiment**

During the month of May the men of the 13th Battalion continued to divide their time between mining, going out on working parties and periods of front-line familiarisation. On May 5th, work began on two mines at Bess Street and on another called Delaney, just north of the Serre Road and facing a prickly portion of the German line called the Heidenkopf, but known by the British as the Quadrilateral Redoubt.

A little way to the south, along the broad shoulders of the Redan Ridge, Lieutenant Cooper paid the price for his adventurous patrol work and was seriously wounded a week later.

Casualties continued to mount steadily largely due to shrapnel wounds, but now the numbers were being swelled by an increasing number of fatalities due to gassing.

For the 14th Battalion, the month of May lived up to its merry title. Freed from front-line duty for the whole of the month, they were at last able to get down to some serious training.

On 16th May the 14th Battalion Pals marched a little way forward to billets in another wood near Bus-les-Artois.

"Bus-les-Artois wood they called it but we called it 'Buzz' Wood. Inside the wood there were canvas

huts between the trees, with the stumps of the trees inside the huts. We had to do spit and polish and get the muck off." **Frank Lindley, 14th Y & L Regiment**

When the Pals arrived in Bus Wood winter had finally breathed its last and the apple and pear trees in the orchards were beginning to show their first hints of blossom. For the first five days the Pals underwent an intensive programme of instruction, as the finely tuned plans for the coming big offensive against the German positions entered their final phase.

There were classes for bombers, special courses for signallers and exercises to sharpen up the men's powers of observation. As well as the small group classes there were larger scale exercises which involved the whole Battalion making a mock attack on a pre-determined objective, while at the same time attempting to make contact with a patient pilot of the Royal Flying Corps.

May 20th. Weather brilliant. In the afternoon an exercise with contact aeroplanes was carried out with the Battalion. An attack was made by a skeleton firing line on a front of 1,500 yards. Red flares were carried by the firing line to signal to the aeroplane the furthest point reached. Brigade HQ were provided with circular ground sheets to indicate their position and four powerful lamps to communicate with the aeroplane.

Method of communication:

When the aeroplane was in a favourable position to observe it fired a white light, upon which red flares were immediately lit in the front line. If successful in discovering the flares, the aeroplane signalled the fact by a pre-arranged code and then proceeded to get in touch with Battalion HQ after which it went away for fifteen minutes. During the interval the front line moved forward about 500 yards. Battalion and Brigade HQs moved forward proportionally. On return of the aeroplane the same procedure was adopted. Another move made forward. On return of the plane after communicating with the front line, obtained connection by lamp and dropped a message within ten yards of HQ and went home.

Satisfactory results obtained for a first attempt. **Extract from the war diary of the 14th (Service) Battalion York and Lancaster Regiment. Public Record Office, WO95/2365**

The Army, it seemed, were doing a thorough job.

During the last week of May the whole battalion were called upon to act as one enormous digging and wiring party for the 210th Field Company of the Royal Engineers. Due to the quality of their trench construction the York and Lancaster digging parties were respected far and wide, but their fame had surely not spread as far as Egypt. Vernon Atkinson however, now fully recovered from his illness and newly arrived from the east, found himself on a digging party within a few hours of walking into Bus Wood.

"They drafted me to the 6th Battalion of the York and Lancaster Regiment from hospital. I said that I didn't belong to that mob. I asked this sergeant if he had any idea how I could get back to my old Battalion. He told me what to do and he said that I would arrive at a place called 'E-taps'. He said 'You'll get to your Battalion from there.' He gave me a paper to certify that I was allowed to travel. He was correct, I did find them at a place called 'Buzz' Wood. The first man that I saw was Sergeant Major Townend. He said to me, 'Who are you?' and I said, Atkinson, Sir, I've been left behind in 'Gippo'. He remembered me. He told me not to go out of the camp because he wanted me for duties. We went up at night to the trenches and they were shelling like bloody hell. We went to a dump and each man got a pick, shovel or scoop. I wondered where we were going. This corporal took us into Babylon trench and told us to clear the water out. It was up to your bloody knees. I said to him 'Have we got to walk in that?' He said to me, 'Oh you'll get used to it, you'll sleep in that lot tonight.' I had this scoop and I had to fill it and throw the water over the trench top. First one went over alright, second one a shell landing nearby blew the scoop right out of my hands. I called out, 'I'm alright 'ere!' And the corporal yelled back, 'Never mind that, you'll have to get it out with your bloody hands now!'" **Vernon Atkinson, 14th Y & L Regiment**

A whole month out of the line had worked wonders for the 14th Battalion. They had been close to the

There is a constant call for working parties behind the lines on the Somme.

front and they had put their backs into any work that they had been asked to do, spurred on by the thought that there would be a fairly safe billet at the end of it. They had also trained hard but, perhaps more importantly, the preceding few weeks had provided an opportunity to recharge exhausted batteries.

The improving weather had gone a long way towards this rejuvenation. On Sunday, May 28th, the hottest day of the year so far, the Pals were given a full twenty-four hours' rest from digging. After church parade some men seized the opportunity to stroll among the mature trees while others did nothing at all except loll in the long grass and listen to the band. Closing their eyes the men's thoughts must have drifted back across the Channel to Locke Park and those golden Sundays before the world was plunged into darkness.

Any flights of fancy were brought crashing to earth the following day when the Battalion were ordered to prepare for a march to the trenches on May 30th.

Chapter Ten

Trench raiders

"We have raided the German trenches with glory. We should be proud to think we were chosen out of the whole Division, especially as we are the youngest battalion in it. We have added to the glory of the York and Lancasters, our name being decorated with one Military Cross – earned by Lieutenant Quest for devotion to duty and self-sacrifice when wounded in three places – and two Military Medals, earned by Privates Clarkson and Russell for gallantry, which consisted of leaving the trenches in broad daylight to bring in a wounded comrade who had been left during the raid."
Letter to Major Carrington from Sergeant C. H. Cawthorne, Second Barnsley Battalion, Reproduced in the Barnsley Chronicle of 15th July, 1916.

FROM THE GOMMECOURT SALIENT, the German front line position ran twisting and turning towards the south-east, passing a thorny pimple known as 'The Point,' until it reached a position opposite the British front line at John Copse. From there it made a sharp turn to the south-west, scrawled its way across the forward slopes of the steady rise leading to Serre village, then down across Serre Road to the Heidenkopf.

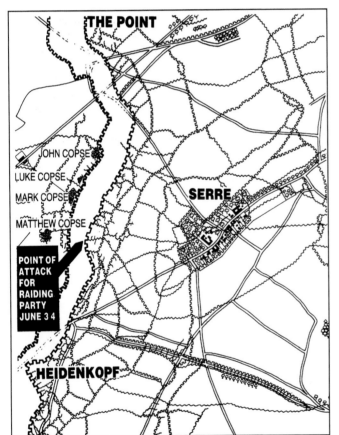

In front of Serre village itself two interesting little bulges swelled out temptingly towards the British lines. Both these small bumps were served at their snouts by communication trenches running back to the second German trench, one hundred and fifty yards behind the first.

The smaller of the two protrusions lay opposite Luke and Mark copses, but the larger faced the British opposite Matthew Copse. That particular portion of the German front line held the dubious distinction of being closer to the British positions than any other part of the German trench system on the Serre sector, excluding forward saps. No-Man's-Land was only one hundred and fifty yards wide at that point.

For that very reason, that small section of the trench was chosen as the target for a raid by a party of men from the 94th Infantry Brigade, more specifically, men of the 14th Battalion York and Lancaster Regiment, the Second Barnsley Pals.

Both the trench raid and its smaller cousin, the night patrol, had been born of the desire on the part of the British generals to ensure that a steady stream

A Bangalore torpedo in position across barbed wire and ready to be exploded. Second Lieutenant Best connected a number of these together to blast a way through the thick German wire. Below and overleaf: *Copies of the actual plans drawn up at the time by Captain Wood.*

of offensive activity flowed in the direction of the Germans. Both were risky, both undertaken under the cloak of darkness, and both were aimed at making the Germans feel that they had no right to be where they were.

The trench raid particularly was conceived as a fillip for the British troops; a means of raising the offensive spirit by giving all ranks an opportunity to engage the Germans after long and tedious months of stagnant trench routine. At the same time it was hoped that the raid would serve as a painful reminder to the German front-line troops that they could be hit quickly and hit hard whenever the British chose to do so.

Apart from the anticipated effects on the relative morale of the armies they also served another purpose – a source of information for the Brigade intelligence officers. Particularly if a few 'gummy-eyed' Germans could be yanked from their dugouts and carted back for questioning and searched for trench maps and pay books.

Any German soldier who died at the hands of the raiders would have buttons, badges and other regimental insignia cut from their uniforms. These, along with the contents of their pockets would be taken back to the waiting arms of eager brigadiers. In short the raids were further acts of terrorism in a war which had already exceeded all known bounds of suffering.

Plans for the raid had been in preparation ever since the Battalion had arrived for its second tour of duty on the Colincamps, Serre sector. The blueprint called for a combined infantry and artillery action, the artillery support coming not only from the 31st Division but also the 29th Division artillery on its right, and the 48th on its left. It was not going to be a half-hearted affair. On the night of the raid the attacking party could count on the support of sixty guns of all calibres, ranging from 18 pounders right up to the 9·2 inch siege howitzers.

As the gunners went to work on their support schedules and calculated their expenditure of shrapnel and high explosive shells, the training of the raiders also began.

Captain Alphonse Wood commanding 'A' Company, was at the forefront of the preparations for the raid. He had taken it upon himself to organise and train the party. To assist him he enlisted the aid of Lieutenant Harold Quest, one of his platoon commanders and Second Lieutenant Best of 'C' Company, the Battalion Scout Officer. Captain Wood next selected nine N.C.O.s and twelve men to operate two pairs of Lewis guns which would protect the flanks of the main party when they were out in No-Man's-Land by sweeping the German parapets with fire. All the men chosen were drawn from men of 'A' and 'C'

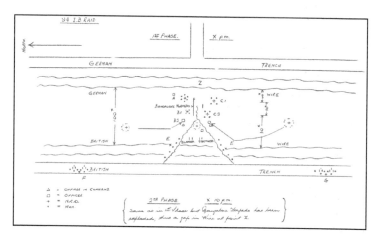

173

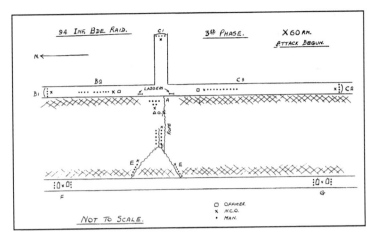

Companies, all that is, except for Private M. Lucas of 'B' Company.

The first item of news that he was able to tell them was that the date for the 'show' had been fixed; 10 p.m. on the night of 5th May, 1916.

"It was some from our Battalion that made a raid on the German lines. Our Officer Best was involved and there was a chap called Fieldsend, a real typical collier lad, a real tough lad in a scrap; and then there was one called Milner, he was a barber. That was the first time that any of our lot had come into direct contact with the enemy." **Charlie Swales, 14th Y & L Regiment**

The time had come to engage the enemy at close quarters and all the long months of training would be put to the test. It was the moment the Pals had been waiting for. On the night of May 5th, some of them would actually leave their trenches and carry the war to the German lines. It did not matter that this was to be a fairly local skirmish when compared with the pitched battles of the previous year, to the Pals it was big enough to show that they were made of the right stuff.

If any secretly feared that they were far too inexperienced for the job ahead, they did not broadcast it. The harsh truth however, was that on May 5th, 1916, the Pals would have had just one month's experience in the fighting zone and out of that month no more than a handful of days in the firing line. Although several of the lads had been lost since the beginning of April the feelings of anticipation mounted as training for the raid got under way.

The first thing that Captain Wood had to do was to split the large group up into seven smaller parties, each designated from 'A' to 'G' and each with a different duty to perform. Every man had to be made aware of his specific role in the overall scheme of the attack. With upwards of seventy men crawling about in the pitch darkness through No-Man's-Land and into the German trenches, Captain Wood had to make sure that all of them knew exactly what they were doing. Any mistakes, any man in the wrong position at the wrong time could spell disaster for the rest of the raiding party.

For some, training meant a little more instruction in the art of clearing hostile dugouts with arms full of Mill's bombs. Other prospective raiders furnished themselves with knobkerries, grisly trench clubs made by mounting a spiked, iron knob on the end of a wooden handle, for use in hand to hand fighting. Such weapons were favoured for their silence as opposed to the use of revolver or rifle, for in the clandestine equation of the raid, silence equalled surprise.

On occasions such as these the hatchet was another favoured tool. Again it was silent in an attack on a person and could also be used to wreck enemy weapons and equipment.

While six of the parties were training with Captain Wood and Lieutenant Quest, the seventh party was placed under the command of Lieutenant Best. It would be their job to blow a way through the German wire. As early as April 5th, the war diary of the 14th Battalion had noted that the barbed wire in front of the German trenches was 'very thick and very high'. The success of the whole enterprise would hinge on their efficiency.

They were to use a device called a Bangalore torpedo, this was a metal tube, usually about six feet long, packed with a high explosive substance called ammonal. It was fired in the usual way by means of a fuse and detonator.

Due to the great depth of the wire to be cut, Lieutenant Best experimented with torpedoes of varying lengths and eventually came up with one that measured sixty feet. Surely, such a device would blast a way through for the raiders.

During the period of experimentation Lance Corporal Critchley of 'C' Company worked closely with Lieutenant Best, aiding and assisting him in joining up the various lengths of tubing. He also practised fixing the fuse and its attendant cable which, on the night, he would have to do in No-Man's-Land amid the thunder of the British bombardment.

Bearing in mind that all the movements had to take place in darkness, both men rehearsed the fixing together of the lengths of tube and the careful poking forward of the bizarre contraption. Time and again they connected the sections as quickly as possible, trying to feel for the contact. To delay on the night might expose the raiders to point blank rifle and machine-gun fire.

On paper at least the plan appeared to be straightforward. By ten o'clock on the night of May 5th, four small parties were to crawl through two gaps cut through their own wire and lie down on the ground about thirty yards out into No-Man's-Land. Two patrols were to be sent out; the first, at nine o'clock and the second at nine-thirty, to ensure that the ground over which the raiders were to advance was free of German troops. The second patrol was also detailed to lay thin white tapes from the gaps in the British wire and take them out quietly up to the German wire at the point where it was to be breached.

After this second patrol had signalled the 'all clear' an intense artillery and trench mortar barrage would fall on the German front, support, reserve and communication trenches, to isolate the garrison in that area of front earmarked for the raid. The barrage would form a box which would prevent the isolated German troops from getting out as well as preventing reinforcements from getting in.

At the same time the guns of the 29th Division would hammer against the Heidenkopf to the south, while those of the 48th concentrated on 'The Point' to the north.

In this way the British hoped to deceive the Germans. With such a fierce barrage falling on their positions they would certainly be expecting something, but with a storm of shrapnel and high explosive spread out over at least three divisional fronts, they would not know exactly where the blow would fall.

After ten minutes of the barrage on the German front line at the point chosen for the raiding party to enter the trench, the artillery would lift its barrage to the second line.

At that point Lieutenant Best and his party were to thrust the Bangalore torpedo under the German wire and blast their way through before the artillery came back to pummel the front line for another half-hour.

Upon the cessation of the hour-long bombardment, the raiding party was to enter the German first trench. Once there, two small groups were to work one either way fifty yards along the fire trench, while another group was to advance up the communication trench for a distance of twenty yards. These groups armed to the teeth with revolvers, bayonets, knobkerries and at least seventy bombs between them, were to barricade the trenches and keep reinforcements at bay. With the blocking parties disappearing around the traverses, Captain Wood and his fellow officers along with the main raiding party, would attempt to wreak havoc among the Germans by throwing bombs into dugouts, smashing machine guns and severing signal cables with hatchets. More importantly they were to take prisoners. It would all be over in about fifteen minutes. A series of red and green rockets bursting colourfully above the British front line would signal the safe return of the raiders with their captives.

The men rehearsed their parts mentally, they rehearsed in their small groups and, as the day drew near, all the groups trained together so that Captain Wood could see how the pieces of his human machine meshed together, and if any of the cogs required a little extra oiling.

By May 2nd everything was ready. Detailed operation orders had been drawn up and copies circulated to all battalion commanders in 94 Brigade, the 170th Brigade of the Royal Field Artillery and to two trench mortar batteries.

On May 3rd a scheme for the artillery acting in co-operation with the raiding party was issued.

Some slight amendments to the operation orders were made on May 4th, to the effect that a sapper of 223rd Field Company of the Royal Engineers was to fire the Bangalore torpedo electrically and that the raiders were to enter the German trench a little earlier than previously planned.

Everybody waited, and then, with just twenty-four hours to go, the whole operation was postponed for 'various reasons'.

For the raiding party the delay was a disappointment, for they had trained hard and had built them-selves up for action; they were left feeling deflated. Their only consolation was that the raid was re-scheduled for the night of June 3rd/4th. This postponement at least appeared to give the Pals a whole

94 Infantry Brigade Operation Order No.38.
-----------------o-----------------

Reference Trench Map, 57 D. N.E.
3 and 4 (parts of) 1/10,000.   3-6-16.
----

1.   A raid on the German Trenches opposite the left section of the Divisional front will take place at 12 midnight, June 3-4. The point of entry will be K 29 b 1200.

2.   The raiding force will consist of 11 N.C.O's. and 70 men of the 14th. York and Lanc. Regt., under the command of Capt. A. Wood, assisted by Lieut. H. Quest and 2/Lt. G.H.T. Best, all of that Battalion.

3.   The force will be divided into the following parties:-
   (a) Wire - cutting party, and hostile}
        trench entrance guard.   } 1 N.C.O. & 6 men.

   (b) Left raiding party (including   } 1 Officer, 2
        blocking party of 1 N.C.O. & 4 men.} N.C.O's. & 14 men.

   (c) Right raiding party (including two}
        blocking parties, each of 1 N.C.O.} 1 Officer, 3
        and 4 men.   } N.C.O's. & 18 men.

   (d) Communication Guard.   1 N.C.O. & 10 men.

   (e) Reserve and Receiving Party (divided}
        into 2 sections, each of 1 N.C.O.   } 2 N.C.O's. &
        and 5 men.   } 10 men.

   (f & g) Right and Left Lewis Gun crews,}
        respectively, each of 1 N.C.O.   } 2 N.C.O's. &
        and 6 men.   } 12 men.

4.   The following Artillery will operate:-
     10   18 pr. Batteries (1 from 29 Div., 7 from 31st.Div.
                and 2 from 48th.Div.).
      4   4.5" Howitzer Batteries (1 from 29 Div., 2 from
                31 Div., and 1 from 48 Div.).
      1   9.2" Howitzer Battery.
      1   60 pr. Battery.
      1   6" Howitzer Battery.
                supplemented by
     10   Medium Trench Mortars.

5.   At 12 midnight an intense bombardment of enemy's first and second lines from K 29 b 46 to K 35 a 22 will be opened by 18 prs. and 4.5" Howitzers of 29th. and 31st. Divisions; 18 prs. and 4.5" Howitzers of 48th. Division will continue bombardment to the North as far as the "POINT". 9.2" Howitzers will fire on QUADRILATERAL. 60 prs. on communication trenches leading from SERRE to 3rd. line. 6" Howitzers on communication trenches between third and second lines.

   (b) At 12-10 am. Batteries firing on German front line between K 29 d 1580 and K 29 b 2325 left to second line and continue. Remainder continue except 6" Howitzers and 8 centre Medium Trench Mortars, who cease fire.

   (c) At 12-40 am. centre batteries return to front line; 6" Howitzers and Medium Trench Mortars re-open fire.

   (d) At 1 am. the 4.5" Howitzers and Medium Trench Mortars cease fire; remainder gradually slacken and cease fire at 1-20 am.

6.   At 12-10 am. party "A" of the raiding force will cut the enemy's wire opposite the point of entry by means of a "Bangalore Torpedo"; immediately after this, parties B and C enter the enemy's trench.

7.   The O/C. Raiding Force will recall his men not later than 12-25 am.; their return to our trenches will be notified to the Artillery both by telephone, and by a series of RED rockets fired from vicinity of Company Headquarters in ROB ROY, west of MATTHEW COPSE.

8.   O/C. 14th. York & Lancs., together with an Artillery Officer from the Left Group, will be at the Company Head-quarters mentioned in para.7 throughout the operations.

9.   Watches will be synchronised at Brigade Headquarters, COURCELLES, at 9 pm. on Saturday, June 3rd.1916.

                         G. Piggott, Capt.
                              Bde. Major,
                         94 Infantry Brigade.

month extra in which to prepare for this, their first face-to-face encounter with the enemy. However, the month of May was given over to training for the 'Big Push', so practice sessions for the raid had to be fitted in with this and the gruelling trips out on digging parties.

The final practice took place on the night of the Battalion's last Sunday in Bus Wood. Not for them the joys of a full twenty-four hours' respite from their hard work of the previous few days. Watched by the Divisional Commander himself, Major General Wanless O'Gowan, they ran through the raid for the umpteenth time. If they didn't have it all worked out now they never would get it right. Surely a whole month had been long enough for several small changes of plan to become imprinted on the memory. True, the artillery bombardment was planned to be much shorter, but now there would be more guns, and this time their shells would fall almost as far back as the village of Serre itself.

As Captain Wood prepared to lead 'A' Company back into the line the next day he received the following message:

Dear Wood,
General O'Gowan spoke to me on the telephone this morning and asked me to let you know how splendidly he thought last night's practice went off; and that your scheme and its attendant technical details, (notably the "BEST" torpedo) will no doubt, shortly become the sealed pattern for raids. Yours sincerely, (Signed) F. S. G. Piggott Brigade Headquarters 29-5-16

On May 30th the Battalion turned its back on the haven of Bus Wood, and after eating dinner en route just outside Courcelles, they tramped into the trenches once more and took over the left sector of the Divisional front from the Accrington Pals.

Nothing seemed to have changed on the other side of the British wire. Still the Pals were plagued with an apparently limitless collection of projectiles of all shapes and sizes, which screeched across No-Man's-Land in angry swarms. This time however, the Pals had a few tricks up their sleeves. This time the Barnsley lads were going to hit back.

On June 2nd, with a little over thirty-six hours to go, the British gun layers began the job of sighting then registering on their targets over in the German lines.

June 3rd, the day of the raid, was King George's birthday and the members of the raiding party were determined to celebrate it by delivering up a few prisoners to Brigade Headquarters.

Just before dusk the raiders fell in outside 'A' Company headquarters which was situated in Rob Roy trench, just west of Matthew copse.

A party of trench raiders receiving last minute instructions.

"My mate Hoppy went on the raid. The officers were camouflaged, there wasn't a shiny button to be seen and they had their faces blacked. They had 'knobbling' sticks and things like that." Frank Lindley, 14th Y & L Regiment

They were indeed a sinister looking mob, standing there with the whites of their eyes flashing out from blackened faces. Their uniforms, covered here and there with sandbags, were fastened together with pieces of string or toggles. Each man had removed every trace of who he was and which unit he belonged to in case he was captured, or worse still killed. All collar flashes, regimental buttons, identity discs, paybooks and even personal letters, had all been bundled together and left behind. Pouches and pockets bulged with bombs – almost every man brandished a knobkerrie or hatchet. Lance Corporal Critchley and six more men were also burdened with several sections of sixty-foot Bangalore torpedo, as well as the fuse, and several pairs of wire cutters.

All went well as they filed down the communication trenches towards the firing line, equipment rattling and clanking as they walked. Everything was going according to schedule.

All they had to do was slip over the parapet, haul their equipment out and start the long crawl forward, through the gaps in their own wire and then wait patiently in the early summer grass that sprouted in No-Man's-Land. They would be there in plenty of time to watch the artillery barrage get under way on the stroke of midnight. After ten minutes of watching the fireworks playing among the German trenches they would crawl forward, place the torpedo, and blow a neat path through the German wire. Then they would go in – it would be as easy as falling off a log, but as soon as they reached their own front line trench, the plan started to go wrong.

The raiding party were due to emerge from the fire trenches just to the south of that portion of the front line held by the 14th

Orders outlining purpose of the raid.

```
O.C. 14th. Y.& L.        (for information).
SECRET.
                        Night of 3/4th.June 1916.
                 --------------------
        Required as soon as possible:-

        1.  Number of prisoners, giving Regiment.
        2.  Approximate damage to Bosche.
        3.  Our casualties.
        4.  Prisoners to be sent under Captain Wood's
            arrangements to No.53 Billet, COLINCAMPS,
            where they will be taken over by the
            Division.
        5.  No interrogation of prisoners to take place
            except name of Regiment, if not obtainable
            otherwise.
        6.  Full details of raid to be rendered by
            evening of June 4th.


Copy sent to Capt.Wood.
------------------                      1-6-16.
```

No.	Rank and Name.	I.D.No.	No.	Rank and Name.	I.D.No.
485	L/C. Critchley.	1	962	Pte. Symons.	39
553	Pte. Dunn. A.H.	2	1191	" Dale. J.	40
491	" McNulty.	3	1134	" Allen. E.	41
1247	L/C. Dryden.	4	170	" Lever. J.	42
580	Pte. Haddock. T.W.	5	78	" Naylor. A.	43
1197	" McKelvey.	6	1284	" Barker. J.	44
567	" Causer.	7	992	" Firth. C.	45
495	" Swaine.	8	101	" Sheridan.	46
77	L/C. Morgan.	9	148	Sgt. Garside. H.	47
530	Pte. Milner.	10	974	Pte. Jubb. J.H.	48
510	" Clay.	11	1116	" Teale. C.	49
1053	" Fieldsend.	12	102	" Shannon. J.	50
		13	1319	" Turton. A.	51
1220	" Martin.	14	143	" Fearn.	52
969	Cpl. Atkinson.	15	161	" Illingworth. G.T.	53
194	Pte. Robinson. A.	16	64	" Jones. E.	54
32	" Davies.J.E.	17	496	" Taylor.	55
181	" McLee.	18	38	" Freeman. H.	56
149	" Galloway. G.	19	171	" Lewis.	57
160	L/C. Iveson. G.	20	29	Cpl. Draisey. J.T.	58
19	Pte. Clare.	21	5	" Ashton. J.H.	59
180	" Maddigan.	22	1320	Pte. Lyons. F.	60
97	" Smith.	23	650	" Beevors. A.	61
984	" Symons. F.	24	947	" Hobson.	62
627	Sgt. Gill.	25	176	" Mallinson. J.	63
1050	L/C. Wilkinson.	26	1327	" Bonds. J.	64
659	" McGuigan.	27	1257	" Ledger. T.	65
571	Pte. Mulligan.	28	68	" Laughton. A.	66
1075	" Wilson. E.P.	29	204	" Sellars. A.	67
1209	" Jackson.	30	1320	" Denmar.	68
1217	" Pepper.	31	34	" Ecclestone.	69
957	" Squires. E.	32	1055	" Appleyard.	70
1073	" Monagan.	33	635	" Denton.	71
636	" Hanson.	34	562	" Popplewell.	72
1223	" Davison.	35	71	" Lucas.	73
1354	Sgt. Johnson. W.R.	36		Sapper Vickers.	
209	L/C. Thomas. L.	37		Capt. A.Wood.	
169	" Lomas. R.G.	38		Lieut./H.Quest.	
				2/Lieut. G.H.T.Best.	

Battalion. On the night of June 3rd that section of the trench system was being manned by the Hull 'Commercials' (10th East Yorkshire Regiment).

Captain Wood had specifically asked for several of the fire bays to be left clear of men to allow his seventy-two strong party a smooth passage over the parapet. If it had been left to the officers of the Hull 'Commercials' his wishes would have been granted. Anticipating a swift and forceful reply to the British barrage and taking into account the dilapidated state of some of their trenches, they desired to withdraw half their front-line garrison into the freshly dug assembly trenches a little way behind.

The higher authorities at Division would have done well to have listened to the suggestions from the officers of the 10th East Yorkshire Regiment, but their requests to vacate a section of the front on the night of the raid went unheeded. It was a decision that had grave consequences for both the Hull men and members of the raiding party.

Reaching the front, progress of Captain Wood's party was hindered due to congestion in some of the fire bays and the minutes were ticking away towards midnight. Several of the small parties slithered over the parapet and across the shell holes out towards the German wire, but some of the men were struggling to get themselves and all their paraphernalia over the 'lid' and into position with just moments remaining.

With hearts thumping and feeling thoroughly flustered, they valiantly attempted to locate and join up with their respective parties already out in No-Man's-Land, but the artillery working to schedule, couldn't wait.

On the dot the British guns opened up and shells screamed and roared over the heads of the disorganised and, by now, unhappy band of men.

For the first few seconds of the bombardment most of the raiders were more intent upon keeping their heads down than on concentrating on their particular role. 2nd Lieutenant Best and Lance Corporal Critchley set about the task they had performed so many times before in training. Section by awkward section they began to assemble the long lengths of Bangalore torpedo and fitted the fuse wire. 2nd Lieutenant Best gave the order for it to be carried towards the German wire and Privates Dunn and McKelvey lugged the long tube forward.

Suddenly, the men picked out the sound of one shell quite clearly above the rest and moments later a premature burst rained searing fragments of metal down onto No-Man's-Land, wounding Lieutenant Quest and several others. From then on the situation began to go from bad to worse.

At ten minutes past midnight the barrage lifted to the second German trench and 2nd

Private William Henry Clarkson

178

Lieutenant Best moved forward to fire the torpedo, but he found it not quite in the correct position. Something was preventing it from being shoved forward and as Private Dunn moved along the joined sections of aluminium pipe he came across the body of Private McKelvey slumped across it.

Heaving McKelvey's body aside Private Dunn hurriedly drove the tube under the German wire and connected the detonator. Taking cover he fired the torpedo, then he leapt up and raced forward through the gap, but after several strides he came to an abrupt halt. Stretching before him, off into the darkness, lay some fourteen feet of uncut wire.

Small parties of raiders collected together where the wire had been blown and they had to wait five more minutes trapped in No-Man's-Land as Lance Corporal Critchley attacked the murderous barbs with a pair of wire cutters.

Roused into action by the opening of the British bombardment Major Berthold and Hauptmann Wetzke of the German 169th Regiment had already called for immediate artillery support to be directed against the British trenches. In the German front line Oberleutnant Hodel in command of the 5th Company of the 169th Regiment, and Fahnrich Arnold, one of his junior officers on trench duty, were also on edge. They still had several patrols out in No-Man's-Land who were cut off by the heavy British barrage. The patrols were only able to return when the British guns lifted their fire from the front line. Both men noticed the barrage switch to the rear trenches and, fearing the worst, Fahnrich Arnold let off a series of red flares, a pre-arranged signal requesting counter fire from his own artillery. The German retaliation was swift and sure, and a curtain of fire descended on the British front line positions.

Back in the trenches held by the Pals, three men were killed and four were wounded. Many more were spared injury as the officers withdrew the men into deep, narrow slit trenches behind the front line. On their right the Hull Commercials suffered badly for they were packed into trenches which were in a poor state of repair. Many of them were buried alive as shells smashed into the parapets and all but levelled most of the fire bays.

Not more than one hundred and fifty yards away, deep within the German wire Lance Corporal Critchley heard a twang as he cut through the last strand.

He was first man through, closely followed by 2nd Lieutenant Best, Lieutenant Quest, and several other men who dashed towards the German parapet, but they were already under fire. Musketier Heinhofer, standing guard on the right flank of the 3rd Company of the 169th Regiment, had suddenly noticed movements as if men were pushing their way through the damaged wire. Due to the pitch darkness, the noise and the smoke and dust of the barrage he had not seen or heard the raiders cross No-Man's-Land, and even now he could not be sure just how many British soldiers were worming their way through the wire towards him. He opened fire and the Pals fired back. They were almost upon him when a shot from the revolver of Lance Corporal Morgan hit him in the hand. Unable to hold his rifle Heinhofer thought it useless to carry on and ducked down into a disused tunnel which had been run out under the parapet as a listening post. The few Pals who had managed to get through the German wire hurled themselves over the German parapet and into the unknown.

By now the highly organised plans, the sketches and rehearsals counted for nothing as the affair further degenerated into a shambles. Instead of the fifty or so men detailed to take the trench in organised groups and carry the raid to a successful conclusion, only a handful of men from mixed parties had actually entered. The rest were tending their wounded Pals out in No-Man's-Land, casualties caused by the British barrage.

Weapons and personalised arms of raiders:
1. *Knotted rope soaked in paint to add weight and stiffen it. Ex-Pals.*
2. *Cudgel carried by Y & L officer.*
3. *Stabbing knife and scabbard.*
4. *Knuckle-dusters, brass. Carried by Barnsley Pal.*
5. *Webley revolver.*
6. *Very Light Pistol.*

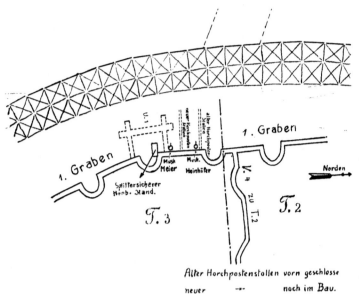

German drawing of the sector raided by the Second Barnsleys and included with their report of the incident. The 'Splittersicherer' is a shrapnel-proof shelter; the dotted lines (U.1) indicate the deep underground dugout. The two sets of dotted parallel lines jutting out towards the German wire are listening posts. The positions of musketiers Meier and Heinhofer are indicated by the two small circles. Sector identifying letters 'T' are changed to 'S' a few weeks later. (Compare with map on page 194)

For three violent and highly disorganised minutes a confused encounter raged in a small sector of the German trench. Dashing along the firm wooden duckboards the raiders frantically searched for anything remotely resembling the entrance to a dugout. Coming across two likely holes they tossed a couple of Mills bombs in.

Amid the momentary flashes of the resulting explosions several revolver shots cracked out. Lieutenant Quest and Lance Corporal Morgan had pursued the hapless Musketier Heinhofer and were shooting blindly down the tunnel at him. Heinhofer was screaming for help and by now he had a leg wound to contend with as well as the wound to his right hand. Where could his fellow sentry Meier have got to?

His comrade Musketier Meier was unconsconcious, blown down into the entrance to a deep mined dugout a little futher along the trench to the south. All was not lost however. Coming up from the depths of the dugout, Musketier Meschenmoser leapt into a splinterproof shelter to the left of the dugout entrance. Meschenmoser heard Heinhofer's cries for help and rushed towards the Pals throwing hand grenades at a few of them standing on the parapet.

After just three minutes Captain Wood realised that it was futile to continue with the raid with so few men. Already the sound of German bombers working their way down the front line and the communication trench could be heard quite clearly above the artillery duel. Following Musketier Meschenmoser out of their deep dugout, Unteroffizier Marzenell and Musketiers Dapp, Kuhner and Meier, who by now had recovered consciousness, were moving towards the Pals and were pushing them back with hand grenades, hurling one after another as long as their supplies lasted.

Suddenly, a German hand-grenade dropped among the raiders and Lance Sergeant Garside received six pieces of shrapnel in his body, and Private Galloway was killed. Captain Wood gave out the recall password. As the word Kantara flew from the lips of one raider to another a dozen Pals climbed and scrambled out of the German trench and scurried back towards the gap in the German wire, leaving the body of Private Galloway behind.

The last man out was Private Symons, half carrying, half dragging the wounded Lance Sergeant Garside, tossing bombs into the German trench behind him as he went.

Now, with German bombs exploding all around and machine-gun bullets hissing through the grass, they made their way back towards safety. There was little point now in being stealthy. Pausing only to pick up wounded colleagues they beat a hasty retreat across No-Man's-Land.

Lieutenant Quest and 2nd Lieutenant Best were the last two men to jump into the British front line. By half past midnight most of the raiding party were accounted for and the wounded men were being sent down to the advanced dressing stations.

By any standards the entire episode had proved to be a fiasco and not all the blame lay at the feet of the raiding party themselves. Certainly they had looked the part, but for all that they were lacking the knowledge of trench fighting to carry out such an enterprise.

Thrown off balance by several hitches as events swiftly overtook them the members of the raiding party never fully recovered.

The affair had failed to achieve its objectives on almost every count. For a start there were no prisoners, and without prisoners there was no information. The sum total of the raiding party's achievements had been the bombing of what they thought were two German dugouts and the feeling that they had shot two German soldiers. The raiding party could by no

Report on Raid by a Party of 14th. York & Lancs.
Regt. during night of June 3rd. & 4th.1916.
----

    1 beg to report that the partial success that resulted
was due in the first place to the excellent work done by Lt.
Quest and 2nd.Lt. Best.   Lt. Quest was wounded in two places
in the five minutes and he carried out his work thoroughly,
and actually shot one German himself in their trenches.
    I cannot speak too highly of the work done by 2nd.Lt. Best
who helped to place the "Bangalore Torpedo" in the German wire
and exploded it, leading his men into the enemy trench and
shooting a German there.   Both were of the utmost assistance
to me in getting our men back on the return journey, and helped to carry our wounded back.   They were last in our trenches
on "N" side of "Warby".
    I did not know till after Lieut. Quest's return that he
had been wounded.
    I cannot speak too highly of the conduct of the following
men.

        485 L/Cpl. Critchley.   )
        553 Pte. Dunn.   )
        580   "   Haddock.   ) C..Coy.
        491   "   McNulty.   )
        148 L/Sgt. Garside.   )
        959 Cpl. Atkinson.   )
        169 L/Cpl. Lomas.   ) A. Coy.
         77   "   Morgan.   )
        962 Pte. Symons. J.   )
        984   "   "   F.   )

            A. Wood,   Capt.
            14th. York & Lancs. Regt.
            ----

means have been certain that they had actually killed the Germans. In fact they hadn't. In the small sector of the trench chosen for the raid, only Musketier Heinhofer had been shot and wounded and Musketier Meschenmoser had been wounded by a grenade splinter in the bombing duel. Further north one man was killed and seven wounded by the British barrage, including Oberleutnant Hodel who had been hit as he had stood on the top to get a better view of what was happening in No-Man's-Land.

No one could say that the Germans had been hit hard. The raid did succeed in one of its aims — the Pals, if nothing else, had been 'blooded'. Fourteen of them had wounds to prove it, Privates Clare, Galloway and Hanson were dead, and the absence of a comforting tick by the name of Private J. McKelvey on the nominal roll, told its own tale as to the uncertainty of his fate. He had last been seen as if dead sprawled across the Bangalore torpedo in front of the German wire. When the dead and wounded from the front line garrisons of both the 14th Battalion and the Hull Commercials were also included, the 'offensive spirit' began to look like an extremely expensive commodity.

For over sixty minutes after the raiding party had returned the British and German guns were still hammering away though they began to slacken as 2 a.m. approached. For the rest of the night the guns remained silent as both sides set to work to repair the damage to the trenches, and the dig out of their buried colleagues.

While the guns were relatively silent the German patrol which had returned a few hours earlier, went out once more to search the ground over which the raiding party had moved. They came across what they thought were three dead bodies. They could find no clue as to which Regiment the dead men were from, but they took back with them five steel helmets, one revolver, one axe, one club, a pair of gloves and a few Mills bombs. Due to heavy British rifle and machine-gun fire the German patrol were forced to leave the bodies where they lay.

After 'Stand to' at dawn one of the Pals noticed a man, alive but obviously wounded, eighty yards away in No-Man's-Land beyond the wire.

After watching the man for some time, someone recognised him as Private McKelvey, last seen by Private Dunn some six hours earlier. By now it was broad daylight, any man who went out to fetch McKelvey would expose himself to the Germans and would face almost certain death. But the wounded man had

Report on a Raid carried out by 14th. York & Lancs.
Regt. on Night of 3-4th. June 1916.
-- ----------------------------

The object of this raid was to gain any information
possible about the German trenches, to secure prisoners,
and to increase the morale of our troops.

The party detailed for this enterprise consisted of
3 Officers and 72 other ranks, with 4 Lewis Guns - and
Artillery.

The hour fixed for the commencement of the enterprise
was 12 midnight.

Every precaution was taken, during training, to ensure
that there would be no hitch ; but, on the night of the
raid, there appears to have been some congestion in certain
fire-bays, from which all the paraphenalia, men, etc. were
to emerge and get into position prior to the commencement
and this was the cause of some of the party being flurried
as the enterprise opened.

The intense bombardment lasting for the first ten minutes does not appear to have been sufficiently intense -
and during this, and before the party moved forward towards
the German trenches, 1 Officer and some men were wounded
by what was thought to have been a premature burst of shell.
A Bangaloe Torpedo (60 ft.long) was sent to make a line
through the German wire, and this was most successful; but,
it was not long enough and therefore about 14 ft. of extra
wire had to be cut by hand, and this was done without any
difficulty. This was fired about 12-11 a.m., and by 12-16
a.m. some of the men had entered the trench, and at this
hour Captain Wood was in his alloted position at the point
of entry.
Here, the detailed order of procedure appears to have
broken down, and instead of the whole of the party detailed to enter the trench doing so, only about 12 men of mixed
parties with Lieut. Quest and 2nd.Lt. Best did so - and
after they had been in the trenches about 3 minutes, Capt.
Wood, who was in command, seeing that it was impossible to
continue further with his few men, recalled them from the
trenches. The men who should have been inside and were
not, were in "No man's land" looking after their wounded
pals.
I am glad to report, with reference to this bombardment, our Casualties were only 3 killed and 4 wounded, and
I attribute this to the fact that the Officers commanding
my Companies took precautions to withdraw the men from the
front line into deep narrow slit trenches a few yards behind.

I would single out the follwoing Officers, N.C.O's.,
and men as deserving of special mention in connection with
this enterprise:-

Capt.A.Wood.
To this Officer belongs the credit of having
trained and organised the whole party. That this
had been done satisfactorily was shewn in the final
practice which was held a few nights prior to the
enterprise taking place, and it was through no fault
of his that the affair was not a total success. He,
on the night of the raid, acted with great coolness
and set a good example to his subordinates.

2nd.Lt.Best.
I can not speak too highly of this Officer.
He was in sole charge of the Bangalore Torpedo used
to cut the wire, and it was he who produced one 60 ft.
in length. He helped to fix the torpedo in position,
actually fired it, and led his party into the trenches.

182

*Private
Henry Clare
14/19, Cudworth*

*Private
George Galloway
14/149, Barnsley*

*Private
Archibald Hanson
14/636, Barnsley*

Left: The bodies of Clare and Hanson are brought back from No-Man's-Land; probably killed by shrapnel from British shells which fell short. They are buried at the Sucrerie Cemetery at Colincamps. Galloway is left behind in the German trench, killed during the hand grenade fight with the men of the 3rd Company of 169th Regiment. Galloway's body is not recovered, he has no known grave. He is remembered on the Thiepval Memorial, Tier 14A, Face 14B.

He showed the greatest dash and resource, and it was through his efforts that the majority of the wounded returned safely.

Lt.H.Quest.

Although wounded in two places during the first 5 minutes of the bombardment, this Officer did not hesitate to go forward, but entered the enemy's trenches, and assisted in controlling those who had entered with him.

77 L/Cpl.Morgan.

This N.C.O. was in charge of the only complete party that entered the trenches, which proved that he had full control of the few men under him.

485 L/Cpl.Critchley.

This N.C.O. helped fearlessly Lieut. Best in the fixing and firing the Bangalore Torpedo and was the first man through the wire after it had been cut.

553 Pte.H.Dunn.

The man, when one of the men detailed to carry the torpedo into position, was wounded, took his place, and assisted L/Cpl.Critchley in cutting through that part of the wire left uncut by the torpedo.

962 Pte.J.Symons.

This man covered the retirement of the party getting out of the trenches by bombing the Communication Trench, and when all were out except 1 wounded man, he helped him to get out of the trench.

In conclusion, and as a sequel to this raid, I attach a special report as to the recovery of one member of the raiding party who had been left in "No man's land" apparently killed.

W. B. Hulke, Lt.Col.
14th.S.Bn. Y.& L.Regt.

been out there unattended for several hours already, and by nightfall it would perhaps be too late to save him.

At least one man had come to a decision. Without hesitation Private W. Clarkson hauled himself over the parapet, went out through the British wire and scrambled over the ground towards McKelvey. Hoisting him on his back he carried him
7-6-16.
back to the wire, but then ran into difficulties.

Seeing Private Clarkson struggling with his precious cargo and perhaps thinking about his poor brother two months earlier, Private Arthur Russell climbed out of the front line trench, dashed through the wire and helped Clarkson to bring their wounded Pal in. Loud cheering from the men of the Second Barnsley accompanied the rescue.

To their credit, and probably out of admiration for the displays of heroism, the Germans never fired a shot, and that in spite of being subjected to the raid only hours before.

For their efforts on that morning in early June both Private Clarkson and Arthur Russell were recommended for the Military Medal.

"I witnessed this act of gallantry on the part of your husband and brought the same to the notice of the Battalion officers with the result as shown. I am sure that you will feel proud of your husband, and well you may be." Letter to Mrs. Clarkson from Second Lieutenant Hirst of 'A' Company, reproduced in the Barnsley Chronicle of 15th July 1916.

"We the undersigned, write a few lines to congratulate you on having a son who by his brave conduct has won the honour and friendship of all his surrounding friends and comrades, not only on this occasion but at different times when he has not been under the eyes of his officers. But he has at last been told that he is to receive the Military Medal for bravery, and we his brother bearers feel it is an honour to us to have the presence of your son amongst us. We are sure you will agree with us in giving credit where it is due and will accept these congratulations." Letter to Mrs. F. Hirst, mother of Private Arthur Russell, from his fellow stretcher-bearers. Reproduced in the Barnsley Chronicle of 15th July 1916.

Later that day the 14th Battalion were relieved by the First Bradford Pals and marched back to the sanctuary of Warnimont Wood. The following day they joined up with the Sheffield City Battalion and the Accrington Pals for the march to Gezaincourt, a village set in the heart of a pleasant valley close to the town of Doullens. Marching along they could not fail to notice the increased volume of traffic travelling in the opposite direction. Above all the Pals noted that there were far more guns on the move than they had seen before.

> *"Up started rumbling the guns, they came up nearly wheel to wheel. A while before the big attack we were short of 'ammo' and the rumour was that all the engineers were on strike, so there was a hold up in making it. I never knew if it was true – it was the bush telegraph working again."* Frank Lindley, 14th Y & L Regiment

When the 'Big Push' finally got under way the war would almost certainly be over in a matter of weeks.

On the way their Corps Commander, General Hunter-Weston, made a point of halting the marching columns to congratulate the raiding party on their 'good show'. It was perhaps a politic move on his part. With so little to show for so many casualties the men of the 14th were probably in need of someone in authority to reassure them that their Pals had not died in vain. After all, they still had faith at this time, in the words of their commanders.

```
        Report on the recovery of No.1196. Pte McKelvey.J. C.Coy,
            14th Y & L, from "No Man's Land" when wounded,
                      by No.20. Pte Clarkson.W.H.
            _____


              After "stand to"on the morning of the 4th June, when a
        raiding party had returned after a visit to the German trenches,
        a man apparently wounded was noticed beyond our wire, some
        80 yards from our trenches.
              After observing the man for some time, he was recognised
        as one of the raiding party reported missing, and without any
        hesitation and with the greatest gallantry, No20. Pte Clarkson.W.H.
        went over the parapet, got to the man who he found to be No.1196.
        Pte McKelvey.J.
              He hoisted the wounded man on his back and carried him in,
        amidst the congratulations of all ranks in the vicinity.
              The Germans probably out of admiration for the plucky action
        of Clarkson, never fired a shot.

                        W. Pust. 2nd Lt.
                   A. Coy. 14th Y & L.
                   ------- - ---


                      4-6-16.
                Pte A. Russell.   304.
            _____

              Helped Clarkson to bring the man in after former got into
        difficulties on getting  to edge of our wire.
            _____
```

Chapter Eleven

Over boys and give them hell

"HOW THE GERMAN LINE WILL BE PIERCED. There are people in England today who seriously believe that any attempt we may make upon the German line is foredoomed to failure, and that the war must end in a stalemate, with the troops standing approximately upon the ground they now hold. We are told that both the Allies and the enemy hold lines so strongly fortified, so perfectly defended, that it is humanly impossible that any breach can be made.

"I make this reference to a view which is held by a very large number of intelligent thinking people because it shows how little we have learnt from nearly two years of war. A defensive chain, like every other chain, is as strong as its weakest link. It is not necessary that we should apply uniform pressure at all points along the line, nor is it possible that if the German gave ground he would give ground falling back at all points at the same time. If you crack the outer crust along a sufficiently wide front, and you put your wedge of troops into that crack and broaden it still further, the unbroken crust is valueless for defensive purposes . . .

". . . The only thing that can bring about a stalemate is lack of the artillery and munitions to reduce the undeniably strong defences which the enemy has erected in France and in Flanders. If we have the guns and munitions the breach can be made, and I am one of those who believe we have the tools." **Barnsley Chronicle 27th May, 1916**

IT WAS ALMOST MID-DAY by the time General Sir Douglas Haig had finished packing and had got round to leaving his chateau near Montreuil for the trip to Boulogne and a Channel crossing to England.

The date was June 6th, and the Pals of the 14th Battalion had been hard at it with the 'spit and polish' for several hours in Gezaincourt as General Haig boarded the quarter past one mail boat bound for Dover. The General endured a stormy passage but on reaching his destination he found that the inclement weather was not the sole reason for the apparent gloom which had descended upon the nation. Writing up his daily journal several hours later, Sir Douglas concluded his entry for the day with the following succinct comments.

". . . Military Landing Officer showed me a telegram from Police stating it was reported that Lord Kitchener and Staff on H.M.S. Hampshire had been drowned. Ship struck a mine and sank. Sea very rough."

A few days later the Barnsley Chronicle, predictably, displayed a good deal more passion in recounting the passing of a national hero.

WAR MINISTER'S TRAGIC FATE

LORD KITCHENER AND HIS STAFF DROWNED

THE NATION IN MOURNING

Since the great European war broke out many sensational and tragic happenings have thrilled the populace, but none of these could compare to the grievous shock inflicted upon this nation on Tuesday when it was announced that Lord Kitchener and the members of his personal staff had been sunk on board H.M. Cruiser 'Hampshire', by a mine or torpedo, off the Orkneys while on the way to Russia.

As in other towns the length and breadth of this country and the countries of our Allies, the

information caused the profoundest sorrow in Barnsley and neighbourhood. **Barnsley Chronicle 10th June, 1916**

If Lord Kitchener's loss was a tragedy for the nation, it was a disaster for the men who were part of 'Kitchener's Army'. After all, many of them had joined up for no other reason than he had asked them to.

In August 1914 his military record had assured him of a reputation unequalled by any other soldier or politician in the British Isles. No one else could have commanded such public respect in the early weeks of the war; but now he was gone. He would never see his volunteer

Final stages of the build-up for the 'Big Push' behind the lines at Mailly Maillet, 29th June, 1916.

Army of miners, clerks, dockers, butchers, bakers and candlestick makers, fight its first major battle; and what a battle it was going to be. The 14th Battalion in Gezaincourt talked of little else and the 13th, although still billetted in Mailly Maillet, would have had to have been walking around with their eyes closed not to have noticed the prodigious quantities of small-arms ammunition, trench mortar shells and Mills bombs being ferried towards the trenches. Nothing, it seemed, was being left to chance.

On the Colincamps sector, by now familiar to the Pals, the 210th Field Company of the Royal Engineers had been toiling since the beginning of the month constructing twelve new stores to hold the extra supplies, eight of them being bomb stores to be sited in 'Eczema' trench. The same Company also had orders to build six observation posts for the artillery and two for use by the 94th Brigade. In an area where lack of fresh water was a problem, work had also begun on the laying of a network of four-inch pipes to take water from a huge tank in Bus Wood towards the front line.

In addition to the labouring going on in the Colincamps area, the 31st Division Staff were busy preparing for every eventuality. Three Divisional compounds were being built three miles behind the front line, to house the prisoners everyone expected to see filtering back from the battle zone. The nearest one to the Pals would be near Courcelles-au-Bois, and would consist of three separate cages, specially designed to hold officers, N.C.O.s and men, suitably graded in size. On a less optimistic note the medical services were girding themselves for an increased flow of casualties and there were plans to dig several wide trenches close to the cemetery near the 'Sucrerie' at Colincamps. With such a grand attack in the offing, the digging of these mass graves was a disturbing but logical necessity.

Billetted well away from the 'Sucrerie' the Pals were to be spared the spirit-sapping sight of the mass graves during the build-up to the battle; on the contrary their spirits were high. They were pleased that at last they were being given the opportunity to take part in Sir Douglas Haig's 'Great Push', a ringing slogan which was shortly to become the title of a popular magazine. They were confident that the 'Great Push' or the 'Big Push' would bring the war to a swift conclusion. When the time came for them to leave their trenches, they would stride out across No-Man's-Land, and keep going, over the German lines and all the way to Berlin itself. For its part the Army had thought long and hard about detailed plans which would bring success to the Pals.

General Haig had already drawn up a broad scheme of attack which he had handed to General Rawlinson for more detailed consideration. The British Commander's desire was for the Fourth Army to attack the tactically important ridges and spurs which lay north of the River Somme and fell into the valley of the River Ancre.

Four of General Rawlinson's Corps were to penetrate the German front-line system between Maricourt and the Ancre leaving the 8th Corps alone to deal with the German positions between the river and Serre, three miles to the north.

As part of the 31st Division, the task of the Barnsley Pals, along with the Accrington Pals and the Sheffield City Battalion, was to capture Serre; no more, no less. It was certainly a tough job which they were being asked to perform. Although the Pals had faced the village several times before on their forays into the front-line trenches they had never actually seen it, but it was there all right; as safe and as strong as ever behind its intimidating defences. Despite their meagre front-line experience the Pals felt they were up to it and they would have to be. The success of the entire Fourth Army operation would rest on them reaching and holding all their objectives.

The 31st Division was to deliver its attack using two of its three Brigades. The 94th Brigade were to take the left of the Divisional front with the Leeds, Bradford and Durham Pals of the 93rd Brigade on their right. The 94th Brigade had been assigned a 700-yard stretch of the front running from the eastern edge of John Copse in the north, down to the southernmost tip of Matthew Copse. This frontage was further divided into two equal stretches of 350 yards between the two battalions chosen to lead the assault. The Sheffield City Battalion were to lead off on the left, side by side with the Accrington lads on their right.

Both Barnsley Battalions were to act as reserves for the leading troops, the men of the First Barnsley Battalion were to be in reserve to the Accrington Pals while the majority of the Second Barnsleys were once more relegated to following in the footsteps of the 'Coffee and Bun Boys' of Sheffield.

Each of the two leading battalions were to advance against the German lines in four waves. The first two waves were to roll steadily, irresistably across No-Man's-Land and engulf the first four lines of trenches which lay in front of Serre. They were to stay there and strengthen their position until the remaining two waves broke over them and swept clean through what was left of the orchard on the outskirts of the village, eventually flushing the Germans out of Serre itself.

Meanwhile most of the Barnsley Pals following in their wake, would be winkling out the few German soldiers who had been caught in their trenches and dugouts as the khaki tide had washed over them. Having taken the village and cleared it of German troops, all that the men of the 94th Brigade were required to do was to make good their gains, turn to face north-east, and shield the northern limit of the Fourth Army's advance with the help of the Pals of the 93rd Brigade. This was where the 14th Battalion would come into its own. 'A' Company in fact would have already followed the four waves of the Sheffield City Battalion as far as the fourth German line and would have started converting a German communication trench running back to their front line, into a fire trench facing north-east.

Moving out of Nairne Street trench, two platoons of 'B' Company were to file into the tunnel leading from John Copse to the German front line, break through the thin layer of topsoil which remained, and begin its conversion into a fire trench, joining it up with the trench garrisoned by 'A' Company. As far as the 94th Brigade was concerned, if all went smoothly they would have stitched up the Fourth Army's left flank one hour and forty minutes after leaving their trenches, with a defensive line running east/west from the north-east corner of Serre back to John Copse. Only then could the Pals watch with satisfaction as the whole of the

The sugar refinery west of Serre behind the British lines. It is here that mass graves are dug ready to take the anticipated casualties from 93rd and 94th Brigades.

Fourth Army turned like a giant cartwheel on the Pals' well greased axle and began to roll north, crushing German resistance as it bowled along.

By some strange quirk of military reasoning the responsibility for ensuring that the advance of an entire army went unmolested on its left flank, was entrusted to men who counted their battle experience in days rather than months.

To the immediate left of the Pals there would be no attack, only two-line holding battalions of the 48th Division who were to lay down a thick, protective curtain of smoke to cover the left flank of the 94th Brigade on the morning of the assault, as the Second Barnsleys and the Sheffielders crossed No-Man's-Land. The Army however, had already taken steps to ensure that the Germans to the left of the Pals were kept occupied on the opening day by arranging a diversion against the Gommecourt salient a mile to the north. Two Territorial Divisions of the Third Army would attempt to nip out the village of Gommecourt and the German trenches which skirted a wooded area in front of the village known as Gommecourt Park.

To the right of the two brigades of the 31st Division would be the 'regulars' of the 4th Division and to their right the Incomparable' 29th with orders to seize Beaumont Hamel. The detonation of 40,000 pounds of high explosive beneath the Hawthorn Redoubt would tear open the door to Beaumont Hamel and help to catapult the whole of the 8th Corps forward to their objectives.

It all sounded like a wonderfully well organised plan but first the troops had to get through the German wire. The members of the 14th Battalion raiding party who had managed to reach the safety of their own trenches in one piece could testify to that. If a sixty foot long 'Bangalore torpedo' could not be relied upon to do the trick and blow a gap to allow less than a hundred men through, what were the chances of cutting the wire adequately enough to allow thousands of men a trouble-free passage on a front of some fifteen miles? Even if that prickly problem were solved there was then the question of just how to deal with the deep, underground shelters full of troops. Both the wire and the deep shelters would have to be nullified prior to the advance if any progress was to be made.

General Rawlinson believed he had the perfect solution to both problems. He would make the artillery do all the hard work by having them shell the German wire and front-line trench system non-stop for five days and nights before the infantry went over. The German troops, their remarkable earthworks and their own artillery, were to be subjected to an unprecedented downpour of shrapnel and high explosive. By the time the infantry made their attack it was hoped that there would not be a man left alive on the other side of No-Man's-Land, and if there were they would be in no fit state to face the leading waves of British infantry.

There were guns and shells in abundance and with the Royal Flying Corps dominating the air and pinpointing the artillery's targets to the inch the Pals would have no cause to worry.

On June 7th, as Sir Douglas Haig treated his wife and children to an afternoon show featuring the 'Bing Bong Brothers' at the Alhambra Theatre in London, the Barnsley Pals put themselves in the hands of their superiors and set about rehearsing their part in the coming battle.

"Training was more or less by word of mouth. We'd been trained to go in one man covering another, but on July 1st we went across in waves. They told us to walk.' **Frank Lindley, 14th Y & L Regiment**

This departure from the usual procedure whereby the infantry 'rushed' the German positions on the lifting of an artillery barrage, was founded on General Rawlinson's absolute faith in the ability of the artillery to pound the Germans into near submission.

Since there would be so few Germans left alive in their trenches and villages, and since their own guns would have long since been reduced to heaps of twisted metal, there seemed little point in rushing. The British troops were to walk instead, in extended lines moving forward at no more than 50 yards a minute; the men two or three paces apart, and each line following the preceding one with about a hundred yards separating them.

Of course, at that pace they would be able to take all their equipment with them to save time in consolidating their gains.

In Gezaincourt the Pals of the 14th Battalion discovered that the Royal Engineers, apart from the one hundred and one other jobs they had to attend to, had found time to lay out a small scale model of the area around Serre, showing the village and all the German front-line system. Not only that, in the fields

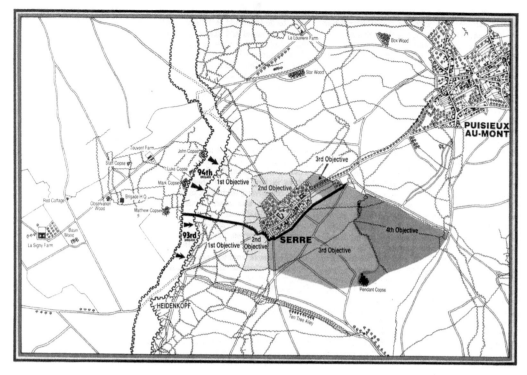

The 31st Division using the two of its three Brigades is to form the extreme left flank of the British 4th Army in its attack on the Somme. 93rd Brigade (Leeds, Bradford and Durham Pals) are to sweep around the fortified village of Serre and end up facing Puisieux au Mont. 94th Brigade is to take Serre, turn to face north-east and shield the northern limit of the entire British attack.

around Gezaincourt they had also marked out a full scale 'mock up' of the same area on ground chosen for its topographical similarity. Rough furrows scratched across the fields, marker tapes and signs traced almost every twist and turn of the German trenches and showed all the 94th Brigade's objectives.

It was hardly the real thing but the Royal Engineers had tried hard to faithfully represent the aerial photographs brought back by pilots of the Royal Flying Corps. The 'mock up' was the only way the Pals were able to rehearse their role.

Almost every day for a week the 14th Battalion practised their attack formations with the Sheffield City Battalion and the Accrington Pals, but their training was seriously hampered by the continued absence of the 13th Battalion due to their tunnelling commitments.

On June 13th the Second Barnsleys marched to Warnimont Wood where, ten days later, they were joined by the main body of the 13th following an advance party who had arrived a day earlier under Major Riall.

At long last all four battalions of the 94th Brigade could begin to rehearse the attack on Serre as one unit, but time was running out.

During the latter part of May and early June, the question of the starting date for the 'Big Push' had been tossed back and forth between the British and French like a tennis ball. The struggle at Verdun and wrangles within the French government had led to Joffre crying out for the British to be ready early and General Haig had agreed. Towards the end of June however the furnace of Verdun was showing signs of cooling. The Germans were to make one last attempt to wrest Verdun from the French, but it would come too late.

They were already doubting the wisdom of pressing their attacks with such disappointing results, and by the middle of June the crisis was all but over. At a meeting of the two Allied commanders on June 17th it was now Joffre's turn to ask for more time, but Haig had pushed ahead with his plans to assist the

French, and by now he saw little point in waiting and perhaps allow the Germans to steal his thunder. They would attack on June 29th; 'Z' day, weather permitting. The date was fixed, all that remained was to choose the hour and General Rawlinson, haggling with the French, chose 7.30 a.m., some three hours after sunrise during high Summer on the Somme.

Not only were the Pals destined to walk into battle, they were to do it in broad daylight rather than at dawn.

Those extra hours of daylight would give more time for artillery observers to spot their targets and for the gunners to put the finishing touches to their bombardment.

The Pals woke up on June 24th to find dull skies and heavy clouds threatening rain. It was 'U' day, the day they would begin full Brigade training on the mock up of Serre near Gezaincourt. By 'Z' day, June 29th, the 13th Battalion would have received a mere four days' training for the biggest battle the British Army had ever faced, and the 14th would have fared little better, having spent just six days more in rehearsing the attack. In spite of their previous training it was a criminally short time in which to prepare for an assault on a village as strongly defended as Serre. As they formed up into their attacking formations and ran through the battle plan they could hear the guns booming as the Pals had never heard them boom before. They had been at it since just after 'reveille' that morning. Well behind the line even the Pals were disturbed by the awesome intensity of the barrage.

"It started then. It started with the little 'uns and then the big 'uns, and then, 'crash', on for days. I think it lasted about seven days, you couldn't tell to the exact day because it was at it night and day and God love me, you didn't know where to put yourself. You were absolutely muddled with the bloody things. Bang, bang, bang, bang. Behind us there were some Navy guns on wagons on a railway line." Frank Lindley, 14th Y & L Regiment

Judging by the incessant rumbling of the guns, clearly audible to people on the south coast of England, it was easy to understand the mood of optimism spreading warmly throughout the British Army. After several long months of being subjected to superior German fire-power in almost every department, the opening of the preliminary bombardment went a long way to raising morale.

Along the 8th Corps front alone there was one heavy gun for every 44 yards, mainly employed in destroying the German trenches, shelters and machine-gun nests with their enormous shells. Every twenty yards or so, there was a lighter field gun, and the burden of cutting the German wire had fallen on the batteries of 18-pounders using mainly shrapnel shells. Cutting barbed wire with shrapnel was a delicate operation requiring a high level of skill and patience and not a little luck bearing in mind the poor quality of some of the shells provided. The 18-pounder shell cases were packed with lead balls which, when exploded in the mid-air by means of a time fuse, sent the bullets whizzing through the wire and blew it away. That was the theory, and with an experienced gunner supplied with sufficient shells of good quality it could be done. Due, however, to a combination of inferior manufacturing techniques resulting in faulty fuses, and inexperienced gunners, many shells exploded too early or too late. The shrapnel balls either dropped harmlessly in No-Man's-Land or the shells exploded in the ground. In both cases the wire was left intact.

The same manufacturing faults were evident among the shells for the heavy guns. A fair proportion of 'duds' left the overworked gun barrels only to signal their arrival in the German rear positions with nothing more harmful than a heavy thud as they buried themselves in the earth.

The artillery bore an enormous responsibility but even after five days and nights they would not be allowed to rest. On the morning of the attack they were to prepare the way for the infantry by moving towards the German rear in a series of rigidly timetabled 'lifts'. It was usual for an intensive barrage falling on the German front line, to 'lift' at zero hour and move back to concentrate on the infantry's first objective for as long as the Army had calculated it would take the attacking troops to get there. The guns would then 'lift' again to the next objective and the infantry would follow.

On the 8th Corps front however, the Army had planned for the artillery to attempt something a little more adventurous to give closer support to the infantry. In the case of the 94th Brigade the field artillery were to 'lift' their barrage from the German front trenches as usual at 'zero' but instead of moving back immediately to the first objective, the barrage was to sweep slowly in front of the troops as far as the fourth German line, lifting at twenty minutes after 'zero' hour to allow the attackers to enter.

There was a strict timetable of movements and that applied to both the infantry and the artillery. There would be little room for error as the barrage moved back to fall on the western edge of Serre twenty minutes after the attack had begun. The orders for the Sheffield City Battalion were quite specific.

"0-28 Third and fourth waves again advance, and pass through the leading line in the fourth German trench approaching as near as possible to our Barrage. Should the first two waves be held up, third and fourth waves will carry them on to the first objective and immediately re-organise for a further advance.

"0-40 SECOND BOUND. The artillery barrage lifts from the Western edge of SERRE village, and the third and fourth waves advance to secure the second objective. 'A' Company after pushing forward bombing parties up communication trenches running to north-west corner of the orchard and round the orchard as far as the barrage permits, will move forward behind 'B' Company occupying the trench running round north-westerly boundary of SERRE village up to point (68), thus forming defensive Rank facing South East . . ." **12th (Service) Battalion, York and Lancaster Regiment. (Preliminary) Operation Order No. 14.**

"Zero + 40. Only small parties of men should be detailed to work through the village itself. All men will closely follow our barrage which will move slowly up the village at a rate of four minutes for the first 200 yards, afterwards lifting at the rate of four minutes for every 100 yards. This barrage finally lifts from the north-east edge of SERRE at 1.20 . . . " **94th Infantry Brigade Preliminary Operation Order No. 45, Public Record Office WO 95/2363**

Orders handed down from the 8th Corps headquarters made it perfectly clear that the set timetable for the artillery could not be altered and that the infantry . . . "must make their pace conform to the rate of the artillery lifts . . . The success or otherwise of the assault largely depends on the infantry thoroughly understanding the 'creeping' method of artillery".

In the case of the Pals, a few days training hardly constituted a 'thorough understanding'. There was of course one major drawback in the artillery operating to pre-determined schedules. If, by some remote chance the infantry did get into difficulty, they would not be able to rely on the artillery for support. Unable to get messages back to Brigade or Division, any troops held up by fierce resistance would be left behind by the artillery bombardment, rolling ever onward according to its timetable. The infantry would be left to sort out their own problems.

On the morning of 24th June however, it was the German troops who were confronted with the problems of how to survive the storm of shrapnel and high explosive being hurled at them from the mouths of the British guns. Undeniably a fair proportion of 'duds' were being fired but even so thousands of shells were exploding with devastating effect on their targets. If Frank Lindley was 'muddled' by the mere sound of the cannonade back in the comparative safety of Warnimont Wood, what of the men who were caught up in its effects?

Sheltering in their deep dugouts and cellars in and around Serre were the men of the 169th Infantry Regiment.

Although there was no such thing as a Pals Battalion in the German Army, many Regiments had strong regional ties. Many officers and men of the 169th Regiment came from the Baden region of south-west Germany, their homes and families in the villages and towns tucked away in the valley of the Rhine, close to the frontiers of France and Switzerland.

As well as its official title, the 169th Infantry Regiment was also known as the 8th Baden Regiment. The Regiment had only come into being during the late 1800s when forty-two new Infantry Regiments were formed out of hitherto half-battalions and placed in the existing German Divisions.

In late 1897 the 169th, (8th Baden), Regiment consisted of two battalions, the first stationed in Karlsruhe; the second in Rastatt. Later the Regiment consisted of three battalions and its troops were stationed in Lahr and Villingen.

At the beginning of the British bombardment the 169th Regiment occupied Serre and the trenches of the front-line system to the west of the village, their positions corresponding almost exactly with the front of

British 8 inch howitzers in action on the Somme. These provide part of the 'Trommelfeuer' on the German positions which lasts seven days.

the 31st Division on the other side of No-Man's-Land. The Regimental front was further sub-divided into four sections which, running north to south, were marked S1-S4. Remarkably the two most northerly sections, S1 and S2, mirrored the two sections of the 94th Brigade's attacking frontage, almost to the yard.

Like the British troops the German soldiers had given a name to many of their trenches for very similar reasons. Their fourth line in front of Serre, the first objective of the 94th Brigade, was known as the 'Tubinger Stellung' named after a town on the River Neckar in Wurttemberg. 'Struensee' trench was named after the commanding officer of the 169th, Major von Struensee, while another senior officer, Major Berthold, also gave his name to a trench south of the village.

North of the 169th Regiment lay the trenches of the 66th (3rd Magdeburg) Infantry Regiment in front of Puisieux au Mont, and further north still, opposite Hebuterne and almost up to Gommecourt Park, was the sister regiment of the 169th, the 170th (9th Baden). Together the three regiments constituted the 104th Infantry Brigade of the 52nd Division.

For the men of the 169th the opening of the British bombardment signalled the onset of a week-long ordeal under what they called the 'Trommelfeuer', the 'drumfire'.

They had sheltered from heavy bombardments before but as the day progressed and the intensity of the barrage persisted it became obvious that this time they were facing something that went far beyond any artillery fire they had previously experienced.

> *"On 24.6 at 6 a.m. brisk enemy artillery fire was brought into action on the whole regiment's sector and the north and south adjoining positions, at first mainly small calibre shrapnel. During the day, however, shells of small and medium calibre also appeared which in the first place were fired against the communication trenches and especially the trench junctions and rear areas. Our own artillery returned the enemy fire at a steady rate over the entire enemy position. Our own troops were held in increased readiness. They all put themselves in position.*

> Note to reader: Keep in mind that German time is one hour ahead of British time.

192

Gas shells or not, there were definite plans to release poison gas from the British line whenever the wind blew towards the Germans.

A short while before the bombardment a large working party of the Hull 'Commercials' had struggled to lug heavy gas cylinders up to special

An 8 inch shell explodes on German positions on the Somme.

emplacements dug out from under the front-line fire steps. Several officers and men of the same battalion found that releasing the gas was a dangerous business. As soon as the German artillery replied to the British fire, many cylinders were buried while others were damaged and started to leak. Often this led to the gas causing more casualties among the British troops detailed to release it than it caused among the Germans.

Nevertheless by midnight of 24th/25th June, after some eighteen hours of shelling, six men of the 169th Regiment were dead, fourteen were wounded and one was missing. For the men left unhurt there was to be no reprieve. Although the shellfire slackened off during the night, at times it became almost impossible for them to distinguish between individual shells bursting and hammering away at their trenches above. The explosions appeared to fuse together in one long thunderous roll, beating out a relentless tattoo on nerves tightening by the minute.

The sound and the fury went on, and on.

Leutnant Schwendemann, who came from Lahr, was the first officer of the 169th Regiment to die during the first three days of the British bombardment. His death along with that of ten other men on 26th June, took the total number of casualties up to twenty-three dead and fifty-three wounded plus the man who had not been seen or heard of since the barrage began. It was indeed a grim time for the German troops, powerless as they were to prevent the loss of their comrades.

There was little they could do except to hope and pray that they would be spared when the bombardment finally stopped, if it stopped at all. Only then would they be able to do something about it. For the moment however the 'Trommelfeuer' raged on above them and it appeared that General Rawlinson's faith in the artillery was being vindicated.

"On 27.6 enemy artillery and mortar fire continues undiminished. The destruction of the trenches,

dugouts and obstacles increases in spite of the constant work of all companies. The 1st Platoon Pioneer Company 104 under Oberleutnant Le Blanc is placed at the disposal of the Regiment again. The whole Pioneer Company 104 is made available to carry out repair work to the right sector; and the two platoons of the 1st Company, Bavarian Pioneer Regiment to the left sector." Extract from the war diary of the 169th Infantry Regiment. Generallandesarchiv Karlsruhe 456 EV 42 Vol. 108

There was obviously a great deal of damage being caused to the German defences. Not only that, eight more men were killed and twenty-five wounded on the 27th June pushing the tally of casualties for the first four days past the one hundred mark.

By now the British guns were concentrating on the rear areas, attempting to smash the dugouts and sever communications. It was all carefully worked out. The systematic shelling of the main communication trenches leading from Serre, along with important trench junctions, effectively isolated the fron- line companies of the 169th Regiment. It was no longer a simple task to fetch and carry rations from Serre itself or to relieve the men who had been sheltering for four long days and nights. It would be a brave man indeed who dared to risk his life by venturing from the comparative safety of his dugout some twenty feet underground to seek food and water. But there were brave men like riflemen Thum from Kaiserslautern, and Benzer, both of the 6th Company. Time and again they risked their lives to fetch food and ammunition for their comrades in the front trenches. Even though Thum received a head wound and Benzer was buried when a shell landed close by, they carried on, making their way forward collecting as much food as they were able to carry.

The men of the 5th Company of the 169th manning the 'Tubinger Stellung', also played their part in making sure rations got through to the companies in front of them. Night after night, taking advantage of the slightly subdued fire, Unteroffizier Franz Maurer and his men would drag food, weapons and other supplies to the front-line trenches. For these men and more, although the British shells were tearing up the earth and shattering their defences, although their heads and ears ached and their nerves jangled with every explosion, the shells could not destroy their spirit. It was a fact of life which became all too obvious to several raiding parties and patrols of the 31st Division during the last few nights before the attack.

As the infantrymen prepared to play their part in the preliminaries by raiding the German trenches, their superiors sat down to draft speeches and messages of encouragement for them.

In the early evening of June 26th, Major General Wanless O'Gowan had concluded a speech to the drawn-up ranks of the Sheffield City Battalion with the bold assertion, '. . . The village of Serre will be taken.' The men of Baden holding the village would not have agreed with him although in this sector

German positions at Serre based upon 169th Regiment trench maps and British aerial photographs.

of the front the Germans were outnumbered five-to-one.

Each night, in common with every other division in the line, the troops of the 31st Division were required to carry out raids and patrols against the German trenches to inspect the damage caused by the shelling, take prisoners and generally cause as much trouble as they could for the weary men of the 169th Regiment.

It was easier said than done. On the night of June 27th, less than two days before the scheduled start of the big attack, the British guns raked back from the German front line trenches to allow a raiding party of the 12th East Yorkshires to cross No-Man's-Land. By now the artillery should have been well on their way to cutting the seven lanes through the German wire which 31st Division orders called for. Instead the East Yorkshires found the wire standing as thick and as daunting as ever. To add insult to injury the Hull 'Sportsmen' found the Badeners to be more than a fair match for them despite their trying ordeal under the British guns. There was no question of them accepting a British raid meekly and they beat the Hull men back amid a shower of bombs and machine-gun bullets.

The men who returned to their trenches told a depressingly similar story to the one recounted by members of a raiding party of the 11th East Yorkshires who, the night before, had aborted their mission almost as soon as it had begun due to the quantity of wire still apparently untouched by the British shrapnel.

Elsewhere on the 8th Corps' front a disturbing picture of large expanses of uncut wire and dogged German resistance was beginning to emerge. A few patrols returned safely with optimistic tales of a few gaps here and there and a good deal of damage to trenches held by mere handfuls of men, but there were many others who had suffered the same demoralising experience as the men of Hull. It was clear to these men at least, that the British batteries had yet to complete their tasks, but the weather was against the gunners. All in all it had been a miserable week for late June. Several thunderstorms bringing heavy rain had already begun to fill up some of the less well drained assembly trenches; both they and the communication trenches assuming the appearance of so many muddy pools of water. Low cloud was seriously restricting the artillery 'spotting' sorties of the Royal Flying Corps, and without the assistance of the aviators in correcting their fire and pinpointing the German guns, the gunners groped and fumbled to find the range of their targets. The pilots were the eyes of the artillery and due to the low cloud and drizzle the artillery had been a little blind as a result. The battered and bruised raiding parties had ample proof of that.

It continued to rain into the early hours of June 28th.

There were now a little over twenty-four hours to go and 94th Brigade Headquarters duly issued the following 'Special Order of the Day'.

"You are about to attack the enemy with far greater numbers than he can oppose to you, supported by a huge number of guns.

"Englishmen have always proved better than the Germans were when the odds were heavily against them. It is now our opportunity.

"You are about to fight in one of the greatest battles in the world, and in the most just cause.

"Remember that the British Empire will anxiously watch your every move, and that the honour of the North Country rests in your hands.

"Keep your heads, do your duty, and you will utterly defeat the enemy." **F.S.G. Piggott, Captain Brigade Major, 94th Infantry Brigade**

Unknown to Brigadier General H.C. Rees, commanding the 94th Brigade, there had been a good deal of soul-searching at Fourth Army Headquarters. The state of the weather had weighed heavy on the minds of the Staff. At 11 o'clock they decided that there was nothing for it but to postpone the attack for forty-eight hours. 'Z' day would now be Saturday 1st July; 'Zero' hour 7.30 a.m.

The postponement drew a sigh of relief from many artillerymen. They would certainly have to spin out their supplies of ammunition over another two days to make sure that they had enough left for the final barrage on the morning of July 1st and the rest of the battle, but at least they could now put more time into cutting the wire. The Royal Flying Corps too were also keen to get busy; buzzing over the German lines in an effort to catch up on all the work they had missed due to the bad weather.

For the troops of the 169th Regiment the postponement only added to their long misery.

Ernest Bell contracts kidney trouble on the eve of the 'Big Push' and is shipped home. His best pal, Harry Gay, takes over his Lewis Gun team and is killed.

The German information was partially correct. Patrolling activity along the 31st Divisional front went on undiminished but the 14th York and Lancasters played no part in it. On the night of the 28th, 29th June they were still safely encamped in Warnimont Wood along with the Pals of the 13th Battalion. Perhaps the Germans had confused the 2nd Barnsley Pals with a patrol of the 12th East Yorkshires who tried once more that night to breach the German wire and failed for a second time.

As far as the identity of the raiding party on the night of the 29th, 30th was concerned, the Germans were absolutely right, albeit misinformed as to the strength of the group. A little before half past twelve a party of four officers and thirty-eight men of the 18th West Yorkshire Regiment, (2nd Bradford Pals), managed to get within thirty yards of the German front line. They got no further. As they had done several times before, the front line companies of the 169th Regiment saw the raiders off with hand grenades and trench mortar fire. The Bradford Pals lost ten men killed and thirteen wounded during the two hours it took for them to regain the safety of their own trenches. Two of their officers were also missing.

On the 31st Divisional front the lengthy casualty returns from the raiding parties with little or nothing to show for them, were by now reaching various Brigade Headquarters with embarrassing regularity, yet the Staff at Corps Headquarters displayed an alarming tendency to dismiss the reports of the raiding parties and patrols as largely unreliable, or simply chose to ignore them completely.

Even such an experienced campaigner as the Corps commander, a man steeped in the ways of military engineering due to his early service with the Royal Engineers, was disinclined to believe fanciful tales of unbroken wire and stiff German resistance.

After a meeting with General Hunter-Weston, a Brigade Major of the 31st Division recalled:

"The Corps Commander was extremely optimistic, telling everyone that the wire had been blown away, although we could see it standing strong and well, that there would be no German trenches and all we had to do was walk into Serre." **Public Record Office, CAB 45/188**

Quite unaware of the failure of many of the raids or their Corps Commander's extreme optimism, the decision to postpone the attack did not unduly affect the Pals in Warnimont Wood beyond causing a certain amount of disappointment at having to wait two more days. They were fortunate to be in a far better situation than several of the assaulting battalions in other stretches of the line, some of whom had been moved up into their assembly positions before June 28th. Those poor 'Tommies' were well and truly soaked in their damp trenches. In the area earmarked for the attack by the 94th Brigade, then held by troops of the 92nd, the communication trenches at Northern Avenue, Nairne Street and Pylon Avenue were rapidly crumbling into nothing more than a slimy morass with water well above knee level in places. In the assembly trenches named 'Monk', 'Campion' and 'Copse', conditions were not much better and German shelling had considerably added to the swift deterioration of the British line. From those dank and dismal ditches the Barnsley Pals would be expected to launch the attack which would break the German Line.

But for Ernest Bell there would be no attack. Fate had decreed that no length of postponement would enable him to play a part in the coming battle. Like his brother George, a York and Lancaster volunteer in the war with the Boers, Ernest too was struck down by a debilitating malady. George Bell's fever had taken his life; ironically, in Ernest's case, the illness probably saved him.

"I was taken ill with kidney trouble in June and was sent back to billets. They brought the doctor and by then I was as big as a balloon; very swollen with fluid. I was a real mess. Exposure to the filthy conditions; the water and being wet through had caused it. Coming from Egypt, a warmer climate, didn't help. It's a wonder many more didn't get it. They sent me straight to hospital in Rouen the week before the 'Push'. The day before the 'Push' they cleared all the hospitals out and sent us all back to England. On July 1st I was on a hospital ship going home. They were getting ready. They must have known what was going to happen. At the time I was annoyed at being ill, having to leave the other chaps. When the doctor came to see me I said, 'I'll be all right', and he said, 'You'll be all right in hospital'." Ernest Bell, 13th Y & L Regiment

Playing cards carried by 'Tiger' Billy Ward of the First Barnsleys.

Ernest's transfer to a hospital in Taplow left a gap in one of the 13th Battalion Lewis gun teams for the 'Big Push', but Ernest himself had been at the forefront of training over four hundred men on the Lewis gun in the event of just such an emergency. The man chosen to go into battle in the place of Ernest Bell on July 1st was none other than his boyhood pal and former workmate, Harry Gay.

In the ranks of the 14th Battalion too, there were men already on their way home to 'Blighty'. The hospital ship *Panama*, which crossed the Channel on June 29th, counted Frank Lindley's pal 'Hoppy' Hobson amongst its precious human cargo.

"Poor old 'Hoppy' got hit in the ribs before the attack and I was glad because I thought if old 'Hoppy' had been with us he might have finished up like most of them did. I didn't hear about it until some time after. Somebody said, 'Thi mate's been hit,' but I could never follow it through." Frank Lindley, 14th Y & L Regiment

There was little the Pals could do during their last day in Warnimont Wood. Their training was at an end. In less than twenty-four hours these 'Kitchener' men of Barnsley would attempt to deal the Kaiser's Army a body blow from which it would never recover. Their long wait was almost over. While some of the men cleaned and re-oiled their rifle bolts for the umpteenth time others were content to while away their time with a pack of playing cards. In shady and secluded spots well away from the prying eyes of the officers, the 'Crown and Anchor' merchants unfurled their linen rolls and went on to make a packet as if it was just another day. Other men sat quietly or walked around the camp, silently pondering on what the following day held in store for them.

In the afternoon Major Guest made a point of strolling over to the Battalion barber Private Crossley for a trim. After all he wanted to look his best and set an example for 'B' Company as he led them triumphantly through Serre at a little after 9 o'clock the following morning. The Major at least was well pleased with his smart appearance. Later it was the appearance of an officer holding a rank far above that of battalion Major which impressed itself on the memory of sixteen-year-old Frank Lindley.

"On the eve of the battle a bloke came. He had a hyphenated name; I believe it was Hunter-Weston. He looked like he'd just stepped out of a band box, all polished up and with red tabs. We were in this clearing in the wood and we all crowded round and he started talking to us. He said, 'Now you men, you will get on the top and you'll walk across with 'port arms'. He thought that we'd blasted all the 'Jerries' away. When they were saying, 'Our guns will tear up the wire so that you can get through', I thought by God I hope so, but no. They'd been uplifted by all this crashing we'd sent over. The 'Heads' thought all that crashing had 'buggered' the Germans but it hadn't, they were so well fixed." Frank Lindley, 14th Y & L Regiment

At long last the time came to move up to the front. Towards seven o'clock on the evening of June 30th, the troops of the 94th Brigade fell in for the march from Warnimont Wood up to their assembly trenches opposite Serre. First away for the York and Lancaster Regiment was the Sheffield City Battalion which moved out of the camp on the stroke of seven. Fifteen minutes later they were followed by the Second Barnsleys who, in their turn, were followed by the First Barnsley Battalion at 7.40 p.m.

Apart from the men like Ernest Bell and 'Hoppy' Hobson who were already safely out of harm's way, there were others who were not preparing to march out that night. In the case of the 13th Battalion, ten officers and 174 men were to remain behind as reinforcements. Around those men the Army would rebuild the battalion should a disaster occur. They could only stand and watch or shout out messages of encouragement as their pals set out. For those 23 officers and 698 other ranks and a similar number in the Second Barnsley Battalion, only a few short hours and a few miles separated them from their destinies.

For the most part the men were quiet as they began their trek along the muddy tracks still wet from the heavy rains a few days earlier. Apart from the dull mumbling of the guns over six miles distant, there was little to keep the men's thoughts from the coming battle, save for the clinking and clunking of their equipment and the soft thud of their mess tins as they swung and struck their haversacks. There was now no bugle band blowing lustily at the head of their columns, no crowd to cheer them on their way and even if there had been, the Pals would have struggled to raise a cheery whistle or swing to the beat of a drum. They needed every molecule of oxygen their lungs could muster just to cope with the weird and wonderful loads some of them had been detailed to carry. Such was the Army's optimism that they were intent on giving the Pals every single item of equipment that they could think of.

"We went into the line during the night before the attack. We'd come up from Bus Wood. We had what they called marching order without packs, just our haversacks on with a little diamond shaped piece of tin tied to it so that the sun would shine on it during the attack and show our position. We all had a bandolier around us and a Mills bomb in each pocket and all our pouches were full of 'ammo'. I also had a telephone in a leather case with big batteries slung over my shoulder on a leather strap. It weighed a ton. I had a coil of signal wire as well, and my gun. I hadn't a feeling for anything." Frank Lindley, 14th Y & L Regiment

"We were earmarked for the attack and at that time we were camped at a place called Authie, well behind the front line. We fell in in fighting order; ammunition, shovels, extra tackle, kitchen sink and all the bag of tricks on our backs. All this for a tot of rum; and it was the real stuff. You only needed one sip and that was it. Of course, the effects had worn off before 7.30 the following morning. It was then 7.30 at night. Then we marched up through the artillery positions into the trenches. It was about a twelve hour job moving up. We were all tired out. Instead of going to attack we ought to have been going to bed! As we passed by the guns, they were firing and then the Germans would fire back." **Charlie Swales, 14th Y & L Regiment**

"I remember moving up that night. We'd got bags of bombs, entrenching tools, full kit including blanket, gas masks, picks, shovels and rifles and God knows what. We'd set off at about 8 o'clock and moved up from a place further back than Mailly Maillet. We'd been having some specialised training in different sections ready for July 1st, and we marched up next morning and got into these trenches at about 6 o'clock. Zero hour was 7.30. We got there and we were licked, absolutely. We'd been walking nearly all night. There was no singing, we were all too tired what with carrying all that lot. It was hard work, all the communication trenches had been bashed about and they were in a right state. When we got into the final positions a lot of the lads sat down on the fire step and went to sleep even though the guns were at it. I know I did." **Harry Hall, 13th Y & L Regiment**

Opposite page:
2nd Lieutenant Frank Potter takes up a command in the Brigade trench mortar battery. Like the majority of officers and men he writes his last letter to be forwarded to his parents on the event of his death in the forthcoming attack. It is reproduced here in full. Frank Potter receives a fatal head wound during the opening stages of the battle.

Mr. Frank J. Potter,
14th (S.) Bn.
York & Lanc. Regt.

France 27/6/1916

My dearest Mother & Father,

This is the most difficult letter I have ever sat down to write. We are going into an attack tomorrow and I shall leave this to be posted if I don't come back. It is a far bigger thing than I have ever been in before and my only hope is that we shall help in a victory that will bring the war nearer to a successful conclusion. I am hoping to have the nerve to keep my end up & to do my share — that is all that worries me at present. Of death I haven't any fear. I have no premonition of anything happening to me, I have every faith that I shall come out safely, but the chances are against one in a big attack & it is as well to be prepared. The worst of war is that one's

people at home have to bear all the sacrifices and suffering. For my part I am content and happy to give my services and life to my country, but it is not my sacrifice, Mother & Dad, it is yours. The one great thing of this war is that it has taught us to appreciate our homes, and to realise our duty to you more, and also the enormity of your sacrifice in giving your sons to our country. At a time like this I couldn't be anywhere else but here. We have all been brought up at home, in school, & church, to a creed which places our duty to our country next to our religion, and I should not have been a true son had I stayed at home instead of coming out here.

Dad & Mother I don't want you to grieve over me, we have done our duty. I hope Eddie & Dick will never have to face the horrors of war and

that they will realise that we are fighting now so that they will never have to do, and that they will grow up to be better sons than perhaps I have been. We have been so long in peace in England that this war has come as a big shock to us all, but I am content and happy Mother that I have done my duty.

I have made a will which as a soldier's will I think is legal and will perhaps save some trouble. I very want you to let Ruth have any of my belongings she may want, and I know that you will do anything in the world you can for her.

My fondest love to all at home
Your loving Son
Frank
xxxxxxx

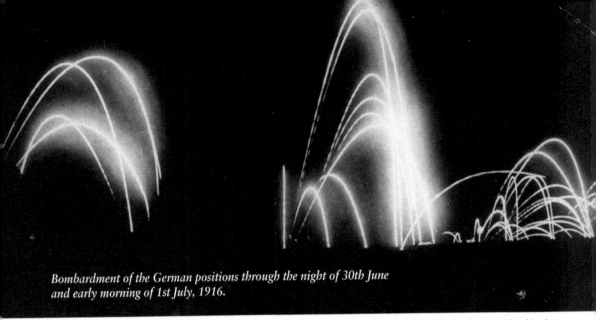

Bombardment of the German positions through the night of 30th June and early morning of 1st July, 1916.

Back at his Headquarters at the Chateau de Valvion in Beauquesne, the British Commander-in-Chief had also been fast asleep even as the Pals had tottered on their way up the line. Before retiring on the night of June 30th General Haig had written up his diary for the day:

> "*The weather report is favourable for tomorrow. With God's help, I feel hopeful. The men are in splendid spirits. Several have said that they have never before been so instructed and informed of the nature of the operation before them. The wire has never been so well cut, nor the Artillery preparation so thorough. I have seen personally all the Corps Commanders and one and all are full of confidence. The only doubt I have is regarding the 8th Corps (Hunter-Weston) which has had no experience of fighting in France and has not carried out one successful raid.*"

General Haig was not the only high ranking officer to harbour doubts about the preparations on the 8th Corps front. The entry in General Rawlinson's diary for the same day contained unnerving misgivings about the state of affairs along General Hunter-Weston's stretch of the line.

> "*. . . The artillery work during the bombardment, and the wire-cutting has been done well except in the 8th Corps, which is somewhat behindhand . . .*"

By the early hours of July 1st however, it was too late for doubts. The outcome of the battle was no longer in the hands of the Generals, it was in the hands of men like Harry Hall, and for the moment at least Harry, exhausted after the long march, slept on.

By the time Harry Hall had moved into position in Rolland trench with the rest of 'B' Company, it had turned five o'clock in the morning. The journey had taken some nine hours in all. Nine hours to walk the six or so miles from Warnimont Wood. The Sheffield City Battalion had made slow progress owing to the wretched state of the sticky country tracks and waterlogged communication trenches and had delayed the Barnsley Battalions following on. The 14th Battalion had entered the trench system near Colincamps at Northern Avenue at midnight, and it took them another two hours to travel the three quarters of a mile to Pylon trench. The 14th had all been in position by 4.30 a.m., half an hour before the 13th Battalion.

Every single man in the 94th Brigade had been hampered by the sheer weight of the equipment he had been given to carry. In addition to all their personal kit, and the bombs, picks, shovels and field telephones; some men were further encumbered by mallets and mauls. Two men from each platoon had a pair of wire cutters dangling uncomfortably from a lanyard in the unlikely event that they would be called upon to do a little extra pruning of the German wire. These men sported a natty band of bright yellow cloth encircling their right arms. It had nothing to do with their rank, it merely served as a mark of identification. If the men were to fall on the battlefield then the yellow armband would mark them out so that the wire cutters could be picked up.

There were other men who carried Bangalore torpedoes, two each for the Barnsley Battalions and some with various markers and flags for the bombing sections. Another two men from each company were also entrusted with the task of transporting two peculiar devices called vermorel sprayers across to the German lines. Originally intended for spraying rose bushes to keep down greenfly, the contraption was filled with a solution which could be sprayed over all and sundry to neutralise the effects of poison gas.

Under the circumstances the Pals of 'B' Company could perhaps have been forgiven for snatching forty winks when they finally arrived at their destination. After all their backs had just borne upwards of six stones in weight for almost nine hours. No amount of rum, not even a reviving mug of hot tea ladled out seven hours earlier during a short halt just west of Courcelles, could keep drooping eyelids open.

Men like Harry Hall and the rest of the weary Houghton Main 'Mob' slept right through the raging of the British guns which had started to increase their fire and by now the German guns had chimed in to add to the bedlam. The German gunners were definitely jumpy. They had begun to shell John Copse and the whole length of the front line on the left flank of 94 Brigade almost as soon as the first hint of daylight had crept over the eastern horizon a little after 4 a.m. The intensity of the shelling demonstrated beyond any shadow of a doubt that the British guns had failed to locate and destroy all the batteries they had been searching for. To some of the men it must have appeared that their own artillery had been doing anything but bombard the German batteries for the last seven days.

For their part the Germans were now quite sure that the British were coming. Their observers had watched the feverish activity of the • weeks of preparation and their front line troops had endured seven agonisingly long days and nights at the hand of the British gunners. The only question which remained unanswered centred on the exact timing of the attack.

Ironically the troops of the 94th Brigade had already gone at least part of the way to furnishing them with the information they required.

Only hours before the Pals had filed up into the trenches a party of the Hull 'Commercials' had crawled out from the front line to cut lanes in the British wire to enable the attacking waves an easy passage into No-Man's-Land. Captain Clarke of the Sheffield City Battalion had then led a handful of men over the parapet to check on the gaps and run out lengths of white tape a hundred yards beyond the wire and parallel to the front line. A few hours later when the leading waves of men filed through the wire in shallow columns, they would use the tapes to correct their lines before setting off for the German trenches.

Captain Clarke's group were back by half past midnight, their mission accomplished. With the coming of the dawn, German observers looking down on the British lines from Serre, could not fail to notice the swathes chopped out of the barbed wire entanglements. The gaps were much wider than the officers of the Sheffield City Battalion would have liked since there had been little attempt to conceal them by staggering the lanes. Not only that, even at such an early hour, the tapes lying just over half way across No-Man's-Land, were plainly visible.

The feeling that the preparations of the 94th Brigade had already served to show too much of their hand to the Germans was not confined to the officers of the battalions within it. Brigadier- General Rees, in temporary command of the Brigade in the absence of Brigadier-General Carter Campbell, was quite certain that they had given the game away, yet he was more concerned with a lack of preparation on the part of the 8th Corps rather than too much.

"A few days before the attack, I pointed out to General Hunter-Weston that the assembly trenches stopped dead on the left of the 94th Brigade and that not a spade had been put in the ground between me and the subsidiary attack at Gommecourt. Worse still, no effort at wire cutting had been made on that stretch either. A child could see where the flank of our attack lay, to within ten yards." Brigadier-General H.C. Rees D.S.O. Temporary Commander of the 94th Infantry Brigade, 15th June – 2nd July 1916. Public Record Office, CAB 45/190.

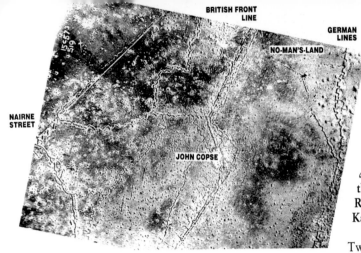

BRITISH FRONT LINE

GERMAN LINES

NO-MAN'S-LAND

NAIRNE STREET

JOHN COPSE

Aerial photograph taken on the morning of 1st July, 1916.

By 3.30 a.m. Major von Struensee, commanding the 169th Regiment, was convinced that he now had all the answers he needed.

"On 1.7. at 4.30 a.m., communique from 104th Infantry Brigade that the already repeatedly announced attack is to be expected at 5.30 a.m. today." Extract from the war diary of the 169th Infantry Regiment. Generallandesarchiv Karlsruhe 456 EV 42 Vol. 108.

Two minutes later the 1st Battalion holding the right sector of the regimental front reported that their patrols had noticed active movements in the British trenches between John and Mark Copses. What the German patrols had witnessed were the trenches filling up with Barnsley and Sheffield men. On the left sector of the Regimental front a patrol of five men led by Vizefeldwebel Ackermann of the 7th Company had actually entered the British front line on the front of the 93rd Brigade at a little after 4.00 a.m. They didn't see another soul, although they could tell that there was a fair amount of activity in the British second line. Moving stealthily along the trench to the north they came across a tightly stretched cord which they could tell ran all the way from the second line up to the front line and continued out into No-Man's-Land. Vizefeldwebel Ackermann cut it up into tiny pieces and then led his patrol back to the German lines.

By the same token the German patrols on the north sector of their regimental front opposite the 94th Brigade had been just as industrious and by 6.00 a.m. the white tapes laid by Captain Clarke of the Sheffield City Battalion had vanished.

As the Germans braced themselves for the coming onslaught signals flew excitedly between regimental headquarters in the remains of an orchard behind Serre village, and the 104th Brigade Headquarters. Since the British were coming it seemed logical for the Germans to want to do something about it. A little before 4 a.m. Major von Struensee had received another message.

"4.50 a.m. Message from the Artillery group 'South', that at 5.00 a.m. a strong surprise attack on the English trenches is to take place." Extract from the war diary of the 169th Infantry Regiment. Generallandesarchiv Karlsruhe 456 EV 42 Vol. 108

But the hour had come and gone and the surprise attack had not materialised.

Even so the German guns continued to pulverise the Pals' positions in spite of the attentions of the British artillery. For the men in the leading waves however, the British guns were just a little too close. All along the front line between John and Luke Copses British shells were pitching short, rearranging the trench architecture and worse still causing casualties among the Sheffielders.

The Barnsley lads of the 14th Battalion's 'A' and 'B' Companies were faring little better. A deluge of shells rained down on a 'mopping up' party consisting of two platoons of 'B' Company under Lieutenant Forsdike and 2nd Lieutenant Strong in Copse trench. Immediately to their left the rest of 'B' Company under Captain Houston, were packed tight into Nairne Street running at right angles to the assembly trenches. In front of them, like a continuous human chain with its links stretching all the way to the front line near John Copse, was the whole of 'A' Company under Captain Roos. Right at the front were the men of Number 1 platoon; and Number 1 platoon were having it rough.

"We all filed up Nairne Street. We were cheek by jowl because we'd had a stoppage. As we stood

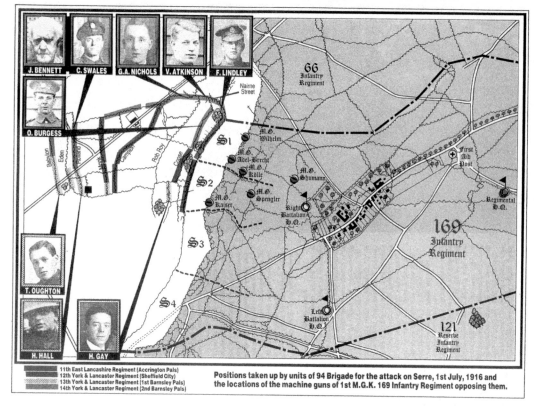

11th East Lancashire Regiment (Accrington Pals)
12th York & Lancaster Regiment (Sheffield City)
13th York & Lancaster Regiment (1st Barnsley Pals)
14th York & Lancaster Regiment (2nd Barnsley Pals)

Positions taken up by units of 94 Brigade for the attack on Serre, 1st July, 1916 and the locations of the machine guns of 1st M.G.K. 169 Infantry Regiment opposing them.

there one of their 'coal boxes' dropped on the top and covered us all. We scattered ourselves out a bit. My knees must have been red raw with the soil hitting me. The next bloke to me started shaking. He was absolutely unhinged, couldn't do a thing. We had to bypass him and travel on because they were shoving us forward. They were 'blotting' us in the rear. I was next to one of our Sergeants, Sergeant Jones, and this salvo of shrapnel came right over the top of us, rattled on our tin hats. Some must have gone down the back of this Sergeant and he was done. I don't know if this Sergeant was dead but he was certainly badly wounded. Blood was coming out of his back between him and his haversack. He had to be shoved back." Frank Lindley, 14th Y & L Regiment

Although Sergeant Jones' fate was not apparent to Frank in the heat of the moment he did survive the shrapnel wounds to his back.

For the men right at the front it appeared that Nairne Street was the only stretch of trench the German gunners were concentrating on. The problem was that it lay so close to John Copse and as Frank Lindley had already worked out the Germans could shell John Copse all day with their eyes closed. The copse was already battered beyond all recognition but now it seemed that the German gunners were intent on erasing it from the map completely. For every shell which poured down onto the area it became increasingly difficult to distinguish just where Nairne Street ended and No-Man's-Land began. To the utter dismay of 'A' Company and the two platoons of 'B' Company, Nairne Street was being systematically flattened. What's more some of the shells causing the damage were coming from their left; from German guns opposite the 48th Division.

A little further back and on the right hand side of the 94th Brigade area, the din was now loud enough to disturb the slumbers of young Harry Hall.

"I woke up and there was hell on. I wondered how ever I'd slept through it, because we'd been shelling them all night and they'd been replying. There were shells whistling and bursting all over. It was hell, absolutely hell." Harry Hall, 13th Y & L Regiment

It was almost as much as Harry Hall could do to think straight.

Back in the gun lines the artillery officers had been glancing anxiously at their wristwatches and as half past six approached they issued orders for the bombardment to move into its final phase. The artillerymen, many of them on the point of physical and mental exhaustion from a week of serving their guns, called on hidden reserves of energy. Lathered with sweat they fired, re-loaded and fired again as quickly as their aching limbs could manage.

Things were hotting up.

Behind Serre the sun was rising into a clear blue sky flecked only with the curling white plumes of smoke from bursting 18-pounder shrapnel shells. Down the long, steady slope in front of the village, the sun's rays slowly reached down and touched the coarse grass in No-Man's-Land and then the tumble down parapets of the 94th Brigade's trenches.

After a clear night, a thin ground mist had risen from the damp earth and its remnants still filled some of the deeper shell holes in No-Man's-Land. It looked like July 1st had all the makings of a glorious Summer's day, the perfect end to a week plagued by bad weather.

"We knew what time they were going to blow the whistles, half past seven. We knew it all before we started, it was passed down somehow. I can remember thinking what was going to happen when we went over. The birds were singing and the sun came up. It was a beautiful day, beautiful. We had the morning chorus before we got the 'other'." **Frank Lindley, 14th Y & L Regiment**

"You could hear the larks at five minutes to seven. You could hear nothing else after that." **Vernon Atkinson, 14th Y & L Regiment**

Soldiers in a support trench during the preliminary bombardment on 1st July a few miles to the south of the Pals.

It was almost inconceivable that such small creatures as birds could have lived through the thunder of the guns and the foul air caused by the fumes from the explosives, let alone be heard quite clearly above the noise of the shells which shrieked over the heads of the Pals.

In Rolland trench, Charlie Swales and the rest of 'C' Company of the 14th Battalion under Captain Edmeades, took his life in his hands and risked a peep over the parapet. He didn't want to miss anything in his first battle.

"There was a light summer mist that morning and I could see over to Gommecourt Wood which was covered in dense smoke as if it was on fire. I didn't look any more, I ducked my head the other road." **Charlie Swales, 14th Y & L Regiment**

There was certainly something going on at Gommecourt two miles to the north. There the waiting waves of the Third Army Territorial Battalions were also pinned down under accurate German artillery fire, but at least that was part of the plan. The Barnsley Battalions should, in theory, have been free of such molestation.

Captain De Ville Smith's 'D' Company of the 13th Battalion formed the very last wave of the attack on the right hand side of the 94th Brigade area. Their job, along with 'C' Company under their South African commander Captain Currin, was to act as reserves for the leading waves. If all went well they would not be called upon to advance across No-Man's-Land at 'zero' hour. All they would have to do would be to walk over the duck-boards bridging their own trenches to fill the positions vacated by the four waves of Accrington Pals and the clearing up and consolidating parties of their own 'A' and 'B' Companies. Even so they would still have to go over the top.

A Lewis Gun team on the Somme.

Like a good many more in Number 14 platoon of 'D' Company, Tommy Oughton was deep in meditation. Keeping his head down in Babylon trench his thoughts turned to his platoon commander Lieutenant Hions. Tall, fair-haired Tommy Hions was not much older than Tommy Oughton himself. An engineer in Castleford before the war, Tommy Hions was one of the nicest chaps Tommy knew. In fact they were more like pals than officer and 'ranker'. Tommy remembered how, a short while earlier, Captain Smith had tried to tear a strip off Tommy Hions for playing cards with his lads. Lieutenant Hions had also wanted Tommy to come out of the signals section and accept two stripes in the platoon, but Tommy knew when he was well off. He stayed where he was. Now as 'zero' hour drew near Tommy reflected on Lieutenant Hions' ability to lead them into battle. As close as they were and as much as Tommy Oughton liked him, the truth was that Lieutenant Hions' experience ran no deeper than Tommy's.

"My feelings were very mixed as we waited to go over. More so with us because we'd had no experience at all from a fighting point of view. We were wondering what it would be like. We had no idea that it would be like it turned out to be. We had no actual front line experience. I know we'd been into the front line, into the saps, but we'd no idea of trench fighting at all. That was the biggest disadvantage we had." **Tommy Oughton, 13th Y & L Regiment**

Mixed in with the members of 'B' Company, Ossie Burgess was mulling over the task allotted to his Lewis gun team in the impending attack. Unlike his pals in 'D' Company of the 14th Battalion in Babylon trench, who were also to act as reserves for the Sheffielders and their own 'A' and 'B' Companies, Ossie had received special instructions. With his Lewis gun team he was to follow the leading waves over at 7.30 a.m., take up a position in No-Man's-Land and stay there until further orders.

"There was only me briefed on the Friday night before the attack. I had to report at these headquarters. I didn't know where it was. There was me and me only. When I got there there were two 'Redcaps' on the door, and one of them said, 'Corporal Burgess? Just wait there'. Then he knocked on this door and said, 'O.K. come in.' There were no lights on. This officer came over and said 'You'll go to this place (pointing at a map) and you'll stay there and on no account fire a shot.' Both Barnsley Battalions were to be side by side and I was to be at the back of the lot. I was to be there in case of emergency. If the Germans started knocking our lads back then I could open fire, but not before." **Ossie Burgess, 14th Y & L Regiment**

It was a mysterious mission to say the least, and was obviously a 'last-minute' arrangement. Ossie kept the details to himself, but by now he was familiar with his weapon. He had been on the Lewis gun since the Pals' stay at Ripon in the late summer of 1915. On the other hand Ernest Bell's friend Harry Gay had been

"Fix bayonets!" At a little after seven o'clock on Saturday morning, 1st July a Lancashire unit prepares to 'go over the top'.

a member of his Lewis gun team for a matter of days. Being in a Lewis team was an unfamiliar role for Harry Gay. After his initial period of regimental training he had gone back to other duties but now, due to his friend's sudden illness, he found himself replacing Ernest at the last moment. Suddenly he was to be pitched into the battle of the Somme at its very outset. With the rest of two platoons of 'A' Company under the command of Lieutenant Maleham behind Copse trench, Harry Gay and his Lewis team were to follow up the second wave of the Accrington Pals as they advanced to the fourth German trench in front of Serre. Their task was to clear the captured trenches of German soldiers as they went. It was all a far cry from his previous employment as servant to Lieutenant George Asquith before he had been wounded.

With a little over ten minutes left before the Pals went over, the British guns growled out in an ear splitting finale to the preliminary bombardment. Not to be outdone, moments later two Stokes mortars tucked away in their emplacements at the heads of two saps in No-Man's-Land, furiously began to cough up shells at a rate of ten per minute each and tossed them into the German front line. Five hundred yards behind the front line, Brigadier-General Rees climbed from the safety of the ten foot deep steel shelter that passed for advanced Brigade Headquarters, to view the spectacle at first hand.

"A splendid view was obtainable from the trench outside, over the whole ground as far as Serre... I stood on top to watch. It was magnificent. The trenches in front of Serre changed shape and dissolved minute by minute under the terrific hail of steel. Watching, I began to believe in the possibility of a great success, but I reckoned without the Hun artillery." **Brigadier-General H.C. Rees**

At the same time wisps of smoke from smoke candles curled up and out of the trenches of the 48th Division immediately to the left of Nairne Street and floated gently over the shell-torn ground in the general direction of Germany. At once the first puffs of smoke drew rifle and machine-gun fire from the trenches of the German 66th Magdeburg Regiment opposite the 48th Division, and the slaughter of the Barnsley men began.

Roused by the cries of their sentries, the German soldiers had more than a good idea that the British attack was about to commence. As the smoke rose higher and crept towards them at a steady two miles per hour, the German troops 'stood-to' on the lower steps of their dug-outs waiting for the 'Trommelfeuer' to lift from their front-line trenches as they knew it surely must. They had worked hard for this moment for a long time; long before the Barnsley Battalions had begun to rehearse the attack on Serre. As the British had done in the fields near Gezaincourt, German officers too had seen fit to reconstruct a part of the battlefield in an area behind Puisieux, shot through with valleys and a disused railway embankment. It was an ideal area for putting the machine-gun crews through their paces. Time and again the crews had worked at manhandling their heavy machine guns from dugouts on hearing the cry 'Everybody out, they're coming'. They had sweated, they had strained, they had almost been driven into the ground by their officers shouting them on with stopwatches in hand, but they had survived. At the end of four weeks they were bursting with confidence. They knew they could have their weapons into position in a matter of moments after hearing the alarm. With the appearance of the smokescreen they also knew that all their training was about to be put to the test.

7.20 a.m. and the British mine beneath Hawthorn Ridge explodes. The ground shudders under the feet of the Accrington, Sheffield and Barnsley men; just ten minutes to go before the whistles blow.

As they had done so many times before, the machine-gunners began to haul their guns up the steep dugout steps and fixed them onto specially constructed wooden mountings.

The riflemen of the Second Battalion of the 66th Regiment were also on the move. Led by Hauptmann Rochlitz they rushed forward onto the destroyed breastworks of their trenches and fired into the smoke as quickly as they could.

Far from being a cover for the leading waves of the Sheffielders and 'A' Company of the 14th Battalion, the smoke had merely served to bring almost every shell and every bullet from the direction of the 66th Regiment down on the heads of the men on the British left flank. With a hail of bullets fizzing through the grass and thudding into the earth around them, the leading men of Number 1 platoon of the 14th Battalion started to make their way over what was left of the parapet in front of Nairne and crawled towards the gaps in the British wire. Wriggling through the lanes they crawled a little further to join up with the left flank of the Sheffield City Battalion, already lying down in their lines one hundred yards out in No-Man's-Land. Everybody waited.

Englander Kommen!

A contemporary German sketch.

At twenty past seven the huge mine so painstakingly prepared beneath the Hawthorn Redoubt, burst open and tore the roof off the Hawthorn Ridge. It took with it three sections of Number 9 Company of the German 119th Reserve Regiment.

"As we were waiting for the whistle, a bloody great mine went up on the right hand side. We saw it going sky high. It was just one huge mass of soil going up over towards our right. It shook all along our line but there were other things going off as well. That mine shouldn't have gone up till we were on the top. As soon as it went off the barrage lifted and the smaller guns lifted too on account of this here mine going up. In the time between that mine going up and us going over, well the 'Jerries' were out. They'd got their guns ready." Frank Lindley, 14th Y & L Regiment

If he had had his way, General Hunter-Weston would have had the mine fired half an hour before daybreak in order to allow his 29th Division to capture the mine crater before the actual assault. The only problem with that particular plan was that German soldiers were past masters at rushing freshly blown mine craters, and what's more the General Staff knew it. Blowing the mine four hours before the attack was definitely out of the question. In their opinion the later the mines were fired, the better. As it stood, twenty minutes past seven was a compromise. Even so the barrage would have to be lifted at that time to enable the troops to take the crater. Orders had been issued to the heavy artillery of the 8th Corps and on the dot they lifted their fire from the German front line. For a few moments the frenzied barking of the heavy guns ceased along the entire length of the 8th Corps front as the gunners prepared to move the barrage to the German rear.

During the brief lull in the heavy artillery barrage and in between the splutterings of the Stokes mortars and the thin 18- pounder barrage, the Pals now began to hear the ominous chatter of German machine-gun fire coming quite clearly from their left. For the Germans of the 169th Regiment the firing of the Hawthorn Ridge mine was the final confirmation that the curtain was about to go up on the Battle of the Somme.

They could hardly believe what was happening. For a full ten minutes before the barrage was due to lift from the German front trenches along the rest of the British line, the Germans opposite the 8th Corps found, to their amazement, that the firing had all but stopped.

With only Stokes mortar shells and shrapnel to bother them they were free to man their trenches once more; free to vent their frustrations on the attacking waves of British infantry.

Already due to the appearance of the smoke, the sentries had been increased and the men not on sentry duty were sitting out of their dugouts with rifles in their arms and bags of hand grenades next to them. Already the Magdeburgers on their right were firing at the British soldiers. Emotions were running high.

"If the English thought that they could wear us out by the unprecedented fire of the past few days they were badly mistaken. Never was the battle enthusiasm and the camaraderie greater than during these days of terror and privation. The most ardent wish that we all cherished was that they would finally come. Everyone was aware of his duty. The look-outs were standing and when the shrapnel flew like hailstones, the action of our Company leader Herr Hauptmann Haufer, acted as a shining example to us all. Almost constantly, day and night, he was in the trench and looked-out; went through the completely battered trenches and spoke in his fatherly manner to his 'children' and awakened the enthusiasm for battle. Who could have hidden their cowardice?. . . Now everyone knows that the hour of retaliation will soon come. Cartridges and hand grenade reserves are made ready; everything is ready . . ." Extract from the war diary of the 6th Company of the 169th Infantry Regiment. Generallandesarchiv Karlsruhe 456 EV 42 Vol. 114

It looked like the Pals were out on their own. Left behind by the heavy Corps artillery they now faced German troops willing and, due to the absence of shellfire, more than able to make the British pay dearly for their suffering.

Many of the German troops could not contain themselves any longer. Braving the trench mortar fire the men of the 3rd and 4th Companies of the 169th Regiment scurried into the front-line trenches and opened a fierce rifle and machine-gun fire on the first two waves of Sheffield and Accrington men lying prone in No-Man's-Land. Others scooped up their bags of bombs, ran forward and hurled them down onto the helpless khaki figures causing dreadful casualties. For almost ten minutes there was little that the British troops could do except to try and burrow into what little cover there was and tilt their tin helmets towards the Germans. The incessant chatter of the machine guns and the bursting of the bombs drilled into the minds of the men as they lay there waiting for the signal to advance. What on earth had gone wrong? Where had the machine guns come from? Why didn't the whistles blow?

All along the straggling miles of the British front line, several thousand seconds hands on several thousand wristwatches ticked off the last few moments before 'zero'. Waiting in Nairne Street, Frank Lindley adjusted his equipment yet again. His weighty field telephone and coil of signal wire were already hanging from his shoulders and somehow he had to manage his rifle as well. Reaching down he checked the position of his entrenching tool for the last time. It was still firmly in place, strapped low across his groin to protect his manhood from a bayonet thrust or a low flying sliver of shrapnel. It was not usual Army practice to carry an entrenching tool in that particular position, but then again Frank had never had too much regard for Army practice, and anyhow, he was simply taking precautions. After all, he was still a very young man.

At last the taunting tittle tattle of the German machine guns was answered by the noise of the British barrage falling on the fourth German line in front of Serre. Not only that, the German artillery were also firing with redoubled intensity, dropping their high explosive and shrapnel shells onto the two remaining platoons of 'A' Company of the 13th Battalion under their monocled Company Commander Captain Gurney in Monk trench. Anticipating the British assault almost to the second, the German counter-barrage rolled slowly forward from the assembly trenches towards the front line and over into No-Man's-Land.

"On 1st July at 8.30 a.m. after one and a half hours of extraordinarily heavy 'Trommelfeuer' there is a pause in the firing on the foremost trenches. Now the English must come! . . . The blue sky laughs cloudless, the whole front forms an uninterrupted gas cloud, our barrage has begun. English pilots courageously circle very low over our position. " **Extract from the Heroic deeds of the 6th Company of the 169th Infantry Regiment in the battles at Serre, 1916.**

Next to Frank Lindley his platoon commander Second Lieutenant Hirst, was already putting the whistle to his mouth. William Hirst was just a month away from his first wedding anniversary. A little more than two years before he had been leading the Wombwell Church Lads Brigade in his spare time, now he was about to lead his men into battle. William Hirst blew his whistle. The shrill call told his platoon that the time had come to advance. Out in No-Man's-Land more whistles were blowing. Some men filled their lungs and bellowed encouragement to their pals, others bellowed to encourage themselves. Orders were bawled out amid the riotous turmoil. The two leading waves of Sheffield and Accrington men struggled under their burdens to lift themselves upright, looked right and left along their lines and set off.

They were followed by the leading men of 'A' Company of

The British attack in the northern sector is faltering under the withering fire of the German Machine-Gun Companies. A patrol crawls out into No-Man's-Land later in the morning of 1st July.

the 14th Battalion who tagged onto the left flank of the first two waves of Sheffielders as they passed. Not far behind the second wave, the four clearing platoons of Barnsley Pals, two from each battalion, were already on their way. On the right Lieutenant Maleham led half of the 13th Battalion's 'A' Company over the top, while Lieutenant Forsdike and 2nd Lieutenant Strong urged on the men of the 14th Battalion's 'B' Company. Lurching forward to drag their heavily laden bodies over the last few inches of the parapet, the bright rays of the early morning sun struck the pieces of tin tied to their haversacks for an instant, and a shower of sparks seemed to flash along Copse trench.

Four hundred yards behind, the third and fourth waves of Sheffield and Accrington lads were striding forward from Monk and Campion in shallow columns to enable them to cross the duckboards bridging the three lines of British trenches which lay ahead.

Following them from Rolland and Babylon trenches, advancing in the same section columns over the open, came 'C' and 'D' Companies of the 14th Battalion, moving forward as far as Campion and Monk. Kitchener's Army was on its way.

"Over there in closed rifle ranks, come the attacking English. Slowly, almost leisurely, they trot along, out of the third into the second, then into the first English trench. From there they proceed to the attack, their light cooking utensils flash in the gunpowder impregnated air." **Extract from the Heroic deeds of the 6th Company of the 169th Infantry Regiment in the battles at Serre, 1916. Generallandesarchiv Karlsruhe 456 EV 42 Vol. 127**

The Pals walked headlong into a flailing maelstrom of shell splinters and machine gun bullets. Shells were bursting so thick and fast that at times it seemed as though they were walking through a thick forest of explosions as columns of earth sprouted in their paths.

". . . as our infantry advanced, down came a perfect wall of explosive along the front trenches of my brigade and the 93rd. It was the most frightful artillery display that I had seen up to that time and in some ways I think it was the heaviest barrage I have seen put down by the defence on any occasion." **Brigadier General H.C. Rees**

"I was in the first wave on the extreme left. Second Lieutenant Hirst was next to me, just to my right. We were almost touching. We scrambled onto the fire step and then on the top. It wasn't long before he got it. I think he got a machine-gun bullet in the head but I only took a fleeting glance. We had orders to keep moving. We were told not to bother with the wounded. I looked around. Our lads were all going on our right, there was nothing on the left. You could see both ways, you could see all the front laid out like a panorama; Gommecourt Wood and Serre all laid out and all these trenches of theirs riding up. We had to go up. They could shoot out of all their trenches but we were down below. It wasn't a steep rise, just undulating, but of course it seemed like a mountain that morning. There was enfilade fire coming from Gommecourt." **Frank Lindley, 14th Y & L Regiment**

"On 1st July when we went over the top there were the First and Second Barnsley Battalions and I was at the back of the lot. When I stepped on to the fire step there were two 'Redcaps', I'd seen one of them before. Well he shook my hand and said, 'Good luck Corporal', and I said, 'It looks as if we want it as well'. We got 25-50 yards, no more; when I heard that a young Lieutenant we'd had in England had been killed; Lieutenant Anderson. Next, my number six, my range finder went out of action. He was shot. Fire was coming from the left and right as well as from the front. The Germans had all their preparations done. When our lot were fighting and travelling up the hill you could see the Germans at the top. As a matter of fact you could see how things were going, but things were going very badly at our place. Very bad." **Ossie Burgess, 14th Y & L Regiment**

"When the whistle went we went up the ladders and began walking across towards Serre, but we were still among our own trenches. At the back of us there were the military police, seeing to it that you didn't miss your turn to go over. As I jumped across one trench I saw my first casualty that

morning, it was the top half of a man – the other half was lying in the bottom of the trench. I don't know if he were a Barnsley lad or a Sheffielder, he must have taken the full blast of the shell. Sheffield City Battalion had been in the front line of trenches. They must have been wiped out by this time."
Charlie Swales, 14th Y & L Regiment

All three Pals were correct in the assumptions they had made. The German troops and their officers had prepared themselves thoroughly for the attack. They could indeed fire out of all their trenches, and were doing so with devastating results. Whole sections of the leading waves were simply melting away as the ranks were lashed by stream after stream of machine-gun bullets. Manning their machine gun in the front line opposite Luke Copse, Unteroffiziers Reiner and Adelbrecht of the 169th Regiment's 1st Machine-Gun Company couldn't fail to hit the lines of Barnsley and Sheffield men advancing steadily towards them in neat rows. It was madness. All they had to do was to make sure that the hungry guns were fed with belt after fabric belt of ammunition, and fire. A little further down the line Fritz Kaiser was doing the same, knocking entire sections of Accrington and Barnsley men down like so many skittles. Even though some of the leading waves of Accrington Pals were but twenty yards from entering the German front line, Unteroffizier Kaiser kept firing, firing; scything down the oncoming lines.

Further back the other guns of the 1st Machine-Gun Company were finding their targets just as easily.

From the second trench right in the centre of the 94th Brigade area, from the third trench and even from the fourth trench, the German machine guns, positioned so as to cover every single inch of ground, wrought havoc among the Pals.

"You couldn't get past a row of them guns all firing together. Our lads were going down in their waves, flop, flop, flop. They were walking across. It was stupid, absolutely stupid. It was all right the Generals saying, 'You'll walk across', even if we'd run across we'd still have been in the same fix because we couldn't have got through their wire. Perhaps one or two would have got through but what good would they have been? You couldn't get to the places where the machine guns were, they were in emplacements. Their wire was bundled up in great rolls with just an odd gap between, not very wide; perhaps two blokes could have got through at once, but there wasn't a chance of that. As soon as you made for that gap it was, 'R-R-R-R-R'. They had their guns on that gap. They knew you couldn't get through them bloody coils, you couldn't have got through for love nor money. As soon as they saw anything that was it. You saw a gap and as soon as you went for it the old machine-gun bullets were floating around like bees round a honeypot. You could hear them whistling past you. You knew you couldn't get through there. All you could do was dive in a shell hole to get out of the 'spray', and the ground was pitted with shell holes because our guns had tried to bust all their wire up, then you had to sort your way through the shell holes to find a way through. I remember the lads laid in rows, just as if they'd gone to sleep there, and the sun flashing on them bits of tin on their backs all down the lines. Some of the lads I recognised; that's so and so I thought. The machine guns just laid 'em out. They must have stopped one or two bullets and it finished them. 'Napoo'. They didn't look to be in a mess. There were some 'lumps' flying about though. Them

A major contributor to the halting of the British attack — the German Maxim 08. Seen here without its usual sled mount — attached to a simple wooden block which facilitates the weapon's speedy manhandling from the deep dugouts and its positioning in the fire trenches. The ammunition boxes, to the right, each contain a canvas belt holding 250 rounds.

that had made for the gaps in their wire were all piled up. Some were hanging on the wire, hanging like rags. Machine-gun bullets were knocking 'em round as if it was washing hung on the line. Legs and arms and everything were flying all over." **Frank Lindley, 14th Y & L Regiment**

Frank Lindley had made the crossing of No-Man's-Land without a scratch, but before the village of Serre that day, he was just one of a very tiny minority who had managed to get as far as the German wire. He had carried on as he had been ordered, ignoring the dreadful screams of his comrades and stepping over the headless, legless, khaki bundles which, moments before, had been human beings. Still the men of the 94th Brigade went on, the following waves striding out with their rifles held at an angle across their chests, only to be met by the same withering fire.

The attack was just ten minutes old.

Back at the 14th Battalion Headquarters in Rolland trench Colonel Hulke and his Staff were trying desperately to make sense of the first few minutes of the battle. If reports were anything to go by it looked as though the attacking troops of 'A' and 'B' Companies on the left flank had got off to a flying start. By twenty minutes to eight, not a single man of 'A' Company could be seen in Nairne Street. The simple truth was that three out of every ten had not been able to leave, they had never reached the parapet of the British front line. Nairne Street was indeed flattened in places, but even so, what Battalion Headquarters had thought to be an empty stretch of trench concealed a good many dead and wounded Barnsley Pals. Many more, as Frank Lindley had witnessed, were already strewn out across No-Man's-Land between John Copse and the German wire, lying among the dead of 'A' and 'C' Companies of the Sheffield City Battalion.

Vernon Atkinson, in 'A' Company of the 14th Battalion, was still in one piece and yet he had never moved. He was not wounded; not physically at any rate, and he hadn't been seized by cowardice. What he was, under the circumstances, was very, very lucky.

"I was standing in this trench and next to me there was this bloke with a machine gun, a Lewis gun. I said, 'Are you all right chum', and he said, 'Yes'. Next minute a shell had lifted him clean away. How the hell it missed me I'll never know but, well, there can't have been one made for me. I didn't go over the top, I never saw anybody go over the top, I just stood in that trench near to where the shell had dropped. I was in an awful state. I must have been there four or five hours in that trench by myself. I had no kit on at all. Where my rifle and equipment went I don't know. All I know is that I saw Sergeant Reg Dunk land there in the trench. He was hit full tilt, done all together, then somebody got hold of me and took me away." **Vernon Atkinson, 14th Y & L Regiment**

Like Vernon Atkinson, Reg Dunk was just one of the many men of the 14th Battalion's 'A' Company who had never left Nairne Street. He had been the toast of the Barnsley Swimming Club when he had fished two of his Second Barnsley Battalion Pals out of the depths of the Suez Canal at Kantara a few months earlier. He had been no less than a local hero. Now no amount of attention on the part of the Army Medical Corps would be enough to preserve him. Reg Dunk was past saving.

On the right hand side of the attack Lieutenant Maleham and almost all his fellow officers and men had suffered the same fate as the leading waves of the 11th East Lancashire Regiment. Scattered among the shell holes and the still rows of Accrington Pals the men of the 13th Battalion's 'A' Company had been cut down within the first hundred yards of No-Man's-Land. Lying out with them was the body of Ernest Bell's friend Harry Gay. The 25-year-old Barnsley Corporation stonemason's battle had lasted a matter of seconds.

Just in front of the German wire the fortunate few who had survived the initial carnage were now seeking the sanctuary of shell holes. Helplessly they could only stare in horror as their pals tried vainly to struggle through the few gaps they could see in the German wire, only to be picked off by the machine-gunners.

In spite of the appalling number of casualties sustained by the leading troops of the 94th Brigade during the first fifteen minutes of the attack, it was by no means always clear to British observers just exactly what was going on in No-Man's-Land. The desolated strip of ground between the lines was shrouded in the drifting dust and fog of battle. Beneath its masking blanket many Pals like Frank Lindley and Ossie Burgess were pinned down by the machine guns and now rifle fire from German infantrymen growing in confidence.

The German riflemen had witnessed the effects of their machine guns on the successive waves of British soldiers and were so exhilarated that they had come up out of their trenches to get a better view and therefore a better shot at the men who were still bravely traversing No-Man's-Land. There were some, like Oberleutnant Emil Schweikert, commanding the 6th Company of the 169th Regiment in the front line opposite Matthew Copse, who were so carried away that they forgot about their wounds. Almost as soon as the leading waves of Accrington Pals had started to advance Oberleutnant Schweikert had been struck by a large splinter from a trench mortar shell, but such was the heat of the moment that he would only accept a makeshift field dressing and that was already soaked with blood. With blood-

A light trench mortar of the type used by Lieutenant Potter's battery. (see page 199)

stained bandages and with a naked upper body he scrambled high on the sides of the front-line trenches and led the firing, screaming encouragement to his men.

There was little to stop him as the British heavy barrage had long since gone creeping off towards Serre, but men like Oberleutnant Schweikert ran the risk of being sniped at by the British soldiers taking cover in shell holes in No-Man's-Land.

For Pals like Frank Lindley, unhurt and with plenty of ammunition, such men provided clear targets.

"I was still dodging from shell hole to shell hole to try and get through their wire. I also tried picking them off, some of the Jerries, because they were on the trench tops cheering their mates on. It was a gift for them." **Frank Lindley, 14th Y & L Regiment**

The machine-gun crews of the 169th Regiment's 1st Machine-Gun Company were also under fire. They could scarcely have believed their luck when they had been presented with row upon row of British soldiers plodding towards them and had proceeded to decimate their ranks. Events were to prove, however, that several of the German machine-gunners were to pay the ultimate price for their positions as the chief executioners of the men of 94 Brigade.

Unteroffizier Adelbrecht was the first to lose his life; shot through the head as he struggled to free his jammed weapon. His gun, in the front line opposite Luke Copse, had been firing without a pause since the sentries had first noticed the khaki waves rising from the ground in front of the British wire. The gun had caused the leading waves of South Yorkshiremen to stagger and falter and finally to veer to the south to escape the sweeping hail of bullets. Now the weapon leader was dead, and next to him lay the shattered body of Rifleman Pfähler, a victim of the premature explosion of his own hand grenade, along with another four wounded men of the team.

One hundred yards behind in the second line, the messages reaching the Machine-Gun Company Commander informed him that the gun was out of action for the time being at least. The Commander, Oberleutnant Faller, quickly assessed the situation, he now had only one operative machine gun, under Unteroffizier Kaiser, in the front line opposite Matthew Copse. He needed another to plug the gap in the front line defences. Without the first line defence there was a danger that the British would enter the trench system, in spite of the other guns and the counter-barrage on No-Man's-Land.

His own weapon, under Unteroffizier Kölle, could not be sent forward as it lay in a central position from where he could observe the progress of the British assault and also how his machine-gun teams were operating. In the trench behind were two guns; on the left was Unteroffizier Spengler and on the right the team of Unteroffizier Wilhelm. Wilhelm's gun was the obvious choice since it could be removed from its present position without upsetting the balance between the right and left of the Company's defensive front.

Oberleutnant Faller issued the order for Wilhelm to take his gun from its position in the third trench opposite John Copse into the front line. No sooner had the gun been installed in its new location and begun firing than Unteroffizier Wilhelm was also hit in the head. There was a moment of confusion as the gun stopped firing.

From the numerous shell holes near the German wire some of the Sheffielders started to throw Mills bombs towards the gun in an effort to silence it for good. Gradually they worked their way a little closer. Unteroffizier Reiner remained calm. He had been with Adelbrecht's team and had remained in the front line to join Wilhelm's crew. Taking control of the situation he ordered the gun to keep firing on the British in spite of the Mills bombs exploding all around. The gun did its work. Within seconds of firing it brought down the York and Lancasters who had taken advantage of the fleeting pause to move forward and they dropped in their heaps in front of the German wire.

The wounded were dealt with separately by the German riflemen.

Some five hundred yards away to the south, Unteroffizier Fritz Kaiser was also having trouble. Soon

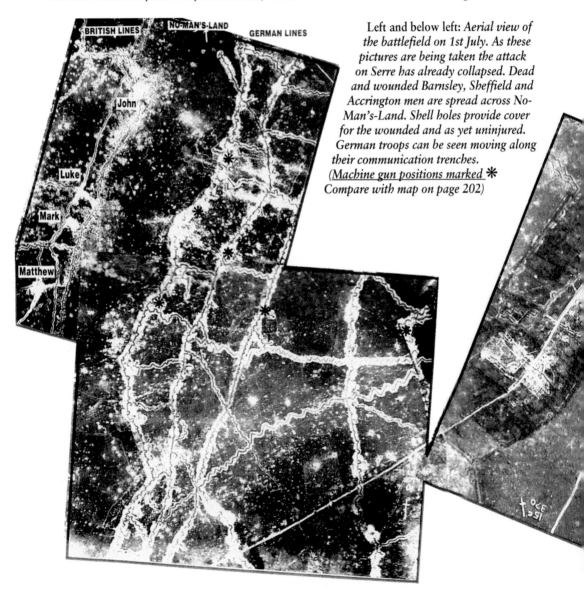

Left and below left: *Aerial view of the battlefield on 1st July. As these pictures are being taken the attack on Serre has already collapsed. Dead and wounded Barnsley, Sheffield and Accrington men are spread across No-Man's-Land. Shell holes provide cover for the wounded and as yet uninjured. German troops can be seen moving along their communication trenches.* (*Machine gun positions marked* ✳ *Compare with map on page 202*)

after his team had brought their gun into position in the front line he had lost Unteroffizier Bursch, Rifleman Keller and his two war-time volunteers Klein and Wälde through a variety of wounds. Now the gun had suddenly and unexpectedly given up the ghost. There was nothing he could do. It would have to be replaced, and if the worst came to the worst the machine-gunners, in their grey-green uniforms, would have to fight as infantrymen alongside their comrades dressed in field grey.

Opposite Luke Copse Unteroffizier Schloss had somehow managed to free the block in the gun which Adelbrecht had died attempting to remove, only to have the firing pin snap minutes later. Removing the casing he realised that there was little he could do there and then. Fearing that the weapon would fall into the hands of the British he ordered it to be rushed back to Leutnant Beyer in the third line. They would try to repair it there. Oberleutnant Faller now had two guns out of action, both from the front line. He was left with only the one weapon under Reiner in the front trenches.

Back at 94th Brigade Headquarters just in front of Observation Wood, Brigadier General Rees was experiencing much the same difficulty as Colonel Hulke had encountered in attempting to unravel the tangled knot of events of the first quarter of an hour or so.

He was quite aware of the tornado of shell, machine-gun and rifle fire his troops had met as they had clambered out of their trenches. The large numbers of dead and wounded covering the ground between Monk trench and the front line, or hanging from the British wire were proof enough of that. He was also quite sure that the leading waves had probably come up against the same volume of fire out in No-Man's-Land, but despite his own misgivings, he just could not be sure how they were progressing. The same blanket of smoke which hid the numerous isolated duels betwen individual British soldiers and the Germans lining the tops of their trenches, was also confounding his own observers, as well as those from Divisional and Corps Headquarters.

Below: The ruined village of Serre with the trench system running through it.

There were no signs of the flashing tin diamonds which were to have traced out the advance in glittering lines of gold and silver moving in quick time across the German lines; no signs of the red and yellow marking flags which the bombers had carried over the top to show how far they had penetrated the trench system; no signs either of Company runners with reports hopeful or otherwise.

Each officer and N.C.O. should have carried a notebook with pages previously marked to show clearly the destination of each message. Unknown to Brigadier General Rees, most of those notebooks were now resting in the breast pockets of dead men or had perished along with their owners amid the blinding fury of a high explosive shell.

Telephonic communication was out of the question. Most of the men who had been carrying the heavy field telephones and coils of signal wire were now dead or, like Frank Lindley had jettisoned them to increase their chances of survival.

Brigadier General Rees was undoubtedly tense, as were Colonel Hulke and Colonel Wilford but after all, there was bound to be a good deal of confusion in the early stages of such a large scale offensive. Surely the tales of doom and disaster on the left flank told by the wounded men of the 14th Battalion already coming back, were the garbled stories of a handful of badly shaken soldiers.

Deaf and blind with regard to the overall progress of the battle, Brigadier General Rees could do little more than trust what he had been able to see with his own eyes, and his eyes told him that despite the bravery of his troops, they were suffering a severe mauling. Obviously the Brigadier's experienced eye told him much more than his junior officers were able to comprehend.

"I have never seen a finer display of individual and collective bravery than the advance of that Brigade. I never saw a man waver from the exact line prescribed for him. Each line disappeared into the thick cloud of dust and smoke which rapidly blotted out the whole area. I can safely pay a tribute also to the bravery of the enemy, whom I saw standing up in their

trenches to fire their rifles in a storm of fire . . . I saw a few groups of men through gaps in the smoke cloud, but I knew that no troops could hope to get through such a fire. My two staff officers, Piggott and Stirling were considerably surprised when I stopped the advance of the rest of the Machine-Gun Company and certain other small bodies now passing my Headquarters. It was their first experience of a great battle and all that morning, they obviously found it impossible to believe that the whole Brigade had been destroyed as a fighting unit." **Brigadier General H.C. Rees**

Although Brigadier General Rees was sure that no man could have got through the heavy fire his men had been subjected to, one of his observers was equally sure that, through a window in the drifting smoke, he had seen a party of East Lancashires on the point of entering the German front line. The Brigadier was left with little choice but to assume that the leading waves, albeit much thinner than when they set out, were still advancing. At a little after a quarter to eight a buzz of excitement swept along 'B' Company of the 13th Battalion in Rolland trench. They were going over.

Harry Hall still felt tired and so did a good many more of Number 6 Platoon, but Major Guest had received orders to follow the Accrington Pals to the fourth German line, and he intended 'B' Company to get there. Colonel Wilford had offered him the choice of leading his men over the top or staying in reserve, but Major Guest had risen through the ranks in another war and he wasn't about to desert the N.C.O.s and private soldiers at the last minute.

Writing in the Chronicle a year later, one Pal of 'B' Company remembered that the Major,' . . . was as cool as the proverbial cucumber'. Clutching his revolver, gazing towards the parapet and occasionally glancing at his wristwatch, Tommy Guest was reported to have spoken what were to be his final words

of encouragement to his men. 'Now boys we have to uphold the honour of the old town and remember, I am the first over the top. Over boys and give them hell.' With that he blew his whistle and 'B' Company started to follow him over the parapet.

Harry Hall could just about see the figure of Major Guest fifty yards or more further down the line, but what with the blur of men scrambling up the ladders it was difficult to see what he was doing, and anyway Harry had himself to think about.

Harry was much closer to his platoon commander Lieutenant Hunter and as the young officer blew his whistle Harry noticed that he was gripping his revolver quite hard. Taking hold of a duckboard which had been lifted from the floor and upended against the side of the trench, Harry Hall heaved himself out of Rolland.

Two hundred yards in front of him the remaining two platoons of 'A' Company under Captain Gurney were climbing out of Monk trench with orders to advance only as far as the British front line, and to stay there in support.

Major Thomas Guest

"*When the time came, up we went and over we went. Major Guest went over in the middle of the Company and we were going over at the sides. We all went over in waves and we crossed over our trenches first. Then we passed through the gaps in our wire which had been cut the night before, but when we got into No-Man's-Land it was every man for himself. After a while you couldn't call the waves straight lines, they were irregular. You had to find your own way across; you'd got to try and pick your spot and get through their wire in front. That was the main obstacle to us. The German wire hadn't been cut and it should have been. I could see fellows struggling to get through and they were picked off on the wire. I only knew that we'd got to get to the German line. That was our only objective, because we were under the impression that there was nobody in there. Our artillery had been shelling that much for such a long time we thought that there couldn't be anybody living in their trenches, but we found out after that as soon as we were nearly there the Germans were up on them machine guns mowing us down as we came.*" **Harry Hall, 13th Y & L Regiment**

Too late the staff at Brigade and Battalion Headquarters had begun to realise that the distances between the attacking waves were far too great, the only benefits falling to the Germans. Gaps of a hundred yards between waves simply gave the German machine-gunners ample time to deal with one wave before turning their guns onto the one behind.

Oberleutnant Faller, in the second German line, only had one operative gun in the front line but he could tell his other guns were firing at the new waves of British troops. He ordered Unteroffizier Kölle in charge of the firing of the weapon to concentrate on the British trenches. Throughout the attack the gun swept back and forth along the assembly positions and then the front line as the steel helmets of the supporting troops showed above the parapets.

At a few minutes before 8 o'clock the 169th Regiment received a message from Haury, one of their observers, that the British were advancing in waves from the direction of Matthew Copse. The waves were almost certainly the Pals of 'B' Company of the 13th Battalion crossing the British front line and stepping into the traversing fire from Oberleutnant Faller's weapon. It appeared the advance was spotted by more than just one observer as the German artillery seemed to redouble its efforts in dropping a curtain of fire across No-Man's-Land. The advance of 'B' Company, which had started off as steadily, 'as if on a drill parade', was cut to ribbons in minutes, but a few men pushed on through the barrage. Out in front Major Guest continued to lead his men. Along with Major Guest, Lieutenant Heptonstall and three other men made their way through a gap in the wire and were within yards of entering the German trenches when Lieutenant Heptonstall felt a sharp stabbing pain in his side and fell into a shell crater. He looked on as the three Pals fell and then saw Major Guest shot in the right leg just as he was about to enter the front line. It was the last anyone saw of Tommy Guest.

Harry Hall was among those still walking forward with bullets and shell splinters singing about his ears and dead and wounded Pals falling all around him. Since there were no waves left he had seen fit to forget all about the instructions to carry his rifle held out in front of him.

"There was none of this 'port arms', not for me anyway. With all that weight we were expected to carry, bombs on one side, entrenching tool on the other, it was carry it how you could. I lost sight of my friends after a while but there were some of us got to their line. There were sections where the wire had been cut. I know there were eight or ten of us went into a section of their line. I didn't know who the men were. We started working our way to the left and right to see how far we could get. Well we'd got into the German front line and that's as far as we got. We daren't go any further. If you'd put your nose up there was another line of Germans in reserve still firing. There wasn't much we could do on our own, because it was only a small section we had broken into. We were under enfilade fire and we had no cover. The word was passed along to get out and get back as quickly as we could. I don't think anybody could have got any further, especially into Serre, the Germans were too strong." **Harry Hall, 13th Y & L Regiment**

Harry Hall and the pitifully few men who had reached the German front line had taken over half an hour to cross No-Man's-Land, and now they faced the dreadful journey once more. It was perhaps the only course of action left open to them apart from trying to take on the entire 169th Regiment on their own. Realising that a mere handful of men could make little headway against German soldiers intent on holding on to their trenches whatever the cost, the men of the 13th battalion climbed out of the German line and began to retrace their steps. They were fortunate to get out alive. The Germans were already massing the 9th, 10th and 12th Companies of their Reserve battalion for a counter-attack. Major Berthold, commanding the 1st Battalion of the 169th Regiment was himself preparing to kick the British out of the trenches for the second time in the space of an hour. Harry Hall and the few 13th Battalion Pals who had managed to get into the German front line were not the first men of the 94th Brigade to do so that morning. Miraculously, in spite of the shells and bullets, small parties of 'W' and 'X' Companies of the Accrington Pals and a few men of 'A' and 'C' Companies of the Sheffield City Battalion, had been seen by Brigade observers to break into the front line on the right and left of the attack a few minutes before 8 o'clock, and had gone on as far as the second line where they disappeared from view.

On the hour Headquarters of the 169th Regiment behind Serre had received an urgent signal from the 3rd and 4th Companies holding the front line.

"Message from Right sector that the enemy has penetrated the first trench S2."

The British had forced their way in and the men of the 3rd and 4th Companies were well aware of the fact

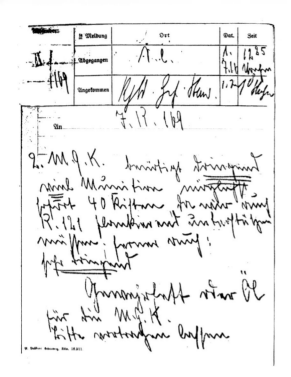

Message sent by 2nd Machine Gun Company at 11.25 a.m. (12.25 p.m. continental time) urgently requesting ammunition. It takes the runner 35 minutes to reach the Regimental Command Post behind the village. Message reads:

*2nd M.G.K. **urgently** requires **as much** ammunition as possible. 40 boxes immediately for we have also to support 121st Regiment on our flank. **Very urgent.** Please send forward gun grease or oil for the Machine Gun Company.*

since it was they who were having to fight tooth and nail to hold on to their positions. In some cases the issue had been settled in fierce hand-to-hand combat as British and German infantrymen fought to the death. Few prisoners were taken by the Germans. A counter-attack had been ordered immediately. Major Berthold had called for his 2nd Company to advance at once from the third trench against the intruders bombing their way along the front line. At the same time he pushed his 1st Company forward to support his right flank, while sections of the 10th Company in reserve in the fourth line, had rushed ahead to assist the 1st Battalion.

It was a wonderfully orchestrated display of strength in depth, in contrast to the lonely and isolated parties of Accrington and Sheffield men holding on for dear life. They never stood a chance.

At twenty minutes past eight, while Harry Hall had been making the crossing of No-Man's-Land for the first time, the first reports of a successful counter-attack were reaching Major von Struensee at Regimental Headquarters.

"Report from 1st Battalion 169 that the first trench is in our hands. Everything is going well."

And three minutes later,

"Reports from Leutnant Winter, 1st Battalion 169 Right and Reserve Battalion, that all trenches are in our hands."

It all seemed too easy. Now, just over ten minutes later, with fresh reports of another British break-in and with another counter-attack under way, it was just a matter of time before similar messages were received regarding the successful eviction of the First Barnsley Pals. Fortunately for his sake Harry Hall had not stayed to find out just how successful the Germans were likely to be.

Although 'B' Company's attack had broken down irrevocably, it was still rumoured that a few Accrington Pals had survived all counter-attacks and had been seen fighting their way towards Serre village. The drifting smoke of battle may have clouded the view of the German positions from the 94th Brigade Headquarters but that did not prevent messages of hope and encouragement pouring in from other sources. An aeroplane reported that men of the 94th Brigade were actually in Serre itself; the 93rd Brigade were said to be forging ahead to the right of the 94th and beyond them the men of the 4th Division were claimed to have overrun four sets of German trenches. Although Brigadier General Rees was convinced that if any of his men were indeed in Serre then they were probably prisoners, both Corps and Divisional Headquarters urged him to throw in his reserves where the leading troops were making progress rather than push them in behind those who were held up. Other reports were coming in of the Germans firing shrapnel into their own front line. If that and the previous reports were true, and the East Lancashires were pushing ahead, they would need help. The heavy German barrage had eased off a little and the Brigadier still had two and a half Companies of the 13th Battalion to throw in behind the East Lancashires.

It was doubtful whether the remains of the two platoons of 'A' Company in the partially obliterated front line were of much use to him. Captain Gurney's small force had been savaged by the German fire during their short journey to their present position, and even now were losing more men under a terrible shower of shells.

In a much healthier state were 'C' and 'D' Companies. They had escaped relatively lightly as they had advanced across the open to fill the trenches vacated by the third and fourth waves a little after half past seven.

Just before nine o'clock, Brigadier General Rees received a message from the 11th East Lancashires asking for reinforcements for their leading waves, and runners were despatched immediately to Captain Currin and Captain De Ville Smith in Copse and Monk trenches.

It hardly mattered that the timetable for the 94th Brigade was now running late; an hour late in fact, and anyway, what did count was that some men had apparently reached the fourth German line, the first objective for the day.

The orders for Captain Currin and Captain De Ville Smith were simply to support the leading waves by advancing and holding on to the first and second German lines, but as events had already shown, nothing was simple any longer.

It was now Tommy Oughton's turn to go over. He had struck lucky on many an occasion as a company signaller, ever since that October day in 1914 when Old Tom Lax had taken a shine to the young Wombwell lad as they had all trooped off up Doncaster Road on their way to the Public Hall. It remained to be seen if his luck would hold. Once more the piercing cries of the officers' whistles called out to the men of Barnsley, and 'C' and 'D' Companies rose from their trenches. Tommy Oughton was one of the last men of 14 platoon to leave Monk trench.

"*The whistle blew and the lads started going, Tom Bradbury was near me and a lad from Staincross who later got to be a parson. Being a signaller I was just in the rear of the others and I followed them. When I went over I didn't carry my rifle, I'd dumped that because I had full kit on, a spare field telephone on my shoulder and a roll of telephone wire for if we gained any objective. There was shelling, rifle and machine-gun fire as we went across. We hadn't a chance. I can't really describe what I saw to tell the truth. There you were, you could see bodies dropping here, there and wondering, is it you next? I saw plenty men I knew drop. No hope at all. Of course we didn't get far before we were knocked back. What made us stop was we got the order to retire. I don't know who gave the order, whether it was Lieutenant Hions or not I don't know. They'd seen all those on either flank retiring and we got word to get back as fast as we could. You had to get back to the best of your ability; drop in a shell hole for a rest and then back again. As we came back that's when I saw 'Devil' Smith's body and he looked to have hardly a scratch on his face. It must have been shock that killed him. There was a shell that had landed not far from him, we could see where it had dropped. You couldn't really call them trenches when we got back, they were blown up that badly. We'd to start and dig ourselves in again. The lads were in a terrible state.*" **Tommy Oughton, 13th Y & L Regiment**

Tommy Oughton was back where he had started. The advance of 'C' and 'D' Companies had lasted but a few minutes. Tommy's experience was remarkably similar to that of Harry Hall, but the difference was that few men of 'C' and 'D' Companies had managed to cross what was left of the British front line. They had run head first into a solid wall of shellfire as soon as they had shown themselves above the parapets. It seemed that the Germans could see everything; every tiny movement that the Pals cared to make.

The order to call a halt to the advance had come directly from the lips of none other than Brigadier General Rees himself, who had ventured out to personally put a stop to what was clearly a hopeless case. Concerned as he was about the East Lancashires said to be deep within the German lines and concerned as he was to consolidate what gains they had made, the few unsubstantiated reports he had received certainly did not seem to warrant the massacre of half a battalion. Even so he had called a halt a little too late to prevent both Companies being reduced to a shadow of their former selves.

Back in Monk trench Colonel Wilford set out to try and organise the men into some semblance of order. His was an unenviable task. Colonel Wilford had earned himself the nickname of 'the swashbuckler' at Brigade Headquarters and had already been to see Brigadier General Rees to tell him that he had been shelled out of two shelters which he had used as his battalion headquarters. On the last occasion Lieutenant Dart, the 13th Battalion Adjutant, had been killed. He was also willing to resume the attack and told the Brigadier,

"As far as I can make out, General, I have two companies left. If you would like me to charge at their head I shall be delighted to do so."

But Brigadier General Rees knew full well that what men remained of the 13th Battalion were in no fit state to do anything other than hang on to their own support trenches.

In stunned silence some of the men like Tommy Oughton were attempting to throw up some form of parapet under the German shellfire which continued unabated. Others clustered on the fire step among the groaning wounded or lay on the floor of the trench in a stupor. There were sections from 'C' Company mixed in with the shattered oddments of 'D' Company, who were now without their Company Commander along with a few stragglers of 'B' Company who had not got as far as Harry Hall. Nobody seemed to know quite what they were doing. That pitifully small, stunned band of men now represented the second line of defence on the right flank of the 94th Brigade. Five hundred yards or so ahead of them, the even smaller band of 'A' Company were cowering under cover of the crumbling parapets of the front line. The whole episode had been a truly horrific 'blooding' for the 13th Battalion. They had scarcely been in the trenches together as a whole battalion since they had arrived on the Western front, and from being part of an attacking force which had been told they would be instrumental in bringing peace within weeks of a 'breakthrough', they were now ripe for counter-attack. The hot sun had barely begun to climb into the sky.

On the left flank of the attack, the beautiful Summer morning was turning into one of the blackest days in the entire history of the York and Lancaster Regiment. Ossie Burgess had duly taken up his position in No-Man's-Land as ordered and from there he had seen a nightmare unfold before his very eyes. He had witnessed the wholesale butchery of both the elite of Sheffield and his own fine Battalion, yet he had not seen one man run away. Still, he had been powerless to do a thing about it. He had told his team that they had to remain where they were until told to move and he had not dared to fire the Lewis for fear of adding to the slaughter. All he could do was lie there and watch it all go horribly wrong.

The Germans were still firing however. The machine-gun which had been taken back to Leutnant Beyer had reappeared in the front line trenches in a depressingly short space of time and despite a makeshift repair, it commenced to fire against the left flank of the 94th Brigade once more.

Frank Lindley had spent a long time dodging the machine gun bullets and trying to get through the German wire but had failed every time. Flitting from shell hole to shell hole as fast as his young legs could carry him, he had searched in vain for a gap that was not already covered by a machine gun. At least no one could say that he hadn't tried. As he jumped into yet another shell hole, little did he suspect that at sixteen years and four months old he was a matter of moments away from a 'Blighty' wound.

"I didn't know anybody in the shell holes I got into. We were all mixed up. There was no conversation, it was self preservation; dive in and risk what you got. There were bags of 'em laid about in the holes, dead of course. The final shell hole I got in was the finish. We were hog tied. There I was studying form and this here 'whizz bang' came over and that put paid to the lot. There were three of us in that shell hole. It came over us and split, I never heard it coming. A piece of shell went right through my thigh and took all my trousers in with it. I looked down and I had no trousers and there was the blood all running out and the piece of shell stuck in my thigh. I thought I'd better go and get it seen to when I'd recovered a little. We were still trying to get through when I got wounded. The orders were, no coming back. I started to roll back over No-Man's-Land towards our trenches. On my way back I dropped into John Copse and I found a Sap head as though our lot had been sapping for a mine there. Well I went in there and had a smoke and there was a bloke, he was wounded somehow, and he was in the door hole. The Germans dropped some shells into the Copse

and some fragments hit his arm and a piece of the hot shell burnt a little hole in my leg as I was laid inside." **Frank Lindley, 14th Y & L Regiment**

Frank had taken refuge in one of the two tunnel entrances which had been dug into the bank behind John Copse. He wasn't in the near end of the entrance to the Russian Sap as that should have been full of the party from 'B' Company of the 14th Battalion and from where Frank was sitting all he could see were a few wounded men like him, taking shelter. In fact there was no sign of two full platoons and they should have been somewhere in the vicinity of John Copse, since they were supposed to have followed the survivors of 'A' Company out of Nairne Street a few minutes after 'zero' hour.

As the remnants of 'A' Company had plunged into the smoke in No-Man's-Land, Lieutenant Fairley and Lieutenant Lowinsky in charge of the Russian Sap party, had been faced with a dilemma.

Instead of filing quickly down towards John Copse and making a start on helping the Pioneers to convert the shallow tunnel into a fire trench facing north, the two young officers quickly realised that the plans had gone awry. Their men were hardly moving, most of them held up under heavy fire from the left in a particularly exposed stretch of Nairne Street. Someone, somewhere, had seen fit to order the men to follow each other at intervals of three paces. Choked as it was with dead, and with some of the less seriously wounded cases beginning to squirm their way back to the advanced dressing station at the far end of Nairne, the order was simply inviting the annihilation of the

Brigadier General Rees, temporary commander of 94th Brigade, holds Barnsley Companies back from further attacks against the German positions as the disastrous failure becomes obvious.

Russian Sap party. They had already suffered casualties from the heavy German shelling of the John Copse area and were now taking more by being in such a dangerous position. Realising the gravity of the situation Captain Houston immediately passed orders forward to clear Nairne as quickly as possible. Captain Houston personally pushed his way down the trench to make sure that the order was carried out. Abandoning all thoughts of intervals and paces every able-bodied man in the Russian Sap party began to push on towards John Copse and the Russian Sap. The defence of the left flank of the Fourth Army rested on them reaching their objective, but they never got there.

At half past nine Lieutenant Lowinsky, badly wounded, appeared at Battalion Headquarters with the news that every officer of the Russian Sap party had been 'knocked out' and that two new platoons must be sent. That was all the information he could give. His wounds were so severe that he had to be sent back for treatment straight away. Colonel Hulke then ordered 2nd Lieutenant Johnson to take two platoons of 'C' Company forward to reinforce the original party or, if they had been wiped out, to consolidate and hold the Sap themselves.

2nd Lieutenant Johnson led his force from Campion trench into Nairne. When they arrived at the flattened stretch he halted the men and went forward alone to locate the position of the Sap and the trench. He found no trace of them and no signs of the original party either.

Back at Battalion Headquarters Colonel Hulke received the woeful message from 2nd Lieutenant Johnson and decided to take a look for himself. Going forward he too soon began to realise that the Russian Sap was no longer to be found in the place where it should have been. Perhaps the whole area had been so levelled that the German shells had caused the tunnel to collapse. In any event he came to the decision that it was quite impossible for the two platoons of 'C' Company to even attempt to reach the spot where the Russian sap had been without running the risk of the total destruction of the whole party. 2nd Lieutenant Johnson withdrew his men and Colonel Hulke went back to his dugout to make arrangements for an officer to try and find another route via Mark Copse. That arrangement was soon forgotten as word was received from Brigadier General Rees to hold 'C' and 'D' Companies back.

The position on the right flank was so tenuous that the Brigadier needed every last man he could lay his hands on as the thought of counter-attack worried all at Brigade Headquarters. Meanwhile all Frank

Lindley could think about was to get back to a first aid post and have his wound attended to. Leaving the entrance to the little tunnel in John Copse he began to pull himself along the ground towards the rear. It was a heart-rending journey.

"It was a drag, dragging at the side of the trenches. It really didn't seem too far. I was sliding over different people that had been done in the other trenches. They'd caught it as bad as we had at the front. While we'd been getting dealt with up there, the Germans had been dealing with the other lot behind us. The reserve lines were peppered. There were no reserves left, they were in pulp. One bloke must have been climbing out of the trench and it had done him across the middle. It left his feet and bottom half in the trench and all his insides were hanging down the side of the trench. I remember thinking, 'So that's what a liver and kidney look like'. It's funny what you think at times like that. There ought to have been something different to that. I found my way down past this dugout that the 'Heads and Tails' were in. There they were, the Boss and his retinue, marching up and down outside this dugout, with white faces, looking over towards the front. I remember seeing Sergeant Major Ascough there. The thought struck me then, if they ask me how things are going over there I should have said 'Bloody well go and find out for yourself', but they never asked. I got by and I got to the end of Nairne Street, and there was a bloke patching you up. It was a bit of an aid post. He had a go at me and gave me a shot for tetanus and then they picked us up and slotted us in a little ambulance feet first, on little shelves, and away we went. What I thought mainly, the very first thing I thought was, 'How the bloody hell are they going to clear this mess up'. Them stretcher-bearers must have thought all Hell was let loose. With a disaster on the scale as it was you wondered how the hell they'd shifted 'em. There's a lot still there, there must be." **Frank Lindley, 14th Y & L Regiment**

Lieutenant Robert Allatt Heptonstall. He is wounded in the attack and waits in a shell hole for an opportunity to crawl back across No-Man's-Land.

Frank Lindley had been one of the lucky ones, in that he had managed to crawl all the way back across No-Man's-Land without sustaining further injury. Harry Hall was another Pal with luck on his side that morning. He had crossed No-Man's-Land twice under heavy fire and had not received so much as a bruise.

"We didn't lose too many going back. There weren't many to lose. There were about fifteen for roll call that morning, fifteen out of about three hundred. They weren't all killed mind. Some were missing, some were still out. Somebody had seen Major Guest fall but didn't know if he was hit and wounded or hit and killed. The wounded came creeping in. The least opportunity they had when they'd recovered their senses they came creeping back." **Harry Hall, 13th Y & L Regiment**

Lieutenant Heptonstall was one of the 'B' Company officers who was alive but still out on the battlefield. He had been one of the last men to see Major Guest alive, but he could not get back to report to Colonel Wilford at Battalion Headquarters. Like many other badly wounded men he was unable to make the journey back to the British lines. He lay in the same shell crater he had fallen into earlier, not daring to attempt the long crawl back across No-Man's-Land. The shell holes were full of men unable to make their way back. Some were so severely wounded that they could not move at all due to extreme pain or weakness through loss of blood. There was also the added danger of German snipers. Even the unwounded were often unable to move in case they attracted undue attention.

Some of the men were under such shallow cover that they dare not reach for their water bottles to slake their raging thirsts for fear of revealing their positions. One of Harry Hall's pals in the Sheffield City Battalion had found cover in a shell hole so shallow that one of his feet stuck up above ground level. It wasn't long before he was hit in the foot. With no treatment available apart from personal first aid packs the dangers of gangrene for men with open wounds were serious indeed, and the longer they stayed out the worse it would be.

The sun beat down mercilessly on them all and there was nothing anyone back in the British lines could do about it. Many of them were so far out that the stretcher-bearers would certainly have perished in attempting to reach them. The slightly wounded and able-bodied would have to wait until after dark before risking the journey back. For many of the rest, darkness would have come long before the sun had disappeared behind Colincamps.

As Lieutenant Heptonstall waited patiently for nightfall he was treated to a gruesome spectacle.

"From my shell hole I could see a dead man propped up against the German wire in a sitting position. He was sniped at during the day until his head was completely shot away." Lieutenant **Robert Allatt Heptonstall, 13th Y & L Regiment**

It was all over bar the shouting at around eleven o'clock, for the Pals at any rate. From the German trenches only stretcher-bearers and wounded were to be seen over in the British lines. On the right hand side of the 94th Brigade, Captain Gurney's small force of 'A' Company of the 13th Battalion were clinging to the front line, together with a few stragglers from 'B' Company who, like Harry Hall, had managed to crawl in without being spotted by German snipers. In Monk trench the survivors of 'C' and 'D' Companies with a few Accrington Pals, a handful of 12th K.O.Y.L.I. Pioneers and several men of the 94 Brigade Light trench mortar battery, held grimly on to what was now the second line of defence.

On the left flank the situation was equally chaotic. Charlie Swales had been in Campion trench since twenty five minutes to eight and his company had lost several men hit mainly by enfilade fire from the positions of the German 66th Regiment on their left. Although they too now formed part of the second British line, their advance had not suffered in the same way as the advance of 'C' and 'D' Companies of their sister Battalion. Nevertheless they were still in a shambles.

"We couldn't see any officers to co-ordinate us into any kind of order so we just dropped into a trench and that was it. A few of us were together when a sergeant rounded us up. I think they were talking about making another attack but they hadn't enough men. I thought at the time that if we had tried to make another attack that would have been it." **Charlie Swales, 14th Y & L Regiment**

On the other side of No-Man's-Land the men of the 169th Regiment would have agreed wholeheartedly with Charlie Swales' assessment of the state of 94 Brigade. In fact they would have gone so far as to say that it had all been over long before eleven o'clock and that they had succeeded in blunting the bright spears of the entire 31st Division as early as nine o'clock that morning.

By ten minutes past nine a messenger was already winging his way to the Headquarters of the 104th Brigade with the good news from Major Berthold that the front line had been purged of British troops for the second time.

Oberleutnant Faller of the 1st Machine-Gun Company was another man who was convinced that the attack had been crushed by nine o'clock, and that the large numbers of dead and wounded littering the deep German front line and piled in front of the wire, would serve as a painful reminder to the British not to try again. He was proud of his men, proud of the way they had stood up to the physical and mental strain of the seven-day 'Trommelfeuer', proud of the way they had stuck to their tasks when the time came for them to act. At no time during the battle had he felt the reins of command slipping through his fingers. Orders had been given and received in a calm, almost businesslike manner, and although he had lost some of his best men and highly trained weapon leaders among the five dead and fourteen wounded out of his 149 strong company, he still felt that the victory was complete.

The same picture was emerging in the trenches opposite the 93rd Brigade a little further to the south, where the 7th Company of the 169th Regiment were holding the front line. Their diarist reported that 'calm gradually came' to their trenches at around nine o'clock and it continued throughout the remaining hours of daylight. The 7th Company diarist was so obviously delighted with the way the battle had gone that he saw fit to show off his literary talents when writing up the report of the actions of July 1st. Towards the end of the entry he inserted a clever play on words, 'Sehre'haben sie gekriegt aber nicht' Serre'. 'They took much but they didn't take Serre'.

But what of the men of the 94th Brigade last seen battling their way on towards the village? What of

Captain Roos and his tiny band of Barnsley Pals of the 14th Battalion's 'A' Company, thought to have entered the second German trench on the left of the attack? What of the Sheffielders and the Accrington Pals?

At 10.27 a.m., Brigadier General Rees had received a telegram from the Headquarters of the 31st Division.

"Following information received. 56th Division from Hebuterne have gone right through, and are flanking Rossignol Wood. 165th Royal Field Artillery Brigade report that infantry has taken Serre. At 9.45 a.m. our men were seen carrying what looked like machine guns in front of Pendant Copse also three or four hundred of our men advancing on the line Pendant Copse-Serre."

And again at 10.50 a.m.

"Another report just received that several of our men have been seen in Serre."

These and subsequent reports of British troops seen to be in and around the village of Serre helped in sowing the seeds of a legend, a legend which was to flourish in later years and tell of how a few men of South Yorkshire or East Lancashire; a few miners or schoolteachers or cotton spinners, had fought on against all the odds to drive a wedge seven or eight hundred yards deep into the German trench system against a highly efficient and battle-hardened German Regiment.

Some may indeed have entered the village, just as thirteen men of the 18th Durham Light Infantry had succeeded in reaching Pendant Copse a little to the south and much, much further than eight hundred yards behind the German front line. Perhaps the men of the 94th Brigade had been cut off with no officers or N.C.O.s to guide them and had suffered the same fate as that which beckoned to the Durham Pals, to be swallowed whole and to end up in the belly of the whale.

The truth behind the legend may never now be told. However, it appears strange that if, as various observers have stated, troops of the 94th Brigade were seen to be in Serre village, that Major von Struensee should issue orders for three companies of his reserve battalion to advance to the aid of the 121st Reserve Infantry Regiment at around nine o'clock. Surely his reserves would have been used against those threatening the village itself.

Sensing that the Württembergers to the south were struggling to contain a break-in by the regular troops of the 4th Division at the Heidenkopf, Major von Struensee came to a decision to despatch the men of his third reserve battalion, who, up until then had been holding the trenches and cellars of Serre and the fourth line immediately in front of the village, up the slope towards the redoubt. At no time had he received a call for help.

Since his 10th Company had already been committed to helping the 1st Battalion of the 169th Regiment, and the 12th Company would have to move up from a position well behind Serre, only the 11th Company were available to move at once.

For the rest of the day the 11th Company were attached to the 121st Reserve Infantry Regiment, Leutnant Friedrich Hoppe's 2nd Platoon playing a major part in driving the mixed force of the 4th Division out of the Heidenkopf towards evening.

For their prompt action in going to the assistance of their beleagured comrades from Württemberg, Major von Struensee was recommended for the Württemberg medal of honour, along with his reserve battalion commanding officer, Hauptmann Engel and Leutnant Fritz Hoppe the commanding officer of the 2nd platoon of the 11th Company, which had fought so long to keep the British out.

The decision to send reserves to the aid of a neighbouring Regiment so early on the opening day of the British offensive was hardly the action of a senior officer threatened with British troops fighting hard on his own doorstep.

For the rest of the morning and well into the afternoon there was little the Pals could do but hang on to their trenches and tend their wounded friends as a heavy German barrage rumbled on into the evening.

Although Major General Wanless O'Gowan continued to badger Brigadier General Rees into sending what reinforcements he had over the top to help the men still thought to be in the German trenches, the Brigadier wisely declined. For a start his Brigade was in no fit state to do anything other than sit tight and he was unwilling to commit more men until he had received definite reports from the front. The only word coming back was that brought by the wounded and by now there were so many of them with the same sorry tale that it was becoming perfectly clear that the 94th Brigade had met with disaster on a grand scale.

Several orders to renew the attack in the afternoon were cancelled as the magnitude of the failure in front of Serre gradually filtered back, first to Divisional and then to Corps Headquarters.

At five o'clock in the evening Captain Currin took what was left of 'C' Company of the 13th Battalion forward to relieve Captain Gurney and the shocked and shattered remnants of 'A' Company who had been holding the front line for more than nine hours. As they worked their way back to Monk trench, trying hard not to step on the bodies of the dead and wounded of two battalions, the weary men of 'A' Company little realised that they were among just 280 men of all ranks who could be accounted for at that particular time.

Towards nine o'clock, as a dust-filled gloom began to weigh down on the British trenches, 'C' and 'D' Companies of the 14th Battalion moved up to relieve the few unwounded men of the Sheffield City Battalion in the front line.

Wounded, fortunate enough to be hit whilst within the British lines are collected by the stretcher-bearers and attended to on the morning of the attack. Wounded crouching in shell holes out in No-Man's-Land are waiting for darkness to fall before attempting the painful journey back.

As darkness fell on the battlefield concealing the movements of the men out in the shell holes, those who could, began to pull, drag or roll their aching bodies back towards the British lines. Lieutenant Heptonstall was one of those who managed to return with the story of how he had seen Major Guest fall before the German front-line trench several hours earlier. Such was the popularity of the 'B' Company commander that some of his men were prepared to risk their own lives by going out to search for him.

"Someone had seen Major Guest fall but didn't know if he had been hit and wounded or hit and killed. They decided to go out and find him that night. There were about four or five of them. They went out but they never came back." **Harry Hall, 13th Y & L Regiment**

Some of the wounded were brought in by Captain Currin and a volunteer search party from 'C' Company. While the rest of the men set to in digging out blocked fire bays and deepening the shallow front line, Captain Currin's party worked long into the night scouring the British lines and No-Man's-Land for dead and wounded and bringing them in under heavy fire.

The 44-year-old South African officer was personally involved in the rescue of some eighty wounded men from exposed positions, acts of gallantry which led to the Captain being awarded the Distinguished Service Order on 25th August, 1916.

For the young men of the 13th Battalion the sight of some of the badly wounded Pals sickened them

No-Man's-Land, British dead litter the field, a common sight along the Somme front on 1st July.

to the very core. Harry Hall had joined up for a change of life, among other things, but the barrels of beer at the end of a long march round Barnsley, the almost carefree days of Silkstone, Cannock, Ripon and Hurdcott and even the fun and games in Egypt had not gone even halfway to preparing them for the concentrated suffering which met their eyes.

Hall was quite convinced that for the moment at least, the survivors of the 13th Battalion had had the stuffing knocked out of them.

> *"Everybody had the same opinion, they'd had enough and seen enough. It was more what you saw than what you experienced. To see fellows coming in maimed, oh it was terrible."* **Harry Hall, 13th Y & L Regiment**

Even as Captain Currin was risking his life to bring in the wounded from their long and painful isolation in No-Man's-Land, Frank Lindley had long since bowed out of the Battle of the Somme.

From the Casualty Clearing Station the ambulance carrying Frank had rattled off somewhere towards the rear. In a swirling haze of pain Frank thought that they passed through Amiens and on to Etaples. Every time it jolted to a halt people would rush forward to offer the parched Tommies a sip of cooling liquid. At Etaples the medical staff were already working like fury to cope with the tremendous numbers of wounded beginning to reach the base hospitals. There was precious little chance of putting the sixteen-year-old to sleep, the order of the day was 'do it'. A doctor yanked the shrapnel out of Frank's thigh and Frank thought the doctor had pulled half his innards out with it. As he began to drift into unconciousness Frank could have sworn he had heard the sounds of someone sawing.

As the minutes ticked by towards midnight and the end of the first day of the Battle of the Somme, Ossie Burgess was still out in No-Man's-Land with his Lewis Gun team. Just as they were beginning to think that they would be out all night they heard the sound of someone approaching. Anxiously they waited and then, unable to stand the suspense much longer one of Ossie's team challenged the oncoming figure. Happily it was a messenger with their long awaited 'further orders'. After being out all day without firing a shot, and helplessly looking on as his battalion had been massacred, Ossie Burgess was told to report back to the original line. Whatever the mission his superiors had in mind, other than being in position to prevent German counter-attacks, it was now long forgotten. There were other things to worry about.

As Ossie turned his back on No-Man's-Land and began to make his way towards the British lines he left behind him a part of Barnsley which had fought and died that day and lay out along the scarred grassy slope in front of Serre. He left behind fathers and sons, husbands, sweethearts and scoundrels, and a wealth of dreams, hopes and memories. The memories had perished along with the men, and most of the men had fallen within the first two burning hours of battle. It was still too early, too chaotic, too mind numbing to try and establish just how many had been lost. For the survivors the problems of trying to stay alive and sorting out the mess among the living overshadowed every other consideration for the time being.

To even contemplate the location of the large numbers of men who officially would come under the category of 'missing' was a headache best left until later. It was impossible to know how many were simply lost, mixed in with other units and were still too shellshocked to know where they were, or how many were still out in No-Man's-Land. In any event, out of the men still out on the battlefield there were an untold number who were wounded and uncared for but still alive, sustained by little more than memories and the hopes which had led many of them to join up in the first place. Those men were definitely out there somewhere and while some of them moaned and wailed in their agony no one heard them. The British guns had started up again, shelling the German front trenches and drowning out the cries of the wounded. There were some men of course who had simply vanished without trace.

It was perhaps an easier task to account for the men who lay dead among the British trenches or who had been brought in wounded but had since died. Captain De Ville Smith's body was found and buried later in a cemetery near Colincamps. Sergeant Harry Scargill was another man whose loss could be accounted for. He had gone over the top that morning but before going very far he had been severely wounded and had lost consciousness almost immediately. The 29-year-old Eldon Street draper, who almost two years earlier had taken up space in the Barnsley Chronicle to assure his clients that his business with the Kaiser would not take too long, had died long before anyone had been able to carry him back to the British trenches.

A few, precious few, of the missing men had been taken prisoner by the 169th Regiment. Among them was Private William Henry Clarkson, hero of the Second Barnsley Battalion and proud recipient of the Military Medal. Less than a month earlier he had risked death by rescuing the wounded Private John McKelvey from No-Man's-Land in broad daylight. Now Private Clarkson was wounded and in German hands. He was one of only two men of the 14th Battalion listed as being taken alive by the Germans, the other Pal, Private William Goldthorpe was also seriously wounded when he was taken. The two men did not spend long in captivity. Both of them died of their wounds on the same day, July 4th, in the same place, a German field hospital at Fremicourt.

Seventeen-year-old 'Tiger' Billy Ward, First Barnsleys, waited for nightfall before crawling back from a shell hole in front of the German wire.

Only two prisoners were mentioned as belonging to specific units in the war diary of the 169th Regiment for July 1st. At ten minutes past eleven in the morning the following entry appears:

"The regiment has caught two prisoners from the 12th and 13th York and Lancaster Regiments (Besides that, in S2 a machine gun captured)."

Twenty-five minutes later the 169th Regiment sent a message to the Headquarters of the 104th Brigade and by that time the two men, probably exhausted and scared out of their wits, had told their captors all they knew.

"According to their statements they must make a breakthrough in the direction of Bapaume at all costs. Losses are heavy."

Already the Germans were starting to piece together the tiny fragments of evidence which would give them a clue as to what the British were up to and, more importantly, what they would do next. They did not need to be told however that the British losses were heavy. They had seen that for themselves. At a rough estimate the 169th Regiment put the British dead at around the two thousand mark on their particular sector, but their figures too were distorted by the wounded left out on the battlefield. Under the circumstances the German figure was a good guess.

By midnight on July 1st Major von Struensee had been presented with a bundle of papers marked 'Secret' which had been taken from the pockets of a dead British officer. They carried the information that the British had '. . . laid great value on the occupation of Serre to secure the northern flank of the attacking Army'. In all, the 169th Regiment took forty-two prisoners along with 4 machine guns. It was reported that the 2nd Platoon of the 11th Company under Leutnant Fritz Hoppe captured 32 men and three Lewis guns during the course of the fighting in the Heidenkopf, yet it is not clear if these men are included in the total number of prisoners taken by the entire 169th Regiment. The low numbers are perhaps some indication of how few men reached the German trenches alive. Even lower was the number of prisoners taken by the entire British 8th Corps.

Just 22 men had made their way through the Divisional compounds on their way to the Corps compound at Acheux. The officers who had waited to interview the prisoners had waited in vain and the labours of the Royal Engineers Field Companies in constructing the cages had been for nought.

The long winding stream of walking wounded travelling in the same direction as the 22 prisoners towards the casualty collecting station at Acheux had been a distinct embarrassment to the 8th Corps. They had been trudging back all day and well into the night the medical staff were finding it difficult to cope with the seemingly endless flow.

Opposite Serre during the early hours of July 2nd, wounded and unwounded Pals would here and there slither to safety into the front-line trenches after their long journey from No-Man's-Land. William 'Tiger Billy' Ward of the 13th Battalion crawled in after being out all day. He was the son of a regular soldier and had been born in no less a place than Colchester Barracks. His father had gone off to South Africa and had been killed in action when William had been five years old, but the first day of the Somme offensive had not claimed the life of the seventeen-year-old miner from Ivy Terrace off Doncaster Road. While he tried to get his bearings and perhaps thought about informing someone that he was still alive, his Company Commander and the volunteers of 'C' Company were still working tirelessly to bring in the wounded out beyond the British barbed wire.

The Battalion Headquarters of the Sheffield City Battalion received a signal during the night to the effect that yet another report had been gathered by Brigade telling of some 150 Sheffielders who were still clinging to a stretch of German front line. Ever hopeful of saving more lives Brigadier General Rees had told the Sheffielders to get in touch with their men and withdraw them, but that was easier said than done. The Sheffielders had but ten unwounded men at Battalion Headquarters and they were runners and signallers. There was nothing for it but to call on the men of the Second Barnsley Battalion. Between half past one and a quarter past three two officer patrols went out with parties of men from the 14th Battalion and crawled across to the German wire. They heard nothing, nothing apart from the relieved gasps of wounded men whom they had stumbled across on their travels, and the German machine guns still sweeping No-Man's-Land.

The report of the men in the German trenches was yet another example of how every line of communication had been severed despite all efforts to repair them.

A few hours earlier General Douglas Haig had jotted down a few of his first impressions of how Lieutenant-General Sir Aylmer Hunter-Weston's 8th Corps had fared on July 1st, based on the reports he had received.

"North of the Ancre, the 8th Corps (Hunter-Weston) said they began well, but as the day progressed, their troops were forced back into the German front line, except two Battalions which occupied Serre village, and were, it is said, cut off. I am inclined to believe from further reports, that few of the 8th Corps left their trenches."

It was quite clear that communications had completely broken down.

228

Chapter Twelve

Talk of the town

FOR CHARLES PLUMPTON AND HIS SMALL BAND of three reporters working at the offices of the Barnsley Chronicle in Peel Square, the first week of July was a trying time.

They were quite aware, as everyone else in the Barnsley area was, that the Barnsley Pals had probably gone over the top with the rest of General Rawlinson's Fourth Army very early on Saturday 1st July, and they were also aware that they would have a certain amount of difficulty in reporting such a major story. Being a provincial weekly meant that their copy could never compete with the immediacy of the national and provincial dailies in keeping their readers abreast of the day to day goings on of the war.

Every day for a week, before the opening of the 'Big Push', Mr. Plumpton and his chief reporter Mr. Allen had dutifully scoured the pages of the national daily papers as well as those of the nearby Sheffield Independent, and had seen the same story crop up again and again. News of the terrific artillery preparations on the Somme appeared to be hitting the presses almost as often as the British shells were hitting the German lines.

While Mr. Plumpton and his team of journalists could not hope to convey the awesome spectacle of the British shelling to their readers quite as graphically as those affluent dailies, who had despatched correspondents to the scene of the fighting, they perhaps had good reason to be pleased with the way events had turned out in the light of the Chronicle editorial comment of July 1st.

> "No doubt good and solid reasons explain why there has been no great spring 'push' all along the Western Front. It would, of course, never do to act in the least degree prematurely in so momentous a matter. It may be assumed, however, that the summer will not pass without the present apparent stalemate being radically changed.
>
> "It does not, of course, follow that the war will end either this summer or even in the autumn, but all the same events seem pointing to very decisive movements which may completely alter the entire outlook of the campaign." **Barnsley Chronicle, 1st July, 1916**

The only problem was that the British Army had chosen to make its 'decisive movement' on the very day that that particular issue of the Chronicle had hit the news-stands of Barnsley. Now Mr. Plumpton, Mr. Allen and the two junior reporters Mr. Smith and Mr. Roycroft, would have almost another week to wait before they could tell their readers what had happened on the Somme. They would have almost a full week in which to digest the deluge of official despatches and press reports regarding the progress of the battle before the next issue of the Chronicle went to press.

As far as the Chronicle was concerned the story of the 'Push' really broke on Saturday 8th July, since that was the first opportunity Mr. Plumpton's staff had to comment on the way the battle was progressing, but they were at a serious disadvantage.

Although the journalists had had a week to take in the pile of official, semi-official and popular reports, they could only write about what they knew, and they only knew as much as the reports told them. They could do little other than regurgitate the news they had been fed with, and if that news loudly trumpeted the initial driving successes of a conquering British Army then that is exactly what the people of Barnsley were given.

THE BRITISH OFFENSIVE

In Barnsley and throughout the kingdom the one topic on every tongue this week is the great Anglo-French offensive. The progress of our gallant troops is being watched with the keenest interest. Tremendous events are developing. Momentous issues are in the balance. The British had struck where the Germans least expected the blow to come. The point selected is in front of the joint where

Peel Square dominated by the Chronicle office block. The setting for a procession of heartbroken relatives clutching photographs of husbands, fathers and brothers officially reported 'killed in action' by the War Office in the weeks after 1st July, 1916.

the British Army links up with the French Forces. The stroke was prepared for by a week's heavy artillery shelling, but as our guns roared equally along the whole of our ninety miles of front, the enemy could not judge by this circumstance precisely where the blow would be delivered . . .

. . . The preliminary British bombardment paved the way to the great success afterwards achieved, for it not only wrecked the enemy's first line trenches, but the second and third line defences also suffered severely. The British left nothing to chance. Raiding and reconnaisance parties with much dash entered the German trenches in order to ascertain precisely what degree of damage was done by our guns. In this way much useful information was gained and many prisoners were captured. Sterner work quickly followed when this preliminary blow was driven home. Serre and Montauban, two important tactical points were soon captured, and comparatively early in the fight even more valuable positions were taken after a sharp struggle. The initial success of defeating the enemy on a sixteen mile front has naturally elated the whole British Army and nation, and aroused the utmost confidence of further triumphs . . . The long talked of advance is now actually in course of accomplishment . . . The progress made along the British front may be regarded as most promising . . . The crisis of the war is at hand . . . With the triumphant British advance the great conflict seems entering upon its penultimate and most momentous phase.

Barnsley Chronicle, 8th July, 1916

Other pages carried reports from a variety of different sources, including some of German origin, which dealt with the ebb and flow of the fighting during the first week of the Allied offensive. The reports reflected the confusion as to just how well the British had fared, particularly with regard to their 'initial success'. It was there for all to see, in black and white. Serre had been captured. Without realising the devastating significance of their words the Chronicle had reported the capture of Serre as a fact one full week after the sons of Barnsley had been bloodily repulsed in front of the German village fortress. They were words which would come back to mock the writers in the very near future as the full story of the Barnsley Pals' part in the fight for Serre became known.

It wasn't that Mr. Plumpton and his staff were lying, they were merely passing on a mixture of fact and fiction which the British Army itself had been unable to separate successfully in the vital early stages of the battle. If General Haig himself had been under the impression that two battalions had managed to get into Serre when he made up his diary in the evening of 1st July, how then could Mr. Plumpton and his staff, sitting at their typewriters in the heart of South Yorkshire, and far removed from the whine of shells and the cries of the wounded, hope to reveal the truth.

What the Chronicle staff were doing, along with many other provincial weekly journalists, was trying to make some sense of events which were of immense importance while at the same time playing their patriotic role in boosting morale and keeping hopes of victory alive.

Even so, things were not quite as rosy as the Chronicle had made out, and the Chronicle recognised this to a certain extent. The same 8th July issue which carried stories of glorious advances over miles of the front also carried an article which served to get all the relatives of the Pals at the front talking, if they weren't talking already. One whole week had apparently not been long enough to clear up some of the confusion, but it had been long enough for rumour and uncertainty to make their way hand in hand across the English Channel in the company of the many wounded soldiers who were shipped home in the first few days.

Vernon Atkinson left France on board the hospital ship *St. Denis* on 3rd July and a day later Frank Lindley was on his way back to England on board the same vessel. The crews of the ships were working overtime crossing and re-crossing the Channel to evacuate the wounded. The stories told by some of the casualties did not seem to match the stories the relatives had read in the papers. Naturally the people at home were worried and unsettled by these new revelations, and elements of the worry and uncertainty had penetrated as far as the coalfields of South Yorkshire.

The Chronicle saw fit to bring the problem out into the open.

THE WAR

GLORIOUS BRITISH ADVANCE

Wild Local Rumours

Up to the hour of going to press the British continue their gloriously successful 'push' in France, begun well over a week ago, and reported at length on another page.

All sorts of wild rumours were yesterday current locally concerning the Barnsley Battalions, and whilst we are not in a position to give them the lie direct, we can authoritatively say that no official news has come through which would in any way corroborate the startling tales afloat regarding the fate of our lads.

Last night's post brought us several postcards briefly recording the fact that some of the members of the Battalions have been wounded and were – at the time of writing – being treated in the dressing stations behind the firing line, but the stories of officers and men being killed in great numbers is unsubstantiated.

During next week – should any news come through regarding the Barnsley Battalions – we shall post the messages on the front window of the 'Chronicle' buildings. In the event of no message being posted it must, therefore, be taken for granted that nothing of outstanding importance has happened. **Barnsley Chronicle, 8th July, 1916**

The Chronicle had gone to great pains in attempting to calm the troubled waters of doubt and uncertainty, but the printing of the article did little to allay the fears of the relatives of the Pals at the front. They naturally wanted to know what had happened to their menfolk and yet their own local paper had confessed that it did not hold any of the answers to their many questions. If anything the article only served to make matters worse. It was a terrible time for the relatives of the Pals, not knowing whether their Tommy, their Harry or their Frank had come out of the 'Big Push' alive.

There may have been uncertainty on the part of the many relatives but there was definite news of one of the 13th Battalion officers. On Sunday, 9th July several members of the congregation at St. Thomas' Church, Worsbrough Dale, were moved to tears as the Reverend Banham chose to preface his sermon with a reference to the death of Captain George De Ville Smith, their former curate.

"It was a source of great pain when on Friday morning I received from the War Office a telegram announcing that our old friend and curate had been killed while on active service in France on 1st July." **Barnsley Chronicle, 15th July, 1916**

The Reverend Banham had received a letter from Captain Smith just two weeks earlier and although it seemed bright and cheery enough, the Reverend informed the congregation that as he had read between the lines he had noted a hint of melancholy. The letter had closed with the hope that the Reverend Banham would not forget Captain Smith at the 'Throne of Grace'.

The War Office telegram concerning the death of Captain Smith was among the first of many which would bear a Barnsley address.

Gradually further snippets of information filtered back to Barnsley but always the news seemed to lack any real substance. At a meeting of Barnsley Town Council on Tuesday 11th July, the Mayor, Alderman Henry Holden, read out a letter from Major General Wanless O'Gowan, commanding officer of the 31st Division, in which he referred specifically to the gallantry of the Barnsley Battalions.

"I am certain you will be interested to know how well the York and Lancaster Brigade fought on Saturday last. All the Battalions, 12th, 13th and 14th York and Lancaster and 11th East Lancashires distinguished themselves by their coolness, dash, and extraordinary bravery. Their advance in face of a terrific bombardment was beyond all praise, and one of the finest performances ever accomplished by British soldiers. I am sure Yorkshire and Lancashire will appreciate the way in which the whole Division behaved."

There was still no mention of heavy losses, or for that matter any denials either, only more of the same ringing praise of the British troops which had been so evident in the early news bulletins. Alderman Holden

The news at last is out and the Chronicle makes it front page news on 15th July, just two weeks after the Pals' abortive attack on the German stronghold of Serre.

sley (

RO' WATH AND I

BARNSLEY, 1123 | VOL. LVIII. NO. 4013   SATURDAY, JULY 15.

LOCAL HEROES FALL IN ACTION.

BARNSLEY BATTALIONS CHARGE THE HUNS

THROUGH SHOT AND SHELL.

OFFICERS & MEN MAKE GREAT SACRIFICES.

Hundreds of troops from Barnsley and district took part in the great British offensive on Saturday, July 1st, in the region of Albert, France, and though they succeeded in carrying out their plans this was done at a great sacrifice of life and limb.

It was about seven o'clock on the morning of the 1st inst. that the order was given for the men of the two Barnsley Battalions, the Territorials, and other regiments to fix bayonets preparatory to leaving their shielded quarters for the move forward. The Germans, it was known, were only about 100 yards away, and no sooner had the Britishers mounted the parapets than they were faced with terrific machine-gun and shrapnel fire. Many officers and men were struck down and the casualty list is sorrowful reading.

Grief-stricken parents, relatives, and friends can take consolation from the reading of the observations made by the General leading the Division and which appears in this issue.

Taking a rough calculation, it may safely be said that fully 5,000 men from Barnsley and the immediate district took part in the great attack. Special mention should be of made our brave Territorials who have been in the thick of it so long ; once again they acquitted themselves splendidly.

Lieut.-Colonel Hewitt has this week received letters from many of the officers of the 13th Y & L (1st Barnsley Battalion), six of whom it is thought were killed and at least as many wounded. These wounded officers vividly describe the attack and say that the Battalion lads performed as coolly as though on parade at Silkstone— a fact which Colonel Hewitt is delighted with, but by no means surprised to hear.

Major T. Guest is reported missing, and Colonel Wilford writes of him : " He was last seen leading a Company into a German trench ; he was shot in the right leg just as he reached the trench ; there is still hope."

Major Kennard, Captain de Ville Smith, and Lieuts. Dart and Hirst were killed ; Capt. Maleham believed to be killed ; Lieut. Sharp reported missing (believed to be killed).

munity of South Yorkshire. He held the bronze medal of the City and Guilds of London Institute in surveying. His death has undoubtedly cut short what promised to be a brilliant career in the mining world. He devoted a great deal of time and interest to the Wombwell Church Lads' Brigade, of which he was Captain for several years.

Lieut. Hirst was married as recently as August, 1915, to Miss Bertha Lockwood, daughter of Mr. and Mrs. S. Lockwood, of Wath-on-Dearne. He was 30 years of age, and the elder son of the late Mr. John Hirst, for many years curator of the Wombwell Cemetery. His only brother, Mr. John Hirst, is now serving as a writer in the Royal Navy.

LIEUTENANT D. FAIRLEY.

Lieut. Duncan Fairley, of the 14th Battalion York and Lancaster Regiment, was the youngest son of Mr. Barker Fairley, Park Grove, Barnsley, and headmaster of St. John's School, Barnsley. Although no official intimation has been received, letters from comrades have conveyed the sad news to Barnsley, and there is no doubt that Lieut. Fairley has made the highest of all sacrifices. He was 26 years old and had had a distinguished and promising scholastic career. After receiving his early education at St. John's School, he gained the Locke Scholarship and a County Minor Scholarship, and proceeding to the Barnsley Grammar School he was successful in matriculating and securing a County Major Scholarship. Lieut. Fairley took his B.A. degree with first class honours at the Leeds University, and subsequently became English master at the Scarborough Municipal Secondary School.

He was in Scarboro' at the time the town was bombarded and had a narrow escape, a piece of shell striking his hat whilst he was in the room.

Early last year Colonel Raley asked Lieut. Fairley to accept a commission in the 14th Battalion York and Lancaster Regiment, and this he accepted, joining on May 18th, 1915. When the Battalion left for Egypt Lieut. Fairley remained behind on Salisbury Plain in charge of a draft of men, and after a period of suspense, when he three times received orders to embark, to be cancelled at the last moment, he left for Egypt. After being only six days in Alexandria Lieut. Fairley went with the Battalion straight to France, where he has been ever since. He had been looking forward to getting leave at Whitsuntide, but this was stopped and the parents of the gallant officer have not seen him since Christmas Day.

The greatest sympathy is felt with Mr. and Mrs. Fairley in their irreparable loss, for their son was known to a very wide circle of friends, and he was held by all in the highest esteem. An able scholar, he gave promise of having a distinguished career as a schoolmaster, and he proved himself during his

FO

PTE. H. ATKINSON

went on to propose that a copy of the letter be placed on record in the minutes, since it characterised 'the conduct of the Barnsley Battalions in the recent advance', and that a copy be sent to every officer and man of both battalions and also to the relatives of those killed in action together with a covering letter expressing the council's admiration and appreciation.

Alderman Rose seconded the resolution and said that he was sure every Barnsley breast would swell with pride at the glorious doings of the Barnsley boys.

The resolution was unanimously carried with enthusiasm.

Alderman Rose was a busy man that Tuesday night. No sooner had the council meeting broken up than he rushed off to attend the Annual General Meeting of the Barnsley Football Club. Once again Alderman Rose referred to the high tributes paid by the likes of Major General O'Gowan to the Barnsley Battalions and said such news was 'better than winning the English Cup'. Even so such news did not tell the whole story. It was left to Colonel Fox, who had relinquished command of the Barnsley Territorials in September 1915, to add a note of caution to the proceedings. Although he supported a resolution to send messages of admiration to the commanders of the Barnsley Battalions he feared that the rumours of heavy casualties might yet prove to be true.

Unlike the members of the Barnsley Town Council and members of the Barnsley Football Club, Colonel Fox had actually faced the Germans in battle and certainly knew what the Barnsley Pals were up against. Just twelve months earlier he had taken his battalion, 1/5 Territorial York and Lancaster Regiment, into a particularly nasty section of the British line. It was the northern corner of the Ypres Salient where the British butted up to the French on the bank of the Yser Canal. The Germans had just been pushed out and the Barnsley and Rotherham men took over the old German trenches, in some instances just yards away from a furious and determined enemy. Colonel Fox's sector was described by the Divisional Commander as the 'worst trenches of the Allied lines'.

Amid brave, cheerful optimism Colonel Fox adopted a cautious tone. The local civic leaders would have done well to have listened more closely to the experienced voice.

Less than a week later the dreadful news was finally out. The flower of the British Army, the flower of Barnsley and the nation, had been scythed down on the rolling uplands of Picardy and the Pals had been at the worst end of the slaughter.

The news of the opening of the Somme offensive, although momentous, had not made the front page of the Chronicle, but the headline it carried on Saturday 15th July was a different matter altogether; it was front page news.

The report was remarkably accurate in its description of the massacre but again the whole truth about the territorial gains was disguised. It would not do to tell the people of Barnsley that their Pals had died without reaching their objective.

To the reporters of Barnsley's other newspaper, the Barnsley Independent, the Pals had certainly not died in vain. Scribbling away in their offices in George Yard off Market Hill, they were intent on presenting the first day of the Battle of the Somme as a great victory for the British Army in general and for the Pals in particular, despite the casualties they had sustained.

On 15th July, the same day that the Chronicle at last broke the news of the Pals' losses, the Independent also devoted several pages to the 'Big Push' and the Barnsley and district 'Toll'. On the back page their headlines were very similar to those of the Chronicle. The Independent too, was keen to tell of 'How the Barnsley Lads Went Into Action', of the 'Gallant Officers and Men' and of the 'Heroes' who had fallen. On other pages, however, the journalists waxed much more lyrical than those of their rival publication just yards down Market Hill.

This strange advertisement is run during the weeks of July in 'The Barnsley Chronicle' along with news and photographs of the slain Barnsley men.

THE TALK OF THE TOWN

Barnsley Boys and the British Push

A Story of Heroes Who Never Looked Back

Imagination must be necessarily feeble in trying to picture the enthusiasm of their charge. The messengers of death had no terrors for these Barnsley Builders of Freedom, who struck hard for God and the Right, while they swept forward – a veritable human avalanche to right inhuman wrongs. Brave men and true fell all too quickly, but their comrades pressed ever onward, ever onward, and never faltered in their stride until the goal was reached. Those that were killed died with a shout of exhultation on their lips and a light of victory shining in their eyes. Those that were wounded suffered pain with never a murmur of complaint, and those that went through scatheless took a heavy toll of the hunted hun, who has no illusions now as to the quality and quantity of the most wonderful volunteer army the world has ever known. **Barnsley Independent, 15th July, 1916**

By mid July the columns of both the Chronicle and the Independent were heavy with obituary after obituary concerning the officers and men who had been killed on 1st July. The Independent went one up on the Chronicle by publishing the first batch of photographs to accompany the lenghty accounts of how the Pals had met their deaths.

There was the fresh-faced 2nd Lieutenant Frank Potter and below him 2nd Lieutenant William Hirst. Further down the column the face of Sergeant Reg Dunk gazed proudly from the page as did that of Lieutenant Duncan Fairley on his right shoulder. In the words of the Independent, they were all part of Barnsley's 'noble sacrifice'.

The obituaries and photographs were far too numerous to mask the heavy losses suffered by the Pals but they could be presented as being part of the high price Barnsley had paid to secure the 'victory' which, even now, the British Army was presumed to be in the process of winning. Such sentiments were little different from those expressed by young officers like Frank Potter during their short lives in uniform.

Frozen forever onto the pages of Barnsley's newspapers the quiescent portraits stood sentinel over the intolerable, unprintable secrets of their death.

"I cannot express in words how I feel for you all at this time. For myself I have lost my best pal . . . Frank of course was with his guns, so I did not see him. The Corporal in the section told me the sad news, and it will be some consolation for you to know that he suffered no pain . . . He gave his life for his country, and no one could do more." **Letter to the parents of 2nd Lieutenant F. Potter from 2nd Lieutenant H. Strong, 14th York & Lancaster Regiment. Reproduced in the Barnsley Independent of 15th July, 1916**

"Second Lieutenant William Hirst, of Wombwell, is another officer in the Second Battalion who fell in the great advance. 'His Battalion', says the Quarter Master Sergeant, 'went into action on the morning of the 1st, and was met with very heavy machine gun and shrapnel fire which caused many casualties among officers and men. Lieutenant Hirst led the company across No-Man's-Land and got into the first line of German trenches, and there he fell. He died as an Englishman – facing the foe at the head of his men." **Letter to the Barnsley Independent from Quarter Master Sergeant Bentley, 14th York and Lancaster Regiment. Reproduced in the Barnsley Independent of 15th July, 1916**

Corporal C. Pickering, 14th Y & L, whose home was at 16 Junction Street, Barnsley was killed. The deceased soldier was 37 years of age and worked at Barnsley Main Colliery. Lance Corporal J.W. Denton has written to Mrs. Pickering conveying the sad news, 'I have written you as soon as we got out of the trenches, and I have been to look at the grave where he was buried. He was put

The Barnsley Chronicle

AND PENISTONE MEXBRO' WATH AND HOYLAND JOURNAL.

VOL. LVIII. NO. 4014   SATURDAY, JULY 22, 1916.   ONE PENNY

Butterfields SALE.

The greatest occasion of the year to save money.

Butterfields (The Drapers), Ltd., 1, Church Street, BARNSLEY.

WONDERFUL.

The opportunity now to buy Drapery at Lessened, instead of Increased, Cost.

Butterfields (The Drapers), Ltd., 1, Church Street, BARNSLEY.

LOCAL OFFICERS AND MEN WHO HAVE FALLEN.

The full impact of the results from the disastrous attack is now hitting the Barnsley people as shown by this front page of the Chronicle.

away very nicely under the circumstances. Charlie was liked by everyone'.

"Leonard Barlow, 13th Y & L, of King Street, Barnsley, has been killed, and three other Pals from the same street have been wounded . . ." **Barnsley Chronicle, 15th July, 1916**

There was still a good deal of anxiety and confusion abroad in Barnsley however, and it didn't help matters for the public to be treated to apparently conflicting reports of the 1st July battle as seen through the eyes of the survivors.

The tone of some of the first eye-witness accounts to be printed in the local journals was in much the same vein as the sabre-rattling journalism of the Independent.

Obviously coming through such a débâcle unscathed was certainly a cause for a good measure of relief, and it was entirely probable that with the passing of a few days those who had survived should come to view their preservation as a glorious achievement.

Like the initial Chronicle reports of the battle many of the letters described the fierce German resistance with some accuracy, yet neglected to tell the whole truth about the horrific casualties and the failure to take Serre. They wrote what they knew would appeal to those at home.

"The sight was magnificent and the camera is the only thing that could tell the real truth of the battle . . . At a certain time arranged beforehand, the whole of the troops mounted the parapet and advanced on the German lines in the finest order. Some fell before the onslaught of the terrific German fire which was concentrated on us by his heavy guns, high explosive and withering machine-gun fire. You could not think that anything like the size of a man could live in it. Still the

235

Darton Soldier Dies of Wounds.

PRIVATE ALFRED BRAITHWAITE.

A Pal comes back to a hospital in England to die from his injuries sustained on the morning of 1st July. His gravestone stands in Darton Churchyard.

boys went on without a look back, and accomplished all that was asked of them. I have never seen a more combined set of daredevils than our own Barnsley Battalions. They are the finest soldiers I have ever been associated with." Letter from 787 Sergeant C. H. Cawthorne, 14th York and Lancaster Regiment. Reproduced in the Barnsley Chronicle of 15th July, 1916

"At 5 a.m. on 1st July we were all in our trenches waiting, with our guns pounding away . . . At 7.30 'over my lads', and up we got and went over. Before we had gone far I saw chums hit on either side of me, and I got bowled over, but it was only a little tap on my right arm. It wasn't bad enough to stop me there, and up I gets and into the line with my chums breasting on. We still had to go over a hundred yards ahead, and just before I got to the German line I got another blow – a real one, too – straight through the right thigh, and I sustained a little mark or two on the left side of my face. I crawled into a shell hole full of pain, but I looked ahead and saw the East Lancashires giving the Germans the time of their life, hand to hand on the parapet. What a shock the Germans got. They squealed like pigs." Letter to the Barnsley Independent from Private Harold Emson, 13th York and Lancaster Regiment. Reproduced in the Barnsley Independent of 15th July, 1916

Writing from his hospital bed in Bristol, Private Emson was obviously convinced that the British Army had given the Germans something to think about despite his wounds, but other 1st July casualties writing from their hospital beds in France and England, were not so sure.

"I have lost my right leg; it is something awful. I hope to get over to England in a day or two. I am very sorry to say that the Barnsley lads have caught it. It was like hell let loose, and I never thought I should get through it alive. Jud Lyons was killed." Letter to his wife from Private W. Hartness, 13th York and Lancaster Regiment. Reproduced in the Barnsley Chronicle of 15th July, 1916

"I was wounded in the Big Push on 1st July. I have a shrapnel wound in my right eye, and two on my left hip. Through my left arm is a bullet wound which had stripped the bone. I also have two pieces of shrapnel in my left arm so you will see that my left side is put out of action.

"Our boys made a gallant stand although I am afraid we lost heavily both officers and men. After a quarter of an hour I was blown off my feet by a German shell. After that I remembered no more until I found myself at our dressing station." Letter to Colonel Hewitt from 1060 Sergeant H. Rimmington, 13th Battalion York and Lancaster Regiment. Recovering from his wounds in Cambridge Hospital, Aldershot. Reproduced in the Barnsley Independent of 29th July, 1916

"I thought there would have been no Germans left after the bashing bombardment our artillery gave them. It was like being in hell. The time came for us to charge, and it was a charge I can tell you! The Germans seemed to be fixed everywhere, popping our men off, but the boys kept on. I was carrying bombs at the time I was hit. I hope to be home at No. 4 Wilberforce Street, Worsbro' Common, before long." Letter from Private T. Tighe, 14th York and Lancaster Regiment. Reproduced in the Barnsley Chronicle of 5th August, 1916

Other letters from survivors seemed to tell a similar story. Private Walter Bygate of the 14th Battalion wrote to say that he had come safely through the 'push' but regretted that many of the Barnsley Pals had been killed or wounded.

The people of Barnsley did not have too long to wait however, before the awful consequences of the

1st July were brought home to Barnsley for all to see. On 14th July the remains of Private Alfred Braithwaite of the 14th Battalion were laid to rest in Darton Churchyard.

Badly wounded on 1st July, Private Braithwaite had already had to have one of his legs amputated by the time the medical services had managed to ferry him across the Channel and had got him as far as St. Thomas' Hospital in London. Although his father had rushed down from Barnsley to be at his son's bedside, there was nothing anyone could do to save his life. He died several days later. His body was brought home to rest in the grounds of the church, where being a regular churchgoer, he had spent many hours before the war.

In the weeks which followed there were many more obituaries and many more photographs of the dead Pals in Barnsley's newspapers. The pages of the Chronicle particularly were black with the closely printed names and details of those who had been killed or wounded on 1st July. Soon there were so many that the Chronicle had to refrain from printing all but the most essential details about the casualties.

The sun may have shone on Barnsley during the last days of July and on into August, but as 'Barnsley Feast' drew ever closer the relatives of the dead Pals never noticed it. All thoughts of sunshine and holidays were banished as whole streets drew down their blinds and families retreated into the gloom of their parlours to mourn their loved ones.

Sergeant Draisey, one of the many missing later to be 'presumed dead'.

It was as though a long and deepening shadow had been cast over the whole town and its outlying districts, and a lingering depression seeped into the very soul of Barnsley. It soaked into the fabric of Barnsley society and, for a time, class barriers were dissolved as families from opposite ends of the social scale grieved over the men who were lost to them forever.

The gloom had descended on the offices of the Barnsley Chronicle and on young Frederick Winford too. Being an office junior at such a tragic period in the town's history was no easy position for a seventeen-year-old since he saw the anguish and distress of the relatives at first hand. Day after day there was a seemingly endless procession of bereaved parents, or wives with children, who had trooped through the doors of the Chronicle offices to take up the editor's offer to print photographs and details of those killed in action.

There was many a heart-rending scene as the precious photographs of proud youths and men newly attired in khaki and taken in some studio in Rugeley or Salisbury, were handed over. There were countless tears shed as Mr. Allen and his reporting staff gently enquired as to the particulars of the soldier's life; his age, where he had worked before the war or how many children he had left behind.

It all went in the Chronicle. Column after column of dead and wounded from the town and the surrounding districts. Under separate headings the Chronicle listed the casualties from Hemsworth and Hoyland, from Darfield and Dodworth, and every week there were more. The lists went on and on and on; ample proof, if any were now needed, that Barnsley and district had suffered heavily in the 'Big Push'. Not all the names were those of Pals of course. There were the other battalions of the York and Lancasters to be taken into account, and the King's Own Yorkshire Light Infantry had suffered heavily, but nevertheless it was much easier to find '1st Barnsley Battalion' or '2nd Barnsley Battalion' printed at the side of the names.

The grief of the families who had received a terse, official telegram from the War Office telling them that a son, a husband, father or brother had been killed in action, was understandable, but at least they had definite news. It was much worse for the relatives of those men who had been reported as 'missing', since the families were trapped in a limbo-like existence, not knowing whether their dear ones were dead or wounded. Some of the reports in the Chronicle were inaccurate. Men listed as missing and sometimes as dead eventually turned up in various hospitals in France and England, but for many families there was no news whatever. They endured a long agonising wait for some word from a fellow Pal or from the medical staff at some hospital; anything to settle their minds. The Chronicle tried its best to throw a life-line to those families who were at their wits' end with worry.

MISSING

The relatives of the appended names of soldiers who are missing would gladly welcome any news concerning them. Will comrades in the respective regiments who have survived and are able to communicate by letter, please do so at once. No charge is made for the insertion in the Chronicle of particulars relative to missing soldiers. **Barnsley Chronicle, 12th August, 1916**

A week later they went further.

'We are now prepared to insert in our columns free of charge, the photographs of soldiers who are officially reported 'missing'. Parents and friends desirous of taking advantage of this offer should leave the photographs of the missing men at the Chronicle office together with the usual details – name, rank, regiment etc." **Barnsley Chronicle, 19th August, 1916**

PRIVATE FRED WALKER

It meant more work for the young Frederick Winford, but it was a job which he would perform willingly.

Among the many worried relatives was Major Guest's wife. Although Lieutenant Heptonstall had seen a bullet strike the Boer War veteran just before he had disappeared from view, no one could say for sure that he was dead. Early reports passed on to the Barnsley Chronicle from the front had gone to great pains to point out that 'there is still hope', but by the beginning of August Mrs. Guest had received more definite news. Colonel Wilford himself had gone to the trouble of writing to the Major's wife at her home in the Isle of Man to tell her that he now presumed her husband to be dead.

"He was last seen leading his company into a German trench and was reported to have been hit in the leg, just as he reached it . . . Our Brigadier, who has seen many fights, remarked that he had never seen anything more splendid than the way your husband led his men through the heavy artillery barrage and intense machine gun fire. He showed an example of bravery and devotion which has been unequalled." **Letter to Mrs. Guest from Colonel E.E. Wilford, Commanding Officer of the 13th York and Lancaster Regiment. Reproduced in the Barnsley Chronicle of 5th August, 1916**

CORPORAL CHARLES WALKER

Private Crossley, the 13th Battalion barber who had cut Major Guest's hair the day before the attack, also mentioned the officer in a letter which was published in the same edition of the Chronicle. It proved that, over a month later, some of the men were still intent on striking a note of optimism. Writing from Woolton Auxiliary Hospital in Liverpool, where he was recovering from shrapnel wounds, he said,

Typifying the kind of tragedy that occurs with the Pals Battalions; three Walker brothers killed on 1st July, Fred (35), Charles (31) and Ernest (33).
'For many years our family chain, Was closely linked together; But O, that chain is broken now. Three links have gone forever.
– From their sister, Fanny

PRIVATE ERNEST WALKER

> *"I picked up a paper the other day with Major Guest's photo in it. He is a man who will be greatly missed by the Battalion as he was a fine soldier and a proper gentleman . . . I must say that it was fine to see the lads go over the top as if on parade; not one faltered, but straight on for a noble cause."*

Down in Buckley Street, Harry Gay's parents had not drawn their blinds but that did not mean they had not suffered almost unbearable agony since they had first heard of the 'Big Push' and a rumour of their Harry's death in action. They had pursued all the avenues they could think of in an effort to find out whether Harry was dead, missing, or wounded. They had even located Lieutenant Asquith, Harry's former officer, who was at Blyth recovering from wounds sustained earlier in the year, in the hope that he could help. Since Harry had been orderly to Lieutenant Asquith it seemed a reasonable line of enquiry to follow.

Sadly it was Lieutenant Asquith who wrote to tell them that after writing several letters himself, he was at last able to confirm that the rumour of Harry's death was true. Mr. and Mrs. Gay and Mrs. Guest endured almost a month of anguish before learning of the fate of their relatives but a response to the enquiries of Mrs. Smith of Lower Thomas Street, Barnsley, came much later. Like Mr. and Mrs. Gay, Mrs. Smith had decided to try and find out what had happened to her son Joseph, and had gone as far as seeking the assistance of the Red Cross to help her in her crusade. She had to wait a long time. It was not until late November that she received a letter signed by the Earl of Lucan on behalf of the British Red Cross and Order of St. John.

> *"Re Private 889 Joseph Smith, 13th Y & L Regiment, Dear Madam,*
>
> *I regret to say that we have received a report which will give you great pain. J. I. Taylor, 979 of Highbury Hospital, Birmingham (home address: 6 Copper Street, Barnsley) states: 'On the 1st July close to the village of Serre, held by the Germans, I saw J. Smith, 889, fixed on the British barbed wires. I called to him to come but he could not. He shook his head. On returning I found Smith's helmet. I think that he could not have been taken prisoner'."*
>
> Barnsley Chronicle, 25th November, 1916

Lieutenant Potter's belongings are returned to the family after his death, by Lieutenant Rawcliffe of the 94 Brigade Light Trench Mortar Battery, Accrington Pals.

Months after the first day of the battle, months after the confusion and turmoil at the front which had left everyone wondering whether all the missing men had been killed, wounded or taken prisoner, Mrs. Smith finally knew what had happened to her son. Her mind could at last rest in her grief. There were other parents however, other wives, other young children who would never learn what had become of their relatives. In due course they would receive a brief communication from the War Office to the effect that, for official purposes, their menfolk were now deemed to be 'missing presumed killed'. In the cases of those families the wondering would last forever.

Meanwhile there had been more local burials of Pals who had been wounded on 1st July and had died of their wounds in England. Twenty-eight-year-old Private Walter Taylor of the 14th Battalion, had succumbed just four days after being wounded and was brought home to be buried in Barnsley Churchyard.

George Rose was buried with full military honours in Worsbrough Dale Churchyard in the afternoon of Wednesday 26th July. He had been wounded in the head by shrapnel and had been transferred to the Cambridge Hospital at Aldershot after crossing the Channel on board the *Panama* on 4th July. He died some three weeks after receiving his wounds. George Rose was well known locally, having worked at Barrow Colliery before joining up, and a large crowd turned up to pay their last respects to the twenty-one-year-old 14th Battalion Pal.

During the months immediately following the 1st July, 1916, the families of the dead Pals were too lost in their grief to ponder on how far that one day would affect the entire course of the struggle on the Western Front and ultimately the war as a whole.

George Rose, 14th Battalion, 2nd Barnsley Pals, returns home with head wounds to die, is buried in Worsbrough Churchyard.

For the time being they were far more concerned in coming to terms with the empty spaces which were now to be a part of everyday life, as street after Barnsley street was left to mourn what would become their lost generation.

In spite of the lengthy casualty lists and the many photographs which appeared week after depressing week, public opinion in Barnsley, indeed in the nation, was still very much behind the 'Big Push'. After all there was no reason to suppose that the papers were telling anything but the whole story.

It is possible that there may have been one or two members of the Barnsley populace who were perhaps beginning to wonder at the reasons behind the long casualty lists and their ominous persistence in the light of what they were being told about the British successes. Few however, cared to broadcast them.

The reality was that the public never read the bitter truth about the abject failure of the 31st Division to capture Serre. Even as the news of the Pals' fate had reached their home town, the Battle of the Somme had inexorably moved into another phase and survivors like Harry Hall had been taken out of the line.

For the people at home, the menfolk killed in action had made a noble sacrifice for 'King and Country'. Everything the public had read, everything they were still reading told them so. It was after all, no less an ideal than many of the Pals had voiced in their first mad dash to join the colours. Although the Battle of the Somme and the Pals had moved on, the tributes continued to make their way across the water.

"France 11th July, 1916.

My Dear Hewitt,

The 13th Y & L have covered themselves with glory, and you who raised the Battalion should indeed be pleased. They have added a page to history.

"The way the Regiment advanced through an intense artillery barrage and machine gun fire to the attack equals any deed done in the War. No faltering or wavering, each man pressing on to his objective as steadily as if on parade.

"Our casualties were very heavy, but we have the consolation they fell in the hour of victory.

A letter sent to every man serving with the Barnsley Pals or to relatives of those killed in action.

"I would like you to let the people of Barnsley know that evey lad who fought that day was a hero.
"The Battalion has been congratulated by many – the Corps Commander, the Divisional General, and by our Brigadier on its Gallantry, and I am the proudest man in France." Letter to Lieutenant-Colonel Joseph Hewitt from Lieutenant-Colonel E.E. Wilford, Commanding Officer of the 13th York and Lancaster Regiment.

Lieutenant-Colonel Hulke was not to be outdone in singing the praises of his Battalion either.

"I want you and the inhabitants of Barnsley and district to know that the men behaved splendidly. Their discipline and determination was magnificent, and though I regret to say that the casualties were heavy you can assure everyone that each man met his death heroically for his King and Country in face of a determined enemy. I have no hesitation in saying that Barnsley should be proud of the knowledge that she produced such men." Letter to Mr. W.P. Donald, Town Clerk of Barnsley from Lieutenant-Colonel W.B. Hulke, Commanding officer of the 14th York and Lancaster Regiment. Reproduced in the Barnsley Chronicle of 29th July, 1916

It all added up to one thing; the Barnsley Pals had definitely 'done their bit', and the Chronicle was quick to underline the fact.

"One of the outstanding features of the great offensive by the British is the dauntless heroism of our Barnsley Boys. Unfortunately there have been casualties. But we are confident that these losses will be borne with Spartan courage, for they are the inevitable price of victory. The brave women folk of Barnsley and district will show the same fortitude under affliction as is being displayed everywhere by the women of England . . . They are buoyed up and consoled by a quickened sense of the just and noble cause for which our soldiers are giving so freely their all, even life itself. How can men die more gloriously than in fighting for the honour and liberty of dear old England?" Barnsley Chronicle, 15th July, 1916

As far as the people back home were concerned that particular question needed no answer, at least for the present.

Chapter 13

The long way home

If you want the old battalion, I know where it is,
I know where it is,
I know where it is.
If you want the old battalion, I know where it is,
It's hanging on the front line wire.

BRIGADIER GENERAL REES had every reason to feel disconsolate as he trudged back through the trench system towards Colincamps in the afternoon of Sunday 2nd July. Only a few hours earlier he had received word that Brigadier-General Carter Campbell had returned from sick leave and was even now on his way to resume command of the 94th Infantry Brigade.

The news had come as a bitter disappointment to Brigadier General Rees. Although he had only been placed in temporary command of the Brigade for a little over two weeks in the place of Brigadier-General Carter Campbell, he had felt sure that he would have been allowed to stay on in view of the traumatic time his men had just come through. It was perhaps reasonable to suppose that the Brigade needed the command of a man who had seen it march into its first major battle and had witnessed its return; a scarred and bloody shadow of its former self. Such a man, it could have been said, would have understood the Brigade more than most in the days which followed but alas for Brigadier General Rees the Army had other ideas. Reluctantly he had bid goodbye to Piggott and Stirling at Brigade HQ and had turned his back on 94 Brigade, leaving a special message for the survivors still clinging desperately to the dilapidated front line and assembly trenches. It was a tribute to the way the men had soldiered on in the face of almost inhuman odds, from a man who would no longer have any influence on their future.

> *"On giving up command of the 94th Infantry Brigade to Brigadier-General Carter Campbell, whose place I have temporarily taken during the great battle, I wish to express to all ranks my admiration of their behaviour.*
> *"I have been through many battles in this war and nothing more magnificent has come under my notice. The waves went forward as if on drill parade, and I saw no man turn back or falter.*
> *"I bid goodbye to the remnants of as fine a Brigade as has yet ever gone into action."*

The truth of the matter was that there was precious little of the Brigade left for the returning General to command and Brigadier General Rees knew it. He had known it for several hours, long before the members of his own staff and the visiting members of the 8th Corps intelligence branch had begun to accept that the 94th Brigade had been all but destroyed. As early as the previous afternoon Brigadier General Rees had come to the devastating conclusion that his two leading battalions had been annihilated and that both Barnsley Battalions had suffered severe casualties. It was still impossible under the circumstances to obtain realistic figures, but as far as the Brigadier General could make out he had only 550 men left out of some 2,600 who had been launched into the attack against Serre.

It was a horrifying estimate and one which Brigadier General Rees would duly convey first to Divisional Headquarters and then to General Hunter-Weston himself. On a day when casualty estimates up and down the entire attack front tended to verge on the optimistic, that of Brigadier General Rees was unusual in its pessimism. The prospect of over two thousand casualties sustained by a single brigade in less than a day was difficult to comprehend but as it turned out the estimate was not too far removed from reality.

Of the assaulting battalions, the Sheffield City Battalion and the Accrington Pals had paid a high price in leading the attack for between them they had lost more than a thousand men killed or wounded out of a total of a little over 1,400. For their part, of the 1,442 men of the Barnsley Battalions who had climbed from their trenches in support of the Sheffield and Accrington men, 175 officers and men had lost their lives. A further 392 were wounded and of these, another thirty-five died during the weeks which followed.

The saga of the Barnsley Pals and the 94th Brigade was but one episode in the story of the 31st Division which, in turn, was just one scene in a tragedy concerning the 8th Corps.

From Serre down to the valley of the river Ancre the British Army had failed to make any impression on the German front-line defences. All along the 8th Corps front the troops were in the same sorry state. Three full divisions of infantry and several units of a fourth, had stormed

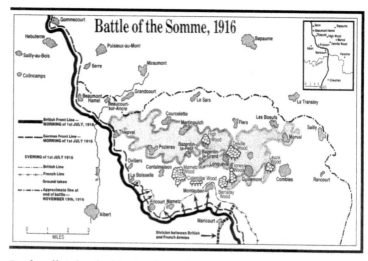

By the official end of the Battle, 19th November, 1916 the British Army is still short of its objective, Bapaume. Serre, the Pals' objective of 1st July remains in German hands.

the German line and had nothing to show for it except stupendous casualties. Not one yard; not one inch had been taken and held save for a tiny perilous toehold which a mixed band of regulars from the 4th Division had chipped out of the Heidenkopf. By the evening of the first day however, they were beyond help.

Crossing the Ancre stream the trail of woe wound its way up onto the Thiepval ridge and down past Ovillers, then across the Albert-Bapaume road as far as Fricourt where the British line twisted and ran out to the east. All along that nine-mile stretch of the line British troops had fallen like nine-pins. The corpses were still out there in No-Man's-Land to prove it. The only success, that of the Irishmen north of Thiepval, shone like a beacon amid the gloom of defeat as the men of Ulster had bulldozed their way across at least three lines of trenches and into the Schwaben Redoubt. They had gone on to threaten the German second line but on a day when the majority of the British troops had not gone far enough, the Ulstermen went too far and ran into the fire of the British guns. The artillery timetables had struck again.

Like the men who battled it out in the Heidenkopf, the Ulstermen held on to their gains in the Schwaben Redoubt all day, but they too were isolated and at the mercy of German counter-attacks. The Germans would not rest until they had their trenches back.

Things had gone much better for the British elsewhere. Down around the bend of the British line at Fricourt it almost seemed as though the men who had attacked the villages of Mametz and Montauban had been fighting in a different battle. At the end of the day the troops were resting in deep German dug-outs well behind the front line, and had good reason to be well satisfied with their outstanding success. Their gains were the exception rather than the rule.

It was not only the Fourth Army which had suffered. The men of the Third Army who had attacked Gommecourt had been cut down in exactly the same way. The diversion had not achieved its objective. The Pals of the 31st Division had not benefitted from the help of the experienced Territorial units to the north.

It was not the fault of the Pals that they had not achieved all that had been asked of them. They had joined the Army to do a job which they were convinced they could accomplish and they had tried so hard that almost two years of training had fallen face down into the dirt of No-Man's-Land within minutes. An entire town had suffered an appalling loss as a result.

The fact of the matter was that the Army had not trusted Kitchener's men in their first major encounter with the Germans and had planned accordingly. The resulting plans had been so rigid that battalions like the Pals were never given the opportunity to display their undoubted talents to the full. The stifling strategy with its ponderous timetables and a plethora of supplies and equipment, had been the Pals' undoing.

The first day of the Battle of the Somme was the blackest day in the history of the British Army. One hundred thousand men had gone over the top carrying much more than a rifle and over seventy pounds of equipment on their backs. The men of the New Army had also carried a boundless enthusiasm and a hope of victory into No-Man's-Land, and more than nineteen thousand men had died in the process. Another thirty-eight thousand were wounded and over five hundred taken prisoner, but they were not the same men in mind or body who had risen from their trenches early that summer morning. Things had changed. The first day of the battle was a tragic lesson for the War Office as scores of families from the same town or city were left without their men, and it ensured that Britain would never again see the likes of a Pals Battalion.

For the Barnsley Pals in particular, the 1st July heralded the decline in the unique local character of the two units. Indeed the process had begun almost as soon as the Pals had moved into the trenches several months earlier but compared with the 1st July the casualties had been but a steady trickle.

Ernest Bell had been shipped home just before the battle as had Frank Lindley's pal 'Hoppy' Hobson, and now Frank himself had joined them. Vernon Atkinson too had departed. Not one of them would grace the ranks of the Pals again. For the men like Harry Hall, Tommy Oughton and Charlie Swales who remained, there was little doubt that the heavy casualties of 1st July would have a profound effect on their battalions. They had seen a good many of their pals, men they had joined up with, men they had trained and been to Egypt with, fall as they plodded on towards Serre. They had seen many more stretchered out of the line never to return to the Pals, if they returned to the trenches at all.

The Barnsley Pals were breaking up.

There were still local men with the reserve companies who would be sent to France to fill up the gaps in the ranks but eventually even that supply of manpower would run dry. All too soon the drafts of reinforcements being sent out to France would be made up of men from all parts of Britain as the Kitchener volunteers gave way to Lord Derby's late volunteers and eventually the first conscripts. These men would not necessarily be from Barnsley or even from the North of England. They would be called up and drilled, wheeled and marched to a base camp in France and then posted to battalions who had suffered heavy casualties. The local flavour of the Barnsley Pals would gradually be diluted. A few Pals would remain but the new men would never really be able to understand just what those who had survived that terrible first day on the Somme had been through together. The new men, no matter how good they proved to be, would never be Pals like the comrades of 1914 and early 1915 had been.

The local ties would become strained and would eventually be severed.

There was also another change afoot, although the surviving Pals would have been hard pressed to identify it in the immediate aftermath of the battle. Harry Hall had felt it as he had watched the wounded men being treated in the trenches during the afternoon of 1st July and Tommy Oughton had felt it too as he had gazed at his ragged and dishevelled comrades crouching under the blistering German cannonade in the afternoon of 1st July. It was a new feeling, a lingering unease with the way the Pals had been managed in battle. Before the 1st July it would have been difficult to find a man who would seriously have questioned the tactical methods of the Army and its leaders but now they were not so sure. It signalled a subtle yet fundamental shift in attitude which would harden into resignation with the passage of time. In short it was the beginning of the end of

A shattered German trench on a sector where the advance meets with some success.

'Kitchener's Army' both physically and spiritually.

> *"We should be about 800 strong when we went over but I reckon there weren't 200 had come back by July 4th. Everyone thought the Somme was going to end the war. I know we were told that if we broke through that would be the end, but I think we were sacrificed for the other part of the line. They never thought the left flank was any good. There was no real bitterness or resentment, although there was plenty of bitter talk, but not really to be causing any trouble. We knew we had been let down by the Generals. It ought to have been them and the German Generals who were put together then we could have watched them fight it out. That's what happens. Them that's responsible for it get away."* **Tommy Oughton, 13th Y & L Regiment**

In the grim days which followed the 1st July it became evident to Tommy Oughton and Harry Hall that what they were living through was not quite the change of life that they had in mind when they had accepted the King's shilling. It was also evident that the German Army was not going to give up the ridges and spurs above the valley of the Ancre without a fight. It was going to be a long and bloody haul for the British Army against men who were driven by a philosophy of holding on to every 'Foot's breadth' of ground. If the British were to advance at all they would have to stride over the bodies of the German soldiers to do so. The collective enthusiasm of a band of men from the same mining town would not, in itself, be enough to break them or to win the war. Sheer enthusiasm was no match for shellfire and machine-gun bullets.

Even so, by 4th July the Germans had translated enough of the various statements of prisoners taken on the front of the 14th Reserve Corps to know that, come what may, the British would keep hammering away on the Somme front.

1. Before the attack

In general it was assumed that a substantial attack on the German lines would take place during the course of the summer. The practice attacks carried out in the rest quarters (jumping out of trenches, planned charging attacks, bayonet fighting etc.) reinforced the assumption.

The men only learnt that the attack was to occur soon when told by the company commanders and, because the officers in the front lines believed their announcement would cause great joy in the ranks, the men were specifically told not to show their feelings in case the enemy nearby deduced something from this. (The men didn't learn of the exact time of the attack until the night before).

The assumption on the part of the officers was not completely justified as the reaction of the men was often divided. The younger soldiers, especially those who had experienced little fighting, were the keenest to fight, but the older ones were anything but overjoyed. Nevertheless, everyone was confident of a successful attack, a feeling shared by the young officers, but not apparently by the older, and especially the high ranking officers. For example General de Lisle, commander of the 29th Division, which had already suffered great losses at Gallipoli, is alleged to have said, 'I am afraid after this affair I may have to take my Division back to England in a Taxi-cab.'

In contrast to this the officers strengthened the opinion of the men that the task would be easy. They told them that the first two trenches would certainly not be manned and would only contain corpses, as the preceding artillery fire would no doubt have wiped out the opposition.

Survivors could only be expected in the third trench, but the trenches were not considered to be very well protected so the English advance would have no trouble in taking them over.

It is therefore no surprise that most of the young troops were looking forward to the attack with great hope and enthusiasm.

2. The attack

During the night of 30th June the Battalions resting behind the front were brought up immediately behind the front position. In contrast to the usual force, which had always been very strong in case of German attacks, there had only been weak 'posts' in the fire and support trenches during the last few days before the attack.

At 6 o'clock on the morning of 1st July (English time), a last meal of tea and meat rations was eaten. The signal to attack was given at 7.30 a.m., a signal which was followed without hesitation. The desire to attack was increased even more by the fact that the men under German artillery fire suffered few casualties, much to their surprise. On the other hand it is admitted that the batteries were every day weakened by German fire. Different prisoners have made independent statements reporting that direct hits brought heavy guns to a standstill, something confirmed by officers taken prisoner. Furthermore prisoners knew of different cases where gun barrels had been destroyed and men lost as a result of shells prematurely exploding in the breech.

The attack was planned to proceed in waves. The companies advanced either in two or four waves. To the left and right of the first waves were hand grenade throwers, behind them the ammunition carriers. The third wave was followed by the Lewis guns; behind the fourth wave came Brigade machine guns, both followed by their ammunition carriers.

These were followed by the carrier troops of the 'Headquarter Company', who carried with them rifle ammunition, hand grenades and scaling ladders. Finally there followed the 'Pioneers' who were to convert the conquered trenches into fire trenches. With small variations, this seems to have been the method employed by the majority of Divisions.

First of all, two battalions from each Brigade were supposed to advance as described above, but this did not always go according to plan, as in many cases one of the front waves were already retreating as the following waves were about to leave their trenches to attack. Even if further progress wasn't stopped by the German wire entanglements which held up surprisingly well in parts, then the force and momentum of the attack flagged in many cases in the face of heavy German infantry fire.

3. After the attack

You could see on the prisoners' faces what a shattering impression this German fire, (rifle and machine gun), and the failure of the attack, had left on them.

Candidly they admired the heroism of the German infantry which had been subjected to the heaviest fire for days on end. The men had expected to storm over empty trenches meeting shattered troops no longer capable of resistance. Instead they came up against officers and men standing openly on the parapets returning devastating fire.

Many times the men did not know what to do, especially those battalions who succeeded in forcing their way deeper into the German positions. Either there followed, quite inexplicably, no support from the battalions behind, or their leaders were incapable of exploiting the success by giving proper orders.

For example the 1st Lancashire Fusiliers and 1st Royal Dublin Fusiliers of the 86th Brigade were sent as the frontal attack. The 16th Middlesex Regiment and the 2nd Royal Fusiliers were supposed to follow. Prisoners taken from the last two battalions claimed that they had completely lost touch with the first two battalions.

The losses must have been great. Of the troops who advanced first it is assumed that the majority of the officers, including the battalion commanders, were lost or wounded. It is agreed that losses were between 50 and 70 per cent. In retrospect the prisoners recognise the courage of their leaders, but it has also become clear to them that the bravery of a leader must be coupled with skill, and this proved, to their great regret, to have been lacking.

The prisoners also seem to be in agreement that those ranks who had succeeded in retreating to their own trenches could no longer be used for the purposes of a repeated attack. The situation and strength of the German positions which they had opportunity to inspect after their capture, had made an enormous impression on them: they do not believe that these could ever be taken, or only with enormous sacrifices.

However, in view of the English character, and in spite of the despondency of the prisoners, who have been discouraged by their failure and unnerved by their efforts, renewed attacks, possibly with increased use of artillery and ammunition, are to be expected. This opinion was also expressed by the educated men among the prisoners. They saw it as a political necessity which simply had to be fulfilled, as too many of England's hopes had been put on to the success of the attack that they could be given up after the first failed attempt!

British dead await burial.

Report compiled from statements taken from British Prisoners taken on 1st July, 1916, and passed to the 1st Battalion of the 169th Infantry Regiment. Generallandesarchiv Karlsruhe, 45 EV 142, Vol. 127

Battalions like the Barnsley Pals had taken on a tough and highly trained force of German conscripts and some of them had succeeded in taking their objectives. In many ways such feats served to prove the worth of the volunteer spirit of 1914 and 1915. Although the first day had been a disaster for the Pals in terms of the horrendous casualties they had suffered, there was never any doubt that the same urge which had driven them to join up would now make them soldier on. Those who remained would learn from their failure. The British Army would need such men in the months and years which were to follow.

Still out on the left flank of the 94th Brigade, Charlie Swales and the rest of the survivors of the 14th Battalion's 'C' Company had 'stood to' religiously in the dim light of dawn on 2nd July, half expecting the Germans to come romping across the shell-torn ground to seize the British positions. They would have met with little opposition but to Charlie's great relief they never came.

> *"We were formed into Companies and took up usual trench duties for the next few days. We were expecting a counter-attack but we hadn't taken anything so the Germans didn't attempt anything. The Germans had also taken a beating from the bombardment. Both sides had had enough."* **Charlie Swales, 14th Y & L Regiment**

Some two hundred yards away on the other side of No-Man's-Land, the men of the 169th Regiment were too busy licking their own wounds to bother about counter-attacking.

They had lost a great deal of men as a result of the British bombardment as Charlie Swales had so rightly assumed but they had lost many more during the great battle of 1st July, although the losses appeared to be comparatively light when compared with those of the British units opposing them. A single German Regiment had managed to beat off the attack of the entire British 31st Division, inflicting some 3,600 casualties at a cost of 141 killed and 224 wounded and missing. Even then, some of those German casualties had been sustained in helping to fight off the men of the 4th Division in the Heidenkopf.

For every German soldier of the 169th regiment who had become a casualty on 1st July, ten British soldiers of the 31st Division had been killed or wounded. In terms of those troops on both sides who were killed the ratio was almost identical. The calculations are staggering considering the numerical superiority enjoyed by the British prior to the battle.

During the night of 2nd July reinforcements of five officers and 45 men arrived in the trenches from Bus and for the next two days those men helped the rest of the Pals to clear the trenches of the morbid results of defeat. Every night the Pals went out to comb the battlefield in the hope of finding more wounded men and incredibly, every night, some were brought back alive. For others there was the task of salvaging valuable supplies of discarded Mills bombs and other items of equipment. By far the most heartbreaking task however, was to assist in the burial of their fallen comrades.

It was a job which went on almost continuously right up to the time the Pals were relieved on the night of July 4th. The men who had missed the battle and had come up to reinforce the line must have wondered what on earth had happened while they had been held back in reserve.

"Bodies were collected according to religions. You couldn't bury a Protestant with a Catholic or anything like that. I didn't carry the bodies. There were men there to fill the graves. It was their job. They used to go round the trenches, collect the bodies and put them in graves where they were found. On the 3rd Colonel Hulke came round and he wanted to go on a tour of the trenches. When we'd finished he said he wanted a rest. There was a bump in the ground which he asked to be flattened out, but when I started to dig, we realised it was a man's body. The Colonel told me to cover it up again quickly." **Ossie Burgess, 14th Y & L Regiment**

There was not one man who was sorry to see the troops of the 1/6th Gloucester Regiment when they appeared in the trenches to relieve the Barnsley Battalions during the night of July 4th.

Along with the rest of the 94th Brigade, or what was left of it, the Pals began one of the longest and most exhausting marches any of them were ever likely to undertake.

Heavy thunderstorms during the day had once more rendered the trenches almost impassable in places adding to the still considerable chaos which plagued the rear positions. Turning their backs on the sound of the guns the Pals slipped and slithered their way back, stopping here and there to allow another stretcher to pass or inching their way carefully around a wounded man who, three days after the battle, was still waiting to be moved. Each man was worn out, wet, filthy and dejected, and it took them all night to cover the seven or so miles to their final destination, the village of Louvencourt.

It was 5 a.m. when the Pals finally shambled into the village. For the first time in days the men could rest safe in the knowledge that there was no danger of them being overrun by the Germans.

At last they could sleep.

Seven miles to the east the Battle of the Somme had already moved into another phase. Operations north of the Ancre, indeed north of the German held village of Ovillers, had been closed down as the Army concentrated on exploiting the gains won by the troops towards the southern portion of the line on the first day. The Pals slept soundly, oblivious to the fact that the battle they had just left behind was gradually slipping into a long and brutal brawl. Always it would be the British who would be throwing the first punches, wearing themselves out as the Germans absorbed them, staggered, but stayed on their feet to hit back. It degenerated into a contest to find out which side would throw the towel in first. The only problem with that, was that it was the men of both sides who were taking it on the chin and by the time the battle ended in November 1916 the slugging match would have claimed some 1,300,000 casualties.

For the time being, however, the Pals were out of it. As far as they were concerned they had left the battle for someone else to deal with. They had done their best and in their present state it was doubtful if they could have carried on even if they had wanted to. The Army was of the same opinion. They thought it prudent to shunt the Pals elsewhere.

Most of the morning of the 5th July was spent in cleaning the mud and the ingrained dirt of battle off their uniforms and equipment. In the afternoon both battalions were ordered to parade prior to their being addressed by Brigadier General Carter Campbell and later, Lieutenant-General Hunter-Weston. General Hunter-Weston was intent on visiting every battalion which had been thrown into the attack on the 8th Corps front to congratulate them on their performance personally.

It was just less than a week since the General had visited the Pals to wish them well in their attack on Serre and as he began to commend them, first on their performance and then on their gallant work in clearing the battlefield, he must have been struck by the haggard faces of the men who listened. What could the General say other than they had done all that they could in the face of a well prepared German Army and that the 31st Division troops could hold their heads high in the company of Regular Divisions like the 4th and 29th. The General considered it an honour to be the comrade of such heroes.

Major General Wanless O'Gowan was also preparing a speech of congratulation which he would deliver at a later date. In it he would emphasise that he too was proud to be their General and that the men should be proud of themselves. He would tell them that every man had done his duty; that they had the stiffest task to accomplish and that they had done it in fine style.

Behind the German lines the leaders of the troops were also busy preparing the first drafts of the messages of congratulation which they were to send to their brave warriors. The commander of the 169th Regiment, Major von Struensee, was concerned to praise his men on their brave resistance and further back behind the lines the commander of the 14th Reserve Corps, General von Stein, had hit upon a novel method of congratulation. The Germans had picked up a copy of the message sent out to all units of the British 8th Corps by General Hunter-Weston, and they used it to reinforce how well the German units had broken the attacks of the British on most of their front. What General von Stein had in mind was to translate the message and reproduce most of it, then beneath it add his own brief statement.

MESSAGE

From
Lieut.-General Sir Aylmer Hunter-Weston.
K.C.B., D.S.O.
To

All Officers, N.C.O.s and Men
of the VIII Army Corps.

In so big a command as an Army Corps of four Divisions (about eighty thousand men) it is impossible for me to come round all front line trenches and all billets to see every man as I wish to do. You must take the will for the deed, and accept this printed message in place of the spoken word.

It is difficult for me to express my admiration for the splendid courage, determination and discipline displayed by every Officer, N.C.O. and Man of the Battalions that took part in the great attack on the BEAUMONT-HAMEL-SERRE position on the 1st July. All observers agree in stating that the various waves of men issued from their trenches and moved forward at the appointed time in perfect order, undismayed by the heavy artillery fire and deadly machine gun fire. There were no cowards nor waverers, and not a man fell out. It was a magnificent display of disciplined courage worthy of the best traditions of the British race.

We had the most difficult part of the line to attack. The Germans had fortified it with skill and immense labour for many months, they had kept their best troops here, and had assembed north, east, and south-east of it a formidable collection of artillery and many machine guns.

By your splendid attack you held these enemy forces here in the north and so enabled our friends in the south, both British and French, to achieve the brilliant success that they have. Therefore, though we did not do all we hoped to do you have more than pulled your weight, and you and our even more glorious comrades who have preceded us across the Great Divide have nobly done your Duty.

We have got to stick it out and go on hammering. Next time we attack, if it please God, we will not only pull our weight but will pull off a big thing. With such troops as you, who are determined to stick it out and do your duty, we are certain of winning through to a glorious victory.

I salute each Officer, N.C.O. and Man of the 4th, 29th, 31st and 48th Divisions as a comrade-in-arms and I rejoice to have the privilege of commanding such a band of heroes as the VIII Corps have proved themselves to be.

H.Q., VIII Corps
4th July, 1916
AYLMER HUNTER-WESTON,
Lieut.-General

The above English order of the day shows what efforts the enemy made to break through our lines. They did not succeed. Greater than the courage and determination of the opponent, were the bravery, resistance and spirit of sacrifice of the 2nd Guards Reserve Division, the 52nd Infantry Division and the 26th Reserve Division. What the combination of artillery and machine guns achieved in defending the assault is described as formidable by the enemy leader.

Auszug aus Tagesbefehl von Generallieutenant Sir Aylmer Hunter-Weston.

An alle Offiziere, Unteroffiziere und Mannschaften des VIII. Armeekorps.

Für den herrlichen Mut, Entschlossenheit und Mannszucht, die von allen Offizieren, Unteroffizieren und Mannschaften der Bataillone, welche an dem grossen Angriff vom 1. Juli auf der Beaumont-Hamel-Serre-Linie teilgenommen haben, gezeigt wurden, die richtigen Worte der Bewunderung zu finden, fællt mir schwer. Alle Beobachter sagen einstimmig aus, dass die verschiedenen Wellen der Angreifer zur festgesetzten Zeit in vælliger Ordnung aus den Græben herauskamen und vorwærts gingen, unverzagt trotz des schweren Artilleriefeuers . . . . . . und tœdlichen Maschinengewehrfeuers. Es gab keine Feiglinge, keine Zaudernden . . . . . . Es war eine grossartige Entfaltung von anerzogenem Mut, würdig der besten Ueberlieferungen der britischen Rasse.

Wir hatten den schwierigsten Teil der Stellung anzugreifen. Die Deutschen hatten mit Geschick und ungeheurem Arbeitsaufwand monatelang ihre Stellungen ausgebaut. Sie hatten ihre besten Truppen da . . . . . und hatten ein furchtbares Zusammenwirken von Artillerie und Maschinengewehren. Durch Euren prachtvollen Mut habt Ihr diese feindlichen Kræfte hier im Norden gefesselt und es dadurch unseren Freunden im Süden, Briten und Franzosen, ermœglicht, ihren glænzenden Erfolg zu erringen. Trotzdem wir nicht alles erreicht haben, was wir erhofften, so habt Ihr doch mehr als mœgliches geleistet und habt im Verein mit unseren noch ruhmreicheren Kameraden, welche ins grosse Jenseits vorangingen, herrlich Eure Pflicht erfüllt.

Wir müssen durchhalten und weiter hemmen. Beim næchsten Angriff werden wir — so Gott will — nicht nur unser mœglichstes tun, sondern auch wirklich grosses erreichen. Mit solchen Truppen wie Ihr, die fest entschlossen sind, in Pflichterfüllung durchzuhalten, sind wir eines glorreich erfochtenen Sieges sicher.

Ich begrüsse jeden Offizier, Unteroffizier und Mann der 4., 29 31. und 48. Division als Kriegskameraden und bin stolz darauf, an der Spitze einer solchen Heldenschar, als die sich das VIII. Korps erwiesen hat, zu stehen.

gez. **Aylmer Hunter-Weston**
Generallieutenant.

Hauptquartier
VIII. Korps
am 4. Juli 1916.

Der vorstehende englische Tagesbefehl zeigt, welche Anstrengungen der Feind gemacht hat, um unsere Linien zu durchbrechen. Es ist ihm nicht gelungen. Groesser als der Mut und die Entschlossenheit des Gegners sind die Tapferkeit, die Widerstandskraft und der Opfermut der Regimenter der 2. G. R. D. der 52. I. D. und 26. R. D. gewesen. Was Artillerie und Maschinengewehre im vereinten Zusammenwirken bei der Sturmabwehr geleistet haben, wird vom feindlichen Führer als furchtbar bezeichnet.

Der næchste Angriff des Gegners wird, dessen bin ich gewiss, das gleiche Schicksal wie der erste Angriff haben.

Der kommandierende General:
v. Stein.

General Hunter-Weston's message to his troops is picked up by the Germans, translated and circulated to their men as a morale-booster.

The next enemy attack will, and of this I am certain, suffer the same fate as the first. von Stein. Extract from the war diary of the 169th Infantry Regiment, Generallandesarchiv Karlsruhe 456 EV 42, Vol. 111

General von Stein had seen fit to omit what he perhaps thought were sentimental references to the Divisions which made up General Hunter-Weston's command.

From Louvencourt the Pals moved on. Their first stop was Gezaincourt, the village in which they had rehearsed their attack on Serre, and a day later they moved on to Frevent. At half past nine the same night they boarded the inevitable cattle trucks for an all night train ride to the north.

"The whole Division moved up to Neuve Chapelle. We were told we were going out for a rest and refit but we didn't, we landed in the line again inside a fort-night – but it was a quieter sector." Charlie Swales, 14th Y & L Regiment

Charlie Swales was annoyed that the Pals were not given long to recover from their ordeal on 1st July. They were in fact given just four days' rest upon their arrival in the area held by the British First Army, before moving up to billets at Vielle Chapelle on 14th

July. The following day the Pals moved up to the trenches and relieved men of the 2/8 Royal Warwickshire Regiment. Both Barnsley Battalions moved up to the trenches together, the 13th Battalion sandwiched between the 14th on their left and the 17th King's Rifles on their right.

The Neuve Chapelle sector was a new experience for the Pals. They had been used to the chalky trenches of the Somme, but the trenches of the old battlefields which lay just south of the Belgian border were totally different.

The whole area had an unsavoury reputation and one which was well justified. It had been a loathsome place even for the earlier British occupants of the sector, and the British decision to launch an offensive on a short stretch of the front in March 1915 had merely exacerbated the situation.

Although a fairly quiet sector when the Pals took over a section of the line just south of Neuve Chapelle, the area was nevertheless a desolate place in which to spend the war. Almost two years of trench warfare plus a major British offensive had conspired to render the region battered beyond belief.

The towns and villages which lay behind the British lines were often no more than heaps of rubble and rusting, broken machinery which were a legacy of the short but furious battle for Neuve Chapelle. It was a damp and smokey region; consisting in the main of an industrial townscape lying between the cotton manufacturing towns of the Lys Valley to the north and the slag heaps of the French coalfield to the south. In the rest areas close to the line the few walls which had escaped destruction were guarded by a profusion of sandbags. It was as though the entire region had sunk into a glum depression from which it was struggling vainly to recover.

The state of the British positions did little to inspire absolute confidence when the Pals finally arrived to take their turn holding the line.

The British front line which ran some five hundred yards east of the heap of debris known as Richebourg L'Avouee, stood on ground which had once been the old German support and reserve lines, captured some sixteen months earlier in the first successful rush of the First Army. When the Pals took over some of the stretches were in a sorry state to say the least, since the trenches ran among low lying, marshy meadows which were not unlike those to be found in Flanders. A stream had once flowed between the British and German front-line trenches and during the Winter months it would swell to a full twenty feet in width and soak the ground for a good many yards on either side.

Unlike the open, well drained uplands of Picardy the soggy nature of the ground had rendered trench digging a laborious task. Whereas the trenches on the Somme had actually been hewn out of the earth, those which ran through the battlefields on the northern fringes of the French coalfield had been built up from ground level using a combination of earth and hundreds of sandbags, which, more often than not, had been filled up with liquid mud rather than soil. The resulting defensive system was an almost continuous line of what Charlie Swales called 'barricades' but which went under the official title of 'high command' trenches.

They had been constructed in the main, during the Summer of 1915 and no account had been taken of the fact that during the Winter months the water level rose to a matter of two inches below the surface. During the Winter of 1915, the British troops holding the trenches of Richebourg had endured a miserable time, soaked to the skin and enveloped in a slimy layer of clinging mud. Many a 'Tommy' of late 1915 had had cause to abandon his gumboots as the mud sucked at his legs.

Even in the Summer of 1916 the ground was so damp that it threatened the stability of the breastworks. Some of the sandbags had been up for so long and had been so wet that their fibres had simply rotted away allowing their contents to spill out onto the ground. Others had just fallen down or disintegrated under the constant pepperings of machine-gun bullets and shrapnel.

High command trenches away from the Somme area. Conditions to which the Pals have to become acclimatised.

It was hardly surprising then, that the Pals viewed their new surroundings with a good deal of suspicion. Their trenches on the Somme, although they had not been palaces, had at least been dug out of the ground, and even they had been demolished by a well placed 'heavy' or one of the dreaded Minenwerfers. The men naturally wondered how long their present accommodation would stand up to a heavy and prolonged bombardment. They didn't have too long to wait before they found out.

As well as getting used to the novel trench design the Pals also had some new names to add to their vocabulary of trench titles. Out went the old familiar names of routes like 'Nairne Street', 'Northern Avenue' and 'Eczema', and in came the new with a distinct flavour of the Capital. Holding the line astride the La Bassee road they found themselves getting to know 'Vine Street' and 'Oxford Street' with the 'Edgeware Road' running between the two.

For the dwindling number of Pals who had survived the attack on Serre the war went on. All the old familiar routines they had learnt in their first four months of trench warfare in France were quickly re-established as they became inured to the idea that the German line was going to take some breaking and that perhaps Lord Kitchener had been right all along.

One thing was certain, at their present strength the Barnsley Battalions were in no position to engage in any further offensive activity. The 13th Battalion for example had moved up to Neuve Chapelle with a strength of 15 officers and 469 other ranks. The 14th Battalion was also desperately short of men but there were various dodges the men could indulge in to trick the Germans into believing otherwise.

> *"One of the Sergeants would say to me 'Come on young 'un, let's go and have a war. Just keep thi 'ead down and don't get hit' and I used to say, 'Aye I'll watch that'. In the daylight, using a periscope, we would spot where one of their sentries would stand, then the Sergeant would lay a stick on the top of the sandbags pointing towards the position where one of the Germans had fired from. Then, from behind the sandbags, I would fire to see if I could get them to fire back. If I managed to draw their fire the Sergeant would fire at the pre-aligned spot. 'I must have slaughtered half o't German Army', the Sergeant used to say. Between us we made it look like the line was active and occupied, when in fact there was anything up to thirty yards from one occupied bay to the next. We were holding a sector of the line as if we were a full battalion – but of course we weren't. We were only the ones who had come out of the Somme attack although there was one good thing; we used to get full rations as if we were the full battalion. We used to live like Lords. If Jerry had known how many were holding that bit of front line he'd have come and taken all the lot."*
>
> **Charlie Swales, 14th Y & L Regiment**

In order to combat the shortage of men the 94th Brigade shuffled its men around. Composite Companies from the various battalions were often attached to the unit which had been ordered to garrison the front line so that an effective level of defence could be maintained. The loaning of men from one unit to another also took place on a Divisional level since the manpower of the 31st Division had been severely depleted as a result of the Somme fighting. The casualties however, continued to rise due to intense periods of German shelling. Although the casualties were slight when compared to those of 1st July, nevertheless the old faces of September 1914 and early 1915 drifted away one by one as men were killed or were returned to England wounded and sick.

Within two days of entering the line the 14th Battalion lost one man killed with Lieutenant McArdle and six men wounded, and the casualties continued to mount steadily for both battalions.

By the end of their first twelve-day tour of duty in the trenches at Neuve Chapelle the 13th Battalion alone had suffered a total of forty-eight casualties. Six men were dead and the remaining forty-two were wounded. Among the wounded were Captain Jack Normansall, one of the first officers of the Pals, with wounds to the face caused by a rifle grenade, and Tommy Oughton's friend Lieutenant Hions.

For the remainder of the month of July and the whole of the month of August the Pals tramped back and forth between their rest billets near Vielle Chapelle and the front-line trenches. Intense bouts of sporadic shelling went on and due to the absence of any drafts of men of any substantial size both battalions remained understrength for the entire period.

Alas, the avowed British Army policy of attempting to raise morale, whilst at the same time keeping the German soldiers on their toes, went on in the Neuve Chapelle sector as it did in every other stretch of the trench line where British troops were to be found in occupation.

Most of the battalions which made up the 94th Brigade took their turn in raiding the German front line to harrass the garrison and seize prisoners. The Army obviously believed that the understrength and rather dispirited battalions which had crawled out of the carnage at Serre would be uplifted by being offered the opportunity to 'get some of their own back'. As the 14th Battalion raid of 3rd/4th June had demonstrated however, the raiding activity, if nothing else, certainly contributed to keeping the Pals below strength.

On 31st August the 14th Battalion lost one officer, Lieutenant G.C. Harbord and two men killed, with 2nd Lieutenant Moxon and two men wounded, in a raid against the German front line. In spite of the losses the raids and patrols went ahead undiminished and their popularity among the rank and file was, to say the least, open to question.

"We were ordered to make an attack. Eighteen of us were detailed to blow our way through the German wire using a Bangalore torpedo. Eighteen were all we could muster. We were to take the first German trench and then send a man back to fetch another party who would come up and consolidate what we had taken, whilst we pushed up a communication trench to their second line. We were to take that and then send another man back to bring up another party to consolidate it while we went on to the third line. When we'd taken that we were to bomb our way so many yards up either side of this trench and hold it at that. I had a large bag full of bombs as I was one of the bombers in that squad. I can remember making the remark, 'We're going to be in bloody Berlin before we've done here'. Jerry was supposed to have been retiring from these trenches but we'd not seen any going. Well we fired the Bangalore torpedo but unfortunately we were a yard short and in the dark my pal who was leading tumbled into the wire at the other end. His clothes were torn to ribbons. We couldn't get through, eighteen men going through as far as their third line. Some bloody General somewhere must have thought, 'Keep the morale of the troops up, keep them on the attack'. I ask you. Eighteen men to storm bloody German positions. He must have been a nut case, somebody out of the asylum. We never got through the wire, all hell broke loose. We got back to our line in penny numbers, one at a time. Sergeant were counting us as we got back in like a lot of stray sheep."

Charlie Swales, 14th Y & L Regiment

By the end of August 1916, both Barnsley Battalions were still something in the region of three hundred men below strength and another of the faces of 1914 had joined the steady stream of original Pals who were leaving their battalions for hospitals in France and England. The waters of the Suez canal at Kantara had almost claimed him and now Tommy Oughton's life was threatened by disease.

"I had dysentery. The doctors told me that I'd contracted it in Egypt then it developed towards the back end of August 1916. Personally I think I got it at Neuve Chapelle. There was a wild orchard and I ate so much fruit there, I think that helped it on. I was certainly in a poor way for the simple reason that letters were sent to my mother from the doctors and padres about my condition until I got a bit better. I must have been so bad they were saying if I didn't get better before long they would give my mother leave to come over and see me. I was in hospital until November. After I came out of hospital I was sent to a camp not far from Newcastle to recuperate."

Tommy Oughton, 13th Y & L Regiment

Tommy was out of the 13th Battalion for good. He would never again see many of the friends he had served with in 'D' Company. Strangely enough 'D' Company was perhaps the one company of the 13th Battalion which had come out of the attack on Serre with a fair number of its men unscathed, unlike 'A' and 'B' Companies which had borne the brunt of the 13th Battalion's part in the action. Tommy Oughton may have been out of the 13th Battalion for good but he was not quite finished with the Barnsley Battalions. He was destined to return to France to join the ranks of the 14th Battalion on recovering from the effects of dysentery, but by then there would be precious few men of Barnsley to carry on the name of the Second Barnsley Battalion.

Tommy Oughton was not the only 13th Battalion man to turn his back on the First Barnsley Pals at the end of August. On the very last day of the month Captain C.H. Gurney who had led part of 'A' Company into action on 1st July, left to take command of the Sheffield City Battalion. Like Tommy Oughton, he would never return.

Early in September both battalions received orders that they would soon be required to help in manning the trenches in yet another sector which had been the scene of heavy fighting in 1915. They were moving to Festubert. In effect all that the battalions were required to do was slide along the trench line a little further to the south.

Lying but a few miles south of Neuve Chapelle, close to the northern banks of the La Bassee Canal, the conditions on the Festubert sector were very similar to those which the men had experienced during the preceding two months in the First Army area.

Moving up to garrison the front line in mid-September the men found that they were once more holding the none too stable 'high command' trenches which squirmed their way through a by now familiar damp and grimy landscape.

Above all however, the Festubert sector was notorious for its high quota of extremely proficient German snipers who commenced to play havoc among the unwary troops of the 31st Division, unused to such a high level of sniper activity.

Whereas British snipers like Charlie Swales were tied to their battalions, moving in and out of the line and even changing sectors when their units moved, the German marksmen stayed on the same sector for weeks on end. Consequently they got to know their sectors like the backs of their hands. Every fold in the ground, every suspect parapet was marked out in the minds of the German snipers. Often they would lie for hours not more than fifty yards from the British line, covering that dangerously low communication trench or the spot where one sandbag was out of place, just waiting for the moment of carelessness on the part of a British soldier. A split second was all that they needed.

In such a fashion did the Sheffield City Battalion lose one of their senior officers, shot through the head when visiting the well known 'Island Posts' on the sector.

The Barnsley Battalion did not have to endure the sniper-ridden trenches of Festubert for too long before they were taken out of the line to prepare for a move to another part of the Western Front.

As the men marched off to the Bethune area very early in October they mulled over the weird and wonderful tales of the new 'Tanks' brought up from the Somme battlefields by the troops who had relieved them. The Battle of the Somme had raged on all through the Summer and into the Autumn, even as the men of the Barnsley Battalions had been holding the line at Neuve Chapelle and Festubert. The British had introduced the tanks in the middle of September and they had been sent coughing and clanking over the increasingly treacherous battlefield towards Bapaume but they failed to achieve as great a success as they perhaps deserved. In trying to salvage some crumbs of comfort from the Somme offensive the Army had thrown the tanks in with precious little forethought as to how best they should be used. The result was that the British had shown their hand and the element of surprise had been forfeited. By early October however the Battle of the Somme was not quite played out. There were one or two more bites at the rotten cherry to be taken before 'General Winter' put a stop to the British attacks for good. The Barnsley Battalions were needed once more on the Somme.

Mutilated tree stumps at Serre.

By 5th October the Battalions had marched as far as Robecq where several days were spent in training, cleaning up and reorganising before they were marched away to Berguette on 8th October. At Berguette the Battalions boarded a train for Doullens along with the Sheffield City Battalion. They were heading for familiar territory. Arriving at Doullens the 13th Battalion marched to Sarton, a settlement which was but four miles west of Mailly Maillet, the village which they had come to know so well on their arrival on the Somme some seven months earlier. The 14th Battalion moved off to renew their acquaintance with Gezaincourt.

By the middle of October the 'bush telegraph' which appeared to keep the British troops so well informed as to forthcoming events, was beating out loud and clear with rumours of another big attack on the old front near Serre.

All Summer long and into the Autumn the British troops had slogged their way north-east towards the elusive prize of Bapaume. A little more than two weeks earlier, on 26th September, British infantrymen had at long last been able to turn and gaze down into the valley of the Ancre from the mass of sludge and shell craters which had once been Thiepval. It had taken them eighty-eight days to capture a hamlet which should have fallen in a matter of hours on 1st July, but eighty-eight days or not Thiepval was finally in British hands.

The Germans holding the line astride the Ancre valley found themselves cupped in the enveloping arms of the British, but the Autumn rains had arrived early and the ground was rapidly developing into a quag-mire. The Germans settled back in their dugouts content in the knowledge that the British would allow them to hang on to the narrow tongue of ground from St. Pierre Divion on the eastern banks of the Ancre, north as far as Serre. The British had other ideas. One more push when the Germans were least expecting it would perhaps drive them out of the valley of the Ancre itself, out of Beaumont Hamel and even out of Serre. All the British needed was just one short break in the weather, and that was on its way.

For the 13th and 14th Battalions in billets at Sarton and Gezaincourt, the arrival of several large drafts of 'Derby' men appeared to add weight to the rumours. Were the battalions being built up so that they could be thrown into the thick of it again? The 13th Battalion received ninety-eight men on 14th October, followed a day later by a further seventy-one. The 14th Battalion fared even better in terms of reinforce-ments. Between the 14th and the 21st October the battalion welcomed a total of 249 Non-Commissioned Officers and men into its ranks. The new men were at once posted to those companies which had suffered heavy losses on 1st July and whose strength had been further sapped by subsequent tours of front-line duty.

The new men of 'B' Company of the 13th Battalion could no longer claim to be part of the 'Houghton Main Mob' as so many of the men who had joined up after the recruiting speeches at the Little Houghton recreation ground some two years earlier were no longer present.

There were however, one or two ex-Houghton Main men left and some like Harry Hall had earned a promotion. In their dealings with the new men those 'old hands' would undoubtedly pass on a little of the Barnsley spirit.

On 18th October both battalions returned once more to their old camp in Warnimont Wood, but it was not the haven they had come to know and love in the early Summer. Gone was the green and leafy peace, the blossom and the warming sunshine and in their place there was mud. Thick brown mud. The entire Colincamps Plain was awash with it due to the early and heavy Autumn rains.

For the rest of October and the first few days of November the battalions ventured out of the dreary surroundings of Warnimont Wood towards the front-line trenches between John Copse and Hebuterne. On their way they passed guns, lots of them; poking menacingly from the endless brown vista and somehow managing to stay afloat above the mire. Their presence was proof indeed that there was some-thing afoot.

The approach to the trenches on the Colincamps sector had been bad enough on the night of 30th June but now many of the communication trenches had simply been abandoned as the mud and the water had moved in to stay. Only one or two selected routes were in use and the pumps being used to keep them clear were working like fury.

Plunging and floundering down waterholes with mocking names like 'Welcome' and 'Whisky', the men of the 13th and 14th Battalions gripped their cold, muddy rifles with equally cold, muddy hands and made their way up the line.

'We were sent down to the Ancre front and moved to Hebuterne. There were six of us with a Lewis gun somewhere on the Hebuterne sector and the trenches were waterlogged. We couldn't man the front line properly, there were just posts here and there. The second and third lines were manned in the usual way. We were in these waterlogged posts for four days, just crouched in the mud for

four days! Our orders were not to fire the machine gun and give our position away but one night a German war dog came towards us, sniffing about. We made up our minds that we were going to shoot it if it came too close. We lay in the mud watching it as it finally made off back towards the German lines. After four days we could barely walk and I had found out that though I could swim in water I couldn't swim in sludge. It was at Hebuterne that I got 'trench feet'. I was then shipped home and that was the end of my service with the 14th Battalion." Charlie Swales, 14th Y & L Regiment

The ruined village of Hebuterne, close to the front line opposite Serre. An uncomfortable billet for the Pals on their return to the Somme in October, 1916.

The 14th Battalion suffered a further thirty casualties during their periods of duty in the front-line swamps of Hebuterne. Harold Quest, the youngest son of the Deputy Chief Constable of the West Riding, was one of them. As a 2nd Lieutenant he had received the Military Cross for his part in the raid on the night of 3rd/4th June, and had been promoted to the rank of Lieutenant by the time his battalion had moved once more to the Somme. He was killed on 3rd November.

At the time of his death Harold Quest's elder brother, Captain Thomas Percival Quest, also a 14th Battalion officer, was in hospital suffering from shellshock.

In between their spells of garrison duty in the trenches the men of both battalions had taken part in several mock attacks around Warnimont Wood, and as the first week of November drew to a wet and bitter close they were well aware that the long rumoured 'push' was imminent.

In the drizzling gloom of the evening of 12th November the battalions squelched their way up from Warnimont Wood to the ruined village of Sailly-au-Bois where they were ordered to stay until further notice.

The men tried hard to make the best of their glum surroundings but it was almost impossible to find a house or a barn left standing. Successive hordes of British troops had seen to it that most sections of the timber framed barns had made their way piece by piece into numerous braziers as the weather had deteriorated.

Some two-and-a-half miles away to the east the four Hull battalions of the 92nd Brigade were already crouching knee-deep in mud in their assembly trenches which stretched from John Copse on the right to Jean Bart trench on the left. Yet again the 31st Division had been called upon to advance and stiffen the left flank of an attack by seven divisions of the Fifth Army on a front stretching from Hebuterne in the north down to St. Pierre Divion in the Ancre valley. This time however, the roles of the Brigades of the 31st Division had been reversed. This time the 92nd Brigade would lead the assault, with the 93rd in support and the 94th in reserve.

The assaulting troops north of the Ancre were to attack from the same trenches which the troops of the Fourth Army had risen from some four-and-a-half months earlier. Little had changed on that stretch of the front in all that time.

The Battle of Ancre was born kicking and screaming with a howl of bursting shells into the inky blackness of a foggy November morning. At a quarter to six the British guns opened up in an overture to the attack and the muzzle flashes of a thousand guns made the entire Colincamps Plain dance with momentary points of light.

On the left flank of the attack the 12th and 13th Battalions of the East Yorkshire Regiment, together with the troops of the 3rd Division on their right, waded into the fog and slime of No-Man's-Land in front of Serre and struggled forward.

All day the Barnsley Battalions waited in Sailly-au-Bois kitted out in full battle order and ready to move at twenty minutes, notice to reinforce the attack. They waited in vain.

One hour after the start of the battle the first cases of walking wounded began to file back through the British trench system and piece by tragic piece an all too familiar picture began to be revealed.

On the left the Hull battalions had forged ahead in spite of the quagmire in No-Man's-Land as far as the German second line, but once there the mud and the Germans had held them up. On their right the men of the 3rd Division had been caught sitting like bedraggled ducks in a mud-bound pond. The machine guns in Serre had picked them off as, with each step forward, they had sunk deeper and deeper into the slough. It was almost a repeat performance of 1st July.

Without the support of the 3rd Division on their right flank, there was no other course of action left open to the men of Hull, now isolated in the German second line, but to retire. Two Lewis gun teams of the Hull 'Commercials' attached to the 12th East Yorkshires held on all day beating off violent counter-attacks, but they had fast run out of pans of ammunition. If they had stayed where they were there was little doubt that the dwindling band of men would either have been killed or captured.

After almost twelve hours of heavy fighting the whole lot pulled out.

By the time the Barnsley Battalions had been ordered to fall in and began the march up the communication trenches towards the front line at ten minutes to four in the afternoon, it was all but over in front of Serre.

There had been precious little daylight to speak of on 13th November and with more fog rolling up from the Ancre and across the Redan Ridge, darkness had already fallen by the time the men were finally in position.

Perched on the crest of the low slope opposite the citadel of Serre glared menacingly out across the black expanse and down on those men of the Fifth Army. Once more Serre had flung back a British attack as a man might have brushed aside a fly with the back of his hand.

There had been some success. On the right of the attack the Germans had been squeezed out of St. Pierre Divion and, at long last, the fortress of Beaumont Hamel had fallen, but the position was not without its complications. Without the protection of the heights of the Redan Ridge and of Serre to the north, the British troops holding the new line astride the Ancre were condemned to spend the Winter months in the flooded valley bottoms, all the time staring up at the German lines above. The territorial gains were hardly worth the price in dead and wounded which the Fifth Army had had to pay to secure them.

Throughout the night of 13th November the men of the Barnsley Battalion ploughed through the mud to rescue the wounded soldiers from the atrocious conditions on the battlefield. The 13th Battalion alone managed to retrieve more than sixty wounded officers and men.

They were the lucky ones. Those who were concealed by the fog and the pitch blackness were left to bleed into the mud or freeze to death as the chill fingers of the approaching Winter groped their way along No-Man's-Land.

For the next few days the Barnsley Battalions shared the holding of the front line with other units of the 94th Brigade and continued to clear the battlefield. By the time they were withdrawn to Sailly-au-Bois on 22nd November the Battle of the Ancre was at an end and so was the Battle of the Somme. The Barnsley Battalions could claim the dubious privilege of being in at the beginning and in at the bitter end. Their own casualties had been mercifully light. The 14th Battalion saw out the 13th November without a single casualty while the 13th lost two men killed and five wounded between the 13th and 22nd November.

For the rest of November and the whole of December the 13th and 14th Battalions divided their time between the waterlogged front-line posts of Hebuterne and cold, damp billets in the rear. Even out in so called 'rest' there was no guarantee that a man would not be called upon to make a trip 'up the line'.

The Royal Engineers were always on the lookout for labour and so the infantry were always called upon to act as working parties. It was nothing that the old hands had not done before.

It was during the last few weeks of 1916 that Charlie Swales paid the price for standing thigh deep in mud for days on end. He had survived the terrible ordeal of 1st July, the rat infested 'high command' trenches of Neuve Chapelle and Festubert, and a second 'push' on the Somme, but now it was disease rather than hostile activity which finally claimed him.

It was at Hebuterne that Charlie got 'trench feet'. After another long soak in the squalid front posts Charlie's feet, when he finally managed to extricate them from his foul, dripping socks and boots, resembled two large, white and wrinkled footballs. They were so badly swollen that on handling them it was quite possible for his fingers to sink in as far as the first joints.

Charlie was shipped home unfit for further service, at least for the moment and another of the original Pals was gone. It was the end of Charlie's service with the 14th Battalion.

Charlie Swales was not alone however, for during the last few weeks of 1916 more men than ever before were reporting sick with a variety of ailments as a direct result of being in a near permanent state of filthy saturation. On the Hebuterne sector, sickness and disease were perhaps as great a threat to the men of the British Army as the Kaiser's troops.

Although the German artillery continued to seek out the British guns and fired on Hebuterne and all the approaches to the front line often causing casualties, disease took away a good deal of men.

In the 14th Battalion's case the loss of men due to disease was partly offset by the arrival of 190 men of all ranks who joined for duty on 19th December.

There was little action to break the treadmill of trench duty and relief, and although the Battle of the Somme was officially over the British Staff were intent on keeping their troops busy over the Winter months.

Two days before Christmas the 13th Battalion staged a large scale raid on the German lines.

Seventy-seven men under the command of Captain L.A.F. Foers and 2nd Lieutenant Midwood, volunteered to cross No-Man's-Land and enter the German trenches.

Under cover of a furious artillery barrage the raiding party tumbled into the German front line but almost as soon as they had scrambled over the parapet a blinding explosion scattered the raiders, seriously wounding 2nd Lieutenant Midwood and injuring seven other men. Owing to the absence of German counter-attackers and judging from the relative inactivity of the German guns it appeared certain that a British high explosive shell had pitched short as in the case of the 14th Battalion raid in early June, 1916.

In spite of this setback the raid went on and the uninjured men of the party made their way along the fire trench looking for dugouts and German soldiers.

Captain Foers demonstrated his knowledge of the German language by shouting "Kommen Sie Mit!" down into the uninviting depths of several dugouts. It was hardly surprising that none of the German soldiers showed their faces even if they had been inside the dugouts and had been able to hear Captain Foers' curt command above the thumping British barrage.

Greeted with silence Captain Foers bounced several Mills bombs down the steps of the dugouts. After several minutes the German trenches were filled with the acrid odour of explosive mixed with smoke which belched from the depths of the underground shelters. Captain Foers duly gave orders for the raiders to retire.

Under heavy machine-gun fire the party scuttled across No-Man's-Land to the safety of their own lines dragging the ominously inert body of 2nd Lieutenant Midwood along with them.

As was the case with the 14th Battalion's raid in June the results of the operation were minimal to say the least. Once again there were no prisoners and no one knew precisely how many Germans had been killed or wounded in the few hectic moments in which the raiders had rampaged along the German trench.

It had been a costly excursion for 'C' Company, with 2nd Lieutenant Midwood and eight men being wounded in all.

At daybreak two German soldiers were sighted huddled under the British wire. Obviously confused by the raid they had fled and had simply been lost in No-Man's-Land. They gave themselves up and after questioning they revealed they were both men of the 8th Bavarian Infantry Regiment. Their capture was added to the four German soldiers taken prisoner in a raid by 'D' Company towards the end of November.

The Germans withdraw and leave the desolate village of Serre to the British.

Shortly after the raid the 13th Battalion were withdrawn from the line and moved back to Rossignol Farm near Coigneux a little way north of Bus Wood, where they spent Christmas Day. Although a gift of 4,400 oranges and half a ton of nuts had been dispatched from Barnsley as a festive treat there would be no rejoicing for the family of 2nd Lieutenant Midwood when they came to mark Christmas Day on their calendars in the years to come. 2nd Lieutenant Midwood had barely been conscious since he had been brought back from the German trenches. He died that day.

Both Barnsley Battalions were still in billets near Coigneux as 1916 gave way to 1917, and as far as their total strengths were concerned they were at least as strong as they had been at any time since setting foot on French soil.

In the case of the 13th Battalion they went into the new year with 26 officers and 946 men but although the uniforms bore the crest of the Tiger and the Rose' of the York and Lancaster Regiment, an increasing number of men inside them were not, and never had been, Barnsley Pals. It was a fact which was recognised by Lieutenant-Colonel Wilford in a letter he sent to Lieutenant-Colonel Hewitt in mid-December. Writing of the trench raid carried out by the 13th Battalion in November he remarked,

> " . . . 'D' Company put up a great performance . . . They are still almost 'all Barnsley' and are far and away my best Company. 'C' Company come next, and they have a good sprinkling still left of the old Battalion. The other two Companies are practically new, but improve daily." **Barnsley Chronicle, 23rd December, 1916**

By the end of January 1917, Tommy Oughton had made a splendid recovery from his bout of dysentery and by mid-February he was on his way once more to France with orders to join the 14th Battalion on the Somme.

If Tommy was expecting to join a battalion holding on to more or less the same trench system he had come to know intimately as a member of the 13th he was in for a surprise.

Dramatic developments were afoot; developments which would not only affect the position on the Somme, but also on a substantial stretch of the Western Front.

Before the Battle of the Somme had ground axle-deep to a halt in the mud of November 1916, the Germans had decided upon the construction of a new and immensely powerful defensive line some twenty-five miles behind their old lines in front of Bapaume.

A new broom was sweeping clean through German defensive philosophy in the shape of a supreme command partnership of Ludendorff and Hindenburg. A policy of non retirement, which the Germans had adopted all through the Summer of 1916 was all very well, but it had crippled the German Army and left it enclosed in a nasty salient. The new partnership thought it wise to prepare a line of defence, stronger and tactically more commanding than their old line; from which the German Army could counter any Allied moves during 1917. What's more they would lay waste to the ground over which they retired, an act of devastation which went under the code name of 'Alberich'. When the British cautiously followed up in the wake of the German retirement they would gain nothing more than a wilderness; complete in its utter desolation.

All through the Winter the Germans toiled on their 'Siegfried Line' even as the Barnsley Battalions were spending their longest period of rest out of the battle zone since arriving in France.

The first six weeks of 1917 was a period of unrelenting frost

British troops are at last free to roam about the 'killing ground' at Serre in March 1917.

No longer 'missing, presumed killed', the grim relics of a battlefield.

and of snow and ice. Over the iron hard ground the battalion would charge in Brigade and Battalion exercises, long miles behind the front line. Although the weather was bleak in the extreme it was much more preferable to the front line and, as the weeks passed, much of the wearing trench fatigue was shaken from the bones and the new men were absorbed into the units.

There was training in all aspects of trench warfare with a greater emphasis being placed on the autonomy of the platoon as the smallest complete unit on the field of battle. The role of the platoon became a key element in future plans for the battalions regarding offensive activity, and the men were trained in all the weapons available to the infantry.

On 25th February, 1917 however, the long period of rest and training was brought to an abrupt end when the 31st Division was moved up to Hebuterne as part of the 5th Corps of the Fifth Army. The word was that a battalion of the Royal Warwickshires had gone over at 5 o'clock that morning and had found Serre to be empty.

It proved to be somewhat of a hollow acquisition.

The Germans had begun their retirement some two days earlier. They had held on to Serre all Winter long and now, when it suited them, they had simply given it up. Slowly, warily, like curious children entering a reputedly haunted house, the British Army crossed No-Man's-Land without a shot being fired. In the distance they heard intermittent thumps and saw pillars of thick smoke rising vertically in the still air as the retiring Germans put a light to their dugouts, destroyed roads and light railway lines. Further back they demolished buildings and felled entire areas of woodland.

As the Barnsley Battalions advanced the skeleton remains of Gommecourt Wood loomed hauntingly on their left. Once an inferno of singing bullets and red-hot shell splinters it was as still as the grave, and that is exactly what it was.

Crossing the one hundred and fifty yards of barren earth to the old German lines the Barnsley men were sickened at the sight of the rows of badly decomposed corpses of British troops who had fallen on 1st July and during subsequent raids and attacks. In many cases, after anything up to eight months of lying exposed to the elements, all that remained of the British dead were skeletons in rotting khaki uniforms, tangled up in the ugly, rusted wire.

Some of the bodies would eventually be identified and the mortal remains buried with dignity, and back in Barnsley one more family might learn of the fate of a male relative.

Tommy Oughton joined the 14th Battalion just before they made their trek across the old No-Man's-Land.

"When I went back to the 14th we were going round the back of the Serre area. It was the time when Jerry was retiring, because we went and followed up through Serre. I remember I went down into their dugouts, had a look around and examined them. They were grand places. They were deeper and as comfortable again as ours. In different parts of the war when we'd knocked the Germans out we used to live in their dugouts. The only disadvantage was that the entrance was facing the shells if we were shelled because the Germans dug them under their parapet. We didn't stay at Serre. It was just a matter of marching through it." Tommy Oughton, 13th Y & L Regiment

The Germans continued to fall back and the Barnsley Battalions followed, sending out patrols to make sure the ground ahead was clear. Often there were brief yet bloody skirmishes as trench by battered trench, farm by ruined farm the British worked their way towards Puisieux and ran across parties of retiring Germans.

The German trench system was an unfamiliar world to the men of the Barnsley Battalions and at the end of each day posts would be established to protect the ground they had gained. The Germans were intent on fighting a stubborn rearguard action to cover their retirement and if that meant going on the attack to eliminate British posts which had crept a little too close for comfort then that is exactly what the Germans did.

On 9th March, Ossie Burgess was in an advanced outpost near Puisieux with twelve other men under the command of Acting Sergeant Wetton, when a German patrol descended upon them.

Back from the Somme, a group of 13th Battalion men. Arthur Edon, wearing souvenir 'picklehaube', is to die of wounds a few months later.

> *"It was round about four o'clock in the afternoon. I was lookout but it was foggy, you couldn't see your hand in front of your face. We were in a dugout and there was a lot of noise. We went to have a look and we could hear talking at the other end of this trench, but we didn't know they were Germans, we thought they were our lads. I says to Tommy Wetton, 'There's something doing down there Tommy, I'll have a walk out and see what's going off.' He said he couldn't understand it. I'd been out two or three minutes when I looked over the top of this trench and I saw this German, then 'whoosh' a grenade went up. He'd thrown a 'tatie-masher' at me. Some of the shrapnel hit him first then it hit me on the hand and on the leg as well. I set off to walk but my leg gave way and I fell over. I must say this, the Germans were very good to me. They picked me up and put me on a stretcher and took me to their first aid post. All the wounded Germans were lying there. I was interrogated three times at three different places. At the third interrogation there were four guards, two at the front and two at the back. They took me to a Colonel with a Belgian interpreter. It was difficult. The Colonel asked me if I wanted a cigarette. He got this cigarette lighter out and it was the first time I'd seen one like that. It was like a revolver. I thought he was going to fire a shot at me. We both laughed. That interrogation went on for over an hour. I told them a pack of lies. I told 'em I knew nothing at all about soldiers but they'd got a first class shot and they didn't know. The night we'd moved up I'd been given another stripe and a needle and cotton to sew it on with. I'd a badge for being a first class shot as well. As we were going up I ripped all the lot off, chucked 'em in a trench and threw a stone on them. By God, it's a good job I did because if they'd got that first class badge, they were offering money for a first class Lewis gunner. I don't know what told me to do it, but I was captured soon after. I spent the rest of the war in prisoner-of-war camps at Minden, Munster and Essen, and then a camp back at Oberhausen."* Ossie Burgess, **14th Y & L Regiment**

Ossie was not alone in being captured. Tommy Wetton was taken along with seven more men of 'D' Company, and by 21st March they were in captivity in Block 3, Group 3, Gefengenenlager, Minden in Westphalia. The 9th March was a costly day for 'D' Company of the 14th Battalion. As well as the men who had been taken prisoner, five men went missing and were later officially deemed to have been killed in action. On the same day 'A' Company lost Privates Ellis and Aldale killed.

The Germans who had routed 'D' Company's post lay in wait for a relieving garrison which, when it turned up, consisted of a party of the 12th York and Lancasters. Another ferocious duel took place and when the dust had settled four Sheffield City Battalion men were missing and five more were wounded. The Germans were obviously not going to go without a struggle.

Ossie Burgess had written to the Chronicle and got his name in print while the Pals had trained in England but when his name appeared again in the Summer of 1917 it was under much less joyful circumstances. The lads in captivity in Minden were in need of much more comfort than a mere melodian could bring.

> *"Four members of the 2nd Barnsley Battalion, who are prisoners of war in Germany and whose*

names are Lance-Corporal O. Burgess, and Privates F. Sherry, C. Turner and F. Rawlings, have written to the Editor stating that they are having a 'rough time of it'. They write: 'We are hoping for a better time as we are just existing and that is all. Up to now we have received no correspondence whatever from England. We have nothing to pass the time away – no cigarettes as these are a thing of the past. This last week or two we have had very cold weather and of course we feel it more with not being well nourished.' These lads, who were captured on 9th March this year on the Somme front state that they will give all the information they can to any persons interested in other boys who were at the same place." Barnsley Chronicle, 11th August, 1917

A group of prisoners of war at a camp in Germany. William Bellin, 2nd Barnsley Pals Battalion is standing, third from the right.

Three days after the capture of Ossie Burgess his battalion was back in billets at Courcelles-au-Bois. There were strong rumours that the Barnsley Battalions were needed in an attack against Miraumont but they proved groundless.

The Germans had pulled so far back that the salient around Serre had been squashed almost flat. When the 7th and 46th Divisions had converged on an ever decreasing front they had squeezed out the 31st Division. There was simply no more room for it on that particular stretch of the Western Front so once more its units were pulled back in reserve. A week later the battalions were marching away from the Somme and the devastation of the Ancre Valley en route for the rear areas in the valley of the River Lys. The weather had changed for the better and the First Army area did not appear to be half as bad as the men remembered it, but then they were well away from the line.

For the remainder of March and on into April both battalions trained hard in the pleasant countryside of the Lys Valley near Merville.

Towards the middle of April they were on the move again, marching south through the French coalfield towards the distant bubbling cauldron of the Battle of Arras. On 1st May they arrived at Maroeuil, three-and-a-half miles north-east of Arras. A day later the 13th Battalion moved up to St. Catherine's and from there made its way into the reserve trenches in what had been the British front line before the opening shots of the battle. When the Barnsley Battalions arrived however, the Battle of Arras, like the Battle of the Somme, had developed into a costly duel of attrition.

A 13th Battalion officer serves out rations in the Gavrelle sector.

It had begun with blazing success at 5.30 a.m. on Easter Monday, 9th April when the Canadian Corps had swarmed up the steep slopes of Vimy Ridge and had driven the Germans from their trenches. On the lower ground to the south the Third Army had been equally successful in breaching the German positions east of Arras and in less than an hour almost the whole of their front line was in British hands along with several thousand prisoners and scores of guns.

In spite of the initial success to the north the offensive began to founder south of the River Scarpe as the attacking troops were checked by heavy machine-gun fire. Waiting behind for the order to push through, the reserves stamped their feet in frustration and behind them the cavalry champed at the bit all day merely adding to the considerable congestion behind the lines.

The cavalry was handed its opportunity two days later. In a little more than forty-eight hours any cherished hopes that the Battle of Arras was to be the final clinching episode of the war had galloped off into the swirling flakes of the last snowfall of Winter to be cut down in a hail of swirling steel in front of Monchy-le-Preux.

Monchy was taken but by then it was too late to salvage lasting results.

Throughout April the British continued to throw troops into the battle although there was little of strategic worth left for them to achieve. A French offensive to the south which opened on 16th April, was, towards the end of the month, in tatters, and although there was no longer any French advance to assist, British troops were pushed into bloody local actions for this very reason.

Men of the York and Lancaster Regiment taking up wire for a night working party on the Oppy-Gavrelle sector.

Thus the Barnsley Battalions became embroiled in the Third Battle of the Scarpe. On their first day in the reserve line the 13th Battalion provided working parties for the Royal Engineers who were busily consolidating ground won at a heavy cost by the 63rd Royal Naval Division near Gavrelle on 23rd April.

It made little difference to the Army that the 31st Division troops were newcomers to that particular section and that they were unused to both the landscape and the enemy trench system, not to mention their own. They were ordered to attack on 3rd May on a twelve-mile front from Fontaine-les-Croissiles to Fresnoy to capture the village of Oppy and the German lines east of Gavrelle.

Fortunately the 94th Brigade were not chosen to lead the attack; that rather dubious honour went to the 92nd and 93rd Brigades on the left and right of the Divisional front, in the company of the 2nd and 9th Division to the north and south.

At 3.45 a.m. the troops went over into a brightly moonlit arena, the silhouette of each man stuck firmly to the incomplete silver disc of an almost full moon. The whole scenario was like a shooting gallery. The German machine guns opened up.

By nightfall on 3rd May the casualty returns from the battalions of the 31st Division which had been engaged were showing figures of two and three hundred casualties, losses which were reminiscent of 1st July, 1916.

On the night of 4th/5th May the Barnsley Battalions moved up to relieve the remnants of the Bradford 'Pals' battalions; if indeed there were any 'Pals' left, in the support trenches near Gavrelle Windmill.

Immediately they were set to work digging a communication trench up to the Windmill spur, a slight eminence which overlooked the German lines to the north-east in the direction of Oppy.

The Germans were intent on making the British keep their heads down on account of the attack the previous day, and all day the Barnsley trenches were drenched with high explosive shells and machine-gun fire.

For three days the shelling continued unabated and inevitably the heavy fire took its toll on the ranks. It was almost impossible to move the wounded out or to get food, water and ammunition in. The tenuous position on the Windmill spur and the lie of the land meant that the battalions were robbed of close artillery support and in effect were out on a limb. The trenches afforded little protection as they ran over recently captured ground and so consisted of little more than a chain of shell holes connected by hastily scratched ditches.

By 21st May after nineteen days of being continuously rotated between the front, support and reserve lines always under heavy fire the 13th Battalion at last reached St. Catherine's near Arras while the exhausted men of the 14th sought sanctuary in huts at Bray.

Both battalions had suffered terrible casualties, among them a commanding officer, Lieutenant-Colonel

*Captain Lewis
Huggard*

Wilford of the 13th was wounded when a long-range shell exploded on Battalion head-quarters situated in a dugout in a railway cutting behind Gavrelle Windmill. Major Courtney-Hood of the 14th Battalion took over temporary command.

The 14th Battalion losses had, however, far outstripped those of the 13th. One hundred and thirteen men had been wounded, among them Captain Alphonse Wood who had recently rejoined the Battalion after recovering from an earlier wounding. Three officers and thirty-three men had been killed and two were missing. It appeared as though simply holding the line on the Arras front was a particularly unhealthy pastime.

The 13th Battalion went into the month of June with a new commanding officer. Lieutenant-Colonel G.B. Wauhope arrived on 1st June to take over the reins of command from Major Courtney-Hood who sidestepped to take command of the 12th York and Lancasters.

For a good deal of the month of June, the battalions moved in and out of the line relieving other units and being relieved in turn on the Rolincourt and Gavrelle, Oppy sectors.

When the 14th Battalion moved back into rest billets at St. Catherine's in the broken northern suburbs of Arras, Major General Wanless O'Gowan took the opportunity of informing them that several units of his Division were to be used in an attack on the German trenches near Oppy Wood.

Oppy Wood was nothing more than an untidy collection of mutilated stumps but it concealed a number of machine-gun nests which had thwarted all attempts at capture during previous nibbling attacks by the British.

The result was that the machine guns in Oppy Wood dominated a tiny salient which threatened the British line. It simply had to be erased.

On 26th June the Barnsley Battalions moved up into the line for the attack which was to be launched at 7.10 p.m. on the 28th. Four days previously 200 or so men of the East Yorkshire Regiment had success-fully raided the German-held Cadorna trench south of Oppy but they had pulled out. This time the British intended to stay.

Each battalion of the 94th Brigade was to be drawn up in line with two companies from each leading the assault. On the right flank was the 14th Battalion and next to it the 12th York and Lancaster Regiment. Further north along the line the 13th Battalion had pushed half of 'A' and 'C' Companies into the front line with the rest in support. The left flank was covered by the 11th East Lancashires.

Lieutenant-Colonel Wauhope was anxious to tour the positions held by his Battalion and with his young intelligence officer of just two weeks, Captain Lewis Huggard, he set off to chart the lie of the land.

Lewis Huggard, the youngest son of the former Pals' chaplain the Reverend Richard Huggard was hit by fragments from a bursting shell and died instantly.

At 'zero-hour' on 28th June, the Battalions of the 94th Brigade rose from their trenches under cover of a brief but ferocious artillery barrage and fairly dashed across the one hundred yards of damp and cratered No-Man's-Land. The leading waves of the 13th Battalion were across and into the German front line within five minutes of climbing from their trenches.

Hardly a shot, hardly a shell had been fired in retaliation and by the time the Germans had recovered enough to send over a

A trench cookhouse near Vimy, 13th January, 1918. A York and Lancaster Sergeant collects hot food.

counter-barrage it was already too late.

The Barnsley Battalions had immediately set about converting their gains into fire trenches and supplies were already on their way across No-Man's-Land.

By 1 a.m. on the 29th, the 14th Battalion was well established in Cairo Alley and by daybreak the entire stretch of the line was bristling with rifles and Lewis guns ready for the expected counter-attack which never came.

Almost a year to the day after the opening of the Somme offensive the Barnsley Battalions had participated in a successful attack which brought congratulations from all quarters. Their action in the encounter earned them the Battle Honour of 'Oppy'.

York and Lancaster Lewis Gun team near Oppy Wood, 1918.

Casualties were unusually low considering the length of occupied trench which was estimated to be of about a thousand yards. The 14th Battalion had but a handful of wounded officers while the 13th fared less well with three men killed, thirty wounded and two missing. The 13th Battalion had taken eighteen prisoners and the Divisional total was near the three hundred mark.

The Battalions stayed in position in the captured trenches during 29th June by which time the Germans had once more begun to pay close attention to the British front and support line. The 13th Battalion lost a further three men killed and eighteen wounded.

On 30th June the Battalions retired to the reserve lines in the railway cutting behind Gavrelle Windmill. They were still in support on the evening of 1st July but what a difference twelve months of trying trench routine and several attacks had wrought. For those who could remember the absolute dejection of that July evening a year ago, here at last was an action that had raised the spirits. Many of their old 'Pals' had not been present to see the battalions take part in an attack which had been a roaring success. It was at least some consolation for the failure of 1st July.

So light was their step that the battalions almost floated out of the line on 2nd July, the 14th Battalion marching up to a camp near Roclincourt while the 13th withdrew to Bray.

The remainder of 1917 was spent in long and tedious hours of trench duty on the sector which faced the German-held villages of Acheville and Mericourt. Occasionally the routine would be broken by a trip up to the line on the famous Vimy Ridge.

On the Acheville sector No-Man's-Land was well over one thousand yards wide in places and although the front could have been described as a relatively 'quiet' sector, constant patrolling by both sides at all times of the day and night contributed to some very frayed nerves.

A York and Lancaster man using a mirror attached to his bayonet keeps a wary eye on No-Man's-Land.

On 16th October at 5.10 a.m. the 14th Battalion were manning the line on the Acheville sector when the Germans heavily shelled their positions. From the opposite side of No-Man's-Land a German raiding party pushed out across No-Man's-Land. Immediately S.O.S. rockets were sent up requesting a counter-barrage but the Germans went on into the shell and rifle fire from the British trenches. The attack was finally beaten off.

Later a patrol led by Lance-Corporal Ridge went out to search No-Man's-Land for wounded Germans and brought in a soldier of the 6th Storm

Battalion. Twenty-seven German soldiers lay dead in front of the British wire.

For Harry Hall, Tommy Oughton and George Armitage Nichols the first three months of 1918 were to bring great changes, as the structure of the British Expeditionary Force was subjected to major alterations.

The heavy losses incurred by the British during the pitched battles of 1917 at Arras, Passchen- daele and Cambrai had led to a severe manpower crisis by the beginning of 1918.

There were growing fears that as the strength of the British Army drained away on the Western Front that of Germany

Corporal Harry Hall, seen here in charge of gas equipment; respirators, alarms and siren, is snapped by Lieutenant Heptonstall.

would increase in view of the recently signed Armistice on the Eastern Front. The situation grew daily more dangerous.

The Army wanted some 615,000 men for 1918 but the War Cabinet claimed they were simply not there and in any event the Army was well down the list when it came to the order of priority for the distribution of manpower.

Claiming that the losses of the British Expeditionary Force could be minimised by standing on the defensive and not embarking on costly attacks, the War Cabinet suggested a reduction of the number of Infantry Battalions in each Division from twelve to nine. In this way the surplus men would be used to bring the remaining battalions up to strength.

The Army were aghast at the idea and said so, but their protests fell on deaf ears. Against the Army's better judgement the reduction went ahead and many of the volunteer 'Kitchener' Service Battalions, for all their intense pride and patriotism of their early days, were the first to feel the sharp edge of the axe.

The 14th Battalion was one of them along with another one hundred and fourteen which were to suffer the same fate.

On 15th February, 1918 the 14th Battalion of the York and Lancaster Regiment made its final train journey of the war under that title to Pernes.

On 16th February it ceased to exist for on that day orders were received for its absorption into Number 4 Entrenching Battalion of the First Army Group. The original 'Pals' who had joined up from the collieries of Barnsley and district would have allowed themselves a wry smile at this strange reincarnation of their old unit. After all the Barnsley lads had always been able to dig.

The remaining two battalions of the York and Lancaster Regiment in 94th Brigade were amalgamated into one numbered the 13th, as were the three West Yorkshire Battalions of the 93rd Brigade. These two units, along with the 18th Durham Light Infantry completed a new-look 93rd Brigade. The 94th Brigade thus ceased to exist. The 11th East Lancashires were transferred to the 92nd Brigade to join two battalions of the East Yorkshire which had been formed upon the amalgamation of the four Hull Battalions. The 4th Guards Brigade formed early in February 1918 completed the shake-up of the 31st Division.

With the 14th Battalion gone, the 13th as its elder, was left to carry on, yet it was no longer a town Battalion with its heart in Barnsley, but a cosmopolitan unit incorporating men from Sheffield and many other parts of the country.

George Armitage Nichols was one of a few 14th Battalion men who were cross-posted to join the 13th and of course Harry Hall was still in the ranks after more than three years with his old battalion. Harry was one of a now very select band of men who had been through the entire adventure with the Barnsley

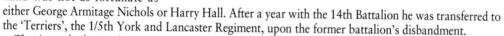

The German offensive of March 1918 takes all the ground won by the British on the Somme in a matter of hours.

Battalions without a single wound.

If nothing else he had certainly had a change of life, almost three-and-a-half years of change to be exact.

Tommy Oughton on the other hand was not as fortunate as either George Armitage Nichols or Harry Hall. After a year with the 14th Battalion he was transferred to the 'Terriers', the 1/5th York and Lancaster Regiment, upon the former battalion's disbandment.

The Army had voiced its grave concern that the reduction of manpower would leave the Divisions stretched and exhausted in the event of heavy and continuous German attacks, and no sooner had George Armitage Nichols and Tommy Oughton settled into their new battalions than the Germans attempted to prove the Army right.

On 21st March, 1918 the Germans launched an awesome offensive against the understrength and, to some extent, unsettled British Army. At the time of the attack the 31st Division was out of the line engaged in training in the First Army Area but as the German attacks continued it received orders at 11.15 p.m. to move to the Third Army Area to help stem the German tide between Bapaume and Arras.

By the afternoon the 13th Battalion was marching up to relieve sorely pressed units of the 34th Division and during the early hours of 23rd March they relieved the 15th Royal Scots in some trenches east of Boyelles.

For the next few days the 13th Battalion was subjected to incessant shellfire and repeated assaults by massed ranks of German troops and although the men succeeded in holding off several of the German efforts slight retirements were made to keep the line intact. By the time the 13th Battalion had been relieved in the line by the 11th Border Regiment and the 2nd King's Own Yorkshire Light Infantry, its casualties amounted to some 400 men.

There was little time to rest when they finally arrived at the village of St. Amand. On 1st April they were marched to Magnicourt and on 9th April they were rushed north up to the Lys where another crushing German blow had been delivered.

Bleary-eyed and exhausted the men of the 13th Battalion reached Vieux Berquin just as dawn was breaking on 11th April. From there they were marched up to Outtersteene, worn-out men in worn out khaki, thronging the road up to the front and pushing against an endless stream of pathetic refugees whose sum total of their existence was lashed loosely to a few rickety handcarts.

They arrived at Outtersteene at 6 a.m. and even as the last few villagers were attempting to salvage their possessions the 13th Battalion went into action.

Just before 7 p.m. the British machine guns clattered out in support of the attack and on the stroke of 7 p.m. the 13th Battalion went over. George Armitage Nichols was with them.

"I got caught going over the top at Outtersteene. I'd just returned from leave in Boulogne and I went straight up the line and went over. Our lads had just started to dig in and we'd got our signal lines run out and had managed to dig a bit of a hole with our entrenching tools to get under a bit of cover. I was just saying to my pals, 'We'll have a bit of 'snap' now we've got our lines run out,' and I'd no sooner said it than Jerry had popped his nose over the top of the trench. He says 'Lose Kamerad'. Of course, we didn't understand but he soon let us know what he meant when he started poking t'bayonet at us. We never went into a camp, we were just behind the lines all the time. When Jerry advanced we went with them; when he retreated after our 1918 'Big Push' we went back with them. All the guards were old men, the young men were up in the line. I did see a lot of Germans when I was taken prisoner, a lot of dead ones. There were a lot of English and Portuguese lying

267

around too. 'Port and beans' we used to call them. For the first week that's all we were doing, collecting the dead in a handcart. The place where we buried them was on a hillside and we put twenty in a grave about three feet deep. We'd put a wooden cross above them with the inscription '20 British soldiers'. The Germans took their boots off them. They took them off us. I had to wear a pair of Dutch clogs. The food was terrible. We used to have a quarter of a loaf of black bread and German sausage. We'd have a bowl of sauerkraut. It was just water with cabbage and two pieces of horsemeat floating on the top. By that time the Germans had very little food for themselves. I was about eight stone when I landed back home, and used to weigh twelve."

George Armitage Nichols, 14th Y & L Regiment

In spite of George Armitage Nichols' capture the attack had been a success, but disaster lay ahead.

On 12th and 13th April the Germans counter-attacked with up to six divisions through a gaping hole to the right of the 13th Battalion. It was a spear through the heart of the 31st Division which penetrated up to a mile and the 13th Battalion were forced to withdraw. All day the retirement continued under fearsome machine-gun fire.

Men were killed and wounded, others got lost as the battalion fought brief rearguard actions. It was absolute chaos.

Harry Hall's run of good fortune finally deserted him that day in early April.

"I was wounded near Bailleul in early 1918. We got into a bit of a fix. The Germans attacked and we'd no reserves behind us. I was sent with five or six men to hold a sector. We went up this sunken road and we were shielded until it went on to the level. They had some snipers in advance of their attack and when we got on the level one of them picked me off. The bullet hit me on the waist, on the left hand side and went through my belt, through my body and out of the belt at the back. I knew I had to get back or be taken prisoner. I doffed all my equipment. There was a Royal Army Medical Corps doctor not far away, and I said to him, 'Is it serious?'. He said, 'Well if you start coughing sit down.' Well, if I'd wanted to cough I shouldn't have done. I set off back and did about three miles and got to a road and saw a little ambulance coming up. When I saw it I flopped over. I can't remember anything else. That shows you what you can do when you're forced. They took me to Rouen for three days. I had nothing to eat but I could have as much Guinness as I wanted. I had three bottles a day. They decided the bullet hadn't penetrated the abdominal wall so there was no damage inside. On the third day somebody came into the ward and said, 'Who wants to go to Huddersfield?', and I said, 'I do'. That was near enough for me."

Harry Hall, 13th Y & L Regiment

The Germans suffer heavy casualties in pushing the Allies back leaving them exhausted and susceptible to counter-attacks which come in August, 1918.

When the 13th Battalion finally arrived at Merris, a few miles south-west of Bailleul, it consisted of just 6 officers and 134 men. The losses were far heavier than the 13th Battalion losses on the Somme. Some 408 men were killed, wounded or missing. Almost two years after the Somme battle the great German offensives of March and April 1918 finally brought the curtain down on the remaining volunteer Pals of 1914 and 1915. The Germans too had suffered horrendous casualties and although they had pushed the British troops back on almost every sector, the British Army never collapsed.

By early August, with the German Army exhausted, the British were able to launch a series of attacks which pushed the Germans back. By early September, 1918 the 13th York and Lancasters were following the German retirement along the River Lys on the Franco-Belgian border.

Tommy Oughton was still at the front with the 1/5th York and Lancaster Regiment. His battalion too were in hot pursuit of the Germans. After weeks on the defensive suffering imponderable casualties, advance proved to be no less costly.

> *"We were more or less in open warfare at that time. Jerry had retired but left so many outposts to cover him. We were advancing up this hill and as we got to the top Jerry was sweeping it with fire. As a stretcher-bearer I stopped to attend a slightly wounded man and my friend, Bernard Earnshaw, went up to the top to attend a man who was badly wounded in the stomach. I was twenty yards further down the slope and the bullets were going over me as they were sweeping the hill top. I was bent down but as Bernard bent down there must have been a machine gun opened up. I'll bet he had fifteen bullets in him, all in the stomach."* **Tommy Oughton, 13th Y & L Regiment**

The last action of the 13th Battalion, the York and Lancaster Regiment during the war of 1914–1918 was an encounter with the Germans as they retired across the River Lys near Warneton at 6 a.m. on 30th September, 1918.

In that final engagement the battalion lost twelve men killed, the commanding officer Lieutenant-Colonel Wauhope and forty-eight men wounded with two missing.

Moving back into Divisional Reserve the battalion was at Renaix when the Germans, having lost all hope of victory, signed an Armistice with the Allies. On the stroke of the eleventh hour on the eleventh day of the eleventh month of the year, the fighting ceased. At last there was peace on the Western Front.

One by one the few remaining Pals of the 13th drifted home as the process of demobilisation commenced.

Throughout December and January small parties of demobilised officers and men would be sent away as the 13th Battalion was broken up piecemeal.

Other old Pals were also finding their own way home from different points on the continent of Europe. For one Barnsley family the return of a Pal caused unexpected joy.

> *"When the Armistice was signed the Germans let us go. I went to meet the British advanced party. Eleven days after the Armistice I was at home, but they didn't know I was living until I got to Hull because the War Office had posted me 'missing presumed killed'. As prisoners we were supposed to send cards home but my family never received any. I wired from Hull that I was coming home. Of course the family thought I was dead. My eldest sister's husband came to meet me at Sheffield and he told me I was on the 'Roll of Honour' at the chapel where I used to go as a lad because I'd been reported 'missing presumed killed'."* **George Armitage Nichols, 14th Y & L Regiment**

As I think of returning to home o'er the sea,
When the war is finished, I'll come back to thee.

Models pose for sentimental postcard photographs. Uniforms are different but hopes and desires are the same. The survivors of four years of slaughter are coming home.

Ossie Burgess was also repatriated after the signing of the Armistice. Arriving in Hull on the same day as George Armitage Nichols aboard the S.S. *Porto*, his return to Barnsley was tinged with rather more sobriety than that of his ex-14th Battalion comrade. Ossie Burgess returned to a different Barnsley than the one which had cheered him off from May Day Green that Christmas night in 1915. It was a community visibly suffering the effects of the War to end all Wars.

"There were no heroes' welcomes when we came back home. You couldn't expect it. There were so many men killed. They told me there wasn't one house that hadn't had a man killed or wounded, and the biggest part of them were colliers." Ossie Burgess, 14th Y & L Regiment

Both Ossie Burgess and George Armitage Nichols had managed to get home for Christmas, even though it had taken them four years to achieve it. Tommy Oughton, demobilised from the 1/5th York and Lancasters was also home for Christmas . . . just.

Christmas 1918 and Tommy Oughton surprises his parents with the best possible present they could hope for. Their lad is home from the war.

"I believe it was the quickest demobilisation there'd ever been. On 23rd December we were still at Dunkirk and then we came across the Channel in the evening and landed at Folkestone. At 10 p.m. we caught a train through London and we were in Ripon by half past four in the morning. In the afternoon of the 24th December we were back at Ripon station where we caught a train to Leeds. I stopped in Leeds with a lad called Jimmy Milburn who liked his ale. We had to make our own way from Leeds. We just caught the last train from Leeds to Barnsley between 10 and 11 p.m. There were no buses when we got to Barnsley so we walked to the end of Doncaster Road to catch a bus from there, but they were all full up. We walked a bit further and who should come round but Lewis Burrows in a van. It was like a mini-bus that used to run on market days and being Christmas Eve it was like a Market day. He dropped us at the bottom of John Street, in New Guinea. We hadn't had time to tell anybody we were coming home. It was perhaps half past eleven and as I walked up the street I could hear carol singing coming from our house. My dad was a violinist and he was playing as it was Christmas Eve. The house was full of relatives and neighbours. I just inched the door open, took my steel helmet from my epaulette and threw it under the table. That stopped all the singing. No one got to bed before 5 o'clock the next morning." Tommy Oughton, 13th Y & L Regiment

Vernon Atkinson and Charlie Swales were also on their way home. Both men had been called up again during the last two years of the war and both men had seen action with other units.

After recovering from 'trench feet' Charlie Swales reported to Sunderland where drafts were being prepared to send to France. It was while he was at Sunderland that he teamed up with 'Brickie' Moore, an ex-1st Battalion York and Lancaster Regular whom Charlie maintained was the 'finest scrounger in the British Army'. Among 'Brickie' Moore's many idiosyncrasies were that he played the trombone, insisted on wearing a white silk handkerchief around his neck and always carried a little bag of tea and sugar which hung from his kit.

In 1917 Charlie and 'Brickie' found themselves in a draft of 80 men bound for Etaples and from there they joined the 7th York and Lancasters, trombone, white silk hanky and all. Charlie served with them until the end of the war.

Vernon Atkinson had moved to Rhyl from hospital in Mexborough and very soon he found himself going much further than the Western Front. One day a group of 'Derby' men were parading on the promenade at Rhyl and Vernon was ordered to fall in with them. It appeared as though Vernon was going out to the battlefield again. He joined the 9th South Lancashire Regiment who were bound for Salonika. He was wounded when an aircraft spotted him running across open ground and the pilot dropped bombs on him.

After a stay in hospital in Malta he was sent back to England and never returned overseas.

There were many of the original Pals who, after being returned to England sick or wounded, never rejoined the Army.

After spending the last five months of 1916 in hospital in Taplow, Ernest Bell then went to Durham and eventually to Sunderland when he was discharged unfit for further active service. Ernest Bell returned to his old job with the Barnsley Corporation.

Frank Lindley had been shipped back to a hospital in Ipswich after being wounded on the Somme, and when his real age had finally become common knowledge one of the nurses had refused to permit him to smoke as he was "too young". After leaving hospital Frank was posted to Pontefract to recuperate with lots of slow marching to bring the strength back to his legs. Even in Pontefract he could not escape grim reminders of war.

"There was a chap died of wounds at Wakefield and they called on us for an escort. We went across to Wakefield with a gun and some ammo. They got this poor chap on a gun limber draped with a Union Jack and drew him to the cemetery, then they lined us up with the guns They dropped him in, played the 'Last Post' and 'Bang'. The bloke next to me nearly fell into the grave. I had to grab him or he'd have been on top of the box. He'd gone. That burst of fire took him back to the trenches." Frank Lindley, 14th Y & L Regiment

Being under the age of eighteen, Frank was ineligible for the armed forces even though conscription had been introduced.

Throughout 1917 and 1918 he had various jobs on an aerodrome in Sheffield and in a munitions factory. With his experience of soldiering he did not altogether take kindly to the half-hearted approach to the work adopted by some of his fellow workers.

"I was on a shell machine putting brass bushes in the shells. There were two youths making these brass bushes and they kept having nights off, so we'd only work perhaps two nights a week and there I was waiting for bushes for the shells. I blew up and told the gaffer. I said, 'There's lads out there want some ammunition and this is happening.' All the shop were against me. In fact they took me off the machine and they had me walking about the factory. They wouldn't give me a leaving certificate. I found myself on a tribunal. One of the main blokes in Sheffield, Sir William Clegg, ran this tribunal. As soon as I'd mentioned I'd been over there he said, 'Give this man his certificate'."
Frank Lindley, 14th Y & L Regiment

With his eighteenth birthday in March 1918, Frank received his conscription papers through the letter box. His father was almost bed-ridden and he was the sole breadwinner for his mother and younger sister. He had responsibilities and decided to seek exemption. He found himself facing another tribunal.

"There were old councillors and officers. I stated my case. I said I didn't mind a bit of soldiering but I've got my family to look after. One of the officers said, 'I want that man,' but a little old man piped up and said, 'You shall not have him. He's done his share'. I just missed being called up." Frank Lindley, 14th Y & L Regiment

SATURDAY. NOVEMBER 16. 1918.

END OF THE WORLD WAR.

ARMISTICE SIGNED BY GERMANY.

Great Rejoicings Throughout England.

At 11 a.m. last Monday came to an end the cruellest and most terrible war that has ever scourged mankind. The Armistice [...] by Germany signing the [...] Here is the text of

is the great object of the Allies and we hope and trust that wish will be early carried out and without delay." (Hear, hear.)

UNITED THANKSGIVING SERVICE.

Sir,—In connection with the end of the war it has been decided to hold Public Thanksgiving Service in the [...]

VICTIMS IN WAR'S CLOSING STAGES.

A CAWTHORNE LOSS.

Monday's glad news of Peace was mingled with sorrow at Cawthorne by the sad news of the death of Sec.-Lieut. T. R. Allott. He went out to France on October 12th, 1918, and was killed in action near Le Incenoy, on November 4th. Mr. Allott, who was in the K.O.Y.L.I., was educated at Barnsley Grammar School and prior to joining the Army two years ago, was on the staff of Messrs. Bury and Walkers, solicitors. For several years he was organist at Cawthorne Westgate Chapel and afterwards at Westgate Chapel. He leaves a widow and one little girl.

Corpl. A. Dunn, Y. and L., son of Mr. and Mrs. J. Dunn, Don Street, Penistone, is in a base hospital in France suffering from gunshot wounds.

Lce.-Cpl. J. Ellin, Y. and L., has been wounded in the thigh and is now in hospital at Oswestry. His home is at 98, [...] Street, Barnsley. This is the second time he has been wounded.

Bombardier B. Lench, R.H.A., has died at [...] Military Hospital from influenza. [...] Street, Stair[...]

MAYORALTY

ALD. W. E. [...]

SPEECHES AT

Last Saturday a [...] Barnsley County [...] mously elected [...] Raley, J.P., as [...] The statutory me[...] Alderman H. E[...] Mayor, and the[...] Councillors Eng[...] non Dr. Horne, [...] Alexander, M[...] Moulstone, Woo[...] Town Clerk (C[...] offi[...]ists.

Alderman T[...] been well said [...] permit[...] of an [...] leader to wh[...] rates. They[...] the man, w[...] the loyalty[...] us to enjo[...] that whor[...] (Hear, hea[...]

SPECIAL GRATIS SUPPLEMENT TO

The Barnsley Chronicle.

AND PENISTONE, MEXBRO', WATH, AND HOYLAND JOURNAL.

VOL. LXI. NO. 3161. TUESDAY, MAY 27, 1919. GRATIS.

RETURN OF THE BARNSLEY BATTALIONS.

CADRE TO ARRIVE ON WEDNESDAY.

CIVIC WELCOME TO TAKE PLACE ON MARKET HILL.

COLOURS TO BE DEPOSITED IN ST. MARY'S CHURCH.

THURSDAY'S GREAT PROGRAMME.

Barnsley has had many memorable military gatherings and processions since the outbreak of hostilities, but they have all been to say good-bye and God-speed to our departing troops.

On Thursday next there will be another, a greater, and a happier procession and gathering on Market Hill.

It will be the day of days for Barnsley, for the inhabitants will at last be able to turn out to welcome back the Cadre and Colours of the 13th Battlion of the York and Lancaster Regiment.

The Battalion was quickly raised in September, 1914, in response to a call for volunteers to uphold their country's honour, and the town's farewell to this and its sister Battalion, the 14th, was made on Thursday, May 13th, 1915, when the "Pals" left Silkstone Camp for Cannock Chase.

None then knew when the local Battalions would return to the town which gave them birth, but few, we venture to think, when they saw their citizen-soldiers on that memorable march to Court House Station, thought that it would be four years to the very month before the members of the 13th Battalion would return victorious, and with colours flying.

The great day, long looked forward to, is at last in sight, and all Barnsley, we hope, will turn out to cheer the representatives of the Battalion, and the discharged and demobilised men who carried the Battalion with honour and glory through many weary months of war and hardship to the wonderful day of Victory.

The cadre of the 13th York and Lancaster Regt. (the original First Barnsley Battalion) arrived at Southampton on Thursday, and at present are at Catterick Bridge.

A telegram was received by the Town Clerk (Mr. W. P. Donald) on Friday, informing the Corporation that the cadre were prepared to come to Barnsley this week, and arrangements were at once made for their reception.

It has been arranged that the full cadre shall arrive in the town to-morrow (Wednesday) noon, and they will be accommodated at the Drill Hall, Eastgate. They will bring with them the King's Colours of the Battalion, presented to them when they went to form part of the Army of Occupation in Germany, and these have to be deposited for safe custody in the Barnsley Parish Church.

The ceremony in connection with the depositing of the Colours will take place on Thursday at 12 noon.

The proceedings will begin at 10.30 a.m., when the discharged and demobilised men of the 13th and 14th Battalions will assemble in the Queen's Grounds. Each Battalion will be inspected by its former Commanding Officers. The inspection, it is hoped, will be carried out by Major-General Hulk (formerly commanding the 14th Battalion), Col. Sir Joseph Hewitt, J.P. (formerly commanding the 13th Batt.), and Col. W. E. Raley, J.P. (formerly commanding the 14th Batt.)

Shortly before 11 a.m., the cadre will march off from the Drill Hall to the Queen's Grounds, and from there they will head the procession of the two Battalions to Market Hill.

Here the cadre and the Battalions will be received by the Mayor (Col. W. E. Raley, J.P.), and members of the Town Council, and His Worship will formally welcome back the men to the town.

The Battalions will move off from Market Hill to St. Mary's Church, and will then form a guard of honour through which the Council and the cadre will proceed to church.

At the Church door they will be met by the Rector (Rev. Canon Hervey, M.A.), and a short service will be held, during which the Colours will be formally handed over to the Rector by Major Goodburn, the officer at present commanding the 13th Battalion.

After the ceremony, the two Battalions will march to the Queen's Grounds, where refreshments will be served. In the event of wet weather, the Drill Hall and St. Mary's Schools will be utilised for this purpose.

His Worship the Mayor desires to make a general appeal to the public of Barnsley to co-operate in the welcome to the men by displaying flags and bunting, especially along the line of route, and by their presence on Market Hill on Thursday morning. There should be a tremendous crowd to witness what will be a memorable and historic gathering.

The accommodation of St. Mary's Church is, of course, limited, and such members of the general public who desire to be present at the service must take their seats before 11.45 a.m.

The feeding of the men will be in the capable hands of the Barnsley British Cooperative Society, and the liquid refreshments will be given by the two local breweries—the Barnsley Brewery and Clarkson's Old Brewery Companies. The arrangements for the distribution of the refreshments is in the hands of a sub-committee consisting of ex-Company Sergt.-Majors Bridge, Morrison, Taylor, and Townend and Councillor W. Barnes.

The general arrangements in connection with the visit will be carried out by the Raising Committee of the Council, of which the Mayor is chairman, and they will have the assistance of Col. Sir Joseph Hewitt, Col. T. W. H. Mitchell, and Col Fox. The provision of a band has kindly been arranged for by Col. Fox.

The line of route from the Queen's Grounds will be: Queen's Road, Kendray Street, Eldon Street, and Market Hill.

The strength of the cadre will be 50 men and 5 officers. It is interesting to note that Major Goodburn, the present Commanding Officer of the 13th Battalion, joined the Second Barnsley Battalion as a Second-Lieutenant on its formation early in 1914, and he has been with one or other of the Battalions throughout the war. The officers of the cadre will be the guests of the Mayor at luncheon at the Queen's Hotel on Thursday at the conclusion of the ceremony at the Church.

Whilst the cadre which will arrive in the town on Wednesday will be that of the 13th Battalion, it will in reality represent both the local Battalions which were raised for Kitchener's Army in the early days of the great war. When the Division in which the Battalions were was re-organised, the 14th was partly merged into the 13th and partly into another Service Battalion of the York and Lancaster Regiment, and there is no longer a 14th Battalion. The Colours to be handed over into safe keeping in St. Mary's Church, are, of course, the actual colours of the 13th Battalion, but the merging of the two Battalions is the reason why the discharged and demobilised men of both Battalions will parade on Thursday.

In order to prevent any misunderstanding, the Mayor wishes it to be distinctly understood that the welcome to the Colour party is quite a separate function from the welcome to be given to the whole of the Barnsley men who have served. This will take place at a later date, when there will be an assembly of all service men for a civic welcome home.

APPEAL TO ALL OLD 'PALS.'

BIG MUSTER WANTED.

The Barnsley Branch of the National Federation of Discharged and Disabled Sailors and Soldiers makes a special appeal to all its members who were originally either with the 13th or 14th Battalions to participate in the reception, and to parade at the Queen's Grounds on Thursday morning. In view of the fact that the inspection takes place at 10.30, the men are urgently requested to be there not later than 10 o'clock.

Uniform may be put on if desired, and a request is made that medals and decorations shall be worn.

All ex-officers, warrant officers and N.C.O.'s are invited to meet at 10, Peel Street, on Wednesday evening, at 7 o'clock, to discuss arrangements concerning Thursday morning's parade.

The civic welcome home to all Barnsley service men, to take place at a later date, will include sailors and soldiers from many regiments. Thursday's ceremony is the Barnsley Pals' Battalion's own particular day, and it is doubtful whether there will be another such opportunity for them to march shoulder to shoulder in Peace as they did in War.

A big muster of "Pals" is required. The authorities want it, and the people want it, and we trust the response to the appeal will be most gratifying.

If you served with the 13th or 14th Battalions, don't be satisfied to look on, but be on parade.

THE OFFICIAL PROGRAMME.

BARNSLEY COUNTY BOROUGH COUNCIL.

NOTICE.

THE CADRE OF THE 13th BATTALION, YORK & LANCASTER REGIMENT WILL RETURN TO THE TOWN FOR THE PURPOSE OF

DEPOSITING THE KING'S COLOURS

IN THE PARISH CHURCH,

ON THURSDAY, MAY 29, 1919.

All Officers and Men of the 13th and 14th Battalions, York and Lancaster Regiment, are cordially invited to attend and take part in the proceedings.

THE PROGRAMME IN CONNECTION WITH THE VISIT WILL BE AS FOLLOWS:

Thursday 10 to 10-30 a.m.

The demobilised men of the 13th and 14th Battalions, York and Lancaster Regiment, will assemble in the Queen's Grounds. Each Battalion will be inspected by its former Commanding Officer.

11 a.m.

The Cadre will proceed from the Drill Hall to the Queen's Grounds, and will head the march of the two Battalions from the Queen's Grounds to Market Hill.

11-30 a.m.

The Mayor and Town Council will receive the Cadre and the men of the two Battalions on Market Hill. The Mayor will address the Cadre and the Battalions.

11-45 a.m.

The two Battalions will march from Market Hill to the Church door, and will then line the route from Market Hill, forming a Guard of Honour for the Mayor and the Town Council and the Cadre.

12 noon.

The Cadre and the Mayor and the Town Council will arrive at St. Mary's Church.

12 noon to 12-30.

Service in St. Mary's Church and depositing of King's Colours. Members of the General Public desiring to attend the Service must take their seats in the Church before 11.45 a.m. The accommodation for the general public is extremely limited. All wounded men unable to walk are requested to take their seats in the Church before 11.45 a.m.

1 p.m.

Battalions will march back to the Queen's Grounds, where sandwiches, beer and mineral waters will be provided for all men taking part in the procession.

The General Public are requested to co-operate in the welcome to the Men by displaying Flags, and by their presence on the line of Route and Market Hill.

W. E. RALEY, Mayor.

PLACING OF COLOURS IN THE PARISH CHURCH

FORM OF SERVICE.

1. National Anthem (3 verses).
2. Te Deum.
3. Lesser Litany, and Prayers.
4. Hymn No. 437 (Ancient and Modern Hymn Book).

4a. Last Post.

5. Receiving of Colours at the Altar Rail.
6. Short Prayer.
7. Hymn No. 391 (Ancient and Modern Hymn Book).
8. Pronouncement of Benediction.
9. Recessional Hymn.

VISITS TO GRAVES IN FRANCE.

It is believed that by the end of July all military restrictions on travelling to France will be removed, and already many relatives are planning to visit the graves of soldiers in the late war zone. Tourist agencies are receiving letters of inquiry on the subject. The latest development is the establishment by ex-officers of a travel bureau. The itinerary consists of a three days' visit to France, with Amiens as the headquarters. It is an excellent centre for the battlefields of Northern France, and all parts of the Somme are within easy reach by motor-car. The bureau make themselves responsible for the traveller at Victoria, and accommodate him in Amiens the same afternoon. Next morning he is driven to the required destination—wherever the grave of his fallen kinsman may be—in a private motor car, and accompanied by an officer guide. The return journey to Amiens is made in time for dinner, and the journey to England is made on the third day, Victoria being reached in the evening. The fees charged for the visit will be for one person 25 guineas, two persons 30 guineas, three persons 40 guineas, four persons 50 guineas, five persons 60 guineas. The visits can be extended beyond the three days at a supplementary charge of two guineas per day per person for hotel accommodation and service, and 10 guineas per day for the use of a private car for two or three persons, and the services of an officer guide. Should a special "rush" visit of two days from London and return be desired, a car with an officer guide can be sent to meet the traveller on arrival at Cailais or Boulogne. The bureau assures intending travellers that "the journey is not by any means an excursion, but a visit made to the graves, in a proper spirit, and with due reverence."

The number of soldiers' graves now identified and registered in France and Belgium is 373,351. The number of other burials reported is 154,828. In many of these cases the burials took place under such conditions that the graves were never found, and in others all markings have been destroyed by shell-fire. During the last month 2,125 such graves have been identified and registered, and it is hoped a considerable number more will be traced. Some considerable time must elapse before all requests for photographs can be met, and the present situation does not permit of a general permission being given to visit graves. Relatives are strongly advised that no visits should be undertaken without first ascertaining from the Directorate of Graves Registration and Inquiries, War Office, Winchester House, St. James's Square, S.W.1, that the grave is registered.

FOOD CONTROL OF THE FUTURE.

The possibility of the retention of food control in some of its forms was foreshadowed recently, and a well-informed correspondent says the Cabinet has just instructed the officials of the Ministry of Food to prepare a Bill for presentation to Parliament this session, giving effect to certain recommendations made by the Consumers' Council. The Bill will, it is said, include a provision whereby tea, coffee, and cocoa must be sold by net weight.

COST OF BUILDING MATERIALS.

The Local Government Board issues the following statement:—It has been brought to the attention of the President of the Local Government Board that the present high market prices of building materials are tending to deter, or to prejudice, the rapid promotion of State-aided housing schemes, and he wishes it to be known that, by organisation and large-scale buying, contracts for the supply of building material have been entered into by the Government which show considerable saving on the ruling market prices. Local authorities and other promoters of State-aided housing schemes obtaining their building materials from or through the Ministry of Supply, will be given the advantage of this economy, which, though difficult to express in a general figure, amounts to from 10 to 15 per cent. on present market prices, and in some cases more. Application should be sent to "The Director of Building Material Supplies, Ministry of Supply, Caxton House Tothill Street, London, S.W.1."

Printed and published by the "Barnsley Chronicle," Limited, at their offices, "Chronicle" Buildings, Peel Square, Barnsley, in the West Riding of the County of York.
TUESDAY, MAY 27, 1919.

Market Hill, Thursday 29th May, 1919. 11.30 a.m. Lieutenant-Colonel Hewitt addresses some of the surviving Pals. The wheel has turned full circle.

Harry Hall just missed being called upon to return to France. After two months in hospital at Huddersfield, he was moved to Blackpool where he spent the greater part of another two months. He was then sent to Clacton-on-Sea. Although he had done more than his bit, it appeared the Army wanted more.

"I went down and they transferred me to the London Regiment. We'd started trench work and I knew there was going to be another 'Big Push'. I thought, by God, I'm going back again. I reconciled myself if I had to go I had to go and that was it. On the day before we went a fellow came in from the orderly room. If you'd been wounded and were in Class 'W' and you'd been a miner you could go home. I'd applied for this before I went to Clacton. Anyway this fellow said, 'Call for your rations and tickets, you're being discharged on Class 'W'. That was it. I didn't start work for a week or two. I thought I'd have a few weeks off before I started." **Harry Hall, 13th Y & L Regiment**

James Bennett had been transferred to the East Yorkshire Regiment during the latter part of 1916 and had been badly wounded in mid-November of that year.

"I remember getting wounded. I put my hand up to my neck and felt the blood running out. I only had a piece of white rag to stem the blood and until I could get them to stop it, blood was running out and down my neck and dropping off my sleeve end. The doctors said I wouldn't live three days. They could see the shrapnel through the rings of my throat. I was eight or nine months before I was discharged. They wanted to make sure I was healed up." **James Bennett, 14th Y & L Regiment**

By 9th May, 1919 the 13th Battalion in France had been so greatly reduced that it was at cadre strength of four officers and thirty-six other ranks. The cadre sailed from Dunkirk on 21st May aboard the S.S. *Moelieff* which docked at Southampton early the following morning. That same evening the last remaining men of the 13th boarded a train for the camp at Catterick.

On 29th May, 1919 the cadre returned to Barnsley to deposit the Battalion colours in St. Mary's Parish Church amid similar scenes of rapture which had accompanied the send-off of Barnsley Pals four long and weary years earlier.

In spite of the sadness which still haunted many families that their men had not lived to see the end of the war, thou-

Marching Pals on their way up Church Street, to St. Mary's Church.

The Cadre march the Battle Honours into St. Mary's Church where they remain to this day.

sands again took to the streets. There was a civic reception and the Education Committee padlocked the school gates for a day. It was a holiday.

Some 900 Pals who had been spared in the conflict, some without limbs and others carrying the appalling wounds they had received in action, turned out for a special parade on the Queen's Ground where, as fit young men, they had trained in their early days.

Shortly after half past ten the Pals of the 13th Battalion were inspected by Lieutenant-Colonel Hewitt who had received a knighthood for his part in raising the Battalion. Colonel Raley passed along the ranks of the Second Barnsley Pals, stopping every now and then to chat to a man wearing a Distinguished Conduct or Military Medal ribbon.

As the Pals stood there, some of them bearing up to the pain they felt in simply standing erect, they couldn't help but think about the gaps in the lines left vacant by their friends who had not returned.

There then followed a march behind the home-coming colours, the cadre with bayonets fixed, following the lively Volunteer Band down Queen's Road and Queen Street towards Market Hill.

Market Hill was packed with people as it had been on so many occasions in the past and presently the thump, thump of the bass drum and the shrill call of brass sent the waiting tumult into paroxysms of babbling anticipation. As the procession swung majestically across the bottom of Peel Square the cry went up, 'They're coming.'

Within minutes the band, the cadre and those Pals who had been able to manage the march, were standing stiff and erect in front of the Mayor.

Silence fell as the Mayor began his speech.

"Officers and men of the two Barnsley Service Battalions, we welcome you here today on this occasion when we are going to say 'Goodbye to the Colours', which were given to the 1st Barnsley Battalion in France . . . You know very well that on the 13th May, four years ago, the two Barnsley Battalions left this Market Hill for the purpose of taking up their training with Colonel Hewitt. . . The lads went to Egypt, then to France – you lads went to these countries and did well until the two Battalions were absorbed in France, and then you did well again at Bullecourt until your ranks were reduced to 200 and after that the Battalion became composed of men from all parts of the country. I hope when we deposit these Colours in the Parish Church today we shall say goodbye to war! (Cheers). We are all looking forward to Peace; we hope we shall have peace abroad, but let us have peace at home, and after we have deposited these Colours let us make up our minds that, after all, this war has not been fought in vain, but that it has brought us nearer together." **Barnsley Chronicle, 31st May, 1919**

With that the crowd erupted, and after a speech by Lieutenant-Colonel Hewitt and a brief medal ceremony the Colours were proudly borne up Church Street towards St. Mary's Parish Church.

The noise was incredible, loud cheers rang out and the Volunteer Band struck up to accompany the cadre up the hill.

At that precise moment with the words of the Mayor still ringing in their ears, the joyous crowds would never have believed it, even if they were told, that with the passing of twenty years another world war more ferocious and horrific than the one which had so recently ended would set light to the globe.

They would never have believed it, but then, they would never have heard above the clamour of the brass band.

Nominal roll

13th Battalion (1st Barnsley) York & Lancaster Regiment

An Unofficial and Incomplete list of
Officers and Men proceeding overseas
– December 1915.

Compiled by Peter Taylor

The Nominal roll of the 13th Battalion York & Lancaster Regiment is far from complete. It has been compiled by our researcher Peter Taylor using the following sources:

Soldiers Died in the Great War 1914-1918 Part 61 – His Majesty's Stationery Office, London 1920

The Barnsley Chronicle – September 1914 – January 1916

The Electoral Roll of Absent Voters, 1918

The York and Lancaster Regiment (The Territorial and Service Battalions 1758-1919) Volume II – Colonel H.C. Wylly C.B.

The compiled list is set out in the following order: Name, Rank, Number and Company (where known).

OFFICERS

Lieutenant-Colonel E.E. WILFORD
Major M.N. KENNARD
Major T.H. GUEST
Captain R. WILKINSON
Captain G. de V. SMITH
Captain C.H. GURNEY
Captain J. NORMANSELL
Captain N.W. STREAT
Captain R.W. CURRIN
Captain E.H. FIRTH
Captain H. DART
Lieutenant G. ASQUITH
Lieutenant H. BUTTERLEY
Lieutenant G.H. HUDSON
Lieutenant C.B. DIXON
Lieutenant R.A. HEPTONSTALL
Lieutenant S. MALEHAM
Lieutenant J.I. COOKE
Lieutenant F.T. COOPER
2nd Lieutenant A. HARROP
2nd Lieutenant E.A. BRAITHWAITE
2nd Lieutenant S.O. SHARP
2nd Lieutenant L.D.R. HUGGARD
2nd Lieutenant M. ASQUITH
2nd Lieutenant T.M. HIONS

ADAMS G.H.	*Sergeant* (22)
ALLEN F.	*Private* (719)
ANDREWS J.	*Private*
ANDREWS W.	*Private*
ARCHER D.	*Private* (30)
ARCHER E.	*Private* (26)
ARDRON H.	*Private* (16)
ARKROYD J.C.	*Private* (13)
ARMITAGE W.	*Private* (33) 'D' Co
ASQUITH J.J.	*Private* (123)
ATKINSON H.	*Private* (1)
ATTEWEL LE.	*Private* (1485)
AUDIN A.	*Private* (1127)
BAGNALL J.	*Private* (133)
BAILEY C.	*L/Corporal* 'C' Company
BAILEY C.H.	*C S M* (138)
BAILEY F.L.	*Private* (143)
BAILEY M.	*Private*
BAKER A.H.	*Sergeant*
BAKER A.H.	*Corporal*
BAKER G.	*Private* (33552)
BAKER H.	*Sergeant*
BAMBRIDGE C.	*C S M* (4930)
BAMBRIDGE E.W.	*Private* (27564)
BAMFORTH B.	*Corporal* (1392)
BARKER E.	*Private* (1360)
BARKER S.	*Private* (155)
BARLOW L.	*Private* (45)
BARLOW W.	*Private* (88)
BARNETT J.	*Private*
BAWCUTT L.	*Private* (75)
BAXTER H.	*Signaller*
BAXTER P.	*Private*
BEARDSALL J.R.	*L/Corporal* (73)
BEARDSHALL W.	*Private* (39)
BEAUMONT A.	*Private*
BECK G.E.	*Private* (102)
BECKETT W.	*Private* (153)
BEDFORD B.	*Private* (54)
BEECHILL F.	*Private* (1076)
BEEVORS J.	*Private* (69)
BEIGHTON G.	*Private*
BEIGHTON J.	*Private* (132)
BEIGHTON W.	*Private* (154)
BELL E.	*Private* (64)
BELL P.	*Private* (1509)
BELTON F.	*Private* (1395)
BENNETT A.	*Private* (1307)
BENNETT F.	*Corporal* 'D' Company
BENSON H.	*Private* 'D' Company
BENSON J.R.	*Private* (62)
BENTLEY J.	*L/Corporal* 'C' Company
BERRY H.	*Private*

BERRY J.	*Sergeant* (125)	COPE R.C.	*Private* (223)
BILLINGTON R.	*Sergeant* (115)	COSGROVE G.	*Private* (1167)
BINGHAM J.	*Private* (313)	COSGROVE W.	*Private* (196) 'C' Co
BIRKINSHAW W.	*Corporal* (146) HQ Co	COTTAM C.	*Private* (189)
BLACKBURN G.H.	*Private*	COTTAM T.	*Private* (224)
BLANCHARD L.	*Private* (1115)	COTTON E.	*Private* (1203)
BLANCHARD L.	*Corporal* (1116)	COUNTEE W.N.	*Private* (229)
BOND F.	*Private*	COX J.E.	*Sergeant* (226)
BOOCOCK J.	*Private* (70)	CRAWFORD H.	*Private*
BOOCOCK T.	*Private* (123)	CROSBY W.S.	*Private*
BOSKWICK A.	*Private* (498)	CROSSLAND A.	*Private* (1275)
BOWEN A.	*Private* (100)	CROSSLAND F.	*Private*
BOYCE S.	*Private* (97)	CROSSLAND J.	*Private*
BRADBURN C.	*Private* (1051)	CROSSLAND J.	*Private*
BRADBURY T.	*Private* 'D' Company	CUNLIFFE J.	*Corporal* (217)
BRADLEY T.H.	*Private* (795) 'D' Co	DALE G.H.	*Corporal*
BRANT W.	*Private* (1235)	DALTON W.	*Private*
BREATHWICK J.	*L/Sergeant* (147)	DANFORTH J.	*Corporal* (863) 13th Band
BRIGGS E.	*Sergeant* (50)	DARBY J.C.	*Private* (237)
BROADHURST T.	*Private* (148)	DARLEY J.	*L/Corporal* (12579)
BROADHURST W.H.	*Private* (1277)	DAVIES J.H.	*Private* 'C' Company
BROCKLESBY E.	*Private* (63)	DAVIS H.R.	*Private* (1173)
BROMLEY G.	*Sergeant* (3/4833)	DAWSON W.	*Signaller*
BROOKS J.	*Private*	DEAKIN A.	*L/Corporal* (248)
BROWN G.	*Private* (77)	DENT J.	*A/Corporal* (266)
BROWN H.	*L/Corporal* (1236)	DIBB A.	*Private* (257)
BUCKLEY G.	*Private* (78)	DICKENS H.	*Private*
BUCKLEY J.	*Private* (1467)	DICKINSON H.	*Private* (255)
BURGIN G.W.	*Private* (93)	DOBBIN	*Private*
BURTON H.	*Private* (1078)	DOBSON H.	*Private* (1300)
BUSWELL R.	*C.Q.M.S.* (134)	DOBSON O.	*L/Corporal* (262)
BUTCHER E.	*Private* (1162)	DODSON C.	*Private* (263)
CARR R.W.	*Private* (1087)	DORMAN P.	*Private* (267)
CARTER A.	*Private* (171)	DOUGHTY F.	*L/Corporal* (253)
CAUNT H.	*Private* (227)	DOUGLAS T.	*Private* (1221)
CHAMBERS C.	*Private* (1178)	DOYE W.	*Private* (1395)
CHAMBERS G.	*Corporal*	DRURY J.	*Private* (1305)
CHAPMAN A.	*Private* (206)	DUNCAN H.	*Private* (1433)
CHARLESWORTH E.	*Private* (204)	DUNCAN H.	*Corporal* (1434)
CHEETHAM J.	*Private* (174)	DUNCAN R.L.	*Sergeant* (252)
CHEETHAM J.	*Private*	DWIGHT S.J.	*Private* (265)
CHILTON H.	*Private*	DYSON A.	*L/Corporal* (14220)
CLEGG J.	*Private* (181)	DYSON E.	*Private* (1222)
CLEVERLEY W.R.	*Corporal* (218)	DYSON H.	*Signaller* (258)
CLOWREY E.	*Private* (1186)	DYSON S.	*Private* (232)
COLES J.	*Private* (225)	EAMES T.B.	*L/Corporal* (286)
COLES T.	*Signaller*	EBBAGE T.	*Private* (228)
COLLINGS E.	*C Qmaster S* (163)	EDER G.	*Private* (290)
COLLISHAW J.	*Private* (158)	EDON A.	*Private* (268)
CONWAY A.H.	*Sergeant*	EDWARDS E.	*Private*
CONWAY T.	*Private* (1423)	ELLIS W.	*Private* (1224)
COOPER A.	*Private* (221)	EMMERSON G.	*Private* (289)
COOPER A.R.	*Private* (228)	EMPSAL H.	*Private* (281)

ENSLIE F.J.	Sergeant (269)	HARRIMAN T.W.	Private (1341)
EVANS J.	Sergeant 'A' Company	HARRIS J.	Corporal (503)
EVERITT T.	Private (36375)	HARRISON	Private (443)
EXLEY F.	Private (291)	HARRISON R.	Private (490)
FAWLEY S.	Private (1517)	HARSTON J.	Private (402)
FEARENS J.	Corporal	HART J.W.	Private (1190)
FEARN E.	Private (1486)	HARWOOD W.	Private (450)
FEARN H.	Private (1232)	HATFIELD H.	Private (1128)
FEASEY F.	Private (1120)	HATFIELD H.	Sergeant (437)
FENTON J.H.	Private (320) 13th Band	HAWCROFT H.	Private (516)
FINAN P.	Private (318)	HAWES H.	Sergeant (433)
FIRTH F.	Private (311)	HAYES W.H.	Private (413)
FIRTH M.H.	Private (588)	HEALD G.	Private (444)
FISHER H.	Sergeant (341)	HEPPLESTONE	Private (461)
FISHER H.	Private (321)	HEWITT C.E.	L/Corporal (506)
FISHER W.	Private (1371)	HEWITT J.W.	Private (486)
FLETCHER W.	Private	HEWITT L.	Private (415)
FORD W.	Corporal (292)	HIBBERT H.	Private
FORT C.	Sergeant (309)	HIRST A.	Corporal (421)
FOSTER S.	Private (1440)	HIRST C.H.	Private (412)
FOSTER W.	Private (335)	HIRST H.	Private (441)
FOUNTAIN H.	Sergeant	HODGSON S.	Private
FOX E.	Private (303)	HOLDSWORTH J.E.	Private (467)
FREE W.	Private (312)	HOLDSWORTH T.	Private (434)
FROBISHER C.A.	Private (1040)	HOLLINGSWORTH E.	Private (496)
GALLOWAY G.	Private (1047)	HOLMES H.	Private (475)
GARNER W.	Private	HOWARTH H.	Private (470)
GARNER W.H.	Private (3788)	HOWARTH J.	Private (457)
GASCOIGNE G.	Private (354)	HOWE A.	Private (468)
GAY H.	Private (363)	HOYLAND L.	Private (428) 13th Band
GIBBONS J.W.	Private (385)	HUBBARD J.	Private (448)
GIBBS J.	Private (364)	HUDSON B.	Corporal (39962)
GIBSON J.	Private (379)	HUDSON H.	Private (1065)
GLEESON W.	L/Sergeant (391)	INSKIP F.	Private (521)
GLOVER H.	Private (147)	IVES E.	Private (517)
GLOVER H.	Private (1432)	JACKSON C.	Private (534)
GOOSE G.	Corporal (393)	JENNINGS W.	Private (1123)
GRAHAM O.	L/Corporal (374)	JEPSON H.	Private (542)
GRAWFORD H.	Private	JOHNSON B.	Private (908)
GRAY W.	Corporal (998)	JONES E.	Private (522)
GREAVES A.E.	Sergeant (1196)	JONES E.A.	Private (63) 'A' Co
GREAVES G.S.	Private (297) 'B' Co	JONES L.	Private (1244)
GREEN J.	Private (353)	JONES N.	L/Corporal (527)
GREEN J.W.	Private (1191) 13th Band	JONES V.P.	Private (529)
GREENHOUGH N.	Private (356)	JOYNER J.E.	Private (525)
GUEST T.	Private (395)	JOYNER J.H.	Private (530)
GUY I.	Private (1479)	KAYE J.	Private (2826)
HALL H.	Private (440) 'B' Co	KENDALL J.S.	Private (554)
HALL J.	Private (1469)	KENNETT W.M.	Private
HARDCASTLE J.A.	Private (1461)	KERSHAW H.	Private (258)
HARGATE H.	Private (445)	KERSHAW W.J.	Private (558)
HARGREAVES J.	Private (473)	KILNER G.E.	Private (548)
HARGREAVES J.	Private (481)	KILNER G.E.	Private (348)

KIRBY H.	L/Corporal (22487)	NAYLOR A.	Private (1007)
KIRK W.	Private (555)	NAYLOR A.	Private (1110) 'A' Co
KNAPTON F.	R S M	NAYLOR H.	Private (81) 'A' Co
KNOWLES A.	L/Corporal (1324)	NEEDHAM E.	Private (1008)
LAKE J.W.	Private (562)	NICHOLSON W.H.	Private (1012)
LANGLEY W.	Private (560)	NICKERSON G.	Private (1018)
LAPIDGE J.	Private (575)	NOWELL F.	Sergeant
LARKIN W.	Private (57)	O'CONNOR W.	Private
LAWMAN A.P.	Private (577)	ODDY W.	Private
LAWRENCE J.A.	Corporal (1092)	OLDFIELD J.	Private (997)
LAWSON H.	Sergeant (567)	OUGHTON T.	Private
LAWTON W.	Private (1207)	OWEN D.	Private
LEADBEATER J.	Private	OXFORD W.	Sergeant (83)
LEAMING J.W.	Private (584)	OWEN H.	Private
LEDGER C.M.	Private (563)	OXLEY S.	Private (995) 13th Band
LEE A.	L/Corporal (565)	OXLEY W.	Private (994)
LEE J.R.	Groom (568)	OXTABY H.	Private (1128)
LEECH T.A.	Private (576)	PAEECE W.	Corporal
LEWIS	Bugler	PAISLEY J.	Private (775)
LILES A.	Private (1407)	PALEY P.	Private (773)
LINDLEY G.	Sergeant (595)	PALMER A.	Private (1072)
LLOYD B.	Private	PALMER W.	Private
LOACH J.	Private (1522)	PARKIN B.	C S M (790)
LOCKWOOD	Private (578) 'A' Co	PARRINGTON T.	A/Corporal (757)
LOWE A.	Private (561)	PARRY T.E.	Private
LYONS G.	Private (564)	PEEL A.	Private (1148) H.Q. Co
MARCHBANKS J.	Private (1233)	PENNINGTON C.J.	L/Corporal (801)
MARSH A.	Private (1314)	PICKERING J.	Private (774)
MARTIN G.	Private (621)	PLEWS J.	Private
MARTIN J.	Private (1297)	PORTER E.	L/Sergeant (779) 'B' Co
MASON T.	Private (653)	POSKITT T.	Private (1139)
MATTHEWS W.A.	Private (614)	POWELL T.	Private
McDEVITT M.	Private (612)	POWER T.	Private
McGUIGAN J.	Private (1282)	POWERS J.W.	Private
McKELVEY H.	Private (638)	POXON A.	Private (1118)
MEE G.H.	Private (1217)	PRENDEGAST J.	Private
MEGGS C.	Private (645)	PRESTWOOD H.	Corporal (785)
MELLER G.S.	Private	PRINCE H.	Private (771) 'D' Co
MESEDALE E.H.	Private (626)	PROCTOR S.L.	Sergeant (783)
MIDGLEY E.	Private (601)	PUGSLEY T.	Private
MILLER H.	Private (620)	QUINNELL H.	Private (1168)
MILLWARD W.	Private (654)	RAMSDEN T.	Private (904)
MONTGOMERY W.	Private (649)	REDFEARN F.	Private (1193)
MORLEY G.A.	Private (1482)	REDGATE J.W.	Private (942)
MORRIS G.	Private (603)	REID E.	Private
MORSON W.	Private (1173)	RENSHAW C.	Private
MORTON H.	Private (275)	REYNOLDS F.	C S M (917)
MOSEDALE E.H.	Private (626)	RICHARDS B.	Private
MOSLEY F.	Private (148)	RICHARDS T.	L/Corporal 'D' Company
MOSS F.	Private	RICHARDS T.	A/Sergeant (936)
MOSS W.H.	Sergeant (625)	RICHARDS T.	Private (1070)
MOXON F.	Private (1276)	RICHARDSON H.	L/Corporal (915)
MULLINS M.F.	L/Corporal (641)	RICHARDSON J.H.	Private (1081)

RICKETTS J.W.	Private (1189)	STREET W.	Corporal (859)
RILEY J.	Private (934)	STRICKLAND F.	Private
RIMMINGTON H.	Sergeant (1060) 'A' Co	STRUTT G.	Private (1049)
ROBERTS R.	Corporal (927)	SWIFT W.	Private (890)
ROBERTS S.H.H.	Private (932)	SWINBURN J.	Private (894)
ROBINSON A.	Private (924)	SYKES E.	Private (1251)
ROBINSON J.	Private (939)	SYKES F.	Private (1154)
ROME A.E.	C S M (1824) 'D' Co	SYKES J.H.S.	Private (865)
ROSE E.	Private (947)	SYKES M.	Private (871)
ROTCHELL J.H.	Private (744)	TALBOT T.H.	Sergeant (952)
ROWE H.	Private (931)	TAYLOR F.	Private (1254)
ROYDS W.H.	Private (492) 'C' Co	TAYLOR G.H.	Sergeant (978)
ROYSTONE A.	Private (1491)	TAYLOR J.T.	Private
RUSHFORTH C.	L/Corporal (1312)	TAYLOR W.	Private (1082)
SAGAR F.	Sergeant (852)	TEALE H.	Private (966)
SAGAR T.	Private (1194)	TELFOR J.A.	L/Corporal
SALMON	Private	THOMAS P.H.	Private (985)
SAMSON T.	Private (874)	THOMPSON H.	Private (1247)
SANDERSON G.	Private (1322)	THOMPSON J.	Private (953)
SANDERSON L.	Private (814)	THOMPSON J.E.	Private (1234)
SAYERS C.	A/Sergeant (841)	THOMPSON W.	Private (1097)
SCARFE G.	Sergeant (1283)	TILSON A.	Private (976)
SCARGILL H.	Sergeant (891)	TIMLIN F.	Private (962)
SCHOLEY C.W.	L/Corporal (881)	TINGLE H.	Private (958)
SCOTT G.W.	Private (819)	TOWNEND F.B.	Private (1220)
SELLARS G.	Private (899)	TOWNEND J.	Private (1431)
SHARMAN J.	L/Corporal (815)	TOWNEND J.E.	A/Corporal (1272)
SHARP J.	Corporal (1302)	TRACEY T.	Private (984)
SHAW A.	Private (279) Cyclist Cor	TUCKWELL H.J.	Private (1287)
SHAW E.	Private (862)	TURNER E.	Private (967)
SHAW G.	Private (860)	TURNER H.	Private (956)
SHAW T.	Private (1306)	TURNER W.	Private (1275)
SHEARD W.	L/Corporal	TURTON L.	Private (975)
SHEPHERD W.H.	C S M (39973)	TUTILL A.C.	L/Corporal (1452)
SHERRIFF S.	L/Corporal (1271)	TYAS C.	Private (955)
SIDDAWAY P.	Private (737)	TYERS C.	Private (1023) 'B' Co
SIMON J.R.	Private (868)	VICTORY T.W.	Private (1136)
SLIRU H.	Private (279)	WADDINGTON W.	Private (692)
SMITH G.	Private (1255)	WAINWRIGHT H.	Sergeant (703)
SMITH G.W.	Private (807)	WALKER E.	L/Corporal (740)
SMITH J.	Private (899)	WALKER W.H.	Private (753)
SMITH T.	Private (829)	WALKER W.H.	Private (740) 'A' Co
SMITHSON A.	L/Corporal (837)	WARD A.W.	Private (680)
SQUIRES J.	C S M (8999)	WARD H.	Private (735)
STACK G.	Private	WARD J.	Private
STANIFORTH J.E.	Private (1149)	WARD W.	Private (680) 'C' Co
STATHER G.	Private (246)	WARDLE G.	C S M (745)
STEELE F.	Private (1497)	WARDLE H.	Private
STEPHEN F.	Private (31273)	WARDLE J.	Corporal
STIMSON W.	Private (897)	WARING J.T.	Private (1323)
STOCKER W.	Private (804)	WATHEY H.	Private
STONER T.	Private (876) 13th Band	WATKIN F.	Private (720) 'D' Co
STORRS E.	Private (873)	WATSON C.	Private (250)

WATSON F.	Private (666)	WIPON J.	Private (1411)
WATSON W.H.	Private (715)	WOOD G.	Private (755)
WELDON G.	Private (682)	WRAITH J-H.	Private (667)
WESTON A.	Private (697)	WRIGGLESWORTH E.	Private (733)
WHERRETT A.	Private (1126)	WRIGHT J.	Private
WHINCUP J.E.	Private (1174)	WRIGHT W.	Private
WHITAKER J.	Private (689)		
WHITE H.	L/Corporal (705)		
WHITEHEAD W.	Private (736)		
WHITFIELD F.	Private (742)		
WILD F.	Private (1172)		
WILDMAN W.	Private (702)		
WILKINSON W.H.	Private (665)		
WILKS D.	Private (719)		
WILLIAMS A.	Private		
WILLIAMS J.	Private (1389)		
WILMOT W.	Private (751)		
WILSON F.	Private (716)		
WILSON V.	Private (706)		
WINTER H.W.	Private (750)		
WINWOOD A.	Private (748)		

Nominal roll

14th Battalion (2nd Barnsley) York & Lancaster Regiment

*The Official roll of Officers and Men
proceeding overseas – December 1915.*

HEADQUARTERS

Lieutenant-Colonel W.B. HULKE	*Commanding Officer*
Major G.A. SANFORD	*Second-in-Command*
Captain A.V. NUTT	*Adjutant*
Lieutenant J. STEWART	*Quartermaster*
Captain G. BOLEY R.A.M.C.	*Medical Officer*
Lieutenant C.H. OLIVER	*M.G.O.*

'A' COMPANY

Captain A. WOOD	*Company Commander*
Captain W.O. HARRICK	*Second-in-Command*
Lieutenant J.B. BROOKE	*Transport Officer*
2nd Lieutenant W. HIRST	*1st Platoon Officer*
2nd Lieutenant H. QUEST	*Reserve Transport Officer*
2nd Lieutenant F.J. POTTER	*Reserve Scout Officer*

'B' COMPANY

Captain T.P. QUEST	*Company Commander (Billeting Officer)*
Lieutenant C.G. KIRK	*Second-in-Command*
Lieutenant H.B. FORSDIKE	*Reserve M.G.O.*
2nd Lieutenant D. FAIRLEY	*Assistant Adjutant*
2nd Lieutenant H. STRONG	*Reserve Bombing Officer*
2nd Lieutenant C.R. CRAN	*Pioneer*

'C' COMPANY

Major F.J.C. HOOD	*Company Commander*
Captain W.C. HANKINSON	*Second-in-Command (Reserve Billeting Officer)*
Lieutenant C.V. FITTON	*Signalling Officer*
Lieutenant H.D. FIELDING	*Reserve Musketry Officer*
2nd Lieutenant R.M.J. MARTIN	
2nd Lieutenant G.H.T. BEST	*Scout Officer*

'D' COMPANY

Captain C.H. ROBIN	*Company Commander*
Captain G.O. ROOS	*Second-in-Command*
Lieutenant F. BROOMHALL	*Musketry Officer*
2nd Lieutenant C.G. HARBORD	*Bombing Officer*
2nd Lieutenant R. GOODBURN	*Reserve Signalling Officer*
2nd Lieutenant A.C.H. CALVERT	

The compiled list is set out in the following order: Regimental Number, Rank, Name, and Company.

No.	Rank	Name	Coy
1	Private	ARMITAGE J.W.	A
2	Private	ASKIN D.	A
3	Private	ACKLAM H.	A
4	C.S.M.	ASCOUGH J.W.	A
5	L/Corporal	ASHTON J.H.	A
6	Private	ARMSTRONG H.	A
7	Private	BROOKE C.	A
9	Private	BEEVERS J.	A
10	L/Corporal	BELLIN Wm.	A
13	Private	BIRCH Wm.	A
14	L/Corporal	BEDFORD E.R.	A
15	C.Q.M.S.	BENTLEY J.G.	A
16	Private	BURNS T.	A
17	Private	BREAR J.	A
19	Private	CLARE H.	A
20	Private	CLARKSON W.H.	A
21	L/Sergeant	COOPER H.	A
23	Private	COWEN I.	A
24	Private	CARR C.	A
26	Private	CROFT G.W.	A
27	Corporal	DAVIS A.	D
28	Private	DAVIES F.C.	A
29	Corporal	DRAISEY J.T.	A
30	Private	DODSON W.G.	A
32	Private	DAVIES J.E.	A
34	Private	ECCLESTONE R.	A
35	L/Sergeant	EARNSHAW W.A.	A
36	Private	EXLEY E.	A
37	Private	FIRTH C.E.	A
38	Private	FREEMAN H.	A
39	Private	FRETWELL W.H.	A
41	Private	GORE J.	A
42	Private	GLOVER H.	A
43	Private	GRIST G.W.	A
44	OR/Sergeant	GLEDHILL T.L.	A
48	Private	GREEN H.	A
49	L/Corporal	GRUNHILL A.	A
50	Private	GILLISPIE E.	A
51	L/Corporal	GIBSON G.	A
52	L/Corporal	HARPER G.	A
54	Private	HAYES C.H.	A
56	Private	HORBURY G.	A
59	Private	HARGATE W.	A
60	Private	HANNON H.W.	A
61	Private	IRONS T.	A
64	Private	JONES E.	A
65	Sergeant	JONES W.	A
67	Private	JONES A.E.	A
68	Private	LAWTON A.	A
69	Private	LOGAN H.	A
70	Private	LYMAN L.	A
71	Private	LUCAS M.	B
72	Private	LINTON W.	A
73	Private	McKENNING W.	A
74	Private	McDONALD G.	A
77	L/Corporal	MORGAN W.	A
78	Private	NAYLOR A.	A
79	Private	NIXON S.	A
80	Private	NEEDHAM G.	A
83	L/Corporal	OXFORD W.	A
84	Private	PINCOCK O.	A
85	Private	PROUDLOVE E.	B
86	Private	PRATT J.	A
87	Private	QUICK J.	A
88	Sergeant	RICHARDSON T.	A
89	Private	ROBINSON A.	A
90	Sergeant	RYAN T.	D
91	Private	ROWDEN W.T.	A
92	Private	RANDLE A.H.	A
93	L/Corporal	RAMSDEN W.	A
95	Private	SHACKLETON A.	A
96	Private	STORRS A.	A
97	Private	SMITH W.	A
98	Private	SHEARD A.	A
99	L/Corporal	SHARP J.	A
100	Private	SHARP J.	A
101	Private	SHERIDAN J.	A
102	Private	SHANNON J.	A
103	Private	SANDERSON M.	A
104	Private	TURNER J.H.	A
105	Private	TURNER R.	A
106	C.S.M.	TOWNEND H.	C
108	Private	TIMMINS J.A.	A
111	Private	WORSLEY W.H.	A
113	Private	WESTMORELAND G.	A
114	Private	WATTS T.	A
115	Private	WILSON E.	A
116	Private	WALKER F.	A
117	Private	ALDERSON H.	A
118	Sergeant	CARROLL J.	D
119	L/Corporal	ALLENBY H.	A
121	Sergeant	ALLDREAD J.W.	A
122	Private	AUDIN A.	A
123	Private	ASQUITH J.J.	A
124	Private	ATKINSON J.	A
125	Sergeant	BAILEY H.	A
126	Private	BURGWIN H.	A
127	Private	BURNS J.J.	A
128	Private	BANKS P.	A
129	Private	BARTLE H.	A
131	L/Corporal	BATTY W.	A
132	L/Corporal	BROADHEAD G.	A

134	Corporal	BRIGGS R.	A	193	Private	RUSHWORTH W.	A
135	Private	BOWER C.W.	A	194	Private	ROBINSON A.	A
136	Private	CONNOR R.	A	195	Private	STUART C.	A
137	Private	CARR A.	A	196	Private	SHERWOOD W.	A
138	Private	DUDLEY B.	A	197	L/Corporal	SMITH J.W.	A
140	Sergeant	DUNK R.	A	198	Private	SMITH H.	A
141	Private	ELLEWAY W.	A	199	Private	SCAIFE W.	A
142	C.Q.M.S.	FEASBY H.	D	200	Private	SHARP W.L.	A
143	Private	FEARN W.	A	201	Private	SHAW C.	A
144	Private	FROST I.	A	202	Private	SNOWDEN F.	A
145	Sergeant	FAWLEY A.	A	204	Private	SELLARS A.	A
146	Private	GREEN G.	A	205	Private	SHARPS S.	A
148	Corporal	GARSIDE H.	A	206	Private	TRAINER J.	A
149	Private	GALLOWAY G.	A	207	Private	TRUEMAN T.	A
150	Private	GREENWOOD J.T.	A	208	Private	TOMLINSON W.	A
151	Private	GILL J.	A	209	L/Corporal	THOMAS L.	A
152	Private	GILBERTHORPE A.	A	210	Private	THORPE W.	A
153	Private	GELDER W.	A	211	Corporal	UTLEY E.	A
154	Private	GREEN F.	A	212	Private	WILLIAMS E.	A
155	Private	HALL W.	A	213	Private	WALSH P.	A
156	Private	HEBDEN J.	A	214	Private	WINTERBOTTOM F.	A
157	Private	HOWARTH C.F.	A	215	Private	WIGGINS J.W.	A
158	Private	HEATLEY A.	A	217	Private	WIDDOP L.	A
159	Private	INSULL J.E.	A	218	Private	WRIGHT J.	A
160	Private	IVESON G.	A	219	Private	WILLIAMS C.H.	A
161	Private	ILLINGWORTH G.T.	A	220	Private	WILDMAN J.	A
162	Corporal	JOBURNS W.	A	221	L/Corporal	WALKER F.	A
163	L/Sergeant	JONES A.	A	222	Private	WOOD J.	A
164	Private	KILNER G.A.	A	223	Private	WILLIAMS J.	A
166	Sergeant	KIRWAN C.D.	C	225	Private	ILLINGSWORTH H.	A
167	L/Corporal	KNOWLES W.	A	226	Private	MARSHALL G.	A
168	Private	LIGHTHOLDER J.A.	A	229	Private	WEST H.	A
169	Sergeant	LOMAS R.G.	A	231	Private	CHALKLEY A.	B
170	Private	LEVER J.	A	232	Private	COBURN J.	B
171	Private	LEWIS W.	A	233	Private	GRAINGER J.E.	B
172	Private	MURPHY E.	A	234	Private	HARAN F.	B
173	L/Corporal	MOORES J.	A	235	Private	HARDISTY E.	B
174	Private	METCALFE J.	A	236	L/Corporal	HORNE H.	B
175	Private	MARSH S.	A	237	Private	HORSEMAN G.H.	B
176	Private	MALLINSON J.	A	239	Corporal	KERRY J.	B
177	Private	MORGAN C.A.	A	240	Corporal	KILLINGBECK J.T.	B
178	Private	MOORES H.	A	242	Private	RANDLE W.	B
179	Private	MOXON R.	A	244	Private	SEPHTON G.	B
180	Private	MADDIGAN R.	A	246	Private	STATHER G.W.	B
181	Private	McLEE A.	A	247	C.Q.M.S.	TAYLOR P.W.H.	B
182	Corporal	MOORHOUSE J.	A	248	Sergeant	TOTTY A.	D
184	Private	NORTON L.	A	249	Private	TYAS F.	B
185	Private	NEEDHAM G.	A	250	Private	WATSON C.	B
186	Private	OLIVER D.	A	251	Sergeant	WHITTAM J.A.	B
187	Private	OUSBY T.	A	252	Private	WILSON T.	B
188	Private	PRESTON E.	A	254	Private	CRUMP H.	B
191	Private	RADLEY G.	A	255	Sergeant	CHAMBERS J.	B
192	Sergeant	REID B.	A	257	L/Corporal	MOUNCEY P.	B

No.	Rank	Name	
259	L/Corporal	ROBERTS R.	B
260	Private	PEAKER L.	B
261	Private	STEELE W.V.	B
262	Corporal	SLATER G.H.	B
263	Private	THOMPSON W.	B
265	L/Corporal	CHILTON H.	B
266	Private	DAVEY T.	B
268	Private	HUTCHINSON T.	B
270	Private	LAMBERT W.H.	B
271	Private	LAW C.H.H.	B
272	Sergeant	LITTLEWOOD W.A.	B
273	L/Corporal	LOVATT W.	B
274	L/Sergeant	MARSHALL H.	B
275	Private	MORTON H.	B
276	Private	MOXON A.E.	B
277	Private	ROSE G.	B
279	Private	SHAW A.	B
280	L/Corporal	STANYON J.R.	C
282	Private	WOOD R.	B
284	Sergeant	BROMLEY J.W.	B
286	Private	BRAMMER J.W.	B
287	Private	ELLIS G.	B
288	Private	JOHNSON G.	B
289	Private	KIDD F.	B
290	Private	MILLS R.	B
291	L/Corporal	SCHORAH E.E.	D
293	Private	WOOLLEY S.	B
294	Sergeant	BIRCHALL T.	B
295	Private	COOKSON C.R.	B
298	Private	STEPHENSON A.	B
299	Private	SUTCLIFFE J.	B
300	Private	UTLEY E.	B
302	Private	GREENFIELD S.	D
303	Private	HAGUE W.	B
304	Private	HAWCROFT A.	B
305	Private	HIGGS J.E.	B
306	Private	HAYES J.	B
307	Private	LEE H.	B
308	Private	MILTHORPE H.	B
309	Private	PARKER W.W.	B
310	Private	SHARPE J.H.	B
311	Private	SMITH H.	B
312	Private	ADDY A.	B
313	Private	BAMBRIDGE A.	B
314	Private	BARROW J.	B
318	Private	HOLLAND G.J.	B
319	Private	HUNTER J.	B
320	Private	JACKSON W.	B
321	Private	MATTHEWS R.J.T.	B
322	Private	MOSS I.C.	B
323	Private	NEAL W.	B
324	Private	PARKINSON A.	B
327	Private	SYKES A.	B
328	Private	THOMPSON C.	B
329	Private	WRIGHT J.	B
330	Private	YORK H.	B
331	Corporal	ATHA J.B.	B
332	Private	HOBSON G.	B
333	Private	HARGATE J.	B
334	Private	HARTSHORNE J.	B
335	Private	JASPER H.	B
336	Private	NEWSOME S.	B
337	Private	PADGETT J.	B
338	Private	STANYON L.	B
339	Private	STENTON H.	B
341	Private	WILLIS F.	B
342	Private	ALDERSON I.	B
345	Corporal	EATON F.	B
346	L/Corporal	GAMWELL M.	B
347	Private	GLEAVE H.	B
348	L/Corporal	HOWARTH J.	B
349	Private	JONES E.	B
351	Private	SUNDERLAND W.	B
352	Private	WHITEHOUSE T.H.	B
353	Private	HALL L.J.	C
354	Private	ALLEN E.	B
355	Private	FINAN J.	B
356	Private	FULWOOD J.	B
357	Private	ATKINSON L.	B
358	Private	McGINN W.	B
360	Private	FRYER A.	B
361	Private	FIRTH W.E.	B
362	Private	MILLARD W.	B
363	Private	BEDFORD S.	B
364	Private	RUSSELL A.	B
365	Private	HINCHLIFFE J.W.	B
367	Private	BIRKETT C.	B
369	Private	BOWLING W.	B
371	Private	BROWN W.	B
372	Private	CARBUTT J.W.	B
373	Private	COE T.	B
375	Private	FALLIS J.	B
376	Private	FLETCHER G.	B
377	Private	GODFREY F.	B
378	L/Corporal	HALL H.	B
379	Private	HODGKISS T.	B
380	Corporal	HOUGHTON W.	B
381	Private	HOUGHTON P.	B
382	Private	HUGHES W.	B
383	Private	JAMES T.	B
384	Private	KNOWLES R.	B
385	Corporal	LATCHEM H.	B
387	Private	LAYCOCK J.W.	B
388	Private	MOXON J.	B
389	Private	NORTON E.	B
390	Private	PARKES E.	B

393	Sergeant	RICHARDSON J.	B	466	Private	HAINES A.	C
395	Private	RUSSELL W.	B	467	Private	HITCHIN R.	C
396	Private	SLATER E.	B	468	Private	JOHNSON T.	C
397	Private	SQUIRES J.E.	B	470	Private	LENG W.	C
398	Corporal	THORNE H.	B	471	Private	PARKER J.	C
399	Sergeant	TILLOTSON T.	B	472	Private	PEACOCK W.	C
401	Private	BALL T.	B	473	L/Corporal	PICKERSGILL F.	C
402	Private	BALLARD A.	B	476	Private	SUNLEY A.	C
405	Private	BARRACLOUGH T.	B	477	Private	WALSH J.	C
406	Private	BROADHURST G.	B	478	Private	WALKER G.H.	C
407	Corporal	BOWEN W.	B	482	Private	BURROWS W.	C
408	Sergeant	CLIFFORD J.	B	483	Private	BYGATE W.	C
409	Private	COLLIER S.	B	485	Sergeant	CRITCHLEY E.	C
410	Private	DOUGHERTY J.	B	486	Private	EVERETT C.E.	C
411	L/Corporal	FITTON J.	B	487	Private	GRAHAM F.	C
413	Private	GOODYEAR S.	B	488	Private	GREEN R.	C
415	Private	GUEST P.	B	490	Private	KEY S.	C
417	Private	HOUGH N.	B	491	Private	McNULTY J.	C
418	Private	JEFFREYS W.	B	495	Private	SWAINE F.	C
419	Private	JONES J.	B	496	Private	TAYLOR W.	C
421	Private	MADDEN P.	B	497	Corporal	WILLIAMS W.C.	C
422	Private	MITCHELL A.	B	498	Private	BOSTWICK A.	C
424	Private	NEWSTEAD J.	B	499	Sergeant	ELLISON T.F.	C
425	Private	OATES A.E.	D	500	Private	PRIESTLEY W.	C
426	Private	POPPLEWELL E.	B	504	Private	WOOD H.	C
429	Private	PRIESTLEY W.C.	B	506	Sergeant	ARNOLD C.P.	B
430	Private	REYNOLDS P.	B	507	Private	BARNES T.	C
431	Corporal	SCHOLEY J.W.	B	508	Private	BARNETT J.	C
432	Private	SMITH H.H.	B	510	Private	CLAY W.	C
434	Private	STACEY E.	B	511	Private	DAVEY H.	C
436	Private	WHITEHEAD J.W.	B	513	L/Corporal	EVERS T.M.	C
437	Private	WILKINSON W.	B	514	Private	FINAN J.	C
439	Private	BOLDY G.	B	517	Private	GRAHAM T.	C
441	Private	BUSSINGHAM C.W.	B	518	Private	GREEN J.W.	C
442	Private	ECKERSLEY G.	B	519	Private	HARDCASTLE T.	C
443	Private	GOLDTHORPE A.E.	B	520	Private	HEATON J.	C
444	Private	HIRST W.	B	521	Private	HYDE T.	C
445	Private	HURD G.	B	522	Private	KIRK C.	C
447	Private	IVES D.	B	523	Private	LAWTON R.H.	C
449	Private	MATTHEWS W.	B	525	Private	LEONARD M.	C
450	Private	McCRUMM W.	D	526	Private	LOVELAND F.A.	C
452	Private	PHILLIPS E.	B	527	Private	KILNER H.	C
454	Private	TATTERSLEY W.	B	528	Private	LOCKWOOD H.	C
455	Private	THOMPSON J.	C	530	Private	MILNER M.	C
456	Private	WARD G.	C	531	Private	NORTON G.	A
457	Private	WOODCOCK W.	C	533	Private	PADGETT G.A.	C
458	Private	ASQUITH A.	C	536	Private	SHAW A.	C
459	Private	BAILEY R.	C	537	Private	SPEIGHT M.	C
461	C.Q.M.S.	BAYFORD C.G.	C	538	Private	TEASDALE D.H.	C
462	Private	BRAMMER G.	C	539	Private	THOMPSON J.	C
463	Private	CHARLESWORTH F.	C	540	Sergeant	TOWNEND E.C.	C
464	Private	CONNELLY J.	C	542	Corporal	TURGOOSE J.	C
465	Private	CROSSLEY H.	C	543	Private	WATERWORTH T.C.	C

544	Private	WILKINSON J.	C	607	Private	HARROD J.	C
545	Private	WRIGHT E.	C	608	Private	HODNETT T.	C
547	Private	BARNARD T.	C	609	Private	JOHNSON G.W.	C
548	Private	BEEVORS A.	C	610	L/Corporal	KEARSLEY H.B.	C
550	Private	BRADLEY S.	C	611	Private	OATES A.H.	C
552	Private	COOK J.W.	C	614	Sergeant	STRUTT W.H.	C
553	Private	DUNN H.	C	615	Private	TENNANT R.	C
554	Private	ELLIS S.	C	616	C.S.M.	BOWER H.	B
555	Sergeant	FARMER F.A.	C	617	C.S.M.	ENGLAND A.	D
556	Private	GREENFIELD F.	C	618	Corporal	BRANT R.H.	C
557	Corporal	HADFIELD D.	C	619	Private	HILTON A.	C
558	Private	HOOSON J.	C	620	Corporal	LINDLEY F.	C
559	Private	HUNT E.	C	621	Private	MILNER H.	C
560	Private	JONES W.	C	622	Private	NOBLE J.W.	C
561	Private	LOWE A.	C	623	Private	PHILLIPS E.	C
562	Private	POPPLEWELL A.	C	624	Private	ROEBUCK W.	C
563	Private	REEVES T.P.	C	625	Private	SUNDERLAND T.	C
565	Private	SHAW G.	C	626	Private	WILLIAMS R.	C
566	Private	BEAVER R.	C	627	Sergeant	GILL W.	C
567	Private	CAUSER H.	C	628	Private	TIGHE T.	C
568	Private	GIBSON E.	C	629	Private	SIMPSON R.	C
569	Private	MARSHALL W.W.	C	630	Private	BATRAM F.A.	C
570	L/Corporal	MORLEY E.C.	C	631	Private	BOWEN W.	C
571	Private	MULLIGAN T.	C	632	Private	BROWN P.	C
572	Sergeant	NOWELL E.	C	633	L/Corporal	BROOKS J.	C
573	Private	RUSHTON W.	C	634	Private	DAWSON C.	C
574	Private	SUTTON R.H.	C	635	Private	DENTON J.W.	C
575	Private	SYKES S.	C	636	Private	HANSON A.	C
577	Private	RODERICK H.	C	637	L/Corporal	HANKS G.	C
578	Private	DICKINSON W.	C	638	L/Corporal	HOWARTH S.	C
579	Private	GREEN J.W.	C	639	Private	HOULT A.	C
580	Private	HADDOCK T.W.	C	641	Private	JONES T.	C
581	Private	LEADBEATER H.	C	643	Private	MYERS C.	C
583	Corporal	WADE W.	C	645	L/Corporal	PICKERING	C
584	Private	WARING J.	C	647	Corporal	ROSCOE G.	C
587	Private	DAVIS R.	C	648	Private	RYDER F.	C
588	Private	FIRTH M.H.	B	649	Private	BEAUMONT F.	C
589	Private	LISLE J.H.	C	650	Private	BEEVORS A.	C
591	Private	BEAUMONT F.A.	C	651	Private	DALEY L.	C
592	Private	BENNETT J.	C	652	Private	FOULSTONE H.	C
593	Private	COE E.	C	653	Private	FRANK J.	C
594	Private	CUNLIFFE T.	C	654	Private	GOODAIR C.W.	C
595	Private	FEATHERSTONE C.	C	655	Private	GOSLING G.B.	C
596	Private	LEE J.W.	C	656	Private	HYDE G.	A
597	Private	MASON A.	C	658	Private	LYNCH B.	C
598	Private	McGINN W.	C	659	Private	McGUIGAN P.	C
599	L/Corporal	RICHARDSON C.J.	C	660	Corporal	PARKIN A.	C
600	Private	SHEPHERD F.	C	662	Private	RUSTON G.	C
601	Sergeant	STOTT G.H.	C	663	Private	SHARPE C.	C
602	Private	WHITE J.	C	665	Private	SHAW E.	C
603	Private	RILEY H.	C	666	Private	SIDDALL R.	C
604	Private	WALKER J.W.	C	667	Corporal	SYKES T.J.	C
606	L/Corporal	GELDER C.	C	669	Private	UTTLEY A.	C

670	L/Corporal	ASPINALL S.	C	740	Private	WINTER W.H.	D
671	Private	BROOKES J.	C	741	Private	BURGESS S.	D
672	Private	DANFORTH E.W.	C	742	L/Corporal	BURGIN J.E.	D
673	Private	HAZELDINE T.	C	744	Private	ROTCHELL J.H.	D
675	Private	HOBSON E.	C	745	Sergeant	PAVIOUR W.	D
676	Private	HOLLING E.	C	746	Private	TAYLOR J.	D
677	Private	HOUGHTON W.	C	747	Private	WRIGHT J.	D
680	Private	NEWTON J.A.	C	749	Private	ATKINSON G.	D
682	Private	STOCKS A.	D	750	Private	BEEVOR W.	D
683	Private	VOLLANS S.	D	751	Private	BERRY T.	D
684	Ll Sergeant	WARD J.A.	D	752	Private	BURGESS O.	D
685	L/Corporal	WETTON T.	D	753	Private	DRINKWATER J.	D
686	Private	WOOD H.	D	754	Private	FINAN J.	D
689	Private	BARRETT W.	D	755	Sergeant	FROST A.W.	D
691	Private	BROWN A.	D	756	Private	GUMMERSON C.W.	D
692	Private	COOPER H.	D	757	Private	HANNAH W.J.	D
693	Private	DUDLEY J.	D	758	L/Corporal	HARMAN R.E.	D
694	Private	FARRAR H.L.	D	759	Private	HEAVERSEDGE R.	D
695	Private	HOLMES V.	D	761	Private	KEY L.	D
696	Private	HORSLEY W.	D	762	Private	LANGFORD W.R.	D
697	Private	HOUSLEY H.	D	764	Private	PARKINSON G.	D
699	Private	LANDERS F.	D	765	Private	ROBINSON J.	D
700	Private	TUTILL A.E.	D	766	Private	SANDERSON J.	D
701	Private	VICKERS H.	D	767	Private	SHARMAN W.	D
703	Private	YATES T.	D	768	Private	SEDDONS J.	D
704	Private	PARKIN C.	D	769	Private	STEPHENSON J.	D
705	Private	PADGETT W.	D	770	Private	SYKES R.	D
706	Private	ROBINSON	D	771	Private	SYKES J.	D
707	Private	SLATER J.T.	D	772	Private	TAYLOR J.	D
708	Corporal	COOPER J.W.	D	774	Private	WALKER M.	D
709	Private	ELLIOTT W.T.	D	776	Private	ALLEN B.L.	D
710	Private	FARMER T.H.	D	778	Private	BLACKBURN F.	D
711	L/Corporal	HALLINAN M.	D	779	Private	BARLOW S.	D
712	Private	HARVEY J.W.	D	780	Private	CLARKSON J.	D
713	Private	LANE T.H.	D	781	Sergeant	HOFTON E.	D
716	Private	SPENCER H.	D	782	Private	HESFORD J.	D
717	Private	TURTON J.	D	783	Private	LOMAS J.	D
718	Private	WALKER H.E.	D	784	Private	POOLE F.	D
720	Corporal	BAILEY G.C.	D	787	Sergeant	CAWTHORNE C.H.	D
721	Private	BULLOUGH E.	D	788	Private	EATON H.	D
723	Private	FAIRHURST H.	D	789	Private	GOUGH B.	D
724	Private	FEARNLEY R.	D	790	Sergeant	OATES C.H.	D
725	Private	GIRDLESTONE W.	D	791	Private	WIGGLESWORTH J.W.	D
726	Private	GRAHAM P.	D	793	Private	BEARDSALL J.	D
729	Private	HOLT J.	D	794	Private	BEASLEY J.	D
730	L/Corporal	MARSDEN J.	D	796	L/Corporal	BROOKS H.	D
731	L/Corporal	MOODY E.H.	D	797	Private	CLEGG J.	D
732	Private	MURRAY J.	D	799	Private	DOUGHTY T.	D
735	Private	SENIOR G.H.	D	800	Private	FISHER A.	D
736	Private	SHEPHERD H.	D	801	L/Corporal	FOSTER J.H.	D
737	L/Corporal	SIDDAWAY P.	D	802	Private	GLEADALL A.	D
738	Private	WALKER W.E.	D	803	Private	LAYCOCK A.	D
739	Private	WHITFIELD W.	D	804	Private	LEEK A.	D

805	Private	POPE J.	D	869	Private	CHANDLER L.	D
806	Private	ROEBUCK W.	D	870	Private	FLETCHER G.	D
807	Private	SIXSMITH T.	D	871	Private	GUNN C.	D
810	Private	WESLEY J.	D	872	Private	HUGHES H.	D
811	Private	WILLIAMS E.	D	873	Private	LOWE R.H.	D
812	Private	BANNISTER J.W.	D	874	Private	SANDERSON J.	D
813	Private	BOULTON J.W.	D	875	Private	SLATER J.W.	D
814	Private	COOPER J.W.	D	877	Private	WINTER R.	D
815	Private	CRABTREE G.H.	D	878	Private	BIBBY W.H.	D
816	Private	FUDGE W.	D	879	Private	EYRE R.	D
817	Private	GAWTHORPE W.	D	880	Private	FARNHILL W.	D
819	Private	HOWLEY R.	D	881	Private	HOBSON G.	D
820	Private	LOVETT J.	D	883	Private	HARDCASTLE A.	D
821	Private	LUTY J.W.	D	884	Private	INESON E.	D
822	Private	MARPLES F.	D	885	Private	TEMPERTON R.	D
823	Private	MORRIS T.W.	D	886	Private	TONKS G.	D
824	Private	BOOTH A.	D	887	Private	ALSTEAD H.	D
826	Private	DAWES H.	D	889	Private	BEDFORD E.	D
827	Private	GALLEAR T.	D	891	Private	BLY J.	D
829	Private	GROSVENOR G.	D	893	L/Corporal	CLARKE E.	A
830	Private	HAWCROFT G.H.	D	894	L/Corporal	COWARD J.	D
831	Private	HOROBIN J.	D	895	Private	CRAWSHAW A.	D
832	Private	KENNY Jas.	D	896	L/Corporal	FINDLOW L.	D
833	Private	KENNY J.	D	897	Private	FIRTH F.	D
834	Private	MILNER A.	D	898	Private	GALLEAR W.	D
836	Corporal	WATSON E.	D	899	Private	GRIFFITHS J.R.	D
837	Corporal	ARMITAGE G.	D	900	Private	HEFFER H.	D
838	L/Corporal	BURLEY A.	D	902	Private	HICKS J.	D
839	Private	BUSSINGHAM A.	D	903	Private	HIRST E.	D
840	Private	BUSSINGHAM J.T.	D	904	Private	NEVILLE E.	D
841	Private	CHAPPELL F.	D	905	Private	PADGETT G.E.	D
842	Private	DAWES W.	D	907	Private	SHERRY J.F.	D
844	Private	DRAKE J.H.	D	910	L/Corporal	TAYLOR A.	D
845	Private	GOLDTHORPE A.	D	912	Private	WOOLLEY J.	B
846	Private	GREEN G.	D	913	Private	BEASLEY R.	D
847	Private	GREEN P.	D	914	Private	BLIGH T.	D
848	Sergeant	HAIGH H.	A	915	Private	COTTON H.	D
849	Private	HAYWOOD J.T.	D	916	Private	DAVIES L.	D
852	Private	JEAVONS F.	D	917	Private	GALLEAR A.	D
853	Corporal	MANNING T.	D	918	Private	MARSHALL C.	D
854	Private	NEWBY J.W.	D	921	L/Corporal	SINCLAIR G.	D
855	Private	SANDIFORD J.	D	923	Private	WELDRICK G.	D
856	Private	STEELE C.	D	924	Private	BENNETT W.	D
857	Private	STRAW R.	D	925	Sergeant	BRAMLEY A.	D
858	Private	WATKIN E.	D	926	Private	CHANDLER F.G.	D
859	Private	WHITTINGHAM A.E.	D	928	Private	HANSON J.	D
861	Private	ASHTON A.	D	929	Private	KENNERLEY W.	D
862	Private	CARTER J.W.	D	930	Private	LAITHEWAITE R.	D
864	Private	GOLDTHORPE W.G.	D	931	Private	MOON E.J.	D
865	Private	LEE S.	D	932	Private	NORTH C.H.	D
866	Private	MARTIN G.	D	934	Private	SCHOFIELD F.	D
867	Private	TYE J.	D	935	Private	SIMPSON J.W.	D
868	Private	ARMSTRONG I.	D	938	Private	WARD J.W.	D

No.	Rank	Name	Coy	No.	Rank	Name	Coy
939	Private	BOOTH J.	D	1009	Private	CRABTREE F.	B
941	L/Corporal	MORRIS F.	D	1010	Private	ELLIS A.	B
942	Private	RUSSELL T.	D	1011	Private	GASKIN J.	B
943	Private	SHARPE J.T.	D	1013	Private	JOHNSON T.	B
944	Private	BELLAMY F.	D	1016	Private	LINDSEY F.	B
945	Private	FINDLOW F.H.	D	1017	Private	LINDSEY W.	B
946	Private	GUEST L.	D	1018	Private	NICKERSON G.	B
947	Private	HOBSON B.	A	1019	L/Corporal	SCATTERGOOD G.	B
948	Private	LINDLEY T.	A	1020	Private	SHARPE F.	B
949	Private	LINDLEY F.	A	1021	Private	STOTT E.	B
950	Private	SPEIGHT H.	A	1022	Private	SWALES C.A.	C
951	Private	WHITAKER A.	A	1024	L/Corporal	WALKER C.	B
952	Private	ALLOTT A.	A	1025	Private	BAILEY W.	B
955	Sergeant	GREGORY C.	A	1026	Private	BELL E.	B
956	Private	SEWARD S.G.	A	1027	Private	BISSELL M.	B
957	Private	SQUIRES E.	A	1028	Private	BRYCE H.T.	B
958	Private	WYDILL J.W.	A	1030	Private	CROSSLAND J.	B
959	Private	ATKINSON A.F.	A	1031	Private	GELDER F.	B
960	Private	BIRD W.	A	1034	Private	JACKSON S.	B
961	Private	HARDCASTLE R.	A	1035	Private	MOORS E.	B
962	L/Corporal	SYMONS J.	A	1036	Private	OGLEY A.	B
964	Private	BAILEY J.M.	A	1038	Private	PICKERSGILL F.	B
965	Private	COOPER A.	D	1040	Private	BATTY J.	C
967	Private	SHAW S.	A	1041	Private	KIRK F.	C
968	Private	WELSH F.	A	1042	Private	OWEN A.C.	C
969	Corporal	ATKINSON A.	A	1043	Private	RILEY J.	C
970	Private	CHESNEY J.E.	A	1044	Private	STENSON J.W.	C
973	Private	FOGG J.W.	A	1046	Private	CREIGHTON H.A.	C
974	Private	JUBB J.H.	A	1047	Private	FIRTH G.H.	C
975	Private	LLOYD C.	A	1048	Private	MASON W.	C
977	Private	ROTHIN C.	A	1049	Private	SHORT A.	C
979	Private	ALLEN A.	A	1050	L/Corporal	WILKINSON C.	C
980	Private	PENTON G.A.	A	1052	Private	FELL J.W.	C
982	Private	HINCHLIFFE A.	A	1053	Private	FIELDSEND F.	C
983	L/Corporal	MOORE A.	A	1054	Private	HAWCROFT F.	C
984	Private	SYMONS F.	A	1055	Private	APPLEYARD F.	C
985	Private	BANNER C.	B	1058	Private	LAX F.	C
986	Private	BLACKBURN C.	B	1059	Private	MANN G.W.	C
987	Private	GOODWIN G.W.	B	1060	Private	MIREE S.	C
988	Private	KIMBERLEY G.	D	1061	Private	NAYLOR T.	C
989	Private	NICHOLSON F.B.	B	1064	Private	THOMPSON H.H.	C
990	Private	WARD T.H.	B	1066	Private	CLARKSON H.	C
992	Private	FIRTH C.	A	1067	Private	COTTINGHAM J.	C
993	Private	PLUNKETT T.	B	1069	Private	FIRTH P.	C
994	Private	ALMOND J.	B	1070	Private	GEESON F.	C
995	Private	GREEN B.R.	B	1071	Private	GOVIER B.	C
999	Private	BROWN J.	B	1072	Private	MILTHORPE H.	C
1000	Private	DAWSON H.	B	1073	Private	MONOGHAN A.	C
1001	Private	GAMBLE W.	B	1074	L/Corporal	SMITH J.W.	C
1004	Private	RICHARDSON S.	B	1075	Private	WILSON E.P.	C
1006	Private	BENNET J.W.	B	1076	Private	WILSON W.H.	C
1007	Private	CHAPMAN J.	B	1078	Private	BELLIS W.	B
1008	Private	COOPER J.R.	B	1080	Private	BOLDY T.	B

No.	Rank	Name	Coy	No.	Rank	Name	Coy
1081	*Private*	BRISCOE B.	C	1174	*Private*	POSKITT W.	D
1084	*Private*	NOBLE L.	C	1175	*Private*	SHAW W.	C
1086	*Private*	HIRST H.	C	1178	*Private*	CHAMBERS C.	B
1087	*Private*	JOHNSON F.C.	B	1179	*Private*	GREAVES W.	A
1088	*Private*	JONES W.	B	1180	*Private*	CROOKS J.A.W.	B
1089	*Private*	GALLEAR N.	D	1181	*Private*	GUEST H.	C
1094	*Private*	ANDERSON W.	A	1182	*Private*	BRADLEY H.	B
1095	*L/Corporal*	ASHTON C.	B	1184	*Private*	EDWARDS R.	A
1096	*Private*	BENNETT J.	C	1185	*Private*	HAIGH W.	B
1098	*L/Corporal*	MARSLAND J.R.	B	1186	*Private*	LONGFIELD G.F.	A
1099	*L/Corporal*	NEWTON J.	B	1187	*Private*	METCALFE H.	B
1100	*Private*	BRAITHWAITE A.	A	1191	*Private*	DALE J.R.	A
1101	*Private*	BROOKES J.	C	1194	*Private*	HAYES B.	D
1103	*Private*	HARRISON G.	D	1195	*L/Corporal*	HEALEY J.	C
1105	*Private*	LINDLEY T.	C	1196	*Private*	HEPPLESTONE J.W.	A
1108	*Private*	PRINCE H.	C	1197	*Private*	McKELVEY J.	C
1109	*Private*	SMITH C.	C	1198	*Private*	PARKIN C.	C
1114	*Private*	THORPE G.W.	D	1200	*Private*	BOYLE J.	A
1115	*Private*	HAWCROFT G.	C	1205	*Private*	BUXTON J.T.	A
1116	*Private*	TEAL C.	A	1207	*Private*	JESSOP J.	C
1119	*Private*	RUSHWORTH T.	D	1209	*Private*	JACKSON A.	C
1122	*Private*	ALLEN J.	B	1210	*Private*	WHEATER E.	B
1128	*Private*	BARLOW J.	D	1213	*Private*	VAUGHAN J.	A
1129	*Private*	KENDREW C.	B	1216	*Private*	ROTHWELL J.	A
1130	*Private*	KILNER J.W.	A	1217	*Private*	PEPPER W.	C
1131	*Private*	MITCHELL W.	A	1218	*Private*	WALKER J.	B
1132	*Private*	WOOLLIN F.	A	1219	*Private*	WARWICK J.M.	B
1133	*Sergeant*	HAYWARD G.	D	1220	*Private*	MARTIN T.C.	C
1134	*Private*	ALLEN E.	A	1222	*Private*	WREND J.	A
1135	*Private*	ATKINSON V.	A	1223	*Private*	DAVISON J.	C
1136	*Private*	COOPER W.	D	1225	*Private*	GRIEVE R.	C
1137	*Private*	LENG H.	C	1227	*Private*	WATKINSON H.	D
1138	*Private*	RIMMER J.W.	A	1231	*Private*	WORTH W.	B
1140	*Corporal*	MARTIN C.	D	1232	*Private*	SYKES W.	B
1142	*Private*	BENNETT T.	B	1233	*Private*	SMITH F.	B
1145	*Private*	HARDY S.	D	1234	*Private*	WHIPPEY E.	D
1146	*Private*	HAYES E.	D	1236	*Private*	HORSFALL W.	C
1147	*Private*	POULTER A.S.	B	1238	*Private*	HYNES P.	B
1148	*Private*	WARD E.	A	1242	*Private*	COOPER J.W.	D
1149	*Private*	STANIFORTH J.E.	D	1244	*Private*	STANFIELD J.	C
1150	*Private*	THOMPSON M.	A	1247	*Private*	DRYDEN R.	C
1151	*Private*	KNUTTON W.	C	1248	*Private*	DOLAN J.	B
1153	*Private*	BLACKBURN S.	B	1251	*Private*	GOODWIN T.	B
1157	*Private*	BLACKER A.D.	A	1252	*Private*	GLYNN J.	A
1158	*Private*	FOX J.	D	1254	*Private*	LEDGER T.	A
1163	*R.Q.M.S.*	SAMPSON J.	A	1255	*Private*	LAWTON W.	C
1166	*Private*	BAILEY D.	B	1259	*Private*	SMITH J.	C
1167	*Private*	FURY F.	B	1260	*Private*	CROSS J.	C
1168	*Private*	HOLMES H.	B	1263	*Private*	HENINGHAN J.	B
1169	*Private*	LOCKWOOD T.E.	C	1264	*Private*	MORTON A.	D
1170	*Private*	HUSSELLBEE W.H.	C	1266	*Private*	WOFFINDEN W.	A
1171	*Private*	KELLY G.E.	A	1267	*Private*	DICKINSON F.	B
1173	*Private*	OWEN P.	C	1273	*Private*	HOLT J.W.	B

1275	*Private*	MERRILLS W.H.	B	1311	*Private*	MERRY J.	D
1276	*Private*	DAVY D.G.	B	1315	*Private*	CHRISTOPHERSON F.	B
1277	*Private*	MARSDEN J.	C	1317	*Private*	LOWE J.	A
1280	*Private*	RENSHAW W.	D	1319	*Private*	TURTON A.	A
1281	*Private*	WOGAN J.W.	C	1320	*Private*	LYONS F.	A
1283	*Private*	BALL G.	A	1323	*Private*	BROADBENT E.	A
1284	*Private*	BARKER J.	A	1327	*Private*	BONDS W.	A
1285	*Private*	STUBBINGS J.F.	B	1328	*Private*	DENMAR W.H.	A
1287	*Private*	BEAUMONT C.E.	A	1330	*Private*	HIGGINBOTTOM R.J.	D
1289	*Private*	CONWAY G.	D	1331	*Private*	KERR W.B.	B
1291	*Private*	FLETCHER J.H.	B	1332	*Private*	LOCKWOOD H.	C
1293	*Private*	HOPKINS J.	B	1337	*Private*	CLARK R.	C
1294	*Private*	LILLEY A.	A	1341	*Private*	BRIGHTMAN E.	C
1295	*Private*	LOMAS J.	A	1400	*Private*	MADDEN E.	B
1296	*Private*	MELLOR J.	D	1450	*R.S.M.*	SMITH A.	B
1298	*Private*	MELLOR A.	D	1354	*Sergeant*	JOHNSON H.R.	A
1300	*Private*	HARDCASTLE E.	C	9724	*L/Sergeant*	CAWTHORNE C.	B
1302	*Private*	WILLIAMSON B.	D	9466	*L/Sergeant*	GODFREY W.	C
1303	*Private*	ELLIS H.	C	22847	*Private*	LEE A.	D
1308	*Private*	DICKINS H.	B	6262	*Corporal*	ROBERTS T.S.	D
1309	*Private*	GARRITY W.	C	2069	*Sergeant*	BUSZARD A.F.	D

Machine Gun Section, 14th Battalion pose with their dummy Vickers machine guns. Private Walter Bygate, second row seated, second from left, sends this postcard to his mother in 1915 prior to his going overseas. "Hope you like my face . . . I look as if I've had a fortune left, don't I?"

Casualty roll

13th & 14th Battalions
(1st and 2nd Barnsley)
York and Lancaster Regiments

*The Officers and Men killed in action
prior to, and on the first day of the
Battle of the Somme.*

Compiled by Stuart Eastwood

13th Battalion men killed before 1st July, 1916

ARDRON Harold *born Barnsley, enlisted Barnsley* Private, 13/16, **April 8th, 1916**

ARKROYD John Cavill *born West Melton, Rotherham, enlisted Barnsley* Private, 13/13, **May 14th, 1916**

ATKINSON Herbert *born Gawber, Barnsley, enlisted Barnsley* Private, 13/1, **June 17th, 1916**

BECK George Edward *born Darfield, enlisted Barnsley* Private, 13/102, **June 18th, 1916**

COTTAM Charles Thomas *born Staincross, enlisted Barnsley* Private, 13/189, **June 21st, 1916**

EAMES Thomas Bates *born Darnall, Sheffield, enlisted Barnsley* L/Corporal, 13/286, **May 24th, 1916**

HARGREAVES Joseph *born Carlton, Barnsley enlisted Barnsley* Private, 13/473, **June 17th, 1916**

HARGREAVES Joseph *born Denaby Main, Doncaster, enlisted Barnsley* Private, 13/481, **May 17th, 1916**

HEPWORTH Arthur *born St. Mary's, Barnsley, enlisted Barnsley* Private, 13/505, **June 4th, 1916**

JONES Norman *born Heckmondwike, Yorks, enlisted Barnsley* L/Corporal, 13/527, **May 5th, 1916**

LEDGER Charles Milton *born Staincross, enlisted Barnsley* Private, 13/563, **April 9th, 1916**

NAYLOR Arthur *born Silkstone, enlisted Barnsley* Private, 13/1110, **June 21st, 1916**

POXON Andrew *born Eastwood, Yorks, enlisted Barnsley* Private, 13/1118, **April 9th, 1916**

RICKETTS William John *born Westbury, Gloucester, enlisted Barnsley* Private, 13/1189, **April 10th, 1916**

STRUTT George *born Dodworth, enlisted Barnsley* Private, 13/1049, **June 18th, 1916**

THOMAS Phillip Henry *born Cinderford, Gloucester, enlisted Barnsley* Private, 13/985, **May 20th, 1916**

THOMPSON James Edward *born Newcastle-on-Tyne, enlisted Barnsley* Private, 13/1234, **April 21st, 1916**

TOWNEND, James Ellis *born Oldham, enlisted Barnsley* Private, 13/1272, **June 17th, 1916**

TRACEY Thomas *born Oldham, enlisted Barnsley* Private, 13/984, **May 26th, 1916**

WILMOTT Ernest *born Cudworth, enlisted Barnsley* Private, 13/751, **April 9th, 1916**

WINTER Herbert William *born Nottingham, enlisted Houghton, Barnsley* Private, 13/750, **April 9th, 1916**

14th Battalion men killed before 1st July, 1916

BEEVERS John *born Liversedge, Yorkshire, enlisted Barnsley* Private, 14/9, **April 8th, 1916**

BLACKER Arthur Dames *born Rotherham, enlisted Barnsley* Private, 14/1157, **June 12th, 1916**

BROADBENT Ernest *born Royston, enlisted Barnsley* Private, 14/1323, **June 4th, 1916**

BURNS Thomas *born Wolverhampton, enlisted Barnsley* Private, 14/16, **April 5th, 1916**

CLARE Henry *born Royston, enlisted Barnsley* Private, 14/19, **June 4th, 1916**

CORCORAN Patrick *born Barnsley, enlisted Barnsley* Private, 14/1499, **April 30th, 1916**

CUNLIFFE Thomas *born Rochdale, enlisted Barnsley* Private, 14/594, **April 28th, 1916**

DAVY Thomas *born Rotherham, enlisted Barnsley* Private, 14/266, **April 6th, 1916**

FIRTH Charles Edward *born Worsborough Dale, enlisted Barnsley* Private, 14/37, **June 2nd, 1916**

GALLOWAY George *born Barnsley, enlisted Barnsley* Private, 14/149, **June 4th, 1916**

HAIGH William *born Elsecar, enlisted Barnsley* Private, 14/1185, **April 7th, 1916**

HANSON Archibald *born Barnsley, enlisted Barnsley* Private, 14/636, **June 4th, 1916**

HARDCASTLE Reginald *born Barnsley, enlisted Barnsley* Private, 14/961, **April 28th, 1916**

HAYES Edwin *born Barnsley, enlisted Barnsley* Private, 14/1146, **June 3rd, 1916**

IRONS Thomas *born Barnsley, enlisted Barnsley* Private, 14/61, **April 28th, 1916**

JAMES Thomas *born Silverdale, Staffordshire, enlisted Barnsley* Private, 14/383, **June 30th, 1916**

JOBURN William *born Broomhills, Staffordshire, enlisted Barnsley* Corporal, 14/162, **April 28th, 1916**

JONES Arthur *born Woolley, enlisted Barnsley* Sergeant, 14/163, **May 2nd, 1916**

KIDD Frank *born Barnsley, enlisted Barnsley* Private, 14/289, **June 4th, 1916**

KNOWLES William *born Denton, Lancashire, enlisted Barnsley* L/Corporal, 14/167, **April 9th, 1916**

LEE Samuel *born Worsborough, enlisted Barnsley* Private, 14/865, **April 30th, 1916**

LOWE Joseph *born Worsborough, enlisted Barnsley* Private, 14/1317, **June 29th, 1916**

MARSHALL Christopher *born Wombwell, enlisted Barnsley* Private, 14/918, **June 4th, 1916**

METCALFE John *born Barnsley, enlisted Barnsley* Private, 14/174, **May 31st, 1916**

MORTON Arthur *born Wombwell, enlisted Barnsley* Private, 14/1264, **April 8th, 1916**

NOBLE Leonard *born Hoyland Common, enlisted Barnsley* Private, 14/1084, **May 11th, 1916**

NORTON Edward *born Barnsley, enlisted Barnsley* Private, 14/389, **May 13th, 1916**

POPPLEWELL Albert *born Crigglestone, Yorkshire, enlisted Barnsley* Private, 14/562, **June 12th, 1916**

RUSSELL William *born Monk Bretton, enlisted Barnsley* Private, 14/395, **April 6th, 1916**

SCATTERGOOD George *born Worborough Bridge, enlisted Barnsley* L/Corporal, 14/1019, **June 4th, 1916**

13th Battalion men killed on 1st July, 1916, or later died of wounds received on that day

BAILEY Frank Leslie *born Swadlincote, Derbyshire, enlisted Barnsley* Private, 13/143, **July 1st, 1916** Clerk, Barnsley Traction Company, 53 Cemetery Road, Barnsley

BARLOW Leonard *born Barnsley, enlisted Barnsley* Private, 13/45, **July 1st, 1916** King Street, Barnsley

BEARDSALL John Reginald *born West Melton, Wath, enlisted Barnsley* L/Corporal, 13/73, **July 1st, 1916** 5 Station Road, Wombwell

BECKETT William *born Ardsley, Barnsley, enlisted Barnsley* Private, 13/153, **July 1st, 1916** Age 19

BOOCOCK Thomas *born Barnsley, enlisted Barnsley* Private, 13/123, **July 1st, 1916** 25 Longcar Street, Barnsley

BOWSKILL John *born Hollinsend, Sheffield, enlisted Sheffield* Private, 12/1710, **July 1st, 1916**

BOYCE Samual *born Barnsley, enlisted Barnsley* Private, 13/97, **July 1st, 1916** Age 34, Miner, Houghton Main Colliery, Havelock Street, Darfield

BRANT William *born West Bromwich, enlisted Barnsley* Private, 13/1235, **D.O.W. August 21st, 1916** Age 31, Miner, Strafford Colliery Married with 5 children, 9 Balgue Row, Barnsley

BUCKLEY George *born Wombwell, enlisted Barnsley* Private, 13/78, **July 1st, 1916** Age 20 Married, 14 Gregg's Row, Stairfoot, Barnsley

BUCKLEY James William *born Barnsley, enlisted Barnsley* Private, 13/1467, **July 1st, 1916** Age 20, Miner, Barrow Colliery, Married with 2 children, 16 Union Street, Barnsley

BURTON Herbert *born Darfield, enlisted Barnsley* Private, 13/1078, **July 1st, 1916** Age 24, Miner, Mitchell's Main Colliery, Married with child, 11 Providence Street, Low Valley, Barnsley

CAUNT Harold *born Warren Chesterfield, enlisted Barnsley* Private, 13/227, **July 1st, 1916** Church Street, Jump, Barnsley

CHAPMAN Arthur *born Dewsbury, enlisted Barnsley* Private, 13/206, **July 1st, 1916** Age 19, 6 Waltham Street, Barnsley

CHARLESWORTH Ernest *born Barnsley, enlisted Barnsley* Private, 13/204, **July 1st, 1916** Age 22, 8 Quarry Street, Barnsley

CLEGG John *born Leigh, Lancashire, enlisted Barnsley* Private, 13/181, **July 1st, 1916** Married with 3 children, 6 Talbot Road, Plant Lane, Leigh

CLOWERY Ernest *born Dodworth, enlisted Barnsley* Private, 13/1186, **July 1st, 1916** Miner, Church Lane Colliery, Snow Hill, Dodworth, Barnsley

COLLISHAW Joseph *born Headingly, Leeds, enlisted Barnsley* Private, 13/158, **July 1st, 1916** Plumber, Grimethorpe Colliery, Married with child, 65 Margate Street, Grimethorpe

CONWAY Thomas *born Contrassna, New Ireland, Ireland, enlisted Silkstone, Barnsley* Private, 13/1423, **July 1st, 1916**

COSGROVE George *born Earlestown, Lancashire, enlisted Barnsley* Private, 13/1167, **July 1st, 1916,** Age 20, Miner, Grimethorpe Colliery, 61 Margate Street, Grimethorpe

COX John Edwin *born Manchester, enlisted Barnsley* Sergeant, 13/226, **July 1st, 1916**

DART Hugh Captain **D.O.W. July 2nd, 1916**

DOBSON Harry *born Barnsley, enlisted Barnsley*
Private, 13/1300, **July 1st, 1916,** Age 18
Barnsley Tramways, 14 Regent Street,
Barnsley

DUNCAN Reginald Leslie *born Malton, Yorkshire,*
enlisted Barnsley Sergeant, 13/252, **July 1st,**
1916, Age 21, Redfearns Glassworks, 25
Pontefract Road, Barnsley

EXLEY Fred *born Barnsley, enlisted Barnsley*
Private, 13/291, **July 1st, 1916,** Age 20 Miner,
Harbrough Hills Colliery, 38 Waltham Street,
Barnsley

FEASEY Francis *born Banbury, Wiltshire, enlisted*
Barnsley Private, 13/1220, **July 1st, 1916,** 3
Lundhill, Hemingfield

FINAN Peter *born Worsborough Dale, enlisted*
Barnsley Private, 13/318, **July 1st, 1916,** Age
28, Married with child, Marriott's Square,
Worsborough Bridge

FIRTH Ernest Hartley Captain, **July 1st, 1916,**
Age 42, Mounthill, Beckenham, Kent

FORD William *born Leeds, enlisted Barnsley*
Corporal, 13/292, **D.O.W. July 2nd, 1916,** Age
32, Miner, Church Lane Colliery, Joseph Street,
Barnsley

FOSTER William *born Darfield, enlisted Barnsley*
Private, 13/335, **D.O.W. July 2nd, 1916**

FREE William *born Hucknall Torkard,*
Nottinghamshire, enlisted Barnsley, Private,
13/312, **July 1st, 1916,** Age 19 Miner,
Monckton Main Colliery, 19 Railway Terrace,
Carlton

GALLOWAY George *born Worsborough Common,*
enlisted Barnsley, Private, 13/1047, **July 1st,**
1916, 43 Henry Street, Worsborough Bridge

GAY Harry *born Barnsley, enlisted Barnsley*
Private, 13/363, **July 1st, 1916,** Age 25,
Barnsley Corporation Highways Dept, 14
Buckley Street, Barnsley

GLEESON William *born Tipperary, Ireland,*
enlisted Barnsley, L/Sergeant, 13/391, **July**
1st, 1916, Age 26 Miner, Barrow Colliery,
Married with 2 children, Copper Street,
Barnsley

GUEST Thomas Heald Major, **July 1st, 1916**

HANCOCK Thomas Wilford *born Ringinglow,*
Yorkshire, enlisted Sheffield, Private, 12/1763,
July 1 st, 1916

HARRIS Joseph *born Thoomakin, Pennsylvania*
U.S.A., enlisted Barnsley, Corporal, 13/503,
July 1st, 1916, Age 30 Miner, Hickleton Main
Colliery, 138 Doncaster Road, Barnsley

HART Joseph William *born Arnold,*
Nottinghamshire, enlisted Barnsley Private,
13/1190, **D.O.W. July 18th, 1916**

HARWOOD Walter *born Upper Wortley, Leeds,*
enlisted Barnsley Private, 13/450, **July 1st,**
1916, Age 21 Miner, Houghton Main Colliery, 1
Edward Street, Sand Hill, Great Houghton, near
Barnsley

HAWCROFT Herbert *born Wombwell, enlisted*
Barnsley Private, 13/516, **July 1st, 1916**

HAWES Henry *born Tankersley, enlisted Barnsley*
Sergeant, 13/433, **July 1st, 1916** Miner,
Houghton Main Colliery, 32 Haugh Lane,
Wombwell

HEWITT Cyril Ernest *born Hemsworth, Wakefield,*
enlisted Barnsley L/Corporal, 13/506, **July 1st,**
1916

HIRST Charles Henry *born Barnsley, enlisted*
Barnsley Private, 13/412, **July 1st, 1916**
Barman, Queen's Hotel, Barnsley, 9 Spring
Street, Barnsley

HOLDSWORTH James Edward *born Wakefield,*
enlisted Barnsley Private, 13/467, **D.O.W. July**
24th, 1916, Age 19 Miner, Houghton Main
Colliery, 27 Industry Road, Stairfoot

HOLLINGSWORTH Ernest *born Houghton,*
enlisted Barnsley Private, 13/496, **July 1st,**
1916, Age 20, 16 New Street, Sand Hill, Great
Houghton, near Barnsley

HOLMES Herbert *born Methley, Leeds, enlisted*
Barnsley Private, 13/475, **July 1st, 1916,** Age
23 Miner, Houghton Main Colliery, Wright's
Avenue, Darfield

HOWE Arthur *born Darfield, enlisted Barnsley*
Private, 13/468, **July 1st, 1916**

HUBBARD James *born Sheffield, enlisted*
Barnsley Private, 13/448, **July 1st, 1916**

INSKIP Frank *born Great Houghton, enlisted*
Barnsley Private, 13/521, **July 1st, 1916**

IVES Ernest *born Darton, enlisted Barnsley*
Private, 13/517, **July 1st, 1916**

JENNINGS William *born Barnsley, enlisted*
Barnsley Private, 13/1123, **D.O.W. July 2nd,**
1916, Age 22 Miner, Barnsley Main Colliery, 13
Waltham Street, Barnsley

KIRK Wilfred *born New Whittington, Staveley,*
Derbyshire, enlisted Houghton, Barnsley
Private, 13/555, **D.O.W. July 31st, 1916,** Age
23, Married, 11 Well Street, Cudworth

LAKE John William *born Darton, enlisted Barnsley*
Private, 13/562, **July 1st, 1916,** Age 23, Main
Road, Mapplewell, Barnsley

LAPIDGE John *born Brotherton, Ferrybridge, enlisted Barnsley* Private, 13/575, **July 1st, 1916**

LEATHER Cyril *born Wombwell, enlisted Sheffield* Private, 12/1727, **D.O.W. July 17th, 1916** Miner, Wombwell Main Colliery, Pearson Field, Wombwell

LEECH Thomas Arthur *born Chester, enlisted Barnsley* Private, 13/576, **July 1st, 1916** Messrs. Qualter and Smiths Foundry, Married, 228 High Street, Worsborough Dale, Barnsley

LILES Arthur *born Stocksbridge, Sheffield, enlisted Silkstone, Barnsley* Private, 13/1407, **July 1st, 1916**

LOACH John *born Hucknall Torkard, Nottinghamshire, enlisted Barnsley* Private, 13/1522, **D.O.W. July 4th, 1916** 58 Doncaster Road, Barnsley

LYONS George *born Barnsley, enlisted Barnsley* Private, 13/564, **July 1st, 1916,** Age 31, Married with 3 children, 13 Highstone Lane, Barnsley

MALEHAM Stewart Captain, **July 1st, 1916,** Age 37, Secretary to Sheffield Wire Rope Co. 15 Endcliffe Avenue, Sheffield

MARCHBANKS John *born Spennymoor, Co. Durham, enlisted Barnsley* Private, 13/1233, **July 1st, 1916,** Age 29 Married, 5 Obelisk View, Bloomhouse Green, Darton

McKELVEY Horace *born Ardsley, enlisted Barnsley* Private, 13/638, **D.O.W. July 23rd, 1916**

MORLEY George Alfred *born Carrington, Nottinghamshire, enlisted Barnsley* Private, 13/1482, **D.O.W. August 1st, 1916,** Age 21 Miner, Grimethorpe Colliery

MOSS William Henry *born Saltaire, Bradford, enlisted Barnsley* Sergeant, 13/625, **July 1st, 1916,** Age 23 Miner, Houghton Main Colliery, Married, 40 Middlecliffe, Little Houghton, near Barnsley

NAYLOR Albert *born Doncaster, enlisted Barnsley* Private, 13/1007, **D.O.W. July 10th, 1916** *(Reported missing by War Office since July 1st, 1916 – Barnsley Chronicle)* Miner, Barrow Colliery, Married with 3 children, 21 Blacker Lane, Worsborough

NEEDHAM Ernest *born Darfield, enlisted Barnsley* Private, 13/1008, **July 1st, 1916**

PAGETT William Henry *born Pitsmoor, Sheffield, enlisted Sheffield* Private, 12/1431, **July 1st, 1916**

PAISLEY John *born Hoyland, Barnsley, enlisted Barnsley* Private, 13/775, **July 1st, 1916** Miner, Wharncliffe Woodmoor Colliery, 24 Summer Lane, Barnsley

PALEY Percy *born Crofton, Wakefield, enlisted Barnsley* Private, 13/773, **July 1st, 1916**

PRESTWOOD Harold *born Burnslough Bridge, Lancashire, enlisted Barnsley* Corporal, 13/785, **July 1st, 1916**

PROCTOR Samuel Lake *born Ryhill, Wakefield, enlisted Barnsley* Sergeant, 13/783, **D.O.W. July 11th, 1916**

ROBINSON Andrew *born Hollingwood, Oldham, Lancashire, enlisted Barnsley* Private, 13/924, **July 1st, 1916**

ROYSTONE Arthur *born Barnsley, enlisted Barnsley* Private, 13/1491, **July 1st, 1916,** Age 21, 10 St. John's Terrace, Buckley Street, Barnsley

SAGAR Thomas *born Worsborough, Barnsley, enlisted Barnsley* Private, 13/1194, **July 1st, 1916** Miner, Wombwell Main Colliery, Married, 8 Wellington Place, Waterloo Road, Barnsley

SANDERSON Louis *born Darton, enlisted Barnsley* Private, 13/814, **July 1st, 1916,** Age 30, Miner, Houghton Main Colliery, Married with child 21, Fife Street, Barnsley

SAYERS Charles *born New Mills, Derbyshire, enlisted Houghton, Barnsley* A/Sergeant, 13/841, **D.O.W. July 2nd, 1916,** Age 42 Miner, Houghton Main Colliery, 13 Jackson Street, Cudworth

SCARGILL Harry *born Barnsley, enlisted Barnsley* Sergeant, 13/891, **July 1st, 1916,** Age 29 Draper, Eldon Street, Barnsley, 5 Harbrough Hills Road, Barnsley

SHARP Stephen Oswald Lieutenant, **July 1st, 1916** Articled Clerk, 'Kenilworth', Avenue Road, Doncaster

SMITH George de Ville Captain, **July 1st, 1916** Curate, St. Thomas Church, Worsborough

SMITH Joseph *born Royston, enlisted Barnsley* Private, 13/889, **July 1st, 1916** Miner, Barnsley Main Colliery, 35 Lower Thomas Street, Barnsley

SMITHSON Alexander *born Moorthorpe, Pontefract, enlisted Barnsley* L/Corporal, 13/837, **July 1st, 1916,** Age 28 Miner, Mitchell Main Colliery, Married with child, Sykes Street, Kingstone, Barnsley

SWIFT Walter *born Monk Bretton, enlisted Barnsley* Private, 13/890, **July 1st, 1916,** Age 31 Miner, Wharncliffe Woodmoor Colliery, Married with 2 children, Hoyle Mill, Barnsley

SWIMBURN John *born Worsborough Dale, enlisted Barnsley* Private, 13/894, **July 1st, 1916,** Age 22 Miner, Barrow Colliery, Station Road, Worsborough Dale

SYKES Edmund *born Walton, Yorkshire, enlisted Barnsley* Private, 13/1251, **D.O.W. July 2nd, 1916,** Hoyle Mill Road, Stairfoot

TEALE Herbert *born Leeds, enlisted Barnsley* Private, 13/966, **D.O.W. July 6th, 1916**

THOMPSON John *born Seaham, Sunderland, enlisted Barnsley* Private, 13/953, **July 1st, 1916**

THOMPSON William *born Hyde, Cheshire, enlisted Barnsley* Private, 13/1097, **July 1st, 1916** Stockport, Cheshire

TILSON Arthur *born Mexborough, enlisted Barnsley* Private, 13/976, **Died at home, July 20th, 1916**

TINGLE Harold *born Barnsley, enlisted Barnsley* Private, 13/958, **July 1st, 1916,** Age 20 12 Park Road, Barnsley

TURNER Herbert *born Worsborough, enlisted Barnsley* Private, 13/956, **July 1st, 1916,** Age 27, Miner, New Monckton Colliery, 62 Cross Lane, Royston, Barnsley

VICTORY Thomas William *born Monk Bretton, enlisted Barnsley* Private, 13/1136, **July 1st, 1916,** Age 37, Miner, Houghton Main Colliery

WALKER Ernest *born Barnsley, enlisted Barnsley* L/Corporal, 13/740, **July 1st, 1916**

WALKER William Henry *born Kingston-upon-Hull, enlisted Barnsley* Private, 13/753, **July 1st, 1916**

WARING John Thomas *born Barnsley, enlisted Silkstone* Private, 13/1323, **July 1st, 1916,** Age 20, Miner, Woolley Colliery

WELDON George *born Wombwell, enlisted Barnsley* Private, 13/682, **July 1st, 1916**

WESTON Arthur *born Fenton, N. Staffordshire, enlisted Barnsley* Private, 13/697, **July 1st, 1916**

WHITAKER Josiah *born Batley, enlisted Barnsley* Private, 13/689, **July 1st, 1916,** Age 23, Miner, Woolley Colliery, Married, 30 Clarendon Street, Barnsley

WHITEHEAD William *born Burnley, Lancashire, enlisted Barnsley* Private, 13/736, **D.O.W. July 23rd, 1916,** Age 42, Married with child, Margate Street, Barnsley

WIDDOWSON John Allison Dean *born Walkley Sheffield, enlisted Sheffield* Sergeant, 10160, **July 1st, 1916,** Age 24, Clyro House, Sutton, Retford, Nottinghamshire

WILLIAMS John *born Barnsley, enlisted Silkstone, Barnsley* Private, 13/1389, **July 1st, 1916,** Age 29, Married with 2 children, Hermit Lane, Higham, Barnsley

WRIGGLESWORTH Ernest *born Hunslet, Leeds, enlisted Barnsley* Private, 13/733, **July 1st, 1916** Miner, North Gawber Colliery, Mapplewell, Barnsley

14th Battalion men killed on 1st July, 1916, or later died of wounds received on that day.

ALLENBY Harold *born Barnsley, enlisted Barnsley* L/Corporal, 14/119, **July 1st, 1916**

ALLSOPP Bertram *born Barnsley, enlisted Barnsley* L/Corporal, 14/1461, **July 1st, 1916,** Barugh Chemical Works, Barnsley, 44 Keir Street, Barnsley

ANDERSON Reginald Dudley Bawawen 2nd Lieutenant, **July 1st, 1916,** Age 20, Wakefield

ANDREW William *born Ashton-u-Lyme, Lancashire, enlisted Barnsley* Private, 14/1425, **July 1st, 1916,** Age 20 Miner, Rockingham Colliery, Elm Street, Hoyland Common, Barnsley

ASKIN David *born Mexborough, enlisted Barnsley* Private, 14/2, **July 1st, 1916** Miner, Grimethorpe Colliery, Married with 5 children, 11 Chapel Square, Worsborough Common

ATHA John Bruce *born Liversedge, Yorkshire, enlisted Barnsley* Corporal, 14/331, **July 1st, 1916,** Age 25, Teacher, St. John's Boys School, Barnsley Married, 1 Nursery Street, Barnsley

ATKINSON Arthur *born Woodlesford, Yorkshire, enlisted Barnsley* L/Sergeant, 14/969, **July 1st, 1916**

BATTY William *born Barnsley, enlisted Barnsley* L/Corporal, 14/131, **July 1st, 1916,** Age 24, Needham Bros. and Brown Foundry, Barnsley, 36 Windemere Road, Barnsley

BEDFORD Samuel *born Darfield, enlisted Barnsley* Private, 14/363, **July 1st, 1916**

BELL Percy *born Wombwell, enlisted Barnsley* Private, 14/1509, **July 1st, 1916,** Age 22, Joiner and Wheelwright, 12 Smith Street, Wombwell

BETTON Elijah *born Gawber, enlisted Barnsley* L/Corporal, 14/1501, **July 1st, 1916,** Age 21, Miner, Church Lane Colliery, Married with 2 children, 6 Mount Street, Barnsley

BIRCHALL Thomas *born Market Drayton, Shropshire, enlisted Barnsley* Sergeant, 14/294, **July 1st, 1916**

BRADLEY Harry *born Monk Bretton, enlisted Barnsley* Private, 14/1182, **July 1st, 1916**

BRAITHWAITE Alfred *born Wigan, Lancashire, enlisted Barnsley* Private, 14/1100, **D.O.W. July 9th, 1916,** Age 23, Miner, Woolley Colliery, Sackup Lane, Darton

BRIGGS Raynor *born Dodworth, enlisted Barnsley* Corporal, 14/134, **D.O.W. July 13th, 1916,** Age 28, Miner, Rob Royd Colliery

BROMLEY John William *born Grimsby, Lincolnshire, enlisted Barnsley* Sergeant, 14/284, **D.O.W. July 17th, 1916** Miner, Monkton Colliery, Married with child, 35 Garden Cottage, Cudworth

BRYCE Harry Thomas *born Dudley, Staffordshire, enlisted Barnsley* Private, 14/1028, **July 1st, 1916**

BURDETT Stanley *born Walkley, Sheffield, enlisted Sheffield* Private, 12/1693, **July 1st, 1916**

CHAPMAN John *born Gawber, enlisted Barnsley* Private, 14/1007, **July 1st, 1916**

CHARLESWORTH James Joseph *born Attercliffe, Sheffield, enlisted Sheffield* Private, 12/1645, **July 1st, 1916**

CLARKSON William Henry M.M. *born High Hoyland, enlisted Barnsley* Private, 14/20, P.O.W. **D.O.W. July 4th, 1916,** Age 32, Miner, Pyewood Colliery, Darton, Married with 4 children, 32 School Street, Darton, Barnsley

COLLIER Samuel *born Ashton-u-Lyme, Lancashire, enlisted Barnsley* Private, 14/409, **July 1st, 1916,** Age 31, Miner, Strafford Main Colliery, Married, 11 Silver Street, Dodworth

CROSSLAND Joseph *born Barnsley, enlisted Barnsley* Private, 14/1030, **July 1st, 1916,** Clyde Street, Pit Field, Barnsley

DENMAR William Henry *born Wombwell, enlisted Barnsley* Private, 14/1328, **July 1st, 1916,** 25 Alma Street, Barnsley

DICKINSON Frank *born Wentworth, Rotherham, enlisted Barnsley* Private, 14/1267, **July 1st, 1916,** Age 27, 50 Firth Road, West Melton, Wath

DRAISEY John Thomas *born Hoyland, enlisted Barnsley* L/Sergeant, 14/29, **July 1st, 1916**

DUNK Reginald *born Barnsley, enlisted Barnsley* Sergeant, 14/140, **D.O.W. July 3rd, 1916**

FAIRLEY Duncan Lieutenant, **July 1st, 1916,** Age 26 Park Grove, Barnsley

FEARN Edward *born Stocksbridge, Sheffield, enlisted Barnsley* Private, 14/1486, **July 1st, 1916,** Nicholson Avenue, Barugh Green, Barnsley

FORSDIKE Harold Brooke Lieutenant, **July 1st, 1916,** Age 20, Sheffield Simplex Works, Tinsley Parkfield House, Norfolk Road, Sheffield

FROST Arthur William *born Barnsley, enlisted Barnsley* Sergeant, 14/755, **July 1st, 1916** Miner, Wath Main Colliery, Married with child, 23 Sunderland Terrace, Doncaster Road

GLYNN John *born Fuam, Co. Galway, enlisted Barnsley* Private, 14/1252, **July 1st, 1916** Miner, Barrow Colliery, Married, St. George's Square, George Street, Barnsley

GOLDTHORPE William Greenwood *born Liversedge, Yorkshire, enlisted Barnsley* Private, 14/864, P.O.W. **D.O.W. July 4th, 1916**

GREEN Benjamin Riley *born Barnsley, enlisted Barnsley* Private, 14/995, **July 1st, 1916,** Redfearns Glassworks, Barnsley, Married with child, Wood Street, Barnsley

GREGORY Charles *born Aspull, Wigan, Lancashire, enlisted Barnsley* Sergeant, 14/955, **July 1st, 1916,** Age 22, Miner, Barrow Colliery, 1 Arthur Street, Worsborough Bridge

HAGUE William *born Dodworth, enlisted Barnsley* Private, 14/303, **July 1st, 1916**

HARDISTY Ernest *born Barnsley, enlisted Barnsley* Private, 14/235, **July 1st, 1916**

HARGATE James *born Barnsley, enlisted Barnsley* Private, 14/333, **July 1st, 1916,** Rylands Glassworks, 5 Freeman's Yard, Doncaster Road, Barnsley

HEAVERSEDGE Roddy *born Higham, enlisted Barnsley* Private, 14/759, **July 1st, 1916,** Age 47, Barugh Chemical Works, Bloomhouse Green, Barnsley

HEPPLESTONE John William *born Barnsley, enlisted Barnsley* Private, 14/1196, **July 1st, 1916,** Great Central Railway, Married with 4 children, 8 St. Bard's Terrace, Dobie Street, Barnsley

HIGGINBOTTOM Richard James *born Apperknowle, Derbyshire, enlisted Barnsley* Private, 14/1330, **July 1st, 1916,** 13 Alma Street, Barnsley

HINCHCLIFFE Alfred *born Leeds, enlisted Barnsley (Heckmondwike)* Private, 14/982, **July 1st, 1916**

HIRST William 2nd Lieutenant, **July 1st, 1916,** Age 30, Surveyor, Wombwell Main Colliery, Assistant Instructor Sheffield University

HOLMES Victor *born Cudworth, enlisted Barnsley* Private, 14/695, **July 1st, 1916,** Age 19, Miner, Grimethorpe Colliery, 12 Ibbott Street, Cudworth

HOLT James William *born Sheffield, enlisted Barnsley* Private, 14/1273, **July 1st, 1916,** Redfearns Glassworks, Barnsley, Gaunt's Yard, Barnsley

HOUSTON Frederick Neville Captain, **July 1st, 1916**

HOWARTH Charles Frederick *born Great Houghton, enlisted Barnsley* Private, 14/157, **July 1st, 1916,** Miner, Houghton Main Colliery, School Street, Great Houghton, near Barnsley

HUGHES Walter *born Stairfoot, enlisted Barnsley* Private, 14/382, **D.O.W. July 14th, 1916,** Age 27 Miner, Grimethorpe Colliery, Sykes Street, Stairfoot, Barnsley

HURD George *born Ardsley, enlisted Barnsley* Private, 14/445, **July 1st, 1916,** 1 Parpoint Cottages, Stairfoot, Barnsley

JACKSON Walter *born Barnsley, enlisted Barnsley* Private, 14/320, **July 1st, 1916,** Age 20, Platelayer, Great Central Railway, 25 King Street, Barnsley

JOHNSON Herbert Richard *born Newington, Hull, enlisted Doncaster (Leicester)* Sergeant, 3/1354, **July 1st, 1916**

JONES Albert Ernest *born Sheffield, enlisted Barnsley* Private, 14/67, **July 1st, 1916,** Age 40, Miner, Woolley Colliery, Married with 6 children, 5 School Street, Darton, Barnsley

JONES Edward *born Spennymoor, Co. Durham, enlisted Barnsley* Private, 14/64, **July 1st, 1916,** 25 Longcar Street, Barnsley

JUBB James Henry *born Worsborough Dale, enlisted Barnsley* Private, 14/974, **July 1st, 1916,** Great Central Railway, Heelis Street, Barnsley

LAISTER Harry *born St. Mary's Sheffield, enlisted Sheffield* Private, 12/1966, **July 1st, 1916,** Age 22, 16 Lancing Road, Sheffield

LINDSAY Frederick *born Barnsley, enlisted Barnsley* Private, 14/1016, **July 1st, 1916**

LISTER William *born Darnall, Sheffield, enlisted Attercliffe, Sheffield* Private, 12/1659, **July 1st, 1916**

LOMAS Robert Graham M.M. *born Litton, Derbyshire, enlisted Barnsley* A/Corporal, 14/169, **July 1st, 1916**

LOVATT Walter *born Swaith Main, Yorkshire, enlisted Barnsley* Private, 14/273, **July 1st, 1916** Miner, Barnsley Main Colliery, Married with child, 16 Wesley Street, Barnsley

LUCAS Matthew *born Barnsley, enlisted Barnsley* Private, 14/71, **July 1st, 1916**

LYMAN Luke *born Hallbrookes, Derbyshire, enlisted Barnsley* Private, 14/70, **July 1st, 1916**

MILTHORPE Herbert *born Barnsley, enlisted Barnsley* Private, 14/308, **July 1st, 1916,** Age 24, Miner, Wharncliffe Woodmoor Colliery, 49 Caxton Street, Barnsley

MITCHELL Wilson *born Woolley, enlisted Barnsley* Private, 14/1131, **July 1st, 1916,** Age 21, 38 Woolley Colliery, Darton, Barnsley

MOORES John *born Wombwell, enlisted Barnsley* L/Corporal, 14/173, **D.O.W. July 3rd, 1916**

MORGAN William James M.M. *born Ince, Wigan, Lancashire, enlisted Barnsley* A/Corporal, 14/77, **July 1st, 1916,** Age 31, Miner, Barrow Colliery, Married with 3 children, Coward's Court, George Street, Worsborough Dale

NAYLOR Alfred *born Worsborough Bridge, enlisted Barnsley* Private, 14/78, **July 1st, 1916**

NICHOLSON Frederick Bland *born Wetwang, Yorkshire, enlisted Barnsley* L/Corporal, 14/989, **July 1st, 1916,** Age 37, Miner, Monckton Colliery, Married, 67 Carlton Terrace, Barnsley

NORTON Leonard *born Barnsley, enlisted Barnsley* Private, 14/184, **July 1st, 1916,** 20 Prospect Street, Barnsley

PARKER Walter William *born Canada, enlisted Barnsley* Private, 14/309, **July 1st, 1916,** 10 Highstone Fold, Worsborough Common

PENTON George Arthur *born Ashton, Derbyshire, enlisted Barnsley* Private, 14/980, **July 1st, 1916**

PHILLIPS Edward *born Hansley, Staffordshire, enlisted Barnsley* Private, 14/452, **D.O.W. July 8th, 1916,** 23 Ask Row, Hoyle Mill, Barnsley

PICKERING Charles *born Dodworth, enlisted Barnsley* A/Corporal, 14/645, **July 1st, 1916,** Age 37, Miner, Barnsley Main Colliery, Married, 16 Junction Terrace, Barnsley

POWELL Thomas William *born Swinton, enlisted Barnsley* Private, 14/1579, **July 1st, 1916,** Age 39, Married with 2 children, 16 Church Street, Cudworth

POWERS John *born Barnsley, enlisted Barnsley* Private, 14/1437, **July 1st, 1916**

REID Bruce *born Birdwell, enlisted Barnsley (Rotherham)* Sergeant, 14/192, **July 1st, 1916,** Messrs. Butterfields, Drapers, Barnsley

RIMMER James White *born Gawber, enlisted Barnsley* Private, 14/1138, **July 1st, 1916,** Miner, Cortonwood Colliery, 38 Mitchell Terrace, Myers Street, Wombwell

ROBINSON Arthur *born Dodworth, enlisted Barnsley* Private, 14/194, **July 1st, 1916,** Miner, Church Lane Colliery, Fife Street, Dodworth, Barnsley

ROOS Gustav Oscar Captain, **July 1st, 1916**

ROSE George *born Wigan, enlisted Barnsley* Private, 14/277, **D.O.W. July 24th, 1916,** Miner, Barrow Colliery, 6 William Street, Worsborough Bridge

ROYSTON Eli *born Barnsley, enlisted Barnsley* Private, 24217, **July 1st, 1916**

RUSHWORTH Walter *born Hoyland, enlisted Barnsley* L/Corporal, 14/193, **July 1st, 1916**

SANDERSON Matthew *born Dodworth, enlisted Barnsley* Private, 14/103, **D.O.W. July 4th, 1916,** Age 32, Miner, Rob Royd Colliery, Married, New Street, Dodworth

SCHOLEY John William *born Barnsley, enlisted Barnsley* L/Sergeant, 14/431, **July 1st, 1916**

SELLARS Arthur *born Barnsley, enlisted Barnsley* Private, 14/204, **July 1st, 1916**

SENIOR Herbert Hartley *born Barnsley, enlisted Barnsley* Private, 14/1622, **D.O.W. July 5th, 1916**

SHANNON John *born Elsecar, enlisted Barnsley* Private, 14/102, **D.O.W. July 4th, 1916**

SHAW John George *born Aston, Sheffield, enlisted Sheffield* Private, 12/1182, **July 1st, 1916**

SMITH Willie *born Hoyland Common, enlisted Barnsley* Private, 14/97, **July 1st, 1916,** 19 New Street, Dodworth, Barnsley

SNOWDEN Frederick *born Cudworth, enlisted Barnsley* Private, 14/202, **D.O.W. July 2nd, 1916**

STORRS Arthur *born Staincross, enlisted Barnsley* Private, 14/96, **July 1st, 1916**

STOTT Edward *born Wigan, Lancashire, enlisted Barnsley* Private, 14/1021, **July 1st, 1916,** Age 33, Miner, Barrow Colliery, Married with 3 children, 1 Green Street, off Vernon Road, Barnsley

SYKES Albert *born Higham, Barnsley, enlisted Barnsley* Private, 14/327, **July 1st, 1916,** Age 19

SYKES Walter *born Shirehampton, Gloucestershire, enlisted Barnsley* Private, 14/1232, **D.O.W. July 9th, 1916,** Great Houghton, Barnsley

SYMONS Frederick *born Platt's Common, enlisted Barnsley* L/Corporal, 14/984, **July 1st, 1916,** Age 24 Miner, Silkstone Colliery

TAYLOR Walter *born Barnsley, enlisted Barnsley* Private, 14/496, **D.O.W. July 6th, 1916,** Age 28, Rylands Glassworks, Barnsley, Highfield Terrace, Barnsley

THOMAS Lawrence *born Hoyland, Barnsley, enlisted Barnsley* A/Corporal, 14/209, **July 1st, 1916,** 119 Snydale Road, Cudworth

THOMPSON Charles *born Bermondsey, Middlesex, enlisted Barnsley* Private, 14/328, **July 1st, 1916,** Painthorpe Terrace, Crigglestone, Wakefield

TURNER Joseph Henry *born Barnsley, enlisted Barnsley* Private, 14/104, **July 1st, 1916,** Age 29, Fruiterer and Drayman, Married with 2 children, 61 Wood Street, Barnsley

TURNER Richard *born Wakefield, enlisted Barnsley* Private, 14/105, **July 1st, 1916,** Age 32, Miner, Monk Bretton Colliery Married with 2 children, 1 Faith Street, Monk Bretton, Barnsley

TURTON Austin *born Mapplewell, Barnsley, enlisted Barnsley* Private, 14/1319, **July 1st, 1916,** Miner, North Gawber Colliery, Married with child, 9 Smithy Wood, Smithies, Barnsley

TURTON John Alfred *born St. George's, Sheffield, enlisted Sheffield* Private, 12/1524, **July 1st, 1916**

WALKER Charles *born Barnsley, enlisted Barnsley* Private, 14/1024, **July 1st, 1916,** Miner, Monk Bretton Colliery, Married with 4 children, 14 Lower Thomas Street, Barnsley

WALKER Frederick *born Barnsley, enlisted Barnsley* Private, 14/116, **July 1st, 1916,** 6 Princess Street, Wombwell

WALKER Frederick *born Tipstock, Leicester, enlisted Barnsley* A/L/Corporal, 14/221, **July 1st, 1916**

WATERHOUSE John *born Hayfield, Stockport, Cheshire, enlisted Sheffield* Private, 12/1327, **July 1st, 1916**

WIDDOP Leonard *born Barnsley, enlisted Barnsley* A/Corporal, 14/217, **July 1st, 1916**

WILDMAN John *born West Leigh, Lancashire, enlisted Barnsley* Private, 14/220, **July 1st, 1916,** Age 20, Miner, North Gawber Colliery, 24 Pleasant View Street, Barnsley

WILKINSON Thomas John *born St. Peter's, Sheffield, enlisted Sheffield* Private, 12/1636, **July 1st, 1916**

WOOLLEY Stephen *born Dewsbury, enlisted Barnsley* Private, 14/293, **July 1st, 1916,** School Street, Hemingfield

YORK Henry *born Royston, Barnsley, enlisted Barnsley* Private, 14/330, **July 1st, 1916,** Age 22

Officers and Medal lists

Compiled by Peter Taylor

Captain Cyril Burton Dixon, M.C. of Jacob's Hall, Kexborough. At the outbreak of war he joined the 13th Battalion. Awarded the Military Cross 27th September, 1917. He died on November 14th, 1918 from wounds he received ten days earlier. One of the last original Pals to die in the Great War. There is a memorial to him in Darton Church.

Officers who served with the 13th Battalion Y & L Regiment during The Great War. It includes medals awarded to individual officers and the date on which they were confirmed in the London Gazette.

ARMSTRONG R.
2nd Lieutenant

ASHWORTH L.
2nd Lieutenant
Died of wounds 12.4.18

ASQUITH G.
Lieutenant *Wounded 9.4.16*

ASQUITH M.
2nd Lieutenant *Wounded 4.4.17*

AYRES F. Captain

BARNES H.B.
Lieutenant
MILITARY CROSS 11.12.16

BEAUMONT C.F.
Lieutenant

BEECROFT C. Lieutenant

BELL A. 2nd Lieutenant

BERRY T.G. Captain

BRAITHWAITE E.A. Captain
Wounded 1.7.16 & 27.3.18

BRIGGS O. Lieutenant

BRODRICK J. Captain

BROWN S. 2nd Lieutenant

BRYSON W. 2nd Lieutenant
MILITARY CROSS 15.10.18

BUFTON E.E.
2nd Lieutenant *Wounded 14.4.18 Died 20.11.18*

BURGESS C.N. Lieutenant

BURPEE B.P. Captain
United States Marine Corps
Attached to 13th *Reported missing 15.3.18*

BURT W.G. Lieutenant

BUTCHER E.E. 2nd Lieutenant

BUTTERLEY H. Captain

CALDERBANK J. Rev. Captain

CLARK R.E. 2nd Lieutenant

CLEMENTS J.H. Lieutenant

COOK F. 2nd Lieutenant

COOKE J.I.
Lieutenant *Wounded 1.7.16*

COOPER F.T. Lieutenant
Seriously wounded May 1916

COWEN J.C. Captain
MILITARY CROSS 15.10.18

CRABTREE W. Captain
Royal Army Medical Corps

CRAGGS P. 2nd Lieutenant
Killed in Action 30.9.18

CURRIN R.W.
Captain *D.S.O. 25.8.16*

DART H. Lieutenant
Died of wounds 2.7.16

DICKINSON L.
2nd Lieutenant *Killed in action 11.4.18*

DIXON C.B. Lieutenant
Died of wounds 14.11.18
MILITARY CROSS 18.2.19

DIXON W.H. 2nd Lieutenant
Wounded August 1916

DRURY A. 2nd Lieutenant
Wounded 30.9.18

DUNCAN J.A. 2nd Lieutenant

ELLIS E. Lieutenant

ENGLAND E.G. 2nd Lieutenant
Wounded August 1916

FIRTH E.H. Captain
Killed in action 1.7.16

FOERS L.A.F.
Captain
MILITARY CROSS 13.2.17

GIBSON H.
2nd Lieutenant *Killed in action 30.9.18*

GILL J.G. Lieutenant

GILL J.L. 2nd Lieutenant

GOODIER V.R.
2nd Lieutenant *Wounded 28.3.18 MILITARY CROSS 2.4.19*

GROGAN V.deL. Lieutenant

GUEST T.H. Major
Killed in action 1.7.16

GURNEY C.H. Captain
D.S.O. 1.1.17
Bar to D.S.O.26.7.18

HANSFORD H.W.B.
2nd Lieutenant
Wounded 24.3.18

HARRISON D. 2nd Lieutenant

HARRISON J.G. Lieutenant

HARROP A. 2nd Lieutenant

HEPTONSTALL R.A. Lieutenant
Wounded 1.7.16

HEWITT J. L/Colonel

HINCKLEYD.R. Lieutenant
Killed in action 13.1.17

HIONS T.M. 2nd Lieutenant
Wounded July 1916

HOLMAN A. 2nd Lieutenant

HUDSON G.H. Lieutenant
Wounded 27.3.18

HUGGARD L.D.R.
2nd Lieutenant
Killed in action 26.6.17

HUNTER L.E. Lieutenant

IRWIN A.E. Captain

JACKSON J.E. 2nd Lieutenant
Wounded 12.9.18

JARRETT H.D. 2nd Lieutenant

JEFFERSON C. Lieutenant

JENKINS G.C. 2nd Lieutenant
Killed in action 3.5.17

JONES G.W. 2nd Lieutenant
Died of wounds 12.4.18

JONES H. Lieutenant

JUDD H.L. 2nd Lieutenant

KENNARD M.N. Major

KENYON P. 2nd Lieutenant

KIRK C.B. Captain
MILITARY CROSS 26.3.18

KNIGHT S.A.W. 2nd Lieutenant
MILITARY CROSS 11.12.16

KNOWLES A.W.
2nd Lieutenant *Wounded 1.7.16*

LEITH S. 2nd Lieutenant

MALEHAM S. Lieutenant
Killed in action 1.7.16

MARTIN C.H. Lieutenant

MARWOOD A.H.L Major

MEIN H. Lieutenant

MIDWOOD M. 2nd Lieutenant
Died of wounds 25.12.16

MORTON P.C. 2nd Lieutenant
Reported missing April 1918

MORRIS L.M. 2nd Lieutenant

NEWHAM A.W. 2nd Lieutenant

NORMANSELL J.
2nd Lieutenant
Died of wounds 10.3.17

O'SULLIVAN Lieutenant

PARKER E. 2nd Lieutenant

PARRY W. Lieutenant
MILITARY CROSS 26.9.17

PHILLIPS W.P. 2nd Lieutenant
Wounded May 1917

PICKARD J.R. 2nd Lieutenant
*Wounded 13.4.18 ex 14th
Bn.*

POPPLEWELL F.
2nd Lieutenant

POWER A.
2nd Lieutenant
Wounded 23.3.18

PRICE E.V. Lieutenant
MILITARY CROSS 22.9.16

PUKESS A.J. Lieutenant
Killed in action 27.6.18

RAE N.D. 2nd Lieutenant

REED E.D.A. 2nd Lieutenant

RIVERS W.L. 2nd Lieutenant

ROBIN C.H. Captain
Killed in action 11.5.17

ROBINSON J.E.
2nd Lieutenant *Wounded
24.3.18*

SEDDALL J. Lieutenant
MILITARY CROSS 18.7.19

SHARP S.O. Lieutenant
Killed in action 1.7.16

SHUTE C.A. 2nd Lieutenant

SIMPSON V.S. Captain
Killed in action 13.4.18

SKIRROW A. 2nd Lieutenant

SMITH D.deV. Captain
Killed in action 1.7.16

SMITH G.S. 2nd Lieutenant
Wounded 13.4.18

SMITH R.J. Captain
Killed in action 1.7.16

SPARROW 2nd Lieutenant

STAFF-BRETT H.W.
2nd Lieutenant *Killed in
action 24.3.18*

STEVENSON H.G.
2nd Lieutenant *Killed in
action 25.6.17*

STIRRUP T. Lieutenant
Wounded May 1917

STREAT N.W. Captain
Wounded 9.4.16

STUART T.C. Captain

SUDBURY E.R.
2nd Lieutenant
Wounded 24.3.18

SWINDIN E. Lieutenant *M.i.D.
28.12.18*

TAYLOR A. 2nd Lieutenant

TAYLOR E.N. Lieutenant

TEEDALE J. 2nd Lieutenant

Military Cross

TONGE F. 2nd Lieutenant
*Wounded 14.4.18 MILITARY
MEDAL 21.10.16*

TYZAACK W.A. Captain

WALLACE M.B. Captain
Wounded 14.4.18

WARD R. 2nd Lieutenant

WAUHOPE G.B. L/Colonel
Wounded 25.3.18 & 30.9.18

WESTBY F.H. Lieutenant

WESTON C.H.B. Captain

WHITEHEAD E. Lieutenant

WILFORD E.E. L/Colonel
*Wounded May 1917 D.S.O.
1.1.17 O.B.E. 3.6.19*

WILKINSON R. Captain

WILLIAMS G.H. Lieutenant
MILITARY CROSS 26.11.17

WINSHURST 2nd Lieutenant

WISE F.M. 2nd Lieutenant

WOOD G.H. Lieutenant

WOOLHOUSE G.
2nd Lieutenant *Wounded
30.9.18*

WRIGLEY J. Lieutenant

YULE J.G. 2nd Lieutenant

*Officers who served with
the 14th Battalion
Y & L Regiment up to
its amalgamation with
the 13th Battalion,
February 1918. It
includes medals
awarded to individual
officers and the date on
which they were
confirmed in the
London Gazette.*

ADAMS T.W. Lieutenant

ANDERSON R.D.B.
2nd Lieutenant *Killed in
action 1.7.16*

ANDREWS H.D.
Lieutenant

BAKEL F. 2nd Lieutenant
Killed in action 20.5.17

BALDRY A. 2nd Lieutenant
Killed in action 4.12.16

BARTLETT D.J.
2nd Lieutenant

BEALES H. 2nd Lieutenant
Killed in action 9.5.17

BELK C.R. 2nd Lieutenant

BELL H. 2nd Lieutenant
Wounded 28.6.17

BEST G.H.T. Lieutenant

BOLEY G. Captain *Royal Army Medical Corps*

BRAMFITT A.E.
2nd Lieutenant

BROOKS J.B. Lieutenant

BROOMHALL F. Lieutenant

BROOMHALL T.H.
Lieutenant

CAIRO J.C. 2nd Lieutenant

CALVERT A.C.H.
2nd Lieutenant

CARRINGTON C. Major

CHALLICE J.W. Lieutenant

CLEMENTS J.H. 2nd Lieutenant

COLES T.H. 2nd Lieutenant

CRAN C.R. Lieutenant

DAWES C.O.B. 2nd Lieutenant

DIXON H. 2nd Lieutenant

DONALD 2nd Lieutenant

DURNAN E. 2nd Lieutenant
Killed in action 16.10.17

DYSON-COOPE R. Lieutenant

EISTON J.J. 2nd Lieutenant

FAIRLEY D. Lieutenant
Killed in action 1.7.16

FIELD W. Captain Chaplain

FIELDING H.D. Lieutenant

FITTON C.V. Lieutenant
MILITARY CROSS 17.9.17

FOERS F. Lieutenant

FORSDIKE H.B. Lieutenant
Killed in action 1.7.16

FOULDS F.O. Lieutenant

FURNISS C.F. 2nd Lieutenant
Died of wounds 16.4.18

GILL E.L. 2nd Lieutenant

GILSON E.N. 2nd Lieutenant
Died of wounds Prisoner of war 5.11.18

GOODBURN R. Lieutenant
MILITARY CROSS 26.11.17

GRAY G.D. Lieutenant
Died 5.5.17

HANKINSON W.C. Captain

HARBORD C.G. Lieutenant
Killed in action 1.9.16

HARBORD R.F. 2nd Lieutenant

HARRICK W.O. Captain

HIRST R. 2nd Lieutenant

HIRST W. 2nd Lieutenant
Killed in action 1.7.16

HOLMES A.E. 2nd Lieutenant
Wounded 1.7.16 Killed in action 18.9.18

HOOD F.J.C. Major
D.S.O. 1.1.18 Attached 12th Bn.

HORSFALL J.R. 2nd Lieutenant

HOUSTON F.N. Captain
Killed in action 1.7.16

HOWE W. 2nd Lieutenant

HUGGARD R. Rev. Captain

HULKE W.B. L/Colonel *M.i.D. 4.1.17, 22.5.17 & 20.12.18 D.S.O. 1.7.17*

HUNT H.P. 2nd Lieutenant

HUTCHINGS D.A.V.B.
2nd Lieutenant

JOHNSON L.W.
2nd Lieutenant

KAYE G.H.C. 2nd Lieutenant

KEATING D.T. 2nd Lieutenant
Died of wounds 21.4.18

KELL W. 2nd Lieutenant
Wounded 1.7.16

KING L. Lieutenant

KIRK C.G. Lieutenant
Killed in action 20.7.18

KIRKBY J.W. 2nd Lieutenant
Killed in action 25.9.16

LOWINSKY R.E. Lieutenant
Wounded 1.7.16

MANATON A.J. 2nd Lieutenant

MARSDEN W.T. Lieutenant

MARTIN R.M.J. Lieutenant

Distinguished Service Order

McARDLE P.P. 2nd Lieutenant
Wounded 17.7.16

McINTYRE D.W.
2nd Lieutenant
Killed in action 28.6.17

McKENNA F.T. Lieutenant

MITCHELL W. 2nd Lieutenant

MOORE C. A. 2nd Lieutenant

MOXON C.F. 2nd Lieutenant
Wounded 31.7.16

NUTT A.V. Lieutenant *D.S.O. 1.1.18*

OLIVER C.H. Lieutenant

PICKARD J.R. 2nd Lieutenant
Wounded July 1917

PITT E.H.P. 2nd Lieutenant
MILITARY CROSS 2.4.19

POTTER F.J. 2nd Lieutenant

PRICE E.V. Lieutenant
MILITARY CROSS 22.9.16

QUEST H. 2nd Lieutenant
Wounded 3.6.16 MILITARY CROSS 27.7.16 Killed in action 3.11.16

QUEST T.P. Captain

RALEY W.E. Major
Resigned due to ill health July 1915

RAWLINGS K. 2nd Lieutenant

ROADHOUSE F.W.
2nd Lieutenant

ROADHOUSE J.C.
2nd Lieutenant

ROBIN C.H. Captain
ROBINSON J.E.
2nd Lieutenant
ROOS G.O. Captain
Killed in action 1.7.16
SAMES H.W. Lieutenant
SANFORD G.A. Major *Wounded 3.4.16*
SCHOFIELD J.J.
2nd Lieutenant
SCOTT-GLASS J. Captain
Wounded 16.10.17
SIDDALL T. Captain
SMITH C.S. 2nd Lieutenant
SMITH E.G. 2nd Lieutenant

SPENCER A. Lieutenant
Killed in action 1.7.16
STAFF-BRETT H.W.
2nd Lieutenant *Killed in action 24.3.18*
STEWART J.
Lieutenant Quartermaster
STOCKLEY P.H. Lieutenant
STORER H.E. 2nd Lieutenant
STRAW F.W. 2nd Lieutenant
Wounded 3.11.16
STRONG H. 2nd Lieutenant
Wounded 1.7.16 MILITARY CROSS 20.10.16
SUDBURY E.R. 2nd Lieutenant

SYLVESTER B.S. Lieutenant
TENNENT D.C. 2nd Lieutenant
TOLCHARD E.P. 2nd Lieutenant
TYLER K.P. 2nd Lieutenant
Wounded 9.5.17
VINER C. 2nd Lieutenant
WALKER R.H. 2nd Lieutenant
WEST G.A. 2nd Lieutenant
WILSON A. 2nd Lieutenant
WOOD A. Captain
Wounded 3.6.16 & 9.5.17
YOUNG E.V. 2nd Lieutenant

List of decorations awarded to the men serving with the 13th and 14th Battalions Y & L Regiment and the date on which they were confirmed in the London Gazette (if known)

DISTINGUISHED CONDUCT MEDAL

ALLEN E. Private 13/14
Date of Award 3.9.18
BECK W. C.S.M. 13/149 *Date of Award 1.1.17*
BLANCHARD L. Private 13/115
Date of Award 20.10.16
BROWN A. Sergeant 14/691
Date of Award 1.1.18
COLES E. Private 7587
Date of Award 2.12.19
DARLEY J. L/Corporal 12579
Date of Award 26.1.18
DYSON E. Corporal 14396
Date of Award 30.10.18
FIRTH C. Sergeant 14/992 *Date of Award 26.6.18*
FISHER H. Sergeant/C.S.M.
13/341 *Date of Award 30.10.18*
FORT C. Sergeant 13/309 *Date of Award 2.12.19*
GIBBS J. Private 13/364 *Date of Award 3.9.18*
HARDCASTLE J. Private 13/1461 *Date of Award 25.8.17*
McVITTIE G. Corporal 13/45275 *Date of Award 16.1.19*
MULLIGAN T. Private 14/571
Date of Award 25.8.17

PARKIN B. C.S.M. 13/790
Date of Award 11.3.20
PARRY W.F. Sergeant 13/760
Date of Award 20.10.16
RIDGE W.H. L/Corporal 15457
Date of Award 5.2.18
ROME A.E. C.S.M. 13/1824 *Date of Award 28.3.18*
TYAS C. Private 13/955 *Date of Award 3.9.18*
WARDLE G. C.S.M. 13/745 *Date of Award 3.9.18*

Allen E. (Smithies, nr. Barnsley)

For conspicuous gallantry and devotion to duty. He showed excellent work as a runner and never failed to deliver a message safely and correctly. On one occasion he was surrounded by the enemy, when he hid in a ditch, concealing important papers in his box respirator, eventually succeeding in crawling away and handing in his message safely.

Beck W.

For conspicuous gallantry and devotion to duty. He organised and led search parties into No- Man's-

Land under heavy fire, and was instrumental in bringing in many wounded.

Blanchard L.

For conspicuous gallantry in action. When severely wounded in the advance and only able to crawl he got his machine gun forward and rejoined the remainder of his team.

Brown A. (Thurnscoe, nr. Barnsley)

For conspicuous gallantry and devotion to duty and consistent good service at all times. He has always volunteered for any dangerous patrol work, and his courage and coolness have invariably inspired confidence in his men, especially in recruits on patrol for the first time.

Coles E. (Market Harborough)

He displayed great initiative and gallantry whilst in charge of a 3 inch Stokes' mortar during the period 22nd October 1918 to 26th October 1918 at Pecq. On the 23rd a heavy enemy trench mortar was firing on our advanced positions. He volunteered to bring his Stokes" gun into action against the enemy minenwerfer. By advancing his mortar to a most exposed position under direct observation by the enemy, he succeeded in silencing the enemy mortar. He alone served the Stokes' mortar until he had fired thirty rounds. Throughout the period, heavy artillery and machine-gun fire was directed against him, and it was entirely due to his audacity and complete disregard of personal safety that the enemy mortar was silenced.

Darley J. (Hillsboro', Sheffield)

For conspicuous gallantry and devotion to duty. An enemy party raided his post and attempted to take him prisoner. Covering him with revolvers, they compelled him to get out of the trench, but seeing one of the enemy in the trench below him, he threw himself onto him and after a severe struggle took him prisoner. The remainder of the enemy were meanwhile driven off by the remaining men of the post. By his bold and determined action he not only defeated the enemy's object but obtained a valuable identification.

Dyson E. (Rotherham)

For conspicuous gallantry and devotion to duty. This NCO was in charge of a party specially detailed to destroy the foot bridges over a stream during a night attack. When the objective of the attack was reached, several of the enemy were observed escaping over the bridges. Corporal Dyson at once charged forward with his party and threw some of the enemy in the river, where they were afterwards made prisoners, bayonetting others, and capturing a machine gun. By his splendid dash and determination he prevented the escape of several of the enemy and the withdrawal of the machine gun.

Firth C. (Worsborough Bridge)

For conspicuous gallantry and devotion to duty. When in charge of the left flank of a raiding party he led his men forward through heavy machine-gun fire, killed a dozen of the enemy, captured two prisoners, and then skilfully withdrew his party. Hearing on his arrival in our lines that there were some wounded lying out in No-Man's-Land he returned at once, and did not come in again until satisfied that all the casualties had been brought in. He showed the greatest gallantry and coolness.

Fisher H. (Barnsley)

For conspicuous gallantry and devotion to duty. When the left platoon of his company lost its commander and sergeant who were severely wounded, he greatly assisted the company commander in rallying it and steadying men. An enemy machine gun held up the advance of the platoon a little later, and he promptly took command, and working round a flank attacked the gun from the rear, personally leading the rush which captured the gun and its whole detachment. His gallantry and prompt initiative and action undoubtedly secured the left flank of the objective.

Fort C. (Barnsley)

On the night of 22nd October 1918, in front of Pecq, he was in charge of a section which was ordered to cross the River L'Escaut, and establish a bridge-head on the eastern side. This necessitated the clearing of a house strongly held by the enemy about 150 yards east of the river. Working round the flank he rushed the house and encountered a party of the enemy near the doorway. A short fight ensued, in which several casualties were inflicted on the enemy, he himself accounting for four with his revolver. At this point a number of enemy who had been inside the house rushed out, forcing him to withdraw his men. Though wounded, he personally covered the withdrawal, and was the last to leave. He showed fine courage and did splendid work.

Gibbs J. (Dukinfield)

For conspicuous gallantry and devotion to duty when on patrol. He and four others went forward with the officer in charge to secure a prisoner. He personally reconnoitred the enemy-posts and when the post was rushed, he disarmed one of the enemy who was about to bayonet the officer in charge. Throughout he set a splendid example of courage and resource.

Hardcastle J.

For conspicuous gallantry and devotion to duty. During an attack he engaged five of the enemy single-handed, killing one and capturing the remainder. Though blown down into the enemy trench by a shell, he continued his duties and bombed a shelter occupied by the enemy. His fearlessness and determination were of the highest order.

McVittie G. (Hebburn)

In an attack, west of Armentieres, on the 18th September 1918, he was in charge of half a platoon detailed for mopping up a farm and enclosure. He was wounded when leaving the assembly trench, but he continued throughout the attack to lead his party with splendid courage and determination. The farm to be mopped up was strongly held and much opposition met with, and his magnificent example in personally killing nine of the enemy with his bayonet warmed up his men to their work, with the result that it was very thoroughly done, and included twenty prisoners taken. Forty enemy dead were counted within the farm enclosure. Although wounded, he remained with his men until relieved sixteen hours later.

Mulligan T.

For conspicuous gallantry and devotion to duty during an attack. He took charge of a bombing post, from which he went single-handed to meet an enemy attack which was advancing along a communication trench. He killed five of them thereby causing the remainder to retire, and displaying very great courage and resource at a critical moment.

Parkin B. (Barnsley)

For conspicuous gallantry and devotion to duty during the enemy offensive in March 1918, when, in command of his company owing to officer casualties, he handled it with great energy and resource. Subsequently, in the recent advances, he showed great courage and initiative in organising patrols, and his utter disregard of danger in an attempt to cross the river Scheldt.

Parry W.F.

For conspicuous gallantry in action. When his section officer was killed he took command, and handled his mortars with great coolness and complete disregard of danger.

Ridge W.H. (E. Rotherham)

For conspicuous gallantry and devotion to duty. After a strong enemy raid had been driven back he asked permission to take out a patrol of four men. In broad daylight he went beyond our wire and encountered a party of the enemy in a shell-hole, who put up an obstinate resistance. The patrol attacked them with bombs, killing four and wounding a fifth, whom the patrol brought in, thus obtaining a valuable identification.

Rome A.E. (Sheffield)

For conspicuous gallantry and devotion to duty. A strong enemy patrol attacked a covering party as it was passing through the wire. He at once left the trench with a few men, and led them in an attack on the enemy and drove them off. He showed splendid coolness and initiative.

Tyas C. (Barnsley)

For conspicuous gallantry and devotion to duty. Although wounded on three separate occasions he refused to leave his Lewis gun, and kept it in action, repelling continuous attacks by the enemy.

Wardle G. (Little Houghton)

For conspicuous gallantry and devotion to duty. When a post was attacked and driven in, this W.O. at once collected all available men and counter-attacked, driving the enemy off and re-establishing the post.

Date of Award 10.8.16

CLARKSON W.H.
Private 14/20
RUSSELL A.
Private 14/364

Date of Award 11.11.16

BEDFORD B.
Private 13/54
CRITCHLEY E.
L/Corporal 14/485
DEAKIN A.
L/Corporal 13/248
DUNN A.H.
Private 14/553
FOX E.
Private 13/303
GARSIDE H.
L/Sergeant 14/148
OXTABY H.
Private 13/1128
STOCKER W.
Private 13/804
SYMONS J.
Private 14/962

Date of Award 16.11.16

BAGNALL J.
Private 13/133
BLACKBURN R.
Private 14/986
GILLESPIE E.
Private 14/50
POULTER A.S.
Private 14/1147
SEWARD S.G.
Private 14/956

Date of Award 19.2.17

BURGIN G.W.
Private 13/93
SAGAR F.
Sergeant 13/852

DODSON C.
Private 13/263
LOMAS R.G.
L/Corporal 14/169

Date of Award 12.3.17

CHEETHAM J.R.
L/Corporal 13/178
GIBBS J.
L/Corporal 13/364
STEWART P.
Sergeant 13/880

Date of Award 26.5.17

COLE S.
Private 13/172

Date of Award 28.7.17

MORGAN W.
A/Corporal 14/77

Date of Award 21.8.17

BENT W.
Private 13/1362
BRIGGS J.
Private 14/1462
FLETCHER J.H.
Corporal 14/1291

HATFIELD H.
Sergeant 13/437
HAYWARD G.
Sergeant 14/1133
HORNE H.
L/Corporal 14/236
SHAW E.
Private 13/862
SUNDERLAND A.
Sergeant 13/888
YATES H.
Private 14/1601
BIRKETT C.
Sergeant 14/367
BREATHWICK J.
L/Sergeant 13/147
MORLEY E.C.
Corporal 14/570
TAYLOR A.
Private 13/1142

Date of Award 19.11.17

HARDCASTLE T.
L/Corporal 14/519

Date of Award 12.12.17

GRAHAM P.
Private 14/726
JOHNSON T.
Private 14/468

Date of Award 17.12.17

MIREE S.
L/Corporal 14/1060

Date of Award 23.2.18

BELLIN W.
Private 14/10
DOUGHERTY J.
L/Corporal 14/410

Date of Award 13.3.18
PICKERSGILL F.
Private 14/473

Date of Award 17.6.18
FIRTH C.
Sergeant 14/992

Date of Award 6.8.18
BEDFORD S.
Private 13/1356

Date of Award 16.8.18
BOLDY F.
Private 13/142
MALKIN T.
Private 13/611
SHEPHERD H.
L/Corporal 13/817

Date of Award 29.8.18
ATKINSON H.
Private 13/1
BELL G.
Private 13/1212
WINTER R.
Private 14/877

Date of Award 13.9.18
MANSFIELD B.
Private 14/1466

Date of Award 7.10.18
RUSHFORTH C.
L/Corporal 14/1312

Date of Award 21.10.18
BEARDSHALL W.
Private 13/39
BIRKINSHAW W.
Corporal 13/146
BOOCOCK J.
Private 13/70
DEBNEY J.
Corporal 13/244
GOOSE G.
Private 13/393
HALL J.
Private 13/407
KNOWLES A.
L/Corporal 13/1324
SMITH G.W.
Private 13/807
WARD H.
Private 13/735

Date of Award 11.2.19
DICKINSON H.
Private 13/255
EVERITT T.
Private 36375
GODFREY F.
Private 14/377

Date of Award 13.3.19
GUY I.
Private 13/1479

Date of Award 14.5.19
JACKSON W.
Private 13/540
TALBOT F.S.
Private 31273
WILKINSON J.
Private 14/1050
WILSON W.H.
Private 14/1076

Date of Award 17.6.19
SHARP J.
Sergeant 14/99
WINSLADE T.
Private 204700

Date of Award 23.7.19
DAVIES G.
Private 13/1058

Date of Award 2.8.19
HUDSON B.
Corporal 39962

Date of Award 20.10.19
FLINTHAM J.
Sergeant 14/1551

MERITORIOUS SERVICE MEDAL

Date of Award 4.6.17
GLEDHILL T.L.
Sergeant 14/44

Date of Award 1.1.18
SHARP J.
Sergeant 13/1302

Date of Award 17.5.19
BAILEY C.H.
C.S.M. 13/138
LAWSON H.
Sergeant 13/567

STRUTT W.H.
Sergeant 14/614

Date of Award 18.1.19
BAMBRIDGE C.
C.S.M. 4830
BAMFORTH B.
Corporal 12/1392
CLARKE N.W.B.
Private 12/71
HIRST A.
Corporal 13/421
LUNN R.
Corporal 22503

MENTIONED IN DESPATCHES

FIRTH C.
Private 14/992 *4.1.17*

JONES T.
Private 13/536 *25.5.17*

HIGGS J.E.
Private 14/305 *25.5.17*

EVERETT C.E.
Private 14/486
21.12.17

FISHER H.
Sergeant 13/341
21.12.17

WARDLE G.
C.S.M. 13/745
20.5.18

BUSWELL R.
C.Q.M.S. 13/134
9.7.19

HALL J.
Corporal 13/494
9.7.19

RYAN W.
C.S.M. 3/4444
9.7.19

SHEPHERD W.H.
C.S.M. 39973
9.7.19

SQUIRES J.
C.S.M. 8999
9.7.19

STIMSON W.
A/L/Corporal 13/897
9.7.19

BELGIAN CROIX DE GUERRE

HARDCASTLE J. Private
13/1461 12.7.18

SUNDERLAND A. Sergeant
13/888 12.7.18

FORT C. Sergeant *13/309*
24.10.19

BROMLEY G. Sergeant *3/4833*
4.11.19

STEPHEN F. Private *31273*
4.11.19

CROIX DE GUERRE

FISHER H. Sergeant *13/341*
19.6.19

NEWTON H. Sergeant *3/3036*
19.6.19

ITALIAN SILVER MEDAL FOR MILITARY VALOUR

GIBBS J. Private *13/364*

ITALIAN BRONZE MEDAL FOR MILITARY VALOUR

FORBES S. Sergeant 34895

Acknowledgments

'Pals' is not my story, nor is it the story of my generation. By the time I was born the old battlefields of 1914–1918 had been under the plough for almost half a century and the rumbling thunder of a second world conflict had been silent for well over a decade.

Nevertheless, as I grew older I became fascinated by photographs in old books, which showed grubby men in grubby clothes and strange, rounded hats, sitting in holes amid surroundings which resembled a rubbish heap.

Later still I learned that these men were British soldiers of the First World War and that my own grandfather, as a lad of eighteen, had been one of them.

I became fascinated by the war he had been involved in and although the experiences of that war belonged to his generation, while he lived the memory of it stretched over the years into mine.

When pressed, which he often was, he would relate a favourite tale of how a small group of men, including himself, had been pinned down all day in a ditch by German machine guns. The story and the strange sounding names of the places he used, 'Vimy Ridge' and 'Passchendaele', gripped my imagination. And then there were his memories of the horses. How those poor dumb beasts had suffered in the wastelands of mud created by man.

I thirsted for more but he was reluctant to tell. Perhaps the full horror of what he had seen made him hold his tongue. Perhaps he thought he was protecting the innocent.

He cried out in his sleep with some long remembered terror, every night until he died. His memories were lost forever.

If the First World War had touched my family it must have touched others and I became interested in the story of the Barnsley Pals Battalions. My grandfather had been a conscript but these men had joined the Army as volunteers. I wanted to know why; and what had happened to them.

My debt to the nine veteran Barnsley Pals who were interviewed for the book is inestimable. Without their help and cooperation there would have been no book to speak of. Unlike my grandfather they were not quite so reluctant to tell of their experiences, although that does not mean to say that the memories they did reveal were any less painful.

For a long time I baulked at the prospect of sitting down to write these few notes of thanks, not because I did not want to, but because I felt that any words of mine would be of meagre recompense for the hours of persistent prying into their past to which they were subjected.

These men allowed a total stranger into their homes and yet exhibited an overwhelming patience and warm-hearted hospitality which left a deep impression on me. Frank Lindley even went so far as to

Jon Cooksey was born in the village of Havercroft, near Royston and attended secondary school in Grimethorpe. During that time he represented South Yorkshire as the Captain of the South Yorkshire Schools Rugby Football Union Under 15 and Under 16 teams. He later studied at Leeds Polytechnic where he gained an Honours Degree in Education. At present he is a teacher of Physical Education and Geography at Swanwick Hall School in Derbyshire. 'Pals' is his first book and he is currently researching material for another – the Barnsley Territorials, York and Lancaster Regiment, during World War One.

allow me to use his electricity when the batteries in my recorder ran flat. I had merely dropped in to introduce myself and left five hours later in the early hours of the next morning.

On the many occasions when I have had cause to visit them again with 'just one more question', they and their families have never failed to make me feel more than welcome. Many is the time I have had to turn down the offer of a 'drop of something stronger' from Mrs. Hall. I would never have got home otherwise.

My greatest fear, as an inexperienced writer, was that since I had been entrusted with their memories, I would fail to do them justice.

To Vernon Atkinson, Ernest Bell, Oswald Burgess, Harry Hall, Frank Lindley, George Armitage Nichols and Tommy Oughton I extend my sincere thanks.

In many ways however the publication of the book is tinged with sadness, for James Bennett and Charlie Swales did not live long enough to read the stories of their comrades. Their passing before the completion of the project, will always be a source of regret, but in some small way they will live on among the pages of 'Pals'. I feel it an honour to have been part of the preservation of their memory.

Mr. John Davies also passed away during the time in which the book was in preparation. His willingness to allow me to examine numerous original documents of a very personal nature helped me to piece together the story of his father, Sapper John H. Davies, the First Battalion Pal killed whilst serving with the Royal Engineers.

Without the generosity of Mr. Davies and his family the story of the Barnsley 'miners' would undoubtedly have lacked substance.

I should also like to express my appreciation to the following people who have kindly given of their time or have allowed me to borrow treasured family possessions for inclusion in the book: Mr. B. Ashton (Accrington District Central Library), Mr. Bates, Ms. Bellin, Mr. S. Bygate, Mr. C. Bradley, Mrs. C. Brooks, Mr. W. Colebourne, Mr. and Mrs. Copley, Mrs. D. Crossfield, Mr. H. Fretwell M.M., Mr. Gay, Mr. D. Gill, Mr. and Mrs. F. Gillott, Mrs. Greenfield, Mr. H. Haywood, Mr. M. Hepworth, (Barnsley Library Local Studies Section), Mr. Hodgson, Mr. C. P. Heptonstall, Mr. R. Hibbert, Mrs. Leak, Mrs. Lee, Mr. G. Marlow, Mr. R. Oldfield, Mr. Oxley, Mr. H. Pankhurst, Mr. R. Potter, Mrs. G. Procter, Mr. S. Race, Mr. M. Reed, Mr. G. Reid, Mrs. E. Rhodes, Mr. W. Ruddlesden, Mrs. J. Strachan, Mr. E. Sutcliffe, Mr. W. Swift, Mr. E. G. Tasker, Mr. R. D. Watson, Mr. G. Whyte, Mr. K. Wilson, Mr. G. Wilson, Mr. F. Winford, Mrs. N. Wood.

I have spoken to Mr. Bill Turner of Accrington several times over the telephone and his knowledge of the Accrington Pals Battalion has helped to clarify several points.

Mr. Ralph Gibson of Sheffield has also given his time freely to speak with me on the subject of the Sheffield City Battalion.

Peter Taylor expended an enormous amount of time and energy compiling the medal lists and nominal rolls. There can be no doubt that all the credit for their inclusion must go to him.

I am also indebted to Stuart Eastwood, late of the York and Lancaster Regimental Museum and now curator of the Loyal North Lancashire Regimental Museum in Lancaster, for his unstinting efforts and assistance in drawing up the casualty rolls and supplying items for photographing.

The Staff at The Imperial War Museum in London have dealt with my many enquiries, both in person and over the telephone, with unfailing courtesy. I should particularly like to thank Mr. R. W. A. Suddaby, the Keeper of the Department of Documents and Ms. A. Commander of the same department. Ms. A. Wootton of the Department of Printed Books and Mr. M. Willis of the Department of Photographs.

Similarly, the Staffs at both the Public Record Office and the Commonwealth War Graves Commission have been of invaluable assistance.

I enlisted the help of my own battalion of volunteers to help with the translation of many pages of what, to me, were incomprehensible handwritten German records.

Sonja Higgins did much of the hard work at short notice and I should also like to thank Lieselotte Barton, Colin Day, Frauke Dunnhaupt and Trevor Stevens. All gave up many hours of their own valuable time in order to help me.

Thanks must also go to Mrs. von Renteln at the West German Embassy in London who helped to put me in touch with the Generallandesarchiv in Karlsruhe.

Frauke Dunnhaupt put me in touch with Hugo Stockter in Wilhelmshaven. His efforts in tracing much valuable German material and sending it to England at his own expense quite staggered me, particularly as he had received only the merest hint of what my project entailed. His efforts truly went above and beyond the call of duty.

Also in Germany Dr. Marie Salaba of the Generallandesarchiv in Karlsruhe has responded promptly to my many communications regarding the War Diaries of the 169th Regiment.

A huge vote of thanks must go to Mary Farmer. She has slaved over page after page of unintelligible ramblings and must have typed out the same words in a different order at least half a dozen times. On every occasion she appeared with beautiful typescript.

At the Barnsley Chronicle, Sir Nicholas Hewitt's enthusiasm helped to generate the project initially, but the bulk of the production work fell on the broad shoulders of the Graphics and Features Department of the Barnsley Chronicle.

In the camera room John Fawcett and Nick Gillott often succeeded in making silk purses out of some very poor sows' ears and produced photographs worthy of being put into print.

Thanks, also, are due to Denise Winstanley who marked all of the proofs and still claimed to have enjoyed reading them.

My parents deserve a special mention for allowing me to stay with them, free of charge, on my extended trips to Barnsley.

For permission to include quotations from *Goodbye To All That* by Robert Graves and *The Private Papers of Douglas Haig, 1914-1919*, I am indebted to the Executors of the Estate of Robert Graves and Robert Blake, Eyre and Spottiswoode.

To Mr. G. Sassoon for releasing the Poem of Siegfried Sassoon.

I should also like to extend my thanks to Mr. Martin Middlebrook for his kind permission to include the quotation of Lieutenant Robert Allatt Heptonstall, which first appeared in Mr. Middlebrook's *The First Day on the Somme*.

Mrs. H. Dodd and Miss A. Rees graciously gave permission for me to quote from the papers of their father, Brigadier-General H.C. Rees D.S.O. which are held in the Department of Documents at the Imperial War Museum.

Quotations from Crown Copyright Records deposited in the Public Record Office are reproduced by permission of the Controller of Her Majesty's Stationary Office.

For permission to quote from the War Diaries of the German 169th Regiment I am grateful to the Directors of the Generallandesarchiv, Karlsruhe, West Germany.

Photographs which are held by the Imperial War Museum appear by kind permission of The Trustees of the Imperial War Museum, whilst those held in the Archives of British Coal are reproduced by permission of British Coal.

Last, but by no means least, I should like to thank Victoria. Without her constant encouragement and understanding over many a long month, I doubt very much whether I would have completed the book at all.

Jon Cooksey

Bibliography

The British Official Histories

ASPINALL-OGLANDER, Brigadier-General C.F. (Compiler) *Military Operations Gallipoli*, Vols. 1-2, (William Heinemann Ltd., 1952).

EDMONDS, Brigadier-General Sir James E. (Compiler) *Military Operations France and Belgium, 1914*, Vols. 1-2, (Macmillan & Co. Ltd., 1925).

——, *Military Operations France and Belgium, 1915*, Vol. 1, (Macmillan & Co. Ltd., 1927).

——, *Military Operations France and Belgium, 1916*, Vol. 1, (Macmillan & Co. Ltd., 1932).

MACMUNN, Lieutenant-General Sir George & FALLS, Captain C. (Compilers) *Military Operations Egypt and Palestine* (H.M.S.O. 1928).

MILES, Captain Wilfred (Compiler) *Military Operations France and Belgium, 1916*, Vol. 2, (Macmillan & Co. Ltd., 1938).

ASHWORTH, A.E., The Sociology of Trench Warfare. *British Journal of Sociology, 1968*, Vol. 19, 407-423.

ATTERIDGE, A.H. *The British Army of Today* (People's Books, 1915).

BARRIE, Alexander *War Underground 1914-1918* (House Journals Ltd., 1962).

BLAKE, Robert (Editor) *The Private Papers of Douglas Haig 1914-1919* (Eyre & Spottiswoode, 1952)

BORASTON, CB, OBE, Lieutenant-Colonel J.H. (Editor) *Sir Douglas Haig's Despatches* (J.M. Dent & Sons Ltd., 1919)

BROPHY, John and PARTRIDGE, Eric (Editors) *The Long Trail* (Deutsch, 1965)

CARVER, R.B.(et al) *A History of the 10th (Service) Battalion The East Yorkshire Regiment, (Hull Commercials) 1914-1919* (A. Brown & Sons Ltd., 1937)

CHURCHILL, The Rt. Hon. Winston S. *The World Crisis 1916-1918*, Part 1 (Thornton Butterworth Ltd., 1927)

COWPER, H.S. *The Art of Attack* (P.W. Holmes Ltd., 1906)

CRUTWELL, C.R.M.F. *A History of the Great War* (Oxford Clarendon Press, 1936)

DUFF COOPER *Haig* (Faber & Faber Ltd., 1935)

FARRAR-HOCKLEY, A.H. *The Somme* (Pan Books Ltd., 1983)

FITZGIBBON, Constantine *Secret Intelligence in the Twentieth Century* (Granada, 1976)

GARDNER, Brian *The Big Push: A Portrait of the Battle of the Somme* (Cassell & Co. Ltd., 1961)

GRAVES, Robert *Goodbye to All That* (Penguin Books Ltd., 1984)

GUINN, Paul *British Strategy and Politics 1914 to 1918* (Oxford University Press, 1965)

HAIGH, R.H. and TURNER, P.W. *Not for Glory* (Pergamon Press Ltd., 1969)

HAMMERTON, Sir John (Editor) *The Great War, 'I Was There': Undying Memories of 1914-1918*. Vols. 1-3 (Amalgamated Press Ltd., 1938)

HEDIN, Sven *With the German Armies in the West* (The Bodley Head, 1915)

HUDSON, R.N. *The Bradford Pals: A History of the 16th and 18th Battalions, The West Yorkshire Regiment* (1978)

ILLUSTRATED Michelin Guides to the Battlefields 1914-1918 *The Somme* Vol. 1 (Michelin & Co. 1919)

LIDDELL-HART, B.H. *History of the First World War* (Cassell & Co. Ltd., 1970)

LUDENDORFF, General E. von *My War Memories, 1914-1918* Vol. 1 (Hutchinson & Co. Ltd., 1936)

MACDONALD, Lyn *They Called it Passchendaele* (Macmillan & Co. Ltd., 1983)

——, *Somme* (Macmillan & Co. Ltd., 1984)

MARWICK, Arthur *The Deluge: British Society and the First World War* (Macmillan & Co. Ltd., 1965)

MASEFIELD, John *Gallipoli* (William Heinemann Ltd., 1916)

——, *The Old Front Line: The Beginning of the Battle of the Somme* (William Heinemann Ltd., 1917)

MATUSCHKA, Edgar Graf von Organisationsgeschichte des Heeres 1890-1918, in MEIER-WELCKER, Hans and GROOTE, Wolfgang von *Handbuch zur deutschen Militärgeschichte 1648-1939* (Bernard & Graefe, Frankfurt, 1968).

MIDDLEBROOK, Martin *The First Day on the Somme* (Penguin Books Ltd., 1984)

MOTTRAM, R.H. *Journey to the Western Front* (G. Bell & Sons Ltd., 1936)

PRIESTLEY, J.B. *Margin Released* (The Reprint Society, 1963)

SECRETT MM, Sergeant T. *Twenty Five Years with Earl Haig* (Jarrolds, 1929)

SELDTE, Franz *Dauerfeuer* (Koehler, Leipzig, 1930)

SPARLING, Richard A. *History of the 12th (Service) Battalion, York and Lancaster Regiment* (J.W. Northend Ltd., 1920)

STOSCH, Albrecht von, (Editor) *Schlacten des Weltkrieges: Somme Nord* Part 1 (Gerhard Stalling, Oldenburg, Berlin, 1927)

TERRAINE, John *White Heat: The New Warfare 1914-1918* (Sidgwick & Jackson, 1982)

TOWNROWE, B.S. *A Pilgrim in Picardy* (Chapman & Hall Ltd., 1927)

WAITE D.S.O., Major Fred *The New Zealanders at Gallipoli* (Whitcombe & Tombs Ltd., Auckland, 1919)

WILKINSON M.C., Captain R.M. *History of the 10th (Service) Battalion York and Lancaster Regiment 1914-1918* (Privately Published, 1938)

WYLLY C.B., Colonel H.C. *The York and Lancaster Regiment: The Territorial and Service Battalions 1758-1919* Vol. 2 (Butler & Tanner Ltd., Printers, 1930)

Unpublished Sources

JONES, Joseph *A Portrait of My Father*

LAWSON, J. *War Memoirs of a Robin Hood*

REES, Brigadier-General H.C. *Private Papers* (Department of Documents, The Imperial War Museum)

WILSON R.N.P. *Letters 1913-1918*